T0326338

ROUTLEDGE LIBRARY EDITIONS: TRADE UNIONS

Volume 2

THE RAILWAYMEN

THE RAILWAYMEN

Volume 1:
The History of the National Union of Railwaymen

PHILIP S. BAGWELL

Routledge
Taylor & Francis Group
LONDON AND NEW YORK

First published in 1963 by George Allen & Unwin Ltd.

This edition first published in 2023
by Routledge
4 Park Square, Milton Park, Abingdon, Oxon OX14 4RN

and by Routledge
605 Third Avenue, New York, NY 10158

Routledge is an imprint of the Taylor & Francis Group, an informa business

British Library Cataloguing in Publication Data
A catalogue record for this book is available from the British Library

ISBN: 978-1-032-37553-3 (Set)
ISBN: 978-1-032-41464-5 (Volume 2) (hbk)
ISBN: 978-1-032-41476-8 (Volume 2) (pbk)
ISBN: 978-1-003-35822-0 (Volume 2) (ebk)

DOI: 10.4324/9781003358220

Publisher's Note
The publisher has gone to great lengths to ensure the quality of this reprint but points out that some imperfections in the original copies may be apparent.

Disclaimer
The publisher has made every effort to trace copyright holders and would welcome correspondence from those they have been unable to trace.

THE RAILWAYMEN

The History of the
National Union of Railwaymen

BY

PHILIP S. BAGWELL

London
GEORGE ALLEN & UNWIN LTD
RUSKIN HOUSE   MUSEUM STREET

PRINTED IN GREAT BRITAIN
in 11 on 12-point Plantin type
BY UNWIN BROTHERS LTD
WOKING AND LONDON

FOREWORD

Hundreds of books have been written about the railway companies which functioned before 1947. Hundreds more have described in great detail the development of the railway locomotive and the evolution of rolling stock and signalling systems. But the companies and their vast and expensive capital equipment would have been worthless without the men to run them. It is therefore surprising that the number of books about the lives and working conditions of railwaymen could be counted almost on the fingers of a man's hand.

Fifty years ago, through the foundation of the N.U.R., the majority of railwaymen were, for the first time, organized in a big industrial union. The last full account of this dramatic development was written over forty years ago by the late Mr George Alcock.

Dr Philip Bagwell's book, which relates the stirring events in the struggle to end inhuman conditions of employment and to gain union recognition, carries the story forward to the Guillebaud Report in 1960 and will, I am sure, satisfy a long-felt need.

To those who would like to know what railway life was like before the days of the union; what happened in the great national railway strikes of 1911 and 1919; and what the N.U.R. did to gain the guaranteed week, holidays with pay and numerous other improvements, I can strongly recommend this authoritative, finely illustrated and well written book. In the last fifty years the organized workers have played an increasing part not only in determining the conditions of employment but also in shaping the very structure of industry. No student of transport can afford to ignore the essential background to industrial trade unionism provided by this excellent book.

S. F. GREENE.

ACKNOWLEDGEMENTS

It would have been impossible to write this book without the encouragement and help given by a great many people.

I owe a debt of gratitude to Mr S. F. Greene, the Assistant Secretaries, Messrs Brassington and Ballantine, and the members of the Executive Committee for entrusting me with the task of writing the history of the N.U.R. Although I have had the benefit of their knowledge and experience, they have left me completely free in the selection of material and the interpretation of events. The opinions I have expressed are entirely my own. It has been a great pleasure to work in such conditions of confidence and freedom.

I would like to thank Mr Branson, Office Manager at Unity House, who from the beginning, encouraged me to undertake this task and throughout gave me the benefit of his friendship and assistance. I am also very grateful to Mr Shell, Head of the Records Department, for help generously given, and to all members of the Secretarial and other Departments who have given cheerful and ungrudging assistance.

I am greatly indebted to the following friends whose reading of the whole or part of the typescript and offering of advice has been greatly appreciated; Messrs J. W. L. Forge and C. R. Sweetingham, Dr E. Hobsbawm and Major G. Blaxland.

The editors of *The Journal of Transport History* have kindly given permission to reproduce a large part of an article I contributed to the *Journal* in 1957.

To 'Studio Briggs', the *Illustrated London News*, the *Daily Herald*, the British Transport Commission and the Co-operative Printing Society Ltd., I am grateful for permission to reproduce photographs.

Mr Harris at Unity House and my colleague Dr Cotgrove gave invaluable assistance in helping with the photographs.

I am grateful to Mr George Ottley and other members of the Staff at the State Paper Room of the British Museum; to the Librarian and Staff at Congress House; and the staff of the British Transport Commission's Historical Archives Departments in London and York, for unfailing courtesy and prompt assistance.

I am very grateful to Sir Leslie M. Thomas, M.B.E., T.D., M.P., for the loan of a large number of bound volumes of newspaper cuttings of the 1919 strike and the activities of the Rt. Hon. J. H. Thomas, P.C., M.P.

More than a hundred branch secretaries and individual members of the N.U.R. have written to me or helped me by personal interview. This help has been invaluable.

I have been given the friendly encouragement and advice of Mr F. Moxley, Editor of the *Railway Review*, who has contributed a valuable appendix to the book.

A*

Miss I. Ellis, to whom I am indebted for the typescript, has required (and displayed) the patience of a saint and the detective skill of a Sherlock Holmes.

Since this book has been written in my spare time, it is only through the co-operation and understanding of my wife that it has been at all possible.

CONTENTS

CONTENTS

ILLUSTRATIONS

CHAPTER I

BEFORE THE DAYS OF THE UNION

The directors are in principle opposed to combination of any description for the purpose of interfering with the natural course of trade. They think that masters and men should be left in every establishment to settle their own terms, and arrange their own differences without foreign interference or dictation.'
'London, Brighton and South Coast Railway Circular', 1852.

I

ONLY a few of the first generation of railwaymen had even a nodding acquaintance with trade unionism. Though there were examples of the organized withdrawal of labour over a wide area of the country in 1848-50, 1860 and 1867, no permanent trade union was established until 1871.

Considering all the circumstances, it is not in the least surprising that this should have been the case. Many men regarded it as a great privilege to work on the railway. The prospects for regular employment and promotion were good in an industry whose labour force expanded from 47,218 in 1847 to 127,450 in 1860 and 274,535 in 1873. Skilled men, and reliable men in the unskilled grades, were difficult to find in the 1830's and 1840's. In a leading article concerning the supply of engine drivers, the editor of the foremost railway journal commented that 'at first the demand so far exceeded the supply that companies were glad to secure servants of this class on any terms, and a driver was no sooner dismissed from one line for misconduct than he found ready employment on another'.[1] In 1839, Capt. Moorsom, the Secretary of the London and Birmingham Railway, was questioned by the members of a Parliamentary Select Committee:

' "The fact is the number of engine drivers is rather below than above the supply and therefore they can dictate their own terms in a great degree ?"

19

'He answered: "At present it is so; that difficulty will of course diminish." '[2]

It followed that railwaymen, particularly in the skilled grades, were able to command higher wages than could be obtained by men of comparable skill in other occupations. In the 1840's engine drivers could earn between 5s 6d and 7s 6d a day and firemen between 3s 6d and 5s 6d, depending on the length of their service. Considering the greater regularity of employment in the railway service these wages of up to 45s and 35s a week were better than the 26s to 33s earned by turners in the Manchester area.[3] The 22s 1d average weekly wage of switchmen, pointsmen and signalmen compared favourably with the cotton operatives' 19s. Although railway porters averaged only 18s 7d a week and worked at least twelve hours a day, they were substantially better off than the agricultural labourers whose wages averaged 11s 6d a week in the North of England and only 8s 5d in the South. Comparing these conditions, men were only too glad to find jobs on the railways. Most men, once they had been fortunate enough to secure such employment, were careful not to jeopardize their positions by such reckless indiscretions as joining a trade union and taking part in strikes.

For their part, the directors of the railway companies used every inducement to secure the loyalty of their employees. Blending persuasion with cajolery, they were better versed in the art of labour management than the majority of the employers of their day. By the end of the nineteenth century they were falling behind, failing to recognize trade unions when many other employers were learning the advantages of collective bargaining; but in the first fifty years of railway growth in Britain their success in dealing with labour problems was remarkable.

From their first appointment to the time of their retirement and death everything possible was done to bind the railwaymen more closely to the service of the companies.[4] Those men who had in their safe keeping large sums of money or valuable goods, were required, on taking up an appointment, to deposit a sum of money as security for their good conduct. The amount of security varied from the £50 required from a clerk earning a salary of £60 to £90 a year to the £1,000 required from a clerk-in-charge earning £160 a year. Ticket collectors and left luggage office attendants were also sometimes expected to deposit a sum of money as security. Where, as was generally the case, the applicant was unable to raise the required sum from his own resources, he was obliged to find someone who was prepared to stand surety on his behalf. A sense of loyalty to a friend and benefactor thus powerfully reinforced a developing loyalty to the railway company in making less likely, not only theft of the company's property, but also any kind of conduct euphemistically called 'insubordination'.

Until the 1870's, when the size of the companies and the numbers they employed grew so large as to make its continuance impracticable, it was customary for the directors of the companies, in rotation, to exercise the privilege of nominating men for vacancies in the service. One hundred and ten of the 135 appointments on the Great Northern Railway between Peterborough and Lincoln in 1848 were made under such an arrangement. Men thus favoured naturally felt under a more direct obligation to their employers than did workmen in other occupations. Many men must have felt that to demand higher wages or better conditions in such circumstances was like biting the hand that fed them.

Most companies thought it desirable to employ only literate men. Even in the literacy tests applicants for employment were required to pass, the attempt was made to instil a spirit of obedience. Those seeking employment on the Great Western Railway in 1837 were required to write these words:

'Zealously strive to excel. Industry is commendable. Perseverance deserves success. Quietude of mind is a treasure.'

The staff of many companies were kept loyal through the promise of an end of the year bonus for good conduct. Captain Moorsom told the shareholders of the London and Birmingham Railway at the A.G.M. in 1842 that it had been the custom of the company 'to make a portion of the remuneration of the most important part of the working establishment— the engine drivers, switchmen and policemen—contingent on their good behaviour'. He reported that the sum of £358 4s 0d had been given in gratuities to 45 engine drivers and 44 firemen in the last half year in amounts of £5 and £3. Between August 1865, and July 1866, 277 signalmen and switchmen employed by the London and Brighton Railway were given bonuses of from £2 to £5. Porters employed by the same company were not given bonuses but each man received his annual increases of pay only if the company had 'no blot against him'.

For those thousands of railwaymen who lived in company-owned 'railway cottages' the risks incurred in engaging in any sort of trade-union activity were greater than ever. For the man who incurred the displeasure of the general manager and directors, it meant not only the loss of employment but also the loss of a home. By 1897 the Midland Railway possessed 2,199 workmen's cottages, 91 of which were occupied rent free, the rents for the remainder ranging from 1s to 20s a week, with an average of 3s 9d. For a man who lived in a rent-free or low-rented cottage, taking part in a strike would very likely lead to the loss of a steady job and his home and the ultimate resort to the workhouse (often called the Bastille by the poor). In May 1871, engine drivers who had struck work on the London and North Western Railway were evicted from their company-owned homes in Camden Town.[5]

The men's loyalty was also secured through their membership of company-sponsored Friendly Societies. There were over fifty such societies in existence on the railways in 1870, and in the case of ten of the largest of them membership was compulsory. By belonging to them the men could claim sick or accident benefit when need arose and in a few cases they were entitled to a small weekly pension on retirement; but the right to full benefits depended on continued employment with the company. According to the rules of the Midland Railway Friendly Society (which were typical of many) men who left the company's service before the expiry of seven years received only 25 per cent of the excess of their contributions over any benefits received, and they were not permitted to continue in membership. Those who had been with the company for seven years or more and members of the Friendly Society for at least five years, were allowed to continue their membership on leaving the company's service, but their sick benefit was reduced from 12s 6d to 10s a week and their death benefit from £12 to £10. The companies thus provided a strong financial inducement to their employees to abstain from risky adventures in trade unionism which might lead to dismissal and loss of benefits.

By numerous other, individually small, but cumulatively important, ways, the ties of loyalty to the company were increased. Some men took pride in wearing the companies' livery and were impressed by the argument of their employers that such free clothing could be worth anything from £1 to £4 a year to the wearer. Other perquisites of railway employment included a limited number of free passes and the purchase of coal for domestic use at reduced rates.

In contrast with the situation at a later date, the railway companies of the period 1830–60 were often relatively small concerns in which it was possible for locomotive superintendents, superintendents of the line and others in authority, to be known personally by many of their staff. These authorities would often display a paternalistic benevolence to those whose work they supervised and this would generate, in return, the personal loyalty of the men. Although the number of men he employed was much larger than the average in a locomotive department of his day, Mr Gooch, the Locomotive Superintendent of the Great Western Railway, was able to command this kind of respect. In the summer of 1862 a Member of Parliament, Mr Cobbett, introduced a Bill for the limitation of the hours of labour of locomotivemen. This attempt led 'A Great Western Engine Driver' to write these words in a letter to *The Times*:

'I am surprised to see by the motion of Mr Cobbett for the protection of engine drivers and firemen, that the Great Western men are classed with those who claim the protection of Parliament. I am requested by the above to say that they have authorized no one to use their names in any petition asking for the protection of Parliament as a body. Some few may have signed such a petition, but only with a view to benefiting their oppressed fellow workmen on other lines, for as long as our respected and esteemed chief superintendent, Mr D. Gooch, is at our head, we want no other protection than his, for we all know that we can get no protection so just and generous as we receive at his hands.

'Your humble servant has served the Great Western Company under Mr Gooch for 22 years and during that time has never heard his name mentioned but with profound respect.'[6]

II

The oft-repeated claim of the directors of the railway companies was that if any man or group of men had a grievance they were entitled to present a petition to their employers who would give it the most careful consideration with a view to rectifying any proved abuses. The General Manager of the London and North Western Railway declared that it had always been the case that 'anybody on the wages staff has an absolute right of appeal to the directors', whilst his counterpart in the Great Western Railway asserted that 'the Directors of the Great Western Railway have always been peculiarly accessible to their staff'. The Secretary and General Manager of the Cambrian Railway claimed that it was 'the rule of the service that every man has the right of appealing first to his superior officer and then, if necessary, to the directors'.[7]

Many of the men's petitions survive in the archives of the British Transport Commission. Sometimes they were individual appeals such as the letter written to the directors of the Stockton and Darlington Railway on January 11, 1838, from Edward Bell, the spring of whose wooden leg, given him two years previously after a railway accident, was now 'almost useless'. His plea that the directors might contribute towards the £2 needed for its replacement met with some success, for the minute of the Company's Committee meeting held the following day reads:

'Agreed: To allow Edward Bell 20s out of the fine box towards the expenses of a new wooden leg.'

On other occasions it was a small group of men who were concerned. The goods clerks at York employed by the North Eastern Railway petitioned their directors on December 3, 1857, calling attention to 'the miserable and totally unfit state of the places occupied ... as offices' and claiming that, on inspection, they would be pronounced 'injurious to health' as well as 'inconvenient to the dispatch of business'. The twenty-three signatories were confident 'an alteration would prove beneficial to the company' as well as to themselves. The petition was given a favourable hearing. After inspection of the premises, the General Manager wrote the words 'This statement is quite correct' by the petitioners' claim that their workplace was unhealthy and, later that month, the board agreed to spend £198 15s od on the building of two new offices.

On January 17, 1862, twenty-one men signed a petition on behalf of 600 workmen employed at Tyne Dock requesting the directors of the North Eastern Railway to subscribe to a new Mechanics Institute. They wrote that a fire had destroyed the old Institute room with its 300 books. As an earnest of their good intentions the men had raised £20 towards the cost of a new building and had collected eighty-seven books. Since there was 'no school for their children nearer than South Shields' they hoped that the directors would contribute something towards the worth-while object. The directors did. At their board meeting on July 4, 1862, they voted £30 'towards the cost of fitting up a building at Tyne Dock as a Mechanics Institute for the use of the Company's servants there'.

On September 20, 1838, eight labourers employed by the Stockton and Darlington Railway at the coal staiths at Middlesbrough, who had taken 'the liberty of attending half a day at the last Stockton races' petitioned against being fined 2s each for this offence and (one would think somewhat tactlessly) at the same time asked for 'an advance of wages of three shillings a week' on the grounds that the 21s a week they were paid was too little to support their families. The Board minutes are silent on the outcome of this appeal.

As might be expected, most petitions were for increases in the rate of wages. Nearly all of these were confined to men of one grade serving on one company's lines. That enginemen employed by six different companies should submit petitions within the space of a few weeks in 1867 was exceptional; the unsuccessful all-grades petition for higher wages on the London, Brighton and South Coast Railway in 1853 was unique in the period before the A.S.R.S. was founded.

Despite the assurance of the directors that the men had a right to petition their employers, it was sometimes found that the organizers of such appeals were marked men whose promotion was subsequently blocked even if they were lucky enough to be retained in the service. Hence it was sometimes the practice to make the petitions 'round robin' ones such as the example shown in Plate 1 facing page 128, so that no one man could be singled out as the leader of the movement. A case which was raised on the Stockton and Darlington Railway, must be well in the running for the record for the quick settlement of a wage claim on the railways. The petition was sent 'by the half past seven o'clock train' on the morning of May 25, 1838, to John Harris, the Engineer. That same day the Committee of the Company considered it and resolved as follows:

'The Waymen of the 1st Division of the line, 43 in number, having applied for an advance in wages from 2s 9d to 3s per day, the Engineer is authorized to allow the same to such men as he may consider deserving.'

A later minute of the Committee dated June 1, 1838, shows that the Engineer decided to advance the wages of seventeen of the men to 3s a day whilst the wages of the remainder were to be advanced to 2s 10d a day.

It was one thing for the directors to give a favourable response to the appeals made by individuals or small groups of men; it was quite another matter when the appeal was from all the men of one important grade. Most appeals of this kind were rejected. This was the fate of the applications made for better wages by the railway police on the London and Greenwich Railway in 1838, the guards on the North Eastern Railway in 1845, the enginemen on the Manchester, Sheffield and Lincolnshire Railway in 1845, the signalmen of the Brighton line in 1865 and the shunters, porters, gatemen and clerks on the Great Western Railway in 1866—to mention only a few of many examples.

III

Men who had petitioned but had failed to obtain redress of their grievances might resort to more extreme methods to gain their ends. It was at this point that the disciplinary measures of the companies were put to the test. Captain Moorsom told the Parliamentary Select Committee in 1839 that he 'considered fines the most efficacious mode of punishment' for the men, though he believed it might also be 'of use to call in the aid of the magistrate and to inflict additional punishment under his authority'. Two directors of the Stockton and Darlington Railway told the same committee that they found no difficulty in controlling their servants. They said—'We fine a man twice; the third time we discharge him.'[9]

At the New Shildon locomotive works of the Stockton and Darlington Railway the rules provided for the following punishments (among others):

'Any workman leaving his work without giving notice to the clerk or the foreman to be fined 1s. Any workman swearing or using abusive language to a shopmate to be fined 1s.

'Should any workman leave his work for the purpose of drinking in working hours, he will be considered as having forfeited his situation.'

Twenty years later the companies' rules were still as strict. At the Darlington works it was the rule that no workman should 'make any preparation for leaving off work such as washing himself, putting on his coat, etc., till the bell rings as the proper signal for so doing'. At the same time the workmen were strictly 'cautioned against the use of profane and improper language'.[10] Engine drivers were fined for unpunctuality, failing to carry proper lights, failing to reduce speed round curves, and many other offences. Joseph Pickering of the Stockton and Darlington was fined 10s on November 16, 1829, 'for carrying passengers on his tender contrary to the bye laws', and John Fardon in the same company's service, an early victim of the lust for speed, was fined 5s on January 15, 1830, 'for furiously driving whilst coming down the run'. In 1865 drivers from Gateshead were complaining to the Directors of the North Eastern Railway that they were being fined for 'late arrival at the terminus' when the delays were due to circumstances beyond their control such as the shortness of platforms making it necessary to move the trains backwards and forwards at the stations.

Discipline on the Taff Vale Railway was perhaps the strictest of all. The rules of that company included the warning that

'... not an instance of intoxication, singing, whistling or levity while on duty will be overlooked, and besides being dismissed the offender will be liable for punishment.'[11]

During the first three decades of railway history, porters were fined for taking tips from passengers. The acceptance of tips was not permitted on the London and North Western Railway until 1857.[12] On May 13, 1838, John Brand, a porter employed by that company at its London terminus helped a gentleman on to a train with his luggage. He was given a sixpenny tip. Immediately, an inspector appeared, demanding to see what the gentleman had put in Brand's hand. On showing the inspector the sixpence, Brand was straightway taken into the office where he was told he had been suspended. Two days later he was ordered to bring in his uniform and was informed that he had been dismissed the service. On June 7th he wrote to the directors asking for mercy and claiming that he had not had time to return the sixpence to the passenger and to explain that he was not allowed to take money, before the inspector pounced on him. Nevertheless the Board of Directors decided against his reinstatement.[13]

It was not that a strict discipline and the imposition of fines necessarily constituted any direct deterrent to trade-union activity. It was rather that those who organized petitions or agitated amongst their mates were liable to find themselves marked men. There were innumerable small offences which might give rise to a caution or the payment of a small fine. A slight misdemeanour which, if committed by an otherwise 'loyal' man might well be overlooked, would, in the case of an 'agitator', lead to punishment.

The support of Parliament was obtained for the directors' policy that the safe working of railway traffic required the maintenance of a strict labour discipline. The Select Committee on Railways in 1839 expressed the opinion that it was 'essential to the safety of the public and to the maintenance of regular intercourse by railroads that companies should have more perfect control over their servants'.

'Where the lives of many persons depend on the good conduct and ready obedience of the subordinate officers, and where the smallest irregularity may be attended with fatal consequences, a system of exact discipline should be encouraged, and powers should be given to the directors for the purpose of upholding their authority.'[14] Under general enactments of 1840 and 1842 any 'engine driver, wagon driver, guard, porter or other person ... found drunk while so employed or who shall commit any offence against any of the byelaws, rules or regulations' was to be brought before the J.P.s 'with all convenient dispatch'. Then on 'oath of one or more credible witness or witnesses' he could be 'imprisoned with or without hard labour for terms not exceeding two months' or given a £10 fine. If the J.P.s considered the offence serious enough, the man concerned could be sent to the next Quarter Sessions whose judge had powers of imprisonment of up to two years.[15] A man would be lucky never to offend against the letter of the law, and there were sufficient byelaws available to 'catch out' those men whose continued service with the company was regarded as undesirable. In the year ending July 31, 1841, seventy-nine of the 700 employees of the Great Western Railway were dismissed. In eight of the cases the cause given for dismissal was 'insubordination' and in a further eight cases it was 'misconduct'. It would be interesting to know exactly what constituted 'insubordination' and 'misconduct' in these cases.

To check 'insubordination' of the trade unionist variety, some of the directors had no hesitation in encouraging men to report on the activities of their fellow employees. George Alcock, who knew many men who had served on the railways before 1870, wrote that in those days

'No man could trust his brother, and this lack of confidence in those working side by side with one another hindered any effective work. They put trust in some men only to find that the holders of the trust carried the information to headquarters.'[16]

In the House of Commons on July 23, 1840, Lord Seymour proposed that 'there should be a registry of servants employed on the railroads' since he believed that it was 'by no means uncommon when a servant was dismissed by one railroad for neglect or misconduct at once to get employment on another railroad'.[17] His assertion may well have been correct at that time as far as some engine drivers were concerned. Perhaps the reason why his proposal for a registry was never taken up by Parliament was that it would have been superfluous. There is evidence that the companies were already notifying each other of the names of employees they had dismissed. On November 7, 1839, Mr E. J. Cleather, Chief Engineer of the Grand Junction Railway, wrote, on behalf of the directors of his company, to the Secretary of the Stockton and Darlington Railway informing him that they had 'recently been under the necessity of discharging several enginemen from their service for acts of insubordination'. 'Feeling the importance of possessing efficient control over this class of men, in which all railways are equally interested,' he appealed to the Stockton and Darlington Board 'to co-operate ... by not readily giving employment to the men who have been discharged'. He was 'authorized to add' that the Directors of the Grand Junction line 'would on similar occasions be ever ready to act reciprocally in a matter which they' considered 'of such importance to all who are connected with railways as well as to the community at large'. The names of the three offending drivers, Evan Edwards, John Cant and George Summerside were given in a postscript.[18]

There can be no doubt that the scales were heavily weighted against any trade-union activity on the railways during the first forty years of their rapid expansion. In view of the odds against them, the actions of those men who did attempt to organize their fellows appears all the more courageous.

IV

The development of British railways in the nineteenth century may be compared with the lurching progress of a motor car driven by a learner driver. Periods of rapid expansion of the railway network were succeeded by sudden checks, then periods of slower advance leading to further incautious plunges forward. Following the phenomenal financial success of the Liverpool and Manchester Railway which for many years after its opening in 1830 paid a steady 10 per cent dividend, there came the first railway mania of 1835-6, when thirty-seven new companies were formed and Parliament authorized the raising of £27,688,000 of capital for the construction of 1,156 miles of track. The unfavourable trade balances and the accompanying crop of bank failures in 1837-8 led to the sudden application of the brakes as far as railway development was concerned. Only two new companies, for the construction of 49 miles of line, were authorized in 1838. By September 1844, with the bank rate down to $2\frac{1}{2}$ per cent and overseas trade prospects rapidly improving, conditions were ripe for the railway mania of 1845-7, when Parliament authorized 576 new companies to raise the huge total of £231,556,000 and to build 8,731 miles of line. In this time of unbridled, unco-ordinated, speculative expansion the investing public went railway mad. So extravagant were many of the projects sanctioned by Parliament at the time that it was found necessary to introduce a special Act of Parliament in 1850, an 'Act to facilitate the abandonment of railways and the Dissolution of Railway Companies', providing for the winding up of uneconomical companies which a few months previously had been given powers to construct 1,500 miles of line. Although the expansion of 1865-6 was not so reckless as that which had occurred twenty years earlier, it had a speculative character, and when the finance house of Overend and Gurney Ltd. of the City of London failed for over £5 million on May 11, 1866, it also brought bankruptcy to the greatest railway contractor in the country, Sir Morton

Peto, and acute financial difficulties to a number of important companies including the South Eastern, the Great Eastern, the London, Brighton and South Coast, and the North Eastern Railways.

Such trade-union action as did occur in the period before 1870 came mostly in the periods of retrenchment and drastic economies which followed the weeks of incautious expansion. The companies then endeavoured to economize at the expense of the men's wages, hours and security of employment and provoked them into an organized, if rudimentary, resistance. The majority of the strikes occurred in the periods 1837-8, 1848-50 and 1866-7, which were alike times of financial difficulty.

It is true that it cannot be said that any sudden need to exercise a greater economy in railway operation was the cause of the first strike it has been possible to trace in the history of British railways. The affairs of the Liverpool and Manchester Railway were prosperous in February 1836, when there was a simultaneous withdrawal of labour by several of its enginemen. The Company Treasurer told a meeting of the Board on February 8th that on the previous Monday, February 1st, a number of the men had given verbal notice that unless the firemen's wages were increased they would all cease work as from the evening of Friday, February 12th. On the morning of Wednesday, February 10th, the Treasurer asked one of the drivers, John Hewitt, whether he still adhered to his intention to strike, and on his replying in the affirmative he (Hewitt) was instantly discharged. Most of the other drivers and firemen struck work at once in support of this first railwayman to be victimized for taking part in an organized movement.

Not all the men who struck work were under written contract with the company, but four of those who were, viz. Charles Callan, Peter Callan, Henry Weatherbury and George Massey, were hauled before two local magistrates who found them guilty of a breach of contract and sentenced them each to a month's hard labour in Kirkdale Prison where they were put to the severe labour of working the treadmill six hours daily. At the next meeting of the Liverpool and Manchester Board on February 18th, a letter was read from the four prisoners who expressed sorrow for their 'offence' and appealed to the directors to intervene to mitigate their sentence. The Treasurer was, however, instructed to reply that the directors had no power to liberate them. A week later a further letter was read, this time from the Chaplain of the jail, pointing out the hardships of working the treadmill and pleading on the men's behalf for more lenient treatment. This time the directors 'were disposed to mitigate the severity of the men's labour' and one of their number, Mr Currie, who was a Chief Magistrate, undertook to convey the feelings of the meeting to the Governor of the jail.[19]

Two of the four prisoners were later employed as drivers on the London and Birmingham Railway where they must have reached the conclusion that one dose of the treadmill was sufficient medicine. In 1842 they were each awarded gratuities of £5 for good conduct.[20]

In the period of retrenchment following the collapse of the first railway mania, two strikes occurred amongst the railway labourers. During the week ended June 2, 1838, there was a strike of labourers employed on parts of the Great Western Railway owing to the contractor being two weeks behind with their wages. Although a squadron of Horse Guards was sent down from Windsor to 'restore order', the men's protest was effective, for arrangements were quickly made to pay off the arrears of wages in three instalments. The men then went back to work.[21] The other strike of sixty Irish labourers employed on the Glasgow and Ayrshire Railway, which began on July 30, 1838, was unsuccessful. The contractors in this case resisted the demand for a wage increase and quickly replaced the Irishmen with Scotsmen![22]

The story of an early attempt of economizing at the expense of the loco-motive staff employed on the North Midland Railway in 1842-3 has been told by Mr Michael Robbins.[23] The line was paying meagre dividends and the shareholders, who suspected wasteful expenditure, appointed a com-mittee of inquiry including the notorious George Hudson, the 'Railway King'. Drastic working economies were recommended. The signatories of the report were brought on to the board of the company and proceeded to discharge some footplatemen and men in other grades. Men who refused to work a thirteen-day fortnight with a compulsory daily run of 146 miles from Derby to Leeds and back, were summarily dismissed and their places taken by men most of whom had been previously discharged with bad characters from other lines. The practice of such false economy provoked the intervention of the President of the Board of Trade who wrote to the Secretary of the Company on February 7, 1843, stressing 'the inexpediency of sudden and sweeping reductions affecting the class of servants upon whose skill and good conduct the safety of passengers depends'. The directors were constrained to provide additional periods of rest for engine-men but they claimed the new men they had taken on were 'fully competent for their job'.

A novel and enterprising, though unscrupulous, method of nipping in the bud a movement for improving working conditions was adopted by the chief clerk of the London and South Western Railway on October 30, 1845. The porters employed by this company at Nine Elms were expected to work from six in the morning until ten or even twelve o'clock at night for a wage of from 18s to 20s a week. On the morning of October 30th, they handed in to the principal overlooker of the goods department a petition for shorter hours or the payment of overtime rates. Immediately the petition was presented, the chief clerk 'went down by express engine to all the stations between London and Southampton' with an agreement for every porter on the line to sign, requiring him to remain at the existing rate of wages and to undertake not to leave the service without a month's notice. The men at the provincial stations signed 'under the belief that the London men had done so'. The chief clerk then returned to London to induce the Nine Elms men to sign by showing them the other porters' signatures. Since under the new agreement the directors were under no obligations to give a month's notice before dismissing their employees, thirty-nine of the London men, despite their attempted browbeating by the chief clerk, refused to sign such an unfair document and were promptly dismissed.[24]

One company which experienced a financial setback in the aftermath of the railway mania of the 1840's was the London and North Western. Its energetic Chairman, Mr Carr Glynn, told the half-yearly meeting of the shareholders on August 11, 1848, that 'it was impossible to conceal from themselves that their capital had received a very considerable check'. The reduction of the dividend on ordinary shares from 9 per cent in 1847 to 7 per cent in the following year confirmed this gloomy statement.[25] The 'remedy' the board decided to adopt at its meeting on June 10, 1848, was 'a gradual reduction of the wages of the artificers in the loco carriage and wagon shops' and a new 'scheme of classification and wages of engine drivers and firemen'. When the details of the new classification were published by the board after its meeting on July 15, 1848, it was apparent that the footplatemen were expected to bear the main burden of the economies. Whereas, under the old system, a conscientious driver could hope to rise from 5s 6d to 8s a day after eight-and-a-half years' service, under the new proposals it would take him between twenty-five and thirty years, for the company proposed to limit to twenty the number of drivers in the new 'special' class where the wage was 8s.

Towards the end of July 1848, 240 footplatemen employed in the Southern division of the London and North Western Railway system—all but six teams of the men employed in the area—handed in their fortnight's notice when they were informed that there was no chance of the old system of promotion being maintained. The strike, which lasted from August 7th–23rd, was conducted by the members of the Locomotive Steam Engine and Firemen's Friendly Society which had been founded in 1839. The men in the London area held daily meetings at the Railway Tavern, Hampstead Road. It was undoubtedly the best organized strike up to that time. The co-operation of men on other lines was sought and it was reported that deputations of drivers from the South Eastern, Eastern Counties, London and South Western and the London, Brighton and South Coast Railways were present at the meeting on August 11th. Three days later a deputation from the men interviewed the M.P.s for Marylebone and told them of the many accidents being caused through the employment of blackleg drivers. Questions were put to the President of the Board of Trade that afternoon in the House of Commons and Mr Carr Glynn, the

Chairman of the Company, who was a member of Parliament, intervened to defend its actions. He asserted that 'the whole of the proceedings' (of the strike) 'had been dictated by a club' but that he was confident that 'the intentions of the club would be frustrated'.[26]

In a letter which Mr McConnell, Locomotive Superintendent of the Southern division of the Company, wrote to Mr C. Steward (one of the directors) on August 1, 1848, he stated that there was 'no doubt' that 'an organized combination' existed among the men which would require 'prompt action and emphatic measures to put down'. The 'emphatic measures' which he took shortly afterwards included the 'borrowing' of 25 men from Woolwich Arsenal and 10 from Thames river steamboats; the switching of 50 fitters from the Wolverton Works to engine driving and the recruitment of 30 drivers dismissed or loaned from other companies' service.[27]

The great weakness of the strike was that it was organized on purely sectional lines, being confined to the footplatemen. No attempt seems to have been made to enlist the support of the other grades who not only continued at work but were even willing to act as strike breakers. On August 7th the Company issued the following instructions to the guards of the Southern division:

'Owing to the appointment of several new enginemen perfectly competent to take charge of the engines but unacquainted with this line of railway, the upper guard on the passenger trains of the Southern division will, until further orders, ride on the footplate of the engine to assist the engine driver and fireman in keeping a lookout for signals. . . . The underguard is to ride in the rear van and take charge of the parcels, etc., a porter being appointed to ride in the leading van of each train.'[28]

After the strike was over the board, at its meeting on September 9th, considered that the 'ready and cheerful manner' in which 'the whole of the guards' carried out these orders in 'the novel and somewhat trying position in which they were unexpectedly placed' merited 'approbation'. It ordered 'that a gratuity be given to each man employed on this extra duty'.

By these means the train services were quickly improved and the strikers were induced to consider any honourable compromise settlement. Mr Carr Glynn must have appreciated the mixed and often unsatisfactory character of his makeshift labour force and on August 21st he asked to see a deputation of the strikers. Eighteen of them met him on the following day and agreed to call off the strike in return for his promise to investigate cases of hardship and to reconsider the classification of the drivers. At a well-attended meeting of the men in the Railway Tavern, Hampstead, that evening, the Chairman, a driver, Jonas Brown, said that 'Mr Glynn's proverbial kindness and liberality to all the officers and servants of the company provided a sufficient guarantee' that he would see justice done to the men. The meeting carried unanimously a resolution in favour of a return to work which also included 'heartfelt acknowledgements' to Mr Glynn for his 'kindness'.

The editor of the principal journal of the railway investors could 'scarcely imagine that this grumbling with bread and cheese to be due to the men themselves'. He believed 'they must have been stirred up to it by some agitating party' who saw 'more advantage to himself in a movement of this kind than it would be of benefit to the men'.[29] This was an interpretation of the origin of strikes which was adopted on numerous subsequent occasions.

The reports of the Company's Locomotive Committee show that the long run objective of the Board to institute economies at the expense of the footplatemen was achieved despite the confidence the men had placed in Mr Glynn. Though the expenses of the department went up in the second half of 1848 'owing to the engagement of a number of new engine drivers in the course of a short time', a year later the Secretary of the committee was pleased to report a reduction of expenses from £13,019 15s 7d to £10,743 1s 8d and gave as the reason for the change that 'more duty had been performed in proportion to the wages paid'.[30] The sectional strike had been a failure.

The settlement of August 21, 1848, did not put an end to Mr Glynn's troubles. There was a further upsurge of discontent on the line in the closing weeks of 1850 when a memorial was sent to Francis Trevithick, the Locomotive Superintendent, from many drivers complaining about the introduction of contracts of three months' duration and about the contradictory instructions the drivers were receiving (a) to oil the working parts of their locomotives well to prevent them from breaking down and (b) to be economical in the use of oil! On Boxing Day the men, once more in the Railway Tavern in the Hampstead Road, after a very long discussion, turned down a proposal for a strike and agreed instead to suggest to the company that a month's notice should be required from either side for the termination of employment. The directors took quick steps to squash the incipient revolt. A statement of a kind known in trade-union circles as 'The Document' was drawn up. It included the following declaration:

'Each man is called upon to state whether he wishes to remain in the service of the company under the existing regulations; if he does, the directors hope to be able to retain him; if not notice must be given to him that his services will not be required after fourteen days.'

When the men went to receive their wages at Camden Station on December 29th, some of them were asked to sign the statement within fifteen minutes, whilst others were allowed half an hour and yet others two days in which to sign. These splitting tactics of the management destroyed the unity of the men and led to the collapse of the resistance.[31]

On the Midland Railway, footplatemen, guards and porters and draymen were affected by the economy drive which followed the period of the railway mania. The wages of the draymen and porters had been reduced by 1s at the end of 1848. When the company proposed to reduce wages again, the porters at Leeds, Derby, Gloucester, Nottingham and many other centres came out on strike on December 22, 1849, rather than accept the proposal that they should be paid a wage of 16s a week. At the same time it was proposed to reduce the guards' wages from 19s to 17s a week, and in consequence, men in the grade also joined the strike. Whilst the guards successfully resisted the attack on their wages and were able to return to work on December 26th on the old conditions since the directors had been unable to find suitable replacements for them, many of the porters went back at the reduced rate of 16s as the directors were rapidly filling vacancies in this grade 'with cheap redundant agricultural labour'. The drivers successfully resisted the proposal that they should do three journeys for the rate of pay formerly received for two, and on December 28th the directors agreed to the men's compromise proposal that the newest driver entrants should be paid firemen's wages during the financial emergency.[32]

On the Eastern Counties Railway, economies took the form of longer trips for the locomotivemen and an increase in the number of wagons per goods train. A martinet Locomotive Superintendent, Mr J. V. Gooch, (not to be confused with the more popular Mr D. Gooch of the Great Western) was appointed to effect economies and tighten up discipline. When, in a train of fifty-six loaded wagons, the cotter in a drawbar broke, the drivers of the two engines pulling the train were fined 2s 6d each though the cost of the cotter was only 3d. Angered by this and other similar punishments a deputation of the drivers saw Mr Ellis, one of the directors, on August 12, 1850, and told him that they had 'unanimously come to the determination to be servants of the board no longer than the 18th day of August, 1850', unless Mr Gooch was 'removed from being the superintendent'. The directors refused to comply with the men's terms and instructed Mr Gooch to accept their notices and find replacements. On August 20, 1850, Mr Gooch wrote to the directors that he had found seventy-seven new drivers and, three days later, Mr E. L. Betts, the Chairman of the company, told the shareholders' meeting that new drivers had been engaged 'from the North and from the South Western Railway' (London and South Western Railway). He wished 'more especially' to thank 'Mr Thornton, the Locomotive Superintendent of the North British line, who put fourteen men off the footplates of his engines' to help them out on the Eastern Counties Railway. A poster black list (see Plate 2, facing page 129) was printed of the drivers and firemen who had gone on strike so that other locomotive superintendents might co-operate in refusing to employ them.[33]

In remarkable contrast with the defeats which were so often the outcome of strikes in the early decades of railway history, was the success of the porters of the Lancashire and Yorkshire Railway and London and North Western Railway in March 1853, and the goods guards, pointsmen and porters of the Midland Railway in March 1854.

With the cost of living rising and railway traffic increasing, the porters at Titlebarne Street Station, Liverpool, struck work on March 18, 1853, for an advance of wages from 18s and 19s to 21s and 22s a week. At first the directors of the company tried to break the strike by bringing in substitute labour from Manchester. However, the newcomers 'proved unequal to their task' and on March 21st, the directors asked the men to return to work at the increased wages. Such a rapidly won success stimulated the goods porters employed by the London and North Western Railway in the area to strike for an increase of their wages from 21s to 24s a week. Although the men were warned that they had broken their contracts and were liable to three months' imprisonment, they stuck to their guns and were able to resume work with improved rates of pay on March 26th. The boom in trade at the time had made these improvements possible.[34]

In March 1854, porters and pointsmen at Sheffield, Masborough and Derby employed by the Midland Railway successfully resisted, by strike action, the attempt of the management to pay them once a fortnight instead of once a week. In Derby the men had canvassed support for their action in the town and their case had 'excited general sympathy', the public subscribing 'a considerable amount of money' to their cause.[35]

How precarious were the gains achieved by sectional action was shown by what happened as soon as trade worsened. In June 1856, the London and North Western Railway reduced the salaries of some of the clerks and the wages of some of the goods porters in the Liverpool area. When 800 men struck, with the intention of getting the wage cuts restored, the company was quickly successful in finding replacements for them. It refused to accept arbitration in the dispute which ended with the men scrambling back to work on the best terms that they could obtain as individuals.[36]

V

In the 1860's the movement for bettering working conditions on the railways covered a wider area and reached a higher level of intensity than ever before. This was partly the response of the railwaymen to the general awakening of labour at this time. In all industrial areas there were increasing protests against the unjust master and servant laws under which a workman who broke his contract was guilty of a criminal offence and could be punished by imprisonment, whilst an employer who committed a similar offence was tried under civil law and was punishable by fine only. Following a conference of trade-union representatives held in Glasgow in 1863, there was set up a 'Committee for the Reform of Master and Servant Laws', branches of which were formed in many parts of the country. Influenced by this agitation, the House of Commons appointed a Select Committee on the Law of Master and Servants in 1866.

In the same year there was an outcry against the trade unions in the newspapers and a demand for a 'tightening up' of the law to limit their powers, following reports of acts of violence against blacklegs committed by some members of small unions in the Sheffield metal trades. The leading trade unionists in the country—those the Webbs styled the Junta—repudiated the violence in Sheffield as quite contrary to their philosophy, and one of their number, Robert Applegarth, General Secretary of the Amalgamated Society of Carpenters and Joiners, suggested a Government inquiry into the incidents, confident that the main stream of the trade-union movement would thereby be vindicated. The Government, however, urged on by the press, opted for a more far-reaching inquiry and appointed a Royal Commission 'to inquire into the Organization and Rules of Trade Unions and other Associations' in February 1867. Many unionists believed that the very right to organize themselves was being challenged.

Working men were also demanding the right to vote in Parliamentary elections—a right which had been withheld from them under the 1832 Reform Act. In this, as in the more purely industrial agitation, railwaymen participated. Among those taking part in a 'Parliamentary Reform' procession to Hyde Park in London on February 11, 1867, were 'a large group of railway servants in their uniforms'.[37]

By the reports of the Board of Trade inspectors on railway accidents the public was being made increasingly aware of the dangers to public safety of excessive hours of labour. One of these inspectors, Colonel Yolland, reported that a contributory cause of a collision which occurred on the London and North Western Railway near Daubhill on January 21, 1865, was the fact that 'the signalman's hours were 5.30 a.m. to frequently after 9.0 p.m.' and that his work included the opening and shutting of gates besides the operation of the signals. Another inspector, Captain Tyler, cited the excessive hours of the signalman at Blackheath box as a contributory cause of the accident in Blackheath Tunnel on December 16, 1864, when eight persons were killed and many others injured. A third inspector, Colonel George Wynne, R.E., declared that 'many accidents occur from men being overworked'.

The editorial board of the *Lancet* played its part in stirring the public conscience. In 1861 it had appointed a Special Commission to inquire into the influence of railway travelling on public health, being mainly concerned at the outset with the welfare of the travelling public. The report of the

Commission revealed, however, that its members had discovered that the most urgent need for reform was in the conditions of employment of railway servants:

'Suppose that men wearied out by long journeys and exhausted by fatigue and want of sleep are ordered, on pain of dismissal, to undertake immediately fresh duties for which they are rendered incapable by previous exhaustion of body and mind. Would it not then appear little short of miraculous if some accident did not result? The worn out engine driver nods, and a hundred lives are in jeopardy; the signalman, dazed by want of sleep, becomes confused, and in a moment the engines are pounding up human beings between them. The acute faculties of the guard are blunted by long unrest, the danger signal passes unnoticed, the brake does not second the efforts of the alarmed engine driver, and next morning there is recorded in the papers another railway accident.'[38]

The Commission noted that cases of signalmen, guards, and engine drivers being employed fifteen hours a day were common, and that the remedy was 'the simple one of fixing a maximum time of work'.

Taking advantage of the more favourable climate of opinion the efforts of the pioneers in railway trade unionism were intensified. In 1860 a Richard Dinnis applied to 'at least six companies' for a 10-hour day on behalf of an Enginemen's and Firemen's Association.[39] But the greatest upsurge of activity came in the years 1866-7 when a number of companies attempted to introduce economies at the workers' expense in order to extricate themselves from their financial difficulties.

In the early months of 1866 the country was in the throes of a major financial crisis, which compelled the Bank of England to raise the bank rate on May 10th to the 'crisis' level of 10 per cent. On the following day the financial house of Overend and Gurney Ltd., failed for over £5 million, bringing to bankruptcy with it the firm of Sir Morton Peto, the biggest railway contractor in the country. Railway companies which had heavy commitments in mileage extensions found it impossible to maintain the old level of dividends, and shareholders of the London, Brighton and South Coast, North Eastern and Great Western Railways, to cite but three instances, were putting pressure on their directors to economize in expenditure.[40]

Economies took the form of longer unpaid overtime and slower promotion for drivers and firemen; the slowing-up of conversion of twelve-hour signal boxes to eight hours; and the failure to employ sufficient guards to reduce overtime (also unpaid) to reasonable limits.

The railwaymen were moved to organized resistance; but, though the movement affected most grades, there was very little co-ordination between the grades. The engine drivers and firemen, the guards, signalmen, and switchmen, and the clerks each formed their own union and presented their demands separately to the boards of directors of the principal companies. The railway clerks were the first to organize. At a meeting held in the St Marylebone Institute in Portman Square, London, on October 11, 1865, a Railway Clerks Association was formed and a committee appointed to compose a list of demands to present to the directors of the principal companies; but there were very few provincial representatives present at the meeting, and the new union failed to recruit new members outside London.[41] The directors were thus able to ignore the clerks' demands with impunity, and nothing more was heard of the union during the important months which followed.

At a 'numerously attended' meeting of guards, signalmen, and switchmen employed on lines serving the metropolis, held in Westbourne Road, Paddington, on January 20, 1866, the Railway Guards, Signalmen and Switchmen's Society of the United Kingdom was formed. Memorials were sent to the traffic managers of the various main-line companies demanding an eight-hour day and wages of 30s a week for signalmen in junction boxes, with 26s a week for straight-road men. None of the companies' traffic managers would, however, recognize the society for purposes of wage bargaining. Nevertheless, the movement must have had some effect, for on three of the leading metropolitan lines increases ranging from 1s to 3s a week were granted to signalmen and guards.[42]

It was now the turn of the engine drivers, whose organization was first started by men employed at New Cross in April 1866. The Engine Drivers and Firemen's United Society, which survived for just over a year, at one time claimed a membership of 15,000 (distributed in sixty-four branches throughout the kingdom), and capital reserves of £50,000, though doubt has been thrown on these figures. It produced its own journal, *The Train*, from its headquarters at 31 Brydges Street, Strand, London, and its president and secretary were Messrs J. Thompson and J. O. Putley.[43] A conference attended by delegates from every important railway in England was held in London in November 1866, when a national programme of demands was agreed. Branches were to petition their directors for a ten-hour day, the payment of overtime, Sunday work to be paid at time and a half, a 150-mile daily maximum for main line drivers, and a 120-mile maximum for those working local lines. Increases of pay were to be negotiated on a company basis.[44]

The directors of the companies were torn between a desire to avoid the heavier working expenses which the acceptance of the men's demands would bring, and a concern that the refusal of those demands might lead to a strike which would cause immediate losses.[45] In the case of the Midland, Great Northern, London and South Western, Great Western and London and North Western Railways the directors decided that the wisest course was to meet the demands of the men,[46] but in the case of the

Brighton line and the North Eastern the extravagant expansionist policy of the preceding months had brought financial difficulties which made more pressing the shareholders' demands for long-term economies and more difficult the recognition of the men's claim. Most of the Scottish companies rejected outright the claims of the union to represent the men.[47]

The Brighton had in 1866 spent nearly £2 million on branch lines and extensions, many of them of poor earning capacity, and in consequence the dividends had fallen from 5¾ per cent in 1865 to 4 per cent in 1866. An influential body of the shareholders was demanding drastic economies in expenditure.[48] Thus when the directors of the company replied to the demands of the union early in March, though they indicated willingness to concede time-and-a-half rates for Sunday duty, they rejected the proposal for a 10-hour day. Instead they proposed a 60-hour week, with overtime at the 8-hour day rate. They also rejected the engine drivers' demand for automatic wage increases at regular monthly intervals. When they learned that the Board were not prepared to compromise on these points the men handed in notices on March 13th to take effect from the 25th of the month. Justifying their resistance to the proposal for the 60-hour week the men, through the columns of *The Times*, declared:

'Under a system of working 60 hours a week they might have to work 15 hours one day and only 5 the next, or it might be possible to keep them on for 20 hours one day, and allow them to be off the next. The detriment to themselves and the risk to the public which were caused by that one day's overwork could not be compensated by the abstinence from labour on the succeeding day.'[49]

On the morning of Monday, March 25th, only a handful of drivers and firemen reported for duty at the depots of the Brighton line. That morning virtually all traffic was stopped between London and the coast towns served by the company. Traffic to and from the Crystal Palace was almost entirely suspended. But the strike was shortlived. All the 400 men who had struck on the Monday were back at work by Wednesday evening. The directors had held an emergency meeting on the Tuesday morning. They telegraphed to managers of other lines asking for engine drivers, but found that very few could be spared. They offered a 'gratuity' of 2 guineas to each driver and 1 guinea to each fireman who stayed on duty, and offered to pay the maximum rates of 7s 6d and 4s 6d a day to any blackleg drivers or firemen who could be persuaded to join the service of the company. These measures were combined with recruitment of men in the managerial grades to run a skeleton service, and an offer to the old hands that if they returned to work before Thursday, March 28th, they would be reinstated, and the directors would promise an annual review of pay of drivers and firemen.[50] Since it was the reluctance of foremen (acting under orders) in the past to promote drivers as rapidly as was warranted, the promise of some reform in procedure, combined with the threat to their livelihood if they stayed out, served to bring the men back to work without a guarantee of a 10-hour day. The strike would undoubtedly have been more successful had other grades besides the drivers and firemen been organized.

Similar reasons help to explain the failure to reach an amicable settlement on the North Eastern, where the most prolonged and bitter strike in the history of the British railways till that time was fought out. The Chairman of the company admitted, when addressing the shareholders at the February meeting in 1867, that when the West Hartlepools line was taken over they had to pay 'nearly half a million pounds from the summer of 1865 to the winter of 1866' and that owing to the changed conditions of the money market 'they had a large amount of money to raise during a time when money was unusually dear'. Consequently dividends of all the constituent companies in the North Eastern Railway group had had to be reduced. As was the case on the Brighton line, shareholders were wanting to know why profits had fallen and were seeking economies.[51]

The drivers and firemen on the North Eastern had been working a basic 12-hour day with frequent unpaid overtime. A deputation of drivers and firemen had met the directors on February 15th, when 'the directors had no hesitation in refusing to accede to the men's demands'.[52]

Consequently, after further exchange of views, 1,042 men gave a month's notice on March 23, 1867. The board, alarmed at these developments, held further discussions with the men, promising a 10-hour day and (so the men understood) a paid shed day once a week. This led the men to withdraw their notices on March 28th. On April 9th, however, when the men at Darlington attempted to claim their shed day this was refused, boys being employed to do the cleaning, at much lower wages than the drivers and firemen would have been paid.[53] The men immediately left work.

A committee of the Darlington engine drivers stated, in explanation of their action:

'We were content to accept the promise of a 10-hour day, and 7s pay with a shed day once a week, leaving the Sunday work and overtime as before. But although these were promised us, we soon found we could place no reliance on it, and were ultimately told they would pay us what they liked and no more.'[54]

There is no doubt that the reason why by April 11th a total of about 1,050 men throughout the North Eastern system had struck work, and the strike was virtually complete, was not simply the resentment of the Darlington men at losing their shed day, but also general resentment that the concessions made on the North Eastern Railway were less than those elsewhere, together with a widespread lack of trust in the word of the directors.

On the day after the strike the Yorkshire sea-coast towns, except Scarborough and Whitby (where there was a skeleton service), had no trains, but the strike was less complete than that on the Brighton line a few weeks earlier. The directors determined not to compromise with the men, but to smash the strike by every available means. They recruited drivers from the Midland, Great Northern, Lancashire and Yorkshire, and London and North Western Railways, and published circulars offering permanent employment at maximum pay to any who would serve as drivers and firemen, provided they did not belong to any union.[55] Sums of £50, £25 and £2 were sent by shareholders to the directors for the benefit of non-striking enginemen. By April 21st the directors announced that the number of applicants for the posts of engine drivers and firemen had been more than enough to fill the vacancies, though no comment was made on the qualifications of the men taken on. At the instigation of the company, the leaders of the strike at Darlington, York, Leeds, and elsewhere were brought before the magistrates and charged with breach of contract on the grounds that they had left their employment without giving the stipulated one month's notice.[56]

All these measures proved effective in breaking the strike, for by April 25th goods services were back to normal, and by the end of the month a full passenger service was in operation.

By comparison, the efforts of the officers and rank and file of the Engine Drivers and Firemen's United Society to support the strikers were of no avail to secure the acceptance of their demands or their reinstatement. A generous attempt was made to support their fellow drivers in the North, the following circular being sent out to all members on April 17th:

'In order to sustain the North Eastern men during their present struggle, the Central Committee have decided that a general weekly levy be made of 3s upon each driver, and 2s upon each fireman. You will, therefore, please call a meeting of your branch immediately, and take steps to carry the resolution of the central committee into effect.

J. Osborne Putley,
General Secretary.'[57]

Although a delegate meeting of over 1,000 men held at Derby on April 28th determined 'pretty unanimously' in favour of recommending to the executive the calling of a general strike, at a meeting held in Leeds the same evening the majority were opposed to extending the strike. In both cases it was agreed to defer a final decision until a special delegate meeting was held in London on April 30th. At this meeting a mood of caution prevailed—fatal to the chances of success of the men on the North Eastern. It was decided:

'That the committee deem it inadvisable, at the present stage of the contest, to ask the men on other lines to withdraw from their employment.'[58]

In the meantime most of the strikers were finding it virtually impossible to be reinstated. It was estimated that no more than twenty-five of the 1,050 who came out were taken back into service.[59] In York only four out of the 100 who struck were taken back, and then only on condition of their renouncing trade-union membership.[60] On May 8th, *The Times* correspondent in York reported that 'many of the old hands are in a miserable plight'. In the circumstances the cases against the strikers arrested in York, Darlington, Leeds and Carlisle were eventually dropped, 'more especially as most of them will be severe sufferers from the loss of their employment'.[61]

What must surely rank as one of the humblest and most pathetic petitions ever presented by a group of railwaymen was signed on June 19, 1867. Headed 'To the honourable board of directors of the Stockton and Darlington Section of the North Eastern Railway' it read:

'We pray you to entertain the humble petition of your humble servants the engine drivers and firemen lately on your section. We have surrendered ourselves to William Bouch, esquire, and are now at his disposal. We had no quarrel with our employers; the course we took was to support the North Eastern men. We were betrayed into a false position and have acknowledged our error already. There were circumstances in the case we were not made acquainted with. We repent of what we have done and promise the act shall never be repeated. "To err is human, to forgive is divine." We cast ourselves entirely on thy mercy. Hoping you will manifest towards us a true chivalrous spirit and have compassion on a fallen foe. And in proportion to your magnanimity, benevolence and humanity on the present occasion, will be our devotion, fidelity and obedience in the future. We petition you, gentlemen, to be so kind, so forgiving and condescending as to pay the money standing to our account. You will be aware, gentlemen, that most of the money was earned in the storm and tempest, whilst exposed to the howling wind and pelting snow.

'P.S. Some of the families are now on the point of starvation. We hope, gentlemen, you will favour us with the money standing to our account. It is now sixteen weeks since we received any from you. And your humble servants will ever pray, etc.'[62]

The directors, however, did not consider it wise to give the men an opportunity to show their 'devotion, fidelity and obedience' in the future. The men's places had been filled.

With the failure of the strike on the North Eastern and the exhaustion of its funds through the issue of strike pay, the despair and despondency of the men, the Engine Drivers and Firemen's United Society ceased to function. From the end of May 1867, there are no further reports of its activities. The campaign to shorten intolerably long hours of labour had not been a complete failure. The advances made in bargaining with some of the companies were retained. But the attempt to form a permanent nation-wide union had failed because there was no serious attempt to co-ordinate the demands of the different grades. The signalmen and guards and the drivers and firemen memorialized their directors at different times, and although the porters of the London and North Western Railway at Liverpool petitioned and struck for higher wages in April 1866, this was purely a local movement without the backing of a national union.

In contrast with the divisions and divided loyalties of the men, the directors of the companies helped each other to stamp out the movement. An example of this was the assistance given to the North Eastern management from the other main line companies in the North of England. The absence of any strike movement in Scotland was in part due to the prompt and united action of the directors of the North British, Glasgow and South Western, and Caledonian Railways, who published a joint statement early in September 1866:

'It having been reported to the directors of several railway companies in Scotland that certain meetings have been held, and that others are in contemplation, for the express purpose "of attainment of our (railway servants) rights, etc.", the directors hereby give notice to the engine drivers, firemen and passenger and goods guards, passenger and goods porters, and pointsmen, that while they, with their several officers, are most desirous of meeting the legitimate demands of their employees, they will most firmly withstand all dictation by the men; and they give notice that any attempt at combination by the respective employees, will be met by the directors in such a manner as may to them seem fit. The directors take this opportunity of cautioning the men in their employ against combination, or joining any union for the avowed purpose of dictating to their employers.

THOMAS K. ROWBOTHAM, General Manager,
North British Railway Company.
W. JOHNSTONE, General Manager,
Glasgow and South Western Railway Company.
C. JOHNSTONE, General Manager,
Caledonian Railway Company.'[63]

Despite the failure to establish an enduring trade union of railwaymen at this stage, the struggles of the years 1865–7 were not without their positive results. By the enactment of the Second Reform Bill in 1867 many railwaymen, among others of the artisan class, gained the right to vote in Parliamentary elections and were thus able more effectively to press for legislative interference on their behalf. Through press reports the public had been made aware of the arduous working conditions of those whose employment was on the railways. Industrially the experience had been valuable, for the men had learned that when sufficiently well organized they could compel attention to their demands. It was now appreciated that when each grade in the service acted independently of the others it could be defeated piecemeal by the enlistment of other grades to break the strike; if they acted together they might succeed. Hence when the railwaymen began once more to organize themselves in December 1871, they formed a union embracing all grades of the service—the Amalgamated Society of Railway Servants.

NOTES

1. *Railway Times*, November 14, 1840.
2. Select Committee on Railways, P.P. 1839, Vol. X, Q. 3210.
3. Sir J. Clapham, *An Economic History of Modern Britain*, Vol. I, p. 550.
4. Many of the details of conditions of service on the railways between 1830 and 1870 are taken from an unpublished University of London Ph.D Thesis 'Railway Labour 1830–1870', written by P. W. Kingsford, to whom I am indebted for permission to quote.
5. L.N.W.R. Locomotive Committee Minute 1108, May 6, 1851.
6. *The Times*, July 31, 1862.
7. Select Committee on Railway Servants Hours of Labour 1890, P.P.. 1890–1, Vol. XVI, Evidence of Messrs Findlay, Lambert and Conacher. Qs. 5488, 5816, 6949.
8. I am greatly indebted to Mr Fowkes of the British Transport Commission Historical Archives at York for letting me examine numerous petitions of railwaymen and for permission to quote from them.
9. Second Report, Select Committee on Railways, P.P. 1839, Vol. X. Qs. 3196, 3211, 4540.
10. Stockton and Darlington Railway: Rules and Regulations to be observed by workmen at New Shildon, August 17, 1833. Ditto Darlington, January 1854.
11. P. W. Kingsford, *Railway Labour 1830–70*, p. 44.
12. Letter from the Secretary of the L.N.W.R. to Charles Stewart, Esq., one of the Directors, dated August 6, 1857. British Transport Commission Archives.
13. L.N.W.R. Board Minutes, June 20, 1839.
14. Second Report, Select Committee on Railways, P.P. 1839, Vol. X, p. 138.
15. Railway Regulation Act, 1840, Regulation of Railways Act, 1842, P.P. 1840 III, p. 427, 1841, III, p. 169.
16. G. Alcock, *Fifty Years of Railway Trade Unionism*, p. 17.
17. Hansard, Parliamentary Debates 1840, Vol. 158, Col. 924.
18. British Transport Commission Historical Archives, York. S.A.D. 8/148/1.
19. Liverpool and Manchester Railway Board Minutes, February 8, 15, 22, 1836. *The Times*, July 29, 1836.
20. London and Birmingham Railway Return of Gratuities to enginemen and firemen for the half year ending December 1842.

21. *The Times*, June 4, 1838.
22. *The Times*, August 4, 1838.
23. M. Robbins, 'The North Midland Railway and its enginemen 1842–3', *Journal of Transport History*, Vol. IV, Number 3, May 1860.
24. *The Times*, November 4, 1845.
25. *Herapath's Railway Journal*, August 12, 1848, pp. 819, 833.
26. *The Times*, August 8–24, 1848; Hansard, Parliamentary Debates, 1848.
27. L.N.W.R. General Locomotive Committee Report, August 9, 1848.
28. *The Times*, August 10, 1848.
29. *Herapath*, August 5, 1848.
30. L.N.W.R. Reports of Locomotive Committee meetings, January 2, 1849, and January 8, 1850.
31. *The Times*, December 23–30, 1850.
32. *The Times*, December 22, 1849; January 2, 1850.
33. *Herapath*, August 24, 1850, p. 816; *The Times*, August 17–22, 1850.
34. *The Times*, March 24, 25 and 28, 1853.
35. *The Times*, March 20, April 1 and 4, 1854.
36. *The Times*, June 19–21 and 26, 1856.
37. S. Maccoby, *English Radicalism*, 1852–86, p. 94.
38. *Lancet*, January 4, 1862.
39. P. W. Kingsford, *Railway Labour 1830–70*, pp. 137–8. The companies were the G.W.R., M.R., L.S.W.R., L.N.W.R., L.B.S.C. and L. and Y.R.
40. *The Times*, March 29, 1867.
41. *Beehive*, October 14, 1865.
42. *Beehive*, January 27, 1866.
43. See P. W. Kingsford, 'Labour Relations on the Railways, 1835–76', *Journal of Transport History*, I (1953–4), p. 69; *The Times*, March 28, 1867.
44. *Darlington and Stockton Times*, April 20, 1867.
45. The strike on the N.E.R. in 1867 is estimated to have cost that company £80,000. G. Alcock, *Fifty Years of Railway Trade Unionism*, p. 28.
46. *Yorkshire Post*, April 8, 1867; *Beehive*, April 20, 1867; *The Times*, March 30, 1867.
47. *Beehive*, September 15, 1866.
48. *Herapath*, May 28, 1867, p. 537; January 20, 1866, p. 67; February 9, 1867, p. 127; May 11, 1867, p. 478.
49. *The Times*, March 27, 1867.
50. *Ibid.*
51. *Herapath*, February 23, 1867, p. 193; August 3, 1867, p. 772; August 4, 1866, p. 853.
52. *The Times*, April 22, 1867.
53. *Darlington and Stockton Times*, April 20, 1867.
54. *The Times*, April 15, 1867.
55. *The Times*, April 17, 1867; *Newcastle Weekly Chronicle*, April 27, 1867; *Yorkshire Post*, April 24, 1867.
56. *The Times*, April 16, 1867.
57. *The Times*, April 17, 1867.
58. *The Times*, May 1, 1867.
59. *The Times*, May 23, 1867.
60. *Yorkshire Post*, April 24, 1867.
61. *The Times*, April 26, 1867.
62. Stockton and Darlington Railway: Humble Petition from Engine Drivers and Firemen, June 19, 1867.
63. *Beehive*, September 15, 1866.

CHAPTER II

THE FOUNDATION OF THE A.S.R.S.

'The worst of it is he can't buy a clear head for a muddled one with overtime sixpences. He can't rub his sleepy eyes with them and make them wide awake.' From an article by James Greenwood *in the* Daily Telegraph, *December 26, 1871, commenting on the condition of a Nine Elms engine driver who had completed 654 hours' work in the previous six weeks.*

'We are not among those who would desire to stimulate or befriend trade combinations or strikes, but we confess that a great part of the excessive labour exacted from railway servants might have been avoided or mitigated if railway servants, like other skilled workmen, had known how to combine for the purpose of striking a bargain with their employers.' From a leading article in The Times, *September 15, 1871.*

I

THERE could be no mistaking the fact that the trade of the country was booming. The Chancellor of the Exchequer said so. In his budget speech on April 20, 1871, he spoke of the 'vitality, soundness and elasticity' of the nation's finances and claimed that the 'commercial prosperity' of the country rested on 'solid foundations'. The chairmen of the railway companies were saying so; and they had every reason for their optimism. Between 1870 and 1871 receipts from goods traffic on the railways rose by 10 per cent and receipts from passenger traffic by over 10 per cent. In the same period the average interest on the total capital of the railway companies rose from 4·19 per cent to 4·43 per cent.[1]

One of the railway chairmen who expressed satisfaction with the trend of business was Mr W. P. Price, M.P., of the Midland Railway. In announcing a dividend of 6¾ per cent to a meeting of the company's shareholders on February 14, 1871, he declared that anyone who gave the accounts 'a fair and impartial consideration' would reach the conclusion that prospects were 'unusually bright'.[2]

46

Although at another shareholders' meeting another, more famous, chairman, Sir E. Watkin, reminded his hearers that it was upon 'that great body of railway servants' that they depended for their dividends,[3] the prosperity of the country and the railway companies brought no bright prospects for the railwaymen. Quite the contrary, in fact. The railway companies cleared the increased volume of traffic mainly by working their existing labour force harder and for longer hours, rather than by increasing the number of men they employed. It was a situation fully understood by the men attending the first general delegate meeting of the A.S.R.S. who wrote in their report that 'the men were overworked to such an extent as to destroy their own comfort and endanger the safety of the public'.

It was on Mr Price's railway, the Midland, that the traffic congestion, with consequent overworking of the staff, was particularly severe in 1870 and 1871. The company employed 2,200 men in the town of Derby alone and it was some of these men who decided to write to their M.P., Mr M. T. Bass, the brewer, to ask him to intervene on their behalf. It was a shrewd decision. Mr Bass had already shown his concern for the welfare of his working-class constituents by providing the money for the construction of public baths in the town and he was known to be a man who did not easily abandon any cause once he was convinced that it was just. Moreover, he was perhaps the most important single customer of the Midland Railway which carried most of the 500,000 Bass barrels and hauled most of the 69,654 Bass railway trucks at a cost to the brewery of over £135,000 annually.[4] The men felt that if Mr Bass asked questions the directors of the railway were bound at least to give them respectful attention.

Mr Bass decided to give the railwaymen his support. At the very same shareholders' meeting at which Mr Price had spoken so optimistically about the 'unusually bright' prospects of the Midland Railway he raised, on behalf of 300 railwaymen who had approached him, the question of the 'excessive labour' imposed on the pointsmen who were on duty twelve and sometimes fifteen hours a day. Engine drivers and guards, he said ' . . . were in an even worse position', the former complaining of 'being kept on their engines for 17, 18, and 19 hours without intermission'. The men were thus rendered incapable of performing their responsible duties in a manner which should ensure the safety of the public. He claimed that these were matters which in the interest of the company demanded 'earnest attention'.

The manager of the company replied that the men had 'nothing whatever to complain of'. It was an answer which satisfied neither the men nor Mr Bass who raised the subject again in a debate on the second reading of the Railway Companies' Bill in the House of Commons on March 15, 1871. He declared that there were thirty or forty drivers of the Midland Railway who, during the previous two months, had worked 'nearly double the time usually assigned to them'. Their normal working day was 10 hours, but they were averaging 19½ hours and in one instance a driver had not left his engine for 29½ hours. The facts could not be doubted for they were 'taken from the books of the company'. The companies disclosed how many persons were killed in accidents involving passenger trains, but he knew that there were hundreds of people killed by accidents to goods trains and that 'the widows and children of the unfortunate victims were left without a penny compensation'.

When Mr Price, the Chairman of the Midland Railway, rose at the end of the debate to defend his company and said that there was 'not a shadow of foundation for the charge' Mr Bass had made, other members laughed. On June 28, 1871, Mr Bass informed the House that 'he had desired his Hon. Friend to point out a single point in which he was inaccurate and his Hon. Friend informed him that he could not'.[5]

The argument between Mr Price and Mr Bass continued in the correspondence columns of The Times. The publication by Mr Bass of numerous examples of excessive overtime working compelled the Midland Chairman to send in his replies, though it was evident that he continued his debate with considerable reluctance. He wrote that he 'doubted the expediency or advantage of public discussion on so delicate a subject as that of the relations between the employers of labour and their servants treated otherwise than as a purely abstract question', and that in any case, he agreed with Adam Smith that all wages were 'naturally regulated' by circumstances.[6] The Times took the side of Mr Bass. It was convinced that railway servants were kept at work too long and that they were insufficiently paid.

The editor of The Times had undoubtedly been influenced to this opinion by the poor record of railway companies in respect of accident prevention in the previous year. The number of accidents reported on in 1870 had been 57 per cent above, and the proportions of passenger killed to the number of journeys made 200 per cent above, the average of the five preceding years. Captain Tyler, an inspector who presented a special report to the Board of Trade on the subject, found that one of the causes of the alarming accident rate was the overworking of the men. He found 'inexcusable' the regular or periodic employment of signalmen for 18, 25 or even 37 hours at a stretch.[7]

Mr Bass had influential support from another quarter—the pages of the Lancet, whose editor bluntly stated that railway companies that overworked their servants were, in fact, 'asking for accidents' and should be made to pay for them when they occurred. The 'average daily labour' of a faulty signalman was 'as important if not more important than the number of hours he had been on duty at the particular moment an accident occurred, since a person would be liable to break down at any time, without it being necessary that he should be specially exhausted at the moment when he did so'.[8]

II

Apart from the thousands of railwaymen who must have heard of these press reports and comments with great interest, three men, at least, were sufficiently concerned to write to Mr Bass about it.

The first of these was John Graham, a pointsman employed by the Midland Railway at Derby. Signing himself 'A railway employee', he wrote to the *Derby Mercury* on March 22, 1871—within a week of Mr Bass's intervention in the Commons—expressing the great satisfaction of railwaymen that at last someone had intervened on their behalf, and pointing out that although the Midland Railway had claimed that no one had been killed on the company's lines in the previous year, he knew of five railwaymen killed from Derby alone during that time. After Mr Bass, addressing a local gathering of the Amalgamated Society of Engineers, had spoken of the hardships of railwaymen, Mr Graham, thinking that Mr Bass had been under the impression that he was addressing railwaymen, wrote to him to thank him for his words whilst at the same time pointing out his 'mistake'; Mr Bass replied that he had been under no misapprehension as to the character of the meeting. In this unusual way a long correspondence and useful friendship was initiated.

A second man to write to Mr Bass was the Rev. W. Griffith, a radical minister of Eccleston, who wrote offering help in any campaign for reducing the hours of labour of railwaymen. He chaired many meetings subsequently held in Derby and other midland towns.

Charles Bassett Vincent, the third correspondent, a clerk employed in the Railway Clearing House in London, was the only one of the three who had had any previous experience of union work amongst railwaymen. In his one-sided account of the origins of railway trade unionism—*An Authentic History of Railway Trade Unionism*—published in 1902, he claimed that in the period of agitation of the years 1865–6 he had helped to form a Railway Working Men's Provident Benefit Society whose objects were to assist members out of employment, to defend them at law and to provide accident benefits. He at the same time contributed a series of articles on overwork on the railways to the Cassell's publication *The Working Man*.[9] He was an eloquent speaker who could attract larger audiences than any other leader of the railwaymen in the early years of the union and he possessed an attractive manner. On the other hand, according to Alcock, 'he lacked initiative, had no wide vision, was self-conscious, and was weak when he should have been strong'. It must have been his reputation as a writer and speaker which influenced the Rev. Griffith and John Graham to suggest to Bass that he should be employed as Bass's agent to address meetings of the men with a view to the formation of a trade union.

Already by July 1871, Vincent was employed full time by Bass, making a tour of inquiry on hundreds of miles of line, on the Midland, London and North Western and the North Eastern Railways, writing letters to *The Times* and organizing meetings.[10] Realizing the immensity of his task, in the autumn of that year he suggested to his employer that a journalist friend of his, James Greenwood, a feature writer of the *Daily Telegraph*, might also be employed to report on working conditions on the railways. The suggestion was taken up, and in October and November, Greenwood, at Mr Bass's expense, travelled nearly a thousand miles on British railways finding out, first hand, details of the working life of the different grades employed. His articles published in the *Daily Telegraph* on December 4, 11, 19 and 28, 1871, whilst being factually accurate, were imbued with compassion on behalf of the unorganized and exploited railway workers.

Perhaps the most moving of his accounts was that entitled 'The Railway Guard' which appeared on December 19th. In it he wrote that it was quite 'the ordinary and common thing' for a guard to be on duty 90 hours in the week and it was 'by no means rare' for him to do 100 hours. Occasionally he was expected to do even 110 or 120 hours work a week. A guard at Leeds told him that one day after he had completed 18 hours' work he was told to take a train to London.

'The tired and sleepy man went to the superintendent and asked to be informed how many hours a day he was expected to work.

'"That's our business", was the official answer, "you've got 24 hours in a day like every other man, and they are all ours if we want you to work them. ..." '

When Greenwood questioned why the man did not complain to the General Manager, the guard replied:

'"That's been done, sir, and I'll tell you how it has worked. As soon as the words are out of your mouth: 'If you please I have come to complain', you are cut short with the question, 'Have you brought your clothes with you?' ... That means your private clothes, which a man would naturally require if he were called on to give up the company's livery on the spot. Well, what can a poor man do with a hint like that flung at him? He's shut up, sir, and only too glad to get out of the office with no more damage than when he entered it." '

For the information of readers who were about to make a customary Christmastide visit to relatives or friends, Greenwood told the story of a guard who went to work at 6.35 p.m. on December 23, 1870, and ended his spell of duty at 2.0 p.m. on December 25th. On December 24th he was found asleep in his brake van standing up by the wheel. There being no relief guard available a porter was sent along to 'cheer him up' and 'nudge' him when he 'dropped off'. Greenwood's comment on this man's case was:

'With all the respect for the kindly admonition contained in the Christmas carol "Let nothing you dismay", I should like to know how the Christmas traveller is to escape the disagreeable sensation now that he is made alive to the possibility that the individual who controls the brake, and on whom the safety of the whole train in great measure depends, may be gaping leaden-eyed and hanging in a state of semi-sensibility over his wheel, only kept from dropping down on to the floor by a friendly "nudging" on the part of the man expressly provided to keep him awake.'

It is conceivable that the pioneers of 1871 might have been as unsuccessful in their efforts to establish a lasting organization as their predecessors were in 1866, had it not been for the help received from influential members of the public. Greenwood's articles were of great value in helping to create an informed public opinion favourable to the foundation of a railwaymen's trade union.

At the same time it is important not to minimize the importance of developments within the labour movement at this time. Starting in Sunderland and on Tyneside, the Nine Hour Day agitation, which had been important in the early 1860's, was renewed early in June 1871. The railwaymen were asked to lend their support to the efforts of the shipwrights and engineers. In Derby the railwaymen played a big part in the formation of a Committee of the Nine Hours League in the town. Whilst supporting the general claim for a 9-hour day their efforts were concentrated on gaining its introduction on the railways. At a meeting held in the town on October 1, 1871, hundreds of railwaymen signed a petition to the Midland Railway directors in favour of a 9-hour working day. When the directors later replied that they could not recognize as valid a petition signed outside the company's premises, the men met in the large mess room of the station and signed a fresh petition there. On the afternoon of Saturday, November 4th, a huge but orderly procession led by five bands was organized. Two huge models of clocks were borne aloft. On one side the hands pointed to 6.0 a.m. and on the other to 5.0 p.m. (presumably two hours were to be allowed for meals). The movement achieved a well deserved success when the directors announced that they would introduce the 9-hour day in the railway workshops from January 1, 1872.[11]

After a mass meeting of 2,000 employees of the London and North Western Railway was held at Crewe and a petition was presented, the directors of that company fell into line with their contemporaries on the Midland and agreed to the introduction of the 9-hour day in the Crewe workshops from January 1, 1872.[12] The Great Northern Railway made similar concessions to workshop men employed at Doncaster.[13]

In the remaining weeks of 1871, Vincent addressed numerous enthusiastic meetings of railwaymen in Leeds, Liverpool, Mansfield, Manchester, Bolton, Wolverhampton, Taunton, Stratford and many other places. At first no attempt was made to establish a trade union; the meetings concentrated on the demands for an improvement in wages and a reduction in working hours. On November 5th, however, a great meeting of 700 delegates from the London and North Western Railway, Lancashire and Yorkshire, and Manchester, Sheffield and Lincolnshire Railways was held in the Free Trade Hall, Manchester. Although it was reported that, with the exception of Vincent, 'each speaker did not give his name for fear of consequences to himself' the meeting carried unanimously a demand for a general advance of wages of 2s 6d a week and the limitation of hours to ten per day. The meeting then went on to consider the formation of a union, being encouraged by the letter which Vincent had received from Mr Bass who promised full support for the movement and a gift of £100 for the initial expenses. But no definite decision was reached in favour of the setting up of a union, it being decided to await the reply of the directors of the companies to the memorial for improved working conditions.[14]

At a meeting of delegates from all grades serving the five railway companies linked to Leeds, held in the People's Hall, Holbeck, Leeds, on November 26th, rules for a trade union of railwaymen which had been drafted by a committee previously, were adopted, and 200 men signed their names as wishing to join. This is the first meeting that can be traced as having made the definite decision to form a railwaymen's union in 1871.

III

In the meantime the London men had not been idle. Early in November a committee had been formed and had drafted rules for a society. Small handbills measuring 4 inches by 2 were surreptitiously circulated, as it was thought desirable to keep the bills as small as possible in order to bring less embarrassment to their recipients and to attract less attention from the authorities. The message on the bills read:

'A meeting will be held at the Winchester Arms, Southwark Street, on Sunday, December 3rd, to further the objects of securing ten hours for a day's labour, payment for Sunday duty, and weekly payment of wages. Chair to be taken at 6 o'clock. Please inform your mates and solicit them to attend.'

The handbills served their purpose well. When Mr Pritchard, a veteran of the campaigns of 1865–6, took the chair at 6 o'clock that Sunday evening he faced an audience of 200 men. The room was packed to capacity. The Chairman explained that the purpose of the meeting was to launch a new Society, the Amalgamated Society of Railway Servants, and to approve the rules. He then called for brief statements from men employed on the different lines serving London. A guard employed on the Brighton line said that in the past six weeks his average working week had been 85 hours. An engine driver, whose minimum hours were 12 per day, had worked 19 hours on both the Monday and Wednesday of the previous week. A signalman, who worked 102 hours 20 minutes in the week commencing November 19th, had been paid his basic wage of 25s and had received nothing for the 30 hours overtime worked. A South Eastern Railway porter said that for working 12½ hours a day for 365 days a year he was paid at the rate of 16s a week. Vincent then addressed the meeting at considerable length, promising the men the full support of Mr Bass. Mr George Chapman, who was announced as the Honorary Secretary of the Amalgamated Society of Railway Servants, read out the objects of the union which were:

'To promote a good and fair understanding between employers and employed; to prevent strikes; to protect and defend members against injustice; to secure ten hours for a fair day's labour and one day's extra pay for eight hours overtime; the payment of the same rate for Sundays; to afford a ready means by arbitration or otherwise for the settlement of disputes; for granting temporary assistance to its members, and to provide legal assistance when necessary; to make special grants to members who desired to emigrate, and to found a superannuation fund for old and disabled members.'

After enthusiastically endorsing the objects of the union the meeting proceeded to discuss the proposed rules, most of which were accepted as drafted, though a few were referred back to the executive committee for modification. The determination of the founders of the union to maintain a high standard of behaviour and a strong sense of responsibility among members was revealed in Rule 12:

'Any member going on duty in a state of intoxication or becoming so whilst in the discharge of his duty shall be reported to the society and fined a sum not exceeding 20s and deprived of all benefits from the society for any period not exceeding three months.'[15]

A further densely crowded meeting of London railwaymen organized by Robert Whitmore of Battersea, was held on the evening of December 8, 1871, at the Lambeth Baths, Westminster Bridge Road. The chair was occupied by the Rev. G. M. Murphy, a well-known temperance advocate, who had the task of reading two letters of apology for absence—one from

Mr Bass and the other from the Archbishop of Canterbury. Some might consider it just as well that Mr Bass was not able to attend, as explosive results can be imagined from a meeting at which a leading brewer shares the platform with a leading temperance advocate; but Mr Bass wrote that he was disappointed not to be present and that although appearances might seem to be against him he 'would do his utmost to destroy intemperance in any shape'.[16] The Archbishop's Commissary wrote as follows:

'The Archbishop of Canterbury will not be able to avail himself of your invitation to be present at the lecture which is to be given by Mr Vincent on December 8th at the Lambeth Baths. His Grace feels with you that it is very desirable that you should all have one day's rest in seven and also that as far as is practicable that day should be Sunday. The Archbishop regrets to find from your letter that in your judgement, according to present arrangements, railway servants are often kept too long at work and that they think their wages are not always sufficient to save them from temptation to be dishonest.

Believe me to be,

Faithfully yours,

C. W. SANDFORD.'

A resolution to petition the various railway companies with lines terminating in London, on behalf of a 10-hour day for all except signalmen and watchmen (who were to have eight), the payment of overtime and Sunday duty, and the raising of porters' and platelayers' wages to a pound a week and the wages of others 'in proportion', was carried with acclamation. When the Chairman interrupted the discussion to read a telegram stating that the Prince of Wales (later Edward VII) was seriously ill, the men stood bare-headed and sang the first verse of the National Anthem.[17]

IV

By the early weeks of 1872 railwaymen were flocking into the union in hundreds each day and dozens of branches were being formed. Given clear and undisputed leadership the union could have forged ahead very rapidly. That this did not happen was due to the jealousy between London and the provinces and the individual jealousies of prominent leaders of the movement.

Branches were most numerous in the London area and it was among their membership that the demand was strongest to establish the union on a firm legal foundation at the earliest moment. As early as November 28, 1871, a small executive committee of London men had been formed and had quickly organized the inaugural meeting on December 3rd. At a meeting called by this committee and held at the General Moore, Stewart's

Lane, Battersea, on Thursday, December 28th, it was decided that George Chapman, a mechanic at the Woolwich Arsenal, who had participated in the 1865-6 movement, organizing the signalmen in South London, should be elected Secretary of the new Society. In recognition of his services as speaker and organizer, Vincent was elected President, although already some were beginning to doubt his trustworthiness.

The hiring of public halls and the printing of leaflets required funds. For the time being George Chapman, who was not very well known outside London, had to be entrusted with the safe keeping of these monies, but until the union was registered with the Registrar of Friendly Societies the members of the union could obtain no redress if any official misappropriated the funds. At the Battersea meeting on December 28th, a porter asked Mr Chapman, who was in the chair, 'If the Society was to be registered under the act?' When Mr Chapman answered that it would be, the porter replied: 'If that was the case hundreds would join because the funds would then be safe.' The meeting then resolved that the council should at once have the Society registered.[18] The London Committee required little prompting. They made application for registration on February 9, 1872, under the names of W. H. Baker, G. Godden, C. Costello, Henry Lacey Smith, G. Harnet, John Mills, Jesse Harmsworth and the solicitor, John Thomas Moss. Registration was granted the Society on March 2, 1872.

It was not the practice of the Registrar of Friendly Societies to grant registration to a trade union until that union had submitted its rules to him and he had found them to comply with the law. Being well aware of this, the London Committee got busy drafting rules, and on Tuesday, January 9th, a fortnight after the Battersea porter raised his important question, they published the results of their labours. The entrance fee was to be 1s 3d and for a subscription of 1s a month, members were to be entitled to unemployment benefit at 10s a week for three months, with 3s a week for a further three months. A five years' member was to be entitled to accident benefit of 5s a week for life and a 10 years' member would qualify for superannuation benefit of 5s a week.[19]

All this had been done without the participation of any representatives from provincial branches and largely without the active support of Vincent who was too busy, with the aid of Mr Bass's funds, addressing meetings and forming branches outside London, to give continuous attention to the business of drafting rules or registering the union. But Vincent was ambitious to become the General Secretary of the A.S.R.S. and was riled at the thought that he could not be in two places at once. In his *Authentic History* he wrote:

'My engagements were increasing, and I was much wanted in the provinces, but matters had arrived at such a stage in London as to render it necessary to prolong my stay; for I wished particularly to make every arrangement, both with regard to the proposed society and newspaper satisfactory before going again into the country, where my engagements would last a long time.'[20]

As an outcome of his divided responsibilities, Vincent had a quickly diminishing influence over the decisions of the London Committee. Resentful at his exclusion from the inner councils of the Society, he increasingly stressed to his provincial audiences the wholly provisional character of the arrangements so far made in London.[21] He urged that no payments should be made to London until after a general delegate meeting had been held and the affairs of the union had been put on a proper footing. He even failed to notify the formation of branches to the London Committee. There were plenty of opportunities for awakening and increasing distrust of the London men. George Chapman spoke little in the provinces and was an unknown quantity, though he seemed imbued with his own importance and he was always asking the branches for more money. When asked by the London Committee to write to Vincent, he had written on December 18, 1871, and ended the letter 'Faithfully and sincerely yours, George Chapman, *Secretary*, A.S.R.S.', when he should have written 'Hon. Secretary (*pro. tem.*) A.S.R.S.'

All the evidence goes to show that John Graham at Derby was a man who put the interests of the union first. Nevertheless he did not accept the authority of the London officers. He distrusted George Chapman and on April 3, 1872, wrote to a friend who had just been appointed secretary of one of the union's branches, that he should 'stick to' his money and 'not let Chapman get the handling of a fraction'.

If Mr Bass had been prepared to accept the office of President of the Society he might have been able to unify the movement, as he had the confidence of both Londoners and Provincials, but in reply to an invitation from Mr Chapman, he wrote from his home on December 27, 1871, that after 'the best consideration' he had come to the conclusion that he would be of more service to the Society by 'preserving a perfectly independent position'. The London Committee then sought a public figure who had means of his own, experience in organization and a spirit of disinterested service on behalf of working men, and they found in Dr J. Baxter Langley, Ll.B., a man who satisfied all these conditions.

Dr Langley was known in London as a radical Liberal who had supported the 10-hours' movement and who was in favour of Home Rule for Ireland at a time when most of the members of his party were opposed to it. He was tactful and clear sighted, being able to grasp the essentials of a situation quickly and to keep the meetings he conducted from wandering from the point. His first appearance at a meeting held on behalf of railwaymen was on January 28, 1872, at the Montpelier Arms, Walworth.

Here he impressed his audience by his eloquence and by his ability as a chairman. Shortly after this, and less than six weeks after Vincent had been made President, the London Committee announced that they had chosen Dr Langley as its Chairman. Although, in the long run, Dr Langley was the most important influence in favour of reconciliation and it was due to him more than to any other person that a permanent split was avoided, the immediate result of his appointment as Chairman was to increase the distrust of the men in the provinces. It did not help matters that Mr Bass, who was a cautiously minded Whig, did not like the politics of the radical home-ruler who had just come into prominence in the affairs of the Society.

The provincial members' distrust of the London leadership would have been more quickly overcome had it not been for the appearance of the *Railway Service Gazette* on the scene. Vincent had suggested to Mr Bass early in December 1871, that it would be a good idea for the Society to have a paper of its own, and on December 9th, Mr Bass replied by letter that he was prepared to help Vincent and Mr Edwin Phillips publish 'a weekly journal to advocate the interests of railway servants'. Vincent and Phillips having estimated the weekly costs of running the paper to be £31 7s od, Mr Bass offered to find the money for a three months' trial. Mr J. H. Brewer, a Master of Chambers in the Queen's Bench, was to make the legal arrangements. The following notice was then issued:

'On Saturday, January 6, 1872, will appear the first number of the *Railway Service Gazette*, a first-class weekly journal especially devoted to the interests of railway officials of the United Kingdom, conducted by Charles Bassett Vincent. Give your orders at once.'[22]

Those who eagerly anticipated the coming of the paper in January were disappointed; the first number did not appear until February 3, 1872, the explanation again being Vincent's inability to be in two places at once. Alcock wrote that 'he (Vincent) wanted to be out and about, to place himself in the limelight, thus having at least equal chances when the final choice of leader was made'. But he could not at the same time be occupying the editor's chair. He eventually agreed that his friend Greenwood should be editor and that Phillips should be the assistant. From the first the new paper put the interests of Vincent and Greenwood before those of the Society as a whole. It was an important stumbling block to all attempts at removing misunderstandings between the two factions of the Society. It gave ample reports of the speeches made by Vincent but refused to publish an important letter from Dr Langley in April 1872. The London Committee and Dr Langley were thus obliged to use the *Beehive*, the London radical weekly edited by J. Potter, as their newspaper. Each party now had its voice; but whereas the *Beehive* was temperate and worked for the unity of the movement, the *Railway Service Gazette* fomented discord.

From the time of his appointment as Chairman of the London Committee, Dr Langley worked ceaselessly and single-mindedly for the reconciliation of the two sides. He succeeded in convincing the committee that compromise with John Graham and the provincial branches was desirable. Mr Bass was also distressed by the rift in the Society and worked for an agreement and to this end invited Dr Langley, George Chapman, Vincent and delegates from Manchester, Derby, Birmingham and other provincial branches to meet him in his London house on March 26, 1872. He also invited the three M.P.s who had recently consented to become Vice-Presidents, Messrs Thomas Brassey, Samuel Morely and D. Straight. Dr Langley assured Mr Bass that all officers elected had been on a temporary basis pending the holding of the first delegate meeting and explained why he and the London Committee thought it was essential to give full legal status to the union. The divided allegiance of the delegates was revealed when delegates from Derby and Birmingham declared that they would have no one but Vincent as Secretary, whilst a delegate from the South Eastern Railwaymen reported support for Chapman. Nevertheless when the meeting ended there were 'cordial expressions of good feeling on all sides',[23] and it was arranged that a further meeting should be arranged to consider the rules of the Society.

When the next meeting was held (this time at the Winchester Arms, Southwark) on April 27, 1872, there could have been serious bickerings from the start. The twelve delegates summoned from the provinces confronted a much larger group of London delegates. The tactful intervention of Dr Langley, however, smoothed over any difficulties. He told the twelve from the provinces that the London men were broadminded and ready to make concessions and, in particular, that they were willing that their representation should be reduced to twelve. He suggested that Mr Graham should take the chair without any loss of voting powers. When Graham declined the offer, Langley was elected Chairman of the meeting. Owing to the hesitations of the provincial branch secretaries about sending their funds to Chapman, a London delegate proposed that until the time of the 'Delegate Meeting, Mr Chapman should collect the London monies only, whilst John Graham should collect the money from all the other branches and forward it to Dr Langley. Since there had been many criticisms of the rules of the Society which had been drafted by the London Committee, it was agreed that the first task of the delegate meeting would be to consider the rules and that any proposals for their amendment would have to be forwarded to the General Secretary (*pro. tem.*) at least fourteen days before the opening of the meeting. It was agreed that the basis of representation at the delegate meeting should be as follows: Any branch having fifty members, or united branches making up that number, to send one representative; branches exceeding 250 to send two delegates; exceeding 300 to send three delegates and no more. Delegates unexpectedly prevented from attending may place their credentials in the hands of any other delegate.

To settle the conflict over the question of the future Secretary of the union, the meeting agreed that an advertisement should be published offering £250 to the most suitable candidate. A selection sub-committee comprising three provincial and three London men was empowered to select the six most eligible candidates whose names would be submitted to the membership. The man gaining a simple majority of votes would be Secretary for the ensuing year. The delegates' expense allowance was fixed at 12s 6d a day, a rule which remained in force until the outbreak of the First World War. It was unanimously agreed that the delegate meeting should open in London on June 24, 1872.

John Graham afterwards wrote of that very successful meeting that 'all provincial delegates (twelve) were satisfied and there is now no division among us'.

As a further effort at conciliation Dr Langley wrote a lengthy letter to the editor of the *Beehive* which was printed on the same day as the Winchester Arms meeting (April 27th). It was a masterly summing-up of the reasons why the London men had proceeded as far as they had with the establishment of the union. The crux of his statement is contained in the following sentences:

'You cannot make any appeal to universal suffrage unless there is previously established and acknowledged a provisional committee which shall have the power of arranging the details of the first delegate meeting out of which the permanent constitution may legally arise. It is the duty of the provisional government to secure the effective expression of the popular will. With this in view, and as a beginning, I accepted the Executive Council formed by the London men, viz. as a provisional government to prepare for the appeal to the suffrages of the whole of the members. It was found necessary, however, to do more than elect a committee. The appeal to members could not be conducted without expense. Who was to receive the funds? The law gave no protection to those funds unless the society was enrolled; but the society could not be enrolled without rules and officers. So these have been elected, and rules prepared and enrolled as a temporary arrangement, to bring the whole affair into legal existence.'

Dr Langley wrote that any mistakes the London men had made could be corrected at the delegate meeting and that he himself sought no office or pay of any kind and was willing to retire as Chairman once the delegate meeting had been properly constituted. Dr Langley by his tact had smoothed the path to the all-important assembly in London.

V

At eleven o'clock on the morning of Monday, June 24, 1872, sixty-two men assembled in the Sussex Hotel, Bouverie Street, near Fleet Street, London.[24] They were the pioneers who constituted the first Great Delegate Meeting of the A.S.R.S. The names and the branches they represented were:

J. Abbott, Bedford, later of Wigston; J. Bull, Broad Street, G. Boon, Camden; G. Billoney, Hull, P. Bannister, Boston; J. Bowley, Wellingborough; T. Baker, T. Burns and R. Salmon, Manchester; J. W. Biggs, A Bladon, and C. Crossley, Birmingham; A. T. Caesar, Doncaster; J. Carter and W. Manston, Stratford; S. Carr, Stourbridge; E. W. Campion, Bermondsey; J. Cordwell, Ardwick; F. Dance, Worcester; H. Dickenson, Salford; D. Dalton and E. Harford, Grimsby; H. Davis, Hereford; T. Evans, Bow; G. Foreman, Toton; J. T. Gladwin, Brighton; W. J. Gwynne, Plumstead; R. Gibson, Accrington; W. S. Grabbam and W. King, South Eastern; J. Graham, Derby; T. Giles, Chester; F. Hornsby, Twickenham; E. Huntington, Newcastle; W. Higgs, Rugby; J. Harris, Longsight; W. Hoe, Sheffield; W. Jeffs, Nine Elms; R. Whitmore, Battersea; H. Kemp and J. Pafford, West End No. 1; E. Lunn, Wakefield; J. Morrish, Merthyr Tydfil; J. Marsden, Manchester; J. R. Peters, New Mills; J. R. Palmer, Gorton; T. Penzer, Wolverhampton; J. Price, Birkenhead; W. Reeves, Crystal Palace; A. Strenton, Burslem; E. W. Sainsbury, Brick Lane; J. Skinner, Dudley; T. Swinburne, Greatbridge; G. A. Skilling, Cardiff; C. Shrives, King's Cross; J. Tucker, Pontypool; C. Turner, March; S. Wyatt, Aberdare; W. Whitehead, Leeds; J. Williams, Newport.

The delegates who were destined to render the most distinguished service on behalf of the union were: E. Harford, of Grimsby, who was General Secretary from February 1883 to October 1897; J. Graham, who was the first full-time organizer and J. Cordwell, who became the Manchester District Secretary.

In addition there were present George Chapman, the General Secretary (*pro. tem.*), Mr Climpson, Treasurer (*pro. tem.*) and Dr J. Baxter Langley, who occupied the chair. The delegates made an early resolve not to waste their time in eating and drinking since it was agreed that business would proceed from 11.0 a.m. to 4.0 p.m. 'with one quarter of an hour about two o'clock for refreshment'.

As soon as the meeting was constituted Dr Langley handed in his resignation from the chair but was immediately re-elected with great enthusiasm by the vast majority of the delegates. Vincent, counting on his pioneering work for the union as being sufficient qualification for admission, handed in his card soon after the meeting started. Dr Langley told the delegates that when Vincent had called on him the previous evening he told him that as he had not taken the trouble to secure nomination as representative of any branch, he (Dr Langley) was not prepared to break the rules to make it possible for Vincent to attend. The delegates upheld Dr Langley's decision by thirty-eight votes to eighteen. Thereupon that gentleman read a brief message of good wishes to the meeting from Vincent.

The Secretary reported that the proceeds of a special levy from the branches fell short of the cost of the meeting by £150, but that Mr Bass had given £50, and several other friends of the movement smaller sums, to meet the deficit.

If the delegates had needed any reminder of the hazards of railway employment (which was scarcely the case) they were given one when, early on in the proceedings, John Graham rose to ask the conference for permission for E. Starr, the Stourbridge delegate, to leave the meeting as he had just received news that his brother had been killed in a railway accident. This permission was granted and accompanied by an expression of sympathy on behalf of the bereaved man.

Dr Langley made yet another, very effective, gesture of conciliation when the meeting divided equally (29–29) on the question of whether the Manchester rules or those drawn up by the London Committee and modified by the Doncaster branch should form the basis of the discussion on the following day. As a Londoner he gave his casting vote in favour of the Manchester rules.

On Tuesday (June 25th), therefore, the delegates got down to a detailed consideration of the Society's rules. The Chairman's recommendation that for the next five years, as a start, the executive should be based on London whilst the annual delegate meeting should meet in different provincial towns was carried by 42 votes to 19.

Rule 2 which defined the objects of the union was unanimously agreed as follows:

'That the objects of this society shall be the improvement of the general condition of all classes of railway employees; temporary assistance when thrown out of employment, through causes over which they have no control; legal assistance when necessary; and to provide a superannuation allowance to old and disabled members; and for these purposes each member shall pay a subscription of 3d per week. All sick, accident and death benefits to be left to the discretion of the branches to adopt and provide for as they may choose.'

There are some notable differences between these objects and the objects as stated at the inaugural meeting at the Winchester Arms on December 3, 1871 (see page 53 above). In the new rules there is no reference to an emigration fund or to arbitration and the prevention of strikes or to a definite programme of hours and overtime rates. Common features of the two statements include the provision of superannuation, legal protection and the granting of an ill-defined 'temporary assistance' to those thrown out of employment.

To encourage a speedy accession of strength to the union it was agreed that the entrance fee should remain at 1s until August 1, 1872, after which it would be raised to 2s.

After a long discussion on the future composition of the executive committee, agreement was eventually reached on the proposal that twenty-one men should be elected from the branches contained within a twelve-mile radius of the city of London and that the President and Secretary of every other branch in the country should be *ex-officio* members who could take part in the discussions 'whenever they chose to attend'. The E.C. was given power to summon the representatives of various branches if the business in hand demanded it, but no member of the union was to be entitled to attend the E.C. and claim expenses more frequently than once in three months. All representatives had to be furnished with their credentials signed by the officers of the branches.

The delegates were under no illusion that they were infallible in the work of constitution making. They therefore appointed a sub-committee of ten (including five from the London and five from the provincial branches) to re-examine the Manchester rules and to report their recommendations on the following day.

The evidence suggests that the majority of the delegates were distrustful of a centralized bureaucracy. They preferred to leave the administration of sick, accident and death benefits to the branches and therefore decided that out of each member's one shilling a month subscription, only one penny should go to a central fund. For the control of the union's finances there were elected three trustees and a Treasurer (Mr Climpson) who together formed a finance committee of four.

On the last day of the conference (Wednesday, June 26th) the delegates considered a request for admission from Canon Jenkins who had been active on behalf of the union in South Wales earlier in the summer. To overcome the constitutional difficulty of his not being the accredited representative of any branch, and as a mark of appreciation for his services, it was decided to appoint him a Vice-President along with Samuel Morley, M.P., Douglas Straight, M.P., and Thomas Brassey, M.P., and Mr Montague Chambers, Q.C., M.P., who had previously accepted a similar dignity.

A noticeable absentee in the list of delegates is any representative from Scotland. It was reported from the chair that a delegate from Edinburgh might have attended had he received longer notice of the meeting, as Mr Bass had offered to pay his fare and his expenses. It is a pity that more attention was not given to securing representation from Scotland. Had this been done it is possible the Scottish railwaymen would not have proceeded in August 1872, to form their own 'Amalgamated Society of Railway Servants for Scotland', and that the uneconomical parallel development of the two societies until their amalgamation in 1892, might have been avoided.

As an expression of gratitude to Mr Bass the delegates all signed the following testimonial:

'To Michael Thomas Bass, M.P.

Respected Sir,

We, the undersigned delegates in meeting assembled, and representing the members of the A.S.R.S. in England and Wales, unanimously concur in the desire to express to you our deep and heartfelt thanks and gratitude for your sympathy for the sufferings endured by the class to which we belong, and for the timely support and invaluable aid rendered by you in the formation of the society, which, we trust, may be the means of improving our social condition and protecting our rights and guarding us against injustice. The universal respect and esteem of railway servants throughout the kingdom will always be yours, and your name will be cherished among them as a household word and enshrined on their grateful memories. We therefore trust that you will allow us to inscribe your honoured name as a patron of the association which owes its existence to your fostering care. Earnestly wishing you better health and praying that your life of usefulness may long be spared to us,

We are, respected dear Sir,

Your faithful and obliged servants.'

Before the close of the proceedings on the last day a number of delegates endeavoured to persuade the meeting to agree to the admission to the union of other members of the working classes besides railwaymen, it being suggested by some that a special class of membership should be provided for men in this category. The proposals were, however, rejected in favour of the policy of membership limited to all grades of railwaymen.

The atmosphere of the meeting was tense when Dr Langley proceeded to announce the result of the ballot of the membership for the election of the General Secretary. The voting was as follows:

Chapman	1,489
Graham	1,137
May	929
Bayley	49
Heath	3
McDonald	3

All the candidates were experienced railway employees. Messrs May and McDonald had written pamphlets and articles on railway matters. Mr Bayley was a traffic manager from Harwich and Mr Heath was employed on the North Eastern Railway at Newcastle-upon-Tyne. It was agreed that John Graham, the runner-up, should be appointed Organizing Secretary.

A notable absentee from the list of candidates was Vincent. Although it seems a remarkable explanation in view of his ambition, the balance of the evidence shows that he failed to send in an application. The advertisement for the post was printed in *The Times* of May 20, 1872, and was worded as follows:

'Secretary wanted. By the Amalgamated Society of Railway Servants, a gentleman to act as General Secretary. Must be over forty years of age, with good address and accustomed to conduct correspondence and keep accounts. A guarantee of £200 will be required. Salary £250 a year. Application, with references and copies of testimonials to be made by letter only to Dr Baxter Langley, 50 Lincolns Inn Fields, on or before May 25, 1872.'

Aware that Vincent might not see the advertisement, Dr Langley telegraphed Mr Penzer of Wolverhampton asking him to tell his friend Vincent about it. Mr Penzer replied that he had urged Vincent to apply. As an additional guarantee the E.C. instructed the sub-committee for the selection of candidates to consider Vincent's application with the others if he had a recommendation from Mr Bass, even though the application was sent in late. No application arrived. Apparently Mr Bass did not urge Vincent to seek election as he wrote a letter of support for May, one of the other candidates. If Vincent had stood for election his intervention would probably have had the result of drawing support from Graham and therefore of making the election of Chapman more certain.

Apparently no efficient check of the voting strengths of branches was made by the sub-committee which permitted the Poplar branch to exercise 600 votes at a time when only 401 men of the branch had paid their entrance fees. Alcock believed that if the voting had been conducted fairly Graham would have been elected; but by no stretch of the imagination can it be claimed that Vincent was a victim of sharp practice.

Just before the Great Delegate Meeting broke up, Mr Stevenson of Burslem proposed that if any delegates happened to get into trouble as a result of their attending the meeting the Society should protect them. The wisdom of the unanimous decision to support this proposal was quickly apparent. On returning to their employment on the following day three delegates, King, who worked on the London, Chatham and Dover Railway; W. E. Campion of Bermondsey and S. Wyatt of Aberdare, were told that as they had attended the meeting in London their services were no longer required.

That their achievements should not go unrecorded the delegates instructed Mr Edwin Phillips, the Editor of the *Railway Service Gazette*, to write the History of the A.S.R.S. up to the conclusion of the first Great Delegate Meeting. For his brief account of less than twenty pages the writer was paid £10.

Their work well done, the delegates merged with the huge assembly of between 2,000 and 3,000 railwaymen that gathered in the Arundel Hall, Arundel Street, Strand, on the evening of the third day of the congress (Wednesday, June 26th). Samuel Morley, M.P., was in the chair and beside him on the platform were Dr Langley, Canon Jenkins, Mr Bass, Lloyd Jones (the Chartist), Vincent and George Potter, the Editor of *Beehive*. Mr Morley in his opening speech 'utterly denied that there were two sides in a question between employers and employed. They had a great common interest and it was the true British position for a manufacturer to take that he should be not only willing but anxious that his men should share in a right degree in the prosperity of the country.'

When Mr Bass stood up to accept the memorial drafted on behalf of the men he was received with the most extraordinary enthusiasm, 'all the men in the room standing on their feet waving hats and cheering'.[25]

Two important resolutions, carried with acclamation, expressed the views of the meeting. The first was moved by Lloyd Jones.

'That this meeting is of opinion that it is desirable for the security of the travelling community that the railway servants should not be overworked or underpaid, that it considers ten hours sufficient for the working day and that six working days ought to count as a week, and pledges itself to support the movement for shorter hours and increased remuneration.'

Mr Cordwell of Ardwick branch moved the second resolution:

'That this meeting learns with satisfaction that a society for the protection of the interests of the railway servants has been formed, and congratulates the delegates who have been sitting in London during the last few days upon their successful efforts to consolidate an association of great national importance.'

VI

However great had been the division and mistrusts in the formative weeks, a union with nation-wide support in England and Wales had now been established. How can we explain the success of the movement in 1871–2 in contrast with the earlier failures of 1865–6?

It was a fortunate circumstance that the foundation of the A.S.R.S. coincided with a period of booming trade. The companies were thus in a position to make some concessions when the first programme of reforms was presented to them by branches of the new union or as an outcome of the meetings held before the union was registered. In the late autumn of 1871, when the flood of petitions began to reach the general managers, a meeting of the Railway Companies Association decided to leave it to each company to settle separately with its staff since 'the circumstances of the several applications appeared to differ and no general rule was applicable'.[26] This decision presents a striking contrast with the close co-operation of the financially embarrassed companies in 1866 in breaking the Engine Drivers' and Firemen's United Society and enforcing worsened conditions of service.

The gains in 1871-2 were not confined to the achievement of a 9-hour day in many railway workshops. The directors of five railway companies serving the Liverpool area agreed on November 25, 1871, to reduce the hours of railway servants employed on Merseyside from sixty-one to fifty-seven per week.[27] On Tuesday, December 5, 1871, 160 porters and carters employed by the Lancashire and Yorkshire Railway at Blackburn suddenly struck work for a 2s a week rise in wages. On the afternoon of the same day the goods manager of the company interviewed the men on strike and offered them an increase of a shilling a week together with a reduction in working hours from sixty to fifty-seven per week. The men gladly accepted this compromise particularly as the manager agreed to their being paid for the day of the strike.[28] In the first week of 1872 the directors of the Great Northern Railway granted three days' holiday with pay to all employees with over a year's service and an increase of 1s a week to all those with over three years' service. Later in January they offered to the London men an improvement in overtime rates and the payment of wages on a weekly rather than a fortnightly basis.[29] Early in February the directors of the Brighton line voted about £2,000 per annum for the improvement of the overtime rates of drivers.[30] On March 2, 1872, the directors of the North Eastern Railway announced wage increases for signalmen and guards of from 1s to 3s a week.[31] On the Great Eastern, wages were increased by 2s a week all round.[32] The strikers on the North Eastern and Brighton lines in 1860 had associated the brief life of a sectional union with defeat, dismissal and, in some cases, penury; the men of 1872 rightly linked the gains they achieved (however small) to the formation of a national union with membership open to all railwaymen.

The second major reason for the success of the movement in 1871-2 was the all-grades character of the union. Although there were jealousies and misunderstandings between the Londoners and the provincial members, there was a marked absence of sectional antagonism. It was a feature of the early months of 1872 that clerks, drivers, firemen, porters, guards, pointsmen, signalmen and many others, flocked into the Amalgamated Union. This was a great and significant improvement upon the sectional organizations of clerks, guards and locomotivemen which had been unsuccessfully attempted six years earlier.

Unlike the unions of the years 1865–6, the A.S.R.S. in 1871–2 received influential and invaluable assistance from sympathizers outside the labour movement. Since the accounts were not properly kept in the early days of the union, it is impossible to give an exact statement of the extent of the financial assistance given by Mr Bass. It is reasonable to suppose that it was well over £1,000, since Edwin Phillips stated that 'in the course of eight months' the inquiries conducted by Vincent cost £600.[33] At various public meetings George Chapman announced that Mr Bass had promised sums ranging from £100 to £300 towards the initial cost of launching the Society. In addition, Mr Bass paid the expenses of the twelve provincial delegates who met the London Committee on March 26, 1872, and he subsidized the *Railway Service Gazette* which was a valuable ally of the movement after the first Great Delegate Meeting. The far-sighted, business-like and tactful leadership of Dr Langley was also of invaluable assistance.

In 1865–6 the railwaymen were without the Parliamentary franchise and in consequence they were able to influence legislation only to a very limited extent. After the Second Reform Bill of 1867 had extended the franchise to include the artisan classes, the opinions of at least the better paid of the railway employees commanded some respect from aspiring politicians. Four M.P.s took a leading part in the formation of the A.S.R.S.; there is no record of similar support for the unions of the 1860's. Moreover, after 1868 the Parliamentary Committee of the T.U.C. had shown what trade unionists could achieve by persistent lobbying in the House of Commons. In 1872 it could be argued that a railwaymen's trade union could exert pressure on M.P.s to introduce long-awaited railway reform.

In 1865–6 the railway system was still expanding rapidly; by 1872 most of the main lines had been completed and the pace of construction slackened. Between 1860 and 1870, 5,104 new route miles of line had been opened—an average of over 500 route miles a year. Between 1870 and 1880, 2,396 new route miles or an average of only 240 miles a year were opened.

Inevitably there was a noticeable slowing up in promotion of railway employees. The fireman waiting more years for upgrading to the rank of driver and the porter finding fewer vacancies for guards, listened more readily to the appeal of trade unionism as a means to the achievement of those improvements in living standards which had formerly come as a result of quick advancement within the service.

Finally there was the public awareness that a contributory cause of the exceptionally high accident rate on the railways in 1870 was the practice of the companies overworking their men to the point where their senses were numbed and their reliability as guardians of the safety of the travelling public was impaired. Hence the remarkable recommendation of *The Times* to railwaymen that they should form a trade union to act as a curb on the companies' abuse of their powers.

Even so there were strict limits to what could be achieved in 1872. That solidarity was not all it should have been and that the resources of the union were meagre was shown by the failure of the strike at Broad Street Station on the London and North Western Railway at the end of July. In May, the London employees of that company had presented the directors with a demand for an increase of wages from 2s 6d to 3s a week. When the company offered between 1s 6d and 2s and the men at their meeting at Milton Hall, Camden Town, on June 10th, accepted the compromise, it looked as if the claim had been settled. However, by July 21st, the men were petitioning the directors for the removal of the London Superintendent, Mr Greenish, who had dismissed two men, Harry King (a clerk) and P. Tarbox (a capstanman) for taking part in the agitation, and who was alleged to have distributed the wage increases unfairly between the men. When the directors refused to move Mr Greenish, 400 goods porters at Broad Street, particularly indignant at the 'spotting' and victimization of two of their colleagues, struck work on July 26th. Although the strikers hid hooks, weights and measures in an attempt to make the strike more effective, and although men at Poplar came out in support, others at Camden Town and Haydon continued at work as did the clerks at all the stations. At a meeting of 800 railwaymen, strikers and their supporters, at the Winchester Hall, Winchester Street, Caledonian Road, on July 30th, the men wore blue ribbons 'as a token of their solidarity'. Dr Langley told the meeting that the men were on the eve of a great victory; but the facts of the situation were very different. Large numbers of blacklegs were coming in from as far afield as Scotland and were rapidly filling the places of the strikers. At another Winchester Hall meeting held on August 1st, Dr Langley announced the abandonment of the strike—a decision forced upon them through 'privation and lack of solidarity'. The directors of the company, meeting at Euston Station the same day, passed a special resolution of thanks to the clerks and others who had remained at work and voted them double pay for the period of the strike.[34] The E.C. of the A.S.R.S., at its meeting on August 26th, resolved to pay £6 to every dismissed striker who wished to emigrate. They had already paid out £500 in allowances to men who had failed to gain reinstatement. This unauthorized strike proved to be a serious strain on the limited financial resources of the union in the first year of its life.

The experience of this failure at Broad Street led George Chapman to write in the First Annual Report of the A.S.R.S.:

'I would take this opportunity of stating that the Council is decidedly opposed to strikes, the Council being of opinion that if railwaymen will only come forward and be firmly united, they would gain that to which they are entitled, without having recourse to any cessation of work.'

There had been a successful delivery of the new infant—the A.S.R.S.—but in his early months of life he was by no means the sturdy child his godparents had hoped to sponsor. There were even occasions in the formative years when they must have feared for his life.

NOTES

1. P.P. 1873, Vol. LVII, p. 653.
2. *Herapath*, February 18, 1871, p. 150.
3. *Herapath*, September 16, 1871, p. 907.
4. *Licensed Victuallers Guardian*, June 1870.
5. Hansard: Parliamentary Debates, 3rd Series, Vol. 205, Cols. 34–37, March 15, 1871, and Vol. 207, Col. 700, June 28, 1871.
6. *The Times*, September 15 and December 17, 1871.
7. General Report by Captain Tyler to the Board of Trade upon the accidents which have occurred on railways during the year 1870. P.P. 1871, Vol. LX, p. 111.
8. *Lancet*, July 29, 1871.
9. C. B. Vincent, *An Authentic History of Railway Trade Unionism*, Derby, 1902, pp. 18–19.
10. Vincent was reported as chief speaker at a meeting in the Temperance Hall, Derby, on July 22, 1871. *Derby Mercury*, July 26, 1871.
11. *Derby Mercury*, November 8, 1871.
12. *Beehive*, November 4, and November 18, 1871.
13. *Manchester Evening News*, November 13, 1871.
14. *Beehive*, November 11, 1871.
15. Reports of the inaugural meeting given in *Daily Telegraph*, December 4, 1871, *Beehive*, December 9, 1871, and Alcock, p. 35. Rule 12 published in *The Times*, December 11, 1871.
16. Alcock, p. 38.
17. *The Times*, December 9, 1871.
18. *Beehive*, February 3, 1872.
19. *Beehive*, January 13, 1872.
20. Vincent, *op. cit.* quoted in Alcock, p. 44.
21. Alcock, p. 43.
22. Alcock, p. 42.
23. *Beehive*, March 30, 1872.
24. This account of the Great Delegate Meeting is based on the report in the *Railway Service Gazette*, June 29, 1872, E. Phillips's *Full Report of the First Great Delegate Meeting of the A.S.R.S.*, and Alcock, pp. 76–90.
25. *The Times*, June 27, 1872.
26. Railway Companies Association: Committee, November 2, 1871, Minute 630.
27. *Beehive*, December 2, 1871.
28. *Mansfield Reporter*, December 8, 1871.
29. *The Times*, January 8 and 22, 1872.
30. *The Times*, February 14, 1872.
31. N.E.R. Circular, March 2, 1872.
32. *The Times*, April 25, 1872.
33. E. Phillips, *op. cit.*
34. *The Times*, June 3 and 11, July 22, 27, 29, 30 and 31, August 2, 1872; *Islington Gazette*, July 23 and 30, August 6, 1872. I am indebted to Mr K. J. Weller of Highbury Branch, A.E.U., for cuttings from this newspaper.

CHAPTER III

THE STRUGGLE FOR SURVIVAL

'The Society must not be in the position of an unarmed state, surrounded by greedy and powerful neighbours; but by throwing away the power to strike they had practically put themselves in this position. They stood unarmed in the face of a powerful army and in their actions had invited the companies to take advantage of them.'
F. W. Evans (General Secretary) January 29, 1879.

I

A GLANCE at the membership figures of the A.S.R.S. during the first ten years of its existence would give the impression that if the union was not actually dying it was certainly, like the legendary old soldier, fading away. At the end of 1872 there were 17,247 members on the books; at the end of 1882 there were only 6,321. The danger that existed of the union disappearing was even greater than these figures might suggest, for by December 31, 1882, slow recovery had already begun. The nadir of the Society's fortunes was reached in September 1882, when it could claim less than 6,000 members. At that time the staunchest supporter of the union could be excused for having grave doubts on its chances of survival.

A large part of the explanation of the decline in membership lies in the provincial members' continued distrust of the Londoners and their reluctance to make available to the full-time officers adequate funds for the efficient management of the union.

These differences between the London members and the provincial members of the Executive Council first came to a head in 1873 on the question of whether the Society should continue to employ George Chapman as its General Secretary. Since the London members came into personal contact with Chapman more frequently, they realized his shortcomings at an earlier date than did the representatives from the provinces. Although there are no doubts as to the honesty and sincerity of the union's chief officer, his failure to keep proper accounts, his factional attitude and

70

his failure to carry out the decisions of the Executive were shortcomings which could scarcely be tolerated. No receipts had been collected for £711 18s 6d expended by the strike committee at Broad Street in August 1872, and a finance committee appointed by the E.C. could not strike a proper balance, having no books to examine but only scraps of paper containing scribbled statements.[1]

Shortly before the second delegate meeting met at the Railway Clock Inn in Manchester on June 27, 1873, Langley told a meeting held in the City Arms, Bloomfield Street, London, that he had resolved to resign from the Presidency of the A.S.R.S. since he found himself 'in the position of a captain of a ship, the men of whom would do nothing but what they liked, and whose first mate would not attend to his instructions'.[2] The Executive agreed with Langley in desiring the dismissal of Chapman, and the finance committee had prepared for the delegate meeting a report which exposed the unsound state of the union's finances. However, the Londoners were in a minority at the delegate meeting and the majority from the provinces resolved not to hear the Londoners' case against Chapman whom they re-elected as General Secretary. Several telegrams were sent from the meeting appealing to Langley to reconsider his decision to resign the Presidency. Although Langley gave eleven reasons for upholding his decision to resign, the most important reason was given in his last telegram to the Conference:

'Final decision. Take no part in the affairs of the Society; re-election of Chapman is the cause.'

At a very critical phase in its history, the union was thus saddled with an incompetent General Secretary largely because the London members of the Executive were not trusted by delegates coming from other parts of the country.

The squabble over the General Secretary continued after the delegate meeting had dispersed. That meeting had resolved that the old E.C. should continue to function until October 1, 1873, when it would be superseded by a new one elected on a different basis. On July 28, 1873, when the old E.C. met for the first time after the delegate meeting, the Londoners, who were in a majority, resolved to suspend Chapman from his office. Meeting again two days later they decided to dismiss him. It was an action which many provincial branches regarded as so unjustified and highhanded that they considered themselves entitled to stage a *coup d'état*. They plotted to seize control of the London offices at 25 Finsbury Square on August 6, 1873. By a coincidence, however, Mr Shrives, the Chairman of the E.C. had, without informing the provincial branches, convened a meeting of the E.C. for the same day and the two parties met, willy nilly. The Londoners wisely decided to be conciliatory and to sit round the table with the 'rebels' from the provinces. The difficult task of keeping order from the chair was given to the newly elected President of the Society, Canon Jenkins. One of the first decisions of the meeting was to carry a resolution for the reinstatement of Chapman moved by the delegate from Bristol, Mr Fred W. Evans. In prolonged discussions which lasted until 11.49 p.m. the provincial delegates learned for the first time some of the shortcomings of their General Secretary. Some were converted to the Londoners' point of view at the meeting, but there was a sufficient majority for Chapman for the meeting to resolve that the Executive Council should be adjourned until October 1, 1873, and that, in the meantime, the business of the Society should be conducted by the President and General Secretary.[3]

When the new E.C. met for the first time on October 1, 1873, they considered a letter from Mr Shrives which contained detailed complaints about the mismanagement of the Society's finances by Chapman; but although they were worried about the absence of receipts, they decided to take no action against Chapman and instead passed a resolution that the money received for the delegate and strike funds in 1872 had 'been used by those concerned to the best of their ability for the good of the Society though no receipts for the same had been taken'.[4] But the more the members of the new E.C. came to grips with the business of the union the more they realized that the old Executive had been right in claiming that, in the interests of the Society, it was necessary for Chapman to go. The General Secretary, they found, had neglected correspondence and there had been 'bungling at every point'. Finally in the autumn of 1874, in a decision of doubtful legality but of practical wisdom, they resolved that the post of General Secretary was subject to an annual election and they invited nominations for the post for the year following October 31, 1874. The result of the election was as follows:

Evans	2,218
Chapman	2,016
Vincent	1,466
Graham	1,348
Bowles	948

Although the validity of the election was challenged by Chapman and his supporters their complaints were set aside by the Executive. Under the new and able leadership of Evans there was now an opportunity of placing the affairs of the Society on a businesslike footing.

II

The new General Secretary, Frederick W. Evans, had started his working life as a clerk employed by the Great Western Railway at Bristol. When the A.S.R.S. was founded he took a leading part in organizing branches as far apart as Plymouth and Salisbury, Weymouth and Taunton. The Great Western Railway rewarded him in January 1874, by giving him a month's notice. Sir Edward Watkin, a prominent railway director, on whose behalf Evans had campaigned in the General Election of November 1873, in return for that gentleman's promise of support for a workmen's compensation bill, thereupon offered Evans a job on one of the three railway companies of which he was Chairman. As, however, it was made a condition of employment that he should not engage in trade-union activity, Evans declined the offer. Watkin subsequently headed a subscription list on Evans's behalf with a donation of £50. In the ten months' interval between his dismissal by the Great Western Railway and his election as General Secretary of the union, Evans as District Secretary of the Bristol region had had considerable success in building up the strength of the branches in that area.

At the Manchester delegate meeting in June 1873, Evans took a leading part in the amendment of the constitution of the union to give enhanced power to the districts and the branches. Recognizing the provincial members' continued distrust of the Londoners and their dislike of the policy of centralizing the union's resources, he proposed a scheme which he hoped would strengthen the provincial members' allegiance to the union and eliminate misunderstandings. Conference approved his plan for the division of the country into eleven districts each containing a roughly equal number of branches and each governed by a committee of local members working in conjunction with a full-time paid secretary. Each district was to elect one member of the reconstituted Executive Committee which would thus comprise eleven members, with provincial representatives filling a large majority of the seats. The Conference further agreed that of the 4d a month each member contributed to the management expenses of the union, 3d was to be retained by the local branches and the district organizations, whilst only a penny was to be allocated to central management funds. The great drawback of such decentralization was that it left the central office starved of funds and impotent to come to the assistance of districts with poor membership figures and poor resources. Some of the eleven districts—the North-East at that time was one—were never strong enough to support a full-time secretary. Weak districts were likely to become even weaker unless they were given a helping hand from outside to put them on their feet. Furthermore, members of the union were likely to be at the mercy of the companies so long as the central funds of the union were too weak to pay compensation to those victimized or to support a strike, where this proved necessary as a last resort.

Evans learned a great deal in the year following the Manchester delegate meeting. He saw the weaknesses of decentralizing the resources of the union. Seven years later he confided in a letter to John Abbot that 'the system was fast preparing the A.S.R.S. for a division into several societies'.

He made a close study of the methods of organization of the Amalgamated Association of Miners, which in South Wales had enrolled a large majority of the miners, and through the fact that it controlled large centrally managed funds was influential in negotiating with the mineowners. That union's success presented a marked contrast with the lack of influence of the decentralized and financially weak A.S.R.S.

In an important article in 'The Future of the Society of Railway Servants' which he wrote for the *Railway Service Gazette* in September 1874, Evans tried to convince the membership of the advantages of pooling their financial resources. He claimed that the A.S.R.S. would be powerless 'without a strong Central Fund immediately available for emergencies'. The union's efforts without one would 'ever be confined to spasmodic but futile struggles of separate branches having no common link of responsibility or connected interest'. The branches were a law unto themselves, often refusing to obey rules or to follow the decisions of the E.C. He believed that it was essential that 'men should be found for enforcing obedience to the rules of the society and that the executive power should be respected by being obeyed'. 'Without discipline' the union was 'a disorganized body'. Nothing could be more injurious to a society than to have branches and district committees 'coolly selecting for approval those rules and decrees of the E.C. which pleased them and resolving to ignore those not in accord with their pleasure'. This was repeatedly happening. If the Society was to be made an effective trade union, contributions would have to be raised from 3d to 4d a week and the number of districts should be reduced from eleven to six.[5]

The history of the first six years of Evans's work as General Secretary is largely the story of his efforts to make the union a strong, centrally directed organization whose decisions, democratically arrived at, were respected by the branches.

The tragedy of the situation was that it took Evans until 1880 to gain the union's acceptance of his major reforms. By this time the prosperous years which had seen the birth of the A.S.R.S. had given place to years of trade depression in which the companies proceeded to withdraw many of the concessions made to the men in 1871–3. When these attacks came, the union was too preoccupied with internal reforms and too financially weak to offer much resistance. Had the changes in organization been effected earlier the union would have been in a better position to meet the employers' challenge in 1879–80.

When he took over from Chapman on November 9, 1874, Evans found the head office 'in a most unbusinesslike condition'. He was unable to obtain an inventory of the property handed over or any intelligible statement of accounts. Pontypool and Reading branches refused to recognize his authority and were contemplating legal proceedings against the scrutineers of the election for General Secretary; Cambridge branch refused to remit any funds to the head office; few branches confined their expenditure to the amounts allowed by the Society's rules and one hundred branches had not sent in balance sheets for the previous year. When the Tonbridge branch closed down the balance of funds was divided amongst its surviving members instead of being returned to the head office.[6]

Evans's first big opportunity for effecting reforms was at the General Delegate Meeting held in the Midland Inn, The Batch, St Phillips, Bristol, on January 12, 1875. Here he pleaded with the delegates to increase the allocation to the central fund by 6d per quarter per member as the Society would be 'powerless as a united body without a strong central fund'. After delegates from South Wales and Manchester had persuaded the delegates that this proposition 'be not entertained', the conference agreed to increase the quarterly levy by 3d only, to cover legal expenses, to help weak branches and to be used for 'any other lawful purpose'. This made possible some improvement in the financial position of the Society but, in Evans's view, it did not go far enough. In his *Railway Service Gazette* article in September 1874, Evans had warned that in a few years' time when foundation members retired, superannuation allowances would become a serious drain on funds, since one superannuated member at 5s a week would 'swallow up the weekly contributions of thirty'. Impressed by these arguments the delegate meeting agreed to increase contributions to the superannuation fund by a penny a week.

It was a hard struggle to persuade the delegates to lessen the power of the districts, but after the reduction in their number to eight had been proposed and rejected, Conference, on the recommendation of a map committee which had studied the question, finally came to a unanimous decision in favour of six. Through the adoption of the new rule that each district should elect two members of the E.C the size of that body was raised to twelve.

The Conference had not gone as far in the direction of reform as Evans had hoped but it had, at least, moved in the right direction. Furthermore, by passing a resolution that instead of holding office for twelve months the General Secretary 'should remain in office during the will and pleasure of the members who should, through the E.C., have power to call upon him to resign', the delegates had given Evans the opportunity to return to the task of reform when the next delegate meeting assembled.[7]

It is possible that already at the time of the Bristol delegate meeting Evans had lost all faith in the district system and was not outspoken against it solely for tactical reasons. Certainly he informed the next meeting of the E.C. that the system was disadvantageous to the weaker areas, particularly to the North-East.[8] By January 1876, he told the E.C. that the reports from branches convinced him that the district system, though costly, had failed to strengthen the operations of the Society or to strengthen weak branches and that whatever successes had been obtained were due to local effort rather than to the form of organization of the Society. The cost of running the scheme, he contended, jeopardized the whole future of the organization. Perhaps the greatest drawback of an arrangement which was made 'to remove the power from London' and to remove 'the great amount of mistrust' which was exhibited in 1873 was that 'the general office might advocate one line of policy' whilst 'each district might advocate one of its own'. The Society was thus like 'a house divided against itself'.[9]

When the fourth delegate meeting of the Society was held in the Royal Hotel, Temple Row, Birmingham, from October 1 to 6, 1877, Evans gained acceptance to his proposal for the abolition of the district system, the Conference agreeing to a policy of central management of the affairs of the union and to the employment of the three surviving paid district secretaries—John Graham, James Cordwell and C. Bassett-Vincent—as travelling secretaries taking their instructions from the General Secretary. In place of the irregular and costly delegate meetings hitherto held it was decided to hold each October an Annual General Meeting of the sixty delegates elected on a district basis. Each A.G.M. was to decide the place of meeting for the following October but the delegates were not to choose the same place at shorter intervals than five years. Special General Meetings (of the A.G.M. delegates) could be summoned by the E.C. 'if absolutely necessary'. The size of the E.C. was raised to thirteen (excluding the President and General Secretary) but for reasons of economy it was decided that it should be elected by the A.G.M. delegates.

Conference was still reluctant to vote a larger quarterly levy for the general funds but agreed to raise contributions by 1s a year specifically for the augmentation of the superannuation fund. An optional sickness and burial fund was established for all members under 50 years of age.[10]

Although the decisions of the Birmingham delegate meeting marked a substantial advance on the reform of the Society's structure and enhanced the powers of the General Secretary and the Executive, the resistance of the branches to a reasonable control over their affairs continued. Despite the fact that the Bristol delegate meeting had resolved that the funds of the branches were 'the common property of the society', many branches resented any interference by the General Secretary in their financial affairs. When Evans wrote to branch secretaries directing them to place sums of between £20 and £30 in the bank he was charged with being impertinent. One branch directed its secretary to make his reply to Evans 'as insulting as possible'. The man did so 'in a characteristic manner'. It required a resolution of conference to instruct branch secretaries to send a quarterly report to head office of their financial position.

So long as the branches continued to defy effective control from head-quarters the temptations for dishonesty on the part of the branch officials remained strong. In 1876 Evans *discovered* deficiencies in the accounts of one in every fifteen of the branches and there may well have been other branches whose malpractices were undetected. In that year the confidence of members of the Oxford, Brighton, Excelsior, Lynn, Pontypool, Aston, Staveley, Ardsley, Stapleford and Bury branches must have been shaken when the branch secretary or treasurer resigned through being unable or unwilling to make good deficiencies.[11] Many of these difficulties were due to the inexperience of branch officials rather than their dishonesty, but this was all the more reason for more effective control, ˙at least for the time being, from head office. The fact that although 4,098 new members joined the union in 1876, 3,475 left it in the same period, is not surprising in view of the mismanagement of so many branches. Evans said that the lack of stability in membership was the 'great weakness' of the union at that time.[12]

Not untypical of the violently fluctuating membership of many branches in the 'seventies was the experience of the Aberdare branch. Of the first hundred members enrolled in the books of this branch, by March 1882 thirty-six 'ran out of benefit', nineteen failed to maintain their contributions, sixteen transferred to other branches, one went to sea, three died from natural causes and two were killed in railway accidents.

III

During the many tedious months in which the organization of the union was being gradually improved, the economy of the country passed from a condition of unprecedented boom to that of widespread depression. The trade of the country in 1872 was officially described as advancing 'by leaps and bounds'; 1873 was a year of 'general prosperity' and in 1874 the country had reached 'the highest point of prosperity'. By contrast, conditions in 1876 were described by the one word 'depression' whilst 1879 saw 'the culmination of distress'.[13]

The Railway Companies' gross receipts from traffic which had increased by over $8\frac{1}{2}$ per cent between 1872 and 1873 decreased by 1·75 per cent between 1878 and 1879 and the proportion of working expenses to receipts which had been 48·8 per cent in 1870 rose to 52·3 per cent in 1879.[14] The companies' dividends were not seriously affected. The Midland dividend was reduced from 6 per cent to 5 per cent in 1876 but was then maintained at 5 per cent for the rest of the decade; the London and South Western Railway fell from $4\frac{3}{4}$ per cent in 1875 to $4\frac{1}{2}$ per cent in 1879; the Taff Vale declared a steady 10 per cent plus 1 per cent bonus and the North Eastern, though less profitable than in the early 1870's, was paying 7 per cent in the depression year 1876. The London and North Western Railway was perhaps most adversely affected. The Chairman of that Company said in 1879 that its financial condition could be compared with 'a man who has been ill in bed for two or three months and gets up to find his clothes too large for him'. The drop in dividend in this case was from 7 per cent in 1873 to 5½ per cent in 1879.[15]

That dividends did not come down further was in no small measure due to economies at the expense of the railway labour force. In 1876 the London and North Western Railway, by introducing the 'trip system' for guards, economized in the payment of overtime for that grade; the North Eastern, the Manchester, Sheffield and Lincolnshire and the Great Western Railway all made men work longer hours before they were entitled to overtime payments; on the Lancashire and Yorkshire Railway many guards were placed in a lower grade and on the Midland Railway the guards were expected to work on Sundays at ordinary rates of pay. Evans told the E.C. in July 1876 that he believed the companies were acting in concert to deprive the railwaymen of the concessions granted in 1872–4.[16]

Because of the defects in its constitution and the character of its policy the A.S.R.S. was virtually powerless to resist the attacks of the companies. Not until 1880 did the union have a protection fund from which to pay strike aliment or compensation to those victimized by the companies, and from the beginning the leaders had declared that the Society opposed strikes. The only group of men to offer any resistance to the companies' economy drive in 1876 were 800 of the goods guards employed by the Midland Railway who struck work on May 18th because of that company's cessation of overtime pay for Sunday duty. When, however, these men asked for assistance from the union, the E.C. declared that they could not be granted donation benefit as the strike was an unauthorized one. Consequently, the men became anxious to resume employment, and most of them returned to work on the company's terms on May 21st. A number of men, including most of the strikers from Burton-on-Trent, slower at returning to work than the others, found their places had been filled. As the rules stood at the time the union was unable to do anything to help them. It must have been poor consolation to the Burton men to learn that the E.C. had (in the significant absence of Canon Jenkins who would have disliked it) passed a resolution deploring 'the recent retrograde movement of the companies and their breach of faith with their servants' and warning that 'should such action be taken in the future' the E.C. would feel itself justified after 'reasonable means' had failed to 'take extreme measures'. Pious resolutions would not bring back lost jobs.

Although the assistance given by people of independent means such as M. T. Bass, Canon Jenkins, Samuel Morley and Earl De la Warr had been valuable in helping to establish the union, the advice on policy which they gave, if conducive to favourable results in 1872–4, was such as to deter the union from effective resistance to the companies' attacks in 1876–9. Canon Jenkins, vicar of Aberdare, who was president of the Society from 1873 until his premature death at the age of 48 on November 9, 1876, was a man of saintly character and great scholarship—he knew ten languages. But he held an almost naïve faith in the identity of interests of masters and men. In his Presidential Report to the E.C. in January 1874, he wrote that 'though the establishment of Joint Stock Companies had tended much to isolate employer from employees, the interests of the two were identical'. He was sure that if they followed a policy of 'peaceful co-operation' their 'reasonable demands would be satisfied'.[17] Earl De la Warr, a Vice-President of the Society, told the members assembled at an anniversary dinner on July 15, 1874, that he believed that in the railway service 'fair and reasonable demands would always meet with a fair and reasonable response.'[18] Mr P. S. MacLiver who, on Evans's recommendation, became President of the Society in January 1877, and who was a wealthy railway shareholder and a proprietor of the *Western Daily Press* and the *Observer*, 'unhesitatingly condemned' all strikes and favoured settling all disputes by arbitration.[19]

Unfortunately not all railway managers and lesser officials were 'fair and reasonable' men any more than were the men they employed. It was reported to the Battersea branch of the A.S.R.S. that many employees of the Brighton line had been told by the company's officials that as long as they belonged to the Society they would never get any promotion; whilst a delegate from Nottingham No. 2 Branch told the E.C. in August 1876, that, since the men at Toton had been threatened with dismissal, the attendance at the Toton branch meetings had fallen sharply, the last meeting being abandoned as only one man turned up.[20] Since the members of the union knew that if they were victimized the union was not in a position to help them, attendances fell off and branches went into dissolution.

Fear of victimization, along with the indifference of many and the disillusionment of some others, helps to explain the poor response of the membership to Evans's one major campaign for the betterment of working conditions by industrial action in this period. In July 1875, the E.C. approved his proposals for a nation-wide campaign for extra payment for Sunday duty. Significantly, he suggested that the appeals to the directors should come from the men and not from the Society as only a tithe of the men were members. Although Evans spent much time, energy and money in addressing meetings up and down the country, the campaign was a flop. He himself told the E.C. in August 1876 that generally there had been 'but little interest manifested' and in any case not 3,000 members of the Society were affected. Consequently it was decided to abandon the campaign.[21]

IV

The experience of largely uncontested withdrawal in the face of the companies' attacks in 1876 caused both those members who regarded the A.S.R.S. as something more than a friendly society, and their General

Secretary, to modify their views on the subject of strike. In September 1875, Evans had helped to compose and to circulate among the branches *The Railwaymen's Catechism*, which included this statement:

'Does the Society encourage strikes? No: it avoids them as an evil to masters and men. But it courts favour from the public and the Press.'[22]

Even in 1875, Evans was not an unqualified opponent of strikes. He told a Birmingham audience on August 18th that year that though 'he was not an advocate of strikes' as they injured both railwaymen and their employers, he recognized that if the men 'were cruelly treated' resort to strikes as 'a mode of enforcing their rights' might be necessary.[23] About a year later he told a Manchester audience that:

'If injustice was heaped on injustice, and wrong upon wrong and if reason was entirely ignored, then they must try strength for strength, for labour had strength equal to capital if put upon its mettle.[24]

It was, however, the renewed attacks by the companies early in 1879 which compelled Evans and the E.C. to consider more urgently the union's policy towards strikes. Though 1876 and 1877 had been years of trade depression, the companies' receipts from traffic had increased. In 1878 and 1879, for the first time for more than a decade, receipts went down and the companies reacted by the introduction in December 1878, and January 1879, of widespread reductions in wages. On the Great Northern the goods men, carmen, passenger guards and others were affected; on the Lancashire and Yorkshire Railway the wages of passenger guards, signalmen, porters and others were reduced by from 1s to 2s 6d a week; on the North Eastern guards and other grades were expected to do an extra six hours' work a week for the same rate of pay; on the London and North Western Railway the trip system was further extended and wages of van boys and telegraph lads were reduced from 10s to 9s a week.[25]

But it was on the Midland Railway where the reductions imposed affected the largest number of grades and aroused the greatest resentment. The reductions on this line were introduced in stages, grade by grade. First the porters' wages were reduced from 18s to 17s a week; then the platelayers' assistants had their wages cut from 19s to 18s; a short while after the goods guards, shunters and horse drivers were informed that their hours would be increased from 60 to 66 per week; the extension of the trip system for guards brought this grade the prospect of an average reduction of 3s a week in their earnings.[26]

As was the case in 1876, it was the goods guards who showed most fight. On the day that the new scales were due to come into operation the men of this grade at Toton sidings left their work and were quickly followed by hundreds of other guards employed on the Midland system. The strike lasted for seventeen days.

What helped to convert the leadership of the union to a more radical policy was the failure of all efforts of conciliation with the company. Mr Allport, its General Manager, whose salary of £4,000 a year was unaffected throughout the dispute, refused Mr Evans's offer (made on behalf of the union) that the dispute should be referred to arbitration. Instead he replaced the strikers with men supplied by the North Eastern Railway, Great Northern and Great Eastern Railway. On January 6th, Mr Bass, who owned over £100,000 worth of Midland Railway stock, wrote a letter to Mr Ellis pointing out that he had looked at the Company's traffic returns and could 'find no adequate excuse in them for reducing wages'. At the time of the strike the company's £100 ordinary stock was worth £121 and a 5 per cent dividend was declared in January.[27] It was circumstances such as these which led Evans to write that 'so far as a strike was justifiable' this one was.

Evans's opinion hardened with the progress of the dispute. When in the early days of the struggle, he told a mass meeting at King's Cross that it was impossible for the Society as then constituted to undertake or support a strike his remarks were 'received with coolness'. On January 22, 1879, he spoke eloquently and passionately to a crowded and enthusiastic meeting held in the Exeter Hall, London. He reminded his audience that it had been a cardinal point of the union's policy to rely on a sympathetic public opinion to help the railwaymen to gain fair conditions of employment.

'And what has public opinion done for us?' he continued. 'It has not stayed for a moment the hands of the companies. Public sympathy we do desire, but looking at what has been done for the goods guards of the Midland, I begin to think it is a poor reed to rely on in the case of necessity. Last week the subscriptions for them amounted to £63 and the bulk of that has been subscribed by railwaymen. You railwaymen are helpless because you are disunited. Some of you know very well that if a man has the courage to speak for his rights or if he has the courage to be the representative of his fellows, he is dismissed from the service. And by the organization of associated railways he is prevented from obtaining employment on any other line. The only other course left—and I speak these words deliberately and with great sorrow, for our Society up to now has declared itself against strikes on railways—is to organize yourselves together in order that you may have the power to inflict on the companies loss for loss, and then your rights will be respected.'

This forthright speech which he ended by quoting Longfellow's *Psalm of Life* was ended 'amidst thunders of applause'.[28] Later on in the meeting, the London railwayman, George Boon, taking his cue from Evans, advised members of the union to make a small weekly contribution towards a strike fund.

At the meeting of the E.C. held within a week of the failure of the goods guards' strike a heart-searching discussion took place on the future policy of the Society. Mr E. Harford, the representative from Sheffield, commented that they were 'in a position of being able to bark but not to bite'. Evans, who when appealed to at the commencement of the strike had declared that men who left work could not claim donative benefit, now suggested that as the men had been discharged for refusing to accept a reduction in wages it was consistent with Rule 14 that this benefit should be paid as from January 10th, the date of their dismissal by the companies. The Executive Committee agreed. On the proposal of George Boon the Committee agreed unanimously to three resolutions. The first regretted that the companies, 'impervious to public opinion', had 'enforced reductions in wages and increased hours'. The second resolution read as follows:

'That as the railway companies have introduced a new element into the treatment of their servants by lowering their wages in times of depression, this meeting refers the question of strikes to the reconsideration of the whole society, so as to place it within the power of men to force the railway companies to give higher wages in times of prosperity as effectively as the companies enforced the reduction. At the same time the Committee declares itself in favour of the establishment of a Board of Arbitration; but until the companies are compelled to submit disputes with their servants to arbitration, and abide by the award, it will be but little advantage to the servants.'

By the third resolution it was agreed to issue to the branches a circular in which the case for a protection fund and an estimate of its cost in terms of weekly contributions would be stated.[29]

The Special Circular, *The Proposed Future Policy of the Society with Draft of Rules for a Protection Fund*, was issued under Evans's name on June 3, 1879. In it the General Secretary wrote that as a result of the members' aversion to strikes and their desire to win public support, they had made their Society a non-striking one. However, public opinion 'had utterly failed to influence the companies', who had 'reduced the wages and increased the hours of their men'. Men who had been selected to represent their fellows had been reduced in grade, removed from place to place or dismissed the service. When dismissed, men had been unable to obtain employment by their being denied a character reference by their former employers. At best, public opinion could exert a *moral* influence. However, the railway companies, by reason of their impersonal character, were, he claimed, callous to *moral* influences and recognized only *material* ones. The men therefore required *material* influence to enable them to assert their rights. So that they should no longer remain 'disarmed in the face of the enemy' they needed a strike fund so that they could 'withhold labour rather than sell it on disadvantageous terms'. Strikes, he maintained, were justifiable when they constituted 'the workman's last and only means of asserting or defending his rights'. They would remain 'helpless' before the 'all powerful companies until they possessed the means and organization to unitedly withhold labour'. Whilst arbitration was 'the true and rational method of settling disputes', the companies would not agree to it so long as their power was unrestricted.

Evans proposed that members should pay 1¼d a week to the protection fund, from which should be paid the cost of any strike undertaken by the Society and the cost of compensation paid to members who had been reduced, removed or discharged from their employment for being the chosen representatives of their fellows in any movement sanctioned by the Society. Out of consideration to those members who were likely to be lukewarm in their support of the proposals, he recommended that at the end of each year any amounts in excess of £5,000 in the protection fund should be transferred to the superannuation fund. He promised that if the men built up a powerful fund, organized themselves so as to act unitedly, and banished any want of friendliness between grades, many men who had until then stood aloof would be attracted to the Society.

The publication of this challenging statement provoked intense controversy in the branches and divided members who were in the Society largely because of the friendly society benefits it provided from those whose main concern was to see the A.S.R.S. become a more aggressive trade union.

When the E.C. called for a report from the branches on their members' attitude towards the new proposals, a majority of the men who expressed an opinion were against the establishment of a protection fund. In the 145 branches who sent in returns 2,531 members were against the fund and 1,416 in favour of it. The most frequent reason given for opposition was that the poorer members of the union 'could not afford to pay more money'.[30] It was a result ominous for Evans's chances of success at the A.G.M. later in the year.

The A.G.M. held at Leeds in October 1879 was one of the most momentous in the history of the union. Attention was chiefly centred on the great debate on the subject of the protection fund. Despite Evans's plea that if they were to adopt the fund there would hardly ever be a necessity for using it since it would serve to prevent rather than encourage strikes, delegates from Peterborough, Cardiff and Bedford and many other branches were unconvinced, though delegates from Southampton, Camden, Brighton and Preston supported Evans and the E.C. A notable contribution to the discussion which helped to sway opinion away from

Evans's view was that made by Mr P. S. MacLiver, the President, who said that when he joined the Society he had no idea that any such scheme was contemplated and he was sure that other influential supporters, like himself, deprecated the proposed changes. The primary principle of their Society was arbitration and he did 'not know a single instance when arbitration had failed'. A hostile attitude to the employers was 'specially to be deprecated' at that time and he was certain that if they attempted to pursue the subject it would end in 'great disaster and disappointment'. Of the goods guards' strike on the Midland he declared that it 'was begun in haste and repented at leisure'.

If Evans made a mistake in tactics at this A.G.M. it was in giving prominence to the financial position of the superannuation fund which, he declared, was actuarially unsound since the scale of contributions was insufficient to cover anticipated liabilities. Although his criticisms of the state of the fund were completely warranted, it might have been a better policy for him to have soft pedalled on this question until the protection fund was established and the members who were disgruntled on account of the ineffectiveness of the union for the protection of their interests had been placated. But in view of the publicity which he had given to the deficiencies of the superannuation fund, Congress set up a special committee to examine the structure of the Society's friendly benefits. In his speech Mr MacLiver used the excuse of the financial difficulties of the Society as an argument against the establishment of the fund and, at the end of the discussion, the Camden representative's amendment:

'That seeing that the whole financial condition of the Society has to be revised, the protection fund question stand over until the next meeting'

was adopted and the introduction of this vital measure postponed for one crucial year.

V

At the time of the Leeds A.G.M. in 1879, the enginemen members of the A.S.R.S., according to Evans, were 'a very large one third' of the membership. If his assertion that half the enginemen of the country were in the A.S.R.S. may be doubted, it was nevertheless true that the enginemen were the best-organized grade in the railway service and that the union had made special allowances for this fact when arriving at a number of policy decisions.[31] At the delegate meeting in October 1877, it was decided not to compel all branches to conform to an 'all grades' pattern since a number of existing branches were composed entirely of footplatemen and it was argued that in some districts footplatemen would not join an 'all-grade' branch. When locomotivemen members were dismissed from the service of the London and North Western Railway for opposing the introduction of the trip system, the E.C. decided to pay them donation benefit at double the normal rate.[32] When the companies began in 1876 and 1878 to withdraw the concessions made to the men at the beginning of the decade, some of the enginemen (whose wages were in many cases double those of porters) felt that the A.S.R.S. was, by its constitution, incapable of defending their interests and they considered that they might be better off organizing themselves on a craft basis. Evans was aware of these rumblings of discontent early in 1879, if not earlier. He warned the E.C. that 'there were those who were urging the formation of other societies of railway servants' on the ground that the A.S.R.S. was 'not defensive enough'.[33] But although the E.C. saw the danger and favoured the immediate introduction of the protection fund, it is doubtful whether a majority of the branches were similarly convinced at the time of the Leeds A.G.M.

During the same week in which the A.G.M. delegates decided to postpone for a year a decision on the protection fund, Sir Daniel Gooch of the Great Western Railway, 'the enginemen's friend', interviewed a deputation of enginemen who were protesting against the company's decision to increase the hours of work of footplatemen from 10 to 12 per day as from October 1, 1879. When the men reminded Sir Daniel that they had obtained 2,000 signatures to a petition on the subject he is reported to have replied:

'Damn the signatures. Have you got the men to back them up?'

The challenge was accepted and on the Great Western Railway and other companies' lines two locomotivemen's societies—the Locomotive and Firemen's National Union and the Associated Society of Locomotive Engineers and Firemen were in the process of formation before the end of 1879.[34]

After the A.S.L.E. & F. horse had bolted, the A.S.R.S. proceeded to shut the door in 1880. At its meeting in February 1880, the E.C. of the A.S.R.S. resolved that there was an 'urgent necessity of the protection fund being speedily established'. Branches, particularly those on the Great Western Railway system which had opposed the protection fund in the previous October were expressing strong opinions in its favour by September 1880; some had even established protection funds of their own.[35] When the delegates assembled in Cardiff for the A.G.M. in October 1880, Evans reminded them that the reduction in wages which some of them had experienced since last they met might have been avoided had Congress voted differently the year before. The resolution, proposed and seconded by enginemen delegates—'That the principle of the protection fund be adopted' was then carried, amid loud cheering, by forty votes to thirteen.[36]

Agreement on the details quickly followed. Members were to pay a penny a week to the fund (bringing the total subscription up to 5d a week). Those who were discharged from employment for taking an active part in any movement by, or under the sanction of, the Society, were entitled to a weekly sum of 12s until they found new employment, though the E.C. could decide to pay a lump sum of £35 in lieu of the weekly benefit. If a member could only obtain new employment at a reduced rate of wages, he would be given an allowance of not more than 5s payable for not more than one year. If any member sought to obtain benefit under false pretences he could be expelled from the Society by the E.C. The second purpose of the fund was to provide strike aliment to members where the Society authorized strike action to prevent a reduction of wages or an increase of hours. The rules of the fund stated that it was the duty of the Society to offer arbitration as a means of settlement of any dispute. If this offer was unnoticed or unaccepted it was to be repeated. Only if the appeal was again ignored or rejected could more extreme action be taken. If a railway company refused to go to arbitration the members concerned could appeal to the E.C. which was then under obligation to take a ballot vote of all members to decide whether or not the strike was justifiable. The strike aliment was to be at the rate of 2s a day or 12s a week, with an additional 1s per week for each dependent child under the age of 12. The E.C. was empowered to grant a lump sum emigration benefit of £8 to enable any member who was unemployed and drawing benefit from the fund to emigrate overseas.

After October 1880, it was thus not possible for a member to claim that the union had power to bark but not to bite. At Cardiff the A.S.R.S. was given the means to invoke sanctions in its bargaining with the companies. The year's delay in adopting these means had, however, been the most important reason for the drop in membership figures from 11,516 at the end of 1879 to 8,589 a year later.

Other decisions taken at Cardiff, though vitally necessary from the point of view of the efficient management of the union, led to a further drain of membership. The failure to reach a positive decision on the protection fund in 1879 led to the defection of nearly three thousand trade-union activists; the winding up of the superannuation fund in 1880 led to the withdrawal of nearly two thousand members who were in the union mainly for the friendly society benefits it provided.

The special committee appointed by the A.G.M. in 1879 to examine the finances of the union endorsed Evans's claim that the superannuation fund was not likely to be self-supporting in the future. An actuary's report, presented to the delegates at Cardiff a year later, provided further confirmation of the unsoundness of the fund's finances. When Evans informed the delegates at Cardiff that if the fund was not wound up the position would be that a few older members drawing 5s a week 'would have handed over to them every penny of the funds' whilst 'a vast majority of the members having equal moral claims' have been left 'without a penny' merely because they were younger, the delegates agreed by forty votes to thirteen to wind up the fund. It was agreed that there should be paid a lump sum of £20 in commutation to superannuated members. It was an overdue decision but one which, on Evans's own admission, caused a 'great number' of the older members nearing retirement to leave the Society and 'to induce others to follow their example'.[37]

The decision to establish an orphan fund, though widely welcomed in the union, involved an increase in contributions by a further $\frac{1}{2}$d and may well have proved the last straw for many members whose contribution, because of the protection fund and orphan fund additions, were, at one stroke, raised from $3\frac{1}{2}$d to 5d a week.

To add insult to injury, in the course of 1880 the *Railway Service Gazette* passed into unsympathetic hands and by the autumn of that year the paper was misrepresenting the aims of the A.S.R.S. and supporting the breakaway locomotivemen's unions. Early in the year, Mr Bass, by now a sick man, sold the copyright of the paper to the Rev. Edward Collett of Retford, Notts. From its first publication in 1872 the paper had never paid its way despite the achievement of a circulation of between 10,000 and 12,000 copies a week; in the course of nine years Mr Bass had paid off debts arising from its publication amounting to nearly £1,000. The first issue published by the new owner appeared on March 19, 1880.[38] Until July 9, 1880, with Mr Edwin Phillips continuing as editor, the paper upheld the policy of the union, but during the ensuing week the Rev Collett sold the paper for £100 to a Mr Dixon of London who was proprietor of the *Grocers Gazette* and who had no particular affection for trade unionism. From July 16, 1880, the paper's editorials cast doubts on the journalistic ability of the editor (Evans) of the recently established *Railway Review* and in particular made fun of his occasional grammatical errors. More serious was the support of the rival unions.[39]

For some time past Evans had favoured the establishment of a weekly newspaper which was under the control of the union. His opportunity came in June 1880, when James Greenwood (the same James Greenwood who had been the first editor of the *Railway Service Gazette*) started editing and publishing the *King's Cross Journal*. When, after the appearance of four issues of the new paper, it did not seem likely to pay its way, Greenwood sold Evans the copyright for £75. Thus Evans produced the first number of the paper under its new title *The Railway Review* on July 16, 1880.

At its meetings on December 31, 1880, and February 16, 1881, the E.C. decided to purchase the copyright of the *Railway Review* from Evans for £75; to make him editor of the paper; to provide him with an editorial assistant; and to inform the branches that the new paper was the official organ of the Society.[40]

To offset the decline in membership and raise the morale of the union, Evans gained the approval of the A.G.M. in October 1880, for the launching of a Nine Hours Movement, and the E.C., in January 1881, approved the expenditure of £1,000 on meetings, deputations and press publicity. In order to involve the membership more consciously in the campaign, Evans persuaded the A.G.M. at Manchester in October 1881, to ask all members to contribute one day's pay towards the expenses of the movement. Unfortunately, the campaign had the exactly opposite effect to that intended. The companies either ignored or decisively rejected the memorial sent them on August 26, 1881, for a nine-hour day for all except signalmen and shunters (for whom eight hours was requested); and the suggestion that they might contribute a day's pay frightened more members out of the Society. The special appeal only realized £568 from 3,000 members. Owing to the unenthusiastic response to its efforts, the E.C., in May 1882, decided to close the movement and return the day's pay to those members who had responded to the appeal.

The complete failure of the Nine Hours Movement caused Evans to lose heart. A fortnight after the E.C. decided to wind up the campaign, Evans wrote a letter of resignation to Mr MacLiver, the President. When the E.C. met and considered the letter on July 19, 1882, Evans gave the failure of the campaign—which he said was 'a personal defeat'—the want of progress of the Society, and the need for economy in management expenses (of which his salary was the biggest item) as the principal reasons for his decision. But when the E.C. unanimously resolved to ask Evans to continue in office he agreed to do so.

In his report to the A.G.M. in October 1882, Evans clearly had doubts about the wisdom of maintaining the union. In commenting on the fact that the membership was 'about 6,000' (it was almost certainly below that figure) he wrote:

'If there was not hope that the society would again recover its numerical strength and thus spread the costs of the movements over a wider area, thereby reducing each one's proportion, it would be the duty of the remaining members to determine whether they were justified in continuing to further objects for the benefit of the whole service at the exclusive cost of the few.'

The disheartened General Secretary could not have found very reassuring the resolution which the meeting carried *nem. con.*:

'That although there seems to be some reason to complain of the General Secretary's past conduct this meeting believes that in the interest of the society it is desirable to overlook the past.'

Evans gained most reassuring support from the Swindon and Battersea delegates who succeeded in carrying the following far-sighted resolution:

'That this congress believes the decrease of members shown in the report is an outcome of the alteration of the constitution by which solvency and better protection have been secured; but believing that the existing basis of the society is a satisfactory one, the future progress must largely depend on the local efforts of the members, and the disposition of the men in the railway service to embrace the true principle of trade unionism, i.e. self help.'

Evans should have taken heart from such a wise and realistic assessment as this, but instead, in a mood of continuing depression, he overworked himself into a nervous breakdown by the end of 1882.

When the E.C. met for the first time in 1883 on February 7th, Evans was not present. The two men who were deputed to visit him in his own home reported that his absence was due to 'mental exhaustion occasioned chiefly by overwork', and the committee charitably resolved 'that one month's leave be granted to the General Secretary', and that Harford should take charge of the office during his absence. Evans failed to return. When the E.C. met again on May 2, 1883, it resolved 'That as the General Secretary has not returned to duty since his month's leave of absence the committee considers he has vacated his position'. By registered letter a copy of the resolution was sent to Evans at his private address. It was a sad end to the career of one of the union's ablest general secretaries.

VI

The only applicant for the vacant post was the 45-year-old Bristolian, Edward Harford, who had been Assistant Secretary in 1882 and Acting Secretary since the beginning of 1883. In his youth and early manhood he had been employed by the Bristol and Exeter Railway (later merged with the Great Western Railway) successively as porter, shunter, signalman, goods guard, passenger guard and inspector. In 1873 he entered the service of the A.S.R.S. as District Secretary of the Sheffield area. With the enlargement of the districts and the reduction in their number in 1875, he lost his employment but retained his membership whilst working temporarily in an iron foundry. He attended the delegate meeting in Birmingham in 1877 and then served on the E.C. from 1878–9, before Evans secured his re-employment as organizing secretary from October 1879 onwards. Though he lacked the brilliance of his predecessor and was a man of stolid rather than mercurial temperament, Harford was a conscientious and hardworking organizer. He was convinced that the Society need not always be engaged in exciting (and expensive) campaigns in order to win support; rather he favoured the painstaking strengthening of union membership at branch level.

In the interval of time between Harford's appointment as General Secretary in 1883 and the important changes made in the Society's rules in 1888 preparatory to an industrial offensive, the membership of the Society crept up from 6,000 to over 10,000, whilst the funds which had amounted to £27,176 at the end of 1882 had increased to £62,186 at the end of 1887. The growth in the membership had been accompanied by a shift in its distribution; in 1887 a much larger proportion of the membership came from the branches in Northumberland and Durham.

The declaration by the North Eastern Railway of a dividend of over 8 per cent in the early 1880's[43] encouraged union members employed on that company's lines to follow up the pioneering work done by Harford in the district in 1879. In 1882 a new and energetic recruit to the Society, William Foreman, started an agitation at Gateshead for improved rates of wages and hours of pay for the footplatemen and goods guards. Although a few concessions were made by the company the demands made on behalf of the mineral guards and the claims made for better overtime rates were ignored. Nevertheless recruitment had been promising and it encouraged Foreman to launch an all-grades movement in the area. At its meeting in May 1883, the E.C. promised the protection benefit for those involved in loss of employment or participating in an official strike.[44] After spending the summer in a recruitment drive Foreman asked the Directors of the North Eastern Railway to negotiate with the All-Grades Committee but the General Manager at an interview granted on October 15, 1883, told him that they would only see the men on a grade basis. Early in December when the company's departmental chiefs did agree to meet the committee of the men they insisted on splitting the men into grades before the start of the discussions.[45] When Foreman started a new campaign early in 1884 Harford, at a meeting with the committee, urged that they should concentrate on the consolidation of the membership as trade conditions were worsening. The only important concession obtained as a result of this agitation was the granting of a minimum period of eight hours' rest between spells of duty.[47] However, the increase of membership in the area had helped to restore the morale of the union.

One outcome of the increased membership in the North-East was a revision of the rules for the election of the E.C. approved by the A.G.M. at Bath in 1884. The membership of the Society was in future to be divided between thirteen equal electoral constituencies each of which would elect one member to the Executive Committee. Each E.C. member was to be elected for one year, was not eligible to sit for more than two years in succession, but could be re-elected again after an interval of three years.[48]

The extension of the Parliamentary franchise in 1884 gave the vote for the first time to tens of thousands of railwaymen in the lower paid grades.

Even before this, at the A.G.M. in Edinburgh in October 1883, delegates from Gateshead had endeavoured to persuade other delegates to agree to establish an election fund. The proposal was rejected by twenty-nine votes to fourteen.

In a printed branch circular issued on February 25, 1885, Harford declared that railwaymen, if they chose, need no longer submit to be legislated for by directors, stock-brokers and others in a higher social sphere who for the most part have little real sympathy with the working classes. Members of the union were requested to answer the following three questions:

1st. Is it desirable that the Society should exert its influence in endeavouring to secure direct representation of railway servants in the House of Commons?

2nd. Are the members of your branch willing to make a voluntary levy towards raising a fund for the purpose? If so, of how much per member per year?

3rd. In the event of the foregoing questions being answered in the affirmative, will the branch appoint canvassers to secure the co-operation of non-members, and collect subscriptions from them?

The result of the inquiry was disappointing to those who were advocates of parliamentary representation. Only 5,441 members out of the 8,460 belonging to the union troubled to vote and of these only 3,335 men in fifty-six branches expressed themselves as favourable to direct A.S.R.S. representation in Parliament. Two thousand four hundred and six members in thirty-nine branches were opposed to such a move. Only forty-seven branches supported an annual subscription. The results of the inquiry were not publicized. When William Foreman endeavoured at the A.G.M. at Leicester that year to carry a resolution in favour of a parliamentary fund built up from a compulsory levy of 6d per member the matter was referred back to the E.C. for them to prepare a detailed scheme.[49]

Next year a sub-committee of the E.C. drafted a plan for financing the fund either by a compulsory levy of 3d a week or a voluntary subscription of 6d. Only 113 out of 178 branches replied to the questionnaire and the results showed strong opposition to compulsory contributions (only 674 out of the 5,583 voting favoured it) and almost equally divided opinion on the merits of voluntary contributions.[50] The subject was removed from the agenda of the next A.G.M. on the somewhat thin excuse that in the interim the Labour Electoral Association had been formed. It was not until the 1889 A.G.M. that there was another big discussion on the subject.

NOTES

1. *R.S.G.*, October 11, 1873, Alcock, p. 101.
2. Alcock, p. 101.
3. Account of the 'Raid on London' taken from Alcock, pp. 107–10.

4. *R.S.G.*, October 11, 1873.
5. *R.S.G.*, September 18, 1874.
6. *R.S.G.*, January 15 and 22, 1875, Report of the General Secretary to the E.C. Alcock, pp. 118–19.
7. The Report of the 1875 Delegate Meeting is given in *R.S.G.*, January 22, 1875.
8. *R.S.G.*, July 30, 1875.
9. *R.S.G.*, February 4 and 9, 1876.
10. *R.S.G.*, October 19, 1877, Supplement reporting Delegate Meeting.
11. A.S.R.S. General Secretary's Report to the E.C. for the half-year ended December 31, 1876, *R.S.G.*, February 9, 1877.
12. A.S.R.S., General Secretary's Report for the year 1876.
13. Royal Commission on the Poor Laws Report 1909, P.P. 1909, XXXVII, p. 350.
14. General Report of the Board of Trade on the Share and Loan Capital of the Railways, P.P. 1880, Vol. LXIV, p. 63.
15. *Herapath's Railway (and Commercial) Journal*, August 5, 12, 19 and 26, 1876, July 12 and August 23 and 30, 1879.
16. *R.S.G.*, August 4, 1876.
17. *R.S.G.*, January 17, 1874. Canon Jenkins's thoroughly unselfish work for the union won him the affection and respect of the men who in 1877 paid for a stained glass window memorial to be placed in Aberdare Parish Church.
18. *The Times*, July 17, 1874.
19. *R.S.G.*, October 10, 1879.
20. *R.S.G.*, March 17 and August 18, 1876.
21. *R.S.G.*, July 30, 1875, August 4, 1876.
22. A.S.R.S., *The Railwaymen's Catechism*, September 17, 1875.
23. *R.S.G.*, August 20, 1875.
24. *R.S.G.*, September 8, 1876.
25. *R.S.G.*, February 14, 1879.
26. *Daily Chronicle*, January 6, 1879.
27. *R.S.G.*, January 24, 1879, February 21, 1879.
28. *R.S.G.*, January 31, 1879.
29. A.S.R.S. E.C., January 29—February 1, 1879. Rs. 1022–4. *R.S.G.*, February 7, 1879.
30. *R.S.G.*, May 9, 1879.
31. *R.R.*, January 7, 1887.
32. *R.S.G.*, October 10, 1877 and October 4, 1878.
33. A.S.R.S. General Secretary's Report to the E.C., February 14, 1879.
34. N. McKillop: *The Lighted Flame*, pp. 13–19. *R.S.G.*, October 31, 1879.
35. A.S.R.S. E.C., February 20, 1880. General Secretary's Report to the E.C., October 1880. *R.R.*, October 15, 1880.
36. *R.S.G.*, October 15, 1880.
37. A.S.R.S. General Secretary's Report to the A.G.M., 1881.
38. *Ibid.*
39. *R.R.*, June 24, 1910, reporting Mr Alcock's interview with Edwin Phillips. *R.S.G.*, March 19 and July 16, 1880.
40. Purchase terms agreed in R. 1464 of E.C. meeting February 16th. See also A.S.R.S. Report and Financial Statements 1882, p. 10. Other decisions in Rs. 1424–7 of December 31, 1880, and 1465–8 of February 16, 1881. *R.R.*, May 13, 1881. Alcock, p. 262.
41. *R.R.*, July 16, 1883.
42. Harford's career outlined in *Trade Unionist*, April 18, 1891.
43. Tomlinson, *The North Eastern Railway* (Newcastle, 1914), p. 754.
44. A.S.R.S. E.C. Minutes, May 1883.

45. *R.R.*, August 10, October 26, and December 7, 1883.
46. *R.R.*, April 18, 1884.
47. A.S.R.S. General Secretary's Report to the A.G.M., 1884, p. 7.
48. A.S.R.S. A.G.M., Bath, October 1884, R. 318.
49. A.S.R.S. A.G.M., Leicester, October 1885, R. 271.
50. *R.R.*, October 15, 1886.

CHAPTER IV

A CHAPTER OF ACCIDENTS

'The greatest sufferers of all and those who receive least attention are simply the companies' servants. There is no concealment attempted for the errors of which the companies' servants are guilty, and for which the poor fellows often pay dearly enough in their own persons. Scarcely an accident happens which is not set down at once to some mistake, or negligence or misadventure on their part. They are in fact the directors' scapegoats; and when it is impossible to deny that some great catastrophe has occurred it is on their shoulders that the entire blame is laid.'
The Times, *leading article, 16th September, 1874.*

'Q.6044. From your general knowledge and experience of railways, what conclusion have you arrived at with regard to the majority of accidents which occur on the railways of Great Britain?'
Mr F. Harrison (General Manager, London and North Western Railway): *'The majority of accidents occur through want of care on the part of the men.'*
Minutes of Evidence, Royal Commission on the Accidents to Railway Servants, 1900.

I

ASK any schoolboy to name the most dangerous of the major occupations in Britain and he would probably mention coal mining and the merchant service. It is unlikely that he would think of railway employment as dangerous, although from the opening of the Liverpool and Manchester Railway in 1830 to the present time, the work of many grades of railwaymen has involved constant dangers to life and limb. In 1906, of every 10,000 railwaymen employed, 8 lost their lives in the course of their work. This figure may, at first sight, seem small when compared with the 55 per 10,000 merchant seamen and 13 per 10,000 miners killed in the same year. But when it is realized that the figure for railwaymen is a general one for all grades of the service and that clerks and station masters are included, the dangers to which other grades are exposed can more readily be appreciated. In the same year, 1906, 27 of every 10,000 goods guards and brakesmen and 26 of every 10,000 shunters employed on the railways were killed whilst on duty, showing that for these grades their work was twice as dangerous as that of miners.

It is not difficult to explain why the hazards of employment in mines are more widely appreciated than are the risks to which railwaymen are exposed in the movement of traffic. When a major mining disaster occurs the sole immediate sufferers are the miners and their families. When a major railway accident occurs it is often the passengers who suffer the greatest number of casualties. Among railway employees the continuous toll of fatalities in their ones, twos and threes to drivers, firemen, goods and passenger guards, shunters, permanent-way men and others is less spectacular and therefore more easily escapes public attention.

The history of accidents sustained by railwaymen is a long and gruesome tale of largely avoidable slaughter and mutilation. Whilst there have been no cases of large scale disaster to railway employees comparable in its effects to the Gresford disaster of September 22, 1934, when 261 colliers were killed, the cumulative effect of very frequent misfortune was indeed impressive. In the quarter century between 1875 and 1899, no less than 12,870 railwaymen were killed and 68,575 were injured. In 1875 the 767 men killed represented a proportion of one in every 334 employed and the 2,815 injured, one in every 89. By 1899 the 531 killed in that year represented a proportion of one in 1,006 and the 4,633 injured one in 115 of those employed, revealing the fact that the earlier accident rate was indeed unnecessarily high. Later figures were to show that a further substantial and rapid reduction in the casualty figures was still possible. By 1920 the number killed was less than half, and the number injured less than a third, of the 1899 figure, though the total labour force was nearly one third greater.[1]

II

When confronted with these very heavy casualty figures the railway managers claimed that there was very little that they could do about it. When asked to state 'the most common cause of accidents' on his line, in 1877, Mr George Findlay, the General Manager of the London and North Western Railway promptly replied: 'I think the neglect of servants.' When asked what class of servants was principally to blame he declared it was the engine drivers and signalmen. Thirty-four years later, as we have seen, another General Manager of the same Company, Mr Frederick Harrison, asserted that 'the majority of accidents occur through want of care on the part of the men'.[2] It was like attributing the spread of an epidemic to the lack of cleanliness of the inhabitants of an overcrowded slum tenement with an inadequate and tainted water supply. The sensible thing for the managers to have done was to have sought the co-operation of the A.S.R.S. to find an agreed policy for reducing the number of accidents. Nothing could have been further from their intention. In their view most trade unionists were irresponsible beings. To co-operate with them would imperil the safe working of the railways. One General Manager, Mr H. A. Walker, expressed the concensus of opinion on the employing side when he said:

'There is no doubt that the most serious effect of the recognition of the trades unions from the point of view of the railway companies would be the lowering of the standard of discipline throughout the railway service. Without a high standard of discipline the safe working of the line would be jeopardized. The entire responsibility for the maintenance of such discipline must rest with the railway companies.'

He was convinced that recognition of and co-operation with the unions would not only be detrimental to the interests of the men but also prejudicial to the safety of the travelling public.[3]

It was, regrettably, all too often the case, at least until after the First World War, that railway management took the view that only by means of an old style military discipline could the safety of the working of the lines be assured. Even many a twentieth-century general manager would not have found so peculiar the view expressed by the famous engineer I. K. Brunel:

'I am not one to sneer at education, but I would not give sixpence in having an engineman because of his knowing how to read or write. I believe that of the two the non-reading man is the best. . . . It is impossible that a man that indulges in reading should make a good engine driver; it requires a species of machine, an intelligent man, an honest man, a sober man, a steady man, but I would much rather not have a thinking man.'[4]

Most railway historians are familiar with Mr George Findlay's opinion expressed in 1893, '. . . that you might as well have trades unionism in Her Majesty's Army as to have it in the railway service. The thing is totally incompatible.'[5]

As a result of their adoption of this 'theirs not to reason why' attitude, railway management lost the invaluable advice on the prevention of accidents which thousands of railway workers were in a position to give as a result of their own experience in working traffic.

Nor did railway management take kindly to the intervention of Government in matters of safe railway working. It is true that from the earliest times the Board of Trade had prescribed some minimum standards in railway construction and operation. For example, under an Act of 1842 it could postpone the opening of a railway if the works or permanent way were in an unsatisfactory condition. Again in 1868 the companies were put under statutory obligation to provide a communication cord between the passenger compartments and the servants of the company in charge of the train. It is, however, noteworthy that the Government was primarily concerned with the safety of *passengers* rather than the safety of railwaymen. A factory act had been passed in 1833 limiting the hours of labour of many textile workers to twelve per day, and further legislation had by 1850 reduced their working hours still further to ten per day. But because of the powerful influence of the railway interest in Parliament the Board of Trade for over sixty years altogether abstained from interfering with conditions of employment on the railways. The accepted view for many decades was that expressed by the Select Committee of 1857 which reported that 'the principle of self interest in its influence on railway companies must be relied on as the best safeguard against accidents'. When, as a result of Mr F. Channing's exposure in the House of Commons of numerous instances of overwork on the railways, Parliament appointed in 1890 a Select Committee on Railway Servants' Hours of Labour, the companies' witnesses were unanimous in opposing any extension of the powers of the Board of Trade. On that occasion Mr G. Findlay said:

'We do not want the Board of Trade to tell us what to do or Parliament to tell us what to do. We surely know our own business better than they can teach us.'

Another General Manager, Mr Lambert of the Great Western Railway, was convinced '. . . it would be a mistake to do anything which would interfere with the responsibilities of the railway companies to the public in the matter of railway safety'.[6]

The concern of Parliament over the long hours and excessive accident rate of railway servants was again aroused in 1900 when a Royal Commission was appointed to inquire into '. . . the possibility of adopting means to reduce the number of accidents, having regard to the working of railways, the rules and regulations made and the safety of appliances used by the railway companies'. The railway companies did not leave the Commission long in doubt as to their attitude to the new proposals. Sir George Gibb, the General Manager of the North Eastern Railway, who, in giving evidence, said he was speaking '. . . on behalf of the companies', declared that '. . . they desired to protest with all their might against such a novelty in railway legislation being introduced'. Asked 'Are you of opinion that any amount of interference on the part of a government department would destroy the responsibility of directors and managers?' he replied, 'Yes, I am.'[7]

That railway managers opposed so strongly any interference either from the A.S.R.S. or the Board of Trade was not due to any innate perversity of character to be found in persons of this type. No doubt railway managers and directors were as kindly family men as the railway servants in their employ. The employers' opposition to outside intervention on behalf of the men is explained rather in terms of railway economics and finances. Far from it being the case that 'the principle of self interest of the railway companies' could be relied on to safeguard the railwaymen against accidents, there is ample evidence to show that this principle was one of the biggest obstacles to accident prevention. The self interest of the railway companies dictated that they should secure an ample return on their capital. But it was often not possible for them *both* to declare a generous dividend on ordinary shares *and* to make adequate arrangements for the safety of railway workers. Safety costs money. A Board of Trade inspector of the railways, Colonel Rich, in commenting on the fact that 187 men were killed in shunting operations in the year 1899 alone, agreed with his questioner that an important way to reduce the danger of accidents was to increase the number of shunters employed. This, he said, was not so simple a matter as might at first appear, for 'it was all a question of expense'.[8] It was generally agreed that the introduction of automatic couplers for railway wagons would help to reduce the casualty figures, but Colonel Rich again hit the nail on the head when he declared 'the problem of automatic couplers in England is financial not mechanical. When you have found the coupler you want its adoption will be barred by the expense involved.'[9] Other examples of the financial stumbling blocks to accident prevention will be cited as the principal causes of casualties among railwaymen are examined.

To the close of the nineteenth century also there was little hope of improvement through the intervention of the Board of Trade. Mr Galt's[8] comment that '. . . the officers of the Board of Trade had no authority to inquire into the treatment of railway servants nor to effect any change if they had' was almost as true in 1897 as in 1877 when the statement was made, except that, in the interim, power had been gained to ask embarrassing questions of the companies on the overworking of their employees and to 'suggest' practical measures to limit working hours of some grades to twelve per day.

As year after year passed and thousands more were added to the total of killed and maimed it was becoming ever more apparent that it was only through their own efforts and the creation of an influential trade union that railwaymen could hope to reduce the terrible toll of casualties. It remains to be seen what the 'irresponsible' body of men in the A.S.R.S. did to make the operation of traffic safer both for those who travelled and those who worked on the railways of Britain.

III

If the vested interests of the companies prevented them from making adequate provision for the safety of their employees it was a vested interest of the A.S.R.S. to advocate the adoption of every means which would reduce the accident rate on the railways. In so far as the A.S.R.S. was successful in its advocacy, it benefited not only the railwaymen but also the travelling public, and in so far as the companies succeeded in Parliament and in the Board Room in resisting the reforms the union proposed, the travelling public as well as the workers on the line stood to lose. The policy of the A.S.R.S. during the first twenty years was one of persuasion and permeation rather than industrial conflicts. *The Railwaymen's Catechism* of 1875 had stated that the Society avoided strikes 'as an evil to masters and men'. The numerical weakness of the union in these years also largely precluded the possibility of vigorous industrial action to secure improved working conditions. Hence if the union was to justify its existence, its officials were bound to place more emphasis on accident prevention.

On the correct assumption that it was necessary to know the extent of the evil before it was possible to set about a cure, the A.S.R.S. began the campaign with a demand for more accurate statistics of railway casualties. Under an Act of 1871 each company was obliged to inform the Board of Trade promptly of every case of death or injury to its servants. The penalty for each instance of failure to send correct information was a maximum fine of £20. During the first two years after the passing of the Act the companies appear to have submitted returns which in many cases grossly understated the number of accidents and less seriously understated the number of deaths. Mr Bass therefore commissioned the then editor of the *Railway Service Gazette* (precursor of the *Railway Review*), Mr Edwin Phillips, to make a thorough investigation of casualty returns, fully in the case of the Lancashire and Yorkshire Railway where the statistics were easier to collect, and by sample in the case of five other major railways. Mr Bass, by publishing Mr Phillips's reports, showed that the Board of Trade returns for 1872 and 1873 were incomplete, that whereas its railway department had reported 39 deaths to the servants of the Lancashire and Yorkshire Railway in 1872, there were in fact 54, and whereas only 73 were reported as injured, in fact there were 1,387. Similar shortcomings were exposed in the figures for the other railway companies. It appears that Mr Chichester Fortesque, the President of the Board of Trade, had demanded an explanation from the Directors of the Lancashire and Yorkshire Company and on receipt of an apology from them had at first decided not to prosecute. When, however, the company continued to send inadequate returns—a fact ascertained from local coroners' reports—proceedings were started against the company by the Treasury's Solicitor. Meanwhile the reports of Mr Phillips had led the editor of *The Times* to declare that the public had 'a right to the fullest information'.

An examination of the figures for casualties to railway servants over the period 1871–1914 brings some startling surprises. The figures of killed and injured made sudden jumps upwards in the years 1896 and 1906–7. The explanation of these reversals of the general trend toward lower casualty figures is that Mr Ritchie in 1895 and Mr Lloyd George in 1906 adopted the recommendation made by the A.S.R.S. for many years that the basis upon which injuries to railwaymen were reported should be extended. Thus the figures for 1896 show an increase of nearly 70 per cent over those of 1895 and those for 1907 an increase of 32 per cent over 1906. Only after this date were there available comprehensive and reliable statistics on accidents sustained by railway servants. The A.S.R.S. had performed an invaluable service to railwaymen and to the public in exposing the inadequacy of the early returns and in demanding more complete and accurate information.

The catalogue of activities of the A.S.R.S. on behalf of safer railway working makes impressive reading. Whilst it is too long to quote fully, the following outstanding activities may be mentioned: the presentation of a petition and memorandum to the Royal Commission on Railway Accidents in 1874, and the evidence given by the Secretary, Mr F. W. Evans, and Mr Harford to the Commission; the organization of a huge procession and demonstration in Exeter Hall, London, on March 14, 1877, when the report of the Commission was published; the publication in 1878 of a pamphlet *Railway Servants: An Appeal to Parliament and the Public*, and its distribution to each member of the two Houses of Parliament; the sponsoring of an exhibition of improved coupling devices at Darlington in 1882; Mr F. Channing's introduction in the House of Commons in February 1886, of the Railway Regulation Bill for the compulsory installation of automatic couplers and other safety measures; the A.S.R.S. sponsored competition for improved coupling devices held at the Nine Elms Goods Yard, London, in March 1886; the presentation of evidence by Mr Richard Bell (General Secretary) and others to the Royal Commission on Accidents to Railway Servants in 1900; the despatch, between 1900 and 1907 of the A.S.R.S. of 463 complaints under the Railway Employment (Prevention of Accidents) Act, 1900, and the successful demand in 1913–14 for the setting up of a departmental committee to examine the adequacy of the Act of 1900.

Signalmen suffered from the excessive nervous strain resulting from long hours and great responsibility. Porters and many others experienced long hours and inadequate pay. The highest casualty figures were sustained by the shunters, goods guards and brakesmen, permanent-way men and drivers and firemen. In the following three sections therefore we shall examine what was done by the A.S.R.S. to reduce casualty figures in three of the most dangerous occupations, shunting, work on the permanent way and driving. Thereafter an attempt will be made to summarize the achievements of the union in the sphere of workmen's compensation and in the relief of orphans. The achievement of the A.S.R.S. in making safer the working lives of railwaymen is therefore best seen in an examination of what was done to reduce the accident rate for those most exposed to danger.

IV

George Osborne, a shunter employed by the Great Eastern Railway at Wisbech said a casual good-bye to his family as he left home to go to work on the morning of January 19, 1898. Although he had seen many of his mates injured in past months, it can scarcely have occurred to him that this might be the last occasion he would see his loved ones. Later that morning, in passing between the wagons of a goods train to read a label on a wagon which was, unfortunately, labelled on the 'far' side only, he was crushed to death between the buffers. Had the wagon been labelled on both sides Osborne would no doubt have rejoined his family that evening.

Less than three weeks later, on February 2, 1898, another shunter, Oliver Child of Gladhold, employed by the London and North Western Railway was likewise killed when passing between wagons. On this occasion it was the necessity to reach a brake on the far side of the wagon which was the cause of death. Had the wagon been equipped with either-side brakes Child also would have seen his family again.

Another shunter employed by the London and North Western Railway, James Allan of Leeds, met his death on September 28th the same year whilst riding on the buffers in the operation known as 'fly shunting'. The method was described 'as a rather risky operation' by a station master witness before the Royal Commission in 1877:

'The ordinary way of uncoupling is that the man stands on the buffers of the two trucks and then puts out his foot or his hand with which he lifts the coupling chain off his hook, and he calls to his driver to come back; he keeps on with one hand and lifts the chain off with the foot, and his other hand ready.'

On August 28th in the same year J. Lowe, a shunter employed by the North Eastern Railway, was killed by being crushed between the buffers when passing between trucks to uncouple.

These are but a few representative cases of the principal ways in which the forty-seven shunters killed on British railways in 1898 met their deaths. The situation in respect of shunting accidents had worsened in the period

1872–98 when the proportion killed each year rose from 3·6 per thousand to 5·08 per thousand. At the close of the nineteenth century shunting was the most dangerous occupation on the railways. In proportion to the numbers employed fatal accidents were more than one and a half times as numerous as among goods guards and brakesmen, and over twice as numerous as among the permanent-way men.

Would shunters Osborne, Child, Allan and Lowe and many others have been killed if the policy advocated by the A.S.R.S. had been enforced by the Board of Trade? It is reasonable to assume they would not.

As early as February 23, 1875, Edward Harford, a prominent member of the A.S.R.S., in giving evidence before the Royal Commission on Railway Accidents, pointed out the dangers of fly shunting and urged the adoption of a stringent law against the practice. However, most companies covered themselves legally by making rules such as Rule 186 of the Manchester, Sheffield and Lincolnshire Railway Company which read:

'In shunting carriages or wagons into sidings they must not be detached from the engine until they are brought to a stand.'

Such rules, Harford said, were 'used against the men in the case of accident' but men who obeyed them were 'abused by some intermediate officials for not getting on the road and getting the work done faster'.[10] Mr F. W. Evans, General Secretary of the A.S.R.S., told the same Commission that a Board of Trade inspector, Captain Tyler, had reported in 1873 that:

'The officers and servants of the companies are too frequently induced, if not compelled, in the absence of necessary means, appliances and accommodation, to disobey printed rules, or adopt hazardous methods of working.'[11]

The General Manager of the Great Western Railway, Mr Grierson, said that there was an instruction in his company that men were not to couple and uncouple trucks in motion. This was 'a caution to the men' but it was 'not laid down in the rules'.[12] Thus both Captain Tyler and Mr Grierson in effect substantiated the evidence given by Mr Harford.

The Society followed up the work of its witnesses before the Commission with the publication in 1878 of the pamphlet *Railway Servants: An Appeal to Parliament and the Public.* Among the seventeen major items of reform it advocated were 'the provision of sufficient siding accommodation for the collection, distribution and working of goods traffic; a sufficient number of servants to be employed; the provision of continuous footboards and the improved coupling of vehicles'. The union considered 'that the Board of Trade should be empowered to require companies to make changes in all matters connected with railways as the Board might consider necessary for the safety of railway servants'. To support their policy the union leaders organized a monster demonstration in Exeter Hall, London, on March 14, 1877. So well was this supported that 2,000 men who could not find a seat in the hall were advised to attend an overflow meeting in Trafalgar Square. A deputation headed by Sir Thomas Brassey, M.P., called upon the President of the Board of Trade, Sir Charles Addersley, who in answer to a demand for more effective safety legislation 'carefully refrained from expressing any opinion and was most successful in evading the questions put by the deputation'. Not a whit deterred, the E.C. of the A.S.R.S. at its meeting in July 1877 resolved to raise a levy of 1s per member to finance further agitation in the provinces. All told the General Secretary estimated that 36,000 persons attended mass meetings in Birmingham, Derby, Manchester, Cardiff and elsewhere in an all out effort to draw attention to the Society's programme. At the same time 130,000 signatures were obtained for a petition sent to the House of Commons.[13]

In December 1881, the E.C. decided that the most constructive way of helping to reduce the accident rate amongst shunters and brakesmen was to organize an exhibition of improved coupling devices for wagons. With the wholehearted co-operation of the Board of the North Eastern Railway, the date of the exhibition was fixed to coincide with the date of the next A.G.M. of the A.S.R.S. to be held in Darlington from October 3 to 7, 1882. The *Railway Review* of September 15, 1882, contained a large advertisement of the exhibition and urged inventors to submit their exhibits. The response was encouraging and the local committee of railwaymen who displayed the entries had no difficulty in filling the Drill Hall with exhibits which came from France, Belgium, Canada, and the United States of America as well as from all parts of the British Isles. Nor was the exhibition confined to coupling devices. Improved brakes, better methods of lighting carriages and goods yards and many other exhibits were shown. Among automatic coupling devices displayed were those of Mr T. Attwood Brocklebank of Shepherds Bush and the Douglas Patent coupling made in Blaydon. Mr David Dale, M.P., a Director of the North Eastern Railway, who opened the exhibition, congratulated the organizers on their most competent work and said that the exhibition was 'probably the first that had been projected, organized and carried out by working men for purely humanitarian purposes'.[14]

The E.C.'s examination of the exhibits convinced them that it was practicable to fit automatic couplers to railway wagons. Apparently the A.G.M. held at Bath in 1884 was also convinced, since it carried unanimously a resolution:

'That this Congress desires to impress upon the railway companies the necessity of adopting a universal system of coupling by which the operation can be performed without the necessity of anyone going between the wagons as we have in the room a remedy which shows it can be done.'

Since in each company the departmental chief had his own pet theory of the best method of coupling and uncoupling wagons it is not surprising that the recommendation of the A.S.R.S. was not adopted.

In 1886 the Society made another major effort on behalf of safer shunting methods. With the co-operation of the Directors of the London and South Western Railway who made the Nine Elms Goods Yard available and loaned twenty trucks to inventors, a competition for improved automatic and non-automatic couplers was held between March 29th and 31st. The Society offered prizes totalling £350 in the two classes, and the entries were judged by the E.C. assisted by Mr Clement E. Stretton, a railway engineer and authority on accidents, Mr Lawrence Saunders, editor of the *Railway Engineer*, and Mr Joseph Stephenson of the North Eastern Railway. Once more some successful automatic coupling devices were displayed. After the judging, a copy of the report on the exhibits together with the list of awards was sent to all the principal railway companies. In most cases, Mr Harford received a formal acknowledgment of the communication. After the lapse of several weeks a further communication was sent to the companies asking the directors whether they would be willing to send representatives to confer with a committee of the A.S.R.S. on the best method of reducing the number of accidents to shunters. Some companies replied that they were seriously considering improving the coupling of their wagons; but nine important companies failed to reply.

It would be a mistake to conclude that the railway managers were completely callous of the loss of life among their employees. They desired to see a reduction in the casualty figures but held the opinion that it was difficult to effect much improvement. In November 1874, the Railway Companies' Association via the Railway Clearing House formed a committee 'for the purpose of regulating on a complete system of uniformity and safety, the working arrangements of the traffic throughout the kingdom'.[15] But after the summer of 1875 nothing further was heard of it. It broke up through the one major difficulty:

'. . . that the agreement which was desired could only be obtained by levelling down the regulations of the better managed lines to those which were less perfectly furnished with appliances conducive to safety.'[16]

The union's spokesman in the House of Commons, Mr F. A. Channing, on February 19, 1886, introduced the Railway Regulation Bill which would have empowered the Board of Trade to compel the companies 'to affix to all vehicles working in goods and mineral trains such improved apparatus for coupling and uncoupling as shall make it unnecessary for men to go between them for that purpose'. The Bill contained provisions for the compulsory introduction of the block system and the interlocking of points and signals, continuous footboards and many other improvements which have since become universally accepted but which at the time aroused a hornet's nest of opposition in railway management circles. The Railway Companies' Association at a special meeting on May 13, 1886, resolved:

'That the consulting solicitors be instructed to ask the President of the Board of Trade to oppose the Bill and that in the event of his declining to do so, the Members of Parliament on the Boards of the several companies be requested to oppose the second reading and that the consulting solicitors be asked to prepare reasons against the Bill.'

A fortnight later the Parliamentary Sub-Committee of the Association formed a select committee of five railway director M.P.s to organize the opposition to Mr Channing's Bill. The fact that the Bill was never enacted is a sufficient testimonial to the success of their efforts.[17]

On the other hand the General Secretary reported to the A.G.M. at Brighton in 1886 that 'on several lines' the general managers had responded favourably to a special request that they should label their wagons on both sides, and on the Midland and other systems the coupling pole was coming generally into use thus rendering it less often necessary for the shunter to have to go between wagons even though with the new method the number of non-fatal accidents increased.

The campaign of the A.S.R.S. was renewed in 1895 when at the A.G.M. held in Manchester the Secretary was asked to write to all railway wagon owners in the country. In his letter Mr Harford pleaded for 'the abolition of all stiff shackles, the adoption of a standard pattern coupling for goods, coal and other wagons, that all such wagons should be labelled on both sides when in transit and that hand brakes should be attached to all horse boxes and carriage trucks'. Hope was expressed that 'the appeal would not be made in vain'. However, although there were fifty-six acknowledgments and sixty-nine favourable replies to the letter, they were mostly from truck owners other than the railway companies. When a follow-up letter was sent in 1896 suggesting a conference between all truck owners and the A.S.R.S., apart from some of the smaller companies, not even any acknowledgments were received from the railway companies.[18] Understandably the proposal for a conference was then dropped. Instead the efforts to persuade the Board of Trade and the Government to act were intensified. The A.G.M. held at Leeds in October 1898 passed two resolutions urging the Board of Trade to compel the companies to make the working conditions of railwaymen safer by following the proposals the union had so often made. Early in 1899, when granted an interview by Mr Ritchie, President of the Board of Trade, Mr Bell explained the policy fully to the Minister who was then convinced of the need for legislation.[19]

Mr Ritchie's Regulation of Railways Bill, 1899, with its proposals for automatic couplings, the labelling of wagons on both sides, and the provision of better brakes for goods trains, though considered not definite enough by Mr Bell, was thoroughly disliked by the companies. At the meeting of the Railway Companies Association on February 22, 1899, it was resolved to send Mr Ritchie a letter stating the reasons for opposing the Bill, while on March 2nd it was agreed that the Minister be asked 'to defer the second reading until later in the session'.[20] Ultimately, the companies were successful in convincing him that the best procedure was to appoint a Royal Commission to find out the facts.

Since the Government of the United States of America had introduced a Safety Appliances Act in 1893, compelling the railway companies there to fit automatic couplers to all their wagons, the Board of Trade sent one of its railway inspectors, Mr Hopwood, to that country in the closing months of 1898 to find out how successful the Act had been in reducing the number of shunting accidents. On December 20, 1898, he reported the success of the measure which had resulted in the halving, between 1893 and 1898, of the number of both fatal and non-fatal accidents to shunters.[21] (Before 1893 the casualty rate was much higher in the United States of America than in the United Kingdom.) The British railway companies having disputed a number of Mr Hopwood's findings, the E.C. of the A.S.R.S. early in 1899 instructed Richard Bell to visit the United States of America to discover whether there was any substance in the companies' claims. Such an action by a none too affluent society indicates the importance attached by it to accident prevention. On his return the union published Mr Bell's findings in a pamphlet entitled *Memorandum upon the use of Automatic Couplers on Railway Stock in the United States of America*, whilst Mr Bell himself told the Commission that in his opinion Mr Hopwood's report was 'a fair and correct one'.[22]

There was a close similarity between many of the proposals made by Mr Bell and Mr J. H. Dobson on behalf of the A.S.R.S. to the Royal Commission, and the recommendations embodied in the report in 1900. The fixing of brake levers on both sides of wagons and the labelling of the wagons on both sides; the abolition of propping and tow-roping; the improvement of the lighting of station sidings and goods yards and the covering of point rods and signal rods where necessary, were all advocated in the report. The union regarded it as most regrettable that the Commissioners were not prepared to urge the compulsory adoption of automatic couplers. The Commissioners declared that:

'"Whilst the application of automatic couplings to railway wagons is most desirable . . . the materials at our disposal do not enable us to make a selection of any particular design and recommend it for obligatory adoption." On the other hand automatic couplers were already in use for some passenger trains on the North Eastern Railway and Mr Bell was satisfied that if the companies were compelled to introduce an automatic coupler within five years one would be found.'[23]

On accidents to railway servants generally the Commission in its report reached the startling conclusion:

'... that the deaths occurring and the injuries sustained amongst railway servants are unnecessarily great in number, and can by means of authoritative action be diminished.'[24]

The Railway Employment (Prevention of Accidents) Act followed later the same year. It gave the Board of Trade power where danger arose 'from anything done or omitted to be done by the railway company or any of its officers or servants, or from any want of proper appliances or plant' to require 'the use of any plant or appliance which has been shown to the satisfaction of the Board of Trade to be calculated to reduce danger to persons employed on a railway'. The disuse of any plant or appliance which brought unnecessary dangers to railwaymen could also be ordered. It was a very big departure from the policy of 'self interest of the railway companies as the best safeguard against accidents', expounded forty-three years earlier, before the influence of the A.S.R.S. could be exerted.

It was important, however, to ensure that the Act did not become a dead letter. With the members of the A.S.R.S. and its officials on the alert there was little chance of this happening. Among the 463 communications concerning the implementation of the Act, sent to the Board of Trade from the head office of the union between July 30, 1900, and February 9, 1907, 162 concerned the lighting of station sidings and goods yards, 65 the protection of point rods and signal wires and 37 the removal of obstruction in goods yards and sidings.

One would have thought it would be a relatively simple matter to carry out the reform listed first on the schedule attached to the Act: 'Brake levers on both sides of wagons.' But there were on the British railways at that time seventy different types of wagon brakes in use, and the history of the Board of Trade intervention with the companies to secure this particular safety measure extends from 1893 (seven years before the passing of the Act) when the companies were urged voluntarily to adopt the reform, to 1911 when a reasonably water-tight rule was finally adopted. Under the terms of the Act of 1900 the Board of Trade on April 27, 1901, gave notice of the new rule (coming into force in a year's time) under which no new wagons were to be built without either-side brakes. When the companies protested that the period of grace allowed was too short, the Board of Trade complied and in January 1902, agreed to two years' notice. The companies then demanded exception to be made in the case of boiler trucks and articulated wagons, with the result that the rule was withdrawn and an amended version issued in December 1902. As repeated amendments again failed to satisfy the companies, Lloyd George, in taking charge of the Board of Trade in 1906, appointed a departmental committee (the Railway Safety Appliance Committee) of three persons; Colonel Yorke (an inspector), Mr R. Turnbull of the London and North Western Railway (for the railway companies) and Mr Bell (General Secretary of the A.S.R.S.). There were undoubtedly technical obstacles to be overcome and many companies had spent thousands of pounds introducing their own particular varieties of brake which did not necessarily comply with the Board of Trade standards, but eventually on November 7, 1911, came the final ruling that wagons were to have brakes which could be applied on either side but released only from the side on which they were applied. In the case of new wagons companies were given six months in which to comply; for existing wagons they were allowed ten years' grace where under 3,000 wagons were owned; fifteen years' grace when the number owned was between 3,000 and 15,000 and twenty years' grace where there were over 20,000 under one management.[25] Though many years had to pass before this source of danger was removed the persistent efforts of the A.S.R.S. on behalf of greater safety did bear fruit. The fatal casualties to shunting staff dropped from 136 or one in every 156 in 1894 to 34, or one in every 444 in 1913.[26]

V

At Syston, Leicestershire, the sun rose in a clear sky on the morning of October 24, 1888. As they strode to their work William Cheeney and John Waring, platelayers employed by the Midland Railway, must have expected a full day's work in pleasant enough weather. But with a fickleness characteristic of the English climate, at about 7.0 a.m. the clear skies suddenly gave place to fog and the men who had already done an hour's work with their gang shifting ballast noted that visibility had dropped to less than twenty yards. The ganger, Henry Drinkwater, a conscientious man, 'highly spoken of not only for his abilities as a ganger, but also for being as a rule more than usually careful to attend to the safety of his men'[27] was keeping a lookout in between giving instructions to his men when, suddenly, at 7.03 a.m. when the gang was about 1,410 yards north of Syston Station, a train burst through the fog. Drinkwater shouted a warning and most of the gang stood clear in the nick of time. Cheeney and Waring, however, who were working at the end of the gang nearest the approaching train, failed to move quickly enough and were mauled to pieces, the driver of the train being quite unaware of any mishap until, on his return journey, he was told of the tragedy. The death of the two men could not be ascribed to any negligence or dereliction of duty on the part of the ganger. The disaster had occurred, so the Board of Trade inspector reported, because 'there were no rules providing for men being posted out to protect gangs'. Furthermore, although the rules of the company referred to 'the precautions which were to be taken for the safety of trains travelling upon the line', there was 'very little reference in them to the safety of the plate-layers themselves'. There was no rule actually forbidding the practice of putting the men to work during fog. After the accident, the ganger, Henry Drinkwater, told Major Marindin:

'I know rule 330. I consider that this rule means that ballast trains are not to be out on main lines during fog. I do not think that rule applies to the men, only to the train.'[28]

The Directors of the Midland Railway in refusing to incur the expense of lookout men for their gangs and in failing to make a rule that gangs should not be employed in foggy weather, despite frequent recommendations to this effect from the Board of Trade,[29] were by no means exceptional in their attitude. George Dalton, a sub-ganger on the South Eastern Railway, when asked in 1900 'What protection have the men when they are at work platelaying?' replied 'None whatever that I know of'.[30] With the large majority of companies the rules were the same. Nor was the fate of the two men, Cheeney and Waring, so very exceptional. Between 1896 and 1900, 573 permanent-way men met their deaths through accidents at work. Though there were fewer fatalities in proportion to the number employed than was the case with shunters, goods guards and brakesmen, it was none the less true that in the early years of the present century out of every twenty permanent-way men who met with accidents nine were killed—a greater proportion of fatal casualties to total casualties than was the case with any other grade on the railways. As early as 1874, in a petition to the members of the Royal Commission on Railway Accidents in 1874, the A.S.R.S. had drawn attention to the need for 'proper accommodation' or space for safety for those whose job it was to maintain the permanent way. This agitation was carried on through the years to 1900 when Richard Bell told another Royal Commission that platelayers should have protection either by the appointment of a lookout man or by a system of warnings by means of an electrical or mechanical appliance.[31] In consequence of his advocacy and the recommendation of Government inspectors, under the Railway Employment (Prevention of Accidents) Act, 1900, the Board of Trade was empowered to frame rules for 'the protection of permanent-way men when relaying or repairing the permanent way'. Such a rule did come into force in August, 1902. Under it railway companies (not the gangers) were to appoint lookout men for each gang employed, a duty they delegated to the gangers. Although some companies had habitually appointed lookout men even before August 1902, when the

Board of Trade in 1907 wrote to all railway companies in the United Kingdom suggesting that 'a whistle of distinctive type be issued to every platelayer employed on the permanent-way', forty-seven companies, including some important ones, such as the North British, refused to supply whistles to *any* of the men, the lookout men not excepted. In consequence such a disaster as that at Parkhead on November 11, 1911, on the North British Railway, when four out of a team of six platelayers were killed in a thick fog by a passing train, was still possible. In this accident the men were killed because the company had failed to comply with Rule 9 of the statutory rules and orders made by the Board of Trade in 1902 and had likewise failed to comply with Rule 273f of the Rules and Regulations for the guidance of officers and men issued by the Railway Clearing House.[32] Apparently, it was still possible for men to be 'turned out on to the railway like a flock of sheep without a shepherd to guide them'.[33] Richard Bell, as the A.S.R.S. representative on the Railway Safety Appliance Committee of the Board of Trade, in 1906 and 1907 did valuable work in advocating the provision of proper safety precautions for platelayers, with the result that the number of fatal accidents fell from the 573 of the period 1896–1900 to 430 for the period from 1906–10, a fall of 25 per cent. At the same time the number of non-fatal accidents fell by 17·5 per cent. Even so the casualties were still excessive. One of the earliest resolutions of the E.C. of the newly formed N.U.R. in 1913 concerned the high accident rate of men employed on the railways.[34] The matter was brought to the attention of the Parliamentary Labour Party which on February 12, 1914, moved an amendment to the King's Speech calling attention to the high accident rate in mines and railways. In the course of the keen debate which followed, a Government spokesman agreed to appoint a departmental committee to inquire into the working of the Railway Employment (Prevention of Accidents) Act, 1900, and to report what amendments, if any, were necessary. Among a long list of improvements recommended by Mr J. H. Thomas of the N.U.R., the principal witness before this Committee, was item 15: 'That the appointment of lookout men should be compulsory.' Thus the N.U.R. was carrying on the prolonged struggle for the more humane treatment of those railwaymen without whose careful work no passenger could expect to travel in safety.[35]

VI

Locomotivemen and the passengers they carry have the closest coincidence of interest in the safe working of the railways. A passenger may feel no immediate inconvenience through any mishap to a platelayer or shunter but he is immediately affected as soon as any damage is sustained to the locomotive or the locomotivemen are injured or killed.

A remarkable feature of the Skipton disaster on the Great Western Railway on December 24, 1874, was that the driver, Richardson, and his mate were not killed though they sustained injuries. In this case some of the passengers were less fortunate as thirty-four of them were killed and sixty-five injured. The immediate cause of the disaster was the breaking of a tyre of one of the coach wheels, but Colonel Yolland who investigated the case, reported that 'if the train had been fitted with continuous brakes throughout its whole length there is no reason why it should not have been brought to rest without any casualty'.[36] In view of the fact that on that part of the Great Western Railway system block signalling had not been introduced the accident might have been even more serious and complicated had it not been for the presence of mind of some of the railway staff who informed the signalmen in the nearest boxes either side of the scene of the accident of what had happened so that succeeding trains were held up. Though this accident had unusual features, mishaps of varying degrees of severity arising from the absence of continuous brakes were common enough occurrences. At the time Colonel Hutchinson, a Board of Trade inspector, told the Royal Commission on Railway Accidents in 1874 that of the eighty-five accidents he had investigated in 1873, thirty-five would have been prevented or mitigated by continuous brakes in the hands of the drivers.[37]

Concerned about the serious loss of life which on occasions such as that at Skipton resulted from the deficiencies of train brakes, the Royal Commission, in June 1875, arranged with the companies a series of practical tests which were carried out at Newark. The Commissioners came to the conclusion that 'a good continuous brake will reduce the stopping distances of fast trains to one third of the distance by which they can be stopped by the present ordinary means'. They recommended therefore that 'every train should be provided with sufficient brake power to stop it absolutely within 500 yards at the highest speed at which it travels and upon any gradient upon the line'.[38] Despite the obvious conviction of the officers of the Board of Trade that continuous brakes were necessary it was at first decided to rely on persuasion rather than compulsion. In a letter to all the companies on January 13, 1877, Mr Farrer, Secretary to the Board of Trade, referred to 'the loss of life and property as shown in recent accidents' and urged that 'the time had come for decisive and harmonious action on the part of the companies', to install efficient continuous brakes. Mr Farrer requested that the companies should keep him informed on the progress made in the installation of continuous brakes.[39] Yet a year later only twenty out of the 119 principal companies in the kingdom had carried out the reform and some of these had done so only partially. The reason in the case of the London and North Western Railway for the failure to follow the advice of the Board of Trade was that the locomotive superintendent was the part inventor and proprietor of an emergency brake which the company had extensively adopted for its rolling stock, even though it wholly failed to meet the requirements of the Board of Trade circulars, particularly one dated August 30, 1877, specifying the characteristics of a good brake. The company were informed that their new brake was unsatisfactory and that a 'heavy personal responsibility' rested with the manager in the event of an accident The company, however, treated the letter with 'a superb disregard'.[40]

Some companies endeavoured to cover up their failure to install continuous automatic brakes by placing the entire blame on the locomotive staff in the event of an accident. On January 24, 1880, an express train came into collision with another train standing at Rutherglen station on the Caledonian Railway. The driver, William McCulloch, applied the Clarke and Webb 'Emergency' brake which failed to act in this, the first 'emergency' in which it was called upon to halt the train. Although no person was killed as a result of the mishap, McCulloch was tried before Mr Sheriff Lees at Glasgow, on a charge of neglect of duty and sentenced to no less than four months' imprisonment. Prior to this he had for thirty-three years held an unimpeachable character of carefulness, attention to duty and sobriety. In all probability no accident would have occurred if the train had been fitted with continuous brakes. When the President of the A.S.R.S., Mr Stewart MacLiver, M.P., appealed in the House of Commons for the release of McCulloch, the Home Secretary reduced the sentence to one of two months.[41] It was poor consolation to McCulloch and other drivers serving sentences for manslaughter to know later that the Clarke and Webb brake had been abandoned as unsatisfactory. In defending its members against such charges the A.S.R.S. was performing a very important task in endeavouring to prevent injustice being done and at the same time in drawing the attention of the public to the fact that the real culprits in such cases were 'the directors and managers who looked from their safe board room upon their wretched servants standing in the dock on a charge of manslaughter'.[42]

In the A.S.R.S. pamphlet Railway Servants: An appeal to Parliament and the Public published in 1878, pride of place in the list of means of safety urgently needed was given to 'automatic continuous brakes'. This was followed by the demands for the maintenance in a high condition of the permanent way, and the extension of the block and interlocking systems. In respect of the introduction of the block systems the companies were making far more rapid progress than they were with the brakes. By 1873 the South Eastern, London, Chatham and Dover, and London, Brighton and South Coast Railways had all double track lines worked on the block system and the record of the London and South Western was also good. Nevertheless between 1872 and 1878 alone there were 112 accidents causing death to a total of twelve persons and injury to 456 more resulting from the absence of interlocking signals and points. In addition there were in the same period fifty-eight collisions which occurred through the absence of a block system, showing that the agitation of the A.S.R.S. was very much to the point.

At the A.G.M. held in Manchester in 1881, the General Secretary of the A.S.R.S. was instructed in co-operation with Mr Courtenay Ilbert, M.P., to draft a Bill for the compulsory introduction of automatic continuous brakes. In the following year Earl de la Warr, the chief spokesman for the railwaymen in the House of Lords introduced the Bill in that House. Although the Bill was given a second reading an impressive array of railway director peers rose to speak against its enactment whilst no railway spokesman supported it, with the inevitable result that nothing more was heard of it that session. When it was rumoured in the following year that the Bill might be taken up again the Railway Companies' Association again went into action. At its meeting on July 10, 1883, it was resolved 'that Lord Colville and the Duke of Sutherland be requested to see Lord Cairns and ask him to oppose the Bill'. Suffice it to say that nothing more was heard of the measure. As we have seen the directors also successfully opposed Mr Channing's Railway Regulation Bill of 1886, which would have given the Board of Trade power to compel the installation of continuous brakes, the block system and interlocking points and signals.

A favourite argument of the opponents of Mr Channing and the union was that the block system bred dependence and carelessness in the railway employees and that more accidents would occur because of the increased sense of security which came with the new method of working. The view of Captain Tyler, a Board of Trade inspector, was however, 'that allowing to the utmost for these tendencies to confide too much in additional means of safety, the risk is proved by experience to be very much greater without them than with them; and in fact the negligence and mistakes of servants are found to occur most frequently, and generally with the most serious results, not when men are over confident in their appliances or apparatus but when, in the absence of them they are habituated to risk in the conduct of the traffic'.[43]

It took the killing of seventy-eight people (of whom twenty-two were under fifteen years of age) in a terrible railway disaster near Armagh in Ireland on June 12, 1889, finally to convince Parliament and the public of the need for legislation on the lines drafted by the A.S.R.S. in 1882. In so far as the Railway Regulation Act of 1889 made compulsory the introduction of continuous brakes, the block system and the interlocking of points, it did represent a vindication of A.S.R.S. policy, but in so far as the provisions concerning brakes applied only to *passenger* trains and not to goods trains, and in so far as the clause for the compulsory introduction of automatic couplers was withdrawn in the face of the opposition of the railway interest, it was clear that 'the main object of the Act was to meet accidents to passengers' whilst 'the other question of accidents to railway servants was not so much in the mind of the legislature'.[44]

When Mr Ritchie brought in his Bill to extend and amend the Railway Regulation Acts in 1899, it included a section which gave the Board of Trade power to compel companies to fit adequate steam or other power brakes to all their engines. As we have seen earlier, the railway companies secured the withdrawal of the Bill and the appointment instead of a Royal Commission of Inquiry. Mr John M. Dobson, Organizing Secretary of the A.S.R.S. in giving evidence to the Commission strongly advocated the provision of adequate brake power being given to all locomotives.[45] That his and others' advocacy had some effect is shown by the fact that under the Act which followed, the Board of Trade was given power to make orders for the provision of 'steam or other power brakes on engines'. But this was by no means the end of the battle. The A.S.R.S. took up forty-five locomotive cases with the Board of Trade between August 1900 and February 1907.[46]

The reason why Eleazer Price, an engine driver in the service of the Rhymney Railway at Cardiff, met his death on May 13, 1889, at the early age of thirty-two was that he was climbing over the tender when his head came into contact with a bridge and he was knocked over on to the permanent way. His death need not have occurred had his locomotive been properly fitted with a box in the vicinity of the footplate to hold the fire-irons. On this subject Mr J. H. Dobson, National Organizer of the A.S.R.S. told the Commission in 1900:

'I do not think men ought to have to go to the back of the tender. I think the boxes ought to be arranged in the front of the tender, so that the men can get what they want by just turning round instead of having to climb over the top.'[47]

It would be possible to cite many other detailed recommendations such as those for the uniform provision of hand rails round locomotives, proper protection for sight feed lubricator glasses on all engines and the provision of more turntables to obviate the necessity of driving engines tender first, made by the A.S.R.S. for many years in the interests of the safety of locomotivemen.

A notable contrast between the attention given to safety measures in factories and on the railways is that, before the First World War, whereas factory inspectors were empowered to make a routine inspection of factories quite apart from the occurrence or non-occurrence of an accident, on the railways the Board of Trade inspectors (apart from the case of the opening of a new line) were expected to carry out an inspection only after an accident had occurred. The A.S.R.S. constantly advocated that the practice of the Board of Trade with regard to railways should be on a par with the practice in mines, factories and workshops. Mr Bell in his Annual Report in 1908 wisely commented:

> 'If instead of having to wait until an accident happens before an inquiry is held, the Board of Trade had the power the same as the Home Office to hold inspections of railways and to enforce the recommendations . . . we should then see a gradual diminution in the number of those annually sacrificed in the interests of private enterprise.'[48]

VII

The hardships associated with the existence of an exceptionally high accident rate on the railways might have been mitigated had it been the practice of the companies to pay compensation, in each case, to employees who were killed or injured. However, it was not until 1897 that companies could be compelled to pay compensation to railwaymen victims of accidents although most companies had accepted responsibility for payment under an Act of 1880. The situation before 1880 was vividly described by F. Harcombe, a goods guard on the Taff Vale Railway. When asked by members of a Royal Commission 'What is the custom with regard to compensation to a man when he is injured in performing his work, or to his widow if he is killed leaving a widow?' he replied, 'I believe the compensation they receive is a nice coffin'. Mr W. Grierson, General Manager of the Great Western Railway said that his company made 'no payment to any servant in the shape of compensation' though it had 'been the custom to make a donation of, say, £10 in the way of a little assistance to the widow'. The London and North Western Railway made a similar payment.[49]

The state of affairs which existed during the lives of the first two generations of railwaymen was ably summarized in the report of the Royal Commission on Railway Accidents in 1877:

> 'Speaking in general terms the company is liable to the public in all cases and to its servants in none.'[50]

Mr Galt, a railway expert, in a special report to the same Commission declared that even the liability of the companies to pay compensation to the passengers failed to ensure the adoption of more safety precautions. He claimed:

> '. . . that the companies' gain, by not adopting the most efficient means of maintaining their lines in a good condition and managing their traffic in a proper manner, far exceeds the loss occasioned by an occasional accident. . . . They calculate on having to pay a certain sum in compensation each year, and the saving they effect is the premium they receive for the risk incurred. . . . So far from it being the interest of the companies to

afford the necessary protection to the public, their respective interests are quite opposed to each other. It is in the interest of the latter to travel safely and that the companies' servants should do their work free from unnecessary danger, but it is in the interests of the former to neglect providing many of the necessary means of safety either for the public or for their own servants. What reasonable hope can therefore exist that the companies will of their own free will knowing the diminution of profit that would result, alter their present course of policy ?'[51]

There was another reason why the principle of self interest of the railway companies could not be relied on to safeguard the lives and limbs of railwaymen. At least by the 1860's many railway companies had grown into giant concerns whose capital was valued in millions of pounds and whose employees could be counted by their thousands and in some cases tens of thousands. The authority exercised by the individual owner manager in the smaller business had of necessity in the case of the large railway companies to be divided and delegated to many agents who, ever since the judicial decision Priestley v. Fowler in 1837, were classed as fellow servants of all the other employees of the company. Thus the companies could generally escape liability to pay compensation to the men by claiming that responsibility for an accident lay with the superintendent of the line, the chief engineer, the foreman ganger, or signalman or some other person in *common employment* with the permanent-way man, shunter or driver who had been injured or killed. The Commissioners in 1877 recognized that railwaymen had strong grounds for complaint when they reported:

'. . . that in numerous cases they (i.e. the interests of the men) are sacrificed from causes and in circumstances which would clearly give a right to compensation, were it not that the law refuses to regard in any other light than as their fellow servants those to whom the companies delegate the master's authority.'[52]

How it worked out in practice was revealed by Mr F. W. Evans, the General Secretary of the A.S.R.S., who said that in the first four years of existence of the union (1872–5) it had only on four occasions proved possible to make the companies pay full compensation. They were all cases where common employment was 'got rid of' through the fact that the servants of one company were accidentally killed by servants of another. Yet in 1874 alone 788 railwaymen were killed at work. Evans told a Parliamentary Committee that as the law stood in 1876 the life of a railway servant was 'of less value than the life of a horse', in as much as however gross the mismanagement which produced the death or injury to a servant there was no responsibility whatever on the company, whereas if a horse was injured or killed 'it cost the company a certain amount of money to replace the animal'.[53]

Understandably one of the chief concerns of the A.S.R.S. in its early years was to secure the abolition of the doctrine of common employment and the introduction of an Employers' Liability Act which would compel the companies to pay adequate compensation to employees injured or killed in their service.

The policy of Evans and the E.C. of the A.S.R.S. on the employers' liability question during the period 1875–80 was thoroughly opportunist. Although in principle an Employers' Liability Bill was preferred which completely abolished the doctrine of common employment and compelled the employers to pay full compensation, the union was prepared to work for a more moderate measure which was a step in the right direction, provided it stood a better chance of enactment. Throughout the period the union had Mr Bass as its patron and another moderate Liberal M.P., Mr T. MacLiver, as its president. Evans consistently supported the efforts of these gentlemen and those of Earl de la Warr in the House of Lords, to pass a Bill which, whilst not satisfying the more extreme reformers, was more likely to pass into law.

Evans's campaigning on behalf of workmen's compensation began when he was Secretary of the Bristol branch of the A.S.R.S. On the suggestion of Mr Bass[54] he campaigned on behalf of a famous Liberal railway director, Sir E. Watkin, in a by-election in Exeter in 1873 in return for that gentleman's promise to introduce an Employers' Liability Bill.[55] Although unsuccessful in 1873, Watkin was returned for another constituency, Hythe, in the general election of the following year. He kept his word in introducing a Bill in May 1874; but both Evans and the Parliamentary Committee of the T.U.C. regarded the Bill as unsatisfactory mainly for the reason that compensation was limited to an amount equal to one year's wages. In the summer of 1875 Watkin introduced another Bill which raised maximum compensation to £300, but despite Evans's support this too was dropped when opposed by the T.U.C. After Alexander MacDonald, the miners' M.P., had introduced another and more radical Bill in 1876, Lord Beaconsfield's Conservative Government offered a select committee of inquiry in return for the abandonment of the new proposal and the offer was accepted.

In his evidence to the Select Committee Evans did not advocate making the railway companies liable to pay compensation in every case of injury or death to their employees. He conceded that the fireman could be regarded as being in 'common employment' with the driver and that where there were two or more guards on the same train they were also in common employment. He agreed that there would have to be a statutory limit to the amount of compensation payable to enable employers to insure against risk.[56]

The railway employers' point of view was put by Mr George Findlay, who was then Traffic Manager (later General Manager) of the London and North Western Railway, and who conceded that his statements were 'in a degree—the general evidence of the companies'. He argued that the middle course such as was advocated by Evans was impracticable. He claimed that it would be 'impossible to stop short of making the company responsible altogether for every accident that might occur to their servants from whatever cause'. He believed that 'almost the entirety of the accidents' were due to the neglect of the workmen themselves. The introduction of full employers' liability would disrupt railway discipline by setting 'department against department'. He warned that if any alteration of the law were made it would no longer be in the interest of the directors to contribute to the funds of the company's provident society which had been functioning since 1871. The railwaymen would be the only sufferers.[57]

Although the majority report of the Select Committee was verbose and not very clear in respect of the ending of the doctrine of common employment, Clause 15 of the minority report stated that the 'negligence of any person exercising authority mediately or immediately derived from the owners' was the negligence of the employer, but employers could not be responsible for negligence of persons who 'though exercising authority, are bona fide employed in actual labour'.[58] Evans made this part of the minority report the basis for his campaign for legislation in 1878. He caused the branches of the A.S.R.S. and many other organizations to sign petitions in favour of employers' liability and he instructed the Society's lawyer to draft a Bill based on the minority report but with clauses intended to make the railway employers responsible for the negligence of drivers, firemen, signalmen and platelayers.[59] From the date of its drafting in the autumn of 1878 and its adoption by Sir Thomas Brassey, M.P., to its acceptance by the newly appointed Liberal Cabinet in May 1880, Evans stuck to this Bill like a limpet. He had to contend with the criticisms of some of the delegates at the A.G.M. in 1878 who, like the T.U.C., supported the more radical Bill being sponsored by Alexander MacDonald. He assured Congress that he thought it 'extremely unfortunate' that the working men of the country supported a man (MacDonald) who was 'so indiscreet and injudicious'.[60] In the spring of 1879 he organized an impressive avalanche of petitions to Parliament in favour of his Bill, the *Railway Service Gazette* of March 28th and April 4th listing over one thousand bodies (branches of the A.S.R.S., trades councils and branches of other trade unions) sending in such petitions to the Lords and Commons.

But the biggest effort of all was reserved for the general election campaign of the spring of 1880. Each of the 200 branches of the union asked the Parliamentary candidates of its constituency the following questions:

1. Will the candidate vote for having a second reading of the A.S.R.S. Bill?
2. Will he support that Bill in preference to the Government's Bill?

Three hundred of the successful candidates (mostly Liberals) sent in favourable answers to both questions. With the support of Joseph Chamberlain, Sir William Harcourt, W. G. Dodson and others who entered the Cabinet, the new Government was won over in the second week in May 1880 to endorse Sir T. Brassey's Bill.[61]

Throughout the passage of the Bill through Parliament, Evans kept in close touch with Samuel Morley, M.P., the spokesman for the union on the Liberal benches. Three out of six amendments proposed by the union were embodied in the Act. One important amendment to the first clause of the Act declared the employer liable to pay compensation in the case of negligence 'of any persons in the service of the employer who had charge or control of any signal, points, locomotive engine or train upon a railway'.[62]

After the Bill became law and before the A.G.M. had met at Cardiff in October 1880, Evans wrote an informative article in the *Railway Review* advising them that although the new measure was to be welcomed since for the first time it offered the prospect of compensation being paid by the companies, there remained the serious loophole that companies who ran provident societies for their employees were entitled to 'contract out' of the Act. Employees of such companies would then be entitled to the provident society benefits but not to the more generous scale of compensation provided under the Act. Hence he advised members of the union that to purchase insurance at the cost of their new right to compensation would be 'to give away the substance in exchange for a shadow'.[63]

The directors of most companies, to their credit, declined to seize the opportunity the Act afforded of contracting out. Three major companies, the London and North Western Railway, the Great Eastern Railway and the London, Brighton and South Coast Railway did, however, decide to make use of the loopholes the Act provided. In the case of the London and North Western Railway, membership of the provident society was made compulsory and the acceptance of its benefits obligatory as a substitute for compensation under the Act; men employed by the Brighton line were given a greater freedom of choice. On the Great Eastern the men were offered strong inducements to contract out but were not obliged to do so.

Mr Moon, a Director of the London and North Western Railway, told a shareholders' meeting of that company held at Euston Station in August 1881, that the men employed by the company had willingly acquiesced in the directors' decision to contract out. Decisions of meetings of the men held at Crewe, Leicester, Liverpool, Wigan, Wolverton, Walford and Camden would suggest that Evans's summing-up of the situation in his report to the A.G.M. in October 1881, was nearer the truth:

'When left to their own free choice a large majority of the men in open meetings repudiated the company's offer, but official influence was then applied. Where that failed, intimidation in hinted or threatened dismissals was resorted to. Officials obtruded at meetings of the men to take down the names of those who were against the company, men were called into offices and warned that the company would not have men in their service who opposed them in this matter. . . . Very many who persisted in standing by the law, and against whom no faults were alleged, were dismissed the service of the company.'[64]

There is no evidence that similar pressure was needed to persuade the men on the Brighton line to accept contracting out.

By 1894 when another Employers' Liability Bill was being considered by Parliament the London and North Western Railway, by lobbying M.P.s, sought to perpetuate the system of contracting out. When the A.S.R.S. endeavoured to rally the company's employees to demand the abolition of the system, the radical M.P. for Crewe, Mr W. S. B. McLaren, declared that his railwaymen constituents wanted to retain the sickness, superannuation and other benefits to which they were entitled under the company's provident scheme.[65] Although, as Mr Harford pointed out, the widow of a driver under the company's scheme would receive only £100, just over half of which came from the employee's contributions, when her husband was killed in an accident and could receive up to £350 compensation under the Act, many men may have preferred the quick and certain payment of sickness benefit of 7s and 14s a week, and an assured and speedy payment of £100 to the widow in the event of accidental death, to the delays and uncertainties of compensation under the Employers' Liability Act, being influenced by the company's warning that in the event of the discontinuance of 'contracting out' the provident society could no longer be supported by the directors.[66]

There were two main reasons why the union campaigned for the abolition of contracting out. Since the benefits provided by the provident societies in the event of accidental death were well below the compensation that could be claimed under the 1880 Act it was held that the companies which had contracted out had a less strong inducement to make every provision for the safety of its employees than did those companies which had not contracted out but had agreed to pay the compensation the courts directed. The fact that during the years 1888–95 inclusive on the London and North Western Railway (which contracted out) one in nine of the employees were killed or injured each year whereas on the Midland Railway (which did not contract out) the comparable figure was one in forty, was the subject of adverse comment. It was also thought significant that in 1895 although in 175 cases out of 287 the recommendations of the Board of Trade to the companies to make modifications for improved safety were adopted, the directors of the London and North Western Railway complied with only fifteen out of the forty-five recommendations made specifically to them.[67]

The second reason why the union disliked contracting out was that it was believed that compulsory membership of the companies' provident societies weakened the men's independence and served to prevent their engaging in 'vigorous collective action'.[68] Mr G. Findlay, General Manager of the London and North Western Railway, admitted that this was the effect of his company's provident society. Before the Select Committee on the Employers' Liability Acts in 1886, the following exchange took place:

'Mr A. O'Connor: What are the terms between the company and its individual employees; at what notice can you dispense with his service?

Mr Findlay: In case of men employed at weekly wages, which most of them are, it is a week's notice.

Q. If a man's services are discontinued what becomes of his interest in the fund; does it cease?

A. It does.

Q. Then you have a pecuniary hold, through this fund, upon every member of the staff?

A. I think we have.

Q. That helps to maintain discipline?

A. It does.'[69]

Thus when in 1894 the House of Lords succeeded in inserting into the Liberal Government's Employers' Liability Bill a clause permitting contracting out, the A.S.R.S. supported the action of the T.U.C. Parliamentary Committee in working for the complete rejection of the Bill. The Liberal Government hesitated to defy this influential opposition and withdrew the measure.[70]

When Mr Joseph Chamberlain's Workmen's Compensation Bill was published in May 1897, it received a cool and guarded welcome from the *Railway Review*. Although the Bill was criticized for the fact that it was intended to apply only to those employed in factories, mines, quarries, engineering works or railways, and therefore did not affect over seven million workers, the important new principle of general compensation was, it believed, deserving of impartial consideration.[71] By the time it became law on July 1, 1898, opinion in the union had become more favourable to the Bill. Although contracting out was to continue, it was made conditional on the Registrar of Friendly Societies certifying that any alternative offered by the employers was on the whole not less favourable to the workmen than the provisions of the Act. It was this clause which obliged Lord Stalbridge to inform the half-yearly meeting of the London and North Western Railway in August 1897 that the directors had decided not to continue to contract out since the company's provident society 'could not exist concurrently with the Government's Act'.[72] Mr Harford declared that despite the survival of the doctrine of contributory negligence and the exclusion from its provisions of 'many of the most important trades in the country' the Act was 'in many respects a useful measure'.[73] Henceforward most injured railwaymen and widows of railwaymen killed in accidents at work were assured of compensation more adequate than had ever been the case before.

VIII

As we have seen it took a long time to persuade Parliament to compel the railway companies to make proper provision for the safety of their employees and to accept responsibility for paying adequate compensation on behalf of those who were injured or killed. In the meantime the number of widows and orphans, whose ultimate prospect was resort to the dreaded workhouse, was increasing each year and humanity demanded that the union should give them immediate practical help.

In the agitation of the years 1865–6 Charles Bassett-Vincent had seen the need for assistance to railway orphans. In 1872 he returned to the subject, suggesting to Mr Bass the desirability of establishing a railway orphanage. He again raised the subject at the Manchester delegate conference on June 27, 1873, when he was authorized, in association with his friend Cordwell, to prepare more detailed plans. In April 1874, the E.C., approving the proposals of the two men, drafted an appeal to the branches which resulted in 200 of them contributing a total of £3,000 for the purchase of an orphanage and the support of orphan children. In the meantime, Vincent and Cordwell had inspected the Port of Hull Orphans Home and had been so impressed that they decided it would be a good plan to establish a similarly run institution. They chose to locate the orphanage in the town of Derby in honour both of Mr Bass and the junior member, Mr Samuel Plimsoll, and because it was geographically central. Shortly afterwards the Mayor of Derby, George Wheeldon, presided at a meeting held in the Town Hall on August 5, 1875, for the purpose of electing a committee and raising more funds.[74]

Using, at first, temporary premises at the corner of Bradshaw Street and London Road, Derby, on January 11, 1875, the orphanage opened its doors to six boys and five girls. More suitable premises were bought and extended in 1877 and a new wing added in 1880.

Soon after the Derby Orphanage was founded the E.C. of the A.S.R.S. lost its control over the committee of management which became dominated by prominent citizens of Derby, some of whom were connected with the Midland Railway. Although contributions were made over to the Derby Committee until the end of 1879, differences of policy led to the withdrawal of the A.S.R.S. from the committee of management of the orphanage in that year.

It was the general rule of the orphanage to admit only one child of the orphaned family; only in very exceptional cases were two children of the same family admitted. Inevitably, this involved the break-up of families. The E.C. of the union preferred keeping families as nearly as possible intact and did not like the idea of concentrating help on one of the children only.

In February 1879, therefore, the E.C. sent all branches a circular in which it was suggested that an orphan fund should be set up under the complete control of the union. F. W. Evans, the General Secretary, subsequently explained the differences between the new scheme and the policy of the Derby Orphanage:

'The difference between them is that ours leans on self-help for its main support; Derby on charity. Ours diffuses the help in the children's home, helping each other alike; Derby bestows all its help on one child, separating it from the family. The help from our fund reaches every family of orphans of members who subscribe; that of Derby reaches only the *one* of the family elected by favour. Derby has spent two-thirds of its income in building and management and but one-third on the orphans. Our fund will not entail 5 per cent of its income on management, leaving 95 per cent for the orphans.'

Influenced by the fact that since January 1st that year the Camden branch had successfully operated its own widows and orphans fund, the A.G.M. at Leeds in 1879 agreed to add a new clause to Rule X: 'That each member shall contribute one halfpenny per week to the Orphan Fund.' The delegates agreed that the fund should commence operations on January 1, 1880. Although the scale of benefits, payable on account of children under 13 was by no means princely—it ranged from 3s a week for a family with one child to a maximum of 7s a week for a family of seven or more children —to the widow, it generally made the difference between maintaining the home, and abandoning it and resorting to the workhouse, or humiliating dependence on outdoor relief granted by the poor law guardians.

Although the orphan fund was primarily intended to help children of railwaymen killed in accidents, in 1883 its scope was extended to include those whose fathers had died from natural causes. In 1888 step-children became eligible for benefit and from 1898 benefit was paid up to the age of 14 years.

The number of orphaned families being assisted rose from 32 in 1880 to 1,239 by the end of 1914. In those first 35 years of the fund's existence, £197,797 1s 0d was paid to a total of 8,740 children.[75] With the fusion of forces the number of children receiving help greatly increased. It reached its peak in 1928 with 6,052 children on the books, but thereafter steadily declined to 1,721 in 1958.[76]

The halfpenny a week from members was never sufficient to meet the payments made to orphans. The union, therefore, earmarked one-third of the interest it received from its investments in railway and corporation stock and in mortgages to supplement the fund. The remainder of the deficiency was more than made good by the voluntary efforts of the branches which in most years realized a sum larger than the proceeds of the halfpenny levy.

Reports of the impressive efforts of the branches to raise money for the orphan fund fill many pages of the *Railway Review* in the years before 1914. The most popular activity was the annual Good Friday or Easter Monday meat tea and concert, although these activities were sometimes preceded by a charity football match. The *Railway Review* published in Easter week (April 23rd) 1897 included three closely printed pages of reports from fifty-four branches of their activities on behalf of the orphans. 'Gracefully served' meat teas were consumed by thousands of railwaymen, their families and sympathizers, who met in church halls, drill halls and guildhalls up and down the kingdom. The record in respect of consumption of ham and tongue must have gone, that year, to the Middlesbrough branch which mobilized 1,717 members and friends for a tea in the crypt of the Town Hall; though the achievements of West Hartlepool which mustered 'about 1,000', and Wolverhampton which mustered 900 for the same purpose, are also worthy of respect. It was reported that Mr Griffith Davies's rendering of 'How vain is the man who boasts in fight' to 600 members and friends of the Cardiff branch was 'quite a treat'. At Normanton in a packed concert hall Johnny Watson 'fairly brought the house down' with his mirth-provoking sketches 'On the back of Granny oh!' and 'The Galloping Donkey'. At Penarth the railway football team which had 'undergone a radical change in its players' beat their opponents Penarth Athletic 'at all points of the game'. Members of the Rugby branch were less fortunate; no sooner had the Steam Shed band led the procession into the street than a cloudburst sent the party scurrying for shelter. This did not prevent them turning out in large numbers to support the evening concert.

It was through such efforts as these that branches of the A.S.R.S. in 1897 raised £4,815 1s 2½d for the orphan fund and helped to maintain 578 orphan families.[77]

Mr F. W. Evans introduced an unusual visitor to the delegates at the A.G.M. at Manchester in 1881 when he described 'Fred, the Railway Dog of England' as 'the latest addition to the Society's official staff'. The dog's presence at the A.G.M. was due to an earlier decision of the E.C. to adopt the suggestion of Guard Climpson, an A.S.R.S. member employed on the Brighton line, that he should buy a dog to be employed as a travelling collector on behalf of the orphan fund. Unfortunately, both 'Fred' and another collie dog bought by Climpson died in the course of 1881. However, a Scotsman, Mr Riddell, presented the E.C. in the spring of 1882 with the third collie 'Help' who was gratefully acknowledged and duly handed over to Mr Climpson. By the time of his retirement in 1889 through deafness and blindness, 'Help' had raised over £1,000 for the orphans. An old shepherd friend of Climpson's at Newhaven looked after the dog until his death, when he was stuffed and placed on Brighton Station where he continued to raise between 12s and 15s a week for the fund.[78]

The only other member of the animal kingdom enlisted to support the orphan fund was a monkey called Jacko owned by the West Brompton branch in 1894.[79]

All too often the image of a trade union held by most members of the public is of an organization which by means of strikes seeks to raise the wages and shorten the hours of its members. Since on the occasion of a railway strike a larger proportion of the public is immediately affected than is the case of a strike in almost any other industry, it has, perhaps, been worth while to demonstrate that although the main and proper task of the A.S.R.S. was to strive for a shorter working week and a living wage for railwaymen, valuable work was also done in making the railways safer for both railway staff and passengers, in striving for workmen's compensation and in caring for the orphans.

Nevertheless it would be unwise to exaggerate the achievements of the A.S.R.S. in the reduction of the accident rate. One of the greatest causes of railway accidents was the overstrain resulting from excessive hours of labour. This is a subject which demands a chapter to itself. There were strict limits to what could be achieved by the numerically weak A.S.R.S. in reducing the length of the working week. Only when, with the formation of the N.U.R. in 1913, the overwhelming majority of the employees was organized in one powerful union which could for the first time bargain effectively with the employers, was the stage set for an impressive reduction in hours and a consequent substantial curtailment of the number of those accidents which were primarily the result of fatigue.

NOTES

1. A.S.R.S. General Secretary's Reports, 1885–1900. Report to the Minister of Transport and Civil Aviation on the Accidents which occurred on the Railways of Great Britain during the year 1957, p. 22.
2. Royal Commission on Railway Accidents, 1877. B.P.P. 1877, Vol. XLVIII, Qs. 30817–8, Royal Commission on Accidents to Railway Servants, 1900, B.P.P. 1900, Vol. XXVII, Q. 6044.
3. Royal Commission on the Railway Conciliation Scheme of 1907, B.P.P. 1912–13. Vol. XVL, Qs. 9083 and 9196.
4. Quoted in Wilson, H. R., *Railway Accidents* (1925) p. 6.
5. Royal Commission on Labour, B.P.P. 1893–4, Vol. XXXIII, Q. 25945.
6. Select Committee on Railway Servants Hours of Labour, B.P.P. 1890–1, Vol. XVI. Qs. 5500 and 5790.
7. Royal Commission, 1900, (as above) Qs. 7343, 7347, 7350.
8. *Ibid.*, Qs. 1978–80.

9. Quoted in 'Lives versus Profits', *New Statesman*, Vol. I, May 31, 1913., p. 231
10. Royal Commission, 1877 (as above), Q. 18218–97.
11. *Ibid.*, Qs. 42, 819.
12. *Ibid.*, Qs. 32778–81.
13. A.S.R.S. General Secretary's Report, 1877.
14. R.R., October 6, 1882.
15. Royal Commission, 1877, Qs. 33, 453. Evidence of Mr Oakley, General Manager of Great Northern Railway.
16. *The Times*, February 25, 1877.
17. Railway Companies' Association Minutes, May 13, 1886. Railway Companies' Association Parliamentary Sub-Committee Minutes, May 27, 1886.
18. Evidence of R. Bell to the Royal Commission in 1900. Qs. 2586–97.
19. *Ibid.*, Qs. 2602–7.
20. Railway Companies' Association, Meetings, February 22, March 2, 1899. Minutes 2247 and 2257.
21. Royal Commission 1900, Appendix D.
22. *Ibid.*, Minutes of Evidence, Q. 2720.
23. *Ibid.*, Qs. 5132, 2920.
24. Report, p. 10.
25. *The Times Engineering Supplement*—Either-side brakes, December 6, 1911.
26. B.P.P. 1898, Vol. LXXXII, pp. 263, 259; 1914, Vol. LXXVII, p. 105.
27. Major Marindin's report on the accident to the Board of Trade, B.P.P. 1889, Vol. LXVII, p. 48.
28. *Ibid.*, p. 96.
29. Major Marindin reported that there were 'many cases' where the Board of Trade had recommended the appointment of lookout men. Royal Commission, 1900. Q. 2426.
30. Royal Commission, 1900. Q. 4725.
31. *Ibid.*, Qs. 2684, 3130–31.
32. 'Platelayers'. *The Times Engineering Supplement*, February 14, 1912.
33. Reports to the Board of Trade by the inspecting officers of the Railway Department on certain accidents. B.P.P. 1912–13, Vol. LXXIV, p. 223.
34. N.U.R. E.C. Minutes, December 1913, R.81.
35. N.U.R. E.C. Minutes, July 1914, p. 72.
36. B.P.P. 1875, Vol. LXVII, p. 308.
37. *Quarterly Review*, January 1878, p. 175.
38. Report of the Royal Commission on Railway Accidents, 1877.
39. Cited in *Railway Servants: An Appeal, etc.*, p. 22.
40. Letter cited in Adams, C. F., *Notes on Railway Accidents*, p. 223.
41. Stretton, C. E., *A few remarks on Railway Accidents*, p. 21.
42. *Quarterly Review*, January 1878, p. 181.
43. Quoted in Adams, C. F., *Notes on Railway Accidents*, p. 177.
44. The statements are those of Mr F. J. S. Hopwood of the Board of Trade to the Royal Commission, 1900, Q. 69.
45. *Ibid.*, Qs. 3190–3210.
46. A.S.R.S. Manifesto to Railwaymen, February 9, 1907.
47. Royal Commission, 1900, Q. 3315.
48. A.S.R.S. General Secretary's Report, 1908, p. 53.
49. Royal Commission on Railway Accidents, P.P. 1877, Vol. XLVIII, Qs. 33895, 32817 and 31034.
50. P.P. 1877, Vol. XLVIII, p. 28.
51. *Ibid.*, pp. 55 and 68.
52. *Ibid.*, p. 27.

53. Select Committee on Employers Liability for Injuries to their servants, P.P. 1876, Vol. IX, Qs. 1031, 935, and General Report by Captain Tyler to the Board of Trade, P.P. 1875, Vol. LXVI, p. 29.
54. R.R., February 25, 1881.
55. *Western Times*, November 22, 1873.
56. P.P. 1876, Vol. IX, Qs. 958, 971.
57. P.P. 1877, Vol. X, Qs. 1295–1305.
58. Majority report. 12 pp. 555 P.P. 1877, Vol. X. Minority Report, *Ibid.*, p. x.
59. R.S.G., October 11, 1878.
60. R.S.G., October 8, 1880.
61. This summary is based on the lucid account contained in P. S. Gupta's 'History of the Amalgamated Society of Railway Servants, 1871–1913'. Thesis submitted for the Degree of Doctor of Philosophy, 1960, Chapter III, Section III. See also A.S.R.S. General Secretary's Report to the A.G.M., 1880.
62. Hansard 1880, Vol. 255, Col. 1157 f. A.S.R.S. General Secretary's Report to the A.G.M., 1880 contains the addition to Clause I of the Act.
63. R.R., September 4, 1880.
64. A.S.R.S. General Secretary's Report to the A.G.M., 1881. Report of meetings in R.R., December 10 and 17, 1880.
65. R.R., February 23, 1894.
66. Details of benefits provided by the London and North Western Railway Insurance Society cited in G. Findlay, *The Working and Management of an English Railway*, p. 78.
   Mr Harford's evidence given to the Select Committee on the Employers Liability Act, 1880. Q. 4591 P.P. 1886, Vol. VIII.
67. Clement Edwards, M.P., *Railway Nationalisation*, pp. 117–18, quoting Board of Trade Accident Returns.
68. R.R., May 29, 1896.
69. P.P. 1886, Vol. VIII., Qs. 2663–6.
70. N. C. Mallalieu, 'Joseph Chamberlain and Workmen's Compensation', *Journal of Economic History*, Vol. X, 1950, pp. 50–4.
71. R.R., May 14, 1897.
72. R.R., August 20, 1897.
73. A.S.R.S. General Secretary's Report to the A.G.M., October 5, 1897.
74. This account of work for the railway orphans is based on an article by C. B. Vincent, 'Railway Reformation', in R.R., March 20, 1885; Alcock, pp. 112 *et seq.* A.S.R.S. E.C. Minutes, April 1874, and General Secretary's Report to the A.G.M., October 1880.
75. N.U.R. Report and Financial Statement, 1914.
76. N.U.R. Orphan Fund, Annual Report, 1958.
77. A.S.R.S. Report and Financial Statement for 1897, p. 19.
78. A.S.R.S. General Secretary's Report, 1881. R.R., March 20, 1885, July 6, 1894. A.S.R.S., E.C., May 10, 1882.
79. R.R., July 6, 1894.

CHAPTER V

1887-1891 THE FIGHT FOR THE FIRST NATIONAL PROGRAMME

'How about food? There is no stopping for that. It's a case of go as you please. The tea is always hanging on the stove and properly inky it becomes. It would do the directors good to drink some out of a lid. And your education? We have to thank the school and mother wit for that. And the church? Trains don't stop there. . . .

'So the upshot seems to be this; for twenty-four to thirty shillings a week you give yourself up body and soul to the public service and a good two-thirds of your life are spent in the guard's van? Yes, it is a common saying that in the winter months a guard never gets the chance of seeing his children. That is the other side of the four per cent dividend.'
Statement of a North British Railway Guard, 1888, in an interview with a reporter of The Scottish Leader.

I

AN inconspicuous ten-line report tucked away at the foot of a column of *The Times* of August 16, 1889, told of 2,500 London dockers who had come out on strike the previous day for a minimum rate of pay of 6d an hour and the guarantee of four hours work per day.

This action of the men of the East and West India docks which attracted such slight notice in the country's foremost newspaper, was to have momentous consequences for unskilled workers in every major industry of the country. Before the successful conclusion of the dispute on September 15th, nearly 100,000 disgracefully paid, impoverished men had joined the original strikers. The principal leaders of the Trade Union Movement of the day had assumed that it was impossible to organize the unskilled, casually employed and ill-paid general labourers. Yet the events of August and September showed that not only had these despised under-nourished mortals power to bring the world's greatest port to a standstill, they were also capable of electing from among their number an able committee which

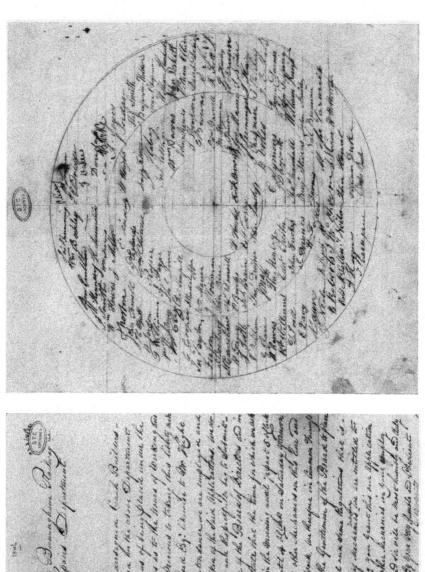

PLATE 1 'Round Robin' Petition, London and Birmingham Railway, 1846

'Black List' of drivers and firemen who struck work, August 1850

PLATE 2

North Eastern Railway Poster, 1868, following the extension of the franchise to better paid working men in 1867

supervised with impeccable honesty the expenditure of the £51,100 contributed by sympathizers, and organized the daily feeding of the 250,000 belonging to families directly affected by the strike.

That the hitherto largely unorganized dockers had by determined industrial action gained practically all their demands was a circumstance not overlooked by hundreds of thousands of other unskilled workers. Within two months of the outbreak of the dock strike the trade unions in the London area alone had recruited 100,000 new members.[1] The enthusiasm generated during the five stirring weeks of the summer of 1889 did not suddenly evaporate. At the end of 1890 there were five trade unionists in the country for every four at the end of 1889.[2]

II

The A.S.R.S. felt the beneficial effects of this revival of trade unionism. Its membership figures, which had fallen to 6,321 in 1882 and had climbed only slowly to 9,589 in 1889, suddenly leaped up to 26,360 in 1890. Gone was the old apathy and disillusionment. If the dockers, who were even worse paid than the poorest paid railwaymen, could gain substantial improvements by aggressive unionism, why should not the porters, guards, signalmen and others enter the fight for more tolerable conditions of employment?

As it happened, one of the obstacles which would have hampered strike action by the union was removed a few months prior to the dock strike. On August 5, 1887, nearly 3,000 drivers and firemen of the Midland Railway struck work after previously handing in their notices. For the past twenty years the locomotive staff of the company had been guaranteed six days' pay a week, though between 1869 and 1873 the men had voluntarily agreed to a 'temporary' suspension of the guarantee as a gesture of goodwill to help the company out of its financial difficulties. On July 15, 1887, the directors, in an official circular, announced that 'men will not be entitled to a full week's pay unless it is actually earned'. The reason given for the proposed change was 'that the system of payment for six days per week when men are not called on duty has been shown by experience to work badly, as it sometimes tends to give enginemen and firemen an interest in shirking work'. Particularly in view of the policy of co-operation with the management which had been followed by the men in previous years, strong resentment was felt at the insinuation that the men were work-shy.

Although Mr Harford had written to the directors asking them to postpone the new arrangements until after they had seen a deputation from the men, the strike was an unofficial one directed solely by the central committee of strikers. However, 600 members of the A.S.R.S. were involved, and there was general support in the union for the Midland men's fight to maintain a guaranteed week. On August 13th, Mr Harford published a circular appealing to all trade unionists to support the strikers. The appeal was unavailing. By August 16th, the strike had petered out through the three principal Scottish companies and the London and North Western supplying a total of 558 drivers and firemen to the Midland. Moreover, many of the strikers had drifted back to work through fear of losing their jobs.[3]

One hundred and eighty-nine members of the union who had been on strike did, in fact, find it impossible to get reinstatement. When they applied at Bradford, Sheffield, Derby and elsewhere to resume work they were bluntly informed that their places had been filled. Their situation posed an awkward problem for the E.C. On grounds both of sympathy for the men and of tactical expediency it would be wise to pay each of the victimized men the protection grant of £35. This was the decision made at the specially summoned meeting of the E.C. on August 30th, when it was also decided to expel some members employed on other railways who had filled the places of the strikers whilst the strike was still in progress. On the other hand, the strike had never been officially sanctioned, partly because the company's notice of the proposed new conditions of employment had been issued on July 15th, just as the normal quarterly E.C. meetings were coming to an end, and partly because the union's rule No. 15 had required the approval of the whole membership by ballot vote before any strike could be authorized.

Thus when the Cardiff delegate at the A.G.M. in October 1887 moved a resolution protesting against the 'misappropriation of funds by the E.C. . . . the said votes being without authority of the rules, and, in fact, a clear violation of them', he was plainly in the right from the strictly legal standpoint. But it can be argued that from both a moral and tactical standpoint the delegates were right in rejecting the Cardiff resolution by thirty-three votes to thirteen. Eight years earlier the failure of the union to give financial support to the many Midland Railway goods guards (sixty-three in London alone) who had not been reinstated after they had struck work to resist a wage cut, and the rejection by the A.G.M. later the same year of the proposal to establish a protection fund, had been partly responsible for the establishment of a new union—the A.S.L.E. & F. At Newcastle the delegates could see that a further failure to give financial assistance to victimized members could lead to a serious decline in the influence of the A.S.R.S.

The conclusion drawn by the members of the Edinburgh and other branches was that the union's rules should be altered to permit the General Secretary and E.C. to act more expeditiously in support of any future strike. The A.G.M. in Preston in October 1888 agreed to a motion from the Edinburgh branch that Clause 8 of Rule 15 should be completely reworded to permit a specially summoned E.C. both to authorize the withdrawal of labour and to expend money in support of the strikers.

Britain's position in the export markets was being threatened by her new industrial rivals, Germany and the United States. On the railways the period of rapid expansion of both mileage and profits had passed. Working costs were rising faster than revenue. The resultant economy drive had indirectly brought about a revision of the rules of the A.S.R.S. which enabled it to be better prepared for the coming industrial struggle.

III

The years 1888 and 1889 were remarkably peaceful ones on the railways, only 199 men being involved in strikes in the latter year.[4] They were years in which the union devised an agreed national programme.

In his report to the A.G.M. in 1887, Mr Harford had included proposals for, and improvement of, railwaymen's hours and wages, 'the attainment of which, would be the first aim and policy of the society'. The principal reforms he proposed were that every man should be guaranteed a week's wages; that with the exception of shunters working in busy yards and signalmen in busy boxes, who should be limited to eight hours, the working day should not exceed ten hours; overtime, including Sunday labour, should be paid at one and a quarter times the normal rate and an agreed scale of wages should be negotiated for each grade. Although no time was provided for a discussion of these proposals at the A.G.M., they did form the backbone of the proposals adopted by A.S.R.S. members on the North Eastern Railway in the following year. The Darlington programme, as it became known, closely resembled Mr Harford's, except that it included the demand for a 54-hour week for shunters and the payment of time and a half rates for Sunday duty.

At the A.G.M. in Preston in 1888, there was hesitation about the adoption of the Darlington programme in its entirety. A Liverpool delegate employed by the Lancashire and Yorkshire Railway declared that some of the engine drivers on his line would receive less pay under the Darlington scheme. The meeting, however, carried by forty-eight votes to three a resolution moved by the Birmingham delegate:

'That this Congress sympathizes with the North Eastern men in their efforts to improve their position and endorses their proposals on the question of time, and recommends the men on other lines to take up the question with a view to making it a universal movement.'

The meeting was prepared to give moral encouragement to men in any district who took the initiative, but there was neither a sufficient sense of urgency nor sufficient agreement on a wages policy to make possible the adoption of a national programme.

131

A year later the atmosphere of the Congress at Hull was entirely different. In the interim in London, gas stokers and dockers had shown what could be achieved with courage and determination. The E.C. had been asked to endorse so many local movements that at its July 1889 meeting it agreed to the proposals from Leeds and Cardiff branches that all members be canvassed to support a 'national memorial on the hours question' which the A.G.M. be asked subsequently to endorse. At the A.G.M. the programme, with its now familiar items of a guaranteed weekly wage, a ten-hour day (except for platelayers, nine hours, and some shunters and signalmen, eight hours) and overtime at time and a quarter and Sunday duty at time and a half rates, was carried 'without a dissentient voice, members rising in their places and shouting and clapping their hands with intense enthusiasm'.[5] Another significant outcome of the 1889 Congress was the decision to appoint Mr Alfred Mears, an ex-driver and victim of the Midland strike of 1887, as an additional organizer to press forward the national programme.

The one big mistake of that memorable A.G.M. was the rejection of a proposal from Mr Holden of the Sunderland branch that a new type of membership with a weekly contribution of 3d should be introduced. This would be additional to, and not in the place of, the existing membership scheme where contributions were 5d a week. It was designed to attract into the union the poorly paid grades, such as the porters and platelayers, who had hitherto remained largely aloof, partly on account of the expense. Mr D. Bunday, in seconding the resolution, showed prescience when he assured the meeting that 'unless they did something in the direction indicated they would have opposition societies springing up'. Mr A. Duffin from Southampton who opposed the resolution did not believe that the introduction of a new class of membership would add a single member to the Society. The view of the cautiously minded delegates prevailed. The resolution was defeated by twenty-eight votes to twenty-five. Within two months of this debate the inaugural meeting of the General Railway Workers Union had been held and a scale of membership contribution identical with that proposed by Mr Holden at the A.S.R.S. Congress approved. Within a further twelve months the G.R.W.U. had recruited 10,827 members to support a policy of militant trade unionism.[6] The new union gained most of its recruits from the railway workshops, the porters, vanmen and rulleymen, grades hitherto virtually untouched by the A.S.R.S., and could therefore scarcely be accused of 'poaching'. Its formation did, however, encourage the members of the A.S.R.S. who were in favour of a more aggressive industrial policy. At the inaugural meeting of the G.R.W.U., on November 19, 1889, the resolution 'That the union shall remain a fighting one and shall not be encumbered by any sick or accident fund'[7] had been carried by a large majority. Especially in towns where there were G.R.W.U. branches, the new unionists acted as an important ginger group to stimulate the staider members of the A.S.R.S. into greater activity.

In 1890 no railway trade unionists could complain about lack of activity or of exciting happenings. The year opened with Mr Harford's dispatch to the General Managers of all the principal railway companies of the 'National Programme' and a request for negotiation on its terms; it ended with the Scottish railways still paralysed by a bitter strike which had begun ten days earlier. The report of the Labour Correspondent of the Board of Trade for 1890 lists seventeen railway strikes in which upwards of 12,000 men were involved compared with the four very minor strikes involving 199 men in the previous year.[8]

The railway managers treated Mr Harford's letter with scant respect. Although some did him the courtesy of a formal acknowledgment, others showed their distaste for the union by failing to reply. In no case was any willingness shown to negotiate on the national programme. Indignation at the brusque rejection of the men's demands was widespread but came to a head principally in the four areas of Ireland, South Wales, the North Eastern Railway and Scotland.

IV

One of the most remarkable developments in this period of the revival of trade unionism was the extremely rapid growth of A.S.R.S. membership in Ireland. Branches of the union were established there from 1885, but largely owing to the particularly scattered distribution of railway employment and the absence of a full-time organizer to bind together the efforts of the local stalwarts, the movement languished. As late as 1888 there were but 190 members in the whole country.[9] Following disagreements between the editor of the *Railway Review*, Mr F. Maddison, and his assistant, Mr W. Foreman, the E.C., in December 1889, resolved to send Mr Foreman to Dublin as organizer *pro tem*. The move proved to be eminently worth while. By the end of February in the following year Mr Harford reported that the Irish membership had increased by 4,000 and that nineteen new branches had been formed in the previous few months.[10] The fact that four new branches had been formed in Dublin alone was indicative of the growing strength of railway unionism in the capital. The curtain raiser of the Irish movement came at noon on January 3, 1890, when there was a lightning strike of guards, porters, ticket collectors and signalmen employed by the Dublin, Wicklow and Wexford Railway. The men demanded a rise of 2s a week with a reduction of hours and improvement in overtime rates. By 11.0 p.m. the same day the company had conceded wage advances of 1s and 2s a week to a number of the men and there was a general return to work, the questions of hours and overtime rates being shelved.

Perhaps it was the partial success of the January strike which led the buoyant-hearted men of Cork to the optimistic opinion that they should float independently an Irish A.S.R.S. In February and March they recruited nearly 400 members to this organization, mostly in the neighbourhood of Cork itself. Elsewhere in Ireland the newly recruited members felt equally strongly that it would be better to remain in one union with their English brothers provided a full-time organizer was appointed to deal with Irish affairs. To settle these differences, a conference of delegates from the Irish branches was held in the Workman's Hall, Wellington Quay, Dublin, on April 15th and 16th. Mr Harford presided. The twenty-five delegates rejected by twelve votes to nine a resolution to establish a separate Irish organization with its own E.C. but agreed to proposals for a full-time organizer for Ireland and the purchase of a central hall for members of the Society in Dublin. In July of the same year the E.C. in London agreed to a proposal for the merging of the Cork Society with the A.S.R.S. whilst the A.G.M. at Belfast agreed to the appointment of Mr Foreman as organizing Secretary for Ireland, normally resident in Dublin.

On April 21st, trouble flared up again, this time on the Great South and West of Ireland Railway. Though the immediate occasion for the strike was the refusal of the Cork railwaymen to handle bacon brought by the Clyde Shipping Company during a strike of carters at the docks, the principal cause of the stoppage was the men's resentment at the introduction of a new and parsimonious classification of the wages of signalmen and guards. Under the scheme, a few long-service signalmen were to be paid 2s a week more than previously whilst the maximum pay for the majority of the signalmen was lowered from 21s to £1. The company hoped to save itself £639 12s 0d a year through this irritating economy. Under a similar scheme for the passenger guards it hoped to save £438.[11] Although the strike was remarkably effective—more than a thousand men were out and the whole of the commerce and trade in South West Ireland was in a state of stagnation—the men were obliged to return to work on May 5th because of the exhaustion of their funds. The company, through the mediation of Archbishop Walsh of Dublin, agreed to consider the men's grievances within fourteen days of the return to work.

After a minor skirmish on the Waterford and Limerick Railway in which the enginemen succeeded in winning a 1s a week rise, battle was again joined with the employers on the Dublin, Wicklow and Wexford Railway on August 9th. The stoppage arose from the refusal of the directors of the company to reinstate two union men who had been dismissed for alleged insubordination. Over 200 porters and signalmen were involved. Mr Foreman declared that both he and the strike pickets were 'very much harassed by the police'. Four of the pickets were arrested and charged with frightening a non-union man. When the magistrates dismissed the case the union, in its turn, brought in a case against the company for illegal arrest and detention. However, the second case was not brought to jury as the union would not have been able to prove that the Board of Directors had ordered the arrest of the men.[12] The strikers' efforts were also hampered by the presence of Government reporters at the meetings called to enlist support for the strike. By such means the strike was broken. At the half-yearly meeting of the company held in Dublin on August 18th, the Chairman, Sir Richard Martin Naish, announced that they had received 'so many applications for employment that he could select men with as much care as if there had been no strike'. He refused to reinstate any of the strikers. Many of those who were refused re-employment emigrated to the United States or to Canada. By a decision of the A.G.M. all applicants for the emigration grant were allowed the full amount of £10. This sum would be more than sufficient to cover the cost of travel for a man and his wife to Canada or the United States. The steerage rates by Dominion Royal Mail Line from Liverpool to Montreal were £4 per person in the 1890's and it was possible to travel steerage to New York for as little as £3.

Although some of the strikers finished up roughing it on the Atlantic passage, the pioneers of the movement in Ireland had some successes to their credit. Not only had the membership greatly increased but the wages of some of the grades employed by the Dublin, Wicklow and Wexford Company and the Waterford and Limerick Company had improved. These successes were sufficient to stir railwaymen elsewhere into pressing their claims for improved conditions.

v

On the North Eastern, progress was very slow after the first presentation of the Darlington programme to the directors. After several interviews between the representatives of the men's committee and the General Manager, the directors, in December 1888, announced their rejection of the men's programme. They said the company could not afford the concessions asked. They also refused to see a deputation. The men replied by organizing mass meetings in all big towns on the North Eastern network. These must have helped to influence the directors who eventually agreed in September 1889, to see a deputation of the men. After three successive meetings the company again announced its rejection of the programme on October 17th, but agreed to leave it to departmental managers, in discussions with grade representatives, to make 'reasonable modification' in the rate of wages. The company began to make concessions on a grade by grade basis. A delegation was informed on January 4, 1890, that the hours of goods guards and shunters would be reduced from sixty-six to sixty per week, that there would be improvement in some drivers' pay and that the number of eight-hour signal boxes would be increased. Whilst these improvements were welcome, the men's committee could see the dangers of such piecemeal advances. Grade rivalry would be intensified. It wisely decided in February to hand over the negotiations to the E.C. and to Mr Harford.

On March 6th, Mr Harford wrote to the directors of the North Eastern suggesting that the questions of reduction of hours and payment for over-time should be referred to arbitration. When the company would not agree to the suggestion the E.C. agreed to the North Eastern men's committee conducting a strike ballot. The result was not encouraging. Less than half the 5,151 ballot papers issued were returned. Of those who voted, 1,688 were against, and only 1,036 for, strike action.[13]

In view of this fiasco, the later decision of the North Eastern Railway Board to agree to submit to arbitration the question of the hours of labour of rulleymen, porters, vanmen and others, is surprising. Both sides agreed to the appointment of Dr Spense Watson as arbitrator even though the major demands of the Darlington programme were not under review. In the meantime impatience with the slow progress of the negotiations was growing, and in November the men's committee conducted another strike ballot. This time a large majority of the voters favoured strike action—2,636 to 551 against—but in one sense the result was every bit as dis-appointing as was that of the earlier ballot as less than a third of the ballot papers issued were returned. The editor of the *Railway Review* declared it to be a 'deplorable collapse'.[14]

The future, however, was not as gloomy as many of the North Eastern men must have feared in November. Within six weeks the situation was transformed by the perseverance of the men of the Northern district of the North Eastern system. They refused to accept defeat. When the result of the ballot was known they again presented their demands and when they received no reply, about 2,000 of them handed in their notices. The North Eastern Directors were too sensible to risk a stoppage at this time of the year. Just before Christmas they agreed to meet not only the men's committee but also Mr Harford and Mr Campion Watson (the General Secretary of the General Railway Workers' Union), who were admitted to the discussions as 'advisers'. The substantial gains which resulted from this first approach to union recognition on the North Eastern included a six-day guaranteed week; an increase of 2s a week in the wages of plate-layers and a 48-hour week for shunters. It was a big step forward and it had been achieved without a strike. That all was settled amicably was in part due to the fact that the Directors of the North Eastern who lived and operated in an area where trade unionism was strong, took a more en-lightened view of co-operation with the A.S.R.S. than did the directors on other railways. The men's success proved a great inspiration to the strikers on the neighbouring Scottish railways.

VI

The story of the movement in South Wales also reveals some dramatic contrasts. The campaign began with the Directors of the Taff Vale, Rhymney and Barry Docks Companies ignoring Mr Harford's requests for negotiations. It ended with his successfully negotiating a favourable settlement with their chosen spokesman. On the day before the strike began he was refused admittance to the Taff Vale Board Room; on the day it ended Mr Inskip, the Chairman of that Company, appearing on the same platform as Mr Harford, complimented him on his reasonableness and negotiating abilities.

The trainmen employed by the Rhymney Railway were the first to take up the cudgels. When their delegates were interviewed by the directors they presented the national programme stressing particularly the guaranteed week's pay and 60-hour weekly maximum. The directors would not accept these proposals and twice rejected an offer to submit the claim to arbitration. From then onwards the directors of all three companies acted together, appointing from among their number a small committee to act on their behalf. The men decided to do likewise. In quick succession, from June 29 to July 11, 1890, the men placed their notices in Mr Harford's hands for him to pass on to the directors at an opportune moment. In contrast with the men on the North Eastern, the railwaymen in South Wales showed remarkable solidarity and resolution. The Taff Vale men tendered 1,082 notices, the Rhymney men 184 out of a possible 194, and the Barry men 217. Over 90 per cent of the men had thus put their trust in Mr Harford and the arbitrament of the strike. Indicative of the determination and sense of unity of the men was the resolution passed by a meeting of Taff Vale railwaymen on July 24th:

'That in the opinion of this meeting when the notices are tendered it is desirable, if the men of one company are allowed to come out on strike, the men of all three do likewise, and do not return to work unless all the companies' employees have received the concessions asked for.'[15]

That it came to a strike was due to the refusal of the directors to negotiate with Mr Harford. Due largely to the intervention of an ex-Mayor of Cardiff, Mr David Jones, a conference between the committee of the strikers and the railway directors was arranged for Tuesday, August 5th. Mr Jones understood and the men understood, that it had been agreed that Mr Harford should be included in the men's delegation. At the appointed hour and rendezvous, Mr Harford accompanied the men. The party was kept waiting, standing in a corridor for an hour like a lot of schoolboys expecting to be reprimanded by their headmaster. They were even denied the common courtesy of being ushered into a waiting room and provided with seating accommodation. After the hour had elapsed they were blandly told that while the directors would be pleased to interview the men, Mr Harford would not be admitted. Naturally, the men declined to negotiate unless accompanied by their Secretary.[16]

That had been the last chance of a settlement, for the men's notices were due to expire on the following day. It was evident that the directors preferred to have a strike rather than see Mr Harford.

The strike which began on the night of Wednesday, August 6th, was the first one officially sponsored by the A.S.R.S. It was remarkably effective. Mr Ben Tillett, who was there to organize the Cardiff dockers, described it as 'the sharpest blow of the year'.[17] The fact was that the valley depended for its livelihood on the export of coal, and the docks and the mines were entirely dependent on the railway. Three days after the strike began the special correspondent of *The Times* reported that 'the stagnation of the trade throughout the whole of South Wales that is dependent on the lines affected by the strike was absolute'.[18]

The men seized every opportunity of demonstrating their unity. By the terms of the contract with the Taff Vale Company, employees were required to hand in their uniforms when resigning the service. Hence on Saturday, August 9th, there assembled a procession of between three and four hundred drivers and firemen at the rear of the Queen Street Hall in Cardiff. The men carried their heavy top coats but many of them decided to wear their sou'westers back to front to protect their faces from the hot rays of the sun as they marched four deep to the General Stores at Cathays Yard where the articles were handed in.

In the Rhondda not a locomotive was to be seen for the duration of the strike. The miners were idle until the goods service was resumed on the railway. (It was not only human beings who felt the effects of the dispute. Rats in the pits, accustomed—with or without permission—to feed on the miners' sandwiches, experienced an exceedingly lean time and would all have perished if the struggle had been a more protracted one.) Many of the miners and their families who, in their earlier years, had been brought up on farms returned to their old haunts to help gather in the harvest.

In face of the complete collapse of trade and the unbroken ranks of the men the railway directors were obliged to negotiate. On Thursday, August 7th, Mr Harford was informed that Mr Inskip, the Chairman of the Taff Vale, who spoke on behalf of all three companies, was willing to meet him together with a deputation from the men. Mr Inskip informed them later the same evening that the companies were prepared to offer a 240-hour guaranteed month in place of the 60-hour guaranteed week. If in the course of that 240-hour month a man did more than fifteen hours' work in a day the excess would be paid at overtime rates. The fact that Mr Harford and the deputation accepted these terms reveals how far they were prepared to go to get a settlement. The vast majority of the railwaymen understandably thought otherwise. At a mass meeting held in the Queen Street Hall, Cardiff, on the morning of Friday, August 8th, only one man voted against the resolution to adhere to the 60-hour week and reject the alternative of the 240-hour month. Speakers at the meeting stressed the harm done to railway passengers and servants alike through a system which made it possible for men to be employed exceptionally long hours at a stretch. The same views were expressed at a monster demonstration of 10,000 people in the Canton Cattle Market on the following Sunday. Two local Liberal M.P.s and Mr Ben Tillett supported from the platform the claim for a 60-hour week. One of the M.P.s, Sir E. J. Reed, offered his services as mediator, only to have them refused by Mr Inskip the same day. Finally, on the afternoon of Thursday, August 14th, Mr Inskip, in a private interview with Mr Harford, informed him that the companies would agree to accept the 60-hour working week with a guaranteed week's pay for all full-time employees. There was one serious omission. The signalmen were not at first included in the agreement and Mr Harford was severely criticized by the E.C. and many of the rank and file for not insisting on their inclusion. In further talks with Mr Inskip he made the omission good by the end of the year.

Speaking from the same platform as Mr Harford before a large audience of railwaymen on the night of the settlement, Mr Inskip referred to the cordial and satisfactory character of the talks they had had. He hoped that by meeting in the way they had that night they might have 'done something towards establishing an altered mode of settling difficulties between employer and employed'. The men gave him three cheers.[19]

That the South Wales strike was so successful was due to the unity of the men. But success was helped by the fact that the entire livelihood of the area was dependent on the mines, the railway and the docks and a closure of one meant the breakdown of all. The strike exposed the antiquated attitude of the railway employers. In the coal mines of the district collective bargaining had been the rule for fifteen years. Many influential local people were angry that the railway directors had disrupted the commerce of the area through their failure to follow the example of the coal owners in negotiating with the men. But if the railway employers gave way to public opinion and the strength of the A.S.R.S. in 1890, the events of 1900 were to show that they had by no means welcomed trade unionism with open arms.

VII

The most dramatic struggle in the eventful year 1890 was the strike in Scotland. Conditions of employment in the Scottish railways had always been more arduous, especially in the neighbourhood of the big cities, than was the case in England. A large percentage of the men were employed in small groups in isolated stations and yards with the result that trade unionism was weak until the revival of 1889–90. Throughout the entire period before the First World War railwaymen in Scotland worked longer hours for less pay than their brethren south of the border.

On the Scottish railways the 12-hour day was 'normal' except for a few signalmen employed in very busy boxes. But long stretches of overtime was the rule rather than the exception, particularly for drivers, firemen and guards on goods trains. Even so the six weeks' strike of December 1890 and January 1891 might never have occurred had it not been for the exceptional circumstances on the North British Railway. The opening of the Tay Bridge in June 1887, and the Forth Bridge in March 1890, greatly increased the volume of goods traffic on the line and created an intolerable congestion in the neighbourhood of Edinburgh. The historian of the company admitted that the Waverley Station became 'dreadfully congested and inadequate',[20] while the conservatively minded editor of the *Engineer* declared that the North British had been 'notoriously mismanaged for some time. The block of traffic at Edinburgh since the Forth Bridge was opened became disgraceful.'[21] Members of the staff of the company had warned the directors of the danger of congestion once the Forth Bridge was opened, but their warnings went unheeded. Only long after the strike was over did Mr McLaren, one of the directors, admit that 'they had not made adequate provision for the sudden expansion of traffic'.[22] The consequence of this gross mismanagement was the placing of an intolerable burden on the staff. In August 1890, many drivers, firemen and guards were employed for 19, 22, 23 or even 25 hours at a stretch. Working weeks of 96 and 97 hours were reported by these grades later in the year. This excessive labour was by no means exceptional. As one of the guards who knew from experience asserted at the time, 'it was the fixing of overwork into a system that was bad'. There is no doubt that through the failure of the company to provide adequate siding accommodation for goods traffic, the men had been systematically overworked for years. Between January 1, 1889, and February 14, 1891, a North British engine driver had worked an average day of 13 hours 40 minutes.[23] Where drivers were not employed under the 'trip' system their overtime in excess of their basic 144-hour fortnight was paid at the ordinary rate of pay. Then the company had no strong incentive to reduce the amount of overtime worked. To cut down running expenses, moreover, the trip system had been greatly extended, a convenient device for dodging the payment of overtime money altogether. Under this system the driver would be allowed a certain time in which to complete his trip and would be paid accordingly. As likely as not he stood as much chance of reaching his destination in the stipulated time as he had (in those days) of reaching the moon. Through fog or delays in sidings whilst passenger trains passed by he would take hours longer to finish the trip. The experience of a Scottish driver in the week beginning January 18, 1890, may be given as an illustration of the typical experience of many:

Time allowed for trip	.	.	.	10	hours
Time taken on Monday	.	.	.	18	hours
Time taken on Tuesday	.	.	.	15	hours
Time taken on Wednesday		.	.	$13\frac{1}{2}$	hours
Time taken on Thursday	.	.	.	17	hours
Time taken on Friday	.	.	.	$15\frac{1}{4}$	hours
Time taken on Saturday	.	.	.	13	hours

Total hours paid for trip, 60; total hours actually worked, $91\frac{3}{4}$; hours worked for which no pay was given, $31\frac{3}{4}$.[24] Similar examples could be quoted for the Caledonian railway.

A guard gave a vivid description of the dangers of systematic overwork when he spoke to a reporter of the *Scottish Leader*:

'I remember once falling into a doze on the seat in the van. A jerk of the train woke me up in a fright. I tried the wrong door in my agitation and thought we were in for a disaster. Luckily there was nothing serious but the sweat was pouring off me, and my nervous system got into a state of collapse. Often the work is done with the men more asleep than awake, and that there are not more accidents is a miracle. After fifteen hours of it the mind falls into a semi-conscious state; and that explains why every now and again a thoroughly experienced, trustworthy man commits some obvious blunder; a driver runs past a signal, or does not pull up soon enough—and can't give any coherent account of the affair.'

The outstanding successes of trade unionists elsewhere in the kingdom put new heart into the Scottish railwaymen. Their appalling working conditions goaded them into activity. In increasing numbers they joined the Scottish A.S.R.S. Since its foundation on March 24, 1872, this Society had a membership of between 1,000 and 3,000 mainly confined to the better paid grades who joined largely for its friendly society benefits. Its rules had been strict. Under Rule 15 'any member going on duty in a state of intoxication or becoming so while in the discharge of his duty' was liable to a fine of 10s. But although it maintained a sturdy independence of the English Society, it was scarcely in a position to influence the conditions of employment of the men. Then came a rapid change. Membership figures, which were as low as 3,350 in December 1888, rose to 6,703 in December 1890. Addressing the Annual Executive Council Meeting in March 1890, the Chairman, William Milne, spoke of unprecedented progress over the past year with eleven new branches established.[25]

The stress in the campaign which followed was on the need for a reduction of the working day. The Society demanded a 10-hour day. Overtime rates at time and a quarter for weekdays and time and a half for Sundays were included as a spur to the companies to keep the working hours of the men within reasonable limits. The ending of the trip system and the guaranteeing of a week's wages were also demanded.

The campaign was launched at a big public meeting in the Trades Hall, Glasgow, on August 18, 1890. The audience carried with acclamation a resolution moved by Councillor Burt:

'That the citizens of Glasgow viewed with regret the lengthened hours men in responsible positions were called upon to work, considered such dangerous to the public, and recommended the Boards of Directors of the Scottish railways to consider the propriety of reducing the same to the limit desired by their employees.'[26]

Many other meetings were held in the principal Scottish cities that week-end.

Early in September, Mr Tait, the General Secretary of the Scottish A.S.R.S., wrote to the companies asking them to discuss the men's programme. The replies received showed uncompromising opposition to any concessions on hours or overtime pay. The Caledonian General Manager in his reply stated that the company had made improvement in the pay of the men seven years previously in 1883 and there was no case for further concessions. On October 19th, Mr Tait offered to submit the questions in dispute to arbitration but the companies turned down the suggestion. The sole positive proposal the companies made was that there should be grade deputations to the directors. The Scottish E.C. commented on November 24th that the procedure of sectional or individual interview had had 'disastrous results in the flower of the delegates afterwards being dismissed',[27] while Mr John Burns described it as 'the massacre of the innocents with Walker (General Manager of the North British) as Lord High Executioner'.[28] Two examples of such dismissals on the Caledonian were given to the Parliamentary Committee in 1891.[29] In a circular to the staff of his company issued on November 15, 1890, Mr Walker declared:

'It may be well to remind our staff generally, that the company has always on the list of applicants for employment, a number of eligible men, which numbers have been increased since the advantages of the sick, accident and superannuation funds have become more generally known and appreciated.'

Inevitably the men were weary of the apparently never-ending and fruitless correspondence between Mr Tait and the directors and angry at the refusal of the companies to go to arbitration. A mass meeting of Glasgow railwaymen held in the Albion Halls on November 23rd, carried by a large majority a resolution to start a strike on December 24th. Similar resolutions were adopted with 'practical unanimity' at Motherwell, Greenock, Falkirk, Edinburgh, Dundee, Perth, Arbroath and Stirling. The E.C. at the time warned the meetings that though they were anxious to see a cessation of labour, they would not favour strike action unless 'a sufficient majority of the membership wanted it. A partial stoppage would result in failure.' By December 7th, 4,173 notices (from a membership of nearly 7,000) had been handed in to the E.C. Since they did not consider this sufficient, at meetings held on December 14th and 21st, they advised against strike action until more support had been obtained.

The Glaswegians were determined to stick to their guns. There was no mistaking the feeling of the monster meeting in the Albion Halls on December 21st. The men were much influenced by the very recent success of the movement on the North Eastern. In the course of one of the speeches from the platform a railwayman shouted out:

'When 1,500 men can do what they have done on the North Eastern Railway what could 5,000 do in Scotland?'

His interjection was greeted with loud applause. Mr Tait told the meeting that the E.C. would prefer they should wait until they had a greater measure of support, but 'if any action was taken, the Society could not stand idly by'. A man from the floor then said:

' "Well, Mr Chairman, I think we ought to take courage and go." He was loudly cheered. Finally "a man in the gallery" moved "that they do not resume work".'

Six hundred and sixty men voted for the resolution and only eighty-one for an amendment that the strike be postponed. The result of the voting was received with 'round after round of cheering, the men rising to their feet and waving hats and handkerchiefs'. After this the meeting was adjourned until later in the evening when results of meetings in other Scottish centres would be known. Apparently, the men elsewhere were encouraged by the decisions of the Glasgow meeting. In most places on the three railways affected—the Caledonian, North British, and Glasgow and South Western—there was a large majority in favour of striking. At Motherwell it was 240 to five.[30] The die was cast. The strike was started that night (21st) without the men observing the stipulated period of notice to the companies.

The Scottish Society entered the battle with meagre resources. Its balance at the bank at the end of 1889 had been £5,438 18s 7d. With strike pay at 10s a week for single men and proportionately more for married men and the number on strike rising within three days to 7,000 this would not last very long. The three companies, though not nearly as prosperous as the South Wales concerns, had substantially improved their financial position over the past twelve months. Their total receipts had risen by over 9 per cent in this period. The Caledonian was paying a steady 5 per cent dividend and the Glasgow and South Western a steady 4 per cent. The North British mismanagement and consequent high working expenses cut down its ordinary dividend to 1¾ per cent, but the companies were likely to help each other in the emergency.[31]

Although there were about 35,000 railwaymen in Scotland, the strike was virtually confined to the goods guards, drivers, firemen, signalmen and examiners who were together about 8,000 in number. At the height of the struggle within a week of its commencement, at least 7,000 of the men in the grades involved, were out.[32]

From the start the weakest link of the strike was the situation on the Glasgow and South Western Railway. Here the traffic congestion and consequent overworking of the men had been much less than on the other two lines. Inevitably there was not the same feeling of bitterness towards the management as had developed on the other lines where the men could not call their lives their own. With equal enthusiasm on each line it is conceivable that the partial character of the strike need not have been a serious obstacle to success but with some of the men initially involved not experiencing as great a sense of grievance against their employers, the existence of a substantial minority of non-strikers did reduce the morale of those not working and the likelihood of a favourable outcome.

If there were weaknesses on the men's side they were not apparent during the first week of the strike when each day brought an increase in the number of the strikers and increasing signs of dislocation of the transport system. All traffic on the City Railway in Glasgow stopped on December 22nd. There was to be no sign of activity here for the next five weeks. Branch line services on all three systems virtually ceased. Carts were being employed to carry goods to Glasgow from as far as thirty miles distant. Five thousand employees of the Singer Company at Kilbowie on the Clyde were out of work as the North British Railway was unable to put on the special trains which normally carried the staff to their factory. As coal stocks at local depots were rapidly depleted and only very partially replenished, the price of coal rose from 20s a ton to what was regarded as a 'famine' price of 40s a ton. Many factory managers decided to accept the inevitable and to make a serious effort to resume production only after the conclusion of the New Year holiday. They were over-optimistic. A week after the Hogmanay celebrations the special correspondent of *The Times* reported that 'next to no trade is being carried on' and that steamers could not sail 'for lack of cargo'.[33]

Leading citizens and businessmen in Glasgow, Edinburgh and elsewhere became gravely perturbed at the effects of the widespread and prolonged disruption of trade. The Lord Provost of Glasgow presided over a well-attended meeting in the City Hall on January 9th, when a committee of prominent citizens was elected to mediate between the two sides in the dispute. A similar committee was elected in Edinburgh a week later.[34] The Glasgow meeting authorized Messrs Harford and Tait to offer mediation terms to Mr Haldane, Q.C., M.P., who was willing to pass them on to the directors of the railway companies. But according to Mr John Burns, Mr Walker and Mr Thompson had 'so wrapped themselves up in the mantle of their conceit which was big enough to cover the Battle of Bannockburn', that they would not consider any terms emanating from the union.[35] Mr Haldane considered the men's terms very reasonable. Though they had proposed a working day of ten hours they had agreed that this clause 'should be interpreted in a reasonable spirit by both parties. The porter at a roadside station would not be treated on the same footing as a porter at a large station.' Overtime at time and a quarter rates was to be paid only after a 60-hour week had been worked. He complimented Mr Tait and Mr Harford on being 'most willing to put the question of recognition on one side' in the interests of a settlement, and he did not see any good reason why Scottish directors should not accept similar terms to those recently accepted by the Directors of the North Eastern, North Staffordshire and Taff Vale Railways.[36] The Edinburgh meeting placed its trust in the Earl of Aberdeen as mediator. The E.C. of the Scottish A.S.R.S. supported the venture and declared that the men would be willing to return to work if, after seeing the railway directors, he could assure them that there would be a reduction of the working week. The directors were not interested in the mediations either of Mr Haldane or of the Earl of Aberdeen. They were confident that they could smash the strike. They refused to negotiate while the men remained out, but promised grievances would be considered on a grade basis when the men had returned to work. To defeat the strike they advanced to the maximum of their wage scales all men who remained loyal to the companies.[37] The Caledonian Company advertised in Belfast for goods guards, promising them free passes to their employment.[38] The North British issued a circular in which it was stated that the company would 'recognize and reward those who had done their duty at this time'. Many blacklegs came from the service of English railway companies. Mr Cooper, the Superintendent of the line of the Glasgow and South Western Company, made a list of strikers and handed it to the company's solicitors so that the men might be prosecuted under the Conspiracy and Protection of Property Act, 1875. Though the cases were subsequently dropped by the court, the fact that such action was initiated may well have deterred men from continuing on strike or joining the strikers.[39] The claim for £20,000 damages later made by the North British on the

Scottish Society was also intended to be a major means of breaking the strike.

For many, the best remembered incident of the strike was the eviction of a number of railwaymen and their families from houses owned by the Caledonian Company in Hope Street, Motherwell. The first attempt by the sheriff to carry out the orders of the company was made at lunch time on January 2nd. As if from nowhere 3,000 persons surrounded ten sites and made it impossible for the sheriff and his two assistants to carry out their intention. The company then tried gentle persuasion. They informed the sixty men affected that if they returned to work the evictions would not be proceeded with. Only two men accepted the offer. On January 5th, fifty men of the 13th Hussars from the Maryhill Barracks were marched into the area and the whole street was cordoned off. This made it possible to carry out the original plan, but it greatly angered a turbulent crowd of between 20,000 and 30,000, in the main composed of coal miners and iron-workers from the surrounding districts, who were striking in sympathy with the railwaymen. Powerless, now, to prevent the evictions, they wrecked a nearby signalbox and smashed the glass roof of the railway station. The Riot Act was read and the police made repeated baton charges to disperse the crowd.[40]

The strike began to collapse where it had all along been weakest, on the Glasgow and South Western. After the Hurlford men returned to work on December 30th, there was 'a general rush for reinstatement' on that company's line.[41] It is true that when a large majority of the strikers on the other lines remained out, John Burns, on January 19th, persuaded over fifty of the Hurlford men to stop work again, but this was only a small check to the drift back to employment. Displaying indefatigable energy, John Burns travelled from one centre to another making impassioned speeches and helping to maintain the morale of the men. At Motherwell on January 5th he told an enthusiastic audience of railwaymen that 'Before the strike was over if necessary they must part with their boots, their coat, their furniture or the house over their heads rather than submit to a tyranny that was becoming intolerable'.[42] In between addressing meetings in Scotland he pleaded with London trade unionists to support the strike. On January 2nd he published an appeal 'To the Workmen of London' for financial help. He was successful in persuading the Amalgamated Society of Engineers to vote a levy of 3d per member. But although these and similar efforts, which brought in £6,000, served to prolong the strike, they were of no avail to bring it to a successful conclusion.[43] By the end of January the companies had recruited enough men to operate most of their normal services. At a big meeting in Dundee on January 26th, the leaders of the union admitted defeat and urged the men to do their best to gain re-employment. On the 29th, a deputation from the men on strike met Mr Walker who promised that the grievances of the men would be discussed within a fortnight. Mr Tait and Mr Harford both signed the manifesto 'To the North British Railwaymen at present on Strike' later the same day. It read:

'Fellow workmen: We have at length received sufficient assurance through a deputation appointed by the E.C. that the company is prepared to give every consideration to the conditions for which you have been contending during the past six weeks and further that everything possible will be done by officials to reinstate every man in his former position, and that no advantage shall be taken of men for anything they may have done during the struggle.

'Under the circumstances we do not see that anything further is to be gained by prolonging the strike and we therefore instruct all men to return to their work on Friday, January 30th, 1891.'

In the evening Mr Harford told a meeting of the men in Edinburgh that the Directors of the North British had agreed to drop the civil action against Messrs Milne and Tait as representing the Scottish A.S.R.S. and to drop all actions against individual strikers. These were the only consolations gained from the settlement. The company did not guarantee to employ any man who had been out on strike. Nor did it make any promises for the reduction of the hours of labour. A similar agreement was made for the Caledonian strikers on the following day.

Though the men had been defeated and had returned to work (where possible) on the terms laid down by the companies, they remained proud of their determined stand for better working conditions. The Standing Committee of the Scottish Society at its meeting on March 12, 1891, decided to order the striking of bronze, silver and gold medallions to be purchasable at 9d, 3s and 21s by those qualified to wear them. The medallion was inscribed on the one side 'Scotch Railway Strike 1890–1' and on the other 'A.S.R.S. for Scotland' with clasped hands in the centre and room for the name of the owner at the bottom.

At the Annual Executive Council meeting held in Aberdeen from June 17 to 19, 1891, both the President, Mr Milne, and the General Secretary, Mr Tait, claimed that the strike had been worth while, Mr Tait claiming that 'it was justified if only to place before the public (who after all are the masters of the railway companies) the degrading and demoralizing conditions which they forced upon their servants'. Since the conclusion of the strike there had been some reduction of hours, whilst Sunday labour which before the strike did not qualify for overtime pay was paid at time and a half rates from March 16, 1891.

Four days after the conclusion of the strike a meeting of directors and shareholders of the North British Railway held in Edinburgh resolved to spend additional funds on extending accommodation for traffic at the

Waverley Station. When this work was completed there were fewer delays and instances of excessive hours were reduced, although for several weeks after the strike there was an extra heavy burden of overtime whilst the backlog of goods traffic was dealt with.[44]

The heaviest burden was borne by those men who were not taken back at the end of January. On May 8th there were still 265 men in receipt of aliment from the union. A large proportion of them came from outlying centres where alternative employment was difficult to find. A week earlier Mr Tait had been obliged to reduce the aliment paid to single men from 10s to 8s 6d and that paid to married men from 12s 6d to 10s.[45] Some of the younger men who could not get reinstatement found appointments on the railways of India and the Argentine, but for hundreds of others the first six months of 1891 were a period of great privation.

Undoubtedly the most important outcome of the struggle in Scotland was the House of Commons debate on January 23rd on Mr Channing's resolution to give the Board of Trade increased powers to fix maximum hours of labour for some grades of railway labour. In the course of the debate a Government spokesman announced the setting up of a Select Committee of the House of Commons to investigate the extent of overwork on the railways and to examine possible remedies. The Scottish railwaymen had performed a valuable service to railwaymen all over the kingdom in focusing the attention of Parliament to this long-standing abuse.

The six weeks' strike was the one major event in the twenty-year history of the Scottish Society. All its resources, and indeed more than all, had been thrown into the struggle. Fourteen weeks after the surrender, Mr Tait reported to the Standing Committee that he had paid none of the accounts for rents, printing, legal expenses, etc., owing to the need to support members still out of work. Those who had been lucky enough to regain their employment had been asked to contribute a day's pay each week, but the response to this appeal had been disappointing. Only £457 had been contributed in this way during which time £6,306 had been paid out in aliment. Sympathizers in other Trade Unions, Co-operative Societies, etc., in Scotland and England had been subsidizing the funds of the Society. The prolonged conflict had placed it in an untenable financial position.[46]

Long before the strike the English and Scottish Societies had negotiated for a merger. The A.G.M. in Newcastle in 1887 had agreed that the E.C. should discuss amalgamation with their Scottish brethren, and it was in accordance with this decision that a Conference of representatives of the two bodies met in Leeds on July 20 and 21, 1888. Although the meeting was very friendly, the talks broke down on the question of rates of contributions. The Scottish representatives would not agree to raise their rate of weekly contribution from 3d to 5d and the English would not agree either to the reduction of the weekly payments or to the introduction of additional, lower scale of contribution. They did agree to exchange information to help each other in the event of strikes and to refrain from poaching on each other's territory. On November 24, 1890, when a strike in Scotland seemed inevitable representatives of the two Societies, together with others from the A.S.L.E. & F. and the G.R.W.U., held discussions in Leeds. They agreed that federation of the four Societies was necessary 'for the purpose of improving the working conditions of the whole of the railway servants'. In the event of a strike they pledged themselves 'to stand firmly together and render all mutual help possible'.[47] The help given by the three non-Scottish Societies after December 21st was vital. Without it the struggle would have been much shorter and less effective.

After the strike was over the case for the amalgamation of the Scottish A.S.R.S. with the larger organization south of the border was infinitely stronger. With the adoption by the Belfast A.G.M. in October 1890 of the new (lower) scale of membership contributions, the principal obstacle which had kept the two Societies apart was removed. Membership of the Scottish Society fell sharply after January and its financial difficulties were acute. It was only a question of time to comply with the formalities. On August 28, 1891, the Standing Committee of the Scottish Society agreed that the Chairman and Secretary should meet their opposite numbers in Newcastle on September 12th. This meeting virtually settled the terms of the merger. A ballot vote of the Scottish membership was conducted between January 23 and February 23, 1892, when a large majority favoured fusion with the English Society. Thus the Scottish Society died an honourable death almost exactly twenty years from the date of its foundation.

VIII

In eventful months between the Newcastle A.G.M. in October 1887 and the A.G.M. held in Birmingham in 1891, the A.S.R.S. had changed its character. In the first seventeen years of its existence it had been a trade union of a friendly society type. It had not sponsored a single strike. Its role was educational, propagandist and ameliorative; certainly not aggressive. If there were differences with the employers, then it was argued it was best that these should be settled by arbitration.

By October 1890, Mr Harford realized the remarkable changes that had occurred. He reported to the A.G.M.:

'We have now, while still adhering to our old principles, adopted methods which are associated with robust and even aggressive trade unionism. . . . We are a trade union with benefit funds, not a friendly society with a few mutual protection benefits, and this cannot be made too clear to members of the railway service.'

The struggles in Ireland, Wales, Scotland and the North East had exposed the inadequacy of the old policy of dependence on arbitration. The blunt truth was revealed by Mr Harford who admitted that 'arbitration was refused whenever offered by the workmen'.[48] The assumption had been that no reasonable man would refuse to settle differences by means of arbitration, and that if the union's claims were just, the arbitrator's award would at least be a partial settlement of those claims. It was perhaps for the very reason that the claims made in 1890 were just and reasonable that the railway directors dared not risk submitting them to an arbitrator.

This critical period which saw the birth of the first national programme brought to a close the era of partial grade-by-grade and district-by-district negotiations. Henceforward the campaigns of the union were to be fought around 'all grades' programmes backed by industrial bargaining strength and not solely by a reliance on advertising the reasonableness of the union's policy and a faith in arbitration. The members of the A.S.R.S. in directing these changes in policy were keeping abreast of developments in the trade-union movement as a whole.

NOTES

1. Speech of John Burns, *The Times*, October 14, 1889.
2. Fourth Report of the Labour Correspondent of the Board of Trade, B.P.P. 1890–1, Vol. XCII, p. 289. Total membership of the 208 unions sending in returns rose from 646,840 to 796,473.
3. *The Times*, August 15, 1887.
4. Reports on Strikes and Lock Outs: Labour Correspondent of the Board of Trade. B.P.P. 1890–1, Vol. LXXVIII, p. 792.
5. *Souvenir History*, p. 61.
6. *The Labour Elector*, January 11, 1890.
7. Webb, S. and B., *History of Trade Unionism* (1920 edition), p. 406.
8. B.P.P. 1890–1, Vol. LXXVIII, p. 792.
9. *R.R.*, October 5, 1888.
10. A.S.R.S. General Secretary's Report to the E.C., February 25, 1890.
11. A.S.R.S. General Secretary's Report to the E.C., May 1890.
12. W. Foreman: Evidence before the Royal Commission on Labour, B.P.P. 1893–4, Vol. XXXIII, p. 327, Qs. 26229–30.
13. *R.R.*, May 2, 1890.
14. *R.R.*, December 5, 1890.
15. *Cardiff Times*, July 26, 1890.
16. *Cardiff Times*, August 9, 1890.
17. *R.R.*, August 22, 1890.
18. *The Times*, August 11, 1890.
19. Details of the South Wales strike taken from the Special Supplement to the *Railway Review*, August 15, 1890, and *R.R.*, August 22, 1890.
20. Hamilton Ellis, *The North British Railway*, p. 133.
21. *Engineer*, February 6, 1891.
22. Select Committee on Railway Servants' Hours of Labour. B.R.P. 1890–1, Vol. XVI, Qs. 9114–5.
23. *Ibid.*, Evidence of Mr Tait. Qs. 439–51, and *Scottish Leader*, June 4, 1888.

24. Letter from Clement E. Stretton, *Engineer*, January 30, 1890.
25. A.S.R.S. (Scotland) Report of the Annual Executive Council Meeting, Hawick, March 19–21, 1890.
26. *Glasgow Evening Citizen*, August 19, 1890.
27. Quoted in Mavor, J., *The Scottish Railway Strike*, 1891.
28. *Glasgow Herald*, January 9, 1891.
29. Select Committee on Railway Servants' Hours of Labour, B.P.P. 1890–1, Vol. XVI, Qs., 8757–61.
30. *Glasgow Herald*, December 22, 1890.
31. A.S.R.S. (Scotland) Report of the Annual Executive Council, March 1890. *The Times*, December 26, 1890.
32. *Glasgow Herald*, December 24, 1890.
33. *The Times*, January 8, 1891.
34. *Scotsman*, January 10 and 17, 1891.
35. *Glasgow Herald*, January 13, 1891.
36. *R.R.*, January 16, 1891.
37. *Glasgow Herald*, December 24, 1890.
38. *R.R.*, January 16, 1891.
39. *Glasgow Herald*, December 25, 1890.
40. *Scotsman*, January 3 and 6, 1891.
41. *The Times*, January 1, 1891.
42. *Glasgow Herald*, January 7, 1891.
43. Quoted in Mavor, J., *The Scottish Railway Strike*, 1891, p. 40.
44. *The Times*, February 4, 1891.
45. A.S.R.S. (Scotland) Standing Committee Minutes, May 8, 1891.
46. *Ibid.*
47. A.S.R.S. General Secretary's Report, 1888, *Glasgow Evening Citizen*, November 25, 1890.
48. A.S.R.S. General Secretary's Report, 1890.

CHAPTER VI

INQUEST ON OVERWORK

'The half-yearly meeting of the General British Railway Company was held yesterday, the Chairman presiding. . . . He was proud to say that they had got on an average, a good working week of 115 hours out of their men all round, and though there had been some complaining and a breakdown here and there, the whole result had been eminently satisfactory. The system of keeping one driver on his engine twenty-five hours at a stretch and of sending a guard back straight off on a fifteen-hour journey had been found to work efficiently; and though some signalmen had protested on not being relieved for nineteen and a half hours, and in one or two instances had alleged that they were not able to totter to their posts and continue their labours, yet their prompt and instant dismissal had had a salutary effect and no insubordination of this kind was likely to be encountered in the future. The saving of expenditure under this head had been therefore a matter for decided congratulation.'
From an article in Punch, *October 6, 1885.*

I

LIKE the may-fly, the A.S.R.S. (Scotland) had taken a comparatively long time to reach maturity; but no sooner had this maturity been attained and its supreme creative effort made, than it quickly passed from the scene. The Scottish Society's supreme effort was the strike of 1890–1 on behalf of a shorter working week. Although that strike killed the Society as an independent body, it so stirred the conscience of Parliament and the British public that they insisted on the enforcement of a reduction of railwaymen's hours of work. Simultaneously with the death of the one organization catering exclusively for Scottish railwaymen came the birth of a policy of Government interference on behalf of railway labour in the United Kingdom.

Mr Channing's Commons resolution in favour of new legislation to empower the Board of Trade to issue orders where necessary to limit the hours of work of some railwaymen had been tabled before the Scottish strike began. But the fact that it came up for discussion on January 23,

1891, whilst that strike was still in progress, gave to the debate a note of urgency and relevance which it would not otherwise have had; and the many newspaper reports on the overworking of the Scottish railwaymen helped to create a public opinion more favourable to legislative interference.

An attempt had been made as early as May 1877, to introduce a statutory limit of twelve hours to the working day of railwaymen. On that occasion, in the House of Lords, the Duke of St Albans had moved the second reading of a Bill which would have restricted the employment of railwaymen to twelve hours in every twenty-four 'except where unforeseen circumstances rendered longer employment necessary'. The purpose of the Bill was to limit only the hours of those engaged in working the traffic, since the main concern of its sponsors was to protect the travelling public from the dangers of accidents arising from the employment of tired railwaymen. Even so this modest proposal was strenuously opposed by other Peers including Viscount Bury, a director of the London and South Western Railway, who declared that if the Bill was passed 'railways would become unworkable'.[1] On account of this opposition the Bill was withdrawn and no further attempt was made to limit working hours of railwaymen for over a decade.

Before 1887 no systematic efforts were made by the Board of Trade to gather information on the hours worked by railwaymen. That department only required information of this kind when there had been a train accident; the hours worked by railwaymen suffering from personal accidents (e.g. while shunting) were not the subject of inquiry.[2]

Early in 1887, with the co-operation and prompting of Mr Edward Harford, Lord De la Warr in the House of Lords moved for a return to be compiled of the hours worked by railwaymen employed by a few large companies in the months of July 1886 and January 1887. Mr Harford and Lord De la Warr together drew up the form on which details were to be supplied. However, the General Managers of the Great Western Railway and the London and North Western Railway (Messrs Lambert and Findlay) complained that the selection of the months of July and January was unfair as the volume of traffic in the first case was high because of the holiday period, whilst in the second case traffic was often unduly delayed on account of fog. On August 9, 1888, therefore, Lord De la Warr carried a proposal for a second return to be compiled for the months of September 1887, and March 1888. After the passing of the Regulation of Railway Act, 1889, the Board of Trade ordered a third and much more comprehensive return (from 108 companies) for the months of September 1889, and March 1890.

The seven-and-a-half hour debate on railway labour in the House of Commons on January 23, 1891, was the first major discussion of its kind in the British Parliament and was valuable as a reminder to the public of the gross overworking of many railwaymen and as revealing the attitude of M.P.s and the Board of Trade towards proposals for legislative interference with the hours of work of adult workmen.[3]

Mr Channing rose from his seat on the opposition back benches at five past four to move the following resolution:

'That in the opinion of this House the excessive hours of labour imposed on railway servants by the existing arrangements of the railway companies of the United Kingdom constitute a grave social injustice, and are a constant source of danger both to the men themselves and to the travelling public; and that it is expedient that the Board of Trade should obtain powers by legislation to issue orders where necessary directing railway companies to limit the hours of work of special classes of railway servants, or to make such a reasonable increase in any class of their servants as will obviate the necessity for overtime work.'

He found valuable shot and shell for his speech from the three Board of Trade returns, claiming that the returns for September 1889, and March 1890, proved that excessive hours of labour were 'not an abnormal incident but a part of a system'. In fact the railways were 'undermanned'. The inevitable corollary of undermanning was the constant recurrence of excessive overtime. He pointed out that in one month there were no fewer than 70,000 instances of over fifteen hours consecutive work performed by railwaymen. He condemned railway management for booking men for hours which, it was known, would be exceeded, 'thereby causing great risks to the public'. The companies were earning dividends 'by saving the wages of the few extra men who ought to be employed if the lines were to be worked on a system tolerable to human nature'. Mr Channing was, however, a radical Liberal, not a Socialist, and he took pains to point out at the beginning of his speech that he was 'not advocating a statutory limitation of the hours of railway workmen'; rather he was working for 'a reasonable extension of the powers of the Board of Trade'. The seconder of the resolution, John Wilson, the Lib.-Lab. M.P. for Durham Mid., revealed at the outset that he approved of the resolution simply because it did not contain 'a proposition that legislation should fix the hours of work'.

The spokesman for the railway companies, Mr Plunkett, a Director of the London and North Western Railway, who was also, as First Commissioner of Works, a member of the Government, claimed with an astonishing *naïveté* that there never had been, and there was not then, 'the smallest difference' between his company and its servants. The 'isolated instances' in which men worked for very long hours were caused by 'circumstances impossible to foresee' as, for example, where a railway engine ran off the line. This was an explanation which provoked the irony of Mr Lockwood, M.P. for York, who said that in 1890, there were 19,098 cases in which engine drivers and firemen worked thirteen hours or over.

He questioned, 'Did 19,098 engines go off the line? Were there 19,000 errors of judgment?'

The situation looked black for the Government for a time when the eminent Sir Stafford Northcote stated bluntly that if Mr Channing's motion 'was met with anything like a *non-possumus*', though he was a 'tolerably staunch ministerialist', he would not feel able to support the Government.

The President of the Board of Trade, Sir Michael Hicks Beach, was reluctant to sanction any further interference with the railway companies. In an endeavour to obviate the necessity for further legislation he had written to the Secretary of the Railway Companies Association, on December 26, 1890—almost a month before the Commons Debate—urging the directors to consider and adopt measures to reduce overwork and requesting them that they should inform him of the action they proposed to take. The reply sent by Mr H. Oakley on behalf of the Association was vaguely worded. Though the companies would be glad to confer with the Minister it was a 'misapprehension' to assume the companies systematically worked their men long hours.[4] Sir Michael Hicks Beach, therefore, confessed to the Commons that he had been 'forced to the conclusion' that more interference was necessary. Nevertheless, he stressed the practical difficulties of immediate legislation on the subject and pleaded that they needed to be better informed of the facts. To this end he proposed to substitute for Mr Channing's motion the amendment:

'That in the opinion of this House the employment of railway servants for excessive hours is a source of danger both to the men themselves and to the travelling public, and that a Select Committee be appointed to inquire whether, and if so in what way, the hours worked by railway servants should be restricted by legislation.'

Despite Mr Channing's protest that members already had sufficient information to provide a basis for action, the House, in a division held just before midnight, approved Sir Michael Hicks Beach's amendment by 141 votes to 124.[5]

A month later the House completed nominations for the twenty-six members of the Select Committee on Railway Servants (Hours of Labour) which included no less than eight railway directors but only two working men (there being no railwaymen M.P.s at the time). The Committee began to hear evidence on March 10, 1891.

II

As might be expected, the evidence given before the Select Committee served mainly to confirm and amplify the facts revealed in the Board of Trade Returns of the period 1886–90.

The Executive Committee of the A.S.R.S., unlike that of the A.S.L.E. & F. wisely decided to play as full a part as possible in the proceedings of the committee as this would give its policy more publicity and increase the chances of its implementation. The General Secretary, Mr Edward Harford, gave clearly stated and well documented evidence. He declared that the 'primary reason' for the formation of the A.S.R.S. was to shorten the hours of labour; hence their great interest in the work of the committee. He cited the case of a man employed by the Great Western Railway at Landon Low Level signalbox who, out of the 310 days ending February 28, 1891, was on duty for one spell of $8\frac{1}{4}$ hours, one of $9\frac{1}{2}$ hours, one of 11 hours 35 minutes, 217 turns of 12 hours and upwards, 28 turns of 13 hours and upwards, 9 turns of 14 hours and upwards, 47 turns of 16 hours and upwards, 2 turns of 17 hours and upwards, one of over 18 hours and one of 20 hours 40 minutes. He gave numerous examples of goods guards, drivers and others systematically employed for hours well in excess of 12 per day.[6]

Other witnesses cited the case of 59-year-old John Gurr who was killed while fog signalling on the Brighton Line near London Bridge on December 31, 1888. At the time of his death he had been on duty for $23\frac{1}{2}$ hours out of the past 30 in dense fog and bitterly cold weather. A goods guard, James Choules, employed by the Midland and South West Junction Railway, was killed whilst shunting on a dark stormy night. At the time of his death he had been on duty for 22 hours and 18 minutes consecutively. In the 27 days immediately preceding his death he worked on 24 days, his average daily working hours being 12 hours 58 minutes. For the last three days of his life the average was 18 hours 46 minutes.[7]

Mr Campion Watson, General Secretary of the General Railway Workers Union, said that wheel tappers on the Great Eastern Railway worked alternate weeks from 8.0 a.m. to 6.0 p.m. and from 6.0 p.m. to 8.0 a.m. but that when they changed hours on a Sunday, one of a pair was on duty for 24 hours without a break.[8] Mr John Clarkson, a mineral brakesman employed by the Caledonian Railway, said that he had worked 13, 14 and 15 hours a day and on one occasion for 20 hours; but working hours had been reduced since the strike.[9]

Not all companies had equally bad records. Since the launching of the national programme by the A.S.R.S. at Hull in 1889 and the publicity given to the men's case as a result of the Scottish strike, several companies revised the working hours of their men. The General Manager of the London and North Western Railway, Mr Findlay, said that as a result of the 'agitation for reform' there had been 'a careful reconsideration of train arrangements'. The Assistant Manager of the Midland Railway said that his company had reduced the booked time of some passenger guards from 15 hours 8 minutes to 12 hours 23 minutes. (This was presumably cited as an example of generosity.) Mr Thompson, General Manager of the

Caledonian, revealed that he had altered the booked times of drivers as a result of complaints made by Mr Tait.[10] Companies with bad records in respect of excessive hours included the North British, the Great Eastern and the Cambrian; companies with better records included the London and North Western, the Midland and the London and South Western.

The main report of the committee published in the spring of 1892 found that, as a rule, excessive hours appeared most frequently on lines with a heavy goods and mineral traffic; they occurred on goods, mineral and cattle trains to a much greater extent than on passenger trains. The committee found that 'in spite of improvement which was admitted by all the witnesses and which (might) be largely due to the inquiry of your committee' it appeared 'from the evidence far more clearly than from the Parliamentary Returns', that there were 'still too many cases' in which 'excessive hours' were 'habitually worked without adequate reason' and that 'no sufficient effort' had been made by the companies generally 'to deal earnestly and thoroughly with the matter'.

III

The recommendations for reform made in the report could scarcely be described as bold and far-reaching. The main proposals were as follows:

'Your committee recommend that the companies should be required, as at present, to make periodical returns of overtime to the Board of Trade; that the attention of any company making an exceptionally bad return should be called to the matter with a view to the hours of work being shortened by the company; and that the correspondence should be published by the Board of Trade. They further recommend that on receiving the report of an accident whether to a railway servant or connected with the movement of trains or rolling stock, which seems to demand further inquiry, the Board of Trade should require the company to state the hours of work of every railway servant concerned in the matter; and that when the Board of Trade has reason to suppose, either from the report of an inspector or from complaint properly made to it by the railway servants engaged in working the traffic that the hours of work of any class of such servants are excessive, a regular inquiry should be held by an inspector of the Board of Trade into the general hours of the servants concerned, and that such inquiry should be followed up, as in the case of the Midland and South Western Junction Railway, until the Board of Trade were satisfied that the hours of the servants had been reduced to a reasonable basis.'

Although these proposals did mark some small advance in the long campaign to reduce overwork on the railways, their weakness was that they suggested what was likely to be a slow and cumbersome procedure and they attempted no definition of what constituted 'excessive' hours.

Furthermore, the committee turned down a proposal for the appointment of a sub-inspector of the Board of Trade whose principal duty it would have been to watch the hours worked by railway employees.[11]

The main reason why stronger measures were not advocated in the report was that the directors and general managers who gave evidence before the committee were of one mind in opposing any increased government interference with the management of the railways, and were generally supported in this view by the eight directors who were members of the Select Committee of twenty-six. By contrast the trade union witnesses held widely differing views on the degree of state intervention they considered necessary.

The directors offered a wide variety of plausible reasons for opposing any state interference with their control over their labour force. Mr Findlay expressed the concensus of their opinion when he said that 'the men must arrange their own matters with the directors'.[12] He foretold dire consequences from any attempt to put a statutory limit on working hours:

'If an attempt were made to put a strict limit to hours the railway companies would be obliged on such occasions either to refuse to carry the mail service and the passenger or parcel traffic or to employ an immense additional staff of trained relief men whose services would not be required at other periods of the year.'[13]

Mr William Birt, General Manager of the Great Eastern, assured the committee that the establishment of fixed hours for railway servants was 'impossible' because the circumstances of railway working were too varied. He claimed that it would be the working classes who would suffer if hours were limited. This company ran forty-nine workmen's trains daily to and from Liverpool Street Station and the margin of profit obtained from that traffic was so small that any increase in labour costs would impel the directors 'to get rid of some of the accommodation' which the working men were given. The same witness considered that a man working fourteen or fifteen hours a day would have 'ample time' to see his children if he started work at one o'clock in the morning![14] Mr Tennant, a director of the North Eastern Railway, stressed the extraordinary fluctuations of traffic on his line as making it impossible to put a fixed limit on men's hours of work; but Mr Harford pointed out that similar fluctuations in the volume of mineral traffic occurred on the Welsh sections of the Great Western Railway and London and North Western Railway, both of which companies had managed greatly to reduce the amount of overtime working of their staff.[15]

Through many decades until the conclusion of the First World War, the railway managers always countered any proposal to interfere with their absolute control over their labour force with the argument that such interference would impair discipline; and strict discipline was vital to ensure safe working of the railways. The managers were true to form on this occasion. Mr Findlay said that if the proposed new powers were granted to the Government 'the men would always be looking to the Board of Trade instead of to their officers, and discipline would be destroyed'.[16]

Perhaps the most telling of the arguments used by the directors was the claim that the men themselves were opposed to a statutory or Board of Trade limitation of their hours. It was an argument used by Messrs Findlay, Tennant and Birt and by Mr Turner of the Great Western Railway. There were two main reasons why some of the men were of this opinion: they sometimes objected to relief if it prevented them getting home at night and they feared the loss of overtime money.[17]

Unfortunately some of the railwaymen witnesses who were members of the A.S.R.S., who had spoken in favour of the national programme and the 10-hour day before the Select Committee met, and were chosen because of these views to give evidence, turned the tables on their sponsors and told the committee they were satisfied with things as they were. Thus, Robert Collingwood, a North Eastern Railway mineral guard who had been an A.G.M. delegate and a member of the E.C. and was in 1891 Secretary of the Tyne Dock branch, admitted that he had advocated the 10-hour day in public meetings but that 'circumstances' had altered his opinion. He told the committee he did not regard an 80-hour week as too much 'under the circumstances' when it was performed. He did not wish Parliament to interfere.[18] Edward Ellis, a goods guard employed by the North Eastern Railway whose working week in the past year had averaged 66 hours 48 minutes was 'perfectly satisfied' with these hours and was opposed to further Board of Trade intervention.[19] William Ellis, a driver employed by the Great Eastern, handed in a petition signed by 1,354 drivers and firemen from twenty-six locomotive depots who were against any State interference with their hours of work, largely for the reason that they believed it would result in their being away from home at night.[20]

Inevitably the presentation of evidence such as this would lessen the chances of achieving the 10-hour day by legislative or administrative action. Nevertheless, the chance of giving some teeth to the recommendations of the committee might have been greater had the trade union officials made some attempt to reach an agreed policy before they appeared before the committee. It is greatly to be regretted that no such attempt was made. In default of it, three different policies were advocated. Mr Harford was not in favour of fixing the day's work of railwaymen by statute even with exceptions for accidents and emergencies. With Mr Channing, he preferred that the Board of Trade should have the power of fixing a limit, where necessary, by order. He was mainly looking for the achievement of the 10-hour day by industrial pressure and collective bargaining. By contrast, Mr Campion Watson, General Secretary of the G.R.W.U., said his men had 'no faith in the Board of Trade; none whatever'; they wanted a legalized 8-hour day. Mr Tait of the Scottish A.S.R.S. took an intermediate view, favouring a statutory limit of 10 hours a day but conceding that he and his Society would accept a 12-hour maximum provided the 60-hour week were not exceeded. Mr Foreman, A.S.R.S. Secretary in Ireland, though originally supporting Mr Harford's view, had recently come to the opinion that a statutory 10-hour maximum was necessary.[21] Confronted with these divided views, the members of the committee could argue that a recommendation in favour of a statutory limit of hours would not be generally acceptable to the railwaymen themselves.

IV

That the management of the Cambrian Railway was among those subject to the severest criticism by the Select Committee was largely due to the untiring energy of Mr Frederick Bather, a miller of Oswestry, who collected abundant evidence of the excessive hours worked by the company's servants. In particular, Mr Bather, by presenting signed affidavits of the men, showed that it was the regular practice of the company to employ some of their men for thirty-six hours continuous duty once a fortnight in the course of a working fortnight of 152 hours.[22]

Inevitably, Mr Conacher, the General Manager of the Cambrian Railway was closely cross-examined on his self-confessed ignorance of the fact that for the past twenty years men had been employed on these 36-hour spells of duty. He was further questioned about an accident which had occurred at three o'clock in the morning on November 6, 1887, when a train had been derailed at the facing points at Ellesmere Junction. Colonel Rich, the Board of Trade inspector who investigated the cause of the accident, commented adversely on the fact that the porter, Humphreys, the only man on duty at the time, had been at his post for nineteen hours. Mr Conacher, when asked to explain these excessive hours, endeavoured to shift the blame to the stationmaster at Ellesmere, Mr John Hood. He told the committee:

'When the accident happened in 1887, the directors blamed the stationmaster for not having made better arrangements with regard to his staff and maintaining discipline, and an intimation was given to him afterwards that he would have to be removed to another station.'[23]

Stationmaster Hood was a man who took pride in his work. By conscientious attention to his duties he had gradually improved his status on the Cambrian Railway which he served for twenty-two years. Starting work in 1869 as a clerk at Llanymenech, he rose to become stationmaster at Criccieth where he served for four-and-a-half years before the directors promoted him to the post of stationmaster at Ellesmere Junction. On the

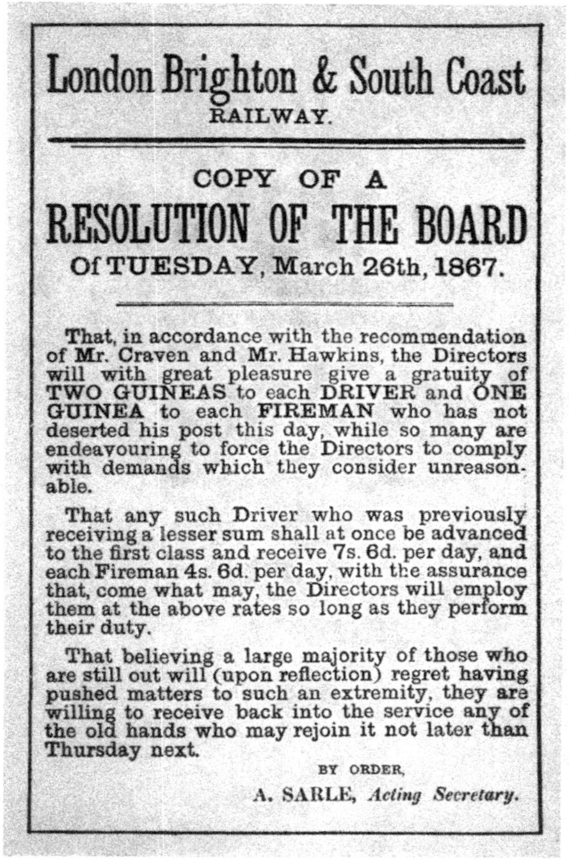

London Brighton & South Coast
RAILWAY.

COPY OF A

RESOLUTION OF THE BOARD

Of TUESDAY, March 26th, 1867.

That, in accordance with the recommendation of Mr. Craven and Mr. Hawkins, the Directors will with great pleasure give a gratuity of **TWO GUINEAS** to each **DRIVER** and **ONE GUINEA** to each **FIREMAN** who has not deserted his post this day, while so many are endeavouring to force the Directors to comply with demands which they consider unreasonable.

That any such Driver who was previously receiving a lesser sum shall at once be advanced to the first class and receive 7s. 6d. per day, and each Fireman 4s. 6d. per day, with the assurance that, come what may, the Directors will employ them at the above rates so long as they perform their duty.

That believing a large majority of those who are still out will (upon reflection) regret having pushed matters to such an extremity, they are willing to receive back into the service any of the old hands who may rejoin it not later than Thursday next.

BY ORDER,

A. SARLE, *Acting Secretary.*

Resolution of the Board of Directors, London, Brighton and South Coast Railway, 1867

PLATE 3

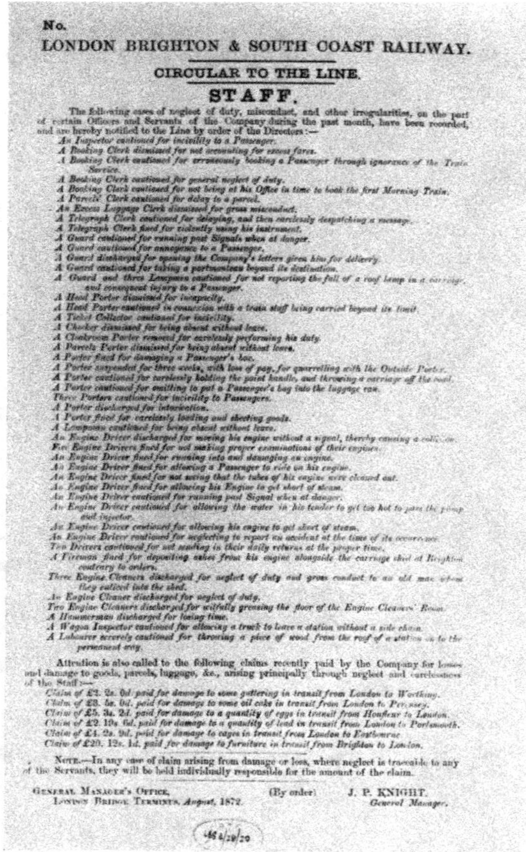

No.

LONDON BRIGHTON & SOUTH COAST RAILWAY.

CIRCULAR TO THE LINE.

STAFF.

The following cases of neglect of duty, misconduct, and other irregularities, on the part of certain Officers and Servants of the Company during the past month, have been recorded, and are hereby notified to the Line by order of the Directors:—

An Inspector cautioned for incivility to a Passenger.
A Booking Clerk dismissed for not accounting for excess fares.
A Booking Clerk cautioned for erroneously booking a Passenger through ignorance of the Train Service.
A Booking Clerk cautioned for general neglect of duty.
A Booking Clerk cautioned for not being at his Office in time to book the first Morning Train.
A Parcels' Clerk cautioned for delay to a parcel.
An Excess Luggage Clerk dismissed for gross misconduct.
A Telegraph Clerk cautioned for delaying, and then carelessly despatching a message.
A Telegraph Clerk fined for violently using his instrument.
A Guard cautioned for running past Signals when at danger.
A Guard cautioned for annoyance to a Passenger.
A Guard discharged for opening the Company's letters given him for delivery.
A Guard cautioned for taking a portmanteau beyond its destination.
A Guard and three Lampmen cautioned for not reporting the fall of a roof lamp in a carriage, and consequent injury to a Passenger.
A Head Porter dismissed for incapacity.
A Head Porter cautioned in connexion with a train staff being carried beyond its limit.
A Ticket Collector cautioned for incivility.
A Checker dismissed for being absent without leave.
A Cloakroom Porter removed for carelessly performing his duty.
A Parcels Porter dismissed for being absent without leave.
A Porter fined for damaging a Passenger's box.
A Porter suspended for three weeks, with loss of pay, for quarrelling with the Outside Porter.
A Porter cautioned for carelessly holding the point handle, and throwing a carriage off the road.
A Porter cautioned for omitting to put a Passenger's bag into the luggage van.
Three Porters cautioned for incivility to Passengers.
A Porter discharged for intoxication.
A Porter fined for carelessly loading and sheeting goods.
A Lampman cautioned for being absent without leave.
An Engine Driver discharged for moving his engine without a signal, thereby causing a collision.
Five Engine Drivers fined for not making proper examinations of their engines.
An Engine Driver fined for running into and damaging an engine.
An Engine Driver fined for allowing a Passenger to ride on his engine.
An Engine Driver fined for not seeing that the tubes of his engine were cleaned out.
An Engine Driver fined for allowing his Engine to get short of steam.
An Engine Driver cautioned for running past Signal when at danger.
An Engine Driver cautioned for allowing the water in his tender to get too hot to pass the pump and injector.
An Engine Driver cautioned for allowing his engine to get short of steam.
An Engine Driver cautioned for neglecting to report an accident at the time of its occurrence.
Two Drivers cautioned for not sending in their daily returns at the proper time.
A Fireman fined for depositing ashes from his engine alongside the carriage shed at Brighton contrary to orders.
Three Engine Cleaners discharged for neglect of duty and gross conduct to an old man whom they enticed into the shed.
An Engine Cleaner discharged for neglect of duty.
Two Engine Cleaners discharged for wilfully greasing the floor of the Engine Cleaners' Room.
A Hammerman discharged for losing time.
A Wagon Inspector cautioned for allowing a truck to leave a station without a side chain.
A Labourer severely cautioned for throwing a piece of wood from the roof of a station on to the permanent way.

Attention is also called to the following claims recently paid by the Company for losses and damage to goods, parcels, luggage, &c., arising principally through neglect and carelessness of the Staff:—

Claim of £2. 2s. 0d. paid for damage to some guttering in transit from London to Worthing.
Claim of £3. 5s. 0d. paid for damage to some oil cake in transit from London to Pevensey.
Claim of £5. 3s. 2d. paid for damage to a quantity of eggs in transit from Honfleur to London.
Claim of £2. 10s. 6d. paid for damage to a quantity of lead in transit from London to Portsmouth.
Claim of £4. 2s. 9d. paid for damage to cages in transit from London to Eastbourne.
Claim of £20. 12s. 1d. paid for damage to furniture in transit from Brighton to London.

Note.—In any case of claim arising from damage or loss, where neglect is traceable to any of the Servants, they will be held individually responsible for the amount of the claim.

General Manager's Office,
London Bridge Terminus, *August*, 1872.

(By order) J. P. KNIGHT.
General Manager.

Monthly Punishment List, London, Brighton and South Coast Railway, August 1872. N.B. Most monthly lists were too lengthy to be printed on one sheet. Note the Telegraph Clerk fined 'for too violently using his instrument' and the two engine cleaners discharged 'for wilfully greasing the floor of the engine-cleaners' room'

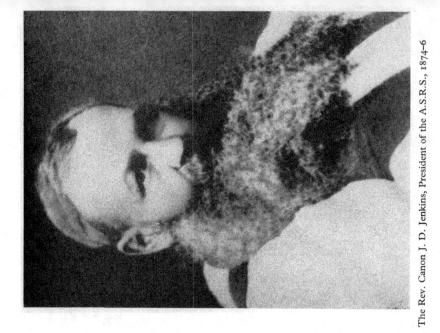

The Rev. Canon J. D. Jenkins, President of the A.S.R.S., 1874–6

M. T. Bass (1799–1884), M.P. for Derby 1848–83, Patron of the A.S.R.S.

PLATE 4

occasion of this move he was presented with a testimonial and a purse of gold by the appreciative citizens of Criccieth. Early in 1888, after again receiving a testimonial and purse of gold, he was transferred to a similar post at Montgomery, where he quickly won the respect and affection of the inhabitants by his unfailing courtesy and his prompt and efficient handling of business. At all three stations where he had been in charge the directors had awarded him prizes in the competitions for well kept stations. The last occasion this had happened was on July 15, 1891, when his station was awarded third prize out of the twenty for distribution among the seventy stations on the line. In view of this fine record he was understandably jealous to maintain an untarnished reputation.

John Hood read the report of Mr Conacher's statement to the Select Committee on the causes of the accident of November 6, 1886, in the local paper of his district, *The Salopian*. He knew the statement to be incorrect, for the general manager and the directors of the company had made no criticism of him in connection with the accident. His employers knew full well the real cause of the derailment of the train; the sleepers at the crossing points were completely rotten. In an effort to escape criticism for negligence, Mr Conacher ordered them to be replaced during the interval of several days before the arrival of Colonel Rich to investigate the reasons for the accident. When the platelayers came to do their job they could not remove the sleepers in the usual way but were obliged to take them out of the ground 'in much the same way as manure is forked'. The general manager, rather than admit such glaring defects in the permanent way, placed the blame on the porter Humphreys whom he dismissed. For publicly expressing an opinion (supported by the editor of the local newspaper and many prominent local citizens) that the defective permanent way caused the derailment of the train, and for agreeing to sign a petition for the reinstatement of Humphreys, Hood had to appear before Mr Conacher in the Company's Office at Oswestry where he was told he had been suspended for a period of fourteen days and would be moved to the station at Montgomery. Ironically enough Hood had on more than one occasion warned the company of the unsatisfactory state of the permanent way although, strictly speaking, it was not his job to do so.[24]

On June 27, 1891, Hood wrote to Mr Conacher asking for permission to write to the local paper to correct the mis-statement and for permission to go to London to give evidence before the Select Committee. Mr Conacher in his reply, sent two days later, wrote that he could not consent to Hood's writing to the papers; he completely ignored the request to appear before the Select Committee. Hood, therefore, wrote again on July 1st renewing his request to visit London and ending up with the plea 'my character is at stake, and I must defend it; surely you will not refuse to allow me a hearing after what has been said of me'. Mr Conacher, however, failed to reply to the letter and in consequence Hood raised the subject with two M.P.s and very quickly received a telegram that he was to appear before the Select Committee of the House of Commons on July 16, 1891.

It took the Select Committee less than a quarter of an hour to hear Hood's statement and to put a few questions to him. He proved satisfactorily that the directors at the time blamed Humphreys for the accident, and he showed that he had tried to obtain a relief man by telegraphing to Mr Conacher at Oswestry, but that Mr Conacher had replied that there was no one to send.[25] The members of the committee gave the matter little thought at the time. Indeed, nothing more might have been heard of Stationmaster Hood had it not been for the obstinacy and vindictiveness of his General Manager.

Soon after Mr Conacher had impugned Hood's character before the Select Committee he realized that he had made a mistake. Considerably later, when further cross-questioned on March 3, 1892, he admitted his mistake to the members of the committee, saying 'Hood was suspended for signing the memorial, undoubtedly'.[26] But he made no apology or correction in the local paper. Had he freely admitted his mistake soon after it had been made and corrected it, there would never have been a 'Case of Stationmaster Hood' and valuable Parliamentary time would not have been wasted.

The General Manager's vindictiveness was revealed by his actions on July 15, 1891, the day before Hood gave evidence in London. He searched through the personal file of Hood's record of service kept at the office in Oswestry and found that two years before there had been a petty dispute with the London and North Western Railway about the payment of 1s 7d for a hamper dispatched by Hood to his son. He therefore wrote at once to Mr Birtwhistle, the official concerned on the London and North Western Railway, 'Please send me all the papers relating to the hamper'.[27] Having by these means obtained what he considered to be incriminating evidence against Hood, he gave it to the directors who decided, on August 6, 1891, to dismiss out of hand, without reasons given, a man who had served them well for over twenty years.

On the morning of August 10, 1891, Hood was attending his duties on the platform at Montgomery station when a relief clerk got out of the 11.37 train and handed him the following letter:

'Secretary and General Manager's Office, Oswestry, August 10, 1891.

I am instructed by the directors to inform you that this company have no further use for your services, and on your handing over the keys and all other property of the company, the bearer, Mr Robert Jones, will pay you a month's wages in lieu of the usual notice, and will take charge of your station from today. The house must be vacated on the 10th proximo. (Signed) J. Conacher.
To Mr Hood, Montgomery.'[28]

The relief clerk would give no reason for Hood's dismissal, and one of the directors of the company who lived at Montgomery, Mr Humphreys Owen, would give no explanation. It was a particularly hard blow to take in view of the fact that the business done at the station had substantially increased in the short time that Hood had been there; but nine months before he had been given a rise because of this good record. Immediately news of their stationmaster's dismissal reached the public in Montgomery, a petition for his reinstatement was drafted and signed by the Mayor, most of the corporation, the vicar, the landed gentry and nearly all the tradesmen of the district, who declared that Mr Hood had shown himself to be 'a capable, civil and obliging agent' who 'had done his utmost to advance the interests of the company'. Hood himself wrote a strong appeal to the Chairman of the company to give him a hearing, and in consequence he was invited to appear before the Board at Crewe on September 30, 1891.

At the outset of the Crewe meeting the Chairman of the company said that the Board thought it desirable that Hood should be given an opportunity to justify *what he had said before the committee*. This, together with the manner of his cross-examination (and the fact that at times several of the directors were speaking to him at once, making it very difficult for the shorthand note-taker to make an accurate report) convinced Hood that he had been dismissed because of his answering the General Manager's charges before the Select Committee. The interview at Crewe appears to have been an occasion for censuring and browbeating a dismissed servant rather than a genuine attempt to ensure that justice was done to a man who had given many years loyal service to the company. At the conclusion of the interview the Chairman said, 'Are there any other points you wish to make statements upon, Mr Hood?' Mr Hood replied, 'I can only say I very much regret going before the Committee. But I feel the matter so deeply, and I hope the Directors will not dismiss me.'[29] After the meeting was over Mr Conacher told Hood he had been dismissed because of what he had told the Select Committee.[30]

The Parliamentary Committee had not given much time or attention to Hood on the occasion of the brief interview on July 16, 1891; but this was a state of affairs which could not be allowed to pass without further investigation. The House of Commons had decided to find out the facts about overwork on the railways and had appointed a Select Committee as its instrument to this end. If working men who dared to appear before such a committee were to be so browbeaten and terrorized that one of them was led to say that he very much regretted giving evidence, the authority of the House of Commons would be undermined and its ability to discover the truth seriously impaired.

In February 1892, therefore, Hood was recalled to London and asked by the Select Committee to give details of his dismissal and of the interview which took place at Crewe. Mr Conacher and the Chairman of the company, Mr Buckley, were also recalled and subjected to further cross-examination. When questioned by Mr Channing, Mr Conacher declined to state the reason for the dismissal of Hood[31] but Mr Buckley denied that Hood was dismissed because of the evidence he had given and claimed that there was ample justification for his dismissal 'on other grounds'. He had sent in a falsified pay sheet in 1887 and the discipline maintained at Ellesmere Junction at that time was unsatisfactory. Above all 'blame could be attributed to Mr Hood as a trusted agent of the company in taking public action for redressing the grievances of the men instead of representing such matters to the management'.[32] He did not convince the members of the committee. In their special report on the case published on March 24, 1892, they concluded:

'That the witness John Hood was by resolution of the directors of the Cambrian Railway Company at a meeting held on the 6th day of August last, dismissed from the service of the Company, mainly in consequence of charges arising out of the evidence given by him before your Committee, and laid before the directors by John Conacher, then manager of the said railway; and further that James Frederick Buckley, John William McClure, a member of this House; and William Bailey Hawkins, Directors of the said company and the said John Conacher did, at a meeting at Crewe on September 30, 1891, held in consequence of the application by the said John Hood for the rehearing of his case, at which the said John Hood was present; call him to account, and censure him for the evidence he gave before your committee, in a manner calculated to deter other railway servants from giving evidence before your committee.'[33]

Just under a fortnight later it was revealed by Mr Channing that it was only by the casting vote of the Chairman (the President of the Board of Trade, Sir Michael Hicks Beach), that the words 'of charges arising out of the evidence' were added to the report. Half the committee were in favour of the stronger original wording that Hood 'was dismissed from the service of the company in consequence of the evidence given by him'.[34]

Although it was manifestly the duty of the House of Commons to bring to book as quickly as possible the men who had been guilty of a breach of privilege, Sir Michael Hicks Beach, speaking in the House of Commons on April 4th, urged delay in the discussion of the case as the Select Committee had not yet reported on the alleged breach of privilege committed by Messrs E. Garrity, John Modral, George Alcock and others who had deprived Robert Collingwood of Tyne Dock and William Ellis of Stratford of their positions as branch officers of the A.S.R.S. as a result (contrary to their promise) of giving evidence favourable to the companies. (The case was shortly afterwards held by the committee to be 'not proven'.) In the brief discussion which followed several members of the committee protested against the proposed delay, and in the same sitting, in the early hours of Tuesday, April 5, 1892, Sir Michael Hicks Beach gave way and he and the House as a whole agreed to the following motion:

'Ordered: That John William McClure to attend this House in his place on Thursday next.
Ordered: That Mr James Frederick Buckley, Mr William Bailey Hawkins and Mr John Conacher do attend this House upon Thursday next at three of the clock.'

Two days later, therefore, the Bar of the House being drawn, the Serjeant at Arms escorted the three gentlemen named while Mr McClure stood in his place on the benches.[35] All four made their obeisance to the Chair, Mr McClure, while stoutly denying any intention of deterring railway servants from giving evidence, expressed 'unqualified regret' if they had unintentionally infringed any of the rules of privilege. Mr Buckley on behalf of the three men at the Bar said that he fully concurred in what Mr McClure had said. The Speaker then called upon the three men to withdraw while M.P.s considered their case.

Parts of Sir Michael Hicks Beach's speech in opening the debate read more like a defence of the Directors of the Cambrian Railway than an impassioned protest against the breach of privilege. He said that it was his strong belief that 'in dismissing Hood the Directors of the Cambrian Railway honestly and bona fide believed that he was not a trustworthy servant of the company'. If the House were 'to censure the directors of a railway for dismissing a servant in the responsible position of station-master' then it would be assuming the conduct of affairs of that company. He proceeded to treat the case purely as one of breach of privilege and moved the resolution admonishing the four men concerned for this offence solely:

'That this House, while recognizing that Mr John William McClure, Mr James Frederick Buckley, Mr William Bailey Hawkins and Mr John Conacher have disclaimed any intention to deter any railway servant from giving evidence before its Committee, and have expressed their unqualified regret for having unintentionally infringed any of its rules and privileges, is of the opinion that the said Mr John William McClure, Mr James Frederick Buckley, Mr William Bailey Hawkins and Mr John Conacher have committed a breach of the privileges of the House in their action towards John Hood and that they be called in and admonished by Mr Speaker for the breach of privilege they have committed.'

It was left to Mr T. P. O'Connor to remind members that the House 'was but a grand Court of Appeal to the nation to which every afflicted man in the country should have the right of full and unrestrained appeal'. He questioned how that right could be secured if 'every person gives his evidence with the halter of dismissal about his neck'. He declared that the House should look 'for acts not words' and that 'a disclaimer on the directors' part' and a 'perseverance in the offence' were 'a mere empty insult' to the House. 'The successors and colleagues of John Hood', he continued, 'are reminded that if they give evidence the directors will get a mere verbal condemnation and remonstrance from this House; but that John Hood will be left to starve'. He therefore proposed to add the following words to the original terms of the motion:

'. . . and this House will not deem that the said Directors and Manager of the Cambrian Railway have purged their contempt until they have re-instated John Hood in the position which he occupied before giving his evidence before this House or otherwise compensated him.'

Mr Cunningham Graham said that the miners had been deterred from giving evidence before the Royal Commission on Labour because of what had happened to Hood. Mr McLaren, M.P. for Crewe, complained that the President of the Board of Trade had chosen the mildest of the three degrees of punishment open to the House (admonition, reprimand and imprisonment). He believed that they should imprison the directors until the end of the session unless, in the meantime, they compensated Hood. But the Government view was supported by the aged and venerable Gladstone who rose from his seat on the front opposition bench to claim that the injury done to the individual was 'not the question put before the House by the Committee' and 'it was not a question that could be satis-factorily disposed of' by them. The offence was 'against the House' and if they accepted the apology—as he believed they should—the offence against the House ceased. Some members who criticized the weak Government resolution nevertheless doubted the practicability of reinstatement as a form of redress for Hood; they therefore supported another amendment moved by Mr Picton calling upon the directors to compensate him financially. With some opposition members following Gladstone into the Government lobbies and others uncertain about the best way of bringing recompense to Hood, the outcome of the voting could scarcely be in doubt. Mr Picton's amendment in favour of compensation to Hood was lost by 189 votes to 245. Mr O'Connor's amendment was defeated by 159 to 274 and Mr Hicks Beach's motion carried by 349 to 70.

Stationmaster Hood was never again employed on the railways. Soon after his dismissal by the Cambrian Railway he was given temporary employment (at a lower salary than the 33s a week, plus rent free house, he was earning as a stationmaster) by Mr Pryce Pryce Jones in his large Royal Welsh Warehouse near Newtown railway station. Though collect-ively the House of Commons, in Mr O'Connor's words, had given a 'bare verbal condemnation and remonstrance' to the Directors of the Cambrian Railway and had not obliged them to pay Hood compensation, many M.P.s and railwaymen sympathizers outside the House as well as citizens of the towns Hood had so conscientiously served, contributed to a fund on his behalf. At a meeting held in the Westminster Palace Hotel on May 12, 1892, he was presented with a cheque for £213 3s 6d by the Chairman, the Labour M.P., Tom Burt.[36] Hood was subsequently elected both to the Urban District Council and the Rural District Council at Ellesmere and was also elected a Poor Law Guardian and a trustee of the Ellesmere Charities—marks of the continued esteem of people who knew him.[37]

The Select Committee considered other cases of alleged intimidation of railwaymen witnesses by the companies but considered they were 'not proven'. In the case of Spinks, an employee of the Great Eastern, the company attributed his dismissal to his falsification of a time book and his arrival late on duty. The E.C. of the A.S.R.S., however, considered that he had been victimized for giving evidence and awarded him the protection grant of £50.

Although it came a long time afterwards—too long in fact to make the correlation clear—the dismissal in February 1895 of George Alcock, a signalman employed by the Great Eastern was believed by the E.C. to be related to the fact that he gave evidence before the Select Committee, although the immediate excuse for his dismissal was a Great Eastern stationmaster's libel action against the *Railway Review* of which Alcock was a trustee. The victimization was made the occasion for a great gesture of solidarity amongst members of the A.S.R.S. who raised £156 11s 5d for Alcock in addition to authorizing (through the E.C.) the payment of the £50 protection grant.[38]

The experience of the Hood case induced Parliament to pass, on June 28, 1892, the Witnesses (Public Inquiries) Protection Act which provides a maximum penalty of £100 fine or maximum imprisonment of three months to every person 'who threatens, or who in any way punishes, damnifies or injures or attempts to punish, damnify or injure any person for having given evidence upon any inquiry or on account of the evidence which he has given on any such inquiry'. To the extent that future witnesses before Royal Commissions and Select Committees could count on a greater measure of security, the sacrifices made by A.S.R.S. witnesses and by stationmaster Hood had not been in vain.

The Hood case also served to keep alive public interest on the subject of railwaymen's hours in the General Election campaign of July 1892. In that campaign 185 candidates (108 Liberals and seventy-seven Conservatives) had replied to a questionnaire concerning their attitude to the regulation of railwaymen's hours of work sent to them by the A.S.R.S. Sixty-eight of the Liberals and only twenty of the Conservatives had declared themselves to be in favour of a statutory limit of ten hours a day. The defeat of the sitting Conservative members at West Islington, Durham and Doncaster was thought to be due to the railwaymen's vote going against them. The Conservative defeat in the elections resulted in the formation of a Liberal Government whose President of the Board of Trade, Mr Mundella, was much more sympathetic to the aims of the A.S.R.S., than his predecessor had been.

V

In view of the divided counsels of the trade union leaders and the companies' strong and united opposition to State interference it may seem surprising that any Act of Parliament came as an indirect result of the labours of the Select Committee.

That the eventual outcome was new legislation was in part due to the failure of the Board of Trade, in the early months of 1892, to persuade the railway managers to make any concessions, as a lesser evil to an increase in Parliamentary control. Neither the Parliamentary chief (Sir Michael Hicks Beach) nor the permanent officials of the Board, favoured Government regulation of hours. Sir H. G. Calcraft, K.C.B., a permanent secretary of the department told the Select Committee that 'the moral force of publicity' was sufficient to expose those companies who employed their men for excessive hours.[39] But with an election pending, the President of the Board of Trade was under strong political pressure to produce some tangible evidence that the Government was taking action to remedy the abuses the committee had exposed. Just before the committee reported he sought an interview with the Secretary (Mr Findlay) and Chairman (Mr Oakley) of the Railway Companies' Association to discover whether the railway managers would agree to the Board being given increased powers to inquire into cases of overwork on the railways. Alternatively, he asked whether the managers would be prepared to make proposals of their own. These suggestions were considered at a meeting of the Railway Companies Association on March 1, 1892, when the keynote of the discussion was 'non co-operation'. Mr Dent of the North Eastern set the tone. He declared that 'the companies must not assent to any interference with the working of the railways. If the companies once gave the Board of Trade the power they now sought it might be quoted against them.' He therefore did not think they would be justified in offering any suggestion. The meeting, and a larger meeting of the Association held a fortnight later, carried unanimously a resolution, 'That the President of the Board of Trade be informed that the companies decline to make any suggestion on this subject'.[40]

When Mr Channing had introduced his resolution in the House of Commons on January 23, 1891, he said that he would 'not press the question of State interference too far' if the companies or the Government suggested the establishment of a board of conciliation. The railway managers were, however, resolutely opposed to any delegation of their authority over the men they employed. Mr Lambert, General Manager of the Great Western Railway preferred 'to face the risks of a strike' rather than to abandon to a board of conciliation the right to determine the hours of labour of his men, and he was supported in his opposition to arbitration by all the other directors and managers who gave evidence before the Select Committee.[41] Even the leaders of the A.S.R.S. were beginning to lose faith in arbitration.[42]

Further legislation was the last resort forced upon a somewhat unwilling Board of Trade by the unco-operative attitude of the railway managers.

At eight minutes to midnight on February 20, 1893, Mr Mundella (who had by this time replaced Sir Michael Hicks Beach at the Board of Trade) 'smuggled through'[43] the House of Commons the second reading of the redrafted Railway Servants (Hours of Labour) Bill and had sent it to a Grand Committee of 103 members of the House. Immediately the Bill was published, Mr Channing and other M.P.s who supported a policy of Board of Trade limitation of hours, invited Mr Harford to put the viewpoint of the A.S.R.S. on the proposed legislation. As an outcome of the meeting, a committee of M.P.s was appointed to seek an interview with Mr Mundella. Mr Harford subsequently claimed that as a result of the constant interchange of views with the Minister, the value of the Bill to members of the A.S.R.S. was 'considerably increased'.[44] In particular, one amendment permitted railwaymen who had cause to complain about being employed for excessive hours to make their complaint to the Board of Trade through their trade union. Nevertheless it is arguable that the Bill was weaker after its passage through Parliament than it had been when first presented and that Sir John Gorst's prophecy in the House of Commons debate on April 24, 1893, that the Act would be 'a dead letter', was nearer the truth than Mr Harford's optimistic assertion that through his concessions Mr Mundella had shown that there had been 'a complete recognition by the Government' of the A.S.R.S.[45] The one alteration which would have given teeth to the Bill was Mr Channing's amendment intended to give precision to the term 'excessive' when applied to the hours of work of railwaymen. He proposed that the word 'excessive' should mean over 10 hours in any 24 in the case of drivers, firemen, passenger and goods guards, porters and signalmen employed in 10-hour boxes and shunters in 10-hour yards; over 9 hours in the case of platelayers; or over 8 hours in the case of signalmen employed in 8-hour boxes and shunters employed in 8-hour yards. But the proposal was negatived after Sir J. Fergusson, Mr Asquith and Sir J. Pease, a railway director, had, according to another speaker, John Burns, treated the House to 'a description of the Arcadian signalman sitting in his box—of course with geraniums and roses growing all round—and working only two and a half hours a day'.[46] The scope of the Bill was certainly restricted by the adoption of an amendment proposed by the Lords and modified by the Commons, to the effect that it was not to apply to any servant of a railway company who was, in the opinion of the Board of Trade, wholly employed in clerical work or in the companies' workshops.

When it finally became law on July 27, 1893 as the Railway Regulation Act, 1893, it provided that 'if it was represented to the Board of Trade by or on behalf of the servants . . . of a railway company that the hours of labour . . . were excessive or did not provide sufficient intervals of uninterrupted rest, the Board of Trade was to make inquiries'. If the Board found there was reasonable ground for complaint it could order the offending company to submit a revised schedule of times of duty of its servants so that the men's hours could be brought 'within reasonable limits, regard being had to all the circumstances of the traffic and the nature of the work'. Companies failing to comply with the instructions of the Board of Trade were to be liable to a fine not exceeding £100 for every day during which the default continued. An annual report of proceedings under the Act was to be made to Parliament.

Since it was clear from the terms of the Act that the extent of its effectiveness would depend on the initiative of railwaymen making complaints either directly to the Board of Trade or indirectly to the Board of Trade via their union, much would depend on whether or not they felt secure against victimization by the companies. Mr Harford therefore approached Mr Mundella to obtain assurances that no man would be in any way penalized for asserting his rights under the Act. This prompted Mr Mundella to write to the Secretary of the Railway Companies Association on September 19th as follows:

'The Board of Trade anticipate that in certain instances representations will be made by or on behalf of a limited number of servants whose cases may appear to present features of hardship, and fears have been expressed that such representations may prejudicially affect these servants with their employers. The Board trust that in order to ensure a fair and equitable working of the Act servants may be given to understand that they may openly and without fear of consequences, make full use of the opportunities which the Act has afforded them of representating any instances of overwork to the Board of Trade.'

Replying on behalf of the Association on November 11, 1893, Mr Findlay opened his letter with a request that 'any companies affected' might 'at once receive copies of representations which may be addressed to the Board of Trade relating to their regulations or practice', and he went on to deny that there was any justification for the suggestion that 'representations made . . . on behalf of any servants may prejudicially affect those servants with their employers'. All railway servants could 'openly and without fear of the consequences make use of the powers of the Act'. The President of the Board of Trade had, however, learned enough from the Hood and other cases to have become sceptical. On February 27, 1894, he replied to the companies that he 'had found it necessary to decline to furnish the railway companies with copies of the complaints received either from their servants or those acting on their behalf'.[47] Had he not stood firm on this point it is likely that what little effectiveness was left in the Act would have disappeared.

At the time of the introduction of the Act, the majority of the members of the A.S.R.S. were prepared to give it a fair trial. Disillusionment grew with the passage of time and the continuance of periods of systematic overwork on the railways. Railwaymen gradually learned how ineffective the Act was in times of brisk trade.

Its first great weakness was that it was permissive in character. The companies were not obliged, as a matter of routine, to submit regularly to the Board of Trade returns of the hours of work of their employees. Only after representation had been made to the Board of Trade by railwaymen or their trade union or other interested parties, was a return called for. It was not until 1902 that the Board of Trade chose to call for a general return of hours worked under the Act. Initially, representations under the Act increased; there were seventy-two complaints (concerning any group from one or two persons to the whole of a given grade employed by a company) in 1894 and 156 complaints in 1895. But thereafter the numbers of complaints steadily declined to ninety-seven in 1896, seventy-six in 1897, fifty in 1898, and so on. In some years there may well have been fewer complaints because there were fewer instances of overwork of which to complain. It was a view of the A.G.M. of the A.S.R.S. in 1904, however, that 'the difficulty of getting representations under the Act attended to had discouraged railwaymen . . . in making complaints',[48] whilst Mr R. Bell, then General Secretary of the A.S.R.S., told the House of Commons that his complaint was that after representations had been made by the men and the Board of Trade had asked for returns, 'the returns were cooked before they were sent in'. On the Lancashire and Yorkshire Railway an instruction had been sent out by the General Manager that 'in making out a long hours return, travelling time, etc., should be deducted'.[49]

It was soon revealed that the Minister did not even possess powers under the Act to prevent companies increasing the normal hours of work of their employees. When Mr Channing asked in the House of Commons on August 9, 1894, for intervention with the Great Northern Railway which had converted a number of 8-hour signal boxes to ten hours, the Minister replied that he could only act if it was represented to him by the men that the new hours were unreasonable.[50]

In two reasonably comprehensive inquiries that were made under the Act it was revealed that at the beginning of the twentieth century there were still thousands of instances of men working in excess of twelve hours a day. The first general return was for the month of December 1902. On this occasion the companies were given three months' notice, which opportunity they used to issue notices telling the officials that the hours of labour were to be kept down. The result was that the number of cases of men working over twelve hours in that foggy month of December was 75,389. The companies were without comparable warning for the next return, for the month of October 1903, which would normally have had less overwork than was the case in December because it was a much less foggy month. Nevertheless, the figure for October 1903 leaped up to 99,586—a remarkable pointer to the survival of excessive hours of work on a substantial scale.[51]

The *Railway Review* had always spoken up for the 1893 Act in the early days of its operation, but on February 15, 1907, the editor felt obliged to comment:

'For some years past every effort has been made to exploit the Act of 1893 to its full advantage, and yet it cannot be denied that, if not a disastrous failure, the success which has been obtained is comparatively slight. . . . Surely even in the darkest days, the number of cases of 20, 21, 22, 23 and even up to 30 hours at a stretch have not been more numerous than they have been seen for two months past on the Great Central Railway, the Midland Railway and the Lancashire and Yorkshire Railway. It appears to be quite useless to supply these lists to the Board of Trade. No permanent results accrue from that course. . . . If it were not for the possibility of sending complaints through the trade unions the Act would be to all intents and purposes a dead letter. . . . In our opinion the Act of 1893 has had a fair trial and has proved a failure.'

More might have been done by the union to replace the law by a stronger one if its supreme governing body, the A.G.M., had given a clear and consistent lead in this direction. At the Birmingham A.G.M. in October 1891, Signalman Longstaff of Newcastle persuaded delegates to vote unanimously in favour of his resolution for a legal 8-hour day. In the following year, however, at the A.G.M. held in London, delegates voted by 30 votes to 12 in favour of the National Programme to be achieved by industrial action. The Glasgow Congress of 1893 passed contradictory resolutions; one favoured the legal enforcement of the 8-hour day, the other followed the Belfast T.U.C. of that year in favouring support for an 8-hour Act which was permissive only. Although in March 1896, the E.C. drafted and submitted to branches a Railwaymen's Employment Bill which combined the 8-hour day with a guaranteed week's pay and was, for this reason, very popular with the branches, the decisions of the A.G.M. continued to fluctuate between the policy of statutory limitation of hours and their limitation by industrial pressure and a 'tightening up' of the Act of 1893. Thus the Bradford A.G.M. in 1904, influenced by a speech from the General Secretary, Richard Bell, rejected a proposal for an Eight Hours Bill and carried instead a proposal to amend the 1893 Act 'so as to compel the railway companies to make returns of all hours over twelve worked by the railway servants'.

After 1906, members of the union and the general public were treated to the distressing spectacle of Richard Bell, one of the union's M.P.s, going into a different division lobby from that of his two colleagues, Messrs Wardle and Hudson, Bell favouring the Liberal Party's policy of strengthening the Board of Trade's powers under the 1893 Act whilst Hudson, supported by Wardle and the Labour Party, introduced an 8-hour Bill for railwaymen in 1908, 1909 and 1910. It is true that personal conflicts of this kind disappeared with the resignation of Richard Bell in 1909 but there was still no agreed policy between the unions. Mr Fox, General Secretary of the A.S.L.E. & F. told a conference organized by the T.U.C. in 1911 to enlist support for Mr Hudson's Eight Hour Bill, that, though his union had an 8-hour day and similar objects in its programme, he had 'no mandate to go to the House of Commons to get it' since they felt that if they asked the companies 'they would be glad to give it'.[52]

Before 1914 only signalmen in busy boxes, shunters employed in busy yards and some locomotivemen employed on main line routes, worked less than sixty hours a week in a normal working week. Only after a large majority of railwaymen had enrolled in the N.U.R. following its foundation in March 1913, and had passed through the experience of the First World War, were their hours substantially reduced to bear favourable comparison for the first time in history with the hours of labour worked in the other principal trades of the kingdom.

NOTES

1. Railway Companies' Servants Bill, 1877, Hansard 1877, Vol. 234, Col. 709 et seq., May 11, 1877.
2. Select Committee on Railway Servants (Hours of Labour) evidence of Mr Courtenay Boyle for the Board of Trade, March 10, 1891. P.P. 1892, Vol. XVI, Q. 43.
3. Debate reported in Hansard, Parliamentary Debates, 1890–1, Vol. 349, Col. 905 et seq., January 23, 1891.
4. *The Times*, January 27, 1891.
5. Hansard, Parliamentary Debates 1891, Vol. 350, Col. 1504, February 24, 1891.
6. Select Committee on Railway Servants (Hours of Labour). Qs. 2173–5, P.P. 1890–1, Vol. XVI.
7. *Ibid.*, Special Report P.P. 1892, Vol. XVI, p. XXVIII and Q. 4004.
8. P.P. 1890–1, Vol. XVI, Q. 3910.

9. P.P. 1890–1, Vol. XVI, Qs. 1241–8.
10. *Ibid.*, Qs. 5266, 8671 and P.P. 1892, Vol. XVI, Q. 2017.
11. P.P. 1892, Vol. XVI, p. vii.
12. Q. 5293, P.P. 1890–1, Vol. XVI.
13. Q. 2353, P.P. 1892, Vol. XVI.
14. Qs. 9440–4, 9466, 9690, P.P. 1890–1, Vol. XVI.
15. *Ibid.*, Qs. 7888–7909 and 2957, 2959.
16. *Ibid.*, Q. 5744.
17. *Ibid.*, Qs. 7885, 5324, 9545 and 1892, Vol. XVI, Q. 2007.
18. Qs. 7077, 7105, 7123, P.P. 1890–1, Vol. XVI.
19. *Ibid.*, Qs. 7580–7603.
20. *Ibid.*, Qs. 8269, 8321, 561–5, 5040.
21. *Ibid.*, Qs. 2609, 3873, 4217.
22. *Ibid.*, Q. 1337.
23. *Ibid.*, Q. 6866.
24. *Ibid.*, Q. 9829. Quotation about the state of the sleepers taken from editorial in the (Conservative) *Salopian and Montgomeryshire Post*, March 26, 1892.
25. *Ibid.*, Qs. 9817–42.
26. Q. 738, P.P. 1892, Vol. XV.
27. Hansard, Parliamentary Debates, 1892, Vol. 3, Col. 945, speech of Mr Lockwood, M.P. for York, April 7, 1892.
28. Q. 6, P.P. 1892, Vol. XVI.
29. Hansard (as above) Col. 953; Speech of Mr Picton.
30. Q. 10, P.P. 1892, Vol. XVI.
31. *Ibid.*, Qs. 674–83.
32. *Ibid.*, Qs. 1118, 1331–8.
33. Select Committee on Railway Servants (Hours of Labour) Special Reports III, P.P. 1892, Vol. XVI.
34. Hansard (as above) Col. 918.
35. Report of Proceedings on April 7, 1892, in Hansard (as above, Col. 883 *et seq.*)
36. *R.R.*, May 13, 1892.
37. *R.R.*, December 18, 1896.
38. *R.R.*, October 25, 1895.
39. Q. 4141, P.P. 1892, Vol. XVI.
40. Minutes of Meetings of the Railway Companies Association, 35 Parliament Street, Westminster, March 1 and 16, 1892.
41. Qs. 6002–19, 8793, 8917, 8265 and 8932, P.P. 1890–1, Vol. XVI.
42. See the evidence of W. Foreman. *Ibid.*, Qs. 5044–6.
43. The words were those used by Sir John Gorst, an Opposition Member in the debate on April 24, 1893. Hansard 1893, Vol. II, Col. 1092.
44. A.S.R.S. General Secretary's report to the A.G.M. 1893.
45. Hansard 1893, Vol. II, Col. 1092 and A.S.R.S. General Secretary's Report, 1893.
46. *Ibid.*, Col. 1103.
47. Railway Companies Association Minutes, November 8, 1893, February 28, 1894.
48. These were the opening words of a resolution moved by Mr T. Williams and carried by the Congress.
49. House of Commons: Hansard, Vol. 157, Col. 570, May 16, 1906.
50. House of Commons: Hansard, Vol. 27, Col. 459, August 9, 1894.
51. House of Commons: Hansard, Vol. 157, Col. 555, May 16, 1906.
52. Report of a Conference on the Railways Eight Hour Bill summoned by the T.U.C. Parliamentary Committee, April 28, 1911; speech of Mr Fox, p. 10.

CHAPTER VII

THE ALL-GRADES CAMPAIGN OF 1897

*'We claim the right to deal with our own servants as we think
expedient.'*
Mr Harrison, General Manager, London and North Western Railway,
December 9, 1896.

I

THE closing years of the nineteenth century were marked by
the increasing militancy of the rank and file railwaymen and their growing support for the A.S.R.S. and by the
simultaneous stiffening of the companies' resistance to the
men's demands for improved working conditions.

Between 1893 and 1896 the forward movement among the men was
largely confined to the best organized grades who believed that their
superior organization improved their chances of wresting improved terms
of service from the companies. One reason why it was possible in 1897
to extend the movement to include all grades was that in 1896 the twenty-
year period of falling prices came to an end. In the period of rising prices
which continued, with few interruptions, from 1896 to 1921, it was
easier to persuade railwaymen that more aggressive industrial action was
needed if a fall in their standard of living was to be averted.

The companies' firm resistance to the granting of concessions in part
sprang from the limitation imposed by the Government in the Railway
and Canal Traffic Act of 1894 on their freedom to raise fares and freight
charges. When this Act came into operation the consent, often reluctantly
given, of the Railway and Canal Commission had to be obtained before
any increase in the companies' charges could be made. At the same time
operational costs were increasing with the necessity of employing more
staff to supplement the labour of those whose excessive hours were being
reduced under the Hours of Labour Act of 1893. In addition the companies
were having to pay more for the materials they used.

In the course of the passage of the Hours of Labour Bill through Parliament in 1893 a deputation of signalmen employed on the North Eastern Railway met the President of the Board of Trade, Mr Mundella, and endeavoured to persuade him to insert a clause into the Bill abolishing 12-hour signal boxes. When the Minister would not agree to their proposal[1] the North Eastern Railway signalmen reverted to industrial activity to gain their ends. At its meeting in May 1893, the E.C. agreed to a proposal made by London signalmen that a national campaign should be launched on behalf of this grade. The North Eastern Railway signalmen, whose programme had been endorsed by the E.C. as early as February 1893, then agreed to merge their efforts in the general movement, and a National Signalmen's Conference was held at Derby in July 1893. The programme launched at this Conference included the abolition of 12-hour boxes and a scale of wages ranging from 25s to 30s a week.[2] Although over 2,000 new signalmen members were recruited to the union within a year, bringing the total of this grade enrolled by June 1894 to 7,000, the campaigners were unsuccessful in achieving their main objectives. When the second, and last, Conference of the National Signalmen's Movement was held in Birmingham on July 9, 1895, it was made clear that the signalmen employed in the less busy boxes had been prepared to accept small, piecemeal concessions in lieu of the major concessions demanded by the union. A great drawback of the movement was that so many signalmen worked in isolated locations where it was more difficult to maintain a spirit of solidarity and militancy.[3]

The failure of the signalmen's movement helps to explain the E.C.'s refusal, by a narrow majority, in September 1895, to sanction a National Goods Guards Movement despite the fact that at this time this grade was the best organized one in the railway service.[4]

Despite these setbacks the organization of these grades improved and the membership of the union increased from 38,119 at the end of 1895 to 44,709 by the end of 1896. After Harford had gained the approval of the E.C. in June 1896 for the redrafting of the rules for the purpose of giving the General Secretary more control over the conduct of movements, he was prepared to view more favourably the demands from the goods guards, shunters, draymen and signalmen for renewed national campaigns on their behalf. At its meeting in June 1896, the E.C. made plans for the holding of a National Goods Guards Conference in Birmingham on November 17, 1896, whilst in September of that year the E.C. yielded to the demands of the draymen and lorrymen for a national Conference of their grade to be held at Sheffield on November 1st. The signalmen's national programme was revived at a meeting held on November 18th.[5] The thirty-five delegates who represented the 2,800 draymen and lorrymen members of the A.S.R.S. at the Conference in Sheffield drew up a programme for a 10-hour day with overtime payments at time and a quarter rates and a guaranteed week for each man on the permanent staff.[6] The signalmen campaigned for their full 1893 programme. The goods guards and shunters wanted a guaranteed week's pay with Sunday duty at time and a half, and overtime at time and a quarter rates, the abolition of the trip system and a maximum 10-hour day for guards and 8-hour day for shunters.

At the end of November 1896, Harford sent circulars on behalf of the guards, shunters, signalmen, draymen and lorrymen to all the companies in the country, requesting a reply to the men's demands by December 8th. Each circular included the names of seven men in the company's service who were prepared to act as a deputation on behalf of the men in their grade. Harford's objective was to achieve national uniformity in conditions for the four grades involved and to gain recognition by the companies of the seven-man delegations as the thin end of the wedge to full union recognition.

Harford's circular to the companies was discussed at a meeting of the General Managers at the headquarters of the Railway Companies' Association on December 2, 1896. It was agreed almost unanimously to present 'a bold front ... to the interference of the Society'. Each company was advised to deal directly with its own employees 'without the intervention of any third parties'. The only dissenting voice was that of the General Manager of the North Eastern Railway who felt that negotiations with the A.S.R.S. were to be preferred to the risks of a strike.[7]

At a meeting of the Great Western Railway Board held the following day it was resolved that 'no answer should be given' to Mr Harford. Instead the draft of a circular to be sent to all stationmasters in the company's service was approved. The circular recorded the directors' determination, in the event of a strike, 'to take immediate steps for filling up such vacancies as may arise'. Stationmasters were 'to personally see each goods guard, brakesman, shunter and signalman' whose name was on their pay rolls and to ask each 'which course they would follow' in the event of a strike. The concluding sentences of the message read as follows:

'In order that there may be no misunderstanding it will be well to read this circular to each man and record his answer in one of the columns provided for the purpose. Should any man decline to give a direct answer please make an entry to that effect between the last two columns.'

Although the carrying out of these orders must have helped to break the back of the movement on this line, there is no evidence that any member of the A.S.R.S. was dismissed for giving a 'disloyal' answer to the question put to him by his stationmaster.

The management of the London and North Western Railway resorted to more extreme measures. No sooner had Mr Harford's circular been received than inspectors from Euston started to travel up and down the company's lines questioning the staff. Fairly typical of those affected was the experience of Mr Wale of Nuneaton, an emergency signalman, working a 66-hour week for a wage of 27s. An inspector came to him on December 1st and asked him if he was contented with his conditions of service. Wale replied 'No, I want the 60-hour week', and proceeded on his way. Two days later, without a word of explanation, Wale was discharged.[8]

Edwin Bancroft, a goods guard with fourteen years' service on the London and North Western Railway, who had served on the E.C. of the A.S.R.S. and was one of the deputation of guards mentioned in Mr Harford's letter to the company, was approached by an inspector, Mr Mawby, on December 3rd. Asked whether, in the event of a strike, he would loyally serve the company or stand by the men, he boldly replied that he would stand by the men. When told that the consequences would be instant dismissal he did not retract his earlier statement and was, in consequence, dismissed on the spot.[9]

Altogether the company dismissed eighty-five of its employees in this way.[10] It was a challenge which the union could not possibly ignore. To keep up the morale of the men involved, the E.C. at its December meeting, decided to send all the organizers and the Assistant Secretary to Longsight, Stockport, Leeds and adjoining centres on the London and North Western Railway from which most of the victimized men came,[11] whilst a deputation of three members of the E.C. was detailed to seek a meeting with the officials of the company.

At first the directors would not modify their first impetuous decision. On December 7th, Mr Harford sent the following reply-paid telegram to Mr F. Harrison, the General Manager of the London and North Western Railway.

'Will you kindly receive a deputation from the Executive Council of the Amalgamated Society of Railway Servants respecting the dismissal of our members by you? Please name a convenient time.'

The reply received on the same day read:

'Cannot receive deputation from your committee. The company will deal direct with their servants as hitherto. It is not correct that men have been dismissed for being members of your society.'

Mr Harrison justified his action to the press and the public by stating that in the Birmingham *Daily Post* of November 18, 1896, Mr Harford was reported as telling a meeting of railwaymen that the majority of the men would tender their notices between December 8th and 10th. The company could not afford to have a stoppage of traffic in the busy Christmas season and therefore steps were being taken to ensure the continuance of essential services. But, in fact, neither the General Secretary nor the E.C. had reached a decision on strike action. The newspaper report was incorrect and Richard Bell wrote to each of the directors on December 11th to tell them that this was the case.[12]

Had they calculated that there would be such a storm of opposition to their action it is doubtful whether the directors would have come to the decision that they did. They got little sympathy from the newspapers. The *Manchester Guardian* described the company's tactics as 'repugnant to common good feeling and common sense', whilst the *London Evening News* declared that although membership of the A.S.R.S. might appear a 'monstrous crime' in the eyes of the Directors of the London and North Western Railway, it was 'not an offence in the eyes of the general public'.[13] Some of the shareholders of the company were far from happy about the high-handed action of the General Manager. Within a week of the first dismissals there had been a decline in value of the ordinary stock by nearly four million pounds.[14] Two prominent shareholders, Mr T. Lough, M.P., and Mr Herbert Samuel (later Viscount Samuel) called on Mr. Harrison at Euston and then wrote a letter to the press supporting the suggestion that 'the company should modify their hasty action by restoring the men who [had] been dismissed'.[15] Furthermore, Mr F. Muddison, editor of the *Railway Review*, was successful via Mr Mundella, in persuading some of the directors to have second thoughts.[16] But it was no doubt the intervention of Mr C. T. Ritchie, the President of the Board of Trade, which was most influential in bringing about a more conciliatory attitude on the part of the company's General Manager. On December 8th, he wrote to Mr Harrison that the reinstatement of the men was an 'imperative necessity'.[17]

The directors of the company were aware that the powers of the President of the Board of Trade to intervene were enhanced after the passing of the Conciliation Act in 1896 and in their reply to Mr. Ritchie on December 10th they began to climb down. The company's secretary wrote that if any of the dismissed men wanted to make any statement or explanation the directors were 'quite prepared to meet them either by themselves or before the Board of Trade'.[18]

Mr Ritchie was aware that the situation was one which called for the utmost tact on his part. If a strike was to be avoided he would have to achieve a quick settlement. This settlement required the co-operation of Mr Harford, but on no account was Mr Harford to see Mr Harrison who still refused to recognize the union. It was a tribute to the diplomacy of the Minister that the whole affair was successfully wound up on December 11th. At the offices of the Board of Trade in Whitehall Gardens, first Mr Harford was interviewed at 10.0 a.m. When he was safely off the premises Mr Harrison arrived shortly before lunch and finally, with Mr Harrison out of the way in the Railway Companies' Association

Headquarters in Parliament Street, Mr Harford returned at 3.0 p.m. to give the union's approval to the agreement. The important part of the agreement, as far as Mr Harford was concerned, was Mr Harrison's promise to reinstate all the dismissed men—a promise which he faithfully kept—and his undertaking that the company would 'receive and consider' any representations which the men desired to make. To help make the agreement palatable to the company Mr Harford conceded that although 'no strike was intended' the company 'had good ground for assuming there would be a strike'.[19]

Mr Harford told a meeting of railwaymen in Manchester two days later that the whole fiasco could have been avoided if Mr Harrison had written him a short letter on November 19th asking whether a strike was intended.

II

The impact of the agreement of December 11, 1896, on the railway trade unions was twofold. On the one hand the morale of the members of the A.S.R.S. was raised through the successful outcome of the campaign to reinstate the dismissed men. Inspired by the victory over the London and North Western Railway and encouraged by the hope of success in the grade movements the E.C. had authorized, 53,500 men joined the union in 1897.[20] On the other hand disappointment with the meagre concessions made by the London and North Western Railway in the weeks following the December 11th agreement spurred the men on to greater efforts. Some of them were taking to heart the words of the leading economist of the day, Professor Marshall, who wrote that 'in order to stand the least chance of holding their own in bargaining, the employees of such a company (the London and North Western Railway) require a stronger union than is employed in any other trade. That is one of the valuable lessons which Mr Harrison has taught the men.'[21]

In the first few weeks of 1897, Mr Harrison sent vague replies to renewed requests from the union that he should meet the seven-men deputations. He failed to grant interviews despite the promise to that effect contained in clause three of the agreement of December 11th. Instead some concessions were granted to come into effect on February 22nd. Pilot guards were to get an 8-hour day and a week's holiday with pay was granted to passenger guards, brakesmen and signalmen with five years' service.[22] Since in Harford's view the company was not keeping its promise to meet deputations of the men, he wrote to Mr Ritchie asking for his intervention. Ritchie sent Francis Hopwood to Mr Harrison who told him that individual applications from the men were being considered. Though the E.C. was thoroughly dissatisfied and regarded Harrison's reply as 'nothing but a subterfuge', Hopwood recommended to his chief that no further action should be taken, and his advice was followed.[23]

Since the Board of Trade was not prepared to intervene to secure even the indirect recognition of the union, Harford and the E.C. were ready to give a more sympathetic response to demands coming from the branches and districts for industrial action. Before there was time to resume national organization of the grades, however, trouble flared up in the region which Harford himself had helped to organize in 1879—the North East. By December 1896, the grade committees of all the principal grades employed on the North Eastern Railway had presented the management with their demands for better working conditions. A mass meeting of the men was held in Newcastle on Sunday, December 27, 1896, to hear the report back of deputations to the Goods Manager, Mr Jesper. He had expressed himself unable to satisfy most of the demands for better pay and shorter hours. The situation began to look serious when a deputation of passenger staff told the directors at an interview they were granted on 30th December that they would be back again if the 10-hour day was not granted.[24]

Just under a month later on January 27, 1897, Mr Gibb, the General Manager, issued a circular with the news that fifty 12-hour signal cabins were to be placed in the 10-hour class and thirty-five 10-hour cabins were to be transferred to the 8-hour class. Goods guards, mineral guards and signalmen were to be paid at time and a quarter rates for Sunday duty and platelayers were to have a rise of 1s a week.[25] Although these were worth-while improvements they were far less extensive than the concessions the men demanded and at mass meetings held in Newcastle, West Hartlepool, York and elsewhere on Sunday, January 31st, great discontent was expressed particularly as the deputations had had no hand in drafting the concessions made by the company.[26]

Under Mr Jesper's new regulations the goods checkers and rulleymen at Newcastle were actually worse off than before, having their hours of work increased. On February 20th, seven rulleymen who had been ordered to start work at 5.0 a.m. did not arrive until 7.0 a.m., their old time of starting. They were at once suspended. When Mr Jesper failed to satisfy a deputation of local A.S.R.S. officials, a sympathetic strike of other goods workers at Newcastle and Gateshead spread rapidly.

Harford was annoyed that an unofficial strike had broken out on Tyneside as he feared that public opinion would be alienated and the national programmes jeopardized. On February 24th, he arrived on the scene of the dispute to try and effect a settlement. The Directors of the North Eastern Railway, aware of his dislike of the strike, offered to meet a deputation of the men with their General Secretary, and promised the reinstatement of the seven men who had been suspended. Harford favoured a settlement along these lines since he believed it would bring *de facto* recognition of the union, but the local railwaymen wanted both a formal recognition of the A.S.R.S. by the directors and a reinstatement of all men involved in the dispute. Growing impatient with the local leaders, Harford signed an agreement with the company for a return to work on March 1st and reinstatement of all except the casual workers. He believed that there would be an opportunity to discuss the broader programme of demands at a meeting the directors had arranged for March 12th.[27]

When the thirty-eight members of the deputation and Mr Harford met the directors on March 12th there was a prolonged discussion, lasting from 11.0 a.m. to 7.0 p.m. on the union's main programme. Sir Joseph Pease, Chairman of the company, declared that the men's programme was a 'very large' one and he pleaded for time to consider it, promising the deputation to meet them again in a fortnight. The men concurred. In the interim the E.C. pressed its offer of arbitration and made itself available for a special meeting if the offer was refused.[28]

A majority of the Board of Directors of the North Eastern Railway, at a meeting held on March 29th, resolved to accept the offer of arbitration made by the union as it was felt that the limit of concessions had been reached but, at the same time, a strike might well be prolonged and costly. When they met the A.S.R.S. deputation the following day they announced their decision to submit to arbitration the main demands of the men for shorter hours and improved pay but to exclude from consideration questions of management and discipline and the locomotivemen's demand for an eight-hour day. If the men could have agreed to the company's proposals on the spot a very unfortunate incident would not have occurred. But the company's refusal to submit the locomotivemen's case to arbitration was regarded as serious and the deputation of the men, therefore, asked for an adjournment until the following day.

March 31, 1897, which should have been Harford's day of triumph, proved to be the day of his downfall. On that fateful morning when the arbitration agreement with the company was to have been signed Mr Harford went to the Board Room 'very much under the influence of drink',[29] and not in a fit condition to carry on business. The members of the deputation who under Mr Harford's leadership would have been prepared to sign the agreement, did not, in the absence of their General Secretary, feel able to sign 'on their own responsibility'. Later, on April 5th, the organizer, Richard Bell, who took over management of the case from March 31st, persuaded the men to endorse the company's plan and to accept Lord James of Hereford as arbitrator.[30]

Some opposition to arbitration was voiced at the A.G.M. of the company in August 1897. Sir Robert Craven of Hull received some applause from the meeting when he said that it was true they knew where concessions to the men were to stop. 'Were they to be the masters or the servants?' he asked. After Sir Joseph Pease from the Chair had challenged the opponents of arbitration 'to put down on paper a calculation of the loss which would result from a six months' strike' the majority of the meeting endorsed the directors' actions.[31]

When Lord James published his award later that month the chief grades to benefit were the goods guards, signalmen and locomotivemen. A number of 12-hour signal boxes were placed in the 10-hour group, locomotivemen, goods guards, rulleymen, porters and permanent-way men were to have their overtime calculated on a daily instead of a weekly basis and there were improved rates of pay for Sunday duty. On the other hand, Lord James refused to concede any grade a guaranteed week's pay for he was impressed by the company's argument that the mineral traffic fluctuated greatly from day to day. If the gains in terms of improved conditions were somewhat meagre, the award was important in that the company for the first time recognized the A.S.R.S. as qualified to speak on behalf of all of its employees. That the company was prepared to go this far along the road to full recognition was all the more remarkable in that there were 8,000 non-unionists among its 18,744 employees, whilst only 1,530 of the 4,135 permanent-way men and only 591 of the 2,024 porters the company employed belonged to the union.[32]

Mr Harford's conduct of the negotiations with the North Eastern Railway was subject to severe censure at the A.G.M. held in Plymouth in October 1897. The delegates agreed to hear the members of the deputation of North Eastern Railway men who expressed the opinion that their local all-grades movement was making good progress and stood every chance of success until Mr Harford arrived on the scene and took control of negotiations out of their hands. Harford's statement of opposition to the strike given to the press in Birmingham on February 22, 1897,[33] his decision to accept the terms of a settlement offered by Mr Gibb, the General Manager of the company, before he had fully consulted the local committee of the men and, above all, his drunkenness on the morning of March 31st, were condemned by the majority of the delegates. Whilst Mr Harford fully admitted his misconduct in attending important negotiations in an intoxicated condition, he asked for the clemency of the delegates on account of his being overworked and ill with influenza and inflammation of the left lung throughout much of the month of February during which time he continued to carry out his duties when he should have been confined to his bed. But the North Eastern men's secretary, Mr James Reed Bell, expressed the view of many of the delegates when he declared that, though Mr Harford had done 'excellent service' in the past, his conduct of the dispute on the North Eastern Railway had entirely shaken the confidence of the North Eastern men in him and that respect and confidence had gone 'never to return'.[34] Consequently a resolution to dismiss Mr Harford from his position as General Secretary was carried by 35 votes to 20 and a more moderate amendment censuring him for his misconduct but mentioning, in mitigation, the poor state of his health, was defeated by 35 votes to 23.[35] On the insistence of Mr James Holmes, congress proceeded to carry by 57 votes to 2 a resolution awarding Mr Harford a pension of a 100 guineas a year for the rest of his life. After it had been further decided to give Mr Harford a month's salary in lieu of notice, Mr Richard Bell was declared appointed General Secretary *pro tem*.[36]

Edward Harford did not live to see another A.G.M. Within three months of his dismissal on January 4, 1898, he died on board the liner that was bringing him back from the United States of America where he had attended the convention of the A.F. of L. as a fraternal delegate from the T.U.C. The greater part of the 59 years of his life had been devoted to the service of the railwaymen.[37]

III

By June 1897, there were so many demands from goods guards, draymen, shunters, signalmen, locomotivemen and many other grades for their movements for better terms of service to be recognized, that the E.C. resolved that the programmes of the various grades should be merged into one and that a joint conference should be summoned at Birmingham to draft an all-grades programme for simultaneous presentation to all the companies in England and Wales.[38] In September the E.C. agreed to hold the all-grades conference on October 11 and 12, 1897.[39] The fact that the companies were at that time 'on the top ... of a wave of prosperity' and enjoyed in 1896 the best year they had had since 1890 no doubt gave an incentive to the grade committees and the national executive to forge ahead with the campaign.[40]

It was a characteristic of the all-grades programme agreed by the 113 delegates at Birmingham that it was the result of an adding together of the separate programmes of the individual grades anxious to achieve a national uniformity of conditions, rather than the collective drafting of a new memorandum to the companies. Among the more important of the demands were the introduction of a guaranteed week for locomotive staff, goods guards, shunters and signalmen; a 10-hour maximum day for work in signal cabins; the abolition of the trip system; an 8-hour day for locomotivemen, shunters and goods staff and a 48-hour week for permanent-way men; improved overtime rates including time and a half rates for Sunday duty; a programme for clerks which included a 42-hour week and a limit of three consecutive years for employment on night duty and wages demands which, if granted, would have brought the rates of pay for all grades up to the most favourable levels of any company in the kingdom.[41]

Although in Mr Harford's rules of 1896 it was provided that final decisions on industrial tactics were to be taken by the General Secretary whilst grade conferences were merely empowered to offer advice to the union's principal officers, the absence of Mr Harford from the scene at Birmingham and the still temporary character of Richard Bell's appointment as his successor encouraged the delegates to decide their own tactics in the conduct of the campaign.

The only major difference over tactics revealed at the Birmingham Conference was that, whereas the majority of the delegates favoured the immediate presentation of all the programmes to the companies, delegates from Spa Road, Newton Heath, Mirfield, York and elsewhere suggested that information should at first be collected on the percentage of men in each grade organized in the union. By implication it was understood that the presentation of demands on behalf of the poorly organized grades should await the achievement of a greater degree of unionization. However, a resolution moved by Mr Shaw of York to suspend operations until such information was obtained was disposed of by a motion to proceed to further business and the delegates proceeded to instruct Richard Bell to submit the united programme to the various companies by October 25th with a request for a reply by November 15, 1897, and a further request that if the companies could not accede to the men's demands they should agree to submit the matters in dispute to arbitration.[42] The conference was to be recalled on November 23rd to hear the replies of the companies and consider appropriate further action.

On Thursday, November 4, 1897, there took place at the headquarters of the London and North Western Railway at Euston Station, one of the largest meetings of railway directors, general managers and other principal officers ever to be held. This assembly of over 200 men had met to consider what should be the companies' reply to Mr Bell's letter enclosing the national programme of the A.S.R.S., and whether they should follow the advice of the railway stockholders' journal *The Railway News* and combine to resist trade-union demands as the engineering employers had done.[43] There were differences of opinion as to the best way of meeting the union's challenge, the North Eastern Railway representatives pressing the advantages of arbitration and conciliation whilst the majority of the general managers took a more intransigent view and even considered a plan for fixing a maximum scale of wages for all outside staff. Eventually the meeting agreed to refer to a committee of the general managers the task of trying to secure the united action of the companies in the event of the presentation by the A.S.R.S. of 'any unreasonable demands'.

The General Manager of the London and North Western Railway, who was completely opposed to any compromise with the union, feared that the presence of the North Eastern Railway officials on the General Managers' Committee would lessen its effectiveness. He therefore summoned an informal meeting of the General Managers of the Great Western Railway, Great Northern Railway, Great Central Railway, Midland Railway and Lancashire and Yorkshire Railway on November 17th when they held 'a long and frank discussion . . . on the best means to be employed by the various companies of meeting any attack from the Amalgamated Society' and agreed unanimously to the following four-point programme:

1. During a strike at a competitive place or places all traffic to and from that place or those places (both competitive and non-competitive) to be divided with an allowance for working expenses.

2. Where practicable, companies to help each other by running trains over each other's lines or working traffic or allowing traffic to pass by other available routes.

3. That companies should at places common to two or more of them agree to a maximum scale of wages at those places, each company paying what it chose within that maximum.

4. The companies should also, when possible, agree at such places on similar action with regard to such matters as hours of labour, rates of pay for overtime, holidays, lodging allowances, house or coal allowances and other privileges.

The agreement was shortly afterwards ratified by the boards of directors of the companies concerned.[44]

In the meantime some of the companies' secretaries wrote their boards' replies to Mr Bell's letter. The majority were simply formal acknowledgments although a number included an expression of the directors' willingness to meet their own men in separate grades. Mr Bell read thirty replies to the adjourned All-Grades Conference in Birmingham on November 23, 1897, but was obliged to add that he had received no acknowledgment or reply of any kind from the management of the Great Eastern Railway, Lancashire and Yorkshire Railway, London, Chatham and Dover Railway, the Rhymney, the Barry and a number of other smaller railway companies. It was also significant that five delegates had been refused leave to attend the conference. A proposal that the delegates should show their determination by instructing the General Secretary to issue notice papers to all branches with 'the date to be left open for him to fill in' when they were returned to head office by December 8th, was decisively defeated by 98 votes to 12. Instead, conference approved by 101 votes to 9 the proposal that Mr Bell should write a second time to the companies again offering to submit the proposals to arbitration and requesting a reply by November 30th. He was to inform the President of the Board of Trade of the action taken by the union and to send out notice papers to be returned to head office by December 6th. It was also agreed by 57 votes to 17 that no strike would be called until 75 per cent of the notice papers were signed and returned.

Mr Bell's second circular letter to the companies despatched on November 25th was considered at a meeting of the companies' general managers on the following day. They were agreed that 'arbitration was entirely out of the question' and the only discussion was on the manner of the reply. By this time the managers of all the important railway companies with the exception of the North Eastern Railway had agreed to adhere to the anti-strike agreement of November 17th.[45]

This was clearly the turning point of the campaign when decisive action either by the union or the Board of Trade was called for if the campaign was to achieve success.

Although the membership of the union increased very rapidly during the closing weeks of the all-grades campaign and had reached over 90,000 early in December, the movement fizzled out by the end of the year when membership figures were falling as rapidly as they had risen a few weeks previously.

Part of the explanation of the failure to clinch the campaign lies in the refusal of the President of the Board of Trade to intervene to persuade the general managers of the companies to meet the union grade delegations. Mr Bell had written to Sir Courtenay Boyle on December 3rd appealing to him to prevail upon the companies 'not to precipitate a disaster', but the reply sent the following day stated the Minister's view that 'no good purpose would be served' by the Board's intervention with the companies. The union was warned that 'any attempt to force the claims of the men by a strike' would be unjustifiable in view of the men's rights under the Hours of Labour Act of 1893 and was told that the Minister had no reason to doubt that the companies 'would listen to and discuss with the men in their employment any matters affecting their interests'.[46] When, however, the leaders of the grade movements acted on Sir Courtenay Boyle's advice a substantial number of them were victimized by the companies. From September 30, 1897 to June 30, 1898, a total of seventy cases of victimization was reported to the E.C.[47]

There is no doubt that at this time the union lacked a clear sense of direction and that this was a weakness which contributed to the failure of the campaign. Richard Bell was principally concerned with the securing of union recognition and was prepared to lead a strike with this as the main aim but he lacked full authority, not being formally elected General Secretary until the following June. Many of the delegates at the All-Grades Conference in Birmingham on the other hand were far more interested in the programme for better wages than they were in the principle of recognition. Opinion was divided as to whether a strike would be effective with union membership limited to 90,000. The editor of the *Railway Review*, Mr F. Maddison, thought 90,000 was not enough to secure success. On the same day that Mr Bell wrote appealing for the intervention of the Board of Trade, Maddison wrote in an editorial on 'The Crisis':

'The victory must be ours, but how soon depends entirely on the strength of the A.S.R.S. With 90,000 members it is within sight; 150,000 would make it a "certainty". It is all a question of the size of the battalions. Are they at present large enough? Candidly we think not. And that alone is why we favour a further period of strengthening of our forces before the final encounter.'[48]

Mr Bell, reading the article that evening, became indignant and impetuously told the press that it had 'given the whole show away'.[49] But Maddison was by no means alone in doubting the wisdom of a strike. Speaking at Battersea, John Burns, though attacking the railway companies and declaring that they had a new version of the Ten Commandments including the injunction 'Six days shalt thou labour for little and on the seventh day toil for nothing', nevertheless advised the men 'not to go in for a general strike'.[50]

The members of the E.C., after they had heard Mr Maddison put his case to them on December 6th, were unanimous in regretting the appearance of the article and expressed the hope that 'in similar circumstances in the future' he would 'consult the General Secretary before going to press'. This was too much for Maddison to stomach and his letter of resignation from the editorship appeared in the *Railway Review* a week after the offending leading article. In it he admitted that he had set himself 'to avert a general strike'. Because he included in the same issue letters from railwaymen sympathetic to his viewpoint, the E.C. adopted Bell's recommendation that he be given a month's wages in lieu of notice and that Mr Edward Garrity, Assistant Secretary, be placed in charge of the paper until a new editor was appointed.[51]

In April 1898, Mr George J. Wardle, a 33-year-old Keighley member of the I.L.P and Methodist local preacher who was serving on the Midland Railway as a clerk, was chosen as the new editor of the review.[52]

The hesitations expressed in the union's newspaper and the firm refusal of the President of the Board of Trade to intervene, influenced some of the national newspapers—which had been favourable to the men's case until December 3rd—to condemn in advance a general railway strike. The radical *Daily Chronicle* urged the railwaymen 'to indulge in no more foolishness about a strike' whilst the *Manchester Guardian* praised the wisdom of Mr Maddison and rejoiced at the 'partial lifting of the clouds of the labour world'.[53]

The action of the E.C. in deciding to ask the grade committees to make their own arrangements to re-submit their programme to the companies can only be interpreted as a retreat from the earlier policy of the simultaneous presentation of the programmes of all the grades. It was significant that following interviews granted by the railway directors the most successful grade was also the best organized one—the goods guards. On the Great Eastern Railway, Great Northern Railway, Midland Railway and Lancashire and Yorkshire Railway their hours were reduced from sixty-six to sixty per week. Apart from this there was an improved grading of many of the signal boxes on the Great Northern Railway and some improvements in pay, whilst the conditions of service of the locomotivemen on the South Eastern Railway were described as 'greatly improved', following the visit of a deputation of the men to the Board Room.

At the end of 1897 the companies could congratulate themselves that they had enjoyed a large measure of success in meeting the challenge of the all-grades programme. According to the *Railway News* the campaign conducted by the A.S.R.S. had had one 'most desirable result'—it had 'broken the old system of isolated action which had in the past left the railway companies unnecessarily open to all sorts of attacks' and had brought about in its place a 'solid combination and uniform action'.[54]

IV

At the same time as thousands of railwaymen were being enrolled in the A.S.R.S. in support of the national programme in England and Wales the strength of the union was rapidly increasing in Ireland. By October 1897, 7,500 men, 53 per cent of Irish railwaymen eligible for membership, had joined the A.S.R.S.—nearly twice the percentage of railwaymen organized in the United Kingdom as a whole.[55] Tevenan, tbe A.S.R.S. organizer in Ireland, believing that the time was ripe for the presentation of the national programme to the Irish companies, circularized them all in the third week of October but received offers to negotiate only from the Great Northern Railway and the Great Southern and Western. He therefore laid plans for a strike on the issue of union recognition. Matters came to a head on the Great Northern Railway where the directors, interviewing delegations of the men on November 22nd and 23rd, refused to negotiate with Mr Tevenan. The men on this line then handed in strike notices to take effect from December 13th.[56] In the meantime the Board of the London and North Western Railway in England had offered to supply men to both the Great Northern Railway and the Midland and Great Western Railway in Ireland[57] and the Great Northern Railway Board, confident that it could defeat a strike, issued a circular to its employees on December 4th warning them of the likelihood of a permanent loss of employment if they struck work. This firm action caused Tevenan to hesitate and to write to the Board of Trade to intervene. When this intervention was refused, the local committee succumbed to the pressure of an unsympathetic public opinion and withdrew the strike notices. Tevenan then withdrew the notices previously handed in to the other Irish railway companies and it looked as if the entire movement had collapsed.[58] However, quite unexpectedly, there were repercussions on one of the lines not at first principally involved in the agitation for better conditions. Early in December 1897 a deputation of the employees of the Cork, Bandon and South Coast

Railway led by Signalman Buckley of Cork Terminus met the directors of the company to discuss the national programme. No important concessions were offered. After the interview the directors sent a private circular to the stationmasters advising them to keep a sharp watch on the subsequent conduct of the members of the deputation.

At 7.30 a.m. on January 13, 1898, a light engine left the station at Cork. Through being preoccupied with his level-crossing duties, Buckley, who was on duty at the time, failed to record the departure of the engine in his train book. Shortly afterwards, whilst he was off duty at home eating his breakfast, he remembered his omission and left his meal unfinished in order to rectify his mistake. But in this short interval the stationmaster had entered his signal box and had examined the train book. A week later Buckley was informed that he had been moved to another box at Ballincarthy Junction where his wages of 14s a week would be 7s a week less than he had been earning at Cork. Shortly afterwards a deputation of forty men pleaded with the directors to alter their decision regarding Buckley but failed to move them. The indignation of the men at what they regarded as the shabby conduct of the directors was expressed at a mass meeting held at 9 Coburg Street, Cork, on January 23rd, when it was resolved that unless Buckley was reinstated in his old post by noon on the following day all the employees of the company would come out on strike. Since the directors did not comply with this demand, a strike, which involved 300 men and was remarkably complete, began on January 24th.[59]

It is indicative of the lower standard of living in Ireland than in England that some of the strikers received a greater income from strike pay at 12s a week plus a shilling a week for each dependent child than they did from their employment on the railways.[60]

Richard Bell was quickly on the scene in an effort to secure the quick and peaceful settlement of the dispute but the company's general manager, Mr Croker, sent a brief negative reply—'I beg to state this company cannot recognize the A.S.R.S.'—to the General Secretary's request for discussions. Instead Mr Croker told the press that the men would be prosecuted if they failed to return to work by noon on January 29th.[61] Not a single man applied for reinstatement,[62] but there was a general willingness to return to work if the directors gave a written guarantee to reinstate Buckley.

Every conceivable means was adopted by the company to try and break the strike. Through the agency of William Collison's National Free Labour Association sixty blacklegs were brought by sea from England but Richard Bell persuaded half of them to accept the return tickets as a present from the A.S.R.S. Neither the offer of 9s a week above the normal rates of pay to gangers nor the 2s a week extra offered to permanent-way men sufficed entirely to replace the men of these grades who were on strike.

Such blacklegs as were employed were accommodated and fed in the stations, a Cork furniture firm providing the bedding whilst a local restaurant undertook the catering.[63] Fourteen men were evicted from company-owned cottages. On February 2nd summonses were issued against twenty-eight of the strikers and a further batch of summonses were issued eleven days later. Before the conclusion of the strike eighty-six cases were tried in the courts. Most of those punished were given fines of £4, but one signalman was sentenced to two months' imprisonment, and at Kinsale on March 9th two pickets were sentenced to fourteen days' imprisonment.[64]

The strike, which lasted fourteen weeks and was of longer duration than any other dispute in the history of British railways, was finally settled after a conference of public bodies, called by the Mayor of Cork on May 12th, had passed strongly worded resolutions asking the men and the company to come to terms. In deference to this wish, and after strong pressure from Mr Tevenan, the men agreed to resume work on May 13th in return for a promise by the company to withdraw all prosecutions and evictions, to support a memorial for the release of the men in jail and to take back as many as possible of the strikers.[65]

Before the strike in Ireland had ended, a dispute arose on the Midland Railway. The draymen and goods workers employed by the company in Sheffield and Leeds had sent a deputation to meet the directors to ask for improved pay and working conditions. Within a week of the interview, one of the leaders of the deputation, Mr Morley, who at meetings of the men had spoken of the possibility of strike action, was dismissed from his employment. Although not more than 3,000 of the 15,000 goods workers of all kinds employed by the company were in the union, the men at Leeds and Sheffield struck work on March 21, 1898, for the reinstatement of Mr Morley. The strike did not have the official backing of the E.C. and Mr Mears, the organizer responsible for that area, was reprimanded by the E.C. for continuing to distribute strike pay after instructions had been received to the contrary.[66] Mr Turner, the General Manager of the company, failed to reply to two letters from Mr Bell pleading with him to reinstate the men whose places he had largely filled with labour imported from other districts. By the beginning of June 1898, the plight of some of the strikers was such as to cause the E.C. to grant £100 to the trustees of the Leeds No. 2 branch 'to relieve the distress'.[67]

The two strikes of the spring of 1898 had been costly to the union. It was largely on their account that the amounts spent on suspension and donation benefit leapt up from £3,118 15s 4d in 1897, to £16,331 12s 7d in 1898. Apart from the expense, Richard Bell thought that the fact that they were spontaneous movements without the initial authorization of the General Secretary or Executive Committee, was damaging to the reputation and influence of the union.[68] He therefore persuaded the A.G.M. at

Leeds in October 1898 to alter Rule XVI. The revised Clause 8 of that rule now read:

'The E.C. shall take a ballot of the men before deciding to cease work or issue notices.'

By this time Bell's authority had been enhanced by his election to the office of General Secretary in June. On the first ballot he had not commanded an absolute majority of the votes:

R. Bell	20,639
W. Hudson	13,461
A. Mears	4,536
E. Garrity	2,854

His victory over Mr Hudson in the second ballot had been substantial, if not overwhelming:

R. Bell	22,671
W. Hudson	14,518
Majority	8,153

The newly elected General Secretary, who was 39 years of age, had collected most of his votes from Wales and the West Country where he had been an A.S.R.S. organizer after his dismissal as a goods guard from the Great Western Railway in 1891. His reputation had been greatly enhanced by his successful conduct of his negotiations with the North Eastern Railway in 1897 but he also had the advantage over Mr Hudson of being temporary General Secretary from October 1897 to June 1898. One of his great merits was his thoroughness. The historian has reason to be grateful for the careful way in which records were kept and verbatim reports taken of important discussions during his twelve-year tenure of office. Mr Bell was unquestionably an able administrator though not so farsighted a tactician as his two immediate predecessors had been.

V

One of Mr Bell's principal tasks in 1898 was to ply the President of the Board of Trade with evidence of the victimization of many of the railwaymen who had led the grade deputations to the directors in favour of the national programme. He aimed not only at the reinstatement of the dismissed men but also at preventing victimization in the future.

One reason for preoccupation with this question was the fact that in 1898 the E.C. awarded protection grants to more than twice as many men as in any previous year. In the six months ending June 30, 1898, no less than fifty-seven men were compensated for being dismissed or down-graded mainly because they had taken an active part in the all-grades campaign.

Another reason for taking up the question with the Minister was that it was Sir Courtenay Boyle's claim made in his letter to Richard Bell on December 4, 1897, that union recognition by the companies was unnecessary since he had 'no, reason to doubt' that the directors would 'listen to and discuss with the men in their employment any representations' the men chose to make. Should any difficulties arise in following this procedure the Board would be prepared to use its good offices.[69] Difficulties had arisen and it was decided to take the Minister at his word.

On May 14, 1898, Mr Bell supplied the Board of Trade with detailed case histories of six active members of the union whom the companies had penalized by dismissal or reductions in their wages during the preceding six months. When Mr Hopwood, head of the Railway Department of the Board of Trade, replied requesting more details, Mr Bell wrote on June 3, 1898, enclosing particulars of twenty-four men who had suffered dismissal or removal to lower paid posts. Typical cases were those of Mr W. E. Bell of Gateshead who was dismissed on May 19, 1898, four days after he had led a deputation of carriage and wagon examiners who were interviewed by the Board of Directors of the North Eastern Railway, and Mr James Lenthall, Secretary of the Goods Guards Committee on the Barry Railway who was given the sack on December 16, 1897.[70]

Later in June 1898, Mr Hopwood wrote to each of the railway companies involved asking them for their explanations for the dismissal of the twenty-four men instanced by Mr Bell. Only the directors of the London and North Western Railway were slow in replying and had to be sent reminders. In a personal interview with Mr Hopwood, the general manager of that company, Mr Harrison, said that the directors did not wish to do more than formally acknowledge the letter from the Board of Trade concerning four men dismissed by the company. After Hopwood had argued that if the company's case was a good one the directors ought not to object to the requests for information, and had warned Harrison of the possibility of a Parliamentary inquiry, a full reply was sent by letter. All the companies' replies were then forwarded to Mr Bell. The letters showed the remarkable unanimity of the General Managers in explaining the dismissal of the men as being due solely to misdemeanours at work or failure of health. In some cases the replies were circumstantial and convincing as were the letters from the North Eastern Railway and the Barry Railway. The reply from the Great Central Railway was much less satisfactory:

'General Manager's Office
July 13, 1898.

'Sir,

I duly received your letter of 27th ult., and have submitted it to my directors at their meeting today.

'I am instructed to inform you in reply that whilst my board is at all times willing, as a matter of courtesy, to give every information to the Board of Trade, they do not think that in questions affecting the discipline of the staff they should be called upon to justify their action to the officials of the Amalgamated Society of Railway Servants.

'The statements made by the Amalgamated Society are altogether inaccurate. The men were dealt with for good and sufficient reasons, apart from their connection with any society, and the same course would have been adopted under similar circumstances, whether they were members of the society or not.

Yours etc.

W. POLLITT,
General Manager.'

It was scarcely to be expected that the E.C. would be satisfied with answers of this kind. Its members sifted with great care individual applications for the protection grant and only authorized payment when convinced, beyond all reasonable doubt, that the dismissed man had been victimized because of his activity on behalf of the union. At the four quarterly meetings held in 1898 the claims of 62 men were granted; those of 17 others were referred to organizers and branches for more information, whilst in 60 cases the grant was refused on the grounds that dismissal or down-grading was not due to the applicants' association with the union.[71]

Although the President of the Board of Trade in a letter to Mr Bell on October 19, 1898, expressed the opinion that 'in every case the men were dismissed for reasons entirely unconnected with the fact that they belonged to the A.S.R.S.' the Minister was pressed to institute a departmental inquiry to probe more deeply into the facts. Support for this proposal came from Mr F. Maddison, a former President of the Board of Trade, who wrote to Mr Ritchie on November 14, 1898, that there was 'considerable ground' for the union's charges against the companies though 'in some instances' they might have 'no foundation in fact'. Mr Ritchie, however, replying the next day, refused sanction for a Parliamentary inquiry though he expressed willingness to discuss the matter with Mr Maddison and some of the men affected. After a further exchange of correspondence, Mr Bell took five of the men who had been discharged to interview Sir Courtenay Boyle on February 7, 1899. Bell subsequently stated that 'Every opportunity was given to the men to state their case'. But it was a hard job to present Sir Courtenay Boyle with a clear-cut case. In his report to the A.G.M. in 1899, Mr Bell wrote that 'owing to the tactics of the companies' officials in dealing with the men, it became a difficult task to get a verdict proving them guilty of direct victimization'. Each of the five men brought as witnesses to the Board of Trade had been 'spotted' for some breach of the rules. It was well known by the companies' chief officials that a number of rules were consistently disregarded in order to speed up the movement of traffic, hence the railwayman who committed no breach of the rules in the course of his career was a rarity. The point was that if a man who was not an active trade unionist was discovered committing a fault he was 'cautioned' or punished by a short period of suspension. If, on the other hand, he was a 'militant', the superintendent concerned might seize the opportunity of dismissing him.

In the case of the London and North Western Railway, the company in the course of the year 1898 dismissed six men who were active members of the union. During his off-duty hours H. G. Jones, a gas fitter of Hockley branch, was collecting up the notices issued by the A.S.R.S. when he was accused of interfering with the other men in the performance of their duties and given the sack. J. T. Roberts, a foreman platelayer of Wigan, was discharged 'for not repairing a road bed as instructed'; Ruben Young, a foreman platelayer of Leeds, told the E.C. that he had been given no reason for his dismissal; J. Skelthorn, a brakesman of Wigan, protested about having his journey extended and was dismissed for 'insubordination'; Robert White of Willesden, an examiner who had been a delegate at both the Birmingham All-Grade conferences and had led delegations of the men to the Board of Directors was dismissed for 'underestimating the damage done to a wagon'; whilst Thomas Ridley of Market Harborough, another examiner, convinced the E.C. that he had been dismissed for an offence which had been committed by someone else whilst he was off duty and not on railway property. All six of these men were awarded the Society's protection grant of £50 although in the same year the E.C. rejected the claims of a further six London and North Western Railway men. An examination of the company's 'Caution' and 'Punishment' books for 1898 reveals that 404 men were cautioned and 205 suspended (mostly for one day) for offences which in most cases were every bit as serious as those committed by the active trade unionists who were dismissed. Thus a man who 'failed to turn up for duty after three days' holiday' and another who 'failed to notify that he was sick' were punished by short periods of suspension; several men who overslept and caused delays in the departure of trains were merely cautioned and shunters who were responsible for wagons leaving the rails were similarly treated.[72] However, it is extremely doubtful whether the Board of Trade officials saw the 'Punishment' and 'Caution' books of the company since the matter was dealt with largely by correspondence and they would not therefore be in a position to compare the treatment meted out to active unionists with that given to other employees.

The long exchange of correspondence between the union and the Board of Trade on this question came to an end on February 24, 1899, when Mr Bell received a letter from Sir Courtenay Boyle in which the Minister wrote that after 'very careful consideration' of the representations made by the men, he had come to the conclusion that no case had been made out which would warrant him complaining to the companies. It is significant that Sir Courtenay Boyle's secretary, Mr Hopwood (who was convinced that leading trade unionists had been victimized) in his original draft of the letter of February 24th, included a short paragraph in which it was conceded that the vigorous action taken by the union would have a 'salutary effect' on the companies. His chief, however, ordered the omission of this part of the letter.[73] On February 25th, the Minister sent a letter to the companies exonerating them from blame and expressing the confidence that the directors would not countenance the dismissal of men for taking an active part as union members in organizing deputations.

Though the offending paragraph had been struck out from the letter of February 24th, Mr Bell's persistence was not without its reward. He was able to report 'a great improvement' to the A.G.M. in October 1899. The number of claims for protection grant for the first three quarters of that year had fallen to 29 compared with 85 in the same period of the previous year,[74] and there were fewer disbursements from the Fund in the three years 1899–1901 inclusive, than there had been in the one year 1898.[75] The vigorous intervention of the union had helped to reduce substantially the companies' practice of singling out for dismissal those men who were active in voicing the demands of their fellow workmen.

NOTES

1. *R.R.*, April 28, 1893.
2. A.S.R.S. E.C. Minutes, August 1893, p. 10.
3. A.S.R.S. 'Report of the . . . National Conference of Signalmen, Birmingham, July 9, 1895.'
4. *R.R.*, November 29, 1895.
5. *R.R.*, November 27, 1896.
6. *R.R.*, November 6, 1896.
7. Manchester, Sheffield and Lincolnshire Railway; Proceedings of Board of Directors No. 30, para. 16920.
8. A.S.R.S. 'Labour's Right to Combine' December 1896, quoting *Daily Chronicle*, December 5, 1896.
9. *Ibid.*
10. A.S.R.S. General Secretary's Report to the E.C., March 1897, p. 6.
11. A.S.R.S. E.C. December 1896, R. 139.
12. *Daily News*, December 11, 1896.
13. *Manchester Guardian*, December 9, 1896, *London Evening News*, December 5, 1896.
14. A.S.R.S. 'Labour's Right to Combine', p. 15.
15. *Daily News*, December 11, 1896.
16. Alcock, p. 286.
17. *The Times*, December 12, 1896.
18. L.N.W.R. Board Minutes, Vol. 16, § 14849.
19. *R.R.*, December 18, 1896.
20. *R.R.*, December 31, 1897.

21. 'A lesson from the London and North Western Railway', *Progressive Review*, January 1897, p. 293.
22. A.S.R.S. General Secretary's Report to the E.C., March 1897.
23. A.S.R.S. E.C., March 1897, R. 47, P.R.O. M.T. 6/978. Files 1868 and 3241 of 1897.
24. *R.R.*, January 1, 1897.
25. *R.R.*, January 29, 1897.
26. *R.R.*, February 5, 1897.
27. *R.R.*, March 5, 1897.
28. *R.R.*, March 19, 1897, A.S.R.S. E.C., March 1897, R. 37.
29. A.S.R.S. Report of Mr Edward Harford's Case at the A.G.M. Plymouth, October 6, 1897, p. 4.
30. *R.R.*, April 9, 1897.
31. *R.R.*, August 13, 1897.
32. *R.R.*, August 27, 1897, quoting a speech of Richard Bell delivered at Crook on August 22, 1897.
33. A.S.R.S., Mr Edward Harford's Case, p. 6.
34. *Ibid.*, p. 34.
35. *Ibid.*, pp. 63, 61.
36. *Ibid.*, pp. 67–8.
37. A.S.R.S. E.C. Minutes, March 1898.
38. A.S.R.S. E.C. Minutes, June 1897, R. 45.
39. A.S.R.S. E.C. Minutes, September 1897, R. 96.
40. *Railway News*, October 30, 1897, p. 632.
41. Grade programmes bound with A.S.R.S. 'Proceedings and Reports', 1897.
42. A.S.R.S. Minutes of Birmingham Conference for Revising National Programmes, held at the Birmingham Arms Hotel, Smithfield, October 11 and 12, 1897, pp. 4–5.
43. Meeting of company officials reported in A.S.R.S. 'General Secretary's Report to the A.G.M., 1898'. *R.R.*, November 12, 1897; L.N.W.R. Board Meeting, November 19, 1897, Minute 15481 and L. and Y. Railway General Purposes Committee of the Board of Directors, November 10, 1897, Minute 6548. Advice to companies to combine given in *Railway News*, October 9, 1897, p. 527.
44. G.C.R. Board Minutes, November 19, 1897, Minute 168, G.W.R. Board Minutes, December 16, 1897, Minute 22.
45. G.C.R. Board Minutes, December 3, 1897, Minute 194.
46. *R.R.*, December 10, 1897, *Railway Times*, December 11, 1897, p. 871.
47. A.S.R.S. General Secretary's Report to the A.G.M. 1908, p. 50.
48. *R.R.*, December 3, 1897.
49. *The Times*, December 4, 1897.
50. *R.R.*, December 10, 1897.
51. A.S.R.S. E.C., December 1897, Rs. 46–55.
52. *R.R.*, April 1, 1898.
53. *Daily Chronicle*, December 4, 1897. *Manchester Guardian*, December 6, 1897.
54. *Railway News*, December 4, 1897, p. 844.
55. Census of England and Wales, 1901; Census of Ireland, 1901, A.S.R.S. Report and Financial Statement, 1898.
56. *R.R.*, November 26, 1897.
57. L.N.W.R. Board Meeting, December 17, 1897, Minute 15522.
58. Tevenan's letter in P.R.O. M.T. 6/808. File 13907 of 1897, subsequent developments recorded in *R.R.*, December 17, 1897.

59. A.S.R.S. General Secretary's Report to the E.C., March 1898, p. 6. *Cork Daily Herald*, January 24, 1898.
60. Richard Bell mentioned this at a meeting of the strikers, *Cork Daily Herald*, January 28, 1898.
61. *Cork Daily Herald*, January 26, 1898.
62. *Cork Daily Herald*, January 29, 1898.
63. A.S.R.S. General Secretary's reports to the E.C., March and June 1898, *Cork Daily Herald*, February 3, 1898.
64. A.S.R.S. General Secretary's reports to the E.C., March and June 1898, *Cork Daily Herald*, March 10, 1898.
65. *R.R.*, May 20, 1898.
66. A.S.R.S. E.C. June 1898, R. 57.
67. A.S.R.S. E.C. June 1898, R. 53. See also A.S.R.S. 'The Strike of the Midland Draymen and Goods Workers at Leeds and Sheffield' Special Meeting of the E.C., April 17, 1898. Verbatim Report 125 pp.
68. A.S.R.S. General Secretary's Report to the A.G.M. 1908, p. 50.
69. Letter quoted in A.S.R.S. General Secretary's Report to the A.G.M. 1898, p. 4.
70. Details of correspondence on the subject of victimization taken from a bundle of files of the Railway Department of the Board of Trade 13525 of 1899, consulted by courtesy of the Public Record Office.
71. A.S.R.S. E.C., March 1898, pp. 43–8; June 1898, pp. 71–5; September 1898, pp. 48–50; December 1898, pp. 48–50.
72. A.S.R.S. E.C. reports for 1898 as above, and L.N.W.R. Railway 'Cautions Book' and 'Punishment Book' for the 1890's, consulted by permission of the British Transport Commission Historical Archives Department.
73. The drafts of the letters are in P.R.O. M.T. 6/911. File 1454 of 1899.
74. A.S.R.S. General Secretary's Report to the A.G.M. 1899, p. 4.
75. A.S.R.S. General Office Accounts for the years 1898–1901, sub-heading Protection Fund Account.

CHAPTER VIII

THE A.S.R.S. AND THE LABOUR PARTY:
TAFF VALE

'The very existence of trade unions is at the mercy of political action. Political action could render trade unionism powerless, or it could make it all powerful. Political action could solve the labour problem for ever, or it could make the labourer a slave in name and in fact. Political action could give us all that we shout for from the trade union platform or it could damn our movement for years to come.'
From a leading article in the Railway Review, *November 25, 1898.*

I

THE A.S.R.S. played a greater part than any other trade union in the formation of the Labour Party. The first stage of the process was deliberately planned—it was an A.S.R.S. sponsored resolution at the Plymouth Congress of the T.U.C. in 1899 which led to the setting up of the Labour Representation Committee in the following year. In the second and third stages the union became involved, quite unintentionally, in two legal decisions of immense importance, the Taff Vale and Osborne Judgments, which ultimately served greatly to strengthen the foundations laid at Plymouth. The role of the A.S.R.S. in these dramatic events is the subject of this chapter.

In its early days the union had been nurtured by prominent members of the Liberal Party. Mr M. T. Bass, M.P., Dr Baxter Langley, Canon Jenkins, Samuel Morley, M.P., and Mr P. S. MacLiver, M.P.—to mention but a few of its supporters—were all well-known adherents of the Liberal cause. Each of the four General Secretaries who served the union in the nineteenth century believed that the interests of railway labour could best be served by the lobbying of sympathetically minded Liberal M.P.s and the support of Liberal candidates at election times. We have seen that as early as 1873, F. W. Evans, who was then secretary of the Bristol branch, campaigned on behalf of the Liberal Railway Director Sir Edward Watkin, in a by-election at Exeter. Seven years later Evans, now General

Secretary, used his Liberal contacts in Parliament to secure substantial modifications of the Employers' Liability Act. His successor, Edward Harford, resorted to much the same tactics to secure amendments to the Railway Regulation (Hours of Labour) Bill in 1892–3.

In those few constituencies where the members of one trade union formed a substantial fraction of the electorate it was possible for trade unionists to stand directly for Parliament and to secure election, provided the goodwill of the constituency Liberal Party was obtained. In the Parliament of 1892–5 there were no less than ten 'Lib.-Lab.' M.P.s— trade-union leaders whose candidatures had been sponsored by the divisional organizations of the Liberal Party. Particularly by those who had been successful at the polls, this was regarded as an eminently sensible arrangement, for the 'Lib.-Lab.' M.P.s had the backing of the Liberal Party machine whilst their unions paid them adequate salaries (since there was no State payment of M.P.s until 1911). These men thought it folly to jettison an alliance with the party which, in most parts of the country, obtained the lion's share of the working class votes. At that time most of them would have been unseated if they had stood independently of the two main political parties.

The absence of railwaymen 'Lib.-Lab.' M.P.s in the nineteenth-century Parliaments was not due to Evans and Harford having different views on Parliamentary representation from those held by their colleagues in the T.U.C. For most of the period the union was too numerically weak to have a significantly large group of members in one constituency and in any case, railway employment was far more scattered than was employment in the coal mines or the cotton mills. It was not for want of trying that Evans and Harford found no entry into the House of Commons. Harford got himself adopted as a Liberal candidate for Blackburn in April 1891, but withdrew when he realized how meagre were his chances of success in a safe Tory seat.[1] Three years later he was adopted as Liberal candidate for Northampton but was unsuccessful in the by-election of July 1895, because the working class vote was split between Harford, J. M. Robertson (a radical follower of Charles Bradlaugh) and the outright Socialist, F. G. Jones, sponsored by the Social Democratic Federation.

In their approach to Parliamentary matters the leaders of the A.S.R.S. were on common ground with other trade-union leaders of their day. Those trade unionists who had acquired socialist convictions and who favoured independent labour representation in Parliament were strongly distrusted by the 'Lib.-Labs.' of the old school. At the 1889 Congress of the T.U.C., Mr C. Convey of Wakefield, an election agent of the Lib.-Lab. M.P., Mr Ben Pickard, declared that his constituents 'would not be willing to accept the gospel of Keir Hardie'. Whilst Mr Pickard 'might not see eye to eye with the Socialists' he [Mr Convey] could assure his hearers that if he *did* 'he would not be member for the Normanton Division'. He went on to deny 'that the Socialist Party had any right to dictate to Mr Pickard what line of Parliamentary conduct he should pursue'. His assertion that all the Socialists really wanted was to occupy 'a house [i.e. the T.U.C.] that has been built up by somebody else', was greeted with laughter and applause.[2] Such formidable distrust of 'doctrinaire' Socialism had to be largely overcome before there could be acceptance of a policy of supporting independent Labour candidatures for Parliament.

By the time of Harford's candidature for Northampton, the rank and file of the union had become much more interested in party politics than was the case ten years earlier when, in response to a circular from head office, only 3,335 members had favoured direct A.S.R.S. representation in Parliament. One sign of awakening interest in the subject was to be seen in the correspondence columns of the *Railway Review* from March to June 1889. Another was the adoption by the A.G.M. at Hull in October of the same year of a declaration in favour of direct A.S.R.S. representation in Parliament—though the resolution was only carried by the narrow majority of two votes, and when Congress turned to consider the means of supporting a railwayman M.P.—a Parliamentary fund—it was tactfully decided to proceed to next business.[3] The delegates to the A.G.M. held in Birmingham in October 1891 again endorsed the principle of direct representation of railwaymen in Parliament and ruled that branches of the union could nominate Parliamentary candidates from whom *one* was to be chosen by means of a secret ballot of the whole membership. Full time officials of the union were not to be eligible. The strength of the opposition to increased participation in politics was, however, revealed in the rejection by a majority of two, of a proposal to establish a compulsory political levy.[4] In the following year, at London, Congress was more clear cut in its decisions. Harford was to be the official A.S.R.S. candidate and he was to be given clerical assistance to enable him to combine the work of an M.P. with that of General Secretary of the union.

By the summer of 1894 when Harford was officially supported by the Liberals in Northampton, feeling in the union on the pros and cons of Lib.-Lab. candidatures had greatly intensified. Opposition to Harford's policy came from two different quarters. In Lancashire, which was in the 1890's a stronghold of both Anglicanism and Conservatism, seven branches and the District Council passed resolutions protesting against Harford standing as a Liberal candidate. Five other branches in other counties took a similar line for the similar reason that their members were in the habit of voting for Conservative rather than Liberal candidates. The consensus of opinion in these conservatively minded branches was that Harford should not expect to get the best of both worlds. If he wanted to stand for election he ought to resign the office of General Secretary. At the other extreme, thirteen branches criticized Harford for not standing as an *independent* Labour candidate. Opposition from this quarter revealed the existence already of some I.L.P. influence within the A.S.R.S.; the Independent Labour Party established in Bradford in 1893 being committed to a policy of independent Labour representation in Parliament.[5]

Thereafter the influence of the I.L.P. within the union greatly increased until its policy was decisively endorsed by the delegates to the A.G.M.s of 1898 and 1899. There were signs that already in October 1894 the President, Mr W. Hudson, was sympathetic to the I.L.P. point of view. He advised the delegates assembled in the Town Hall in Newport (Mon.) to 'raise one common standard for the cause of labour . . . alone clear and distinct from either of the two political parties'.

The ablest member of the I.L.P. at that Congress was, however, Tom Peacock, the delegate from Newcastle who successfully intervened in the debate to defeat (by 26 votes to 17) a resolution that Harford's candidature at Northampton should be supported 'irrespective of either political party'. A short while after, Peacock moved and carried by 27 votes to 21, a resolution that Harford's candidature be declared valid only if he remained completely independent of both the major political parties. Peacock's final triumph that day was to carry, by the overwhelming majority of 42 votes to 2, a resolution which stressed the independent character of *all* A.S.R.S. candidates.[6]

The Socialist influence in the trade councils and among some of the smaller unions was increasing to such an extent that the moderates in the T.U.C. became alarmed. At the 1895 Congress the Lib.-Labs. succeeded in gaining approval for new standing orders by which at future congresses the voting strength of the unions would be strictly proportional to their membership (the bloc vote) and trades councils and independent politicians would be excluded from participation. This decision was a blow to the I.L.P. faction within the A.S.R.S. which was aiming at converting the T.U.C. to its policy of independent Labour representation in Parliament as it was a well-known fact that the textile workers' unions and the miners, which had the largest membership figures, were Conservative or Lib.-Lab. in their politics. That opinion was divided within the A.S.R.S. was revealed by Harford's welcome to the T.U.C.'s decision and his comment that the speeches of the 1896 Congress of the T.U.C. were 'practical and not dreamy',[7] now that the socialist politicians and the representatives of the trades councils were excluded.

Although, at the A.G.M. held in Manchester in 1895, the Socialists and their supporters among the delegates carried by a majority of two votes a resolution that the union should maintain its political fund to finance Parliamentary candidates,[8] the battle was far from being won. In his annual report of 1895, Harford asserted that:

'. . . direct labour representation has nothing to gain by wantonly ignoring, much less repudiating, the political party willing to co-operate with us for a common object.'[9]

Little progress was made by the reformers in 1896 and the early part of 1897. There was no major discussion on Parliamentary representation at the A.G.M. in October 1896.

After October 1896, however, some able members of the I.L.P. secured election to the E.C. They included T. R. Steels (Doncaster), E. Bancroft (Stockport), B. Kirkby (Batley), J. Turton (Southport), and K. J. Perry (Stratford, East London). Together with J. Miller of Parkhead, Glasgow, who had been elected in the previous year they formed nearly half the committee.[10] Through their ability and determination they were able to win sufficient support from the other members of the committee to carry the day on a number of important occasions. At the June E.C. in 1897, in defiance of official opposition, Steels carried a proposal that in place of the old method of the Executive Committee and General Secretary choosing the union's representatives to the T.U.C., such delegates should in future be elected by the whole body of the membership on the basis of one delegate for every 10,000 members. In October of the same year the A.G.M. approved this change by thirty-five votes to five. This change was an essential precondition for the success achieved at the Plymouth T.U.C. two years later, as the Socialists on the E.C. of the A.S.R.S. rightly calculated that the new method of election of A.G.M. delegates would bring to the front the members of the I.L.P. in the union who were more coherent and outspoken than the general run of the membership.

The I.L.P. faction in the union went on to achieve even greater successes in 1898 and 1899. They were undoubtedly helped by the appointment in April 1898 of George J. Wardle as editor of the *Railway Review* since he strongly supported their cause in its leader columns. From September 9, 1898, regular contributions appeared in the paper from a keen socialist advocate of independent labour representation who, although he passed under the pseudonym of 'The Candid Friend' was not 'candid' enough to disclose his identity until March 14, 1902! Mr Philip Snowden—for such was 'Candid Friend's' real name—pointed out that trade unionists had been 'content to try to get what they wanted by forcing unwilling hands to do it'.

'The trade unions are the mediums through which labour has collective voice. Let the trade unions then, form a political party to do the political work required for the emancipation of labour.'[11]

For two months in the winter of 1898-9 a battle was fought in the correspondence columns of the *Railway Review* between E.C. member Steels, who claimed that the best policy for organized labour to pursue was to hold itself 'entirely aloof from both the great political parties' and to return independent members to the House of Commons, and 'Franchise' who argued that when the workers desired their own emancipation they could have it 'without a single direct representative' since 'the government in power be it Tory or Liberal could not refuse demands which were just and right'.[12] Most of the correspondents who wrote down their views following the conclusion of this single combat thought that Steels had had the better of the argument.[13]

Furthermore, the course of events in the industrial world seemed to bear out the contentions of the reformers who were arguing that employers were combining both inside and outside Parliament, and it was therefore necessary for labour to secure a truly independent voice in the House of Commons. From its foundation in 1893 the National Free Labour Association, with the financial backing of the Shipping Federation—an association of the principal shipowners formed in 1890—was supplying employers in a large variety of industries with replacement labour for men out on strike. When the Employers' Federation of Engineering Associations was founded on Tyneside in 1896 it had but thirteen employer members. When the Federation was reorganized in the winter of 1898 it had 290 members pledged to help each other in resisting wage demands.[14] After a meeting held in London on November 15, 1899, the Employers Parliamentary Council was formed to organize employer M.P.s to defend their economic interest in legislation. Less than a fortnight later a large munitions firm placed £35,000 at the disposal of the new organization.[15]

The defeat of the All-Grades Movement of 1897 helped to convert some members of the A.S.R.S. to the State socialist programme of the I.L.P., and the long drawn out character of the negotiations with the Board of Trade on the victimization question seemed to some to underline the importance of independent Labour representation in Parliament.

In the first five years of the history of their party, the propagandists of the I.L.P. had not made much headway in South Wales. Most of the miners there kept their allegiance to the Liberal Party. In the spring and summer of 1898, however, the Welsh colliers fought a bitter and unsuccessful strike against the sliding scale, a scheme by which wage rates fluctuated with changes in the price of coal. In Leeds on October 6th that year, a smartly dressed 23-year-old delegate from Newport (Mon.), J. H. Thomas by name, speaking for the first, but by no means the last, time at an A.G.M. of the A.S.R.S., told of his experiences as chairman of a relief committee. He reminded his hearers that it was the refusal of the leading colliery owner of the district, Sir William T. Lewis, a prominent Liberal, to accept arbitration, which caused the strike to drag on for twenty-one weeks at the cost of near starvation to the miners' families. The dispute had cost the A.S.R.S. £12,000 in donation benefit paid to South Wales railwaymen thrown out of employment by the coal strike. In the 1895 General Election the colliers had enthusiastically hauled the carriage of one Liberal candidate, Mr Clifford Cory, a distance of seven miles. Yet when the coal strike was over this same gentleman was the first to offer his congratulations to Sir William T. Lewis.[16] These experiences helped to increase I.L.P. membership amongst both miners and railwaymen in the area.

The votes of the delegates from Wales were invaluable as tipping the scales in favour of a resolution which was carried by the A.G.M. of the A.S.R.S. on October 5, 1898:

'That the time has now arrived when the A.S.R.S. should be directly represented in Parliament by the General Secretary, who shall be *independent of either political parties*, and when engaged at the House of Commons his duties at the General Office shall be performed by the Assistant Secretary, and additional temporary assistance engaged at the General Office if necessary. The election expenses to be paid from the funds of the Society assisted by voluntary subscriptions'.[17] (*Our italics.*)

It looked at first as if a by-election at Rotherham would provide the earliest opportunity for the implementation of this resolution. On the day after it had been passed, Conference accepted unanimously a suggestion from the Rotherham Trades Council that the union should provide a candidate. Richard Bell was chosen. But the plan misfired. Just over a week later the *Railway Review* reported that the members of Trades Council had had second thoughts and had decided that there was 'insufficient time to wage a successful campaign in the borough'. Mr Bell was, no doubt, greatly relieved. Had he contested the election it would have been a three-cornered fight—a prospect he did not relish since he was a radical Liberal rather than a Socialist.

The decisions of the A.G.M. were thoroughly disliked by the London District Council of the union. In the London area trade unionists and Fabians such as Sidney Webb, had a friendly understanding with the Liberals and co-operated with them to return 'Progressive' candidates in the local elections. At its meeting on October 18, 1898, therefore, the London District Council appointed a deputation of four of its members 'to interview the official whips of the Tory, Liberal-Unionist and Liberal Parties', to discover their attitude in respect of working-men M.P.s. On November 8th, the deputation was interviewed in the House of Commons. The Tory Whips declared that, before being accepted as one of their Parliamentary candidates, Mr Bell would have to agree to the party programme and be accepted by the local Conservative Association. The Liberal Whips were tactful enough not to require such definite pledges. They offered to find Bell a constituency and left him a free hand as to his programme provided he could obtain the support of a constituency party.[18] There is no record of any interview with the Liberal-Unionists.

When the E.C. met on December 5, 1898, it discovered that the initiative taken by the London District Council was strongly resented by the Southport and Wigan branches and it proceeded to pass a strongly worded condemnation of the L.D.C. for its 'irresponsible and unauthorized action' which was 'a violation of the letter and spirit' of A.G.M. decisions.

The A.S.R.S. Parliamentary representative 'must hold himself absolutely independent of both political parties'. This decisive rap on the knuckles was followed, in March 1899, by Steels's drafting for the Doncaster branch a resolution for submission to the next T.U.C. to be held in Plymouth in September 1899. This historic declaration was worded as follows:

'That this Congress, having regard to its decisions of former years, and with a view to securing a better representation of the interests of labour in the House of Commons, hereby instructs the Parliamentary Committee to invite the co-operation of all the co-operative, socialistic, trade union and other working organizations to jointly co-operate on lines mutually agreed upon, in convening a special congress of representatives from such of the above named organizations as may be willing to take part to devise ways and means for securing the return of an increased number of labour members in the next Parliament.'[19]

The surprising thing was that every member of the E.C. voted for this resolution except W. G. Loraine of West Hartlepool, who voted against. But the support which known Lib.-Labs. such as Green and Tye gave the resolution is perhaps explained by the vague phrase 'an increased number of labour members'. Steels had carefully avoided including that uncomfortable word 'independent'.

When James Holmes, A.S.R.S. organizer for South Wales and the West Country, was chosen as one of the union's delegates to the T.U.C., Steels's resolution was ensured an enthusiastic backing. Holmes was an I.L.P. member and perhaps the ablest speaker the railwaymen possessed.

Yet the prospects did not at first appear at all bright when at an early stage of the proceedings at Plymouth, Congress gave an unfavourable reception to a proposal that each affiliated union should contribute $\frac{1}{2}$d per member towards a Parliamentary Election Fund. Holmes and James Sexton (from Liverpool) who moved and seconded the A.S.R.S. resolution had little hope that it was going to be carried. Though Holmes spoke eloquently, Mr Ashton from the floor declared confidently that not one trade unionist out of ten thousand would take any notice of his proposal. Another opponent declared that though the sponsors of the resolution had worked like horses they talked like asses. When the President began to announce the result of the voting there was a breathless silence. He slowly read: 'Five hundred and forty-six thousand for the resolution, against four—' but he got no further. The next moment men were on their chairs raising their hats and cheering with indescribable enthusiasm. It was only considerably later that most delegates learned that the vote against the resolution was 434,000.[20] The first phase of a long battle for independent Labour representation in Parliament had been won through the determined leadership of the socialists in the A.S.R.S.

II

The events of the next twelve months were to show that the battle was by no means over. The narrow victory of the Socialists at Plymouth was a reminder that many trade unionists remained unconvinced of the wisdom of forming a distinct and independent group of M.P.s in the House of Commons. In the interval of five months between the T.U.C.'s acceptance of Holmes's resolution and the London Conference which formed the Labour Representation Committee, the Annual Report of the powerful Yorkshire Miners' Association was published. It was indicative of the sort of obstacles that had yet to be overcome:

'We should like to ask our members why we should be called upon to join an association having only one object in view, viz. that of providing means for other trades to send representatives to the House of Commons. Why should we be called upon to find money, time or intellect to focus the weaknesses of other trade unionists to do what you are doing for yourselves ?'

The A.S.R.S. was almost alone among the larger unions in being strongly committed to the I.L.P. policy. The attempt of the moderates in the union to reverse earlier decisions was decisively defeated at the A.G.M. at Liverpool in October 1899. The delegates from Derby, where Richard Bell had been adopted as Labour Parliamentary candidate with Liberal support, simply tried to delete the phrase 'independent of either political parties' from the resolution of the previous year. Their action aroused a hornets' nest of opposition from the delegates, culminating in the comment from J. H. Thomas (this year representing Swindon) that 'for a working-man's representative to bind himself to any particular party was suicidal'. At the end of a lively debate the resolution was 'negatived by acclamation, by an overwhelming majority'.[21]

According to the historians of the Labour Party, the members of the A.S.R.S. 'were virtually the sponsors of the Conference',[22] held in the Memorial Hall, Faringdon Street, London, on February 27 and 28, 1900. Certainly one of its delegation of four, G. J. Wardle, editor of the *Railway Review* seconded the vital resolution in favour of 'a distinct labour group in Parliament who shall have their own Whips, and agree upon their policy'.[23] A further sign of the union's involvement was Richard Bell's election to the first Executive Committee of the L.R.C.

The A.S.R.S. was, along with the Gasworkers, the second trade union to affiliate to the L.R.C., being beaten by a short head by the Steel Smelters. It was on March 15, 1900 that Richard Bell wrote to Ramsay MacDonald informing him of the unanimous decision of the E.C., reached the day before, but Hodges, the Steel Smelters' Secretary had written his letter two days earlier. Will Thorne's letter on behalf of the Gasworkers reached Ramsay MacDonald by the same post as the letter from Richard Bell.[24]

However, all the Miners' Associations except that of Lancashire and Cheshire, and all the more important textile-workers' unions remained aloof. At the Memorial Hall Conference there were delegates from less than a third of the trade unionists in the country. When, a year later, in February 1901, the first annual conference of the L.R.C. was held, a prominent delegate from the I.L.P. group, Philip Snowden, was all too well aware of the prevailing 'feeling of despondency' of the meeting. 'It looked as if this new effort was going to share the fate of previous attempts to secure the direct representation of labour.'[25] Something was needed to shake the majority of the trade-union leaders out of their complacency, and it was the action of members of the A.S.R.S. on the Taff Vale Railway in South Wales which provided the stimulus.

III

On August 14, 1890, when Mr J. Inskip, the Chairman of the Taff Vale Railway, had spoken from the same platform as Mr Harford on the value of co-operation with the A.S.R.S., industrial relations on that railway had been as harmonious as on any railway in the country.[26] Ten years later they could scarcely have been worse.

One reason for this deterioration was a change in the management. With the change in management went a change in the directors' policy concerning union recognition. Ammon Beasley, who became General Manager of the company in November 1891, was described by *The Times*'s industrial correspondent as a 'strong man' whose characteristic fault was 'a stiffness of backbone' which could be carried to extremes.[27] Whilst Mr Beasley was ready at all times to meet grade deputations of the company's employees, he did not like trade unions. He believed they already had too great an influence and he determined to deprive them of any part in negotiations on conditions of service. Had Mr Inskip remained as Chairman it is likely that he would have curbed the anti-union policy of the General Manager, but unfortunately he resigned his position soon after Mr Beasley's arrival. From 1895 onward the office of Chairman was held by Mr R. L. G. Vassall, a man who was 'most decidedly' of the opinion that it would be unwise of the directors to recognize the union in any way, since he believed trade unions were 'a very pernicious body as regards railway companies'.[28] With men of these opinions in the key posts it is scarcely surprising that there were frequent rumblings of discontent on the company's lines in the period 1893–1900. In addition the area was such an industrial 'house that Jack built' that the coal strikes of 1893 and 1898 seriously depleted the railway companies' revenues and brought severe hardship to the railwaymen as well as the miners. As soon as the 1893

coal strike began the company issued a circular announcing the abandonment of the guaranteed 60-hour week introduced in the agreement of
August 1890. Although the coal strike was practically at an end by September 9th, the guaranteed week was not restored until many weeks later and
Mr Beasley refused to convene the Standing Committee of the men. He
subsequently tried to justify his decision not to summon the committee
by saying that he found it really consisted of 'delegates and representatives
of the Amalgamated Society'.[29] Angry mass meetings of the railway
employees were held in Cardiff on September 17, October 22 and December 3 and 10, 1893, when protests were made against arbitrary dismissals of
a number of men. A resolution passed on December 3rd referred to Mr
Beasley's assertion that 'the whole staff was combined in an endeavour to
frustrate his management' as a 'most unwarrantable accusation'.[30]

In May 1895, further angry meetings were held because 120 men—
more than a tenth of the labour force—had been dismissed whilst 238
men were working over sixty hours a week. On this occasion the directors,
prompted by a resolution carried at a mass meeting of the men, gave way
and agreed to take back the dismissed men.[31] Just over three months
later, however, there began a five weeks' strike of the company's fitters
in protest against new piecework rates which had not been negotiated
with the Amalgamated Society of Engineers to which most of the men
belonged.

Behind the economy drive and the imposition of a more rigid labour
discipline was Mr Beasley's concern to improve the financial position of
his company. From the time of its opening in 1840 until the emergence of a
serious competitor—the Barry Railway—in 1889, the Taff Vale Railway
had been a gold mine to its shareholders. No other important railway in the
country paid such consistently high dividends. In the ten years before
Mr Beasley's appointment they had averaged $12\frac{3}{4}$ per cent a year. So
profitable had been the concern, that in 1889 a conversion of the ordinary
stock was effected, holders of every £100 of the old stock being given £250
of new stock in exchange. But the competition from the Barry Railway and
to a lesser extent from the Rhymney Railway, knocked the gilt off the Taff
Vale dividends, since Taff Vale Railway coal freights had to be brought
down from $\frac{3}{4}$d to $\frac{1}{2}$d a ton mile if custom was not to be lost.[32] In 1891, the
year when Mr Beasley took over the management, the ordinary dividend
had fallen to $2\frac{1}{4}$ per cent (equal to $5\frac{5}{8}$ per cent on the old stock) and working
expenses equalled 59 per cent of gross receipts. Egged on by a share-
holders' committee under the leadership of Mr George White, Mr Beasley
succeeded in forcing down working expenses to 57·7 per cent by the end of
1899, making it possible to raise the dividend to a level equal to $8\frac{1}{8}$ per cent
on the old stock.[33]

When trouble again brewed up on the line in the winter of 1899–1900
the country was at war with the Boers. The coal of South Wales was in

great demand for the ships of the fleet and its price soared from 8s 10½d a ton at the end of 1897 to 18s 6d two years later. By the summer of 1900 it sold at between 25s and 30s a ton, but the railway companies were still carrying it for 8d a ton for the average run of sixteen miles from the pits to the docks—just as they had done in 1897. In so far as there was an economic cause of the Taff Vale strike in August 1900, it sprang from the failure of the Directors of the Rhymney Railway to seek a modification of a twenty-one year agreement to carry the coal and iron ore of the Cyfarthfa and Dowlais companies at specified rates.[34] Neither the Barry Railway nor the Taff Vale could raise their freight charges for coal, for all three railways were in competition and an increase in their rates above the level charged by the Rhymney Railway would have led to a loss of custom and to merchants complaining to the Railway Commissioners. There were reasonable grounds for some increase in the freight rates, and had the railway companies co-operated to put pressure on the mining companies it is fair to assume that they could have won the right to charge more. From an increased revenue they could then have paid their men better wages. But the Taff Vale Railway Directors whose wagons carried three-quarters of the eighteen million tons of coal mined in the area[35] had most traffic to lose and were not on good terms with the Directors of the Rhymney Railway. The result was that in this war-time boom colliers were getting better pay, coal owners (at least temporarily) enormous profits and shipowners were reaping higher freights. Only the railwaymen stood largely unbenefited.

The sharp rise in the cost of living in the first nine months of the war provided the spur for the renewed agitation of the South Wales railwaymen in the winter of 1899–1900. On August 15, 1900, Mr Holmes, in an A.S.R.S. circular distributed in the area, claimed that the average railway-man's living expenses had risen by 5s a week since the war began.[36]

Despite the fact that Mr Vassall attributed the agitation which began in September 1899 entirely to 'the movements of the Society'[37] there is much evidence that it originated as a rank and file movement under the leader-ship of a Taff Vale signalman, Moses Jones. However, in the first phase of the movement up to March 1900, the movement was supervised, if not initiated, by Mr Bell and the E.C.

At a mass meeting held in Cardiff on October 1, 1899, a Joint Com-mittee of all grades employed on the Barry, Rhymney, Taff Vale and Cardiff Railways was elected. By the end of the month the men had achieved such a good state of organization that Richard Bell gave his sanction to the joint and simultaneous presentation of demands of all four of the railway companies. Each of the general managers received a letter on November 16th containing proposals for improved rates of pay for the principal grades. Thus guards were to rise from 26s to 33s after six years' service, brakesmen from 20s to 25s after five years, whilst all signalmen's wages were to be advanced by 3s a week and twenty-three signal cabins were to be upgraded from ten hours to eight hours. The only replies received to this letter were simple acknowledgments from the Rhymney and Cardiff Railways. The Taff Vale and Barry Railways sent no reply.

The E.C. considered the situation in South Wales at its meeting in December 1899, and instructed the Secretary to offer to submit the questions in dispute to arbitration. If the companies failed to reply within six days a ballot on the question of strike action would be taken. As the four companies replied at the end of the year with acknowledgments only, a mass meeting of 1,800 men was held at Park Hall, Cardiff, on January 14, 1900, at which it was decided, with only two dissentients, that unless the companies agreed to meet representatives of their employees within seven days, notices would be handed in. Again the companies replied with simple acknowledgments; there was no offer to meet deputations or to resort to arbitration.

This was undoubtedly the tactical moment for an effective strike. Richard Bell told a packed and enthusiastic meeting of the men on January 28th that from the notice papers handed in to him, from 91 to 97 per cent of the men employed by the four companies were in favour of a strike. Had these notices been handed in to the companies there would have been effective control over the movement and breaches of contract would have been avoided. But Bell advised the meeting to give the companies another 'seven to ten days' to reconsider their position. The meeting reluctantly agreed.

When the Barry and Rhymney Directors learned from Bell of the impatience of the men they agreed to meet their deputations on February 1st and 2nd. The Directors of the Cardiff Railway agreed to see a deputation later that month. As an outcome of these discussions wage increases of up to 4s a week were granted to signalmen and some other grades. Although Mr Beasley met deputations of signalmen, brakesmen and guards employed on his line on February 9th, and small concessions were made to some of the guards and signalmen, the basic increases of 2s a week and the 8-hour day were refused. Thus the position at the beginning of March was that on three of the railways important concessions had been made; the demands of the Taff Vale men were largely unsatisfied.

A large meeting of the men on March 11th, therefore, decided that if at least 90 per cent of the employees on the four lines voted by ballot in favour of a strike by March 19th, strike notices would be handed in. By now, however, the psychological moment had passed and a number of the men had already received advances in their wages. It is not surprising that when the result of the ballot was announced by Mr Bell on March 22nd, the percentage favouring a strike fell to between 72 and 81—below the 90 per cent minimum agreed to eleven days earlier. The E.C. passed a resolution deprecating the result of the ballot which it said reflected 'no credit on those affected'. For just over three months less was heard of the South Wales movement.[38]

During this quieter period the Joint Committee must have reflected on the effects of Richard Bell's intervention. The more ardent of its members regretted that they had not taken the bull by the horns on January 28th when over 90 per cent of the men were willing to strike. They resolved that when the spirit of militancy returned to the district they would manage the movement themselves, not waiting for the consent of the General Secretary or the E.C. The one official of the union they did greatly respect was James Holmes, the local organizer, who by his energy and eloquence had brought large numbers of the men into the union and had had a lot to do with the successes on the Barry and Rhymney Railways in February and March.

The immediate occasion for the outbreak of the Taff Vale strike on August 19, 1900, was the treatment given to one of the employees, Signalman Ewington of Abercynon, who was 45 years of age, had served the company for twenty years and had an excellent record. However, he was a leading member of the A.S.R.S. in the district and in February and March headed deputations of his grade which were interviewed by Mr Beasley. On April 28th, Ewington was told by his stationmaster that he would have to move to another signal box at Treherbert about sixteen miles from his present home. The company claimed that this was a normal promotion move since the pay at the Treherbert box was 2s a week above that of the box at Abercynon. Ewington did not wish to move. Financially he would, in fact, have been worse off on balance since at Abercynon he was doing two secretarial jobs in his spare time which brought him in an extra 5s a week.[39] Far more important, however, was his domestic situation. In a letter to Mr Harland, superintendent of the line, he pointed out that he had ten children all under 17 years of age and that as his wife was unwell, three of his relatives were helping to look after the youngest of the family. He pleaded to be allowed to stay where he was. His stationmaster was, however, informed by Mr Harland that it was 'not a question of what Ewington wishes' but that he was 'required to move to Treherbert . . . and must be removed forthwith'.[40]

Shortly afterwards Ewington fell sick with rheumatic fever and was not able to return to work until July 24, 1900. In the meantime both his old post at Abercynon and the post at Treherbert had been filled. When he was interviewed at the Superintendent's office, Mr Harland told him that he had brought his troubles on himself and that he should be ashamed of himself for continually causing disturbances amongst his fellow workmen. Not being satisfied with his treatment, Ewington applied for an interview with the directors who saw him, together with two of his mates, on August 11th, and offered him the post of sick relief signalman covering seventeen boxes in the Aberdare valley at the same wage as he was receiving before he was ill. He did not consider this post was as good as the one at Abercynon even though he could still live in the same town; and when he asked the members of the Joint Committee they advised him to refuse the directors' offer. He therefore wrote to the directors asking to be restored to his old post. If at first glance, it appears that Ewington was making a 'mountain out of a molehill', that, after all, he had not been dismissed and he was not being asked to accept any reduction in wages, that it was scarcely justifiable to bring the trade of the area to a standstill just because of the supposed grievance of one man, it is worth bearing in mind other facts of the situation.

When the whole incident was investigated in detail before Mr Justice Wills in the King's Bench Division in December 1902, Mr Beasley and the counsel for the prosecution failed to produce—though they were invited to do so—two witnesses, Messrs Ponsford and Black, who could have helped to elucidate the management's reasons for wanting to move Ewington in April 1900. They also declared that an important letter from Mr Harland to Mr Ponsford had been 'lost'. In his summing up of the case, Mr Justice Wills stated that he did not think that Ewington's claim to have been victimized was satisfactorily denied by the witnesses for the prosecution. He saw in the incident 'a great deal of the sort of thing which would raise the strongest feelings on behalf of the men'.

Further, it was not the normal practice of Taff Vale management either to *oblige* a man to accept a promotion (in such cases the job would be offered to the next in line of promotion) or to make a permanent appointment in the place of a sick man.

No doubt it would have been conducive to peace if Ewington had followed the advice of both Mr Bell and Mr Holmes and had given the job of relief signalman a trial for a month, as agreed by the company. But the members of the Joint Committee, being familiar with earlier cases of victimization, were convinced that in this case also an injustice had been done. Their general feeling was: 'Here is a man who has put forward our case and has acted for us, and now he is suffering and we will stand by him.'

Considered on its own, and given a satisfactory machinery for joint consultation between employers and employed, it is unlikely that there would have been a strike over the Ewington case. Superimposed on a sense of grievance through unsatisfied wage claims it helped to fan the flames of revolt.

On July 29, 1900, the movement to secure better wages and shorter hours on the Taff Vale Railway was resumed when at a public meeting held in Pontypridd a resolution in favour of a 2s a week rise for signalmen and a $\frac{1}{2}$d an hour increase for brakesmen, shunters and guards was enthusiastically carried. The meeting also resolved that notices would be handed in if Ewington was not reinstated in his old position by August 6th.

Mr Holmes, in a stirring speech, said that if the men had any grit they would not allow the company to defeat them again. 'It was not a matter of intelligence but courage', he said.

Nevertheless there was a danger that the men, acting impetuously, would fail to act together. In a letter to the *South Wales Daily News* a week later, Holmes advised the men to delay handing in notices until August 13th so that they would all go in together. But the men seem to have taken more notice of his remark in a speech reported on another page of the same paper, that the present was a 'golden opportunity' to demand their rights.[42] Contrary to Holmes's advice, 363 notices—representing about 90 per cent of the signalmen, brakesmen and guards but comprising less than a third of those employed by the company—were handed in on August 5th. They were due to expire on the 19th of that month. Four hundred more notices were handed in a week later, but since these were not due to expire until August 26th there could be no simultaneous withdrawal of labour without a breach of contract. Holmes had failed to assert his authority over the movement and to impress on the Joint Committee with sufficient forceful- ness the necessity of the men acting together and keeping on the right side of the law. These shortcomings on the organizer's part distressed Richard Bell who greatly resented Holmes's failure to enforce the union rules (for prior E.C. approval of all handing in of notices) and his failure to keep the movement within legal bounds. When, at a later stage, it came to a trial in the courts, Bell insisted on Holmes's defence being separated from his own.

Even after the notices had been handed in to the company the strike might well have been averted had Mr Beasley been prepared to do one thing—discuss the outstanding differences with Mr Holmes. He allowed a deputation of signalmen to see the directors on August 14th and a deputation of the locomen to meet the directors on the following day; but when asked on August 17th whether he would meet an all-grade depu- tation accompanied by Mr Holmes he replied by wire:

'I am prepared to see any reasonable number of the company's servants and give full and careful consideration . . . but I regret I cannot receive officially or unofficially any person not in the company's service.

Beasley.'[43]

The editor of the principal journal of the railway stockholders was sure that Mr Beasley would sooner have resigned his position than have surrendered on the subject of union recognition.[44]

Mr Holmes made two more efforts for peace. When interviewed by members of the Cardiff Chamber of Commerce on August 15th, he sug- gested that the men's proposals for improved pay and conditions should be submitted to an arbitrator acceptable to both Mr Beasley and himself.

On August 17th, Mr Beasley told the Chamber of Commerce that he could not agree to this proposal. Mr Holmes's second concession—that he would not insist on his accompanying a delegation of the men, provided Mr Beasley would agree to meet one representing all grades—fell through on the following day when the all-grades delegation interviewed by Mr Beasley insisted on having Mr Holmes or Mr Taylor (another A.S.R.S. official) with them before they would negotiate further.[45] In the meantime both the Liberal *South Wales Daily News* and the Conservative *Western Mail* deplored Mr Beasley's refusal to meet Mr Holmes.

Since March 22, 1900, neither Richard Bell nor the E.C. had played any part in the South Wales railwaymen's movement, but when a strike seemed imminent, Mr Bell went down to Cardiff on August 17th, with the backing of Mr Ritchie, President of the Board of Trade, and tried to secure an interview with Mr Vassall, the Taff Vale Chairman. Mr Vassall said 'No'.[46] Returning to London empty handed, Mr Bell called a special meeting of the E.C. for Sunday, August 19th, at 10.0 a.m. That day, with two delegates from the Taff Vale railwaymen present, the committee deliberated for six and a half hours, finally passing by seven votes to five the following resolution:

'The Executive have just decided, after hearing the evidence of the deputation from the Taff Vale railwaymen, and seeing the correspondence relating to the dispute, that they cannot but conclude:

1. That the conduct of the men in taking action prior to obtaining the consent of the Committee was most condemnatory.

2. That by the removal of signalman Ewington the management of the Company have acted arbitrarily and have incited the men to their present act.

3. Having regard to both sides of the issue we, as the Administrators of the Society, decide that every effort be made by the General Secretary and others we may appoint to bring the dispute to a speedy termination.

4. We have, after careful consideration hereby decided to support the men financially.'

Whilst the E.C. was in session in London, James Holmes was telling a mass meeting of 1,300 men at Pontypridd that the arbitration that would now take place would be 'the tribunal of rusty wheels and rusty rails'. Those about to assume picketing duties he advised not to exceed the limits of the law though 'there were many ways of persuading men'. In support of a resolution that the men should stop work as one body at midnight almost every hand in the building was raised. The men had determined to strike irrespective of whether the union's executive decided to give them financial support. It was only after the die was cast that

Holmes, near the conclusion of the meeting, received a telegram containing the E.C.'s decision.

At midnight between August 19th and 20th, 1,227 men went out from the employment of the Taff Vale Railway. Five hundred and sixty-four of them had given no notice and a further 400 inadequate notice. In normal times the company gained 70 per cent of its revenue from coal but in the first three days of the strike no mineral trains ran and even on the last day of the strike, August 31st, only a quarter of the number of the mineral trains normally run was in service, despite the importation into the district of a large number of blacklegs to fill some of the places left vacant by the withdrawal of 98 per cent of the labour force. The strike was undoubtedly the most complete yet organized on any railway in Britain.

When Mr Bell arrived in Cardiff on the morning of the first day of the strike bent on arranging a settlement as quickly as possible, he found the men in a very determined mood. He was a man whose mission was peace at almost any price whilst the powers behind him—the rank and file—were in a warlike mood. Had Mr Beasley been less a man of inflexible principle he would have accepted Mr Bell's offer—made by letter on the afternoon of his arrival in Cardiff—to discuss the conditions for a return to work. In fact the two men never met throughout the whole course of the strike and subsequent settlement.

Before the strike began Mr Beasley had resolved that if he was not able to run his railway with the old labour force he would raise a substitute one, if necessary recruiting men from all parts of the country. He inserted advertisements for men in a large number of newspapers, even sending one to the *Railway Review* which the editor decided to print free of charge! (He added a column expressing the hope that no man or railway company would be foolish enough to aid the Taff Vale Railway.)[47] His main source of supply of 'free' labour was through the company's two guinea a year membership subscription to William Collison's National Free Labour Association in London. Collison undertook to 'break the back of the strike' in forty-eight hours for the modest fee of £100.[48] Had he thought the strike would last longer than two days he would have charged more. As it happened he had a reserve of men collected in anticipation of a strike on the Great Eastern Railway. This had not materialized, and 197 of the men were switched to service on the Taff Vale. When he was cross-questioned about the strike after it was all over, beyond stating that there were 'one or two questions at issue', he could not tell what were the grievances of the men. During the ten years in which his organization had operated he had broken up some 300 strikes and this was merely another incident in the campaign to smash the tyranny of trade unions. Though Mr Collison supplied men from places as far apart as Hull, Glasgow, Manchester and Newcastle the bulk of the men came from London.

Mr. Beasley's determined effort to run his railway with blackleg labour not only incensed the old employees of the company and led some of the more impetuous of them to commit occasional acts of violence and intimidation, but also made it far more difficult to settle the strike.

For many of the blacklegs the strike provided an interesting diversion in an otherwise humdrum life. A free trip to Cardiff with ample free refreshment provided did not come a man's way every day of the week. For ten days a brisk business in inducement and counter-inducement went on, the National Free Labour Association paying all expenses from London and other centres to Cardiff, and the A.S.R.S. meeting all expenses of the 166 men out of the 197 who were persuaded to return to their homes.[49]

Although the Locomotive Superintendent of the company had handbills printed informing all new men that the vacancies had been caused 'in consequence of the staff in the grade having sent in their notices'[50] not all Collison's recruits saw them before being sent to Cardiff. The experience of one of them who spoke with 'a strong Cockney accent' was recorded by a reporter of the *South Wales Daily News* who interviewed him in the Strike Committee room at the Colbourne Hotel:

'I was in a lodging house in Kings Cross Road. A gentleman walked in at half past nine and said: "Do you want work?" I said "Yes". He said: "Come and have a quart of beer." I said: "That's me." So when I went he said: "Have you got any mates?" I said: "Any amount", and I fetched fifteen and we had a good soak of beer and plenty of tobacco. We went by the underground to Addison Road and from Addison Road he gave us a ticket and brought us to Bristol. . . . We got into the train again and came to Cardiff. When we got to Cardiff they locked us in on both sides. A young fellow came up and said: "Do you know what you are doing?" and gave us a bill. I said: "It's a strike!" and then someone shoved him away. . . . The officials asked me to do some labour, and I said: "I don't know how to do it." '

Another group of Londoners were told: 'It's only a trip down to Cardiff; you will be back again in a few days. You don't need to work.' When some protested that they had had no railway experience the gentleman replied: 'It does not matter; we only want the men.'[51]

All the local branches of the A.S.R.S. played a part in organizing the return of the blacklegs. The expenditure of the Penarth branch shows payments for the following items:

'Cab, blackleg to Cardiff; dinners self and clerk; two old drivers to Cardiff and dinners; blackleg and escort to Weston (Super Mare) Pier tolls and refreshments; refreshments for blackleg gang 17 in number, brought from Cardiff to discharge boat.'

Merthyr Tydfil branch books recorded expenses of 'blackleg J. Dawson, 1s 6d; capture of two blacklegs at Merthyr station and escorted to headquarters, Cardiff, 7s 3d'. There is no record of any man being successful in making the free return trip from his home to Cardiff and back more than once!

Those blacklegs who reached the outposts of the Taff Vale system and who were persuaded by the pickets not to take part in the attempt to break the strike, were first sent to Cardiff where they were met by members of the men's committee who then arranged for their return to their homes. On the other hand, a large number of Collison's men got no farther than Cardiff on their outward journey. At 2.0 a.m. on August 23rd, Richard Bell met a group of forty men on the Great Western Railway station at Cardiff on their arrival from London. Since many of them had been unaware that a strike was in progress he had no difficulty in persuading twenty-eight of them to take the next train back to London. After being given 'a good feast' and their return tickets—at the expense of the A.S.R.S. —they were found comfortable seats on the same Great Western Railway coach in which they had come down.[52]

Although Mr Beasley arranged for blacklegs to arrive in the early hours of the morning in the hope that they might escape the attentions of the pickets, his careful planning was of little avail. Each evening strikers placed detonators on the rails at the approaches to Cardiff so that the pickets were warned of the arrival of newcomers by the unholy din that was created.

Throughout the eleven days of the strike, Mr Beasley was a frustrated and angry man. Not only were many of his new recruits slipping through his hands, but it was also a depressing fact that many of those who escaped the attention of the pickets or who remained unmoved by their arguments, were found incapable of performing the tasks assigned them and had to be returned to their homes. After the strike was over Mr Beasley admitted that although 400 men came to Cardiff from all parts of the country and even from Scotland (where a 'Free Labour Federation' recruited men from Glasgow) only 'about 190' were found suitable.[53] To add to his difficulties in running the line, a total of 847 pickets were employed by the union, day and night, each man being paid 6d per shift of eight hours in addition to his usual strike pay. Mr Vassall complained that the pickets were in evidence 'pretty well everywhere where you turned a corner', whilst his locomotive superintendent confirmed that the picketing was 'so very efficiently done' that the loyal men 'could not go anywhere without the pickets were out'.[54]

Because of the daring initiative shown by some of the pickets the working life of a blackleg was not such a bed of roses as some of the Free Labour Agents had led them to believe. Collison described the experience of a harassed locomotiveman:

'On the Taff Vale Railway from Quakers Yard to Abercynon there is a very steep incline with an extraordinary gradient of one in forty, and the mineral trains slow down until they go at a walking pace. Strikers used, in the darkness, to dodge themselves on to the line and besmear the rails at intervals of about one hundred and fifty yards with black grease. When mineral trains were passing they would then, taking advantage of their railway knowledge and the darkness of night, uncouple a wagon here and there in a large train. The result was that when the Free Labour driver put on steam to get up the incline, the wheels of the engine used to skid and revolve as if they had been endowed with perpetual motion. The strikers managed to be near at hand in large numbers to view these gyrations of the wheels of the engine, and used to jeer the Free Labour men unmercifully. The latter could neither go backward nor forward in more senses than one. When they had the line sanded and looked round, they used to get on a bit; but feeling lightness about the trains, that now seemed to go so easily, they would stop the engine and get off to see what was wrong. To their dismay and utter confusion, they would find that instead of the large train they started out with, they had only half a dozen of wagons. . . . But the engine driver's place was at his engine, and thither he would go. But even the engine he would find had taken the dumps, and would not act. Truth to tell some of the strikers had tampered with it during his absence. Little wonder if the poor fellows used to think that they would rather be under a turnkey in Newgate than driving an engine on the Taff Vale Railway.'[55]

Although Mr Bell had warned the strikers that their picketing was to be conducted 'without any violence of any description'[56] and Mr Holmes had advised them not to break the law and on two occasions was himself injured in protecting blacklegs from receiving rough treatment,[57] some of the strikers defied their union leaders and by a few acts of violence did great harm to the union cause.

One of the Taff Vale drivers who did not come out on strike was William Cook. When he went to work on August 21st, eight men got over a fence, rushed on to his engine and tried to force him to put out the fire. Cook caught hold of the string of the whistle and signalled for help. He was rescued by a number of policemen. He claimed that when he was at work again on August 23rd stones and rotten eggs were thrown at him.[58] Most of the other cases complained of by the company were of men being 'watched and beset' without violence, although there were instances of guards, lampmen and signalmen being violently handled.

When Mr Beasley consulted the company's solicitors with a view to gaining an injunction to restrain both Bell and Holmes and the union from 'watching and besetting' the company's premises, the Great Western Railway Station at Cardiff and the non-strikers residences, they advised him that since the passage of the Trade Union Acts of 1871 and 1876 it had been assumed that such an action could not be entertained against a trade union in its registered name. Nevertheless Mr Beasley was determined and optimistic. He believed the acts of violence committed by some of the men and the words of a circular issued under Mr Bell's name would influence legal opinion to grant his wishes. The 'bill' which had been seen by the Cockney interviewed by the reporter of the *South Wales Daily News* was worded as follows:

> '**STRIKE ON THE TAFF VALE RAILWAY**
> Men's Headquarters,
> Cobourn Street,
> Cathays.
>
> There has been a strike on the Taff Vale Railway since Monday last. The management are using every means to decoy men here who they employ for the purpose of blacklegging the men on strike.
> **DRIVERS, FIREMEN, GUARDS, BRAKESMEN
> AND SIGNALMEN ARE ALL OUT.**
> Are you willing to be known as a
> **BLACKLEG?**
>
> If you accept employment on the Taff Vale that is what you will be known by. On arriving at Cardiff, call at the above address where you can get information and assistance.
>
> **RICHARD BELL,**
> General Secretary.'

Mr Beasley knew of the Lyons *v.* Wilkins case which came before the courts between 1896 and 1898 and he was aware that Mr Justice Byrne had ruled that picketing which took the form of 'watching and besetting' was illegal and that to call a man a 'blackleg' was a form of intimidation not permitted by the law.[59] Mr Bell had not only agreed to the use of the term 'blackleg' but also consented to its being printed in capital letters. In any case Mr Beasley thought it was worth trying, and an injunction against Bell, Holmes and the union was applied for on August 23rd.

One form of punishment Mr Beasley could inflict at once. The day the strike began, letters were sent to all strikers who occupied company-owned cottages ordering them to vacate their homes 'forthwith' since contracts with the company had been terminated. These evictions were carried through despite the fact that rents had already been paid for the week commencing August 20th.[60]

In the meantime Richard Bell made strenuous efforts to secure a return to work on honourable conditions. He was anxious to secure a speedy settlement for he was aware that the company had already started legal proceedings against 208 of the men who had broken their contracts. A big obstacle was, however, the refusal of both Mr Vassall and Mr Beasley to meet him to discuss terms. When the Mayor of Cardiff, Councillor S. A. Brain, read of Mr Bell's failure to establish contact with the other side in the dispute he had an interview with some of the Directors of the Taff Vale Railway hoping to persuade them to change their minds. He had no success.

Shortly afterwards, Mr Hopwood of the Board of Trade arrived in Cardiff to mediate in the dispute. His work was helped by the appearance of two letters in *The Times* on August 24th. One was from James Inskip, former Chairman of the Taff Vale Railway who wrote that it was lamentable that the directors had not taken the one step (i.e. negotiation with Mr Bell) which would have averted a daily loss of hundreds of thousands of pounds. The other letter was written by Sir W. T. Lewis, one of the most influential industrialists in Cardiff, who advocated the establishment of a Conciliation Board for the railways of South Wales. After the appearance of these letters the Taff Vale Directors were under strong moral pressure to make some concessions, and on the following day they published their terms for a settlement. They agreed to the question of Signalman Ewington being referred to the Board of Trade for arbitration; they undertook to re-employ as many as possible of the strikers immediately and all of them within two months and to guarantee their full pension rights; the claims of the men would be considered in various grade deputations and the legal proceedings taken against the men would be abandoned.

The stumbling block which led Mr Hopwood to abandon his attempt at mediation and to return to London on August 27th, and which caused the continuation of the strike until the end of the month, was the question of the blacklegs. The company was reluctant to get rid of them all quickly by the payment of compensation; the men's committee would not accept the proposal that some of the blacklegs would continue to be employed on the railway for two months after the strike was over as this would have meant unemployment for the old servants of the company. It was at this point that Sir W. T. Lewis intervened again—an intervention made possible by the fact that the Vice-Chairman of the Taff Vale Railway, Mr Russell Rea, disagreed with the rest of the Board in that he was more favourable to the union. In informal conversations between Mr Bell, Mr Holmes, Mr Rea and Sir W. T. Lewis, the differences between the two parties were narrowed down.[61]

Late at night on August 30th a settlement was reached. The company agreed to take back all the strikers within one month; to accept the Board of Trade's arbitration on Ewington; to guarantee the men's pension rights and to stop all legal proceedings against the strikers. A Conciliation Board was to be set up for the South Wales railways 'if possible' by October 31, 1900, and the claims of the men could then be placed before it.[62] The strike was at an end and normal services were in operation by September 1st.

As for Signalman Ewington, the President of the Board of Trade found that he had been treated 'quite liberally' by the company. When he wrote to Mr Harland asking what his position was after the strike, he was informed that he had rejected the offer made to him earlier by the directors. He therefore concluded that he was not wanted and decided to take up employment as a coal miner.[63]

The men heard nothing more of the proposed Conciliation Board. When the directors considered the question on November 6, 1900, they accepted Beasley's advice and decided that they could not 'depute the management of the staff to any outside body'.[64] In February 1901, the company still had not kept its promise about getting rid of the imported workers— seventy-six of them were working on the line at that time.[65] In an interview Mr Beasley granted the men on January 28, 1901, he bluntly informed them that it was the directors' intention to keep the imported men at all costs. He excluded from discussion the question of a Conciliation Board.[66] Inevitably, the men felt that they had been cheated and there were demands for a renewal of strike action.

IV

On the day the Taff Vale strike ended, Mr Justice Farwell granted an interim injunction against Messrs Bell and Holmes restraining them from all forms of picketing in the dispute except 'the communication of information' to non-strikers. On September 5th he made a further statement extending the injunction to the *union* and declaring that a union could be sued in its registered name. Of Richard Bell the judge declared that he had 'put his name to a most improper circular' which was a 'distinct threat' to the imported labour. On the question of the possibility of suing the union he stated:

'Has the legislature authorized the creation of numerous bodies of men, capable of owning great wealth and of acting by agents, with absolutely no responsibility for the wrongs they may do to other persons by the use of that wealth and the employment of those agents? I do not think so.'

The E.C. of the A.S.R.S. was aware that, although they had only academic interest in respect of the Taff Vale dispute now that the strike was over, the decisions of Mr Justice Farwell had the greatest importance to the trade-union movement. At its meeting in September 1900 it was decided to lodge an appeal and to ask the General Secretary to write to the Parliamentary Committee of the T.U.C. for its support in fighting the case. Within twenty-four hours of the judge's statement of September 5th, the T.U.C. passed a resolution instructing the Parliamentary Committee to write a letter to all unions warning them of the dangers arising from the decisions and asking for contributions on behalf of the appeal.

To the delight of the officials and members of the A.S.R.S., when the appeal was heard by the Master of the Rolls, Lord Justice Collins and Lord Justice Sterling on November 12th, judgment was given in favour of the union and the findings of Mr Justice Farwell were reversed. The Master of the Rolls declared that he 'could find nothing in the Trade Union Acts' which stated that 'a trade union was liable to be sued in its registered name'. The Lord Justices Collins and Stirling agreed with him.

Although the Taff Vale Company's solicitors advised that no further action should be taken, the determined Mr Beasley decided to take the case to the House of Lords. There was a delay of eight months before the, by now familiar, arguments were gone over once more. Finally on July 22, 1901, the five law lords found unanimously in favour of the company, largely repeating the reasons given by Mr Justice Farwell on September 5, 1900.

When the terms for a settlement of the strike were being negotiated between Mr Hopwood of the Board of Trade and Mr Vassall, the Taff Vale Railway Chairman, the latter agreed, in a letter written on August 28th, that 'all legal proceedings' would be discontinued once the strike ended. This promise was repeated in the final terms of settlement with the men on August 30th. On the following day the union's solicitors wrote to the company's solicitors stating that it was understood that all legal proceedings against 'your client's servants or their representatives (Trades Union or otherwise)' were to be withdrawn. The exemption was the question of the injunction on which the union wanted 'a friendly fight'. On September 1st, the company's solicitors replied that the company had agreed to withdraw all pending summonses, but they made no mention, either way, of summonses against the union.[67]

Although Richard Bell feared that the company would apply for damages, it looked at first as if they had decided against any such application. The Lords' judgment, which declared that a union could be sued, was delivered on July 21, 1901, but it was not until December 13th of that year that a claim for damages against the A.S.R.S. was lodged by the company.

Immediately Bell learned of the company's intention, he resolved that the defence of Holmes should be separated from the defence of the union and its other officers. Unfortunately, Bell and Holmes, being of such different temperaments, the one cautious, moderate and calculating, the other warm-hearted and impetuous, completely lacked confidence in each other and rarely consulted together. Bell even went so far as to supply the officials of two branches, Accrington and Liverpool No. 1, with information on Holmes's activities which were in violation of union rules. These branches then appealed to the E.C. to refuse to pay Holmes's defence costs, and when the E.C. turned down their suggestion they applied for, and obtained, an injunction against the union to restrain it from spending funds on Holmes's defence. A 'Holmes Defence Fund Committee' with J. H. Thomas as Secretary, raised £1,172 11s 6d by voluntary subscriptions from unions, trades councils and individuals in quick time and this more than covered the £1,000 paid to the solicitors responsible for Holmes's defence.[68]

The company put in a claim for damages amounting to £24,626 and the hearing of the case in the King's Bench Division of the High Court of Justice lasted from December 3 to 19, 1902, the verbatim report extending to 724 foolscap-size pages. There was a marked contrast between the remarks made by the presiding judge, Mr Justice Wills, about Bell and about Holmes. His impressions of the character and ability of Bell were 'very favourable'. Holmes's conduct he found 'impossible to excuse'.[69] The jury took but ten minutes to find on all counts against the union. By the end of February 1903, the amount paid in damages was settled out of court, the Taff Vale Railway agreeing to accept the sum of £23,000, in settlement of all claims. The cheque (as shown in photograph in Plate 6, facing page 289) was paid on March 23, 1903. The total cost to the union was £42,000.

The decisions of the Lords on July 21, 1901 and of the jury in the damages case on December 19, 1902, brought jubilation to many railway directors. Mr Vassall told a shareholders' meeting in August 1901 that the importance of the Lords' judgment to all employers of labour could not be exaggerated. The business of an employer could always be carried on provided he could obtain a requisite supply of labour, but when men were 'intimidated in such a manner as to prevent them fulfilling their engagements' the difficulty of obtaining an adequate labour force was greatly increased. Such interference and intimidation had been resorted to by the trade unions:

'Trade unions had considered they could perform such illegal acts with impunity but now if they attempted to do so they would be answerable for the consequences, and liable to make good from their funds the loss thereby occasioned to the employers. It was evident in the face of their judgment, they would not act in the future as they had done in the past. Their power to promote and engineer strikes would be most seriously crippled and he thought most properly so.'[70]

'In recognition of his services' Mr Beasley was paid, in the spring of 1903, a gratuity of £1,000 by the Taff Vale Railway Company. A year later he received a further £1,000, a pair of silver candelabra and a pendant brooch for his wife from an 'Employers Testimonial Committee'.[71] Meeting on May 18, 1903, the Council of the Railway Companies' Association resolved that 'the sum of £5,000 be paid to the Taff Vale Railway Company as a contribution to legal expenses'.[72] Perhaps it is not surprising that by the beginning of the year 1905 the Taff Vale Railway, according to its Chairman, was paying 'the highest dividend on any railway in the country'. It was at the rate of $3\frac{3}{4}$ per cent (= $9\frac{3}{8}$ per cent on the old stock).

V

Mr Beasley and Mr Vassall believed that they had seriously crippled the power of labour—and they were proud of their achievement. At first there seemed to be no doubt that they were right. A London newspaper editor's comment, made on the day after the company won its claim for damages, showed how far-reaching the consequences of the legal judgments were:

'A strike under these conditions becomes nearly impossible, and without the ultimate right to strike—however cautious it may be in using it—a union is impotent.'[73]

The whole legal position of trade unions was now uncertain. Whilst striking was still legal, almost all forms of picketing, without which strikes are necessarily ineffectual, were not. A union was not a corporate body in the same sense as a joint stock company; it could, and at the same time could not, be sued. It was even asserted that a trade union was an illegal association and that the right of combination, which had been assumed guaranteed for many decades, was an illusion.

The insecure position of trade unions was reflected in the number of trade disputes occurring in the years 1903–5 inclusive. Since these were years of rising prices, one would have expected an increased number of stoppages caused by the effort to prevent wages dragging behind prices. Instead the number of strikes per year was only half that of the decade of the 1890's.[74]

Nevertheless, despite the fact that, in the short run, it seemed as though Messrs Beasley and Vassall had achieved an outstanding success, in the longer run the Taff Vale judgment and the experience of the years of insecurity which followed it taught the majority of British trade unionists a lesson on the advantages of independent labour representation in Parliament. When, on August 1, 1901, Keir Hardie asked the Conservative leader, Balfour, in the House of Commons whether his Government would introduce legislation to give trade-union funds the protection they had had for thirty years, Balfour said 'No'. The prospect of Liberal support did not seem much brighter. Ramsay MacDonald was quick to seize the opportunities provided by the new situation. Within a fortnight of the judgment, he sent a circular to the trade unions on behalf of the Labour Representation Committee. In it he claimed that 'The recent decision of the House of Lords . . . should convince the unions that a Labour Party in Parliament is an immediate necessity.'[75]

The A.G.M. of the A.S.R.S., meeting shortly afterwards in London, reached unanimously the similar conclusion that the remedy lay 'in electing as law makers and administrators those who have a practical knowledge of industrial work'.

In 1902 and 1903 the majority of the unions which had stood so cautiously aloof from the L.R.C. in the first year of its existence, resolved, by large majorities, to affiliate. The decision of the engineers was taken in February 1902, by a five to one majority. The vote of the 100,000 strong Amalgamated Association of Operative Cotton Spinners taken later that year 'was heavily in favour'. The Furnishing Trades Association, the Amalgamated Society of Carpenters, Cabinetmakers and Joiners; the London United Brassworkers Society and many others had followed suit within eighteen months.[76] Between 1900–1 and 1903–4 the number of trade unions affiliated to the L.R.C. rose from forty-one with a membership of 375,931 to 165 with a membership of 969,800. Moreover, at the inaugural conference of the L.R.C. in February 1900, the proposal to levy the unions at the rate of a penny a member in order to start a Parliamentary fund had been rejected, without a discussion, as 'premature'. The Conference in 1903 carried the same proposal by a large majority and agreed in addition to pay a quarter of the returning officers' fees incurred on behalf of each Parliamentary candidate approved by the L.R.C. Elected members were to be paid a salary of £200 a year.

With the great augmentation of the funds at the disposal of the L.R.C. it proved possible to give financial support to fifty Labour candidates in the General Election of January 1906. Twenty-nine of these candidates were successful. In the previous General Election in 1900—before the Taff Vale judgment—only two Labour candidates had been returned. Whilst it is true that nineteen of the successful candidates in 1906 owed a great deal of their success to an understanding between the Liberal Party manager, Herbert Gladstone, and Ramsay MacDonald on the avoidance of three-cornered contests in a limited number of constituencies, the big bargaining counter which Ramsay MacDonald possessed in the discussions which led up to that agreement was the fact that the L.R.C. now commanded a potential three-quarters of a million votes. Had it not been for the action of the members of the A.S.R.S. in South Wales he would not have been in a strong position to make such a pact.

It was after the assembly of the new Parliament early in 1906 that the long-run effects of the Lords' decision of July 21, 1901, were most strikingly seen. The previous Government had appointed, in 1903, a Royal Commission on Trade Disputes; but its report did not appear until shortly after the Liberal electoral landslide. Partly because the Commission only contained one member favourable to Labour—Mr Sidney Webb—and did not contain a single trade unionist, the report did not go nearly as far in its recommendations for reform as the new Labour members would have wished. Sir Henry Campbell-Bannerman's Liberal Government nevertheless proceeded to draft a Bill based on the Commission's recommendations. It was at this point that the Government was taken by surprise. In the House of Commons, one after the other of its own supporters, and even some Conservative members, rose to say that they had made pledges in the election campaign to support a more generous measure of reform. Thereupon Keir Hardie produced another Bill—The Trade Disputes Bill—which according to a member of the Cabinet, Lord Haldane, 'passed easily' since the Government 'could not resist the numbers pledged to it'.

Thus within five years of Mr Vassall making his confident speech to the Taff Vale shareholders, the Trade Disputes Act was on the statute book. It fully legalized peaceful picketing and declared that inducing a breach of contract was not actionable if done in pursuance of a trade dispute. The unions' funds were to be fully protected. The most sweeping clause of all exempted trade unions from legal action:

'An action against a trade union whether of workmen or of masters, or against any members or officials thereof on behalf of themselves and all other members of the trade union in respect of any tortious act alleged to have been committed by or on behalf of the trade union, shall not be entertained in any court.'

There were no further £1,000 presents for Mr Beasley!

VI

In the same year—1900—which saw the birth of the Labour Representation Committee, a meeting of wives and daughters of members of the A.S.R.S., held in Crewe, decided to set up a Railway Women's Guild.

The objects of the new organization agreed at the first meeting of the Central Organization Committee (renamed the Executive Committee in May 1902) held on August 31, 1901 were:

'... to afford means of social intercourse amongst the wives and daughters of railway workers of the district; to render such assistance to any of its members as may be necessary; to co-operate with the local branch of the A.S.R.S. in any worthy object they may undertake.'

The Guild had very modest beginnings. In the first year of its life thirty-four branches were formed and the total funds handled by the Central Organization Committee only amounted to £13 17s 3d. That subsequent progress was so satisfactory was largely due to the devoted and energetic work of the able Hon. General Secretary, Mrs Mary A. Macpherson, B.A., of 66 Chancery Lane, London, who was known to many readers of the *Railway Review* by her pen name 'Margery Daw'. By the time of the 5th Annual Conference of the Guild, held in Hull in June 1904, she was able to report a membership of nearly 2,000 distributed in sixty-three branches.

It would be wholly erroneous to conclude from a perusal of the Guild's objects that its members were solely concerned with such activities as providing refreshments at concerts and other social occasions promoted to raise money for the orphan fund, although this work was of great value. Sometimes the wives of railwaymen were more appreciative of the value of a trade union than were their menfolk. The Central Organization Committee, at its first meeting, resolved to inform Mr Bell, the General Secretary of the A.S.R.S., that 'the Women's Guild recognizes non-society men's wives as members of the Guild because they are often good workers and influence their husbands in many cases to join the Society'.

The claim of the A.S.R.S. to have played a leading part in the foundation of the Labour Representation Committee could be matched by the claim of the Railway Women's Guild to have taken the initiative in the foundation of the Women's Labour League. At the 6th Annual Conference of the Guild held at Masbro' on May 28, 1905, Mrs Bellamy of Stockport, who had earlier that year helped to form a Women's Labour League in her home town, gained the unanimous support of the delegates for the following resolution:

'That this Conference is strongly in favour of the true principles of Labour Representation on our local governing bodies and in the House of Commons and pledges itself to do all in its power to return direct representatives of Labour.'

Mrs Bellamy also gained the support of the Conference for a second resolution:

'That this Conference requests the National Labour Representation Committee to take immediate steps to form a National Labour Women's Committee, and requests our Secretary to send this resolution to the L.R.C.'

As an outcome of these decisions, Mrs Macpherson and other members of the Guild accepted an invitation from Mrs J. R. MacDonald, wife of the Secretary of the L.R.C., to attend a meeting at 3 Lincoln's Inn Fields, London, on March 9, 1906, when it was decided to form the Women's Labour League.

Ever since that time the Women's Guilds have concerned themselves with the big political issues of the day as well as with matters more limited to the railway industry, and the A.S.R.S. and N.U.R. delegates at the most recent annual conference demanded the transfer from road to rail of 'heavy and dangerous traffic', protested against the Immigration Bill as being 'tainted with racial prejudice' and opposed the resumption of testing of nuclear weapons.

For more than sixty years the Guilds have been a tower of strength to the local branches of the union.

NOTES

1. Report of the Labour Electoral Congress, 1891, *Blackburn Times*, July 18 and 25, 1891.
2. Quoted in Hobsbawm, E. J., *Labour's Turning Point*, p. 97.
3. *R.R.*, October 4, 1889.
4. *R.R.*, October 16, 1891.
5. *R.R.*, August 24; September 7, 1894.
6. *R.R.*, October 5, 1894.
7. A.S.R.S. E.C. Minutes, December 1896.
8. *R.R.*, October 11, 1895.
9. A.S.R.S. General Secretary's Report to the A.G.M. 1895, p. 8.
10. I am very grateful to Dr P. S. Gupta for this 'breakdown' of the E.C. membership in 1897.
11. *R.R.*, September 9, 1898.
12. *R.R.*, December 16, 1898, January 13, 1899.
13. Correspondence columns of the *Railway Review*, February and March 1899.
14. Saville, J., 'Trade Unions and Free Labour; the Background to the Taff Vale Decision' in *Essays in Labour History*, edited by Asa Briggs and John Saville, pp. 337–9. Ludlow, J. M., 'The National Free Labour Association', *Economic Review*, January 1895, pp. 110–18; *R.R.*, January 13, 1899.
15. *R.R.*, January 13, 1899.
16. *R.R.*, October 14, 1898.
17. A.S.R.S. Decisions of the A.G.M., October 1898, p. 11, R. 61. The report in the *R.R.* (October 7, 1898, p. 13) states the resolution to have been defeated by 32 votes to 31. Although the official report of the A.G.M. does not state by what majority the resolution was carried it may be assumed from the balance of speeches in the debate, that the voting was 32 to 31 *for* the resolution.
18. *R.R.*, November 11, 1898.
19. A.S.R.S. E.C., March 1899.
20. *R.R.*, September 15, 1899, *Labour Leader*, September 16, 1899. *R.R.*, October 20, 1899, 'The Trade Union Congress', by J. Holmes.
21. *R.R.*, October 13, 1899.
22. Bealey, F. and Pelling, H., *Labour and Politics, 1900–1906*, p. 25.
23. *R.R.*, March 9, 1900. Ramsay MacDonald: 'Labour Representation Conference Report.'
24. A.S.R.S. E.C., March 1900, R. 25. Bealey and Pelling, p. 36.
25. Viscount Snowden: *Autobiography*, p. 94.
26. See p. 139 above.
27. *The Times*, August 23, 1900.
28. In the High Court of Justice King's Bench Division Taff Vale Railway Company *v.* A.S.R.S., December 5, 1902, Qs. 781, 784, p. 154.
29. *Ibid.*, Evidence of Mr A. Beasley, Q. 27. *R.R.*, December 15, 1893. At a mass meeting held in Cardiff on December 10th a letter was read from Mr Beasley who declined to meet the Standing Committee.
30. *R.R.*, September 22, October 27, December 8 and 15, 1893.
31. *R.R.*, May 10, 24 and 31, 1895.
32. *R.R.*, September 27, 1895.
33. *R.R.*, August 24, 1900.
34. *South Wales Daily News*, August 22, 1900.
35. Statement of Sir Edward Clarke in T.V.R. *v.* A.S.R.S., December 3, 1902, p. 2.

36. Bealey and Pelling, p. 56. A.S.R.S. 'The Taff Vale Case and the Injunction', p. 37.
37. T.V.R. v. A.S.R.S., December 5, 1902, Q. 777.
38. This account of the movement up to March 22, 1900, is based on A.S.R.S. E.C. Minutes, December 1899, and March and June 1900, and on Sir Edward Clarke's statement to the court on December 2, 1902.
39. *South Wales Daily News*, August 8, 1900.
40. T.V.R. v. A.S.R.S. Statement of Mr Rufus Isaacs, K.C., quoting a letter from Mr Harland.
41. *Western Mail*, July 30, 1900.
42. *South Wales Daily News*, August 6, 1900.
43. *Western Mail*, August 18, 1900.
44. *Railway News*, quoted in *R.R.*, September 7, 1900.
45. *Western Mail*, August 7 and 18, 1900.
46. T.V.R. v. A.S.R.S. Statement of Mr Rufus Isaacs, K.C., p. 444.
47. *R.R.*, August 17, 1900.
48. T.V.R. v. A.S.R.S., December 9, 1902. Evidence of W. Collison, Qs. 2747–2849.
49. T.V.R. v. A.S.R.S., December 11, 1902. Evidence of Mr H. M. Ingleden, Q. 4822.
50. *Ibid.*, Evidence of Mr T. H. Riches, Q. 1070.
51. *Ibid.*, Quoted by Sir Edward Clarke, p. 37.
52. *Ibid.*, Evidence of R. Bell, Q. 5075.
53. Royal Commission on Trade Disputes, P.P. 1906, Vol. LVI, Q. 1061. *South Wales Argus*, August 24, 1900.
54. T.V.R. v. A.S.R.S., December 5 and 8, 1902, Qs. 1095–7, 1114.
55. W. Collison, 'Apostle of Free Labour' (1913), p. 152 f., quoted in Bealey and Pelling, pp. 61–2.
56. Quoted by Mr Eldon Bankes, K.C., T.V.R. v. A.S.R.S., December 4, 1902, p. 79.
57. *Ibid.*, December 16, 1902, Q. 6238.
58. P.P. 1906, LVI, Appendix on acts of intimidation committed by the strikers.
59. Saville, J., *op. cit.*, p. 347.
60. *South Wales Argus*, August 21, 1900.
61. *South Wales Argus*, August 30, 1900.
62. *The Times*, September 1, 1900.
63. T.V.R. v. A.S.R.S., Evidence of Signalman Ewington, Qs. 5917–20.
64. T.V.R. Board Minutes, November 6, 1900.
65. *Railway News*, February 16, 1901.
66. A.S.R.S. General Secretary's Report to the E.C., March 1901, p. 11.
67. Letters quoted by Mr. Rufus Isaacs, K.C., in T.V.R. v. A.S.R.S., December 11, 1902, p. 394.
68. Alcock, pp. 312–14.
69. T.V.R. v. A.S.R.S. Mr Justice Wills's summing-up, December 19, 1902, pp. 719, 704.
70. *Herapath's Railway Journal*, August 16, 1901, p. 831.
71. Bealy and Pelling, p. 71.
72. Minute 2,778, Railway Companies' Association, May 18, 1903.
73. *Echo*, December 20, 1902.
74. Webb: *The History of Trade Unionism* (1920 Edition), p. 603.
75. Quoted in Bealey and Pelling, p. 77.
76. Philip P. Poirier: *The Advent of the Labour Party*, p. 141; H. J. Fyrth and Henry Collins: *The Foundry Workers, A Trade Union History*, p. 108.
77. Hansard, Parliamentary Debates, 1901, Series 4, Vol. XCVIII, Col. 877.

CHAPTER IX

THE A.S.R.S. AND THE LABOUR PARTY:
THE OSBORNE CASE

'*They have gone into politics. You cannot blink the matter; that is what it is; these trade unions have gone into politics.*'
Mr C. E. E. *Jenkins, K.C., Counsel for the prosecution, in W. V. Osborne* v. *The Amalgamated Society of Railway Servants, July 21, 1908.*

'*When we were a feeble party, suffering only failures at the polls, we were doing nothing wrong; but when we became successful . . . all the right of former years suddenly became illegal . . . The objection is not to our taking part in politics, but to our politics. The objection is to labour politics and to Socialism.*'
J. R. Clynes, M.P., House of Commons, August 6, 1912.

I

THE affiliation of the majority of the trade unions to the Labour Representation Committee, the remarkable success at the polls in 1906 and the passage of the Trades Disputes Act were outstanding successes for the Socialists. They did not go unchallenged.

The Taff Vale judgment had helped to convince many, but by no means all, trade unionists of the advantages of independent Labour representation in Parliament. Many trade-union leaders continued to remain suspicious of 'intellectual' and 'arm chair' Socialists and preferred to maintain an old-established working alliance with the Liberal Party rather than to venture into an uneasy partnership with the new organization. There was very little common ground between the General Secretary of the A.S.R.S. and the Secretary of the Labour Representation Committee, J. Ramsay MacDonald, who was once described by Richard Bell as 'a Labour member who has never laboured in his life'.[1] On the other hand, those who put their socialist convictions first and their trade-union interests second grumbled about the limited objectives and lack of vision of the 'pure and simple' trade unionists. Through the columns of the I.L.P. newspaper, Keir Hardie complained that the leaders of unionism were 'concerned with petty matters of precedent and little selfish interests instead of being moved by the large human issues'.[2] It was the political careers of two A.S.R.S. officials, Richard Bell, the General Secretary, and Walter V. Osborne, the Secretary of the Walthamstow branch, which inadvertently helped to reconcile the differing viewpoints expressed in the industrial and intellectual wings of the movement and to cement still further the alliance between the trade unions and the Labour Party which has remained a unique feature of the British political scene for more than half a century.

II

Since neither Keir Hardie nor Ramsay MacDonald desired to imperil the success of their new venture by dragooning Labour M.P.s, the first constitution of the Labour Representation Committee was drafted in deliberately vague terms. The London (1900) constitution declared that the objective sought was:

'. . . a distinct Labour group in Parliament, who shall have their own whips, and agree upon their policy, which must embrace a readiness to co-operate with any party which for the time being may be engaged in promoting legislation in the direct interest of Labour, and be equally ready to associate themselves with any party in opposing measures having the opposite tendency.'[3]

Ramsay MacDonald described this as an 'open, free constitution' drafted with 'the distinct understanding that it should be obeyed in the spirit'.[4]

When the Derby Trades Council adopted Richard Bell as its Parliamentary candidate for the borough in 1899 the Labour Representation Committee had not yet been formed. Shortly after its foundation, however, Bell agreed to fight the election under its auspices since he felt no conscientious scruples in endorsing its constitution and joining the Executive Committee. On October 3, 1900, he was elected as the junior member for Derby and was the first railwayman to enter the House of Commons. His expenses in the campaign had been met entirely from the general fund of the union, from which his Parliamentary salary of £200 a year was also paid, since there was no State payment of M.P.s at that time.

In many respects Richard Bell proved to be an admirable M.P. He was extremely conscientious and hard working and never hesitated to intervene to secure the redress of grievances. In the ten weeks ending January 21, 1902, he made no less than forty-one representations to Ministers concerning the excessive hours of work of railwaymen.[5] It soon became apparent, however, that his conception of independence differed substantially from that of the majority of the leaders of the L.R.C. His understanding of the duties of a Labour M.P. was similar to that of a whole generation of Lib.-Lab. M.P.s. He believed he should sponsor measures which protected the interests of the members of his and other trade unions. Whichever party was most likely to give support to such legislation was the party for the time being to support in the House. In ninety-nine cases out of a hundred this would be the Liberal Party. The fact that Bell had been adopted as Parliamentary candidate before the new party came into existence encouraged him to adopt an individualistic line. He told Ramsay MacDonald in 1904, 'I owe nothing to the L.R.C., which had nothing to do with my return'.[6]

The I.L.P. leaders, on the other hand, wanted a complete break from the policy of hanging on to the coat tails of the Liberal Party in Parliament. They viewed with increasing concern the appearance of the railwaymen's leader on Liberal Party platforms. The more distressed they became the more Bell seemed to take pleasure in defying them. At the end of December 1902, he wrote to the *Newmarket Weekly News* urging working men to vote for the Liberal candidate in the Parliamentary by-election in the area. Less than a month later he was writing to the *Liverpool Echo* urging support for another Liberal by-election candidate. He told a meeting of his constituents that he had voted 'on every issue' in Parliament with the senior member for the division, the Liberal, Sir Thomas Roe.[7]

Richard Bell believed that he had excellent reasons for acting as he did. At the time of his first election to Parliament, only one other candidate who stood on the L.R.C. ticket—Keir Hardie—was successful. What possible influence on legislation could be exerted by two members who insisted on cutting themselves adrift from the progressive wing of the Liberal Party? He told the E.C. of the union in March 1903, that his policy of working with the organized group of forty 'progressives' (including twelve trade unionists) in the House was more fruitful of beneficial results than would be a policy of isolationism. Among other things, their chances of success in the ballot for private members' Bills would be twenty times as great.

In vain did Keir Hardie and Ramsay MacDonald point out that the support that Richard Bell obtained from the Liberals was simply due to the fact that they were then the opposition party. A study of the history of Liberal Governments would show that they were, at times, as deaf to the claims of the working men as were the Conservatives, and it was for that reason that a new, fully independent, party was needed in the House of Commons. This was the vital need of the time. If those who stood on the L.R.C. ticket did not conform to the spirit of the original 'open, free constitution' of the L.R.C., then to secure the all-important objective of an independent Labour group, the constitution would have to be revised

H*   233

and a new, more exacting pledge of support would have to be obtained from candidates and M.P.s.

Accordingly, in February 1903, the third annual conference of the L.R.C., meeting in Newcastle, carried by 659,000 votes to 154,000 a resolution which declared it to be 'absolutely necessary' that members of the E.C., M.P.s, and candidates run under the auspices of the committee should 'strictly abstain from identifying themselves with, or promoting the interests of, any section of the Liberal or Conservative Parties'. It was also decided that M.P.s should abide by the majority vote of the group and that if they did not do so they should resign. The decision to raise a levy on affiliated bodies of 1d per member per year made available to the executive at least £2,500 a year for the payment of those M.P.s which it sponsored. At the same time it became possible to enforce a greater measure of discipline since those M.P.s who consistently acted out of sympathy with the majority of the party could not be expected to have any claim on the funds of the organization.

From the Newcastle Conference onwards Richard Bell became more and more adrift from the policy of the L.R.C. and the policy of his own union. In the light of these circumstances it is remarkable that he kept his seat in Parliament and his office in the union as long as he did. It was not until the winter of 1909–10 that he resigned from both.

Before the Newcastle Conference, Bell had often departed from the spirit of the constitution of the L.R.C., but since he had not violated the letter, it was difficult for MacDonald to proceed against him. Such action was possible under the Newcastle constitution which Bell, in his characteristically blunt manner, described as a 'preposterous' one.[8] But although Doncaster No. 1, Doncaster No. 2 and Ormskirk branches protested to the E.C. about the General Secretary hob-nobbing with Liberal leaders, the E.C. was content to advise him to use the 'utmost discretion' in helping other Parliamentary candidates whilst the A.G.M., in October 1903, did not even discuss the question.[9]

In his actions in connection with the Norwich by-election in January 1904, Bell did not display that 'utmost discretion' the E.C. had recommended. The constituency L.R.C. group in Norwich had adopted G. H. Roberts of the Typographical Association and the I.L.P. to fight the election against both Conservative and Liberal opposition. The A.S.R.S. branch in Norwich gave its support to Roberts and the branch secretary wrote to Bell asking him to come and speak on his behalf. Bell replied expressing 'extreme regret that no arrangements had been made to avoid splitting the progressive and free trade vote' and declining to speak on behalf of the Labour candidate. The letter was much publicized by the newspapers which interpreted it as giving support to Mr Tillett, the Liberal candidate. Although Bell in his letter had not directly advised the members of the A.S.R.S. branch in the city to vote for the Liberal candidate, when the election resulted in Tillett's victory he was unwise enough to send the new M.P. a telegram which read: 'Great triumph for progress. Hearty congratulations.'[10] Bell's intervention was regarded both by the Norwich Socialists and by the Executive Committee of the L.R.C. as having very harmful effects on Roberts's candidature.

Within a short while of the Norwich election the E.C. of the union received a request from the executive of the L.R.C. that it should accept a deputation comprising Ramsay MacDonald and David Shackleton, M.P., to discuss Richard Bell's political activity. A prolonged discussion was therefore held at the headquarters of the union at 72 Acton Street, Grays Inn Road, on March 17, 1904. The two Labour leaders politely, but persistently, searched for a compromise whereby Richard Bell could be induced to sign the constitution of their party. Bell would not yield an inch. He stoutly defended his actions over the by-elections and declared that he did not intend to be 'bound or rendered powerless' by the constitution the Socialists had drafted. He declared that if he signed the constitution 'no work would be done' by him in Parliament of any benefit to the union. When he became the candidate at Derby the conditions laid down by the L.R.C. were acceptable but now they were asking him to sign a 'new contract'. He said he preferred men of the kind of John Burns and Sir Charles Dilke 'to a heap of Philip Snowdens'. In the end he threw down the gauntlet: 'If you lay it down that I must sign the constitution of the L.R.C. of course I shall no longer be a candidate.'[11] This confronted the members of the E.C. with a dilemma. Either they must support their General Secretary and ignore the requests of the L.R.C. executive, or they must support the L.R.C. and lose the valuable services of the one railwayman M.P. In the event they passed the responsibility of making a decision to the A.G.M. A resolution was passed thanking MacDonald and Shackleton for their attendance and promising to let them know their final decision on the matter.

When the subject was thrashed out in debate at the A.G.M. in Bradford in October 1904, Congress decided that the best way out of the dilemma was for the union's delegates at the next annual meeting of the L.R.C. to submit proposals for the modification of the constitution to make it less rigid. The resolution which was passed by the narrow majority of thirty votes to twenty-nine expressed appreciation of Bell's 'excellent work' as an M.P., whilst admitting that some of his actions had been indiscreet. Pending the amendment of the 'too stringent' L.R.C. constitution the General Secretary should be allowed to continue as the union's representative in Parliament 'on the same conditions as heretofore'.[12]

These plans came unstuck when the L.R.C. Conference met at Liverpool the following January. The changes proposed by C. H. Ramsay on behalf of the A.S.R.S. seemed temptingly simple and sensible. Where there was no Labour candidate in a constituency the Executive or Annual Meeting of the Party should have power to sanction support being given to candidates of the Liberal or Conservative Parties. The assumption was that only those candidates who were in favour of a new Trade Disputes Bill legalizing picketing and protecting union funds would be supported. Nevertheless, after Philip Snowden had pointed out the dangers of returning a candidate to Parliament because he was sound on one particular measure, and the anomalies that would arise through supporting a Conservative in one constituency and a Liberal in the next, the resolution was decisively defeated on a card vote.[13] The attempt to bend the constitution of L.R.C. to take account of the domestic difficulties of the A.S.R.S. had ended in failure.

Since the differences between the L.R.C. and Bell had not been resolved, the latter stood as an independent candidate backed by the Derby Trades Council in the General Election of January 1906. He was again returned as junior member for the borough; but on this occasion he was joined in Parliament by two fellow members of the union who had been elected on the L.R.C. ticket, Walter Hudson, who was returned at Newcastle, and George Wardle, who was successful at Stockport.

In the new House of Commons Richard Bell's position became increasingly untenable. The L.R.C. group in the old Parliament, even with the augmentation of its strength through by-election successes, had comprised no more than five members. It was then plausible for Bell to maintain that strict independence of action was less profitable than a working arrangement with the Liberal opposition. In the new Parliament there were no less than twenty-nine members who had accepted the 'preposterous' constitution of the L.R.C. (now renamed the Labour Party). It was too large a group to be dubbed as isolated and ineffective. Furthermore, in the old Parliament there had been no other A.S.R.S. M.P. with whom Bell's Parliamentary conduct would be compared, whereas in the new Parliament, through the loyalty of Hudson and Wardle to union and Labour Party policy, Bell was exposed on more than one occasion, through voting in a different lobby in the House of Commons, as defying the majority decisions of the A.G.M. of the A.S.R.S.

When the E.C. of the union in June 1906 agreed to recommend to the A.G.M. an alteration of the rules to make membership of the Labour Party obligatory on all the union's Parliamentary candidates, and when the A.G.M. in October of the same year carried the amendment by thirty-seven votes to twenty-two, Bell knew that it was impossible for him to continue as one of the union's M.P.s beyond the lifetime of that Parliament.[14]

In the Parliament of 1906–10 Bell continued to follow the path of collaboration with the Liberal Party which was the only one in which he had confidence. He aimed to achieve the recognition of his union by the railway companies and he believed that the best way of attaining it was by supporting the companies' plans for amalgamations provided clauses were inserted into the railway Bills to safeguard the interests of the railwaymen. In collaboration with Lloyd George he hoped to secure a more stringent enforcement of the Railway Servants (Hours of Labour) Act of 1893. In the pursuit of these aims he was supremely egotistical and self-confident regarding his fellow members, Hudson and Wardle, in a manner not far short of disdain. His attitude to those who criticized him in Parliament or in the union was summed up by George Alcock who knew him well:

'This way was *the* way, and to question it was something like challenging the old divine right of kings. He had not enough velvet on his glove. He did not give the soft answer that turneth away wrath. He had the touch of the autocrat. He aimed at success and took the path he thought best to achieve it; and all who stood in his way lacked intelligence.'[15]

One illustration of Bell's lack of co-operation with Hudson and Wardle can be seen in the columns of Hansard for March 1907. Owing to the industrial boom, many men employed by the Midland, Great Central, and Lancashire and Yorkshire Railways were being employed for excessively long hours. In collaboration with W. E. Harvey, the Liberal M.P. for Derbyshire (N.E.) and after consultation with Mr Lloyd George, the President of the Board of Trade, Bell sponsored a resolution in the House of Commons urging the Board of Trade to appoint additional inspectors for the railways and to make specialized inquiries into the hours worked in selected congested areas. This would amount to a more effective enforcement of the Act of 1893. Unaware of Bell's behind-the-scenes negotiations, Wardle and Hudson, on behalf of the Labour group, proposed a far more radical amendment providing for stricter limits to be imposed on the hours of labour of railwaymen. At the end of the debate Mr Bell was one of the tellers in the Government lobby while Messrs Wardle and Hudson were tellers in the other lobby counting up the Labour members' votes. Bell's policy had been at variance with A.G.M. decisions whilst the actions of the other two members were in accordance with union policy.[16]

Mr Bell's Parliamentary report to the E.C. later in March was a one-sided account which quoted his own speech and the speeches of Messrs Harvey and Lloyd George at some length, but merely cited the terms of the amendment standing in the name of his two colleagues Hudson and Wardle. These last two felt obliged to submit a separate report on their action in the debate in order to prevent misrepresentation, and the E.C. ruled that in future the three M.P.s were to submit a *joint* report.[17] Even this arrangement did not work smoothly. In March and September 1908, Hudson and Wardle were complaining that Bell was from time to time drafting the Parliamentary Report without fully consulting them.[18] After vainly endeavouring throughout two entire sessions of Parliament to arrange regular friendly collaboration with Mr Bell, the other two members wrote him a joint letter on January 31, 1908, asking him when he proposed bringing the group together as he was instructed to do by the A.G.M. at Middlesbrough in October 1907. They received a rude reply on February 5th in which Bell wrote expressing the wish that if they had something to say they should see him in the House and that they should 'not apply such childish procedure by writing as if they were all miles apart'.

Bell's final break with the union came in 1909 over his attitude to two Parliamentary Bills, one for the amalgamation of the Great Northern, Great Central and Great Eastern Railways and the other for conferring extended powers on the North Eastern Railway.

The union's policy with regard to railway amalgamation had been repeatedly affirmed since October 1894, when the A.G.M. at Newport (Mon.) passed a resolution in favour of the nationalization of the industry. The policy had been reaffirmed as recently as October 1907, by the supreme governing body.[20] The accepted procedure adopted by Labour M.P.s was to block railway Bills as a sanction for obtaining better working conditions for the railwaymen concerned and as a means of airing the party's policy on nationalization. When the three railways' Amalgamation Bill first came before the House of Commons in 1908, Bell, Hudson and Wardle each submitted blocking motions. After the Second Reading of the Bill, however, without consulting or informing his colleagues, Bell had some conversations with representatives of the companies and the Board of Trade. Lloyd George then agreed to insert new clauses into the Bill protecting railwaymen against dismissal, assuring their pension rights, etc., and Bell, in return, agreed to drop his opposition to the measure. Although the Bill was subsequently withdrawn at the request of the companies, indignation was expressed in the South Shields and other branches at the General Secretary's failure to adhere to the policy of the A.G.M. When the E.C. considered the incident in June 1909, it endorsed the action of Hudson and Wardle in voting against the Bill and decided to report the action of the General Secretary to the forthcoming A.G.M. All three of the M.P.s were asked to attend at Leicester to explain their actions.[21]

No sooner had the storm over the Amalgamation Bill died down than another blew up over Bell's attitude towards the North Eastern Railway Bill. In 1897 the North Eastern Railway had crossed swords with the T.U.C. through the directors' opposition to railway clerks joining a trade union. At that time Bell had caused some resentment by agreeing with the company that it was unsuitable for 'confidential' clerks to be enrolled in the A.S.R.S. When the Company's Bill was drafted in 1909, the Railway Clerks Association (whose foundation was closely associated with the 1897 incident) obtained the co-operation of the T.U.C. and the Labour Party in putting pressure on the North Eastern Railway to drop its opposition to trade unionism among its clerks. It was agreed that if the company did not co-operate its Bill would be opposed in the Commons.

On July 14, 1909, the day before the debate on the Second Reading of the North Eastern Railway Bill, Mr Bell, entirely off his own bat and without the authorization of the Railway Clerks Association or the Parliamentary Labour Party, met Mr Butterworth, the General Manager of the company, and reached a compromise agreement with him. Mr Butterworth undertook to remove all obstacles to all but 300 of the 6,000 clerks employed by the North Eastern Railway joining a trade union. Mr Bell thought that this was an important concession and that it would be wise for Mr Walkden, the General Secretary of the Railway Clerks Association, to accept it. On the following day the trade union and Labour members who were supporting Mr Summerbell's blocking resolution were amazed when Mr Bell rose to speak in favour of the Bill, justifying his action by referring to his talks with Mr Butterworth the day before. Mr Wardle was thunderstruck to hear Mr Bell say: 'Of course we do not take in clerks in our organization',[22] and a few minutes later he was on his feet reminding the House that he had joined the A.S.R.S. when he was a clerk employed by the Midland Railway and that it was still the policy of the union to admit clerks.

For his action on this occasion Mr Bell was censured by the T.U.C. to whom he apologized and admitted that he had been indiscreet.[23] In June he refused to discuss his Parliamentary conduct over the North Eastern Railway Bill with the E.C. on the grounds that resolutions for his resignation were already on the Agenda of the A.G.M. and he ought not to be tried twice for the same offence.

The Annual General Meeting at Leicester in October 1909 was an unhappy occasion since it resulted in the union losing the services of a General Secretary who had served it with ability, if not always with wisdom, for more than twelve years. Richard Bell wanted the discussion of his case to take place in public session so that he would have the support of most of the daily press for his 'statesmanlike' policy in Parliament. The majority of the delegates, however, did not like the idea of the union's domestic difficulties being given full publicity in the newspapers. It was therefore decided (as one delegate expressed it with unconscious humour) 'to discuss the matter openly and above board, *in camera*'![24] Because congress would not agree to his plan to have a public debate, Mr Bell declined the opportunity given him to state his case although he listened to the whole of the discussion and occasionally interjected somewhat bitter comments. A delegate from Leeds Central Branch, Mr J. G. Pye, moved a resolution asking the General Secretary to resign his position 'owing to his opposition in the House of Commons on the Amalgamation Bill, the North Eastern Railway Bill, and also his general conduct'. He thought that the delegates had to decide whether the Society should be 'a one-man organization or an organization for the benefit of the whole of the members'. After the resolution had been seconded, Mr A. Law of Newton Heath No. 1 moved an amendment in favour of the appointment of a Parliamentary Secretary who should relieve the General Secretary of all but his industrial duties. It was a compromise which would have overcome the difficulty of the split between Bell and his two colleagues in the House of Commons whilst retaining Bell's services as an able administrator in the industrial sphere. After over six hours' debate the resolution was defeated by 32 votes to 25 and the amendment carried by 32 to 25.[25]

Although the A.G.M. had given Mr Bell an opportunity to continue in the service of the union there was so much bitter feeling on both sides that the arrangements proposed in Mr Law's amendment would never have worked. The union agreed to the printing and circulation of an eight-page statement of his case by the General Secretary, who claimed that it was his refusal to hand himself 'over to the Socialists body and soul by signing the Labour Party ticket' that was the cause of all the differences which had arisen. The executive thought this statement so partisan and unfair that they published a brief reply.

Early in December the E.C. granted the General Secretary one month's leave of absence because of the excessive strain of work of the preceding twelve months. The letter of resignation sent by Bell to the E.C. on December 31, 1909, whilst he was still on leave, was not unexpected, and at its special meeting in January 1910, the E.C. accepted the resignation unanimously whilst recording its thanks for the 'great and valuable services' that the General Secretary had rendered.

Although Bell's resignation in 1906 would have met with widespread regret, since his valuable work in securing the North Eastern Railway arbitration award in 1897, and the passage of the Accidents Act in 1900, his sponsoring of necessary amendments to the rules and his work in the administrative reorganization in 1902–3 were much appreciated, by the end of 1909 few branches, apart from those at Walthamstow, Exeter and Derby, expressed regret at his departure.

Just over a fortnight before his letter of resignation to the E.C., Bell wrote to A. R. Flint, the Secretary of the Derby Labour Association, announcing 'with great reluctance' his decision not to stand again as Parliamentary candidate for Derby. He gave as his principal reason the limitations imposed on trade unionists' political activities by the injunction granted in the Osborne Case.[26] Within a month, the ex-M.P. for Derby had received an offer from the Rt. Hon. Winston Churchill, President of the Board of Trade, of a post at the Central Office of the Labour Exchanges, and he had accepted with gratitude.[27]

Following the General Secretary's resignation, nothing further was done about the earlier decision to appoint a Parliamentary Secretary. The only applicant for the post was a Mr W. H. Morley who gave as his address the West Ham Union Workhouse.[28] No record survives of Mr Bell's comments on this application!

Within a month of the publication of Mr Bell's letter to Mr Flint, J. H. Thomas had been returned as Labour member for Derby in the General Election of January 1910. At the same time Messrs Hudson and Wardle were re-elected for their old constituencies. From then onwards the A.S.R.S. Parliamentary group worked harmoniously together. The experience of Mr Bell's stormy Parliamentary career had taught two valuable lessons—the difficulty of the General Secretary combining successfully his Parliamentary and industrial duties and the impossibility of much effective Parliamentary action on behalf of railwaymen when the union's M.P.s were of different political persuasions.

III

Although the case of Richard Bell was significant in helping to determine the policy of the Labour Representation Committee in 1903–4, the political behaviour of the General Secretary of the A.S.R.S. was mainly of importance in the affairs of his own union. By contrast the activities of one of the union's branch secretaries had immense repercussions on the whole Labour movement.

Walter Victor Osborne of 77 Barrett Road, Walthamstow, started his railway career in 1890 as a porter employed by the Great Eastern Railway, his trade-union career as a member of the General Railway Workers Union and his political career as a member of the extreme Socialist organization, the Social Democratic Federation. By the turn of the century he had changed his employment to become head porter at Clapton, his union to become a member of the A.S.R.S. and his politics to become a member of the Walthamstow Liberal Association. For all this apparent instability Osborne was regarded by his fellow lodger, George Alcock, as 'a man of probity and upright character'[29] who made almost a fetish of his conscience but possessed a remarkable determination and singleness of purpose. His consistency of policy in trade-union and political affairs in the period 1903–14 stands in marked contrast to his earlier vacillations.

Osborne, and the members of the Walthamstow branch of which he was Secretary, supported official A.S.R.S. policy on Parliamentary representation during the whole of the period 1889–1900, i.e. they favoured the union being represented in Parliament and its M.P. being supported from the funds, provided the candidate chosen remained a purely trade-union candidate. As late as February 18, 1909, the Walthamstow branch of the A.S.R.S. passed the following resolution:

'That this branch approves of Parliamentary representation on a voluntary basis, and agrees to accept donations for that purpose, provided that each member of this Society who represents a constituency in Parliament is placed on an equal footing regardless of any political tests.'[30]

From March 1900 onwards, however, the branch and its Secretary, along with a number of other branches of the union, came to be more and more out of sympathy with the decisions of the E.C. and the A.G.M.

There is no indication that Osborne took any particular dislike to the decision of the E.C. to affiliate to the Labour Representation Committee in March 1900. Although from this time onwards some of the funds of the union were earmarked as affiliation fees to the new party, the sums involved were not large and individual members of the union were not called upon to contribute a special levy.

A different principle was raised in December 1901, when the E.C. decided to recommend to members a levy of 1s per member per year for a Parliamentary Representation Fund and resolved to conduct a ballot early in 1902 in the hope of obtaining rank and file support for its proposal.[31] The result, announced in March 1902, was disappointing in that only 29 per cent of the membership voted, but was regarded as satisfactory in that 89 per cent of those voting favoured the levy and only 11 per cent opposed.[32] A special sub-committee of five members of the E.C. was then appointed to 'draft a scheme of Labour Representation'. In June 1902, the recommendations of the sub-committee were endorsed by the E.C. for submission to the A.G.M. in October. The proposal was that the Parliamentary representation fund should be formed and maintained by voluntary subscription at the rate of 1s per member a year, the money to be paid quarterly and forwarded to the Central Office with the quarterly dues. The two principal objects of the fund were to be 'to provide for additional direct representation of railwaymen in the House of Commons' and 'to contribute to the Labour Representation Committee such sums as the E.C. or the A.G.M. should from time to time direct'. Since it was to be a *voluntary* levy and it was provided that a 'separate account' should be kept of the fund there was still no sign of opposition from the Walthamstow branch which read of the proposals in the June 1902 E.C. report. In October of that year the time of the A.G.M. was so taken up with other business that none was left for a detailed consideration of the problem of Parliamentary Representation. Instead a sub-committee of five (quite distinct from the sub-committee of the E.C. appointed in March) was chosen from the A.G.M. delegates, the E.C., the Rules Revision Committee and the Standing Orders Committee to complete the drafting of a scheme for Labour representation.[33] Since the important work of Rules Revision could not be dealt with in the limited time available for the A.G.M. it was decided to recall the delegates as soon as possible after the Taff Vale judgment had been delivered and to complete all outstanding business in London.

When the adjourned General Meeting met in the Holborn Town Hall, London, early in January 1903, the delegates not only approved a complete revision of the rules but also agreed to the Scheme of Labour Representation presented to them by the A.G.M. sub-committee. The scheme was different in two very important respects from that endorsed by the E.C. in June of the previous year. In the first place it provided that no candidate should contest a constituency unless his candidature had been endorsed by both the local Trades Council and the Labour Representation Committee. Secondly, in place of the *voluntary* subscription proposed in June 1902, the subscriptions to the Parliamentary fund were to be *obligatory* on all members. Each candidate elected was to be paid £250 a year plus third-class return fare to his constituency.

Despite these radical changes in the conditions of the union's Parliamentary representation, the delegates agreed unanimously to instruct the sub-committee to be responsible for embodying its recommendations in the rules. This was done in March 1903.[34] The complete set of revised rules, including the new provisions concerning Parliamentary representation, came into force on July 1, 1903. Thus the situation from the summer of 1903 was that each member of the union, whatever might be his politics, was under obligation to give 1s a year towards the financing of Parliamentary candidates or M.P.s who had the support of the L.R.C.

The first protest about the new arrangements came from the Whitby branch which objected to a compulsory levy and urged that a vote of all the members should be taken on the question; but the E.C. ruled that it had no power to alter the decision of the supreme governing body of the union.

The first sign of a protest from the Walthamstow branch came at the A.G.M. at Peterborough in October 1903. The branch proposed to amend the resolution of the A.G.M. of 1894, so that it would read that 'the General Secretary should hold himself independent of any of the political parties' (instead of *either* of the political parties). Had it been carried, it would have amounted to a repudiation of the union's support of the L.R.C. and an endorsement of Richard Bell's Parliamentary policy, but the proposal was turned down.[35]

Osborne, therefore, summoned a meeting of his branch at which the question of the compulsory levy, Bell's political line and the Newcastle constitution of the L.R.C. were all discussed. The branch then carried a resolution in favour of a union ballot on the question of affiliation to the L.R.C. and a stop on the further payment of the levy until the dispute concerning Mr Bell's political policy was satisfactorily settled.[36] By June 1904, the E.C. had received requests from fifty-three other branches in favour of a ballot on the question of affiliation, but it was decided to let the members consider the question until the time of the A.G.M.[37]

At Bradford, in October 1904, the anti-socialists achieved a temporary victory. Not only did Congress agree not to press Richard Bell to sign the L.R.C. constitution, but also it was decided to amend Rule XIII, Section 4, Clause 4, to strike out the requirement that all A.S.R.S. candidates should have the endorsement of the Trades Council and L.R.C. and to substitute the words: 'All candidates shall be finally selected by a ballot of the members; the candidates receiving the largest number of votes shall be the candidates to contest constituencies.'

Nevertheless, in view of the fact that the E.C. had selected three socialist members of the A.S.R.S., Messrs Hudson, Wardle and Holmes, as Parliamentary candidates and the members of the union were paying the Parliamentary levy to help them with their campaign expenses, the Walthamstow branch sent a lengthy protest to the E.C. in March 1905. As Mr Osborne, in his covering letter to Mr Bell, mentioned that the branch would appeal to the law courts on the legality of a compulsory political levy, the E.C. wisely decided to take Counsel's opinion on the subject.[38]

Messrs J. H. Thomas, J. R. Bell and Richard Bell, who were deputed by the E.C. as a sub-committee to obtain an authoritative statement on the legality or otherwise of the levy, immediately determined that they would ask the best Counsel they could find to pronounce on the question. Mr Thomas therefore wrote to one of the most distinguished lawyers of the day, Sir Robert Reid (who later became Lord Loreburn and Lord Chancellor). He enclosed a copy of the rule book and asked Sir Robert whether he would be prepared to answer six questions about the legality of the rules concerning Parliamentary representation. Sir Robert replied that he would be willing to render his services—at the usual trade-union rates! At this stage it was pointed out by one of the sub-committee that Sir Robert Reid was well known for his Liberal sympathies and that his opinions on the subject in question might be regarded by some critics as biased. One of the sub-committee then said 'Who is there on the other side we could have?' and the name of Sir Edward Clark, a distinguished Conservative lawyer, was suggested. Thus the two men were asked to give a joint opinion to such questions as whether the A.G.M. could legally impose a compulsory levy to defray the expenses and support members of the A.S.R.S. elected to Parliament; whether part of the proceeds of the Parliamentary fund could be given to the L.R.C.; whether the contribution from the members could be enforced 'for any political purpose whatsoever'; whether a ballot of all the members was necessary to sanction a compulsory political levy; whether a member who refused to pay the political levy could be deprived of the friendly society benefits to which he would otherwise be entitled and whether a member who did not pay the political levy could be expelled from the union.

The two lawyers submitted their unanimous opinion to the E.C. on May 31, 1905. Owing to the fact that the rules for Parliamentary representation were not passed *at an annual general meeting* they believed the union had no power *at that time* to compel the payment of a levy and devote the proceeds to paying its M.P.s and its affiliation fee to the L.R.C.

But these were immediate technical difficulties that could be overcome by a proper observance of the rules. On the broader question of the interpretation of powers under the Trade Union Acts of 1871 and 1876, they were agreed that the A.G.M. could, by rules duly made, impose a compulsory contribution to support the union's M.P.s. They believed that the E.C. had 'a large discretion' in the way the political fund was used. They could see no necessity, under the rules, for a special ballot to be conducted. If penalties, such as deprivation of other benefits or expulsion from the union, were to be imposed for failure to contribute to the Parliamentary fund, they would have to be specified in the rules which would then be legally enforceable.

The E.C. now felt confident that since they had an assurance from two distinguished lawyers whose political opinions—to use the words of J. H. Thomas—were 'absolutely at variance', the union's expenditure of money on political objects was perfectly legal. To be doubly sure, they not only submitted to the A.G.M. the amendments to the rules exactly as suggested by the two learned Counsel, but they also decided to conduct a ballot of the entire membership on the question whether arrangements for a 3d a quarter Parliamentary levy should be embodied in the rules or not.[39]

The result of the ballot, revealed at the September 1905 meeting of the E.C., was a more convincing indication of the opinion of the members on the subject of Parliamentary representation than was the case with the earlier ballot in 1902. On this occasion the number voting was 26,762, or about 50 per cent of the membership; of these 21,713, or about 81 per cent were in favour of including in the rules provisions for the raising of a compulsory Parliamentary levy of 3d per quarter per member, and 4,825, or about 18 per cent were against.[40]

Mr Osborne was a delegate at the Sheffield A.G.M. in October 1905 when the resolution:

'That this conference accepts the decision of the recent ballot and agrees to the principle of a levy of 3d a quarter for the purpose of Labour Representation being embodied in the rules.'

and an amendment:

'That the cost of providing for Parliamentary Representation shall be met out of the present contributions, thus obviating the necessity for the levy recommended by the E.C.'

were both the subject of debate. Although Osborne spoke forcefully in favour of the amendment and against the resolution, the amendment was defeated by 55 votes to 3 and the resolution carried by 55 votes to 1.[41] Congress proceeded to approve the alterations in the rules as advised by Sir Robert Reid and Sir Edward Clark. There could be no mistaking the fact that those who desired it to be a condition of membership of the union that members should give financial backing to Labour M.P.s had received overwhelming support, and that everything possible had been done to ensure that the decision was reached democratically. Nevertheless, Osborne was far from satisfied. Speaking on another resolution favouring dis-affiliation from the L.R.C., he warned the union of further tribulation to come:

'Rather than that their members should be coerced, every resource of civilization would be availed of including application for a legal injunction. Let them have Parliamentary representation as much as they liked, but let it be by and under the control of their own people.'[42]

Three months later when the E.C. met for the first time after the A.G.M. it was informed that the persistent Mr Osborne had lodged an appeal to the Registrar of Friendly Societies against the revised rules, but that the Registrar had decided that they were in order and had regis-tered them accordingly.[43]

There the matter might well have rested had it not been for the remark-able result of the General Election in January 1906.

The success of twenty-nine of the L.R.C. candidates and the subsequent formation of the Parliamentary Labour Party heartened the Socialists in the union and impressed the waverers. So substantial a group of M.P.s might well influence the trend of legislation. The case for making it obligatory on the union's M.P.s to join the Labour group in Parliament was much stronger than it had been before the election. In June 1906, therefore, the E.C., prompted by requests from the Ormskirk and Grimes-thorpe branches, agreed by nine votes to four to recommend to the A.G.M. an alteration to Rule 13 by the addition of the words: 'All candidates shall sign and accept the conditions of the Labour Party and be subject to their Whip.'

In vain did Richard Bell warn the delegates at the A.G.M. in October that 1906 'was not the year for alteration of any rule',[44] that the rules had been revised in the previous year, and that under Rule 18 (which concerned the method of introducing amendments) it was provided that rules could only be altered every third year and then only on the recommendation of at least twelve branches. It was true that the rules also said that if the E.C. recommended an alteration of the rules as 'a matter of urgent necessity' they could be altered by *any* A.G.M. However, the E.C. in recommending to the delegates at Cardiff the alteration of Rule 13 had brought in no plea of urgency. Nevertheless, the majority of delegates did not consider Bell's objection sufficiently important and carried the clause, as amended, by forty votes to two.[45] Conference had gratuitously provided Osborne with more ammunition.

Had it not been for the attention drawn to the Labour movement by its remarkable success at the polls in January 1906, Osborne's protest might have died away through lack of financial support. The emergence of a strong Labour group in the House of Commons caused some alarm in capitalist circles. The *Daily Mail* noted how:

'. . . these working men by the simple device of collecting one penny per month per man from their trade unions, [had] placed themselves on so firm a financial basis that they are able to meet the representatives of capital on even ground at the polls. . . . Their present success will be found to prove the beginning of a movement that will require much watching by capitalists of all conditions.'[46]

Although the *Daily Express* at first took a benevolent attitude towards Labour's success, claiming it to be reasonable that 'as other members have means to defray their own expenses, so the Labour organization should continue to pay their representatives as before',[47] it was not long before the paper changed its tune to one of violent opposition to the political levy. Sir Alexander Henderson, the Chairman of the Great Central Railway, who was at this time thinking in terms of large scale railway amalgamation as a means of economizing in labour power and curbing the power of trade unions, had a strong financial interest in the *Daily Express*.[48] From September 5, 1906, this newspaper conducted a sustained campaign to protect 'honest trade unionists' who were standing up to the 'pernicious doctrines of the Socialists'. Every day for more than a month the paper's largest front page headline warned readers of 'The Fraud of Socialism'. Great prominence was given to a letter from Percy R. Gayton, a member of the Exeter branch of the A.S.R.S. who protested that his enjoyment of the Society's sickness and other benefits was conditional upon his paying 1s a year to the Parliamentary fund.[49] Next day it was reported that Gayton's letter had struck 'a responsive note among the sane and practical working men'. Mr Bell, who had been interviewed as 'a typical representative of the best in sober, solid trade unionism', claimed that the most Independent of the Labour M.P.s were those who were free of the Labour Whip.

At this point Osborne took advantage of the publicity offered by this mass circulation daily newspaper to ask for financial support for legal action against his own union. In a letter to the paper written on September 16, 1906, Osborne claimed that it was the duty of the Government to protect the political freedom of the subject. He expounded the intricacies of his political philosophy:

'That Socialism is diametrically opposed to trade unionism. The latter exists for trade purposes; the former would abolish trade. That Trade Unions would regulate wages, while Socialism would abolish wages.'

The Walthamstow branch of the A.S.R.S., he wrote, would test the case against the union 'if only the funds can be obtained from a private or public source'. If these funds were forthcoming then 'a test case against the Amalgamated Society of Railway Servants would be a test case against the whole system'.[50] Further appeals were made by Osborne in the paper on September 21st and 27th. His purpose was 'to defeat the advancing Socialist army' by depriving it of its 'war chest'.

By the end of September 'sufficient funds were forthcoming' to enable Osborne to open his test case.[51] Owing to his good fortune in being elected to the Walthamstow Borough Council in April 1906, Osborne had already come to be on friendly terms with Mr Wilkinson, a fellow councillor, who was a solicitor with a practice in the City of London. Wilkinson undertook to conduct the case, and immediately the courts were opened in October 1907, caused the writs to be issued. By this time Osborne claimed to have raised £250. At its meeting in December 1907 the E.C. was informed of the issuance of the writ by Osborne against the Society to test the validity of the compulsory Parliamentary levy.

IV

Mr Jenkins, K.C., Counsel for the Prosecution, used two main arguments against the union in presenting his case to Mr Justice Neville in the Chancery Division of the High Courts of Justice on July 21 and 22, 1908. Firstly, he contended that the alteration of the rules under which the Parliamentary levy was authorized by the A.G.M. in October 1906 was invalid. Rule 18 of the union read:

'No new rule shall be made, nor shall any of the rules herein contained be amended, altered, or rescinded, except by the Annual General Meeting every third year.'

Rule 13, which concerned the Parliamentary levy, had been amended by the A.G.M. in 1905. By Rule 18, therefore, it was not possible for the union legally to alter the rules concerning Parliamentary representation until 1908. The action taken by the A.G.M. in 1906 was therefore *ultra vires* or beyond the scope or authority which the union possessed at that time.

Mr Jenkins's second argument was that his client objected to the funds of the Society being handed over to a society (by which he meant the Labour Party) which was 'frankly socialistic'. He was not objecting to the Parliamentary fund as such:

'Mr Justice Neville: "Is your point that although they may vote for Parliamentary representation they may not institute a fund for it?"
Mr Jenkins: "I don't care about that. They may provide for representation

and have a subscription for purposes of furthering the objects of the union. What I say is that they cannot use the funds of the union for the purpose of furthering Socialism." '[52]

The Judge had so little difficulty in disposing of either of these two arguments that he did not need to call upon the Counsel for Defence to reply or to produce the witnesses on behalf of the union. What it amounted to was that Osborne had claimed against the Society on a technicality and on a difference of political opinion but not on the basis of profound principle. On the first argument that the rules made in 1906 were invalid, the Judge was impressed by the fact that the Registrar of Friendly Societies had registered the rules as correct after their amendment by the A.G.M. in 1906, and that in a very similar case which had come before the courts a short while previously—Rosenburg v. Northumberland Building Society —the Judge had taken the registration of the rules to mean that they were effectively operative even though there had been a violation of the proper procedure for their amendment. As to Mr Jenkins's second complaint that the union had 'gone into politics' (by which he meant Socialist politics) the Judge was equally unconvinced. It seemed to him that if you accepted the right of the executive of the union to spend money to promote the interests of the members by legislative enactments, it was 'a question of policy' whether those interests were best promoted by obtaining the return of purely trade-union candidates or by the support of that party in the State which seemed to the majority of the members of the union to be most worthy of its support.

'The trade unions, if they please, are at liberty just as much to affiliate themselves and to support the Socialist Party as they would be to affiliate to and support, if they pleased, either the Unionist Party or the Liberal Party. Once given the right to spend their money to promote their interests in the House of Commons, I think the question of how they could do so is surely a question of policy with which the court will not concern themselves.'[53]

The Judge admitted that in coming to his decision he had been influenced by the judgment given by Mr Justice Darling in the very similar case, Steele v. the South Wales Miners Federation, heard in 1907, when Steele, a miner, had failed in his appeal against the payment of a political levy.

After a comparatively brief summing up of the case, therefore, Mr Justice Neville declared that Osborne's action had failed and that he must pay costs. The adverse judgment delivered on July 22, 1908, put Mr Osborne on the horns of a dilemma. Either he must abandon the whole case and allow the continuance of what he regarded as the injustice of Liberal and Tory members of the A.S.R.S. being obliged to contribute to the funds of the Labour Party, or he must take the advice of his Counsel and appeal against Mr Justice Neville's judgment on such broad grounds of constitutional principle that in the very process of righting a wrong he might endanger political privileges—such as returning trade unionists to Parliament—which he still wished to retain. Apparently it was the decision of the Miners Federation in the late summer of 1908 to affiliate to the Labour Party which made Osborne go to his solicitor and tell him 'we must go the whole hog'. By their action, the miners 'had destroyed all that he desired to retain of Parliamentary representation' and he no longer felt any compunction in taking the risks of an appeal on more sweeping grounds.[54]

When Mr Osborne's attack was renewed before the Master of the Rolls in the Court of Appeal on November 12, 13 and 16, 1908, it was based on much more far-reaching and formidable arguments. Mr Jenkins, Counsel for the Prosecution, now stood as the defender of the constitutional rights of the ordinary citizen who was oppressed by powerful combinations of unscrupulous men. His main contention on this occasion was that it was *ultra vires* for a union to pay for Parliamentary representation as such. Much less was heard about Socialism. It was contrary to the interest of the State that a representative should be the mere mouthpiece of the vested interests who paid him. The fact that the union had violated its own rules was made a secondary consideration. Mr Jenkins was given encouraging tips on how to conduct his case by the Master of the Rolls and Lord Justice Fletcher Moulton. When Mr Peterson came to conduct the case for the defence he was subjected to a gruelling cross-questioning by Lord Justice Farwell:

'You alter the whole of our representative constitution if you are going to allow people to be driven in this way and to say that they can be compelled to vote in this way.'

Despite a very able speech for the defence by Mr Clement Edwards', who claimed that those who had framed the Trade Union Acts of 1871 and 1876 had not intended to restrict the rights of unions to return members to Parliament, judgment was given against the union. Lord Justice Fletcher Moulton declared that any agreement to bind a candidate to a political party was 'void as against public policy'.

On December 11, 1908, the E.C. came to the unanimous decision to appeal to the House of Lords which Osborne described as 'the last refuge of the Socialist!'[55]

Why did the union, with the eager co-operation of the Joint Standing Committee of the Parliamentary Committee of the T.U.C., the Labour Party and the General Federation of Trade Unions,[56] decide to take the case to the highest court of appeal in the realm? There were two main reasons. On grounds of equity it was regarded as grossly unjust that the vast resources of capital should be available to the secret funds of the two major parties of the State—the Liberal Party and the Conservative Party—but that the infant Labour Party, which fully disclosed the origin of its funds each year, should be denied, by a legal action, its principal source of income. A Government White Paper published in December 1908 revealed that in the course of that year railway companies had contributed £277 11s 1d to ratepayers' associations for the purpose of influencing local political policy.[57] Railway companies paid their directors generous salaries and then arranged for them to be nominated for Parliamentary constituencies. In the Parliament of 1900–6 there were no less than fifty-three railway directors to look after the interests of railway capital. Although their number in the House of Commons was reduced to twenty-one in the General Election of 1906, there were still seven times as many of them as there were railwaymen.[58] If there was nothing wrong in railway directors being paid their salaries while they sat in Parliament why was it wrong for the A.S.R.S. to pay those of its members who were elected? The second reason was that, for a whole generation, trade unions had financed political activities of all kinds from sending deputations to Ministers to supporting their own M.P.s in Parliament, and the legality of these actions had not been in question. Was it not therefore reasonable to assume that the decision given in the Court of Appeal was an aberration from the long run trend of the legal recognition of the political activities of trade unions? Surely it was not unrealistic to hope that the House of Lords might redress the balance upset by the lower court?

Events were to prove the trade-union leaders wrong in their estimate. When the A.S.R.S., acting on behalf of the Labour movement as a whole, brought the case before the Earl of Halsbury and Lords MacNaughten, Atkinson, James and Shaw in the House of Lords on July 22 and 23, 1909, it became apparent from the drift of the argument, that the decision of the Appeal Court was not likely to be reversed. On this occasion the argument mainly centred round the intention of the legislature when passing the Trade Union Act of 1876. The appellants maintained that the definition of a trade union contained in that Act was an identifying rather than an 'exhaustive one'—that enough was stated about the nature of a trade union to distinguish it from other organizations, but that no attempt was made to specify everything that a trade union might legally do. The fact that no mention was made in the 'objects' clause of the right to provide sickness and other benefits, was regarded as indicative of the fact that no exhaustive definition had been attempted, for nobody questioned the right of a union to provide these benefits. Osborne's Counsel, on the other hand, claimed that all things that it was lawful for a trade union to do had been defined in the Act. The financing of Parliamentary candidates had not been mentioned: therefore such activities were *ultra vires*. Besides this it was entirely contrary to public policy that an M.P. should be the paid servant of any outside pressure group.

It was not until December 21, 1909, that the five law lords published their verdict. They were unanimous in dismissing the appeal made by the union. The Earl of Halsbury and Lords Atkinson and MacNaughten declared the Parliamentary fund of the union to be *ultra vires* because Parliamentary Representation had not been mentioned in the Act of 1876. Lord Shaw had some doubts under this head. Lord James of Hereford was, of the five, in the best position to give an authoritative opinion on the intention of the legislature in 1876 since, as Sir Henry James, M.P., he had helped to frame the Act and steer it through Parliament. It is therefore significant that he gave an unequivocal opinion that the 'objects' clause of the Act was 'not a clause of limitation or exhaustive definition'. However, all the lords were in agreement on what they regarded as the far more important constitutional issue, taking very strong exception to the union's rule that its Parliamentary candidates should be members of the Labour Party and, if elected, should be subject to that Party's Whips in the House of Commons. Lord James thought that this meant that the union's M.P. undertook 'to forgo his own judgment', while Lord Shaw spoke the mind of them all when he said that the rule was 'fundamentally illegal and in violation of that sound public policy which is essential to the working of representative government'.[59]

Osborne, who was present to hear the verdict, 'That the appeal be dismissed with costs', declared, 'That is the end of the Seven Years' War'.

With scarce concealed delight, *The Times* commented that, coming as it did on the eve of a General Election the decision would be 'peculiarly inopportune' to those who would now have to look to voluntary subscriptions instead of 'forced exactions'.[60]

The full significance of the judgment was not everywhere immediately appreciated. But within a year, twenty-five injunctions had been granted against as many trade unions to prevent them paying the election expenses of Parliamentary candidates or salaries for their M.P.s. The income of twenty-four Labour M.P.s was affected.[61] Furthermore it was not only Parliamentary representation that was barred. David Shackleton, the weavers' M.P., informed the House of Commons that he had been told on very high authority that if he was to bring a deputation of cotton weavers to Westminster to interview a Minister of the Crown, he would have to bear the expense himself. Unions could not assist in any shape or form the funds of a political party at local election level.[62] Sidney Webb believed that not political action alone but 'any work of general education; the formation of a library; the formation or management of University Extension or W.E.A. classes; the subscriptions for circulating book boxes; the provision of public lectures; the establishment of scholarships at Ruskin College, Oxford, or any other college' were plainly *ultra vires* and illegal.[63] Mr Osborne had been so intent on getting rid of the bathwater of Socialism that he had also succeeded in throwing out the baby of all forms of non-industrial trade unionism—a baby for which he still held some lingering affection. He had been so concerned to prevent the union doing what he thought was wrong that he had succeeded in preventing the great majority of its members doing things it thought were right.

V

A question which was everywhere being asked in the Labour movement at that time was—How was Osborne, a head porter earning 23s a week and maintaining a wife and family, able to take a case to the High Court of Chancery, one of the most expensive tribunals in the land? The simple answer given by many of Osborne's contemporaries was that he was backed by the capitalists. The Webbs wrote that he was 'liberally financed from capitalist sources'.[64] Will Thorne, the gasworkers' M.P., said that the railway directors and shareholders were backing the action.[65] All this Osborne strenuously denied. In a letter written to the *Morning Post* on October 7, 1910, he claimed to have approached the T.U.C. with an offer to allow them to appoint some independent person to investigate the matter and test his bona fides. He received no replies to his two letters. He also wrote to the E.C. of the A.S.R.S. inviting its members to send a competent person to examine the accounts of the Walthamstow branch. At its meeting in September 1908, the E.C. rejected by nine votes to four a proposal that Richard Bell should send an auditor to examine the branch books. On November 10th, Osborne wrote to Mr Bell to inform him that his branch books and accounts 'were always at his disposal for inspection'. In a further letter written on December 6, 1908, Osborne claimed that such contributions as he had been able to collect had been by approaching individuals 'without any conditions whatever attached'. He was quite willing to submit a statement to the next quarterly meeting provided that the case was 'then settled'. It may have been because of this condition attached that the committee did not agree to examine the books of the branch.[66]

Alcock was told by a member of the branch that when the case was concluded, Osborne gave the branch an account of 'every individual subscription'. When Alcock expressed disbelief, he was shown one of the collecting books in which members of the Durham Lodge of Miners had subscribed a total of 29s 6d. Osborne printed and circulated an audited balance sheet for the appeal to the House of Lords which shows that he collected £384 19s 6d by public subscriptions and he recovered costs amounting to £523 19s 3d. The biggest item on the expenditure side was the solicitor's charges amounting to £853 19s 3d. However, these are only the accounts in connection with the Lords' appeal. On Osborne's own admission he had raised but £250 when the case opened before Mr Justice Neville. As this first (adverse) decision was not reversed until four months later a number of people had to wait for payment from Osborne until he recovered costs equal to £1,016 at the conclusion of the hearing in the appeal court.[67] Did someone act as guarantor so that Osborne was able with confidence to proceed to the appeal court? Perhaps the answer will never be known.

The fact that Walthamstow branch officials, after the dissolution of the branch in June 1910, returned some of the books but repeatedly refused to return the remainder, may or may not be an indication that Osborne's accounts would not bear examination.[68]

One thing can be stated with confidence: without the publicity given to his case over many months by the *Daily Express* it is very improbable that Osborne would have had the means at his disposal to conduct the case.

The direct money cost of the Osborne case to the Labour movement can be more precisely stated. The bill for the A.S.R.S. for the preliminary legal charges up to the decision of the Court of Appeal was £2,619 15s 8d. The cost of the appeal to the House of Lords was borne by the whole Labour movement and amounted to £4,477 3s 6d. The union's full legal costs in dealing with Osborne came to £5,306 8s 11d.[69] The indirect cost of the judgment to the union and the Labour movement through the loss of the Parliamentary levy was very much greater.

VI

Although at this moment of triumph on December 21, 1909, Osborne had said that it was the end of a Seven Years' War, this was far from being the case. The union got no peace from its Walthamstow branch for many months to come. Shortly after the Lords' judgment, Osborne instructed his solicitor to hold the trustees of the union responsible for ensuring that the £4,000 which was then standing in the Parliamentary fund was not used to support any of the union's Parliamentary candidates.[70] He also wrote objecting to the payment of Walter Hudson's salary and threatening further court action if it was not stopped, since he was occupied as an M.P. and not a union organizer. He wrote again to warn the E.C. that if it acted on the resolution of the A.G.M. of October 1909, and proceeded to appoint a Parliamentary Secretary, this would be an evasion of the injunction granted against the union.[71] When, early in the new year, the E.C. received a letter from Osborne's solicitor advising it how to dispose of the balance in the Parliamentary fund its patience was nearly exhausted. A resolution was passed warning Osborne that a 'continuance of his vexatious interference' which was obviously intended to 'injure and break up the effective progress' of the Society would be met by expulsion.

There being no respite (the trustees being next to have to endure Osborne's nagging letters) the E.C. reached the unanimous decision under Rule 9, Clause 14, in June 1910, to expel Messrs Osborne and Addison from the union and to dissolve the Walthamstow branch.[72] But still Osborne would not let go. On July 26, 1910, his solicitor served a writ against the union to rescind its decision to close the Walthamstow branch and expel two of its members. After a hearing lasting two days in November 1910, Mr Justice Warrington dismissed the case with costs, his main reason being that the Trades Union Act of 1871 prevented the action being maintained. Not being satisfied with this decision Osborne, having first written to *The Times* asking for financial support from the public,[73] took the case to the Court of Appeal which overruled Mr Justice Warrington's judgment in March 1911. The union then took steps again to appeal to the House of Lords and a day was fixed for the hearing of the case. But before the time appointed for the hearing, the union received a letter from Mr Osborne's solicitor, and after some negotiations it was agreed that all litigation on either side should be withdrawn in return for the union paying £650 to Mr Osborne's solicitor. The E.C. wisely reached the conclusion that if it won the case in the House of Lords they might not be able to recover the money from Osborne and that it might well cost more to prosecute the case than the union could recover from Mr Osborne. Thus came to an end a spate of litigation which had started in October 1907, and had lasted over four years.

Though he had ceased litigation, Osborne continued his political activity against the Parliamentary levy of trade unions right up to the outbreak of the First World War. He posted a copy of his pamphlet 'Trade Union Funds and Party Politics' to every M.P., he set up a 'Trade Union Political Freedom League' with its headquarters in his own home and intervened in by-elections in the London area. When a by-election was fought at Walthamstow in November 1910, Osborne urged his supporters to vote for the Conservative candidate rather than for Sir John Simon, the Liberal candidate, whom he did not regard as being sufficiently outspoken on the political levy. The local Labour group urged their followers not to vote for Simon because they did not regard his views on this subject as progressive enough! On a heavy poll Simon was elected with an increased majority. As the World War approached Osborne was to be heard speaking against the Trade Union Act of 1913 at meetings organized by the British Constitutional Association.[74]

VII

Faced with the sudden drying up of its source of income for political activity the union took emergency measures to make good the deficiency. In the summer of 1909 the Railwaymen's Parliamentary Representation Association was formed as a purely voluntary body with George Wardle, M.P., as Secretary. Members of the union were invited to make voluntary contributions to this fund and on December 13, 1909, all members were asked to inform the General Secretary by January 3, 1910, whether they desired their past contributions to the compulsory Parliamentary fund to be refunded or transferred to the new voluntary fund. By September 1910, 24,174 members had indicated their willingness to transfer the money standing in their name to the new fund and the trustees were thus able to pay over a cheque for £1,080. By such means as this the salaries of the union's three M.P.s were paid.

In the meantime the T.U.C. Parliamentary Committee, the E.C. of the General Federation of Trade Unions and the E.C. of the Labour Party had been active in exerting Parliamentary pressure. On November 10, 1910 a Special Conference of the combined Labour forces on the subject of the Osborne judgment was held in the Caxton Hall, Westminster, to prepare a case to be presented to the Prime Minister. In the Prime Minister's reception room at No. 10 Downing Street the following day, the press reporters found it difficult to take notes as the room was so crowded with the forty members of the deputation. Messrs Shackleton, Robinson and Gee stressed the serious restrictions imposed on the trade-union movement by the Osborne judgment. Mr Asquith in his reply conceded the importance of maintaining the direct representation of labour in the House of Commons and hoped to be able to announce the decision of the Government in a very short time.[75]

The members of the deputation did not have as long to wait and see as did deputations who saw the Prime Minister on behalf of other causes.

The Government's decision took the form of the Parliament Bill which introduced the payment of M.P.s (£400 a year) and became law as the Parliament Act in 1911. This reform, though welcomed by Labour M.P.s, was certainly not regarded as the final answer to the Osborne judgment. As Mr George Barnes explained to the House of Commons on November 18, 1910:

'Payment of members is all very well when you get there, but you have to get there first, and to get there a very considerable sum of money has got to be paid in the way of entrance fee.'[76]

David Shackleton told the House more precisely what that entrance fee had been in his case. The total expenses of his election campaign in January 1910 had been £1,160 including £320 for Returning Officer's expenses.

The final remedy only came with the Trade Union Act, 1913, which provided that trade unions could spend money on political objects, given the fulfilment of three conditions. A majority of the members would have to approve the political objects of the union in a secret ballot; the political fund would have to be kept entirely separate from the general fund and any person who had an objection to contributing to the political fund should have the right to 'contract out' of such payment by signing a form in which he indicated this intention.

Just as Mr Beasley's determined opposition to trade unions had served in the end greatly to strengthen their industrial power, so Mr Osborne's dogged opposition to the Parliamentary fund served greatly to strengthen the attachment of the trade-union movement to the Labour Party. When Osborne began his campaign in 1903, the trade-union M.P.s committed to support the Labour Representation Committee were a small minority swamped by the 'Lib.-Labs.' By the time the spate of litigation over the Osborne case ceased, only three Lib.-Lab. M.P.s survived whilst there were fifty M.P.s accepting the Whip of the Labour Party. Few votes at the Trades Union Congress have been so overwhelming as the vote in September 1910, on the resolution in favour of a new trade-union Bill which would include the legalization of the political levy. The figures were 1,717,000 for and 13,000 against.[77] The fact that one of the law lords involved in the Osborne judgment, Lord Shaw of Dunfermline, was a Liberal, and that the Liberal Government took until 1913 to bring in the Trade Union Act helped to sway trade-union opinion away from the Liberal Party. From a different angle, the Osborne judgment contributed to the unity of the Labour movement by teaching those M.P.s who set more store on Socialism than they did on Trade Unionism, which side their bread was buttered. The sudden drying up of the Parliamentary fund gave such leaders a more lively realization of their dependence on the trade unions.

VIII

In the course of the turmoil over Osborne and a General Election, the union acquired both a new General Secretary and new head offices. With the resignation of Richard Bell in December 1909, the E.C. appointed Mr James Edwin Williams (Assistant Secretary) as General Secretary (*pro tem.*). The result of the subsequent ballot announced in June 1910 was as follows:

Mr J. E. Williams	24,567
Mr W. Hudson, M.P.	17,970
Mr W. Hart	1,244

Mr Williams obtained an overwhelming majority of the votes cast in his native Wales and in Scotland; Mr Hudson would have won, hands down, if the election had been confined to the North East (from which he came) and to Ireland where he had served as an organizer. Mr Hart was the chief clerk at the Head Office.

The new General Secretary, who was 53 years of age, had joined the Pontypool branch of the A.S.R.S. as early as 1875 when he was employed as a signalman. Although he had lost a leg in a serious accident in 1877, this did not deter him from taking an active interest in union affairs or from participating in local politics. He was Secretary of the Pontypool branch for twenty-five years. Early in 1903, Mr Williams had been elected to the post of Assistant Secretary then vacant through the resignation of Mr Garrity. A man of sterling character and much charm, he was held in profound respect and affection by the membership.

Mr Williams's election caused a vacancy for the post of Assistant Secretary which was filled in September 1910, after Mr J. H. Thomas had scored a clear majority over the combined votes of both his opponents:

J. H. Thomas	20,113
W. Hart	10,411
G. W. Brown	5,710

G. W. Brown, who was a fireman member of Hull No. 2 branch, was well known for his left-wing views.

The condition of the Head Office of the Society at 72 Acton Street, Grays Inn Road, London, W.C.2, in 1908 was like a successful holiday-maker's overfilled suitcase—bulging at the sides, or to use the more sedate language of the E.C. at the time, the accommodation was 'taxed to the utmost'. With monotonous regularity the periodic visit of the scrutineers was followed by the illness of at least one of their number due to their having to work in a cold, concrete-paved basement built on a level with the drains. Among the reasons for the overcrowding in the office were the centralization of the funds in 1903, the passage of the Railway Servants (Hours of Labour) Act of 1893 and the Railway Servants (Prevention of Accidents) Act in 1900, and the introduction of the Conciliation Scheme in 1907. Richard Bell therefore made a strong recommendation to the E.C. in December 1908 that alternative accommodation should be sought. The E.C., complying with his wishes, appointed a sub-committee of five to confer with the trustees and make recommendations.

Early in 1909, the Building Committee, hearing that a site between Euston Road and Gower Place, which included houses numbered 193–203 inclusive in Euston Road and houses numbered 37–43 in Gower Place, was up for sale, negotiated for its purchase at £18,500. Early in 1909 the work of demolition was started and the whole building was completed in time for the opening by Sidney Webb on September 17, 1910. Although the building was erected to a height of three floors the external walls and foundations were designed to carry an additional floor if this was later found to be necessary. The Euston Road elevation was erected with polished Cornish granite and the Gower Place elevation was in red brick with Portland stone dressings to all openings. The total cost of the building including decoration and permanent furnishings amounted to £30,474 2s 0d and it was erected by trade-union labour throughout.[78]

Starting off at the Winchester Arms, Southwark, in December 1871, the Head Office staff had spent a short time in no less than six other premises before finally reaching stability at Unity House.[79]

Mr Sidney Webb's hard-hitting speech, delivered on the occasion of the opening of Unity House, caused a rumpus in the Board of Governors of the London School of Economics of which he was Chairman. He blamed the Government for indifference in dealing with the problem of overwork on the railways and for deliberate delay in the introduction of the payment of M.P.s, and he spoke of the 'colossal ignorance' of the judges involved in the Osborne case. He urged railwaymen to demand a minimum wage of 24s a week and a maximum 10-hour day. Lord Claud Hamilton, Chairman of the Great Eastern Railway, was so indignant, that without waiting to discuss the matter with Sidney Webb or even giving him notice of his intention to resign, he wrote a letter to *The Times* announcing his resignation from the Board of Governors. The same ill-mannered procedure was followed by two railway general managers, Messrs Oliver Bury of the Great Northern Railway and James Inglis of the Great Western Railway, who resigned from the Board of Governors at the same time. Lord Claud Hamilton wrote that since he had 'always understood that the teaching of economics necessarily inculcated respect for established law and order' without which no civilized society could prosper, he considered the 'holding up to contempt and ridicule' the highest legal court in the kingdom a 'singularly mischievous' course of action. In his courteously phrased reply a week later, Sidney Webb denied that membership of the governing body of the School made obligatory abstention from all controversial speech making, and he cited examples of strongly opinionated speeches delivered by Lord Claud Hamilton.[80]

It was certainly appropriate to the spirit of the times that Sidney Webb's speech was not simply confined to the customary polite pleasantries. The opening of Unity House was symbolical of the fact that the organization of railwaymen had greatly improved and that in future they would insist on having a much greater influence on the policy of the industry.

NOTES

1. *Daily Express*, October 3, 1906. R.R., October 5, 1906.
2. *Labour Leader*, September 16, 1899.
3. Report of the Second Annual Conference of the L.R.C., p. 30, 'Constitution of the Committee'.
4. This is how he described the situation to the E.C. Meeting of the A.S.R.S. on March 17, 1904. A.S.R.S., *Mr Bell and the L.R.C.*, p. 94.
5. Bealey and Pelling, *Labour and Politics, 1900–1906*, p. 201.
6. A.S.R.S., *Mr Bell and the L.R.C.*, p. 123.
7. Bealy and Pelling, p. 139. *Derby Daily Telegraph*, November 18 and 19, 1903.

8. In an interview with *Daily News* reporter, February 24, 1903.
9. A.S.R.S. E.C., March 1903, p. 15 and R. 24. Decisions of the A.G.M., 1903.
10. A.S.R.S. E.C., March 1904, pp. 119–20. *Labour Leader*, January 30, 1904.
11. A.S.R.S. E.C., March 1904, *Mr Bell, M.P. and the Labour Representation Committee* (Verbatim Report), p. 134.
12. A.S.R.S. A.G.M., October 1904, R. 29.
13. Report of the 5th Annual Conference of the Labour Representation Committee, January 1905, pp. 47–9.
14. A.S.R.S. E.C., June 1906, R. 24 (amended); A.G.M., October 1906, R. 33.
15. *Fifty Years of Railway Trade Unionism*, p. 403.
16. For the Debate, see Parliamentary Debates, March 13, 1907, Fourth Series, Vol. CLXX, Cols. 890–923, and *R.R.*, March 15, 1907.
17. A.S.R.S. E.C., March 1907, R. 14.
18. A.S.R.S. E.C., March 1908, p. 21, R. 19, and September 1908, pp. 7–11, R. 6.
19. A.S.R.S. Agenda and Decisions of the A.G.M., Leicester, October 1909, Appendix I, the A.G.M. and Mr Bell, M.P., p. 39.
20. A.S.R.S. A.G.M. Middlesbrough, October 1907, R. 5.
21. A.S.R.S. E.C., June 1909, Rs. 10 and 11.
22. *R.R.*, July 23, 1909, p. 10. Parliamentary Debates 1909, Vol. VII, Cols. 2378–411.
23. Report of Proceedings at the 42nd Annual T.U.C., Ipswich, September 1909, pp. 111–19.
24. *R.R.*, October 8, 1909, p. 11.
25. A.S.R.S. Agenda and Decisions of the A.G.M., Leicester, October 1909, Appendix I. The A.G.M. and Mr Bell, M.P., p. 77.
26. *R.R.*, December 17, 1909.
27. A.S.R.S. General Secretary's Report to the A.G.M. 1910, p. 11.
28. A.S.R.S. E.C., December 1909, p. 7.
29. Alcock, p. 340.
30. *R.R.*, February 26, 1909.
31. A.S.R.S. E.C. December 1901, Rs. 22 and 23.
32. A.S.R.S. E.C. March 1902, p. 3, Scrutineers' Report.
33. A.S.R.S. Decisions of the A.G.M. Swansea, October 1902, R. 12.
34. A.S.R.S. Decisions of the Adjourned Special General Meeting, January 1903, Rs. 42, 43. A.S.R.S. E.C. March 1903, p. 10.
35. A.S.R.S. Decisions of the A.G.M. Peterborough, October 1903, R. 43.
36. W. V. Osborne, *My Case*, p. 15.
37. A.S.R.S. E.C. June 1904, R. 21.
38. A.S.R.S. E.C. March 1905, R. 23.
39. A.S.R.S. E.C. June 1905, pp. 16–28, and Rs. 20–24. A.S.R.S. Presidential Address of J. H. Thomas to the A.G.M., October 1905, p. 23. Parliamentary Debates, May 5, 1927, Series 5, Vol. 205, Col. 1873, for speech by J. H. Thomas in which he recalled the incident.
40. A.S.R.S. E.C. September 1905, p. 8.
41. A.S.R.S. Decisions of the A.G.M. Sheffield, October 1905, R. 66.
42. Quoted in Alcock, p. 336.
43. A.S.R.S. E.C. December 1905, R. 17.
44. *R.R.*, October 5, 1906.
45. A.S.R.S. Decisions of the A.G.M. Cardiff, October 1906, R. 38.
46. *Daily Mail*, January 17, 1906.
47. *Daily Express*, January 17, 1906.
48. *R.R.*, October 2, 1908.
49. *Daily Express*, September 1906.

50. W. V. Osborne, *My Case*, p. 18, and *Daily Express*, September 17, 1906.
51. W. V. Osborne, *op. cit.*, p. 23.
52. *The Times*, July 22, 1908.
53. *The Times*, July 23, 1908.
54. W. V. Osborne, letter written to the E.C. of the A.S.R.S., December 6, 1908, quoted in the E.C. Minutes, December 1908, p. 51.
55. A.S.R.S. E.C. December 1908, R. 25. Osborne's statement taken from *My Case*, p. 36.
56. By R. 24 of E.C. December 1908.
57. P.P. 1909, Vol. LXXVII, p. 51.
58. *R.R.*, February 9, 1906.
59. In the House of Lords between the A.S.R.S. and W. V. Osborne, December 21, 1909. Judgment, pp. 165–82. Lent by courtesy of Mr F. Donlon of the E.C. of the N.U.R., 1961.
60. *The Times* (Leading Article), December 22, 1909.
61. T.U.C. Parliamentary Committee, 7th Quarterly Report, December 1910, p. 28.
62. Parliamentary Debates, April 13, 1910, 5th Series, Vol. XVI, Col. 1356.
63. S. Webb, *The Osborne Revolution*.
64. *History of Trade Unionism* (1920 Edition), p. 608.
65. *The Times*, December 23, 1909.
66. Letters in A.S.R.S. E.C. December 1908, pp. 49–53. Explanation of E.C.'s refusal to examine Walthamstow branch books given in Alcock, p. 340.
67. T.U.C. Sheffield, September 1910, p. 110. Costs of the Osborne judgment balance sheet *re* the appeal to the House of Lords printed in Alcock, p. 343.
68. A.S.R.S. E.C. December 1910, R. 31.
69. *Ibid.*, and A.S.R.S. Report and Financial Statements for 1910, p. 34.
70. *R.R.*, December 31, 1909.
71. A.S.R.S. E.C. December 1909, pp. 27–37.
72. A.S.R.S. E.C. June 1910, R. 29.
73. *The Times*, December 9, 1910.
74. *The Times*, April 13, June 2, October 27, November 3, 1910, February 4, 1913.
75. T.U.C. Parliamentary Committee, 7th Quarterly Report, December 1910, pp. 25–34.
76. Parliamentary Debates, November 18, 1910, 5th Series, Vol. 20, Col. 120.
77. Report of Proceedings at the 43rd Annual T.U.C. Sheffield, September 12–17, 1910, p. 157.
78. A.S.R.S. E.C. December 1908, pp. 122–3, February 13, 1909, pp. 3–4, March 1909, pp. 109–10. June 1909, p. 106. September 1909, p. 113, General Secretary's Report to the A.G.M. 1909, pp. 12–17, E.C. March 1911, pp. 93–5.
79. To reassure those who might otherwise be unjustifiably shocked by this statement it may be as well to mention that the other premises in the order of their occupation were 308 New Cross Road, S.E., later the site of Deptford Town Hall; 25 Finsbury Square, E.C.; 306 City Road; 55 Colebrooke Row; the Club and Institute Union, Clerkenwell Road, E.C.; and 72 Acton Street, Grays Inn Road; Alcock, p. 267.
80. *The Times*, September 19, October 18 and 25, 1910.

CHAPTER X

THE ALL-GRADES MOVEMENT OF 1906-7
AND ITS OUTCOME

I

THE cost of living rose steadily in the ten years which elapsed between the all-grades movement of 1897 and that of 1906-7. In 1905 alone it rose by 4·5 per cent whilst wages, rising by only 2·6 per cent, failed to keep pace.[1] Until the Taff Vale decision was reversed in the Trade Disputes Act of 1906, industrial action to rectify this state of affairs was difficult and dangerous, but with the restraints of the law eased there was a notable upsurge of union activity in the second half of 1906.

It is easy to understand why the A.S.R.S. was not immune from this general trade-union revival. Railwaymen had a greater cause to be restive than did men in most other occupations. Over the period 1886-1906 their weekly wage rates increased by only 5 per cent compared with increases of 18 per cent in the building industry, 23 per cent in cotton manufacturing and 26 per cent in engineering.[2] The average weekly wage of railwaymen at 24s 7d was lower than the rate for each industry listed in a Board of Trade Survey in 1906-7.[3] Yet their labour was becoming each year more productive. The use of larger capacity trucks and more powerful locomotives made possible the carriage of 11,300,000 tons more goods in 1905 than in 1904, though train mileage decreased by 400,000 miles. The greatly increased volume of traffic was conveyed by some 200 less engines and sets of men. The increased strain imposed on firemen who, in the case of the larger locomotives had to shovel nearly double the quantity of coal without being paid a penny more, may well be imagined.[4]

An examination of the financial position of the leading railway companies during 1906 revealed that this increase in productivity together with the revival of trade, had resulted in an improvement of profits. During the first half year of 1906 the nineteen largest companies made an addition of £566,000 to their net earnings, an improvement of nearly 12 per cent in the amount available for distribution in dividends on ordinary stock compared with 1905.[5] A reputable financial journal declared in the autumn of 1906:

'We consider that the railway stocks are a more tempting purchase than they have been for years.'

When it went on to assert that:

'The companies can meet the wishes of those men who are performing harder and better work than hitherto, and can remove the discontent which the men feel. The cost of doing so is relatively small, and the additional sum can easily be provided out of increased earnings.'[6]

it is not surprising that active branch members felt that the time was propitious for a big campaign for improved conditions.

II

When the members of the E.C. at their June 1906 meeting were confronted by a demand from thirty branches for the launching of a national all-grades campaign they decided to sanction the movement and to instruct Richard Bell to make arrangements for three separate all-grades conferences for England and Wales, Scotland, and Ireland.[7] The A.G.M. at Cardiff carried unanimously a resolution supporting the campaign for the improvement in the hours and wages of railwaymen and appealing to the 'nons' to join the ranks.[8] A great conference of 573 English and Welsh delegates was held at Birmingham from November 26 to 28, 1906, whilst similarly well attended and enthusiastic meetings were held in Glasgow and Dublin in October.

In their all-grades programme the delegates at these conferences demanded 'that eight hours constitute the standard day for drivers, firemen, guards (goods and passenger), shunters, signalmen and platelayers, and that ten hours should be the maximum working day for all other classes of railwaymen'. They claimed that 'no man should be called upon to "book on" more than once for one day's work and that no man should be called out for duty with less than nine hours' rest'. They asked for an overtime rate of time and a half with a minimum rate of time and a quarter for Sunday duty, Christmas Day and Good Friday being regarded as Sundays. They staked a claim for the guaranteed week:

'That independent of Sunday duty, a week's wages be guaranteed to all men whose conditions of service compel them to devote their whole time to the companies.'

Because wages were disgracefully low they asked for an immediate advance of 2s a week for all grades with, in addition, a London allowance of 3s a week. Among the other important items were the proposed abolition of the trip, tonnage and classification systems and the demand that signalmen should not be called upon to take fogging duty.[9] Undoubtedly it was the demand for union recognition which was to be given the greatest emphasis and to attract the greatest attention in subsequent months. The provisional committee appointed by the all-grades delegate conferences resolved that 'The time has arrived when the members of the Society insist on the recognition of Mr Bell and other head officials by the railway companies, to negotiate on their behalf and, further, that we do not enter into negotiations with any company in connection with this programme without full recognition'.[10] At their meeting in December 1906, the E.C. gave priority to the question of recognition in the belief that once this had been achieved the numerical strength and hence the bargaining position of the union on the all-grades demands would be greatly increased.[11]

When the actions of the leadership of the A.S.R.S. during 1907 are examined, what appears remarkable is the patience and perseverance displayed in the approach to the companies. Before a reluctant decision was made to organize a strike ballot, three separate attempts—spread over a period of seven months—were made to persuade the railway directors to negotiate. A fourth attempt was made whilst the strike ballot was being conducted three months later.

The first attempt was made on January 18, 1907, when a copy of the all-grades programme was sent to each board of directors in the country with a request that they should receive a deputation from their men led by an official of the A.S.R.S. Mr Bell's letter failed to bring any positive results. The chairmen of the leading companies consulted one another and agreed in principle to a common stand against the recognition of the union, although each board made its own decision as to the form that the reply— if any—would take.[12] Some, in fact, decided to ignore the union completely, others sent a formal acknowledgment, whilst the majority offered a brief explanation of their reasons for refusal. Typical was the reply received from the General Manager of the Great Eastern Railway on January 30th:

'Dear Sir,

In reply to your letter of the 18th instant, I am instructed by my directors to inform you that they decline to admit of the intervention of any third party between them and the company's employees, who are well aware that they can, through the proper channels, address the directors on any question they desire, and that any petition from them always receives the most careful consideration.

Yours truly,

J. F. S. GOODAY.'[13]

The decision to make a second approach to the companies was taken at a special meeting of the E.C. on February 4th and 5th when Richard Bell was asked to write again renewing the request for discussions. This action was taken on February 22nd. Such replies as were received were brief and uncompromising in tone.

At joint conferences held in June and July between the E.C. and the all-grades provisional committees of Birmingham, Glasgow and Dublin, it was decided that the directors should be given yet one more chance to change their minds, and consequently on July 20th Richard Bell wrote a third time emphasizing that it was not the intention of the union, if given recognition, to interfere with questions of discipline. Only after it was seen that the replies to this further appeal were as unsatisfactory as the earlier ones, did the E.C., at its September meeting, reluctantly decide to conduct a ballot of the membership to ascertain opinion on strike action to enforce the all-grades programme. Ballot papers were to be returned by October 28th.[14]

During the summer, hundreds of meetings in support of the programme were organized. The railwaymen's day of that summer was on May 12th when at railway centres all over the country about 150,000 railwaymen took part in meetings and processions. In London 20,000 men, kept in step by the music of twelve bands, marched from the embankment to Hyde Park where they were addressed from three platforms, from one of which Mr A. G. Walkden of the Railway Clerks' Association spoke in support of the movement. Mr Lowth, Secretary of the General Railway Workers' Union, supported the Manchester demonstration. Many of the rank and file of the A.S.L.E. & F. supported these and other efforts.

Early in 1907 the head office staff had been exceptionally busy collating information on wages and hours received on over 4,500 sheets of paper from hundreds of individuals and branches. The outcome, 'The Railwaymen's Charter' or Green Book, was a masterpiece of publicity which showed that over 100,000 men employed on the railways—an estimated 39 per cent of the total—had a standard weekly wage of under £1 0s 0d a week whilst only 11 per cent of those employed were paid in excess of 30s a week. Only just over 7 per cent of the railwaymen had an 8-hour day, two-thirds worked a basic 10-hour day and over a quarter a 12-hour day. Though the railway companies in the Red Book published by the *Railway News* challenged the accuracy of those statements, they were proved to be correct in a Board of Trade survey published in 1912.[15]

While the strike ballot papers were being prepared and despatched, Richard Bell, always the peacemaker, composed a fourth letter. Having gained the strong impression from the close similarity of many previous replies that the companies were in collusion, he decided this time to write to the Secretary of the Railway Companies' Association, with a request for an interview to discuss what was implied in the demand for union recognition.

At the meeting of the council of the Association held on October 11th, the Chairman, Lord Stalbridge, in opening a discussion on Mr Bell's letter, expressed the hope 'that on this matter there would be unanimity among the companies', in refusing the offer. He was not disappointed. The matter was disposed of with 'comparative promptitude'. The council unanimously approved a letter drafted by the association's solicitors and containing the statement: 'Even if my council considered such a meeting desirable they could not under the powers conferred upon them, take any action in a matter which affects the relations between each individual company and its own staff.'[16] At a public meeting in Paddington shortly afterwards, Richard Bell criticized the casuistry of the directors in these words:

'When the men appealed to the companies individually they met collectively and decided what they should do. When the men communicated with the companies collectively they replied they had no power to deal with the question collectively and that each company must deal with its men individually. If that was not playing the game of bluff with a serious question, what was it?'[17]

The union was up against a brick wall. Only the strike remained.

III

It is necessary to look elsewhere than in the replies of the railway managers to Mr Bell's letters to find the main reasons advanced for the refusal to recognize the union. Lord Claud Hamilton, Chairman of the Great Eastern Railway, addressing the half-yearly meeting of the company in July, took it upon himself to justify on behalf of the companies (as a whole), the refusal to recognize the union. He asserted that 'full control by the directors was essential for the maintenance of strict discipline'[18] and that the division of control with the union would impair both discipline and safety. The union reply to this argument was that discipline and safety on the two railways whose directors had recognized the Union, i.e. the North Eastern and the District, was better than on railways where there was no union recognition. He denied the right of the A.S.R.S., 'which only included a minority of the railway servants', to speak on behalf of the majority. This was undoubtedly the strongest argument in the companies' case and explains the union's determined efforts to boost membership throughout 1907. But it was to some extent nullified by the practice of some companies in exerting pressure, by direct or indirect means, on their employees to renounce union membership. Richard Bell, in a speech at St Pancras Town Hall on October 17, 1907, cited one instance of this kind. Inspector Rollinson, a member of the A.S.R.S. of fourteen years' standing, received a letter from his manager in the Midland Railway informing him that since 'as a member of the A.S.R.S.' he 'ceased to be a free agent', he was to 'stand on one side' as an inspector and do the work of a goods guard at his present rate of pay.[19] What was strange was that it had taken the company fourteen years to recognize the great dangers inherent in Inspector Rollinson's membership.

Another favourite argument of the companies was summed up in a statement made by the General Manager of the London and North Western Railway on January 31, 1907:

'The rules of the company provide that any servant, if he feels himself aggrieved, can appeal to the Board through his superior officer, and all appeals of the kind receive, at the hands of the Board, full consideration. This rule is well known to the staff and acted upon by its members.'[20]

Whilst it would be inaccurate to deny that any improvements were obtained by the method of petition and deputation, Richard Bell expressed a widespread opinion of the inadequacy of the approach when he cited numerous examples of delays and frustration. In July 1903, goods guards, signalmen and shunters on the Great Western Railway endeavoured by petition signed by nearly 1,000 men in each of those grades to get some improvement in their conditions. In November 1903, an interview took place, but nothing was conceded; and in March 1904, a further appeal was made for another interview. Finally, in April 1904, a refusal of this request was received. He cited similar instances of unsuccessful appeals from other grades on the London and North Western Railway, the Midland Railway, and the Great Eastern.[21] In view of such experiences it was unlikely that the men would be greatly impressed by their employers' arguments.

IV

When asked in October 1907, 'Are you in favour of handing in your notice to withdraw your labour at a given time in order to secure representation by the Society's officials to negotiate the full national programme as decided by your delegates at the Conferences?' 76,925 members of the A.S.R.S. voted 'yes', 8,773 'no', whilst there were 2,436 spoilt papers (mostly through the failure of the voter to state his grade or company). The majority of these voters favoured the strike. The total membership of the union at the time was 97,631.

Though a smaller proportion of the members of the General Railway Workers' Union voted in a parallel ballot, the vote was even more decisive with 3,025 for, and only 84 against, strike action.[22] The result of the A.S.R.S. ballot was declared at a monster rally held in the Albert Hall, London, on Sunday, November 3rd. The Hall was filled to capacity. A crowd, mostly railwaymen, and estimated to total 30,000, so congested the street outside, that a worried policeman, seemingly unaware of the identity of its occupant, diverted down Exhibition Road a motor car taking the King of Spain to Buckingham Palace.[23]

The day before the rally the E.C. had met with the intention of fixing the date for the commencement of the strike, but Richard Bell was able to inform them that he had received that morning from Lloyd George, then President of the Board of Trade, an invitation to the E.C., the President and the General Secretary to meet him at the Board of Trade offices at 3.30 p.m., on November 6th. The E.C., therefore, decided to defer further action until after that date.

In fact there was little likelihood of a strike. Lloyd George, who worked with the greatest energy to achieve a peaceful settlement, must have had fresh in his mind the fate of Lord Stanley who, as Postmaster-General in the Conservative administration in 1905, had stubbornly refused to compromise with the Postal Association and the Post Office Trade Union and had been defeated in the General Election early in 1906. Recognition of the unions had quickly followed the change of Government.[24]

Although the A.S.R.S. programme gave priority to the question of recognition, the rank and file were unaware of the fact that Richard Bell confessed to Mr G. E. Askwith (later Lord Askwith), Assistant Secretary in charge of the Railway Department at the Board of Trade, that 'he was not going to press for recognition if he obtained a satisfactory method of dealing with grievances, consideration of the programme and more opportunity for the men to deal with the condition of their lives.'

Naturally enough Mr Askwith passed on this information to his chief. Richard Bell's action is all the more remarkable in view of the priority in the campaign given to the question of recognition and in view of the fact that he alone of the sixteen members of the Parliamentary Committee of the T.U.C. did not have his union recognized by the employers.[25]

The attitude of the directors, with the exception of those of the District and North Eastern Railways, who recognized the union, in consistently maintaining a blank refusal to negotiate, became increasingly unpopular with the public and the newspapers. The *Daily News* considered the directors' attitude 'untenable'; the *Daily Mail* believed that they had made 'a tactical blunder in refusing to meet Mr Bell'; the *Daily Chronicle* concluded that 'one of the most unfortunate decisions in the history of British industry' had been taken by those in charge of the railways; the *Daily Graphic* feared that they 'were in some danger of losing the support of public opinion'; the *Economist* had no doubt that 'the directors had acted wrongly in refusing to confer' and that 'they would not satisfy public opinion in the country if they persisted in a blank negative'. Almost alone among the great daily newspapers, *The Times* opposed the union's claim. Whilst, with unconscious humour, it conceded that 'a little addition to weekly wages would be acceptable' it was convinced that 'the bulk of the men are undoubtedly satisfied with their present conditions'.[26] On the other hand, from his pulpit at the Westbourne Park Baptist Chapel, the famous preacher, Dr John Clifford, claimed that 'it was surely a condition demanding investigation that men responsible for the lives of hundreds of persons should be working eighteen hours a day'.[27]

In view of this formidable barrage of criticism it would have been very unwise of the leading railway directors and managers to have refused the invitation of Lloyd George to meet him at the Board of Trade on October 25th. Seventeen chairmen and twelve general managers in fact attended on that occasion.[28] At these initial discussions Lloyd George, armed with the information received from Mr Askwith, was able to tell them that 'he would not press, and they would escape, recognition',[29] but that they must accept a conciliation scheme, the details of which would be left to them. When further meetings were held on November 1st and 2nd the directors and managers were represented by a committee comprising the chairmen of the six principal companies. Finally, on November 6th, Lloyd George saw the six chairmen at 11.30 in the morning and then both the chairmen and the union delegation (comprising the E.C., the General Secretary and the President) at 3.30 in the afternoon. The company chairmen, however, refused to meet in the same room as the union leaders and Lloyd George had, in consequence, to flit from one group to the other to keep abreast of developments. Both sides to the dispute signed the agreement later that same evening.[30]

V

In view of what has hitherto been written on the origin and authorship of the conciliation scheme of 1907 it is as well to emphasize that although it was publicized as Lloyd George's scheme, it was, in fact, largely the work of Mr Sam Fay, General Manager of the Great Central Railway. His memorandum, embodying the main principles of the scheme as finally adopted, was accepted by the six chairmen who submitted it to Lloyd George on November 6th. The finishing touches were added by Sir Hubert Llewellyn Smith, Permanent Secretary of the Board of Trade.[31] When the representative of the railwaymen appeared for the first time at the Board of Trade on the afternoon of November 6th, they were presented with a cut and dried scheme which, they were told, was the last word on the subject. According to one report,[32] they were given twenty minutes to decide either to accept the agreement or to take the responsibility for rejecting it and declaring a general strike on the railway system. When they asked for time to consult the membership of the A.S.R.S. they were told that the decision must be made there and then. Even if many drivers could be counted on to come out on strike, the support of A.S.L.E. & F. members was, to say the least, doubtful, as on February 5, 1907, at an early stage on the all-grades campaign, Mr Fox, their General Secretary, had written to the Railway Companies' Association, 'Please note Mr R. Bell is not authorized to negotiate for us'.[33]

Interviewed by the *Financial Times* later on in the campaign, Mr Fox had said: 'The points of difference between the Amalgamated Society headed by Mr Bell and the Engineers and Locomotive Society, of which I am Secretary, are very material and such that we cannot possibly fall in with their programme.'[34]

Thus the conciliation scheme of November 6, 1907, reflected the opinion of the more moderate railway chairmen—Lord Stalbridge dissenting—and *The Times*, in summing up the situation, was able to declare that:

'The basis of the scheme agreed on is entirely in accordance with the companies' expressed views as to the best means of dealing with their employees, i.e. by direct representation from the men concerned—and that being so, they can well afford to concede to the other side some minor points in the formulation of the scheme for carrying that principle into effect.'[35]

If it had been announced as a scheme drafted by Mr Sam Fay and sponsored by the six leading railway chairmen it would have stood little chance of acceptance by the railwaymen. As Mr Lloyd George's scheme, however, it could be advocated as a brilliant 'compromise' imposed on both directors and union officials by a determined and public spirited President of the Board of Trade. In any event this manœuvre had every appearance of success. The press was almost unanimous in its praise of the Minister. Both the *Daily News* and the *Daily Chronicle* carried the front page headline 'Peace with Honour!', the *Morning Post* declared that 'Mr Lloyd George deserves well and will receive the congratulations of his countrymen', the *Star* assured its readers that he was 'the most popular man in the country'; the *Daily Express* had reason to be more than usually pleased since the dispute had been 'settled definitely on the lines which the *Express* had laid before the public'.[36] Thus at least four persons claimed paternity of the new offspring—Mr Sam Fay, Mr Lloyd George, Sir Hubert Llewellyn Smith and the editor of the *Daily Express*; but despite the self-assurance of the last-named, the best claim was Mr Fay's.

The principal feature of the first Railway Conciliation Scheme was the establishment of two types of Board of Conciliation on each railway company. Sectional boards were to deal with problems arising in the principal grade groupings, e.g. the locomotive drivers, firemen and cleaners would form one grouping and signalmen and pointsmen another, and the board would be composed of the elected representatives of these grade groups and the nominated representatives of the company, in equal numbers. The area of the larger companies was to be divided into districts with sectional boards in each district. The competence of these boards was to be confined to 'rates of wages and hours of labour'. Questions of discipline could not be discussed. The Central Conciliation Board in each company, consisting of representatives of the company and one or more representatives chosen from the employees' side of each Sectional Board, was to endeavour to reach a settlement if there was no positive outcome at the Sectional Board level. If neither Sectional nor Central Conciliation Boards could reach a settlement, the subject of difference was to be referred to arbitration. If the two sides were able to agree on a single arbitrator the matter would be decided by him; in default of such agreement an arbitrator was to be appointed by the Speaker of the House of Commons or the Master of the Rolls. Matters of interpretation of the scheme were to be settled by the Board of Trade or, at the request of either party, by the Master of the Rolls; the arrangement was to last for a minimum of seven years since the termination of the scheme required one year's notice and such notice might not be handed in until November 6, 1913.[37]

One of the principal reasons why the companies accepted the scheme was that they regarded it as an *alternative* to recognition of the union and in no way as a first step to collective bargaining. Lord Claud Hamilton, Chairman of the Railway Companies' Association, claimed that, 'The union, of course, is not recognized in any way. Not a loophole, so far as I can see has been left open for them.'[38] While Mr Beasley, General Manager of the Taff Vale Railway was even more explicit when he said: 'My company accepted the scheme as an alternative to recognition . . . I do not think it would have ever been accepted by my board at all events, if it had not been so understood'.[39]

Both these statements were true in so far as, under the agreement, only full time employees of the company concerned were permitted to represent railway labour in both Sectional and Central Conciliation Boards, an arrangement which effectively excluded the full-time union officials from the Conciliation Boards from 1908-11 inclusively, though the railway directors were, at the same time, free to choose full-time advocates to state their case before the boards. There was one tiny loophole however. When the scheme came into operation, full-time union officials were allowed to state the men's case to the arbitrators. Lord Claud Hamilton spoke for the majority of the directors when he declared that: 'What we wanted, and what Mr Lloyd George wanted in the interests of the public, was the certainty of industrial peace and quiet on the railways for a fixed period.'[40] The sacrifice of the final say on matters of hours and wages to the decision of an arbitrator would be worth while if accompanied by the prospect of freedom from strikes for at least seven years.

Sir Guy Granet, General Manager of the Midland Railway, made a wider assertion of the agreement when he assured the Commissioners in

1911 that: 'A solemn bargain was made, backed by the Government, that *for seven years* from 1907 the question of recognition should not be pressed upon the railway companies, and that that substituted scheme should be given a fair trial.'[41] (Our italics.)

The union leaders denied that they were committed to refrain from pressing for recognition during this period, a point of view which was upheld by the Commission in its report:

'Whatever may have been understood by the companies we have no evidence before us to enable us to say that the men understood it to be an essential condition of the agreement that the question of recognition should not be raised during its term.'[42]

It is more difficult to understand why the conciliation scheme was accepted by the union. Richard Bell gave his reasons for signing the agreement in a special article in *Reynolds News*:

'The machinery is not as perfect as I would wish or endeavoured to secure, but, if properly used by our members, a good deal can be obtained through it. A good driver can often get more work out of a deficient engine than a bad driver can get out of a perfect engine.'[43]

In a letter to branch secretaries he claimed:

'If the machinery is efficiently and properly used, we may look forward with much confidence to obtaining great improvements in the present conditions of the men.'[44]

The E.C., no doubt influenced by the statement by Lloyd George at the interview on November 6th, 'that he had got the railway companies, after much difficulty, to agree to the proposals he was about to submit to them', agreed, with only two dissentients (Messrs Brodie and Emblem) to accept the scheme as an 'honourable settlement' which they trusted the membership would give 'a fair trial'.[45]

The Bensham branch in a resolution to the December 1907 E.C. opposed the settlement on the grounds that 'Mr Bell failed absolutely in the all-grades movement negotiations, inasmuch as he was a party in the signing of a document drawn up by the Railway Chairmen's Association, which practically excluded our General Secretary or any other official of the A.S.R.S. from taking any prominent part in the future in any movement the rank and file may decide upon', and demanded a ballot of the membership to decide whether Mr Bell should continue as General Secretary. The committee rejected the resolution on the grounds that its premises were 'not correct'. It 'accepted the whole responsibility for the settlement'.[46]

On the other hand seventy-six branches wrote to the General Secretary expressing approval of the terms of settlement.[47]

Whilst there is strong reason to believe—if what happened in 1911 is any guide—that there would have been a loyal and widespread response to a strike call, there was widespread relief that the strike with all its dangers of permanent loss of employment as well as temporary reductions in income, was avoided, even though this relief was mixed with resentment at the inadequate character of the settlement. No doubt many members agreed with the editor of the *Railway Review* when he wrote:

'With the railwaymen it was largely a case of "Hobson's choice". They were confronted with a position in which refusal, even if it were wise, was extremely difficult and they decided to take what was offered and do their best to make the new departure a success.'[48]

NOTES

1. A. L. Bowley, *Wages and Income in the U.K. since 1860*, p. 30.
2. A. W. F. Rowe, *Wages in Practice and Theory*, pp. 8–9 and 12.
3. Report of an inquiry by the Board of Trade into the earnings and hours of Labour of the Workpeople of the U.K., B.P.P. 1912–13, Vol. 108, p. x.
4. These facts are taken from the A.S.R.S. General Secretary's Report to the A.G.M. 1906.
5. *R.R.*, August 24, 1906, quoting the *Statist*.
6. *Statist*, September 29, 1906.
7. A.S.R.S. June E.C. 1906, R. 60.
8. A.S.R.S. A.G.M. 1906, R. 14.
9. A.S.R.S. December E.C. 1906, p. 52.
10. A.S.R.S. General Secretary's Report to the A.G.M. 1907.
11. A.S.R.S. December E.C. 1906, R. 44.
12. Midland Railway: Board Meeting, March 15, 1907, Minute 9699. The Chairman reported having consulted other companies.
13. A.S.R.S. 'National All-Grades Movement', May 1, 1907.
14. A.S.R.S. September E.C. 1907, R. 36.
15. See above, Note 3.
16. Railway Companies' Association: Minutes of Meeting of Council, October 11, 1907. *Financial Times*, October 12, 1907.
17. *The Times*, October 17, 1907.
18. *The Times*, July 31, 1907.
19. *The Times*, October 18, 1907.
20. Royal Commission on the Railway Conciliation Scheme of 1907. B.P.P. 1912–13, Vol. 61, Q. 8975.
21. *The Times*, November 4, 1907.
22. *The Times*, September 24, 1907.
23. *R.R.*, November 8, 1907.
24. See Hansard 1905, Vol. 148, Col. 1354 *et seq.*, July 6, 1905.
25. *Spectator*, October 14, 1907; Lord Askwith, *Industrial Problems and Disputes*, p. 126.
26. *Daily News*, October 15, 1907; *Daily Mail*, October 15, 1907; *Daily Chronicle*, October 12, 1907; *Daily Graphic*, September 23, 1907; *Economist*, October 19, 1907 and September 21, 1907; *The Times*, October 3, 1907.

27. *British Weekly*, October 31, 1907.
28. *The Times*, October 26, 1907.
29. Lord Askwith, *Industrial Problems and Disputes*, p. 121.
30. *The Times*, November 1–7, 1907.
31. L.N.W.R. Special Board Meeting, November 5, 1907, Minute 22117. G.W.R. Board Meeting, November 21, 1907, Minutes 3 and 4. G.C.R. Board Meeting, November 8, 1907, Minute 3887. Lord Askwith, *Industrial Problems and Disputes*, p. 122. *Stock Exchange Gazette*, November 14, 1907.
32. *Manchester Guardian*, August 18, 1911.
33. A.S.R.S. June E.C. 1907, p. 61.
34. *Financial Times*, September 25, 1907.
35. *The Times*, November 8, 1907.
36. All the quotations are from the issues of November 7, 1907.
37. For a fuller version of the scheme see Appendix 'C', G. D. H. Cole and R. Page Arnot, *Trade Unionism on the Railways*.
38. *Railway News*, November 9, 1907.
39. Royal Commission on the Railway Conciliation Scheme of 1907, B.P.P. 1912–13, Vol. XLV, Q. 10634.
40. As above, Q. 10011.
41. As above, Q. 12912.
42. As above, Report, p. 42.
43. *Reynolds News*, November 10, 1907.
44. A.S.R.S. The National Movement, Letter to Branch Secretaries, November 16, 1907.
45. A.S.R.S. Special E.C. Meetings, November 6 and 7, 1907, Rs. 5 and 6.
46. A.S.R.S. December E.C. 1907, R. 39, p. 52.
47. As above, p. 51.
48. *R.R.*, November 15, 1907.

CHAPTER XI

THE RAILWAY CONCILIATION SCHEME
OF 1907

'The scheme was intended to be a safety valve. The companies had insisted on sitting on it, and there was found to be an explosion.'
J. H. Thomas, M.P., interviewed by the Liverpool Daily Post, *August 7, 1911.*

I

THE parties signatory to the agreement of November 6, 1907, undertook to carry it out for at least seven years. By 1911 it had been scrapped and replaced by another. Why did this attempted reconciliation end in failure?

Neither party had accepted the 1907 Conciliation Scheme with any enthusiasm. At the time, the majority of the railway directors saw no necessity for any departure from the established practices of individual bargaining over wages and working conditions. When Mr Glover, the Assistant General Manager of the Great Western Railway was asked, 'Do you think that the old method of dealing directly with your men was preferable to any scheme of either conciliation or arbitration ?' and replied, 'I do', he expressed an opinion shared by most directors.[1] It was mainly for a negative reason—that it gave the companies the promise of 'the non-recognition of trade unionism'—that the chairmen and managers signed the agreement. It was rather from a desire to secure 'a settled condition in the labour world' than from any appreciation of the need for better working conditions for the men, that old practices in wage negotiations were modified and the new scheme adopted. One of the best known of the railway chairmen, Lord Claud Hamilton, admitted that he had 'hesitated about signing' and had only consented after Mr Lloyd George had spoken to him personally. Even then he signed 'with the firm conviction that any question of recognition was to be delayed and not brought up to the surface again until the expiration of the period of the scheme, namely seven years'.[2]

Although Richard Bell accepted the scheme with more conviction of its merits, he had resigned his position as General Secretary of the A.S.R.S. by the end of 1909, and his belief in its virtues was not long shared by his E.C. or by his successor as General Secretary. Had the union leaders taken part in the drafting of the agreement they might have felt a more fatherly interest in its preservation, but both Mr Thomas and Mr F. Lowth, Secretary of the General Railway Workers' Union, testified that they were handed the completed document and were 'under pressure'—the strong desire to avoid a national strike—to accept.[3] In so far as the rank and file of the union accepted the conciliation scheme it was not by virtue of its inherent merits but through a resolve to give it a trial to see whether it produced results in the form of an amelioration of working conditions.

The agreement had been given the name 'Conciliation Scheme' but it is doubtful in the case of some of those responsible for its operation, whether the spirit of conciliation was present.

II

The union officials and the majority of the directors did, however, resolve to give the new boards a fair trial, and there were few complaints of delay in their establishment. As late as August 1910, there was a strike on the West Clare Railway in Ireland through the failure of the company to implement the scheme. A more serious case, because of the greater number of men involved, was the delay on the Caledonian Railway where the conciliation machinery was not set up until December 3, 1908, a delay particularly inexcusable in view of the fact that the Vice-Chairman of the company was one of the original signatories of the scheme.[4] With the large majority of the companies, however, the Sectional and Central Conciliation Boards had been set up by the end of June 1908.

The election of the men's representatives to the Sectional and Central Conciliation Boards were of considerable interest as they served to show to what extent railway workers desired union men to represent them. A week before the final meeting at the Board of Trade in November, Lord Claud Hamilton, Chairman of the Great Eastern Railway, had issued a manifesto to the effect that:

'His men desire to be protected from the domination and tyranny of an irresponsible body which . . . has not at heart their real interests.'[5]

Under the rules of the conciliation scheme it was not possible for full-time officials of the unions to represent the men. Yet within a few weeks of the publication of the manifesto, in the secret ballots for the election of the men's panel on the Sectional and Central Conciliation Boards on Lord Claud's railway, a majority—seventeen—of those elected were members of the A.S.R.S., whilst six of the remaining fifteen successful candidates were members of the A.S.L.E. & F. On other large railways the A.S.R.S. victory was more complete. In April 1908, it secured the return of fifty-five candidates for the sixty seats on the Midland Railway and fifty-eight out of the sixty-four elected on the London and North Western Railway. In the country as a whole the A.S.R.S. secured the return of 694 candidates for 860 seats on the Sectional Boards and polled 233,793 out of a total of 341,904 votes cast. The men appear to have been so eager to subject themselves to 'tyranny' that in England and Wales 93 per cent of all votes for both Sectional and Central Boards went to candidates of one or other of the four unions catering exclusively for railwaymen. In Scotland over 81 per cent voted for such union candidates and in Ireland over 89 per cent.[6] Although the Conciliation Boards came to be disliked through the delays and annoyances with which they became associated, they provided a valuable training ground for the local leadership of the A.S.R.S. to advocate the union's policy. Many non-unionists were drawn into the life of the union through what they saw of the work of A.S.R.S. members on the Conciliation Boards.

III

It was when the conciliation machinery began gradually to creak into motion that the complaints from the men's side multiplied. The agreement of November 6, 1907, had specified that:

'Before a Conciliation Board can entertain any proposal for change in the rates of wages or hours of labour of any class of employees, an application for such change must previously have been made in the normal course through the officers of the department concerned.'

The 'usual course' had varied from company to company. Whilst with many companies it had been the requirement that a petition, signed by a substantial body of men, should precede or accompany the deputations to the general manager or directors, with some there was no insistence on the petitions, the general manager being willing to meet the deputations sent from a mass meeting of the men. After the Conciliation Boards were established, however, there was a widespread insistence on petitioning even where the practice had lapsed prior to 1907, the Great Western Railway being one prominent example. When on March 29, 1908, Mr A. Eatough of Nottingham presented a claim for improved conditions of service for the locomotive men of his area of the Midland Railway, backed by a petition to the locomotive superintendent of the company, he was told that petitions should first have been submitted to the *district* locomotive superintendents. Though this was a departure from precedent it was insisted upon and caused considerable delay in the consideration of the men's claims. A similar procedure had to be followed in the goods department of the company. On the Great Eastern Railway officials organized a counter petition affirming that:

'. . . the signatories are perfectly satisfied with the relations which have always existed between the directors and the staff and do not desire any intervention by either conciliation boards or any other means which would prejudice those relations.'[7]

But this did not prevent the establishment of the Conciliation Boards; it merely caused confusion and delay.

It was conforming to the letter of the agreement rather than to the spirit of conciliation when some companies pursued delaying tactics with regard to the meeting of the Conciliation Boards. The terms of the agreement were that the management were to reply within the space of two months to applications for improved conditions of service received from the men. On the Lancashire and Yorkshire Railway, the General Manager received such an application on March 19, 1908, and replied to it on May 18th, agreeing to meet a deputation of the men in a month's time.[8] Whilst, admittedly, this was an extreme instance, it was not an isolated one. The adoption of such tactics generated suspicion on the men's part of the good intentions of railway managers. The clause in the agreement which stated that meetings of the board were not to be held in the months of July and August did not help to expedite matters. As an example of the slow working of the conciliation scheme the experience on the Great Eastern Railway may be cited:

Department	Date of Application	Date of meeting of Sectional Board
Superintendent's department, e.g. Signalmen, Shunters, Guards	March 20, 1908	October 15, 1908
Electrical Department . .	March 25, 1908	October 22, 1908
Goods Department . . .	April 7, 1908	December 2, 1908
Permanent Way Department .	April 7, 1908	October 22, 1908
Locomotive Department .	April 14, 1908	December 15, 1908[9]

Whilst most companies did not seek to interfere with the men's freedom of choice of their representatives, the fact that a few managers used their influence to try to secure the election of non-union men to the boards or even tried to intimidate the union candidates, created a bad impression. At a meeting of the Great Western Railway Board on January 9, 1908, it was resolved:

'To provide for free conveyance for such members of the boards as might be able to give an assurance that they would not receive payment from any outside source.'

On other railways, notably the London and North Western Railway, non-unionist candidates were given special facilities to further their candidatures, being allowed free passes, time off and the assistance of officials in the distribution of their election circulars.[10]

A locomotive department sectional board secretary elected by the men on the Great Western Railway received a letter from Mr G. S. Churchward, the Locomotive Superintendent, on March 25, 1908, in which he was told that:

'. . . if you and those you represent are not satisfied with the conditions in my department, I shall be pleased to receive your notices'

and the General Manager of the Great Eastern Railway told a deputation on November 8, 1909, that:

'. . . the time has come when we must put a stop to dissatisfaction and agitation, and if we find men going round the line creating dissatisfaction I shall have only one duty, a painful duty, and that is to ask him to resign.'[11]

It proved necessary for Richard Bell to question the President of the Board of Trade in Parliament on May 28, 1908, concerning the dismissal of two elected delegates of the Midland Railway Conciliation Board, who had taken part in a mass meeting on Parliament Hill, Hampstead Heath. After a prolonged discussion between Richard Bell, the General Manager of the Company and the President of the Board of Trade on June 3rd, the men were reinstated.[12] It was another illustration of the fact that participation as a trade unionist in the work of the Conciliation Boards was not the best way of gaining promotion in the service.

The provision that applications should first be made 'in the usual course' was no doubt intended by the Board of Trade to encourage quick settlement of claims. In practice, the knowledge that there were now subsequent stages of negotiation to the men's deputations tended to make petitioning, deputations, and even in many cases appeals to the Sectional and Central Conciliation Boards mere formalities. Thus a machinery designed to expedite the settlement of claims served in fact to lengthen the time taken for a settlement. The members of the Royal Commission on the conciliation scheme recognized these changed circumstances when they declared in their report:

'No doubt the companies, in accordance with the terms of the agreement, required the presentations of the petitions and the holding of conferences between the men and their officers. But these proceedings would appear to have been very much a matter of form, and to have been carried out only as a necessary prelude to placing the points of difference before the Sectional Board. In many instances reference to the Sectional Board seems to have been again a matter of form. Central Board proceedings were much of the same character, and as already stated, the final destination of the demands in many of the cases which arose in the earlier period of the operation of the scheme, was arbitration.'[13]

Although on some railways, such as the Lancashire and Yorkshire, agreement was reached at the Central Conciliation Board level, in most cases the men had to wait until the award of an arbitrator before they could expect any improvements. By the end of 1909 when the majority of those awards had been issued it was apparent that by them the men had obtained no major improvement in pay or important reduction in working hours. The conclusion of the General Secretary of the A.S.R.S. in 1911, Mr J. E. Williams, was that whilst:

'In some few instances there had been substantial concessions, taken as a whole the application of the awards had left a large number of men a great deal worse off than they were before we went to arbitration.'[14]

Taken as a whole he did not think the expenditure of the £30,000—which the union's share of the expenses of the scheme came to—was worth it. Why had this unhappy state of affairs come about?

IV

The unfortunate fact was that precisely during the time the arbitrators were preparing their awards, the repercussions of the financial crisis of the United States of America of 1907–8 were being felt in the United Kingdom. Trade had been flourishing before 1907 and it was to recover during 1910, but it was undoubtedly depressed in 1908–9. Whatever may be the case today, at that time there was no better barometer of the industrial climate of the country as a whole than the volume of goods traffic on the railways. In 1908 the nineteen principal railway companies carried 19,200,000 tons less of minerals and 5,100,000 tons less of general merchandise than in 1907, and in consequence experienced a decrease in their goods receipts of £2,300,000. Receipts from passenger traffic did not increase sufficiently to offset this decline.[15] A capable and experienced General Manager, Mr Sam Fay of the Great Central Railway, confirmed the adverse effect of the trade recession on the settlement of the railwaymen's claims when he declared:

'In 1908 from, one may say, January 1, 1908 trade went down with a bang, and the railways in common with the traders suffered a very severe reduction in revenue. As an example, the four principal lines running from

London to the North, i.e. the London and North Western Railway, the Midland Railway, the Great Northern Railway and the Great Central Railway, showed a decrease of gross receipts during the year 1908 of nearly £900,000 as compared with the previous year. This state of things continued in 1909. . . . There is no doubt that the settlements which were arrived at in 1908 and 1909 were to some extent tinged by the pessimism which existed at that time in the railway world.'[16]

To add to the embarrassment of management the price of coal rose 22 per cent in 1909 compared with 1908.[17] There can be no doubt that these were among the most important reasons for the meagre character of the arbitrators' awards, or that many of the detailed complaints against the companies sprang from the insistent demand for economy pressed upon the general managers in a time of trade depression. Consistent with the aim of maintaining what were regarded as reasonable dividends on ordinary stock, it proved impossible for arbitrators to raise the living standards of the railway workers to any appreciable extent. The incompatibility of the system of private ownership of the railways with the provision of a living wage for railwaymen was again manifested in this period. It was no accident that the Railway Nationalization Society was formed in 1908.

Of the improvements brought about by the arbitrators' awards, the introduction of a uniform rate of time and a quarter pay for overtime and time and a half for Sunday duty, for all principal grades previously excluded from these rates on the London and North Western Railway, Midland Railway and Great Western Railway was of importance. On the Midland there was recognition of the arduousness of firemen's duties on the bigger locomotives in the provision that where the heating surface of the firebox was over 1,500 square feet they were to receive an extra 1s 6d a week. On the London and North Western Railway capstanmen were given an advance of 2s a week, and the hours of work of goods staff, draymen and lorrymen were reduced to 54 per week. On the Great Western passenger guards with over four years' service were to have their wages increased from 27s or 28s a week to 29s.[18] In general, however, the awards were in the nature of a 'tidying up' of conditions of service and a removal of anomalies. Awards were naturally most meagre where the financial position of the company was weakest. Thus the award of Lord Gorrell for the men on the Great Eastern was classed as 'disappointing' by the editor of the *Railway Review* since there were 'practically no alterations in the rates of wages', whilst Richard Bell said that it 'could not be considered as satisfactory' though 'probably the arbitrator took into consideration the financial position of the company which was not so favourable as that of other companies'.[19] Richard Bell made a fair summing up in his Annual Report in 1909 when he wrote that, 'It cannot be said that any of the awards contain anything approaching the full demands of the programme'.[20]

Had the arbitrators' awards been put into effect promptly and in a liberal spirit it is likely that the rank and file of railwaymen would have been prepared to accept with patience the meagre improvements they brought. In the more straightened financial circumstances of 1908 and 1909, however, the railway management resorted to cheeseparing economy at the expense of the men. One example of such tactics was the splitting up of the hours of duty following an arbitrator's award of a 54-hour week, so that the letter of the award was complied with but the men affected continued, in fact, to be on duty more than 54 hours. Mr Chorlton, General Secretary of the United Pointsmen's and Signalmen's Society, asserted that he had numerous cases reported to him of companies 'shifting the men about and manipulating the hours' in order to effect economies.[21] Mr J. T. White, a Midland Railway fireman, said that his employers had split up the work of signalmen, passenger guards and goods shed men (among others) to avoid the necessity of paying the time and a quarter rate for overtime decreed in the arbitrator's award.[22] Another favourite dodge with some companies was to regrade the men so that higher rates of wages need not be paid. On the Midland Railway, goods loaders in goods sheds were displaced by goods porters paid at a lower rate. Numbertakers, awarded a 54-hour week by the arbitrator, Lord Cromer, were renamed sidings porters who were required to work a 12-hour day. At Leicester, in July 1910, head shunters were regraded as train receivers, thus having their hours raised from eight to ten. At Burton-on-Trent the 170 grain porters working a 60-hour week for an 18s wage, were awarded a 54-hour week without loss of pay. The company, thinking this new hourly rate 'excessive', dispatched the permanent men to other stations and filled their places by temporary men paid 16s 11d a week. As much as one-third of all the goods depot men of the company were 'temporaries' and as such outside the competence of the conciliation scheme.[23] After the award of Lord MacDonnell for the Great Northern Railway, the company reclassified a number of 8-hour signal cabins to the 10-hour group and others from the 10-hour group to the 72-hour group. When the men declared that this was an incorrect interpretation of the arbitrator's award the General Manager refused to discuss the matter, claiming that the award was the property of the company. When Lord MacDonnell gave his interpretation of the dispute on April 14th he largely supported the men's case.[24] On the London and North Western Railway economies in engine drivers and firemen's pay were effected by the introduction of the trip system.[25]

Genuine misunderstandings and mistakes could be expected on the initiation of any large scheme of the scope of the Railway Conciliation Scheme of 1907 but Mr J. E. Williams, the General Secretary of the A.S.R.S., was convinced that 'an arrangement had been made by the companies to act concertedly' to interpret the awards in minimal fashion and also to claim the exclusive right of their interpretation. In none other of the 262 conciliation and arbitration schemes covering nearly two million workers in operation in the country, had it been thought necessary to lay down procedures for the interpretation of an arbitrator's award, but it was apparently necessary for the railway scheme.[26] When the Secretary of the men's side of the Central Conciliation Board of the London and North Western Railway requested from the company a meeting of the Central Conciliation Board to consider the interpretation of the arbitrator's award he received a letter in which the company stated:

'As the whole of the matters in question have been referred to an arbitrator and his award received, the functions of the Board are absolutely discharged, and it is for the company to carry out the award according to their interpretation of it.'[27]

There were disputes in the North British, the North Staffs, the Caledonian, the Great Northern, Great Eastern and Midland Railways arising from the prolonged refusal of the companies to discuss in the Central Conciliation Boards the interpretation of the arbitrators' awards. Eventually after Mr Williams had written to the Board of Trade and had seen the Assistant Secretary of the Railway Department about the matter, and Mr J. H. Thomas, M.P. had questioned the Minister in the House, the companies one by one capitulated and agreed to a meeting of the Central Boards.[28] In the meantime, however, men who were entitled to advances in pay, had them withheld, in some cases for months or even years. Lord Cromer had made his award for the Midland Railway on April 1, 1909, but it was only in July 1911, after prolonged stonewalling, that the company agreed to the resubmission of disputed points to the arbitrator who, on the 28th of that month, gave his decision that the company had acted contrary to the spirit of the award, and that men he had intended to receive a 2s a week increase of pay should now be given it together with two years' accumulated arrears.[29]

A further serious disadvantage of the conciliation scheme was that agreements reached at the Sectional or Central Board level, or awards of the arbitrators, were binding in most cases for at least four years. In the case of most of the large companies, agreements and awards were to stand until December 31, 1913. The earliest opportunity for revision occurred on the Highland Railway where the agreement expired on December 31, 1911. On the other hand the arbitrator's award on the North British Railway was made binding until March 25, 1915.[30] In most cases in which arbitration was necessary the men's programme was dealt with once for all in six years.

Such an inflexible arrangement would have been easier to justify had the cost of living fallen and the trading position of the companies remained depressed. But the cost of living continued to rise and the companies' business showed remarkable improvement in the years 1910–11. Following the sharp fall in mineral and general merchandise traffic in 1908–9, the receipts from both, as well as from passenger traffic, increased in 1910–11 as follows:

Receipts in £s. 000,000s

	1909	1910	Increase % 1910 over 1909	1911	Increase % over 1910
Passenger traffic . .	51·2	52·7	2·9	53·9	2·3
Goods traffic . .	59·5	61·5	3·4	63·3	2·9
Mineral traffic . .	28·4	29·2	2·8	29·7	1·8
General merchandise traffic . . .	29·6	30·7	3·8	32·1	4·4

Though the receipts from the carriage of general merchandise were the highest ever in 1910, this record figure was surpassed in the following year. The cost of coal at pithead prices which had been exceptionally high at 8s 11d a ton in 1908 fell to 8s 2½d in 1910. During the first half of 1910 the net revenue of the companies increased by £827,000 or 5·8 per cent, an improvement which continued throughout 1910 and 1911. Because the wages and hours of the railwaymen were fixed (in a period of depression) for at least four years, the improvement in earnings of the companies went largely in the form of increased dividends. The ordinary dividends of every major company—with the exception of the Great Northern and the Great Eastern where they were stationary—were increased in 1910. Thus the Great Western Railway increased its dividend from 3½ per cent to 4 per cent, whilst the increase on the London and North Western was from 4¾ per cent to 5½ per cent and on the Midland from 4¼ per cent to 5 per cent. Had the increase in the net revenues in the years 1910–11 been distributed in the form of increased wages rather than increased dividends it would have enabled each railwayman to receive a rise of 2s a week. But with the average weekly wage at the end of 1910—25s 9d—a penny less than at the end of 1906 (25s 10d) it is scarcely a matter for surprise that up and down the country discontent with the results of railway conciliation was growing. In its operation the scheme appeared to be conciliation to the companies but scarcely so to their employees.[31]

v

The years 1907–11 were remarkable for the virtual elimination of competition in railway transport in many areas of the country. When during 1908 and 1909 a comprehensive agreement for the pooling of traffic and the elimination of wasteful competition was entered into by the Boards of the Great Northern, Great Eastern and Great Central Railways, Mr W. M. Acworth, a foremost authority on railway economics, declared that the result would be 'that competition in the East of England will be absolutely non-existent from the Channel to the Tweed'.[32] The Caledonian and North British Railway Companies started a pooling agreement early in 1908. A few months later a similar agreement was reached between the Midland and London and North Western Railways. In 1910 came a working agreement for the pooling of competitive traffic between the Great Western and London and South Western Railways.[33]

A prominent reason why ten railway directors had entered into these agreements was to economize in the labour force. Whilst economies in traffic operation were welcome in the national interest and were not opposed at any time by the union, they reduced the security of employment of railwaymen in areas where there had been an overlapping and duplication of services, they reduced the prospects of promotion for younger men and they increased the pace and intensity of labour. One of the railwaymen M.P.s, Mr G. J. Wardle, demonstrated to a Parliamentary Committee that over the period 1899–1908 labour costs as a percentage of gross receipts declined where companies had adopted pooling agreements.[34] With the introduction of more powerful locomotives and larger capacity trucks 'American' methods of rationalization were being introduced on British railways. The able Assistant General Manager of the London and North Western Railway, Mr H. A. Walker, stated in 1911 that in recent years his company had increased the loading in its goods wagons 'by something like 33 per cent'.[35] Mr J. H. Thomas told the A.G.M. of the A.S.R.S. at Carlisle in 1911 that as a result of such changes there were 6,000 less enginemen and firemen in the country than there were in 1901, despite the fact that a million tons more traffic was being handled and millions more passengers being carried.[36]

Such developments raised innumerable problems of redundancy, re-grading, increased physical and nervous strain on those operating the traffic, and new dangers to life and limb. But the changes came virtually as 'Acts of God' over which railwaymen had practically no control. When the new Churchward 'Pacific' locomotive *The Great Bear* was introduced on the Great Western in 1908 the drivers and firemen found that 'an uncomfortable feature of the engine was the shortness of the footplate from front to back' thus making the heavy labour of stoking the boiler even more arduous. On the 'Star' locomotives of the same company the inside mechanism was 'very difficult to reach for lubrication and adjustment'.[37] Had railwaymen of the day been treated as something more than mere 'servants', and had there been real co-operation between labour and management, such difficulties might never have arisen. But the Conciliation Boards were limited in scope to discussion of wages and hours, it being assumed by the companies that their competence did not extend to matters of discipline and organization. Thus the experience of their working lives was convincing many working on the railways that the Conciliation Scheme was a stumbling block, not only for the reason that it failed to bring satisfaction of demands for improved wages and shorter hours, but also because it was far too limited in its scope. These were particularly the feelings of younger men, whose promotion was being blocked through circumstances beyond their control.

VI

A government closely in touch with the trend of opinion on the railways would have taken heed of the increasing signs of discontent with the working of the 1907 Conciliation Scheme. At a delegate meeting held at Stratford on August 8, 1910, an 'All-Grades protest Committee' of Great Eastern Railway employees was formed to organize propaganda meetings throughout East Anglia in favour of a radical amendment of the scheme. A meeting of the men's side of the Central Conciliation Board of the Midland Railway on the 24th of the same month urged the E.C. of the A.S.R.S. to work for the introduction of a better scheme.[38] The June E.C. had, in fact, passed unanimously a resolution which stated that: 'The unrest that is so evident at the present time amongst the railway workers . . . has been created largely by the vexatious attitude of many of the railway companies towards the working of the scheme of Conciliation and Arbitration agreed in 1907. We take this opportunity to explain to the public that unless the spirit as well as the letter of the aforementioned agreement is observed more fully in the future than it has been in the past, this committee will have to seriously consider the advisability of repudiating the scheme agreed to in 1907.'[39]

A copy of this resolution was sent to the President of the Board of Trade who thus had warning fourteen months before the national strike of August 1911, of the growing discontent with the conciliation arrangements. The A.G.M. later in 1910 endorsed the opinion of the E.C. and passed a resolution which stated that: '. . . the Conciliation Scheme . . . as at present constituted, is inimical to the interests of members, by preventing them taking advantage of the changes in methods that are continually being introduced by the railway companies.'[40]

On the left wing of the union, the syndicalists, becoming more vociferous and influential, were pointing out that in many cases arbitrators earning £52 10s 0d a day were ruling that men earning as little as 16s, 17s, 18s or 19s a week were to get no more.[41] But the Liberal administration, preoccupied with the struggle over the People's Budget, with the German naval challenge and many other questions, appeared not to be unduly perturbed about the state of labour relations on the railways and required the prompting of a national railway strike before it could be persuaded to make any improvements in the conciliation scheme.

With the settlement of 1907 the term Conciliation Grades as applying to all those grades in the service whose wages were fixed by Conciliation Boards, came into frequent use. The principal groups which did not come into this category were salaried and supervisory staffs and shopmen.

NOTES

1. Royal Commission on the Railway Conciliation Scheme of 1907, Minutes of Evidence, B.P.P. 1912–13, Vol. XLV, Q. 11575.
2. As above, Q. 10048. For similar views of other directors see answers to Qs. 91636 and 12464.
3. As above, Qs. 1935, 763.
4. A.S.R.S. September E.C. 1910, pp. 73–4. Royal Commission, as above, Q. 67.
5. *Daily News*, October 24, 1907.
6. *R.R.*, March 27, 1908. A.S.R.S. September E.C. 1908, p. 74. Mr J. H. Thomas, evidence before the Royal Commission, Q. 1979. A.S.R.S. General Secretary's Report, 1908.
7. J. H. Thomas: evidence Q. 1943. R. Bell, letter to the Rt. Hon. Winston S. Churchill (President of the Board of Trade) May 18, 1908.
8. J. H. Thomas: evidence, Q. 1936.
9. J. E. Williams: evidence, Q. 81.
10. G.W.R. Board Meeting, January 9, 1908, Minute 13. A.S.R.S. June E.C. 1908, p. 58.
11. J. H. Thomas: evidence Qs. 1992, 1986.
12. A.S.R.S. June E.C. 1908, p. 71.
13. Report of the Royal Commission on the Railway Conciliation Scheme, BP.P. 1911, Vol. XXIX.
14. J. E. Williams: evidence Q. 272.
15. *R.R.*, August 27, 1909.
16. Evidence before the Royal Commission, Q. 11813.
17. Bradshaw: Railway Manual 1909, Vol. XI.
18. *R.R.*, February 12, April 9 and June 18, 1909.
19. *R.R.*, August 27, 1909. A.S.R.S. June E.C. 1909, p. 84.
20. A.S.R.S. General Secretary's Report 1909, p. 42.
21. Royal Commission: Minutes of Evidence, Qs. 5467–8.
22. As above, Q. 1181.
23. Evidence of J. T. White and Isaac Brassington (organization of the G.R.W.U.). Qs. 1095–6, 1107–9, 4841.
24. A.S.R.S. General Secretary's Report 1910, p. 41; March E.C. 1910, p. 64.
25. Royal Commission: Evidence of Arthur Bellamy, Qs. 2875–84.
26. A.S.R.S. General Secretary's Report, 1910.
27. *R.R.*, April 23, 1909.
28. A.S.R.S. September E.C. 1910, p. 60. Hansard, June 30, 1910. Session 1910, Vol. 18, Col. 1232.
29. *Manchester Guardian*, August 18, 1911.
30. BP.P. 1910, Vol. LXXX, p. 39, 'Statement of settlements regarding questions as to rate of wages and hours of labour of railway employees that have been effected under a scheme for conciliation and arbitration arranged in accordance with the agreement of November 6, 1907'.

31. Companies' trading returns taken from: 'Returns of Capital Traffic, Receipts and Working expenses of the Railway Companies of the U.K.' BP.P. 1911, Vol. LXX, pp. 685 *et seq.*, and 1912–13, LXXV, pp. 5 *et seq.* Figures for wages taken from 15th Abstract of Labour Statistics. BP.P. 1912–13, Vol. CVII, p. 620. See also Sir Leo Chiozza Money's speech in the Commons debate for the possibility of the 2s rise. Hansard 1911, Vol. 29, Col. 2305, August 22, 1911.
32. 'Railways and the State'. Reports of the British Association 1909, p. 781.
33. A.S.R.S. General Secretary's Report 1909, pp. 34–5; 1910, p. 20.
34. Departmental Committee on Railway Agreements and Amalgamations. BP.P. 1911, Vol. XXIX, pt. 2, Qs. 16625–65. A.S.R.S. June E.C. 1910, p. 7.
35. Royal Commission on the Railway Conciliation Scheme 1907, Minutes of Evidence, Q. 9056.
36. *R.R.*, October 6, 1911.
37. W. A. Tuplin, *Great Western Steam*, pp. 64, 59. I am indebted to Mr Philip Unwin for this reference.
38. *The Times*, August 10 and 25, 1910.
39. A.S.R.S. June E.C. 1910, R. 64.
40. A.S.R.S. A.G.M. 1910, R. 16.
41. C. Watkins in No. 11. *The Industrial Syndicalist*, 'Conciliation or Emancipation', May 1911.

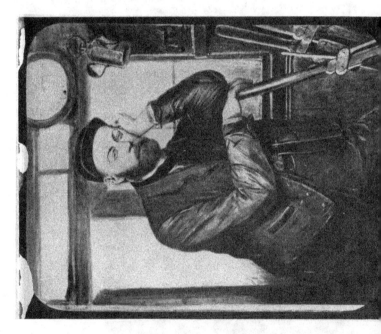

PLATE 5

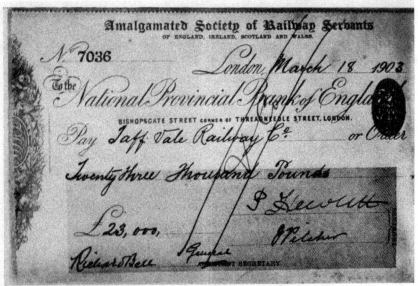

The Taff Vale Cheque, 1903

PLATE 6

Walter V. Osborne

CHAPTER XII

1911—THE FIRST NATIONAL RAILWAY STRIKE

'Suddenly, in August 1911, the pot boiled over.'
Webb: History of Trade Unionism, *1920 Edition, p. 528.*

I

IF the state of labour relations on the railways in the summer of 1910 was sufficiently serious for the E.C. of the A.S.R.S. to warn the Government, it had certainly not improved by the summer of 1911. The sudden boiling over in August 1911 is in part attributable to the fact that by this time the price of foodstuffs was 14 per cent above the level of 1900.[1] Particularly with the many thousands of porters, engine cleaners and others earning 18s a week, or less, there was bound to be a breaking point. But it would be a mistake to attempt to explain the outbreak of the first national railway strike solely with reference to the fall of real wages of railwaymen. Real wages had also fallen in 1909 and 1910 when there was no significant demand for strike action. Nor can the outbreak be explained as arising solely from the failure of the Conciliation Boards to produce satisfactory results, though by this time it is true that they were the subject of widespread disillusionment.

Not much importance can be attached to the view of one of the leading general managers who gave as one reason for the strike, 'the hot weather, which is causing many men who ought to be reasonable to lose their heads',[2] even though the summer of 1911 was the hottest and driest within living memory and the Greenwich Observatory recorded a shade temperature of 100° F on August 9th, for the first time since records began there in 1841. The excessive heat may help to explain particular incidents in the strike, such as the overturning in a Liverpool street of a brewer's dray and the consumption of barrels of beer at a time and place other than those envisaged by the brewer,[3] but it can scarcely be advanced in serious explanation of unsatisfactory labour relations in a major industry. The men almost certainly voted to strike again—the ballot figures were not disclosed—early in December when the temperature had sunk from the dizzy heights of August and when, according to any climatic theory of the origin of strikes, calmer counsels should have prevailed.

That the pot boiled over on the railways in August 1911 was largely due to the fact that it had first boiled over on the docks. In June of that year a national seamen's strike organized by Tom Mann's recently formed Transport Workers' Federation was so effective that the Shipping Federation was compelled to concede practically all the men's demands. The strike movement spread like wildfire to the dockers who were demanding that their 'tanner' an hour, won as long ago as 1889, should be raised to eightpence. In this case, as with the seamen, militant industrial action paid dividends and substantial concessions were made to the men. The railwaymen, particularly those serving in port areas, were inevitably drawn into these struggles. There were numerous instances of their sympathetic action on behalf of the seamen and dockers. Thus the Cardiff Strike Committee was warned by Great Western Railway men of an attempt to send strike breakers to the city by rail, and during the first fortnight in August when the port of Liverpool ceased to function as a result of the dock strike, the railwaymen refused to handle goods from the ships. For this action they received a vote of thanks from Tom Mann.[4] The achievement of the underpaid dockers in defeating the powerful employers' federation and in refusing to be cowed by the dispatch by Mr Winston Churchill of two warships and 7,000 troops to the Merseyside was an 'eyeopener' to the thousands of railwaymen employed in the area. Besides being caught up in the strong emotional fervour of the Liverpool 'General Strike' the men employed by the Lancashire and Yorkshire Railway in the city had their own particular grievances for which they sought a remedy. Their wage rates were below those paid by the other railway companies serving the area and they worked longer hours. When appealed to, the General Manager had said that as the agreement reached in the Central Conciliation Board was still operative, he was not prepared to meet the men to discuss their claim for a 2s a week rise for all grades and a reduction of hours from 60 to 54. Consequently 1,200 of the goods porters employed by the company struck work on August 5th. Within three days there were 2,500 railwaymen out in the city, the strike being extended through the fact that 'the men marched from one station to another calling out groups of men as they proceeded'.[5]

It was a feature of the situation on the railways in late July and early August that in an ever increasing number of centres the men were taking the law into their own hands and coming out on strike without waiting for authorization from the union executives. Thus on July 23rd, a strike of crane lads, goods porters and horse shunters at New Holland on the Great Central Railway rapidly spread to other centres and other grades on that railway. On August 10th, the strike wave spread to the Great Western when goods workers and carmen at Paddington left their work to be joined shortly after by men at Bristol. By this time many more men employed by the Lancashire and Yorkshire Railway in Manchester, Newton Heath and elsewhere had joined those who first came out in Liverpool, whilst in Glasgow the surface men employed by the North British Railway had extended the movement into Scotland.[6] The national railway strike of 1911 was, in fact, a 'soldier's battle' with 50,000 men, or about a quarter of the total force, ultimately involved, already engaging the enemy before the General Staff belatedly took over control.[7] The General Manager of the Great Central Railway, viewing these days in retrospect, declared 'the leaders had to race to get up level with the men'.[8] It was reported as another unusual feature of the strikes that non-unionist strikers seemed to be in the majority.[9] Nor were the strikers who were unionists confined to the members of one union. General Railway Workers Union men were out at Manchester and A.S.L.E. & F. men out at Liverpool, Paddington and other centres. It was abundantly clear by Monday, August 14th, when the strike had spread to Sheffield, Birmingham, Cardiff, Warrington and Rochdale—to mention only some of the places affected—that unless the union leaders intervened their authority would be undermined.

II

The Executive Committees of the A.S.R.S., A.S.L.E. & F., G.R.W.U. and U.P.S.S. were therefore summoned by their general secretaries to attend a joint meeting at the Engineers Hall, Liverpool, on Tuesday, August 15th, to consider what action should be taken. They reached unanimous agreement to a resolution which gave the railway companies twenty-four hours in which to decide 'whether they were prepared immediately to meet the representatives of the unions to negotiate the basis of a settlement'. In the event of their offer being refused they would have 'no alternative but to respond to the demand being made for a national railway stoppage'.[10] They must have been influenced in making this decision by the knowledge that, failing a national stoppage, it was likely that the union funds would be whittled away through a continuation and extension of the numerous local stoppages that had already occurred. Given the continued refusal of the employers to negotiate, perhaps it was better that there should be one big fight with some prospect of success than a succession of profitless local skirmishes.

The Government was obliged to act quickly. On receiving the news of the resolution from Liverpool, the President of the Board of Trade, Mr Sidney Buxton, requested the managers of the main railway companies to meet him at his offices on the following (Wednesday, 16th) morning. He asked to see the railway union leaders on the afternoon of the same day. The managers went to the interview already inclined to favour a showdown with the men. 'The General Manager of a leading Railway Company' interviewed by the correspondent of *The Times* two days earlier said:

'We have come to the conclusion that there are occasions when in our own interest and in the interest of the public it is better to have a battle and fight the matter out than to keep on adopting an attitude of surrender. ... We are willing to go through the inconveniences of a strike, and we can assure to the public all ordinary services—provided only we can get reasonable protection for our men.'[11]

At the Board of Trade they were to receive just such an assurance. Interviewed after the meeting, Sir Guy Granet, General Manager of the Midland Railway, spoke with confident assurance:

'The Government at our conference today have undertaken to put at the service of the railway companies every available soldier in the country.
'In this dispute the Government and the railway companies are necessarily working together ... we have got to stand firm, and if the men wish it, there will be a fight to a finish. The companies are prepared even in the event of a general strike to give an effective, if a restricted, service.'[12]

The Government, in advance of any negotiations with the unions, had given the companies a written *carte blanche* to call upon the troops.

When the union general secretaries met the President of the Board of Trade that same afternoon, he handed them a list of five questions concerning the reasons for the unions' ultimatum. Replies expressing dissatisfaction with the conciliation scheme and demanding union recognition were returned shortly afterwards. When they learned that the Government had promised troops to the companies the general secretaries considered the situation so urgent that they sent a telegram to Liverpool where, in response to the call, the union executives immediately packed their bags and took the night train to London. They arrived 'at Euston at six o'clock the following morning (17th). At 8.30 a.m., the joint E.C.s were in conference at Unity House, Mr J. Ramsay MacDonald also being present by invitation. At about the same time an emergency session of the Cabinet was held at No. 10 Downing Street. All this was preparatory to the decisive conference at the Board of Trade at 10.0 a.m. when the Prime Minister, accompanied by the President of the Board of Trade, spoke to the executives.

Mr Asquith said that the replies the union leaders had given to the previous day's questions hinged on the alleged shortcomings of the conciliation scheme. Therefore it was 'of first and most essential importance to establish or disprove by impartial investigations the soundness of the statements' the unions had made. Hence it was proposed 'to appoint immediately a Royal Commission to investigate the working of the conciliation agreement, and to report what amendments, if any, are desirable in the scheme with a view to promote a satisfactory settlement of the grievances'. This was all the Government offered. The head of the railway department of the Board of Trade who was present at the interview thought that it was a bad mistake of the Prime Minister that he did not explain 'the exact form of the Royal Commission and its intended speedy inquiry'. He was sure the union leaders assumed that, like most other Royal Commissions, its proceedings would last months or even years and that the proposal was merely a time-consuming device. But it was the 'take it or leave it' manner of the Premier which most impressed this witness, since it made 'the jaws of the Northerners stiffen'. The whole statement was delivered in 'to say the least no conciliatory tone'. When the men's leaders indicated that they did not consider the proposal for a Royal Commission adequate the Prime Minister murmured, 'Then your blood be on your own head', and the meeting broke up.[13] At three o'clock that afternoon the union executives sent their formal reply to the Prime Minister in a resolution which read (in part):

'The workers of the railway companies are entitled to the same treatment from their employers as workmen employed by other employers of labour, and as this joint meeting has already urged the employers to meet us with a view to a discussion of the whole position, which if agreed to by them would settle the whole matter, we refuse to accept the responsibility which the Government has attempted to throw upon us. . . . With the full sense of the grave step we are taking, we feel satisfied that our duty to those we represent compels us to refuse the offer of His Majesty's Government, and reluctantly revert to the decision of this body on Tuesday last.'[14]

Immediately following the dispatch of the reply to the Government, a deputation from the executives proceeded to the House of Commons where the Parliamentary Committee of the T.U.C. and the Parliamentary Labour Party in joint session adopted a resolution pledging support to the railwaymen.

Later that afternoon the following telegram was sent to nearly 2,000 centres:

'Your liberty is at stake. All railwaymen must strike at once. The loyalty of each means victory for all. (Signed) Williams, Fox, Lowth, Chorlton.'

To expedite their dispatch, the telegrams were distributed between a number of post offices in the Euston area. The fact that the telegram was signed by the general secretaries of all four of the unions must have raised the morale of the strikers.

III

The result of the appeal 'staggered the executive committee (of the A.S.R.S.) themselves'.[15] At St Pancras the strike telegram reached the goods yard at 7.43 p.m. After a hurried conference emissaries ran up and down 'the bank' and whispered to the various groups. By eight o'clock all but a handful of the 400 men employed had left the yard. Although at Paddington the strike was effective from 9.0 p.m. and at Victoria 'most of the platforms were entirely deserted, at London Bridge no man left work until the 18th and at Waterloo, where the Irish Guards were much in evidence, there was little response to the strike call. But the hundreds of telegrams received at Unity House and the newspaper reports indicated that the strike was very effective in the industrial districts of the Midlands, South Wales and the North. The *Manchester Guardian* headline: 'Manchester and the Strike. Almost complete stoppage of traffic', and the telegrams received from Sheffield: 'Wheels stopped: exceeded all expectations'; Nottingham: 'All grades are out'; Wigan and Middlesbrough: 'All men out here'; Walsall: 'Solid to a man'; Doncaster: 'Line paralysed'; Rugby: 'Traffic practically stagnant'; and Newport (Mon.): 'All grades coming out; great enthusiasm'—to cite only a small sample of those received—would seem to cast grave doubt as to the accuracy of the Home Office statement of Saturday, August 19th, which read:

'So far as the present information goes considerably more than two-thirds of the railwaymen are remaining at their posts. Numerous applications are being received by the railway companies for employment. The companies report that the defections have not been in excess of expectations.'

The effectiveness of the strike was increased through the sympathetic action of the miners. From Nottingham *The Times* reported that difficulties had increased through the action of the colliers holding up many trains on the Mansfield Branch of the Midland Railway. At Dowlais 5,000 miners decided not to work until the railwaymen's demands were met. From Wellingborough it was reported that: 'Women actively showed their sympathy with the strikers.'[16]

Some idea of the degree of effectiveness of the strike in the different areas of the country may be obtained from the following figures showing the decline in railway companies' receipts as a result of the cessation or restriction of services during the two days the strike lasted:

Decline in total receipts from Goods and Passengers for the week in which the strike occurred.[17]

Barry Railway	37%
Lancashire and Yorkshire Railway . .	35·4%*
London and North Western Railway .	29·6%
Great Central Railway . . .	29·3%
Taff Vale Railway	28·8%
Great Western Railway . . .	28·4%
North Eastern Railway . . .	21·7%
Midland Railway	21·2%
Great Eastern Railway . . .	13%
London and South Western Railway .	2·7%
South Eastern and Chatham Railway .	2·7%

The response of the men to the strike call is all the more remarkable in view of the many inducements offered to those who were prepared to stay at work. The Managing Director of the London Underground Electric Railway circularized officials, 'Please inform staff that men remaining loyal throughout will receive double pay'. Similar offers were made by the managements of the Central London and Taff Vale Railways, while on the Midland a bonus of 50 per cent of wages was offered. Subscription lists for 'loyal' railwaymen were opened on the Metropolitan and Southend and District Railways. Free beer was plentiful, for the 'right types' of railwaymen only, at many station restaurants. The Great Northern and Midland companies fed and housed non-strikers on their stations so that they need not encounter the pickets.[18] Above all the Government mobilized 58,000 soldiers for disposal in the areas affected by the strike. Already on August 14th the Press Association's correspondent reported that 'all P.O. telegraph lines' were 'blocked with hundreds of telegrams to soldiers recalling them to duty in connection with the strike'. Large areas of the country were placed under martial law. At 4.30 p.m. on August 19th, on the orders of Mr Winston Churchill, Home Secretary, a telegram was sent to the Chief Constable of every county and the Lord Mayor or Mayor of every city having a separate police force situated within the disturbed areas. It read:

'The Military authorities have been charged with the duty of protecting the railroads and of all railwaymen who continue at work, and the General Officers commanding the various military areas are instructed to use their own discretion as to whether troops are, or are not, to be sent to any

*Here the strike was widespread before August 18th.

particular point. The Army regulation which requires a requisition for troops from a civil authority is suspended.'[19]

In answering questions in the House of Commons, the Home Secretary attempted to justify these extreme measures by stating that acts of violence had occurred in Liverpool and Llanelly. It is true that there were scenes of violence when police and soldiers endeavoured to clear goods from the central stations at Liverpool. However, the strike committee there issued a manifesto which disclaimed connection with rowdyism and violence, asserted that such acts of violence as had occurred were the work of 'rowdy youths to be found in any big city', and called upon 'all who wished well to the men to refrain from all violence themselves and to check it on the part of others'.[20] Though there were violent scenes at Llanelly the loss of life occurred only when the arrival of troops goaded the crowd to throw stones. The soldiers, retaliating, killed two persons. Mr J. H. Thomas believed that 'the indiscriminate use made of the police and military had aggravated the difficulties'[21] in re-establishing peace, and his opinion would appear to be confirmed by the situation in Manchester. Before the soldiers arrived at one of the principal stations of the city the five police officers on duty were able to see that 'everything was proceeding smoothly'. The arrival of the soldiers created such excitement that it then required thirty-five police to maintain order. The Lord Mayor had not asked for any troops and the first intimation he had of their coming was a telephone message from General Burnley who was in command of the forces in the district.[22] In London, where there were no significant acts of violence, the 15,000 to 20,000 troops were almost as numerous as the strikers. It is difficult to escape the conclusion that the ostentatious placing of sentries with fixed bayonets at the entrances to the main line termini and the flamboyant establishment of an army signalling station on the Golden Gallery of St Paul's Cathedral was intended rather to impress the strikers with the odds against them and to cow them into surrender, than to protect those who wished to continue at work. Giving the military authorities a completely free hand to help break the strike on the railways was also creating a significant precedent for, if the salutary rule of not employing soldiers except at the request of civil magistrates could be abrogated in the supposed interests of the railways, it could be abrogated in other interests too. Mr Keir Hardie was right in saying that the law of England had been broken in the interests of the railway companies.

As against all these blandishments all that the union leaders could offer was strike pay at the rate of 10s a week to members of the four unions participating, a gratuitous allowance of 6s to non-union members who came out, and the distinct possibility—if previous experience was anything to go by—of failure to get reinstatement after it was all over. Nevertheless an estimated 200,000 came out on strike.

It must have been a particularly trying time for the strikers' wives striving to make do on even less than the usual housekeeping money. It was perhaps just as well for the chances of success of the strike that not all of them adopted the attitude of one who wrote to the press as 'A striker's wife' in the following terms:

'Sir,

'My Bill came out on strike . . . . I knew it had happened the moment he came in at the door with that smile I dread to see on his face. . . . He never used to look like that till they puffed him up at the meetings, that he was born to be a leader of men.

'He came home with his two thumbs in his waistcoat pockets, and his pipe in his mouth—both ominous signs. As a rule he waits till he is washed and has had his tea, till he lights his pipe. It is only when he is in an excited mood that he swaggers into the house like an idle lord. Then my heart sinks low and I wait for bad news. A woman often knows things without being told.'[23]

IV

Despite the apparent great odds against the unions, within forty-eight hours of the companies' confident statements that, with ample backing from the Government, they would be able 'to give all the services necessary', both Government and companies had climbed down and the railway managers were doing what they had said they would never do—talking over the questions in dispute with representatives of the unions. What were the reasons for this impressive *volte face*?

First it must be emphasized that in so far as the strike was successful it was due to the close co-operation of the unions. During those stirring days the newly built Unity House lived up to its name. All four unions recruiting men from grades concerned with the movement of traffic acted as one. All decisions the executives made concerning the strike were unanimous. The general managers found themselves unable to recruit strike-breakers from the membership of the Railway Clerks' Association, despite the fact that its policy was the avoidance of strikes and the attempt to gain redress by 'Parliamentary action and publicity'. One of the Assistant Secretaries of the Association, Mr W. E. Hill, reported that 'the membership had been asked by a number of companies to do the work of the various grades which are on strike . . . but without exception they had refused to do so'.[24] Some managers, before the strike, had promised as the worst eventuality 'a good skeleton service'. As a result of this union solidarity some of the skeletons were extremely unimpressive specimens. The *Railway Gazette* issued the day the strike began observed that so far as the railway companies were concerned 'one of the most serious symptoms of the labour unrest' was 'the *rapproachement* that has been effected, temporarily at least, between the A.S.R.S. and the A.S.L.E. & F.'

Secondly, the Government climbed down because the repercussions of the strike on industry were more extensive and serious than had been envisaged. From Manchester it was reported that 'mills, collieries and workshops were closing down one after another owing to the lack of coal',[25] a state of affairs due in part to sympathetic strikes of miners and in part to the inability of the railway companies to get the coal carried to the factories. At this time motor vehicles could form no substitute for the railways since there were but 120,000 of all kinds in the country. Had the strike continued there was a strong likelihood that the South Scottish miners—including those the Prime Minister represented in his Fifeshire Constituency—the South Wales miners—on whom the Navy depended for coal—and the engineers, would have joined the strike.

Thirdly, with a serious international situation developing over the gunboat *Panther* incident in Morocco, Lloyd George, trading on his reputation as a mediator in the 1907 crisis, was able to convince the members of the Cabinet, particularly Mr Asquith and Mr Churchill, who had sponsored the strong line in dealing with the unions, that if the policy of 'batons, bayonets and bullets' was continued over the week-end the Government might be in danger of falling in the autumn.

In the fourth place the railway managers' antiquated attitude of blank refusal to meet the leaders of the unions was as unpopular with large sections of the public and the press as it had been in 1907. Although *The Times* was hostile—its headline read: 'Labour Agitation Gone Mad'—the editor of the *Manchester Guardian* believed the demands of the men were 'broadly reasonable', *The Westminster Gazette* considered that the railway managers had 'to make up their minds at this stage whether they consider organized or unorganized labour the better condition for their industry. Unorganized is apparently, for the moment, their answer. . . . We believe this to be a profound mistake.' The *Daily News* pertinently asked: 'What possible harm can come of two parties meeting in a room? The labour leaders are not lepers; there is surely no physical pollution in their presence even for a railway director.'[26] Hence Mr Lloyd George's plea that on grounds of patriotism and in view of the serious international situation it was urgent to settle the strike by negotiation, may not have been altogether unwelcome to the railway managers. As an added inducement they had the Chancellor's promise that they would shortly be given Parliamentary powers to raise their charges to the public if this could be shown to be justifiable after wage increases had been granted.

Finally, the union leaders required no persuasion to induce them to sit round the same table as the railway managers since this was what they had been advocating for years past, in the belief that once they were recognized it would lead to a great increase in their membership, and hence their bargaining strength. Messrs MacDonald, Henderson and Roberts for the Labour Party were also strongly in favour of calling off the strike.

On the morning of Saturday, August 19th, Mr Lloyd George and Mr Sidney Buxton interviewed the companies' representatives to consider the terms of a settlement. From three o'clock that afternoon, the union leaders, for the first time in history, participated in round table discussions with the spokesmen of the railway managers as a whole. It is not recorded that there were any immediately calamitous consequences. What was eventually agreed by 11.0 p.m. when the parties went home, was that in return for a promise of reinstatement of the strikers without suffering any penalties, a speedy convening of the Conciliation Boards to reconsider the men's claims and the promise of a special Commission of Inquiry, the union leaders agreed to call off the strike and 'to use their best endeavours to induce the men to return to work at once'. It was understood that the Commission would be instructed to report speedily and that it would not be a Royal Commission of the slow-moving type.

In a manifesto to the men urging them to accept the agreement and to return to work the general secretaries of the unions expressed confidence that as a result of the appointment of the Commission 'before many weeks' were over railway workers would have 'won a charter long enjoyed by every other class of the community'. It was not going to be easy to persuade men who had demonstrated their power in a way that had surprised even themselves, to accept terms not so very different from those which had been rejected a few days before. Many reports reaching Unity House from the provinces were to the effect that the strikers would not accept the settlement reached in their name by the Executives. Thus at a mass meeting held in the Town Hall of Newcastle-upon-Tyne it was resolved that there should be no return to work until the men had gained an 8-hour day and an advance of 2s a week. At a meeting of 3,000 railwaymen in Manchester only six hands were raised in favour of acceptance. On the other hand, a report from Edinburgh told of a large meeting unanimous for return to work. Of perhaps decisive importance was the unqualified success of the leadership of all four unions at a huge rally in Hyde Park, London, where 20,000 railwaymen, addressed from six platforms, carried overwhelmingly a resolution 'to return to work and to trust the railway leaders to give effect to the spirit and letter of the agreement'. The men were influenced by the argument of Mr J. E. Williams, General Secretary of the A.S.R.S., who said that 'the fight had not been waged for monetary considerations. They fought for a principle, and that principle was that until the officials and executives of the organizations were recognized they would be compelled to continue the strike.' He claimed, somewhat prematurely, one would think, that the principle of recognition had been secured the night before the meeting. Mr Thomas at the same meeting was confident that the dispute would 'sweep out of existence all the petty tyranny'. The railway companies were 'not going to have a second dose of it' as the first dose had taken effect. The remarkable fact was that by Monday the railway services practically everywhere, except on the North Eastern, were almost back to normal.

v

Mr W. Hudson, M.P., at the Hyde Park meeting said that he had been given an assurance that the Labour Party in the House of Commons would be given a fair representation on the Commission. In fact, of the five Commissioners one, Mr Arthur Henderson, was a Labour M.P. and another, Mr John Burnell, had been General Secretary of the Amalgamated Society of Engineers from 1875 to 1886 before serving as chief labour correspondent at the Board of Trade from 1893 to 1907, could be considered as a moderate man sympathetic to labour. Two others of the Commissioners, Mr C. G. Beale, a solicitor employed by the Midland Railway, and Mr Thomas Ratcliff Ellis, Secretary of the Mining Association, represented the interests of the employers. The 'impartial' Chairman was the Rt. Hon. Sir David Farrell, K.C.B., K.C.V.O., who had been Permanent Under-Secretary for Ireland between 1893 and 1902. It has been said that at the time of its appointment in the week following the strike the Commission was tacitly instructed to consider favourably the viewpoint of the men, Mr Keir Hardie even stating specifically that it was 'loaded' to report in this direction. It seems reasonable to assume that Mr J. H. Thomas, M.P., must have had some grounds for his confident assurance to his audience at the Hyde Park rally on August 20th that 'before three months had gone by no deputation of railway employees desiring to see the companies' officials would go unaccompanied by the officials of the A.S.R.S.'[27]. By the time the report was presented on October 20th, however, the German peril had blown over and the Government felt less urgency in satisfying the demands of railway labour. As one unfriendly critic put it— 'the devil was no longer disposed to play the monk'.[28] It was this change in the political situation which helps to explain the mixed character of the recommendations of the report.

On the favourable side was the proposal in paragraph 29 of the revised scheme for Conciliation Boards that:

'The employees' secretary shall be chosen by a majority of the employees' side of the Conciliation Board, who may select him from any source they please, and shall determine the length and condition of his office subject to the provisions of this scheme.'

Gone was the old requirement that the men's secretary had to be a full-time employee of the railway company. In his evidence before the Commission Mr J. E. Williams had argued that it was illogical to permit a union official to act as advocate for the men before the arbitrator (as had been the practice since 1908) but not to permit such advocacy in the Conciliation Boards.[29] The new proposal revealed the Commissioners had accepted the soundness of this argument and in doing so had brought the union a stage nearer full recognition by making it possible for full-time union officials to represent the men in the Conciliation Boards. Another improvement suggested was that the employers should be required to reply to petitions within twenty-eight days instead of within two months as was previously the case. It was also suggested that either side could summon a meeting of a Conciliation Board at fourteen days' notice. The period of validity of agreements was to be limited to twelve months, an arrangement which would help to prevent the recurrence of the situation in 1909 and 1910. The scheme was to operate for three years until November 1914, after which either side could give twelve months' notice to terminate it.

On the other hand some of the recommendations were regarded by the A.S.R.S. as being so unsatisfactory that the report as a whole was considered unacceptable. Under the old scheme there had been a working rule that before a petition could be considered by the company it would have to be signed by at least 10 per cent of the persons in the grade affected. Under the report it was laid down that signatures from 25 per cent would be required. In view of the scattered distribution and irregular hours of much railway labour the fulfilment of this requirement would have made much more difficult the satisfaction of claims for improved terms of service. The Commissioners proposed to expedite the working of Conciliation by accepting the arguments of Mr Albert Fox and nearly all the general managers and directors who gave evidence in favour of retaining the Sectional Boards but abolishing the Central Boards as superfluous. The witnesses from the A.S.R.S. had, by contrast, advocated the substitution of one composite Conciliation Board for each railway on the lines of the scheme successfully operated on the North Eastern Railway from 1897, and the provision of a national board composed of representatives from the men's trade unions and the railway companies, to which questions not settled at the composite boards could be referred. Mr W. Hudson, M.P., in his evidence had pointed out that in his long experience since 1888 he had found that the employers preferred to deal with the men sectionally, settling one class of men on one basis and another class of men on another basis. He believed that railwaymen had 'so much in common on the question of standard hours, overtime rates, Sunday rates and other matters on which they had agreed to fight as fundamental principles' that these matters could more effectively be dealt with as a whole in a composite board. Sectional Boards he believed were 'unnecessary and cumbersome'. In view of the Commission's decision in favour of sectionalism it is understandable that Mr J. H. Thomas said that the report was bitterly disappointing and that Mr C. T. Cramp declared it was 'a bitter farce'.[31]

On this occasion there was a large identity of viewpoint between the branches of the A.S.R.S. and their national officers. On October 27th, the *Railway Review* reported that the 'overwhelming majority' of branches condemned the scheme and that of sixty branch reports so far to hand not one was really favourable. At a joint meeting of the E.C.s of the four unions on November 1st it was reported that many of the branches of A.S.L.E. & F., the G.R.W.U. and the U.P.S.S. also repudiated the new proposals. On the following day the joint E.C.s decided to forward to the Prime Minister a resolution which declared that unless the scheme could be amended there would be no alternative but to reject it entirely. An immediate meeting between the companies' representatives and those of the men was urged. Mr Vaughan Nash replied for the Prime Minister on the following day to the effect that the railway employers refused to meet the men's representatives on the grounds that, prior to its meetings, the companies had agreed to abide by the recommendations of the Commissioners. Minor modifications could be introduced on a company basis once the scheme was put into operation. The E.C.s, finding their proposal for discussions turned down by the companies, carried unanimously a resolution: '. . . to take a ballot of all members as to whether they are prepared to accept the findings of the Royal Commission, or whether they are prepared to withdraw their labour in favour of recognition of the trade unions and a programme for all railwaymen to be agreed upon by the members of this committee.'[32] Voting papers were to be returnable by December 5, 1911.

The railway directors were prepared to see the country involved once more in a national railway strike rather than that they should consent to meet the union leaders round a conference table. This time they resolved to make more detailed preparations to break the strike. A volunteer police force was organized with its headquarters in London. Its members were to be 'available like light infantry' to serve anywhere in the country where trouble was anticipated. The companies also agreed to eliminate competitive services and to carry out a reorganization of the official and clerical staff who would be called upon to do duty in signal boxes and elsewhere.[33] It was this dogged refusal of the company directors to meet the union officials which prompted Mr J. Ramsay MacDonald to move the resolution in the House of Commons on November 22nd:

'That in the opinion of this House, a meeting should take place between the representatives of the parties on whose behalf the Railway Agreement of August 1911, was signed, to discuss the best mode of giving effect to the report of the Royal Commission, and the House asks the Government to use its good offices to bring both sides into conference without delay.'

Mr Leif Jones, Member for the Rushcliff Division of Nottinghamshire expressed the majority view when he said that:

'The obstinate refusal of the railway directors in the country to meet the representatives of the trade unions has gone far to convince the public that the railway management is not in the hands of level-headed business-like men. . . . We, who are neither trade unionists nor directors of great businesses but simply members of the public, see in the coal trade, in the cotton trade, in the iron trade—the great masters of industry—welcoming trade unions, co-operating with trade unions, working with trade unions, and we do not understand why the directors of the railway companies decline to follow what seems to us this wise plan.'[34]

He, and other similar speakers, influenced the House to carry the resolution without a division.

The now inevitable meetings between the representatives of the companies and of the men took place between December 7th and 11th when the draft conciliation scheme was revised in some important respects. The objectionable Clause 2 as drafted by the Royal Commission was altered to permit agreement on a lower minimum for signatures to a petition. In fact, if both sides agreed, the petition could be dispensed with altogether. The employers, who under the original proposals could suddenly confront the men's side of a Conciliation Board with a demand for a wage cut, were now to send written notification to the men's side of such intention at least a month before the date of the next meeting of the Conciliation Board. Section 9 which defined the functions of the boards 'to deal with questions relating to rates of wages, hours of labour or conditions of service, other than matters of management or discipline, of all wage-earning employees engaged in the manipulation of traffic and in the permanent service of the company' was left unaltered. It represented an improvement over the 1907 scheme in so far as 'terms of service' were included as a legitimate subject of discussion, but it made specific what had been assumed under the old scheme—the exclusion of matters of discipline and management from the purview of the boards. Perhaps the most momentous decision was to confirm the abolition of the Central Conciliation Boards and to place the main work of Conciliation in the hands of the Sectional Boards, the final say in the event of disagreement being with the Chairman-Arbitrator, appointed by the Board of Trade. This arrangement served to crystallize the method of settlement of claims on a grade by grade basis rather than on an industrial basis. It accentuated grade consciousness which was inimical to the interests of railwaymen as a whole as it enabled the companies to pick and choose and pit the members of one grade against another. It tended to give a new lease of life to sectional unionism. It was a tragedy that this happened in the very year of the greatest triumph of united trade-union action by the railwaymen.

Opinion in the branches of the A.S.R.S. was very divided about the merits or demerits of the new scheme and on the question as to whether the officers of the union had acted wisely in signing the agreement on December 11th. The *Railway Review* reported 'a strong element of discontent' at a large meeting addressed by Mr J. H. Thomas at the Mechanics Large Hall in Nottingham on December 17th. Many of the audience wanted him to reveal the result of the strike ballot ending on December 5th, but in order not to embitter relations with the employers further he declined to disclose the figures though he had them in his pocket. He believed with the President, Mr A. Bellamy, that the best arrangement possible in the circumstances had been achieved. The E.C. at its meeting in March 1912 took a similar view. With only four dissentients, they rejected the appeal made by Swansea and 101 other branches for the summoning of a Special General Meeting of the union to deal with 'the recent railway crisis, the action of our officials in connection therewith and the future position of this society', on the grounds that since the agreement was now signed 'no useful purpose would be served'.[35]

Perhaps the more accurate measure of the division of opinion within the union is to be found in the voting on a resolution submitted by the Clay Cross Branch at the A.G.M. in Dublin in September 1912. The motion that: 'This Conference declares itself against all such conciliation schemes as are now being imposed on the workers by the employing class and its capitalistic backers in the state, and instructs the E.C. to give the necessary notice to terminate the existing scheme at the earliest possible moment', was defeated by 37 votes to 19. This minority vote represented the peak of syndicalist influence in the union in the pre-war period. However, the E.C., just under a year later, whilst not adopting the extreme view expressed in the Clay Cross resolution, did accept unanimously the recommendation of its sub-committee that the General Secretary should write to the men's secretaries of the Conciliation Boards suggesting they should give the appropriate notice to the employers of their intention to terminate the existing scheme with a view to submitting an amended one.[36]

VI

It was an illusion to imagine that merely by revising a piece of negotiating machinery it would be possible to ensure a decent standard of living for railwaymen whilst the railways remained under private ownership. That is why the A.G.M. for many years had regularly passed resolutions in favour of the national ownership of the railways, and the railwaymen M.P.s had sponsored Bills in Parliament in 1906 and 1908 with this object in view. But it is nevertheless worth while to discover the effects of the first national railway strike and the adoption of an improved conciliation scheme on the standard of living of the railway workers.

The records show that within a year of the two-day strike there was a perceptible, if only slight, improvement in the wages and hours of the men. In the first half of 1912 there were increases in wages on every major line in the country with the exception of the Taff Vale, the North Eastern, Great Central and South Eastern and Chatham Railways. By an agreement reached on the Great Eastern on January 19, 1912, 5,000 signalmen, porters, ticket takers and carmen received increases of wages from 1s to 4s a week. By an agreement made on August 16, 1912, for the London, Brighton and South Coast employees, signalmen were to get increases of from 1s to 2s a week and the hours of goods shunters were reduced from ten to nine per day. All permanent-way men on the South Eastern received a shilling rise starting from August 14th. On the Great Central also in August a number of 12-hour signalboxes were reclassified as 10-hour boxes and some signalmen received increased pay. On an October 1912 award, goods and passenger guards on the Great Northern had increases of 1s a week. On the Lancashire and Yorkshire Railway, drivers' and firemen's pay was raised 3d a day. The result of these and other concessions was that the average wage of railwaymen which had been 25s 9d in 1910 was 27s 4½d in 1912.[37] On the other hand most railwaymen continued under the burden of a 60-hour minimum working week. In both wages and hours they entered the period of the First World War substantially worse off in respect of hours and wages than the employees of any other major occupation with the exception of agriculture. It will be seen that only with more complete unionization of the men and a policy of trade-union unity was this unsatisfactory state of affairs rectified.

VII

The railway strike of August 1911 had immense repercussions on the British Labour movement. Its effects on trade unionism on the railways will be the subject of the next chapter; its impact on the wider sphere of co-operation between major industrial groups must now be considered.

The railwaymen's fight for union recognition helped to reveal the great interdependence of railwaymen, miners and transport workers employed in the docks. We have seen that during the strike the miners in Nottingham and Dowlais took sympathetic action in support of the railwaymen. At the same time thousands of dockers and miners were thrown out of work through the sudden cessation of movement of coal on the railways.

Having experienced the benefits of sympathetic action from miners and transport workers, many railwaymen wanted to show their appreciation in a practical way during the dock strikes in 1911 and 1912 and the national coal strike which began on March 1, 1912. The success of the Cardiff dock strike in the summer of 1911 was partly due to the strike committee being warned by Paddington branches of the A.S.R.S. of the dispatch of blacklegs by rail. In March 1912, A.S.R.S. branches at Marylebone, Neasden and elsewhere were demanding that the E.C. should summon the Joint Executives of the three railway unions in order that the railwaymen should 'join hands with the miners'. The E.C. did not consider it wise to adopt the suggestion as the miners' executive had not asked for help, but it did advise members of the union to refuse to carry any coal which was 'intended to take the place of coal mined by men who were out on strike'.[38]

At the same time the executive was under pressure from other branches who wanted the union to affiliate to the Transport Workers Federation which organized many of the dock workers. Several branches were warned that it would be against the rules of the union for them to join local branches of the Federation unless and until the governing body had sanctioned such action in a national agreement. Liverpool No. 3 branch wanted the union to summon a conference of transport and railway unions 'with a view to the formation of a gigantic industrial union'.[39]

Understandably, Mr Williams, the General Secretary, and most members of the executive, being more acutely aware of the financial cost to the union of the August strike, were more cautious than the rank and file about committing the union to affiliate to other bodies or to engage in sympathetic strikes. Railways were closely related to every major industry in the country. A general policy of sympathetic strike action in support of other workers' demands would have brought financial ruin in those pre-war years of intensified class struggle. Mr Williams told the E.C. in June 1912 that the transport workers' strike had caused him 'considerable anxiety' since he had received 'numerous applications from members . . . asking for advice' on how they might help the dockers. Even the A.G.M. delegates, generally less cautious than the permanent officials, gave careful consideration to 'the many and varied circumstances in which railwaymen were involved in industrial disputes', and, in order to avoid 'sectional and local outbursts', instructed Mr Williams at Carlisle in October 1911, to approach the Parliamentary Committee of the T.U.C. on the question so that an 'agreed policy' might be formulated.

However, it was as a result of the initiative taken by the miners rather than the belated discussions in the T.U.C. that the Triple Industrial Alliance of railwaymen, transport workers and miners came into being. After the national coal strike of March 1912, the object of the Miners' Federation of Great Britain was to arrange for the simultaneous termination of all district agreements so that, in the event of a dispute, all miners could act together. The decision of the Federation's Annual Conference at Scarborough in October 1913, to instruct the executive to approach the E.C.s of the N.U.R. and T.W.F. with a view to co-operative action, was a logical extension of this policy to a wider field.

In March 1914, the E.C. of the N.U.R. was unanimous in accepting the miners' invitation. At a conference held in the Westminster Palace Hotel,

London, on April 23, 1914, sixty-one delegates from the three groups agreed on the general purposes of the alliance and appointed a sub-committee of six to draft the details of a scheme. The outbreak of the Great War delayed ratification but at a further meeting in the Westminster Palace Hotel held on December 9, 1915, its constitution was approved by representatives of the three organizations.

Such moderate leaders of the N.U.R. as J. H. Thomas, J. E. Williams and G. J. Wardle had no intention of surrendering the autonomy of their union nor did they wish to commit it to the automatic support of the demands of their alliance partners. The Constitution of the Alliance provided that 'complete autonomy' was to be reserved 'for any one of the three bodies to take action on their own behalf'. Whilst joint action might be taken when two out of three of the executives agreed to such a course at a specially convened joint meeting, there was no obligation (other than a vague moral one) on any of the unions to submit a dispute to the Alliance. The N.U.R. leadership supported the new venture in the hope that sympathetic and local strikes might be reduced to the minimum. It was certainly not their aim to intensify the class struggle by using every strike in the coalmining, dock and railway industries as an occasion to draft reinforcements to the strikers from the million and a half trade unionists covered by the agreement.

The delegates to the A.G.M. of the N.U.R. held at Swansea in June 1914 had more idealistic and ambitious aims which they expressed in their resolution of support for the Alliance. They believed that the union of forces would 'encourage the growth of greater solidarity and a vast improvement in the social condition of the workers and be a powerful lever in the cause of working class emancipation'.[40]

The contrast between these lofty aspirations and the infinitely more limited view of the agreement held by the leadership was only brought to light when the Triple Alliance was put to the test in the post-war years.

In the interim, however, a working agreement was reached with the Dock, Wharf, Riverside and General Workers Union (a constituent union of the Transport Workers Federation and forerunner of the Transport and General Workers Union), as a result of a meeting of its executive with the E.C. of the N.U.R. in March 1914. A division of spheres of influence was agreed whereby the N.U.R. largely confined itself to recruiting the men employed by the railway-owned docks and canals. Though the establishment of a strict line of demarcation presented great difficulties, the broad division of spheres of action established just before the First World War has been followed ever since.

NOTES

1. Clapham: *An Economic History of Modern Britain*, Vol. 3, p. 475.
2. *The Times*, August 15, 1911.
3. *The Times*, August 10, 1911.

4. A.S.R.S. Report of Special E.C. Meeting, August 15, 1911.
5. *The Times*, August 7, 8 and 14, 1911.
6. A.S.R.S. Report of Special E.C. Meeting, August 15, 1911.
7. *Railway Review*, August 25, 1911.
8. Royal Commission on the Railway Conciliation Scheme of 1907. BP.P. 1912–13, Vol. XLV, Q. 11833.
9. *Liverpool Daily Post*, August 9, 1911.
10. A.S.R.S. Report of Special E.C. Meeting, August 15, 1911.
11. *The Times*, August 15, 1911.
12. *Railway Gazette*, August 18, 1911.
13. Askwith: *Industrial Problems and Disputes*, p. 164.
14. *Railway Review*, Special Editions, August 19 and 22, 1911. I am indebted to Mr J. A. Pentley of Welwyn Garden City for copies of these papers.
15. *Railway Review*, August 25, 1911.
16. *The Times*, August 18, 1911. *Manchester Guardian*, August 19, 1911. *Railway Review*, August 19, 1911.
17. *Railway News*, August 26, 1911, p. 473.
18. *The Times*, August 17, 1911. *Railway Review*, August 22, 1911. *Railway News*, August 26, 1911.
19. Correspondence between the Home Office and the Local Authorities relating to the employment of the military during the railway strike of August 1911. BP.P. 1911, Vol. XLVII, p. 730.
20. *Liverpool Courier*, August 12, 1911.
21. Hansard, 1911, Vol. 29, Col. 2304, August 22, 1911.
22. *Manchester Guardian*, August 22, 1911.
23. *Daily Telegraph*, August 22, 1911.
24. *The Times*, August 17, 1911.
25. *The Times*, August 18, 1911.
26. *The Times*, August 16, 1911. *Manchester Guardian*, August 11, 1911. *Westminster Gazette*, August 17, 1911. *Daily News*, August 19, 1911.
27. *Railway Review*, August 22, 1911.
28. *New Age*, November 23, 1911. *Railway Review*, August 22, 1911.
29. Q. 132.
30. For the evidence of Mr Fox and the general managers and directors, see Qs. 418–24, 9658, 10324, 10385, 11068, 11836 and 12647. For Mr Hudson's views see Qs. 5972 and 6267.
31. *Railway Review*, November 10, 1911.
32. Report of Joint Conference of E.C.s at Unity House, November 1, 4 and 6, 1911.
33. *The Times*, December 5, 1911, Special article, 'Railway Unrest. Preparations by the Companies.'
34. Hansard 1911, Vol. 31, November 22, 1911. Cols. 1327 and 1256.
35. A.S.R.S. March E.C. 1912, p. 96, R. 49.
36. A.S.R.S. September E.C. 1913, Rs. 46 and 47.
37. Sixteenth Abstract of Labour Statistics of the U.K., p. 93; BP.P. 1914, Vol. LXXX. A.S.R.S. September and December E.C.s 1912.
38. A.S.R.S. March E.C. 1912, Rs. 3 and 5.
39. N.U.R., E.C. March 1914, p. 179.
40. N.U.R., E.C. March 1914, R. 75. T.U.C. 18th Quarterly Report, June 1914, p. 69; 22nd Quarterly Report, December 1915, p. 51; 'National Joint Conference, Minutes of Proceedings at a Conference of the M.F.G.B., N.U.R., and T.G.W.F., December 9, 1915', 30 pp. N.U.R., A.G.M. 1914, R. 13.

CHAPTER XIII

THE FOUNDATION OF THE N.U.R.

'*The conception of industrial unionism held by the N.U.R. is that the nature of the product of any industry determines the definition of the industry in so far as it applies to the organized workmen who are employed in any capacity in or about the undertaking. The railway, providing transport as it does, must be regarded as an industry. All those whose labour in any way contributes to the carrying on of this industry are either railwaymen or railwaywomen, and thus being part of the industry, their conditions are ultimately governed by the facts and prosperity of the carrying concern which does produce transport as its chief commodity for sale.*'
C. T. Cramp, *Industrial General Secretary, N.U.R. 1920–31, General Secretary 1931–33.*

I

THROUGHOUT the forty-one years of the life of the A.S.R.S. the maxim that divided organization resulted in weakened bargaining strength was widely recognized by the membership. When it was formed in 1871, the fact that the new organization was called the *Amalgamated* Society of Railway Servants indicated a concern, at least on the part of some of the founders, to avoid the pitfalls of sectional organization so manifest in the struggles of 1866–7.

That railwaymen were aware of the urgent need for united action was shown by the fact that between 1890 and 1913 there were no less than twelve major attempts at the fusion of forces. Throughout this period railwaymen's leaders repeatedly stressed the imperative necessity of railwaymen combining to meet the ever more concentrated strength of railway capital.

How difficult a task was it to bring all railwaymen under a unified command?

After 1897 there were five unions which catered exclusively for railwaymen and had a significant membership. Of these the A.S.R.S. was not only the oldest but the largest in terms of membership and industrial and political influence. The Society would be more correctly described as a 'most grades' rather than an 'all grades' one, since it did not recruit railway shopmen, and little serious effort had been made to bring in the poorly paid casual workers such as the outside porters and the draymen, as it was feared that they might impair the soundness of the benefit funds. Although there had always been some railway clerks in the union they were never a large group. In 1904 for instance, only 369 out of the 63,749 employed on the railways were members.[1]

Because of its predominance in numbers and its policy of recruiting all at least of the traffic grades it is understandable that this union's policy was one of amalgamation rather than federation.

It was the belief of the leaders of the A.S.L.E. & F., a union that was founded in 1879, that locomotivemen stood to gain more by working through their own organization rather than merging their fortunes with other grades, most of whom were not so well organized and therefore not so effectively prepared for industrial action as were the footplatemen. Nevertheless, through this period there were fewer locomotivemen enrolled in the A.S.L.E. & F. than there were in the A.S.R.S. In 1904 the membership of the A.S.L.E. & F. was 11,500, whilst there were 18,546 men in the footplate grades enrolled in the A.S.R.S.[2]

The third union, the United Pointsmen's and Signalmen's Society, was founded in 1880 as a craft union concentrating on its friendly society benefits. It never enrolled as many men of the grade as there were in the A.S.R.S. In the early 1900's the Society had just over 3,000 members, whereas the A.S.R.S. had 7,909 men of these grades enrolled in its books in 1904.[3] Although the leaders of the U.P.S.S. generally fought shy of schemes for outright amalgamation and expressed their preference for federation, they were more open-minded on the question than were the leaders of the A.S.L.E. & F.

The General Railway Workers Union, founded in 1889, was the nearest approach of any of the five to an all-grades union. Its Rule No. 2 read:

'That the workers of all grades employed on or in connection with the Railways of the United Kingdom of Great Britain and Ireland, shall be eligible to become members of the Union.'

It was largely for this reason that the policy of the union was to support amalgamation rather than federation. Though membership of the union was *open* to all grades, in practice it was largely confined to the grades now grouped together in the category 'goods and cartage', a fact reflected in the low subscription rate of 2d a week which was regarded as appropriate for men with very low' weekly earnings. In 1906 about 800 out of the 5,831 members of the union were employed in the railway workshops.[4] Though this was a very small number, it was significant, since the G.R.W.U. was the only railway union to recruit members from the workshops.

The foundation of the Railway Clerks' Association in 1897 was the outcome of the refusal of Mr Gibb, the General Manager of the North Eastern Railway to permit the company's clerks to enrol in the A.S.R.S. and of Richard Bell's conceding that confidential clerks, at least, could not be expected to enrol in his union. From a very small beginning with less than 300 members at the end of 1897 the membership figures gradually rose to nearly 10,000 in 1900.[5] One of the chief differences between the R.C.A. and the other unions was the greater reluctance of its members to strike. The fear of being swamped in a large union by a majority of members who were less closely dependent on the management, led the leaders of the Association to eschew amalgamation schemes in favour of a federation in which scope for independent action would be greater.

This brief survey of the varying origins and policies of the five principal unions functioning at the beginning of the twentieth century reveals how complicated and arduous a task it would be to achieve a fusion of the forces of railway labour.

II

From the time of its foundation to its merger with the A.S.R.S., the G.R.W.U. took the initiative in sponsoring schemes for closer co-operation among or amalgamation of the railway unions more often than did any of the others. Within one year of the holding of the inaugural meeting of the new union, its General Secretary, Campion Watson, wrote to the E.C. of the A.S.R.S. with a proposal for amalgamation. If this action seems difficult to understand, the explanation probably lies in the fact that after experiencing considerable success in recruitment in the London area— from which 52 per cent of the members came by the end of 1889—slower progress was made when attention was directed to membership drives in areas such as the North East where the rival union was already firmly entrenched. Furthermore, the two unions were at least agreed in their opposition to sectionalism and in their awareness of the dangers of dividing the forces of railway labour. But in the few weeks of life of the new organization its leaders had been outspoken in their criticisms of the leaders of the A.S.R.S. Confronted with Campion Watson's proposals, the E.C. of the A.S.R.S. turned them down, giving as its reason Watson's abusive speeches about the older organization.[6]

In October 1890, it was the turn of the A.G.M. of the A.S.R.S. to take the initiative. Meeting in Belfast it instructed Edwin Harford, the General Secretary, to approach the various railway servants' trade-union societies with a view to 'the adoption of a working agreement, in order to secure a combination of members of all societies in any movement, undertaken to improve the condition of railway workmen'.[7] The response to Harford's letters was disappointing. The only fully co-operative reply came from the

Secretary, H. Tait, of the Scottish A.S.R.S. The Executive of the A.S.L.E. & F. at its meeting in March 1891, dissuaded T. Sunter, the General Secretary of that Society, from attending the conference, and because of internal discussions over a change of leadership of the G.R.W.U., no delegate was sent from that union. Thus, although the merger with the Scottish Society went ahead and was completed by 1892,[8] nothing could be done for the time being to bring closer co-operation among the other societies.

By the autumn of 1891 there had been a change of leadership of the G.R.W.U. and at its October meeting the executive decided to appeal once more to the A.S.R.S. to support a conference to discuss fusion. But a few days later the delegates of the A.G.M. of the A.S.R.S. were persuaded by Harford to reject the proposal since it would involve the introduction of a new 2d a week membership scheme which he said the G.R.W.U. regarded as an essential pre-condition for the merger.[9] Harford had become General Secretary at a time when thousands of members were leaving because of the failure of the union to maintain the superannuation fund, and one of his main concerns ever since was to ensure the soundness of the union's finances. He feared that if a large number of members was enrolled at a new rate of subscription of 2d a week the ultimate effectiveness of the union as a fighting organization would be impaired. However, a few weeks later John Burns proposed to the annual conference of the G.R.W.U. a merger of all railway trade unions[10] and this time the A.S.R.S. gave a favourable response. The E.C. at its meeting in February 1892 appointed a sub-committee to meet an equal number from the other union. At the subsequent discussions the main concern of the delegates from the A.S.R.S. was with the solvency of funds, whilst the delegates from the G.R.W.U. were concerned lest the cautiousness of the A.S.R.S. and its reluctance to admit the poorer paid railwaymen to membership should destroy the fighting spirit of the new organization. However, these fears were largely overcome and a scheme for the merging of the two organizations was unanimously agreed. The new union was to be called The National Railwaymen's Union which was to admit all the members of the two unions at their customary rates of subscription (2d a week for G.R.W.U. members and 3d or 5d a week for members of the A.S.R.S.). All new recruits to the union would have the alternative of joining on the 3d or 5d scales only. The two full-time paid officers of the G.R.W.U. were to be taken on to the strength of the new organization at their existing rates of pay.

It was greatly to be regretted that this scheme did not materialize. The Executive of the G.R.W.U. had second thoughts about it and suggested modifications, but the death blow was delivered by the delegates of the A.G.M. of the A.S.R.S., who in October 1892, turned down the proposal to change the name of the Society and rejected also the plan to employ the full-time officers of the other union.[11]

In May 1893, the leadership of the G.R.W.U., prompted by its rank and file, again proposed discussions with the older Society. The E.C. of the A.S.R.S. responded by stating its willingness to interview for thirty minutes a deputation from the G.R.W.U. The interview was held on the afternoon of May 18, 1893, but had no positive outcome, through the refusal of the A.S.R.S. to admit members at a lower subscription than 3d a week.[12] Despite these rebuffs, at branch level, relationships between the members of the two unions remained friendly. In February and March 1895, joint committees of the two Societies were formed in the London and Manchester areas with the result that at the annual meeting of the G.R.W.U. held in May, delegates debated a resolution in favour of a new approach for the merging of the unions. The proposal was defeated by one vote.[13] A year later the proposal was again defeated, this time by the casting vote of the chairman.

The determined supporters of amalgamation tried once more at the A.G.M. of the G.R.W.U. in May 1898, and on this occasion were successful. They instructed their executive to approach all the other railway unions to make arrangements for a conference to prepare a scheme for unification. The E.C. of the A.S.R.S. acceded to the request and appointed four representatives to meet those chosen from other unions; but the A.S.L.E. & F. and the U.P.S.S. declined to join in the attempt.[14] Despite this setback, the conference of the representatives of the A.S.R.S. and G.R.W.U. was held at the head offices of the A.S.R.S. on August 14, 1898, when very friendly discussions took place. They agreed unanimously to the merging of the funds of the two societies and to the A.S.R.S. taking over responsibility for paying benefits. Sufficient time was to be allowed for the G.R.W.U. members to transfer to the 5d or 3d a week scale of contributions. In view of the fact that the A.S.R.S. had need of more organizers, the decision of the E.C. in September 1898 not to employ the officers of the other union was shortsighted. It certainly prevented the quick adoption of the plan, even though it was approved by the A.G.M. of the A.S.R.S. in the following month. In December 1898, the E.C. atoned for its earlier mistake and agreed to further meetings. At the conference held in Manchester on January 1, 1899, it looked at last as if all difficulties would be resolved when the entire scheme of fusion was agreed by delegations of both sides. It was not to be. The snag on this occasion was the attitude of the membership of the G.R.W.U. The response to a ballot on amalgamation was extremely disappointing. Only 724 voted for the plan and 574 against. Manifestly the majority of the members had serious doubts or were indifferent. Afterwards Bell, in his report for the year, noted with some satisfaction that since the A.G.M. of the other society had conceded that there was not enough support for the fusion plan, a number of the branches of the G.R.W.U. had seceded and joined the A.S.R.S. The foremost reason for the indifference and distrust of the

G.R.W.U. membership was the disinclination of the leaders of the older society to recruit shopmen, draymen and casuals. Until 1912 it remained the policy of all general secretaries of the A.S.R.S. to leave the recruitment of shopmen to the Amalgamated Society of Engineers or other craft unions.

III

These many setbacks notwithstanding, the changed conditions in the industry were obliging the rank and file of all railway unions to co-operate with each other in the defence of their living standards. Towards the close of the nineteenth century the railway companies, facing sharply increased running costs with the rise in the prices of coal, iron and steel, and largely prevented from increasing their charges because of the provisions of the Railway and Canal Traffic Act of 1894, drew closer together to eliminate competitive waste and to combine in resisting trade-union demands. Characteristic of the new policy of standing together in adversity was the anti-union agreement of November 17, 1897, signed by the general managers of five major companies.[15]

In November 1899, Mr H. Pollitt, the Locomotive Superintendent of the Great Central Railway—one of the companies participating in the above agreement—confronted the footplatemen of the company with new conditions of service less favourable to the men than those operating since 1890. The men were to operate a 60-hour week instead of a 10-hour day with each day standing by itself and overtime at the 8-hour rate. With membership fairly evenly divided between the two unions the problem was how most effectively to resist the worsening of living standards. The locomotive staff at Mexborough led the way. At a well-attended meeting held on November 12, 1899, the members of both societies present were united in a determination to resist the new conditions of service. They also carried a resolution favouring the amalgamation of the two societies. A similar joint meeting with a similar outcome was held at Sheffield a fortnight later.[16] The unity of the men of these grades had some beneficial results; on February 3, 1900, a conference of the men held at Sheffield was informed that the directors had consented to keep the 1890 conditions of service with less serious modifications than those originally proposed.[17]

From this movement sprang the decision of the A.S.L.E. & F. Conference in December 1899, to sponsor a federation between the two societies. In a letter to Richard Bell, Mr Sunter, the General Secretary of the Associated Society, reported an 'earnest desire' of the conference delegates that 'the two societies of engineers and firemen should try to understand each other more fully than has been the case in the past'. The E.C. of the A.S.R.S. recorded its 'entire approval' of the desire for federation on the part of the other union and complied with the suggestion

314

to nominate a team of ten men to meet an equal number of men from the A.S.L.E. & F. At the same time the E.C. gave its blessing to the co-operation of locomotivemen at local level on the Great Central Railway.[18]

The conference, which was held at Leeds on January 3, 1900, was conducted with goodwill on both sides and resulted in agreement on a seven-point plan of federation which was to be submitted to the membership of the two societies for their approval. All movements concerning locomotivemen were to be conducted by joint meetings of members of that grade and backed by the E.C.s of both societies. Programmes for improved conditions for other grades were to be subject to the approval of the E.C. of the A.S.R.S. only, though the Associated Society was to be kept informed and its support solicited. If movements came to the point of a strike the approval of 75 per cent of the membership of the joint committee was required before the strike was to be started.[19]

Two months later the E.C. of the A.S.R.S. instructed branch secretaries to call special meetings to give members the opportunity of deciding whether they were in favour of federating or not. By June it was clear that the branches had been very slow in responding. Meetings were held in only 155 branches out of 620, whilst only 4,912 members out of 60,000 voted. Four thousand, one hundred and thirty-six favoured federation and 668 opposed; the rest were neutral. The E.C. therefore resolved to give the branches another three months' grace to rally support for the scheme. The outcome was that a total of 323 branches (including those which met before June) held special meetings which were attended by 8,941 of the members. Of these, 7,160 favoured federation, 1,563 were against and 218 were neutral. The response was no more enthusiastic in the A.S.L.E. & F. where out of a membership of 9,050 only 1,673 voted in favour. Confronted with this vast sea of indifference the E.C.s of both societies decided to drop the scheme, the E.C. of the A.S.R.S. expressing the opinion that some such plan was 'most imperative for the amelioration of railwaymen'.[20]

Two major developments of the early years of the twentieth century caused special concern to locomotivemen; the introduction of bigger locomotives and the electrification of the Metropolitan line and other lines in Lancashire and the North East. The former slowed down the rate of promotion of firemen and the latter in some cases dispensed with the services of firemen altogether. In the course of 1901 and 1902, there was co-operation at branch and district level on the Midland Railway, Great Western Railway, Lancashire and Yorkshire Railway, Great Central Railway and Great Northern Railway between locomotivemen of the A.S.L.E. & F. and the A.S.R.S. Since at the beginning of 1903 there were 14,000 locomotivemen in the A.S.R.S. compared with 11,000 in the A.S.L.E. & F. it is not surprising that the initiative for closer working at national level came from the older society. At the adjourned General Meeting of the A.S.R.S. held in London in January 1903, the delegates instructed the E.C. to sponsor arrangements for the federation or amalgamation of the two societies.[21]

The conference of fourteen A.S.R.S. and fourteen A.S.L.E. & F. delegates which met in Leeds on May 18, 1903, as a result of the A.S.R.S. initiative, resulted in the acceptance of a scheme of federation almost identical to that sponsored by the Associated Society in 1900. A joint committee of five men from each society was to operate the scheme although they had to obtain the consent of both executive committees before any movement or strike could be authorized.[22] At the A.S.L.E. & F. triennial delegate conference which immediately followed the joint conference, strong support for the federation scheme was expressed by Mr J. Drummond who deplored the fact that they 'who prided themselves on being acute level-headed men should continue to throw stones at each other'. The resolution in support of federation was carried by 57 votes to 6.[23] In October, the A.G.M. of the Amalgamated Society accepted the scheme by 43 votes to 12, whilst at the same time expressing the hope that it would 'pave the way for an amalgamation'.[24]

The scheme encountered heavy weather from its inception. In the first place economic conditions were not very favourable for an improvement in working conditions and the Taff Vale judgment made strike action very risky. Secondly, Bell was reluctant to authorize a locomotivemen's movement alone because he feared that the benefits in terms of recruitment would go to the Associated Society. This is illustrated by what happened in the winter of 1903–4. The E.C. of the A.S.R.S. at its meeting in December, learned of requests from twenty-two branches for a combined movement with the Associated Society for improved conditions for locomotivemen employed by the Lancashire and Yorkshire Railway. One branch on that line (Bury No. 1) had requested sanction for an all-grades movement. Bell persuaded the E.C. to support the all-grades rather than the locomotivemen's programme. In accordance with the federation agreement he wrote to Mr Fox, the General Secretary of the A.S.L.E. & F. seeking the support of that society, but Mr Fox replied on January 6, 1904, that his executive did not sanction an all-grades campaign. According to the rules of the federation that should have been the end of the matter. Instead, Bell permitted the continuance of the all-grades campaign on the railway and thus succeeded in annoying the executive of the Associated Society which threatened to repudiate the scheme altogether unless the A.S.R.S. complied with its rules. In reply the E.C. of the A.S.R.S. expressed an 'emphatic opinion' that it had not acted in a manner contrary to the letter or spirit of the federation scheme.[25] The unfortunate episode ended with the Associated Society not getting its locomotivemen's movement and the Amalgamated Society dropping the all-grades campaign whilst at the same time asserting its right to decide which movements it should sanction.[26]

The further deterioration of the relations between the two societies seeking to operate the federation scheme can in large measure be explained with reference to the character and objectives of the two general secretaries. Albert Fox, General Secretary of the Associated Society, was distrustful of all-grades movements as he did not believe that it was possible to achieve a high degree of organization among the lower paid grades which would, in a general movement, act as a drag on the effectiveness of organization of the better paid grades. He viewed the agreement with the A.S.R.S. as a means of obtaining backing for the locomotivemen's demands rather than as the instrument for the general improvement of railwaymen's conditions. Mr Fox possessed an irascible temper which, in Alcock's view, was due to his suffering from 'a sluggish liver'.[27] At conferences with delegations from the other union it led him to say things which he must afterwards have regretted but which undoubtedly embittered relations between the two executives.

Richard Bell regarded the federation scheme as a stepping stone on the way to amalgamation and as a means of strengthening the campaign for union recognition which was the objective dearest to his heart. His high-handed and dictatorial manner aroused increasing distrust in the ranks of the Associated Society.

Had it not been for the efforts of the moderate men such as J. H. Thomas of the A.S.R.S. and F. Drummond of the A.S.L.E. & F. who were prepared to give and take and anxious to make co-operation effective, the scheme might well have broken down much earlier.

It was due to Mr Thomas's skilled advocacy that the E.C. of the A.S.R.S. agreed in March 1904, to attend a joint locomotivemen's conference under the federation scheme.[28] When the conference met in the Essex Hall, Strand, London, on May 10, 1904, however, Richard Bell proved a big stumbling block to agreement. Distrust was generated at the start through his denying receipt of a draft locomotivemen's programme which Albert Fox claimed to have sent him. The programme, which included demands for a guaranteed day and week, with a maximum 120-mile trip for passenger trains and 100 miles for goods trains, and a scale of pay ranging from 6s a day to 8s a day over five years for drivers and from 4s a day to 5s 6d a day over five years for firemen, was approved by a large majority of the delegates but treated very cautiously by Bell. Whilst he conceded its justice he doubted its expediency. He claimed that of the 49,639 drivers and firemen in the country, 15,662 were members of the A.S.R.S. and 11,500 in the Associated Society. Allowing for, perhaps, 1,500 men who might be members of both societies, this meant that scarcely more than half the locomotivemen were organized. The cost, which he estimated at £781,350 per year, was such as to make the programme 'inopportune'. Bell's speech was packed with facts, but it was of a character to disillusion some of the delegates.

A further meeting of the Joint Executive Committees held in Leeds on October 9, 1904, was more harmonious, since the delegates were agreed that the response to the locomotivemen's programme had been apathetic. Complacency, apparently, was not something that arose in the 1950's, for one delegate, Mr Clarken, said the response he received from the men was, 'I'm all right, what have we got to bother about'.[29] It was agreed that the two executives should meet together again when they considered that 'sufficient unity of purpose' existed in the localities.[30]

Despite the apparent improvement in inter-union relations, sufficient distrust had been generated to cause persons of both sides to be disloyal to the spirit of the agreement. In the *Locomotive Journal*, the organ of the A.S.L.E. & F., locomotivemen members of the A.S.R.S. were asked to leave their union *en bloc* and join the A.S.L.E. & F.[31] On October 20, 1904, Mr Fox wrote to a fireman member of the A.S.R.S. at Nottingham advising him to bring his mates over to the Associated Society.[32] The complaints made by the Associated men were that when Mr Bell was asked by the Chairman of the Metropolitan District Railway, Mr C. T. Yerkes, in October 1904, to discuss labour problems arising from electrification, he failed to notify Mr Fox. At subsequent meetings with the Board of Directors at which both Mr Bell and Mr Fox (with supporting deputations) were present, the question of retaining two men in the motor cab was discussed. It was afterwards contended by Mr Fox and his executive that Mr Bell had not consulted with them properly before they were interviewed by the directors and that at the interview he had treated Mr Fox as of little importance since he only represented 160 of the men. Furthermore, it was asserted that Mr Bell had not argued very strongly in favour of retaining the two men being kept in the motor cab. Although Mr Bell denied these accusations and pointed out that he had interviewed Mr Bonar Law, the President of the Board of Trade, to put the case for the locomotivemen,[33] Mr Fox repeated his very one-sided criticisms in a circular—No. 17—which was issued to all the branches of his union and which was used for recruiting members from the A.S.R.S. To make matters worse, at a conference of the E.C.s of the two societies held in London in July 1905, members of the Associated Society at first denied the existence of the circular although Mr Holmes and Mr Bell produced overwhelming evidence of its existence.[34] Owing to inadequate liaison between the executive of the A.S.L.E. & F. and the editor of the *Locomotive Journal*, continued denial of the existence of the circular proved impossible. On page 389 of the *Locomotive Journal* for August 1905, the following report appeared under the heading 'Bristol Branch':

'That this branch, having heard read the General Office circular No. 17, condemns the action of Mr Bell in not supporting Mr Fox in his endeavour to secure the abolition of one man in the motor-house on the

District Railway, and also calls attention to the working of the steam motors on the different railways.'

The exposure of such breaches of good faith completely undermined confidence. Inevitably, the London meeting in July 1905 reached the conclusion that the national programme for locomotivemen should 'stand in abeyance'. J. H. Thomas was scarcely guilty of exaggeration when he declared that the movement had been an 'absolute farce'.[35] Although the federation scheme was not officially buried it was certainly dead. In September 1905, the E.C. of the A.S.R.S. expressed the opinion that competition had proved 'disastrous' and urged the forthcoming A.G.M. to offer amalgamation as the only solution.[36] The A.G.M. adopted the suggestion and also empowered the E.C. to call a conference for the purpose of 'uniting the whole forces of railwaymen'. On October 23, 1905, Albert Fox wrote declining the offer of amalgamation which he declared bordered on 'frivolity'. Instead he suggested that all locomotivemen should join the Associated Society.[37] But although some of the locomotivemen members of the A.S.R.S. were distrustful of Richard Bell, they were thoroughly disillusioned about Albert Fox. The experience of federation had convinced them that amalgamation was the only way to progress.

An attempt—which would have been better not undertaken—to hold another joint meeting was made on November 23, 1906. In August of that year the Associated Society had published a pamphlet in which Mr Fox had pulled no punches in his criticisms of Mr Bell and the meeting was called to sort out differences arising from its publication as well as to discuss an industrial programme. The delegates could not even agree on an agenda, and the meeting broke up with Richard Bell declaring the A.S.L.E. & F. pamphlet to be 'libellous, untruthful and malicious', as members of the Associated Society, shouting out 'Liar' and 'Traitor', left the room with Bell still speaking.[38]

An ex-General Secretary of the A.S.R.S., Mr Fred W. Evans, wrote with wisdom in 1899 of the proposed federation scheme:

'To be effective . . . there should be agreement of purpose and principle between the bodies professedly uniting. Without it strength and effectiveness may not be increased, and discord may be emphasized by near neighbourhood.'[39]

It was precisely because there had been no agreement of purpose and principle that the federation scheme had, most unfortunately, broken down.

IV

Whilst the federation scheme was being effectively torpedoed in a battle of personal invective, more constructive proposals for uniting the forces of railway labour came from the G.R.W.U. whose delegates, meeting in

June 1905, declared themselves in favour of amalgamating with other railway trade unions. An invitation to attend a conference with this object in view was accepted by the A.S.R.S. and the R.C.A. At the same time as Mr Lowth of the G.R.W.U. was writing to the other unions, Mr Bell was carrying out the instructions of the A.G.M. of the A.S.R.S. and making similar approaches. The outcome was a conference attended by representatives of the A.S.R.S., G.R.W.U., U.P.S.S. and R.C.A. held in the Deansgate Hotel, Manchester, on February 3, 1906. The A.S.L.E. & F. were invited but declined to attend.[40] Instead Mr Fox wrote to the E.C. of the A.S.R.S. asking all locomotivemen to join the Associated Society. He was possibly not surprised to receive notice of the unanimous rejection of this proposal.[41]

The Manchester conference was conducted in a businesslike fashion and with goodwill and friendliness on the part of each of the nine delegates. They found no difficulty in agreeing unanimously to the proposition that the amalgamation of all railway trade unions would be greatly to the advantage of all railwaymen and they surmounted the difficulty about different rates of contribution by agreeing to three scales at 5d, 4d and 2d a week. On this occasion also there was no stumbling block with regard to officials, it being agreed that all of them should be found employment at their existing rates of pay in the new society. But agreement foundered on the question of the shopmen. The General Secretary of the G.R.W.U. reminded the conference that they had recruited 1,500 men who were employed in the railway workshops and they could not throw them overboard in any scheme of amalgamation. Richard Bell, whilst admitting that hundreds of applications came each year from carpenters, joiners, coach builders, boilermakers and others employed on the railway who wished to join the A.S.R.S., said that they had been repeatedly refused membership. The reasons for this refusal was that 'they were not railwaymen' according to his union's definition of the term. He was supported in this view by another A.S.R.S. delegate, Mr Topping, who admitted that they *could* have had a large influx of shopmen members since the maximum A.S.R.S. subscription was 5d a week compared with the 1s a week paid by members of the Amalgamated Society of Engineers. He did not think it would be fair to the craft union to 'poach' its members and he saw no possibility of altering the constitution of the A.S.R.S. to admit shopmen into membership. Hints of difficulties about the participation of the R.C.A. in any merger were dropped by its Secretary, Mr Challener, who stressed the 'special status' of the clerical staff and declared that 'among their members there was a wholesale dread of strike policy'. Mr Chorlton, General Secretary of the U.P.S.S., was mainly concerned with the solvency of the sickness and out-of-work benefit funds and therefore doubted the wisdom of admitting the unskilled grades and shopmen who formed the bulk of the membership of the G.R.W.U. His

G. Chapman, General Secretary, A.S.R.S.,
1871–October 1874

F. W. Evans, General Secretary, A.S.R.S.,
October 1874–February 1883

E. Harford, General Secretary A.S.R.S.,
February 1883–October 1897

R. Bell, J.P., M.P., General Secretary
A.S.R.S., October 1897–January 1910

J. H. Thomas, P.C., M.P., General Secretary, N.U.R., June 1916-
August 1931

PLATE 8

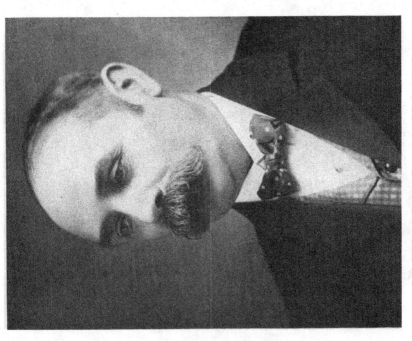

J. E. Williams, General Secretary A.S.R.S., N.U.R.,
January 1910-June 1916

union's annual meeting shortly afterwards vetoed participation in any amalgamation.

In view of the opposition from the U.P.S.S. and the A.S.L.E. & F., and the refusal of the A.S.R.S. to admit shopmen, the E.C. of the G.R.W.U. reluctantly decided to drop the plan for amalgamation. It was feared that if a limited scheme of amalgamation was attempted, excluding the shopmen, there was a distinct possibility of another trade union being established exclusively for the men of that grade.[42] The E.C. of the A.S.R.S. found that there was 'no genuine desire for amalgamation', only 'a wish to perpetuate sectionalism' and it saw no point in continuing the negotiations whilst this remained the case.[43]

It would have been damaging to the reputation of the U.P.S.S. merely to reject a scheme for amalgamation without offering an alternative. This alternative, a federation of all railway trade unions, was offered to the other societies in the course of 1907. At the Annual Meeting of the U.P.S.S. held in Edinburgh on May 13, 1907, a resolution in favour of this policy was carried by a large majority. The E.C. of the A.S.R.S. at its June meeting considered an invitation received from Mr Chorlton, the General Secretary of the U.P.S.S., and replied that it could not act on such a major issue of policy without the authority of the A.G.M.[44] In the meantime, Albert Fox took up the idea with the possible intention of organizing a powerful grouping of all the railway unions apart from the A.S.R.S. in order to undermine the influence of Bell and strengthen sectional organization. He persuaded T. Lowth of the G.R.W.U. to agree to a conference of all unions except the A.S.R.S. to be held in the Deansgate Hotel, Manchester, on October 5, 1907. Mr Chorlton for the U.P.S.S., however, insisted on the A.S.R.S. being represented. Owing to the fact that the A.G.M. of the A.S.R.S. had not yet assembled, James Williams, the Assistant Secretary of that union, attended the Deansgate Hotel conference only as an observer. Even so, a large part of the time was taken up discussing a proposal made by Mr Moore of the A.S.L.E. & F. that the meeting should exclude Mr Williams. If they wanted peace, he declared, they should 'exclude the thorn'. Eventually, Mr Moore agreed to drop his proposal and the delegates came to the more sensible decision to adjourn the meeting until October 19th to allow time for the A.G.M. of the A.S.R.S. to appoint a delegation.

When it resumed with the addition of the six delegates from the A.S.R.S., the conference was the most representative of any of its kind ever to be held, since there were delegates present from the small Railway Telegraph Clerks Association as well as from the five larger societies. The meeting appointed a committee comprising two delegates from each society to draft a scheme of federation to be presented to a subsequent plenary meeting for approval. Aware of the great disadvantages which sprang from disagreement between the railway unions, the Parliamentary

Committee of the T.U.C. wrote to Mr Chorlton before the meeting asking him to allow a deputation consisting of David Shackleton, F. Chandler and A. H. Gill to be present. On October 19th, the Chairman of the meeting allowed David Shackleton to speak. His plea for unity behind the all-grades programme won the support of the delegates, even Fox agreeing at the last minute to a resolution that 'no further deputation be appointed to wait upon officials or directors' (of railway companies) 'unless accompanied by an official T.U. representative'.[45]

The day after Fox had given his support to the plan for securing union recognition by the companies, he addressed a meeting at the Euston Theatre, London, in which he said that the A.S.L.E. & F. had 'nothing to do with the movement of the A.S.R.S.' since it involved 'asking for a reduction' of enginemen's wages.[46] This was a blatant misrepresentation and could not be allowed to pass unchallenged. At its December 1907 meeting the E.C. of the A.S.R.S. decided to appeal to the Parliamentary Committee of the T.U.C. to arbitrate on the right and wrongs of the dispute between the A.S.L.E. & F. and A.S.R.S. In its report on the case presented on February 19, 1908, the Parliamentary Committee severely criticized Fox, stating that his actions during the crisis over the campaign for union recognition were not justifiable. It ordered the Associated Society to pay the costs of the inquiry.[47]

This further evidence of the untrustworthiness of the General Secretary of the A.S.L.E. & F. was regarded as the last straw by the members of the Amalgamated Society. The experience of the failure of the federation scheme with the Associated Society had already predisposed the executive to favour amalgamation as a more satisfactory method of securing unity of action amongst railwaymen, and now another federation scheme had encountered heavy weather. At its December 1907 meeting, therefore, it resolved that it could not sanction the society's delegates proceeding any further with the federation plan. Amalgamation, it believed, was the only solution.[48]

Meanwhile the delegates of the other societies met again in Manchester on December 14, 1907, and drafted a fourteen point scheme for federation to which all railway trade unions were invited to adhere. Provision was made for co-operation between the unions in the presentation of the different grades' demands before the recently established Conciliation Boards. But the scheme stood no chance of success with the largest railway trade union standing aloof. The E.C. of the A.S.R.S. in March 1908 declared that any scheme for federation with any society that catered for the same grades as it did, was against the fundamental principles of the union whose objects were 'to secure all improvements through an amalgamation of all grades'.[49]

All the effort of the A.S.R.S. was thereafter directed to the aim of achieving an amalgamation of all railway unions. The A.G.M. at Glasgow in October 1908, noting 'with apprehension' the 'pooling' and merger plans of railway companies, was unanimous in instructing the E.C. to prepare a scheme for the consideration of all railway unions.[50] Richard Bell, with characteristic promptitude, wrote to the general secretaries of the four other unions on October 9, 1908, but received a prompt and favourable reply only from the G.R.W.U., whose E.C. nominated four men to confer with the representatives of the A.S.R.S. The Executive of the A.S.L.E. & F. did not consider the question until the first week in January 1909, and then declared that it had no mandate to act until the triennial meeting of delegates had been held in the following May. The Executive of the U.P.S.S., meeting on February 26th, decided not to participate in any conference 'owing to the overwhelming vote of branches against any amalgamation'. The General Secretary of the Railway Clerks' Association, Mr A. G. Walkden, wrote that whilst his organization was not opposed in principle to a merger, there were difficulties of a kind 'not encountered by other organizations' which stood in the way. Faced with such an unpromising set of replies, the E.C. of the A.S.R.S. decided to postpone the date of the conference until after the A.S.L.E. & F. was in a position to give an authoritative answer to the invitation. In fact, the delay made no difference. The triennial conference of the A.S.L.E. & F. decided that it was against amalgamation with any other than locomotivemen though it was prepared to join a federation with societies catering for other grades. Reluctantly, the E.C. of the A.S.R.S. decided to go ahead with a conference with the G.R.W.U. alone.[51]

It was not until December 12, 1909, that twenty-three delegates from the A.S.R.S. and G.R.W.U. met under the chairmanship of Mr A. Bellamy, President of the A.S.R.S. at that Society's Acton Street Headquarters in London. After two days of give and take, full agreement on a plan for the merging of the two unions was reached. An old stumbling block to unity was removed when the delegates of the A.S.R.S. showed their willingness to admit to membership existing shopmen members of the G.R.W.U. and all shopmen who had not served an apprenticeship— to qualify them as craftsmen. The G.R.W.U. delegates had two very strong arguments which helped to persuade the delegates of the other union to change their minds on this question. By December 1907, 2,513 out of a total membership of 6,061 of the G.R.W.U. were shopmen, and it was therefore impossible for them to accept any scheme which excluded men of this grade. Secondly the character of employment in the workshops had been changing rapidly in the last few years. One G.R.W.U. delegate said:

'They did not want joiners so much in the shops now as they did handymen, who could knock together the parts made by machinery. In his opinion they ought to lay before the members of each society a scheme whereby they could take into the ranks of a railway union all men employed by railway companies, irrespective of grade or trade and recognizing that the man sweeping the floor was as much a railway worker as the man wearing a gold braided uniform.'

Another delegate declared that circumstances had so altered that it would be difficult to find out where the skilled man left off and the unskilled man began.[52] Such unqualified handymen were ineligible for membership of the Amalgamated Society of Engineers, the Blacksmiths Society or other craft unions and would remain unorganized and a menace to the bargaining strength of railwaymen as a whole unless they were recruited into a railway union.

The concession made by the G.R.W.U. at the conference was to promise to abstain from further recruiting of men employed on private railways and on canals.[53]

The removal of all differences in policy enabled a sub-committee of the conference to agree on a scheme of contributions and benefits, and on the employment of all paid officials of the two societies in the new organization.

It must have been a great disappointment to those who had laboured so successfully at the Acton Street Conference that the membership of the G.R.W.U. failed to ratify the agreement. By trade-union law at that time the consent of two-thirds of the membership to the proposed change was required. When the vote was taken early in May 1910, only 1,153 members supported the scheme compared with 1,972 who opposed it and 3,154 who did not return their voting papers. Mr Williams, by this time General Secretary of the A.S.R.S., attributed the failure to the appearance of a left wing newspaper, *The Railway Worker*, which criticized the leadership of the A.S.R.S. and circulated widely among the members of the G.R.W.U.[54] The strongest opposition to the merger came from the union's branches at Leeds, Darlington, Gateshead and Heaton, whilst there were overwhelming votes for acceptance in Brighton, Eastleigh, Ancoats and Newton Heath.[55]

In spite of the dashing of hopes, the effort had not been made entirely in vain. The Acton Street Conference had brought a very important advance in the policy of the A.S.R.S., which had accepted the idea of enrolling at least a large proportion of the men employed in the railway workshops. The leaders of the two unions had established a friendly understanding which proved invaluable in the crisis of 1911 and the negotiations which followed it.

In November 1908 Mr A. Law, a driver belonging to the Newton Heath No. 1 branch of the A.S.R.S., who became a member of the E.C. in 1910, wrote a letter to the *Railway Review* in which he expressed the opinion that in its relations with sectional unions the A.S.R.S. had arrived 'at the buffer stops'. He suggested that it might be possible to end the deadlock by keeping to the amalgamation plan but working it 'on the departmental principle' of allowing locomotivemen to manage their own affairs, except that, in the case of a strike by any section of railwaymen, the E.C. should have the final say on policy.[56] The proposal provoked a lively, three months' long, discussion in the correspondence columns of the *Railway Review*. When the Newton Heath No. 1 branch proposed that amalgamation on the departmental principle should be the basis for discussion at the inter-union conference on the fusion of forces, the E.C. promised to give the suggestion its 'earnest and careful consideration'.[57] The proposal had come too late to repair the damaged relations between the Associated Society and the A.S.R.S.—the former having rejected the whole idea of amalgamation at the triennial meeting of delegates in May 1909—but its advancement was of value in preparing the ground for the more profitable negotiations of 1911–12. Had the scheme been submitted and worked out in detail five years earlier when the federation scheme was under discussion and whilst relations between the two largest railway unions were still friendly, the prospect for unity would have been brighter.

V

How was it that a problem which over the years 1890–1911 appeared insoluble seemed to be well on the way to solution in 1913, and that the number of important railway unions was reduced from five to three in the eighteen months following November 1911?

The answer lies in the shining example of united action which was given by union leaders and eagerly followed by their rank and file in the national railway strike of August 17–20, 1911.

An attempt has been made to explain the origins and course of that strike in Chapter X. Here the important fact to emphasize is that 50,000 railwaymen felt so frustrated at the failure of the Conciliation Scheme of 1907 to produce improvements in wages that they resorted to unofficial strike action. The leaders of the railway unions then felt obliged to act promptly and together if they were to retain control of the situation. The General Secretaries and Executive Committees of the A.S.R.S., A.S.L.E. & F., G.R.W.U. and U.P.S.S. who met together in the Engineers Hall, Mount Pleasant, Liverpool, on August 15, 1911, were well aware that they had not come for an academic discussion on the relative merits of federation or amalgamation. The necessities of the industrial situation had compelled them to act together to control the strike movement.

The outstanding feature of the situation preceding, during and after the strike was the unprecedented unanimity of the leadership of the four unions *on the main issues* involved in the strike. Characteristic was the statement included at the end of a resolution passed by the Joint Executives at Liverpool before the strike began:

'We further decide that this conference *cannot be divided* to consider any overtures that may be made by any Government Department.'[58] (Our *emphasis*.)

This is not to say there were no divisions of opinion within the leadership. There were men such as C. T. Cramp and C. A. Henderson of the A.S.R.S. Executive who were Marxists; moderate Labour men like J. H. Thomas and Lib.-Labs. like J. E. Williams and T. Dudgeon, the President of the U.P.S.S. The essential point, however, was their unity on the major decisions in the conduct of the strike and subsequent negotiations. Through that demonstration of unity, the railway companies, which since their inception had stubbornly refused to sit round the same table with the representatives of the unions, were for the first time induced to do so.

Successful and often enthusiastic co-operation between men of different unions also occurred at branch and district level. A mass meeting of railwaymen from all four of the unions held at Kings Lynn expressed the hope that all railwaymen would 'endeavour to bring about the unity amongst the rank and file that has been shown among their leaders during the recent crisis'.[59] A similar meeting in Coventry emphatically appealed to the joint executives immediately to draft a working agreement; at Sheffield, a Sheffield and District Federation of Railway Unions was formed; and men at West Ham declared, 'There can surely be no more disunity after this'.[60]

In that week of August 1911, both leaders and rank and file went through a completely new experience which brought a fundamental change of outlook to many of them. Perhaps the most remarkable was the change of policy of the leaders and membership of the U.P.S.S. Mr Fitzgerald, the President of the Society, travelled home to Manchester from London after the strike was over in the same compartment as Mr Bellamy, the President of the A.S.R.S., and a delegate of the G.R.W.U. The other two said to him: 'The next thing is one union for all railwaymen.' As he had his doubts on the wisdom of such a policy at the time, he withdrew from the discussion to the corner of the compartment, not wishing to add a discordant note. But when he got home he noticed 'on every hand a distinct change in the feelings of railwaymen who had worked together and pulled together in that period of stress'. From then onwards he was converted. He saw that the best thing that could happen to the signalmen was 'to get inside a single union'.[61]

Also influencing the movement for union amalgamation was the teaching of the syndicalists who advocated workers' control of industry and the organization of all employees on an industrial rather than a craft basis.

The Industrial Workers of the World (popularly known as the I.W.W. or 'Wobblies') in the United States of America put most emphasis on the need for one big union in each industry whereas the French syndicalists emphasized 'direct action' and workers' control. Tom Mann, who travelled widely in the United States of America, Australia and France before returning to England in 1910, welded together these ideas and expounded them in a new monthly journal, *The Industrial Syndicalist*. The eleventh issue of the journal, appearing in May 1911, was devoted to the railway situation and was written by Charles Watkins of the Clay Cross branch of the A.S.R.S., a man who was to be an A.G.M. delegate in 1912 and 1913 and to play a big part in the final negotiations for fusion. 'The great need of the hour', he wrote, was 'one union for railwaymen' which would result in 'The actual control of working hours on the railways by the men themselves, through their industrial organization; and later still this same organization will be entrusted by the community to control the entire railway system in the community's interest'.

Whilst it would be a mistake to over-emphasize the importance of the spread of syndicalism as an influence in the consolidation of railway trade unionism, it would be just as much a mistake not to take it into account as a doctrine fervently held by a minority of active and influential members of the A.S.R.S. and N.U.R.

Although the Joint Executive Committee of the four unions had adjourned 'for an indefinite period' on August 24, 1911, the railwaymen's dissatisfaction with the Report of the Royal Commission on the Railway Conciliation Scheme brought it into being again on November 1, 1911. The foundation of the N.U.R. was the outcome of the renewed activity of the Joint Executives.

The question of a more permanent alliance of the railway trade unions was opened at the November 1911 meetings by two members of the Associated Society, Oxlade and Hill, who moved:

'That the feelings of this Joint Executive Committee be taken re the necessity of discussing the question of federation.'

The majority of those present considered a more definite step forward could be taken. They rejected the Associated Society's resolution by 28 votes to 14 and then carried by 29–13 an amendment moved by A. Law (the A.S.R.S. member who had made his name by advocating departmental organization in an amalgamated union) and couched in the following terms:

'That this Joint Executive Committee decide to consider the question of fusion of forces of a permanent character, and appoint a sub-committee to draw up a scheme to be submitted to a full meeting of the joint body to be convened as early as possible.'[62]

Agreement was quickly reached on the appointment of the sub-committee comprising three members of the executive of each society and the four general secretaries. The editors of the union journals were respectfully asked to exclude from publication any matter which would tend to cause a division in the ranks of the organized railwaymen.[63]

The crucial decisions on the future of trade unionism on the railways were reached when the sub-committee of sixteen men—four from each of the four unions—met at the Albion Hotel, Piccadilly, Manchester, on December 28, 29 and 30, 1911. The two big issues discussed by the delegates were whether a federation of unions organized on a craft basis or a merger of existing unions into one big industrial union best suited the needs of railwaymen. For consideration were a 'Suggested Scheme of Federation of the Railway Servants Trade Unions', drafted by Albert Fox, and a proposed scheme submitted by the A.S.R.S. re Fusion of Forces.[64]

Those delegates who had had great hopes of achieving a lasting agreement between the four unions could be excused feeling a great sense of despondency after Messrs Fox and Coombes had, at the outset of the discussion, stated the viewpoint of the Associated Society.[65] The leaders of this sectional union were in no mood for compromise. Mr Fox led off with the blunt statement:

'We are here with powers to discuss a scheme of federation and federation only. . . . If you are going to start talking about amalgamation we shall have either to withdraw or sit dumb. . . . I am a sectional man and a sectional man I remain. . . . Amalgamation, in my opinion, is an impossibility and I am afraid it would be a disaster to the railwaymen in general.'

The last triennial delegate meeting of the A.S.L.E. & F. held in 1909 had ruled that the executive must not discuss amalgamation with anybody but locomotivemen. They insisted that they were bound by that decision. In vain did Mr Cramp point out that if each of the delegates came prepared to discuss only his own union's scheme there would be no progress; in vain did Mr Fitzgerald and Mr Chorlton of the U.P.S.S. remind Mr Fox that 'things had been altering' since 1909, that the rank and file were expecting that the feeling generated in August (1911) would 'have some root for all time' and that they of the signalmen's union had decided not to let their last delegate meeting's decision in favour of federation deter them from considering *any* scheme for united working of the unions. The four Associated Society delegates remained unmoved. To the pleading of Mr Williams that railwaymen were 'determined that the divisions of the past must be obliterated' Mr Fox replied that he represented an organization which had 'come to stay'.

Nevertheless, when a resolution, 'That this committee proceed to discuss in detail the various schemes now before the meeting' was carried without any opposition being voiced, it was assumed by some of the delegates that the Associated Society men had relented. Since discussion of a scheme of amalgamation did not necessarily imply endorsement of it, and since the ultimate decision would rest with the membership in a ballot vote it was hoped there would be a consideration of both plans.

For a day and a half, therefore, detailed consideration was given to Mr Fox's suggested 'Scheme of a Federation of the Railway Servants Trades Unions'. It required that all locomotive enginemen, firemen and cleaners should join the A.S.L.E. & F.; all railway clerks should join the R.C.A.; all guards, shunters and 'those normally promoted to guards' should join the A.S.R.S., whilst all carters, platelayers, etc., were to join the G.R.W.U. Although the grades were to be separately organized, any movement for improved conditions had to be approved by each executive committee. Mr Cramp reminded the delegates that in country districts the A.S.R.S. had many branches in which men of *all* the grades in the service were enrolled. These would disintegrate if Mr Fox's plan were followed, for the numbers employed in each grade were too small to be organized in branches of sectional unions. Despite this disadvantage of the scheme, the A.S.R.S. delegation contributed to the discussion on the improvement in its drafting. At midday on December 29th, unanimous agreement was reached on the final draft of the federation plan to be submitted to the Joint Executives.

No sooner had the first part of the work of the meeting been completed than the members of the Associated Society's delegation announced their intention to withdraw from the discussions. Messrs Lowth, Williams, Fitzgerald and Chorlton appealed to them to reconsider their decision, but without any success. Mr Wride, the President of the A.S.L.E. & F. claimed that 'not a branch' out of the 266 branches of the union had recommended a consideration of amalgamation and that his E.C. had very recently upheld the 1909 conference decision against a merger with any group except locomotivemen.

The delegates from the other three unions then carried the following resolution, moved by Mr Ingham of the G.R.W.U.:

'That this sub-committee learns with sincere regret that the representatives of the A.S.L.E. & F. have stated that they intend to withdraw from this movement and refuse to consider any other scheme of fusion of forces connected with the railway trade unions, especially considering they were present when it was unanimously agreed to discuss in detail the various schemes which were before the meeting.'

When Mr Williams, in a last minute effort at reconciliation, urged that it was not cricket for the Associated Society's representatives to withdraw after the other delegates had spent so much time in consideration of the federation scheme, Mr Fox was unrepentant. He claimed that it was a misrepresentation to say that they had allowed the other twelve men to use their energies in amending the federation scheme since they were by no means anxious to have it amended. 'It would have done for us just as it was', he said.

With the four members of the Associated Society absent, the remainder of the delegates proceeded to a consideration of the A.S.R.S. 'Scheme of Fusion'. The first clause, giving the name of the new organization, and the third clause, defining those eligible for membership, provided the greatest controversy. The original draft of the first clause read:

'On and after a date hereinafter to be agreed there shall be established an organization which shall be entitled "The National Union of Railwaymen".'

Mr Lowth did not like the use of the term 'Railwaymen'. Since his union recruited some women, he proposed an amendment that the new union be called 'The National Union of Railway Workers'. Mr Bellamy then explained that the intention was to form a *new* union which could be joined by members of the existing railway unions. They had deliberately avoided the term 'railway workers' because care had been taken to avoid including in the title a single word found in the names of the existing unions. In this way any suspicion that one union was *absorbing* the others might be removed. The existence of such suspicions had been one cause of the breakdown of negotiations for amalgamation in the past. He believed that in a short time it would, in law, be taken to mean that women were also included when the term 'railwaymen' was used. Mr Chorlton was quick to grasp the merits of Mr Bellamy's case. He said:

'We have to recognize the fact that instead of our being amalgamated with the Amalgamated Society or the Amalgamated Society with us, or with any other organization, we must look upon this question as though all four societies . . . eventually are going to cease to exist and become a new organization altogether.'

This generous and far-sighted statement from a man who had spent twenty-five years of his life organizing a craft union for signalmen set the tone of the subsequent discussions. Satisfied with the explanation given, Mr Lowth withdrew his amendment.

In the absence of a spirit of goodwill and compromise the discussions could easily have foundered on the question of the delimitation of membership in the new union. The third clause in the A.S.R.S. draft read:

'Any persons permanently employed, or any extra men continuously employed for a period of twelve months, on any railway in the United

Kingdom shall be eligible for membership, provided he is not eligible for membership in any existing craft or skilled trade organizations.'

Since Mr Lowth's union had a much broader basis of recruitment than had the A.S.R.S. he proposed the complete deletion of Clause 3 and the substitution of the words:

'All persons employed on railways or by railway companies shall be eligible for membership.'

To justify the proposed change Mr Lowth stressed that there were 10,000 shopmen members of the G.R.W.U., 2,700 of them in the City of York alone. There would be no chance of the A.S.R.S. scheme being approved by their shopmen members if Clause 3 remained unamended.

These remarks distressed Mr Williams who had not yet accepted the concept of industrial unionism. He believed it was 'never intended' that a railwayman's union should cater for shopmen. 'A fitter has no more to do with the working of a railway than a shoeblack in the street', he said. If they accepted Mr Lowth's amendment they would be in conflict with at least twenty other unions and the object of their deliberations—to replace competition by co-operation—would be unattainable.

The situation was saved by Mr Cramp who tactfully came to the support of Mr Lowth by declaring that there was 'undoubtedly . . . a very necessary tendency for men to organize by industry instead of by trade', and expressing the hope that they would work on that basis. After Mr Kelly of the G.R.W.U. had warned that unless the A.S.R.S. scheme was modified to admit shopmen to membership, his union would probably vote for federation rather than fusion, a modified version of Mr Lowth's amendment —which now read, 'That all persons employed on or in connection with the railways or allied service of the United Kingdom shall be eligible for membership'—was carried by ten votes to one. The biggest hurdle had been cleared.

The remainder of the draft was accepted without difficulty and with very little amendment. An executive of twenty-four members (compared with the thirteen man executive of the A.S.R.S.) was to be chosen from the six electoral districts into which the country was to be divided. Mr Law's plan for departmental organization was followed in the provision that within each of the six electoral districts there were to be four departments, viz. locomotive; traffic; goods and engineering and permanent way. Thus each important group employed on the railways would be ensured fair representation on the executive. Departmental sub-committees of the executive were to be given responsibility for the conduct of business incidental to movements for improved conditions, but all movements required the sanction of the full executive. Centralization and sectionalism were to be harmonized and given their proper function and scope.

The sub-committee decided to submit both the federation scheme and the amalgamation scheme (with their amendments) to a meeting of the Joint Executives in January 1912. Owing to the absence of the A.S.L.E. & F. delegation, it was decided not to consider the details of the G.R.W.U. programme for improved conditions, although agreement was reached on the need for an 8-hour day and union recognition by the companies.

The Executive of the A.S.L.E. & F. was not present when the sub-committee's report was presented to the Joint Executives of the other three societies at Unity House on January 16, 1912. Mr Lowth had made every effort to secure the participation of Mr Fox and his executive, but without success. Telegrams and letters had been sent suggesting January 11th and then January 16th and 17th as dates for the resumed discussions, but Mr Fox had replied stating that the dates were unsuitable and that his executive could not, for the moment, suggest an alternative date. When the other unions, anxious to complete the business, decided on January 16th and 17th, Mr Fox wrote complaining that the meeting ought not to have been fixed until it was convenient for each union's delegation to attend.[66] However, it is highly improbable that agreement would have been reached with the Associated Society if the date of the meeting had been further postponed to meet their convenience, for Mr Fox informed Mr Lowth in a letter written on January 8, 1912, that his executive were unanimous in declining to discuss 'any scheme of amalgamation'.[67] He also told a *Daily News* reporter that the A.S.L.E. & F. would not be represented at the conference, unless it was agreed beforehand that 'only federation and not amalgamation' were to be discussed.[68] Mr Fox, apparently, had learned a different lesson from the experience of co-operation during the August 1911 strike. Whereas the leaders of the U.P.S.S., G.R.W.U. and A.S.R.S. were led to a strong conviction that amalgamation was desirable, in a speech delivered soon after the settlement, he declared:

'We have proved conclusively that there is no need for the amount of emphasis laid upon the question of amalgamation. Certainly we have proved that collective action can be taken with even more effect through the medium of federation than can be expected through amalgamation.'[69]

The three executives, therefore, expressed their 'deep regrets' at the decision of the A.S.L.E. & F. and proceeded to consider in detail the scheme which Mr Williams had submitted for the A.S.R.S. In making amendments to this scheme the door was left open for 'any existing railway trade union' to join at a later date. The biggest concession in principle was made by the A.S.R.S. delegation which removed the clause excluding skilled craftsmen from membership of the new union. Thus the amended Clause 3 read:

'Any person employed on any railway or in connection with any railway in the United Kingdom shall be eligible for membership.'

When this principle was accepted in the afternoon of January 16, 1912, the foundations of the N.U.R. as an *industrial* union had been laid. The three general secretaries were then given the task of drafting a uniform ballot paper to enable the members of the three societies to vote their acceptance or rejection of the fourteen-point Scheme of Fusion which the Joint Executives had approved.

The result of the ballot of the 23,211 members of the G.R.W.U. announced on May 11, 1912, showed a more than two-thirds majority in favour of amalgamation.

In favour of the terms of Fusion	15,986
Against	110
Spoiled papers	37
Blank papers returned	200
Papers not returned	6,878[70]

In the case of the U.P.S.S. the necessary two-thirds majority was only obtained after two ballots had been held among its 4,101 members.[71] It proved a much harder task to obtain the necessary majority in the case of the A.S.R.S. The special meeting of the E.C. of that body held on April 15th learned with dismay that, although out of a total membership of 116,516 at the end of 1911, 67,844 had voted in favour of fusion and 860 against, more than a third of the ballot papers had not been returned and the necessary two-thirds majority in favour of fusion had not been obtained. It was therefore decided to extend the period during which ballot papers could be returned to May 31st in the hope that the necessary quota of votes would be obtained.[72] Even then it was touch and go. When the scrutineers came to add up the votes, early in June, they found that even by adding the votes that had come in up to and including May 31st, there were still only 76,312 affirmative votes and this only amounted to 66·4 per cent of the membership. They therefore gained the approval of the E.C. for opening the 2,451 ballot papers received on June 1st and 3rd (after the official closing date) and 226 ballot papers which arrived late because they were sent by mistake along with the ballots for A.G.M. and T.U.C. delegates. By adding in these unconstitutional stragglers the affirmative vote was raised to 78,953, or 68 per cent, and the situation was saved.[73]

The A.G.M. of the A.S.R.S. held in Dublin in October 1912 considered in camera the whole question of the fusion of forces, Messrs Lowth and Chorlton being present and taking part in the discussions. The E.C. and the officers of the union were urged to complete their efforts at the earliest possible moment and a small Rules Committee of seven men was appointed to make recommendations for the rules of the new trade union for consideration by the Joint Executives early in 1913.[74]

So expeditiously did the rules sub-committee work that it proved possible to summon the A.G.M. delegates to a special Fusion of Forces meeting at the Holborn Hall, London, on Monday, February 10, 1910. The main work of this conference, which extended over four days, was to gain the acceptance of the delegates to the new rules. For the sake of convenience it was arranged that the delegate meetings of the G.R.W.U. and the U.P.S.S. should meet at the same time in different rooms of the same building and that when each of the three unions had considered the rules separately the three groups of delegates should then meet together in the large hall for final negotiations.

A difficulty that could have caused a breakdown in the negotiations was tackled at the beginning of the A.S.R.S. S.G.M. The President, Mr A. Bellamy, said that he had received a letter from Mr Lowth expressing his members' grave concern over the report of an interview which Mr J. H. Thomas gave to a reporter of the *Daily Citizen*, a Labour newspaper, on January 23rd. On the day before the appearance of the *Daily Citizen* report, the *Daily Herald* had contained a 'scoop' article containing an analysis of the proposed new constitution of the N.U.R. Particular pleasure was expressed in the fact that membership was to be 'open to all persons working on or in connection with any British railway company' and that 'carters, clerks, engineers, boilermakers, coachmakers and every class of worker employed on a railway' would be admitted to membership. In his interview with the *Daily Citizen* Thomas described the *Daily Herald* comment as 'absolutely inaccurate', and declared that it was never intended that the new union should take into its ranks those who properly belonged to other organizations. Mr Lowth had received resolutions from 'a considerable number' of branches of the G.R.W.U. protesting about Mr Thomas's statement and he told his E.C. on February 9th, that if the statement was correct it would prevent the adoption of the fusion plan. The E.C. of the G.R.W.U. called upon its forthcoming delegate meeting to repudiate the statement.[75] On February 14th the delegates of the G.R.W.U. requested of the A.S.R.S. to pass a resolution which upheld the principle embodied in Rule 1, Clause 5, that membership of the new union was to be open to all railwaymen. Pending the fulfilment of this request, Mr Lowth wrote, the G.R.W.U. Congress stood adjourned.

The incident gave the syndicalists in the A.S.R.S. the opportunity to secure a clear pronouncement by congress of a policy of industrial unionism. By 44 votes to 12 congress rejected a proposal that the admission 'of engineers, boilermakers and others' was not intended under Rule 1, and by 45 votes to 11 it carried a resolution moved by C. Watkins of Clay Cross that the rule 'meant what it said' that 'any workers employed on or in connection with any railway in the United Kingdom' were eligible for membership of the new union.[76]

Having settled this important matter of principle, the A.S.R.S. congress proceeded to the herculean task of considering over 900 amendments to the draft rules proposed by branches. The Standing Orders Committee boiled these down to 228, each of which was considered separately and, where necessary, voted upon. There remained a further twelve amendments proposed by the U.P.S.S. and G.R.W.U. to consider before the task was completed, and then only on the understanding that there would be an opportunity to revise the rules in 1914.[77]

At five minutes past five on the afternoon of Friday, February 14, 1913, the final stage of the work of fusion was completed with the signature by the three presidents, the general secretaries and some of the other officials of the unions of the three copies of the deed of agreement. After listening to eleven speeches and much applause, the delegates joined hands and sang 'Auld Lang Syne' with much gusto, whilst, as the meeting was dispersing, some of the bolder spirits sang a stanza of the 'Red Flag'.

To commemorate the official inauguration of the National Union of Railwaymen as from March 29, 1913, a monster demonstration was held in Hyde Park, London, on the following day. It was the greatest demonstration of railwaymen ever held. At 2.30 p.m. in fine, mild, spring weather, thousands of men marched from the Thames Embankment to one or other of the four temporary platforms erected in the park. At 5.15 p.m. the speeches being completed, the bugler of the Camberwell Silver Prize Band sounded a call for the passing of a resolution urging non-unionists to join the N.U.R., which was carried by acclamation by a crowd of 50,000 people.[78]

VI

The new organization started with a membership of 180,000 men of whom nearly 24,000 had been members of the G.R.W.U. and 4,101 members of the U.P.S.S. whilst the remainder had been members of the A.S.R.S. The membership was grouped in 1,083 branches of which eighty-one were former branches of the U.P.S.S. and 160 former branches of the G.R.W.U.[79] The salient difference between the N.U.R. and its largest predecessor was that it was the first serious attempt at organizing an industrial union. G. D. H. Cole, the Labour historian, described it as: 'A new model as influential for the twentieth century as the Amalgamated Society of Engineers had been for the Victorian Age.'[80] The Webbs wrote that the new organization rejected both localism and sectionalism. They believed that the new constitution passed by definition 'even beyond industrial unionism . . . into what has been termed "employmental unionism",' in that it sought 'to enrol in one union not merely all sections of railway workers but actually all who are employed by any railway undertaking'. Not only railway shopmen but waiters and other domestic staff of railway hotels, printers of tickets and timetables, and even those who made crutches and wooden legs for disabled railwaymen were recruited into membership.[81]

To ensure a fair representation of these diverse grades, the executive committee of twenty-four members was to be chosen from the six electoral districts into which the country was divided whilst within those districts the grades were to be divided into four departments as follows: 1. Locomotive Department; 2. Traffic Department; 3. Goods and Cartage Department; and 4. Engineering Shops and Permanent Way. The Annual General Meeting of sixty delegates, elected on the single transferable vote system, was to be the supreme governing body of the union, but the Executive Committee, under Rule 13, had power 'to inaugurate, conduct and settle all trade movements' between the members and their employers. The General Secretary was to remain in office during the will and pleasure of the majority of the members who could dismiss him at an Annual or Special General Meeting. The new union had no difficulty in finding useful jobs for the officers of the unions it had superseded. Whilst Mr Williams continued as General Secretary he was helped by the ex-secretaries of the G.R.W.U. and the U.P.S.S., Mr Lowth and Mr Chorlton, who were appointed Assistant Secretaries in addition to J. H. Thomas who had held such a post since 1910.

However, it would be a great mistake to think of the new union as merely being the sum of three formerly separate parts. The inspiration of successful co-operation between the unions in the 1911 strike and the attainment of a greater measure of unity of organization in 1913 led tens of thousands of railway workers to become trade unionists for the first time in their lives. All the unions experienced rapid increases in membership, but the increase was greatest in the case of the A.S.R.S. and the N.U.R. Immediately following the foundation of the N.U.R., so many forms of application for membership were received at Unity House that extra staff had to be employed to deal with the rush. When 1,934 forms of application were received in the week ending April 19, 1913, it was regarded as a remarkable achievement, but this record was easily surpassed in the autumn. No less than 4,052 new members were recruited in the week ending October 10th.[82] It was through such unprecedented gains that the membership rose from 180,000 at the time of fusion to 273,362 at the end of 1914. At the same time the membership of the A.S.L.E. & F. rose from 19,800 in 1910 to 32,800 at the end of 1914 whilst that of the R.C.A. rose from 19,151 to 29,394 in the same period. After the summer of 1911, railway labour was imbued with a new spirit which rapidly transformed the industry from being among the weakest in trade-union organization to one of the strongest. In the autumn of 1913 the Labour Correspondent of *The Times*, writing as one with 'a long and wide experience of trade-union affairs', declared that he had 'never seen branch meetings so well attended or so enthusiastically conducted as was then the case in the N.U.R.'.[83] Prominent at this time were the activities of the West Ham branch 'Flying Squad' whose enthusiastic members spent their leisure hours roping in recruits at stations 'along the line'.

It is not surprising that there were many members of the A.S.L.E. & F. and the R.C.A. who favoured amalgamation with the N.U.R. or that the majority of the members of the N.U.R. felt that the task of consolidating railway labour would not be completed until the two remaining independent unions were brought into the fold. Although at the R.C.A. conference in 1911 a resolution favouring the Association taking the initiative in establishing a federation of railway unions was defeated, as a result of some clerks being employed in strike-breaking in August 1911, the leaders of the A.S.R.S. and the R.C.A. considered ways of avoiding the repetition of such practices in the future. In December 1913, the two unions reached agreement through the Executive of the R.C.A. promising to do its utmost to restrain members from acting as strike breakers whilst the E.C. of the N.U.R. promised to do what it could to prevent clerks being penalized for refusing to blackleg. That the agitation for amalgamation was continuing in the R.C.A. was shown by the fact that a resolution supporting such a policy was on the agenda of the A.G.M. in 1914. The conference decided to postpone debate on the question; but three years later it was debated and a resolution in favour of discussions on the subject with the N.U.R. was carried. Because branches of the A.S.L.E. & F. continued to demand the reopening of negotiations for amalgamation, the delegate conference in 1914 decided that resolutions on amalgamation should 'not be placed on the agenda of any future conference unless sent in by no less than twenty-five branches'.

VII

One result of the rapid increase of membership was the (temporary) decrease in the amount of funds per head and the consequent weakened financial position in relation to a national strike. In September 1913, with approximately 250,000 men in the N.U.R. one week's strike pay for a national strike would have absorbed £150,000 out of a fighting fund which did not exceed £160,000 (though total funds exceeded half a million pounds). As the union grew larger it became more difficult for its full-time officers to keep fully in touch with opinion in the branches where the membership was increasingly influenced by syndicalist doctrines. With more than half the labour force enrolled in unions for the first time in the history of the railways, railwaymen were less prepared to tolerate the abuses of officialdom, and a series of local incidents which often led to unofficial strikes was the result. Three examples of these must suffice.

Mr Nichol Knox, a mineral driver employed by the North Eastern Railway at Newcastle-upon-Tyne, came off duty on the afternoon of October 26, 1912, and consumed a light meal consisting of tea and bread and butter. Five hours later between 9 and 9.40 that evening he drank two small glasses of rum and hot water, costing twopence a glass, at a public house in Newcastle. Later that evening he was arrested by a police-man and charged with being drunk. At the hearing in the Newcastle Police Court some weeks later, the bench declared that the evidence on both sides was unsatisfactory, but they imposed a fine of 5s for drunken-ness and made Knox pay the costs. Early in December, Knox was in-formed by Mr Vincent Raven, the locomotive superintendent of the district, that on account of his having been found guilty he was being reduced in grade to a pilot driver which would involve a reduction in wages of 9s a week. A mass meeting of 700 Gateshead railwaymen, hearing of these developments, voted by an overwhelming majority to come out on strike on December 7th in support of Knox's reinstatement, even though Mr J. E. Williams, General Secretary of the A.S.R.S. strongly advised them to remain at work. The strike over what the London *Evening Standard* described as 'The right to get drunk' spread rapidly over much of the North Eastern system and 3,500 men were out by December 9th. Before the strikers returned to work on December 14th, the trade of the region had been seriously affected, shipments at Tyne Dock, Dunston and Blyth were almost completely suspended, coal mines were closed and Palmers rolling mills at Jarrow were idle.[84]

The men who seemed to have acted so impetuously denied that they had behaved in an irresponsible manner. They believed they had two strong grounds for supporting Knox; they seriously doubted whether he was, in fact, drunk on the night of October 26th and strongly suspected that there had been a miscarriage of justice, and since at the time of his arrest, Knox was not due back on duty for another thirty hours, they denied the right of the company to punish him for his behaviour when he was off duty. Before this case, Knox had an unblemished record of thirty-seven years' service for the company.

On December 10th, Mr J. H. Thomas, M.P., in the House of Commons, asked Mr R. McKenna, the Home Secretary, to order an inquiry into the Knox case, and this suggestion was quickly adopted. On December 13th, Mr Chester Jones, the Home Office Commissioner who conducted the inquiry, reported that the evidence he had heard on the two previous days had 'totally failed to satisfy him' that Knox was drunk and disorderly or that he was drunk and incapable, or that he was drunk at all in what for want of a better definition of the term we may call the Police Court sense of being drunk'.[85] On the same day the Home Secretary granted Knox a free pardon and the strikers agreed to return to work on the basis of his full reinstatement, though they themselves forfeited six days' pay. The strike had been important as illustrating the inadequate scope of the conciliation scheme which excluded matters of discipline from the purview of the Conciliation Boards, and as revealing the enhanced spirit of militancy and solidarity of the railwaymen.

The second strike, less well known, took place at Leeds on July 4, 1913, as a result of the fecundity of a hen in transit at the North Eastern Railway joint station in that city. A porter in moving a crate of live hens noticed that one of the birds had laid an egg. He slipped his hand through the bars of the crate and removed the egg to place it on his barrow for safety. A railway detective at once arrested the porter and took him and the egg to the railway police station. Within a few minutes all the staff employed at the station were on strike. The district superintendent, hearing of the incident, ordered the release of the porter and immediately the rest of the staff returned to duty. The last that was heard of the egg was that it remained, the subject of earnest discussion, on the table in the superintendent's office. It is not known whether the porter or the superintendent had a boiled egg for breakfast the following morning.[86] In respect of the quick action of the men in the face of what they regarded as an injustice to one of their mates the incident was characteristic of many others which occurred in this period.

Guard Richardson, employed by the Midland Railway, was the central figure in another dispute which arose in February 1913, but very much more was at issue than the treatment of one man. On many British railways in the early years of the present century the power of the subordinate officials had been increased through the introduction of American methods of train control. On the Midland Railway before January 4, 1909, the loading of goods and mineral trains was left in the hands of goods guards to arrange in accordance with the company's Rules and the Appendix to those rules. From January 4, 1909, however, what was known as the train control system came into operation. Under it, although the rule book and appendix remained in force, district controllers were to arrange the loading of trains in their control area.

On January 17, 1913, when working a goods train from Nottingham to Sheffield, Richardson was ordered by the foreman at Chesterfield (an intermediate station at which the train was booked to call) to put on his train three additional wagons for conveyance to Sheffield. Richardson knew that Rule 253 of the company stated that 'The guard in charge of a train must satisfy himself before starting and during the journey that the train is properly loaded, marshalled, coupled, lamped, greased and sheeted, that the brakes are in good working order, and that the train is in a state of efficiency for working'. He also knew that the Appendix stated that for goods trains of more than eighteen wagons proceeding from Sheffield to Chesterfield via Dronfield a fifteen- or twenty-ton brake would have to be provided. With the three additional wagons, Richardson's train would have had the equivalent of thirty-six loaded wagons. Since he was only provided with a ten-ton brake he refused to add the extra wagons. For his refusal to obey verbal orders which were in conflict with the printed instructions of the rule book, Richardson was given fourteen days' notice from a company he had served for twenty-one years.

On February 17, 1913, less than a month after Guard Richardson had disobeyed the foreman's orders, another guard of a mineral train left Storries Hill, Cudworth, for Gowhole sidings with sufficient load for a ten-ton brake; but in the course of the journey, on foreman train controller's orders, given in violation of the conditions laid down in the Appendix to the Rules, more wagons were added, bringing the total on the train up to forty-five. In this case, the guard obeyed the verbal orders rather than the printed rules. Shortly afterwards the train broke loose at the second wagon from the engine and the rear portion of the train ran off the rails at the catch points.

The dismissal of Guard Richardson was an issue which brought together once more and for the last time the Executives of the A.S.R.S., G.R.W.U., U.P.S.S. and A.S.L.E. & F. which met at Unity House on Wednesday, March 5, 1913. The Chairman, General Manager and Secretary of the Midland Railway were informed by letter of the demand for Richardson's reinstatement together with the request for the company's undertaking that in the future, when men were asked to vary any printed rule, written authority for such change should be provided. Two days later an official statement from the company's office at St Pancras showed that the directors had taken a reasonable view of the question at their meeting at Derby earlier in the day. They recognized that it was possible, under the regulations then in force, for an employee to fear that he might suffer injustice if an oral instruction which had been given to him and which was in conflict with a printed instruction, was subsequently denied. They agreed both to reinstate Richardson and to revise the Appendix to the Rules to prevent the possibility of similar misunderstandings in the future. On the following day the Joint Executives, meeting again at Unity House, noted with satisfaction the remedies the company proposed to adopt and expressed the hope that better relations would prevail between the company and its employees in the future.[87]

The three cases cited showed the need for union-management consultation in matters of railway discipline. From its inception on March 29, 1913, the National Union of Railwaymen was within striking distance of achieving this objective.

NOTES

1. A.S.R.S. National All Grades Movement, England and Wales (1906). Comparison of number employed with the membership in principal grades, September 30, 1904.
2. *Ibid.*, and N. McKillop, *The Lighted Flame*, p. 79.
3. Statement by S. Chorlton, General Secretary, U.P.S.S.; Proposed Federation of Railway Trade Unions, Official Report of Conferences ... Manchester ... October 5 and 19, 1907, p. 9.
4. G.R.W.U. Executive Committee Meeting Report, January 26, 1907.
5. R.C.A. Annual Report, 1926, p. 109.

6. A.S.R.S. E.C. February 1890, p. 12.
7. Quoted in George J. Wardle's *Enginemen and the A.S.R.S.* (1905), p. 6.
8. See above, p. 148-9.
9. *R.R.*, October 16, 1891.
10. *Railway Express*, December 10, 1891.
11. *R.R.*, October 14, 1892.
12. A.S.R.S., E.C. Minutes, May 1893, p. 16.
13. *R.R.*, February 22, March 15 and May 24, 1895.
14. A.S.R.S. General Secretary's Report to the E.C., June 1898.
15. See p. 185-6 above.
16. A.S.R.S., E.C. December 1899, p. 15.
17. A.S.R.S., E.C. March 1900, p. 54.
18. A.S.R.S., E.C. December 1899, Rs. 4 and 14.
19. A.S.R.S., E.C. March 1900, p. 6.
20. A.S.R.S., E.C. March 1900, R. 14 (amended), June 1900. R. 9 (amended).
21. A.S.R.S., S.G.M. January 1903, R. 48.
22. Conference of Delegates of the A.S.L.E. & F. and A.S.R.S. with respect to Federation, held at Leeds Trades and Labour Hall, May 18, 1903, p. 25.
23. A.S.L.E. & F. Triennial Delegate Conference, Leeds, May 19–23, 1903. Report.
24. A.S.R.S., A.G.M. October 1903, R. 24.
25. A.S.R.S., E.C. December 1903, R. 42. March 1904, R. 44. June 1904, R. 32.
26. A.S.R.S., E.C. December 1904, Rs. 52 and 49.
27. *Fifty Years of Railway Trade Unionism*, p. 595.
28. A.S.R.S., E.C. March 1904, R. 42.
29. A.S.L.E. & F. and A.S.R.S. Meeting of Joint Executive Committees . . . Leeds, October 9, 1904, p. 36.
30. *Ibid.*, p. 43.
31. *Locomotive Journal*, Vol. XVII (1904), p. 321.
32. A.S.R.S. and A.S.L.E. & F. Joint Meeting of the E.C.s, London, July 21 and 22, 1905, p. 139.
33. *Ibid.*, p. 81.
34. *Ibid.*, p. 90 and A.S.R.S., E.C. September 1905, pp. 31–5.
35. *Ibid.*, p. 185.
36. A.S.R.S., E.C. September 1905, R. 42.
37. A.S.R.S., E.C. December 1905, p. 37.
38. A.S.R.S. and A.S.L.E. & F. Joint Meeting of the E.C.s of both societies at the Essex Hall, Strand, London, November 23, 1906, p. 10.
39 Cited in *Enginemen and the A.S.R.S.*, by George J. Wardle (24 pp.), 1905, p. 8.
40. G.R.W.U., E.C. Minutes, October 29, 1905, A.S.R.S., G.R.W.U., U.P.S.S. and R.C.A. Re amalgamation. Report of a Conference . . . Manchester, February 3, 1906, p. 3.
41. A.S.R.S., E.C. June 1906, R. 31.
42. A.S.R.S., General Secretary's Report to the E.C., June 1906.
43. A.S.R.S., E.C. June 1906, R. 30.
44. A.S.R.S., E.C. June 1907, R. 44.
45. Proposed Federation of Railway Trade Unions, Official Report of Conferences, Manchester, October 5 and 19, 1907.
46. A.S.R.S., General Secretary's Report to the E.C., March 1908, p. 29.
47. A.S.R.S., General Secretary's Report to the E.C., March 1908, pp. 31–2.
48. A.S.R.S., E.C. December 1907, R. 32.
49. A.S.R.S., E.C. March 1908, R. 26.
50. A.S.R.S., A.G.M. October 1908, R. 23 and *R.R.*, October 9, 1908.

51. A.S.R.S., E.C. June 1909, Rs. 43 and 44.
52. A.S.R.S. and G.R.W.U., 'Re Amalgamation'. Report of a Conference held at the Head Offices of the A.S.R.S., December 12 and 13, 1909, pp. 4–6.
53. *Ibid.*, p. 21.
54. A.S.R.S., E.C. March 1910, p. 18.
55. G.R.W.U. Ballot re Amalgamation. Scrutineers' Report, May 10, 1910.
56. *R.R.*, November 13, 1908.
57. A.S.R.S., E.C. March 1909, R. 35.
58. A.S.R.S., A.S.L.E. & F., G.R.W.U. and U.P.S.S. Report and Decisions of the Joint Conference of the Executive Committees . . . Liverpool, August 15th and 16th. Unity House, August 17–24, 1911 (32 pp.), p. 6, R. 9.
59. *R.R.*, August 25, 1911.
60. *R.R.*, September 1 and 8, 1911. *The Railway Clerk*, January 1914.
61. Speech of Mr Fitzgerald at the S.G.M. of the A.S.R.S., Holborn Hall, February 14, 1913. *R.R.*, February 21, 1913.
62. A.S.R.S., A.S.L.E. & F., G.R.W.U., U.P.S.S. Report and Decisions of the Joint Conference of the Executive Committees held at Unity House, November 1st–6th, R. 54.
63. *Ibid.*, Rs. 57 and 56.
64. A.S.R.S., A.S.L.E. & F., G.R.W.U., U.P.S.S., 'Report and Recommendations of the Joint Conference of the sub-committees re Fusion of Forces held at the Albion Hotel, Piccadilly, Manchester, December 28, 29 and 30, 1911' (8 pp.).
65. *Ibid.*, p. 5.
66. A.S.R.S., G.R.W.U., U.P.S.S., 'Report and Decisions of the Joint Conference of the Executive Committees . . . Unity House, January 16 and 17, 1912, Correspondence', pp. 8–16.
67. *Ibid.*, p. 12.
68. *Daily News*, January 9, 1912.
69. Quoted in N. McKillop, *The Lighted Flame*, p. 95.
70. G.R.W.U., E.C. May 11, 1912, p. 570.
71. U.P.S.S., Annual Report and Balance Sheet, 1912, A.S.R.S., E.C. September 1912, p. 3.
72. A.S.R.S., Special E.C. Meeting, April 17, 1911, R. 1.
73. A.S.R.S., E.C. June 1912, p. 8.
74. A.S.R.S., Agenda and Decisions of the A.G.M., Dublin, October 1912, Rs. 12 and 15.
75. *R.R.*, February 14, 1913; *Daily Herald*, January 22, 1913; *Daily Citizen*, February 23, 1913. G.R.W.U. General Secretary's report to the Executive Council, February 8–9, 1913, p. 767. Executive Council Minutes, February 8, 1913.
76. *R.R.*, February 14, 1913.
77. A.S.R.S. Suggested Amendments to Draft Rules of the N.U.R. considered at the S.G.M., February 1913.
78. *Daily Citizen*, March 31, 1913. *R.R.*, April 4, 1913.
79. *R.R.*, April 4, 1913. N.U.R. General Secretary's Report to the E.C., April 1913, p. 5. Grouping for the E.C. (The U.P.S.S. and G.R.W.U. branches are incorrectly indicated here). U.P.S.S. Report and Balance Sheet, 1912.
80. G. D. H. Cole, *A Short History of the British Working Class Movement*, Vol. 3, p. 93.
81. Webb, *History of Trade Unionism* (1920 Edition), p. 531.
82. *R.R.*, April 25, October 17, 1913.
83. 'Labour on the Railways', *The Times*, October 11, 1913.

84. This account of the Driver Knox strike is based on reports in the *Northern Echo*, December 3, 7 and 10, 1912; The *Evening Chronicle* (Newcastle), December 7, 10 and 13, 1912; the *Newcastle Daily Chronicle*, December 9, 10 and 14, 1912; the *Northern Mail*, December 10 and 11, 1912; the *Illustrated Chronicle*, December 9, 1912, and *R.R.*, December 13 and 20, 1912.
85. *Newcastle Daily Chronicle*, December 16, 1912.
86. *Daily Mail*, July 4, 1913; *R.R.*, July 11, 1913.
87. *R.R.*, February 28, March 7 and 14, 1913.

CHAPTER XIV

THE FIRST WORLD WAR

'Think what the railwaymen are doing. An immense number of men have been taken from the railways; but the railways are carrying now a volume of trade such as never has been carried on our railways before. That is nothing but silent heroism, as necessary and as great a contribution to victory as the work of the seamen or soldiers.'
Lord Selborne, quoted in the Railway Review, September 4, 1914.

I

THE N.U.R. had insufficient time to exert its newly-won strength to win better working conditions from the companies before the guns opened up on the western front in August 1914. Once the firing started the campaign for the 8-hour day and 5s a week advance in pay, approved by the E.C. on May 14th, was shelved. There was no prospect of a major advance in this direction until the guns were silenced.

Although proposals for radical alterations in the railway conciliation scheme were under consideration earlier in the summer, the E.C. at its first quarterly meeting after the outbreak of the war resolved to ask the Board of Trade and the companies for the continuance of the existing scheme. When a meeting was held with the railway managers on October 1, 1914, both sides agreed that the existing arrangements should continue 'provided that either the railway companies, the N.U.R. or the A.S.L.E. & F. may give six weeks' notice to determine the agreement'. Both sides further agreed that 'all existing contracts and conditions of service' should remain in operation, and that 'no new arrangements' should be made by the companies either with deputations or Conciliation Boards during the suspensory period. This was the railway 'truce' which was to be operative until ended by the action of the E.C. on November 12, 1918.[1]

Thousands of railwaymen who could have claimed that their work was of outstanding national importance and that this gave them a legitimate excuse to escape enlistment in the armed forces, nevertheless flocked to the recruiting stations in the early days of the war. By September 4, 1914, the railway managers felt obliged to plead with the Cabinet to stop the flood of volunteers. As a result by the end of September no railwayman was allowed to enlist without the permission of his company officials. A release tribunal on which the N.U.R. was represented was set up to prevent abuse in the release of men in accordance with a system of priorities. It worked fairly. Although there were nearly 650,000 persons employed on the railways the tribunal received only forty letters of protest up to June 1917.[2] In the last year of the war the demands of the army increased, and, under protest from the companies, more men were released. Eventually 184,000 railwaymen joined the forces, 40,000 of them serving in the railway troops. 18,957 railwaymen lost their lives whilst serving in H.M. Forces.[3]

Inevitably, so substantial a depletion of the labour force would have imposed a far heavier burden on those who remained even if the volume of work had not increased. In fact the goods and passenger traffic increased greatly in most regions. Mr W. Montgomerie, the Barrhead signalman who at the A.G.M. in London in 1917 was frank enough to admit that the train service in his area was very restricted and that in consequence he was having 'the best time he had ever had in his life', was exceptionally fortunate. For the vast majority the war brought longer hours, greater responsibility and a seemingly hopeless struggle to raise wages sufficiently to offset a constantly rising cost of living. In June 1917, the Chairman of the London and North Western Railway, told his shareholders that a staff, 12,000 less in number than in 1914, was carrying an additional million tons of goods a year. At the same time the understaffed Taff Vale Company was keeping its drivers on duty for twenty hours at a stretch and then bringing them back to work after only nine hours' rest.[4] The editor of the *Railway News*, often regarded as the spokesman for the companies, declared in the summer of 1915 that, having parted with 80,000 men, the managers were left with the 'absolute minimum' for efficient working.[5] Three years later they had parted with an additional 104,000. It is true that 55,942 women were employed during the war, compared with only 4,564 in July 1914, as porters, cleaners, ticket collectors and even signalwomen. It remained the fact that the men were given more work and more responsibility without—for many grades—an advance in real wages. From May 1916, staff employed in Eastern and Southern areas of the country laboured under the additional handicap of a partial blackout. By order of the Field-Marshal Commanding-in-Chief, Home Forces, 'in districts threatened by hostile aircraft, railway lights other than signal lights' were to be 'reduced to the minimum necessary for the continuance of the traffic'. Railway establishments and trains actually running were to be rendered 'as inconspicuous as possible'.[6] The inconvenience and danger caused to shunters, brakesmen, guards and drivers—to mention only some of those affected—can well be imagined.

Lord Claud Hamilton, Chairman of the Great Eastern, whose standards were exacting, and who had not acquired a reputation of unstinting praise to his men in the past, paid a tribute to 'the loyal and ungrudging co-operation of the whole of the staff' who had 'behaved splendidly throughout the course of the war'.[7] Lord Kitchener's comment that in the transportation of the British Expeditionary Force 'all grades of the railway services had laboured with untiring energy and patience'[8] was as true of the tedious later years of the war as it was of the exciting opening week. Towards the end of the war, Sir Albert Stanley, the President of the Board of Trade, declared in the House of Commons that the country owed 'a genuine debt of gratitude' to all those employed on the railways for the 'immense amount of hard work' they were doing and 'the long hours in which they were engaged'.[9]

II

Immediately on the outbreak of hostilities Mr Asquith's Government put into operation plans for the State control of the railways which had been under discussion with the leading general managers since November 5, 1912.[10] By an order in Council made under Section 16 of the Regulations of Forces Act, 1871, a Railway Executive Committee comprising ten leading general managers under the chairmanship of another, Mr H. A. Walker, of the London and South Western Railway, was given full authority to utilize the railway resources of the country for the successful prosecution of the war. The Government, for its part, undertook to guarantee the companies the net revenue they had earned in 1913—a record year. The *Economist's* comment on the agreement was that 'the railway shareholders' had been 'most generously treated by the Government'.[11]

The E.C. of the N.U.R. was quick to notice that although the financial position of the shareholders was a first consideration of the Government, there had been no mention of the position of the men. At its September meeting it was 'strongly of opinion that this arrangement to be equitable, should cover the full maintenance of the standard of ordinary conditions of the men', with 'no disturbance of the guaranteed week or reductions in staff during the period over which the guarantee extended'.[12]

In the House of Commons, Mr J. H. Thomas seized the opportunity provided by the Prime Minister's statement that the Expeditionary Force had been conveyed to France 'without loss of man or beast' and that the arrangement with the companies was an 'admirable' one. He submitted that it was 'a most one-sided arrangement', for whilst the shareholders were guaranteed their dividends the railwaymen were not guaranteed a full weekly wage. Mr Asquith gave one of his 'wait and see' answers which could not have been completely convincing to railwaymen with some experience of railway management in pre-war days. He said:

'Of course we will inquire into the matter, but I am quite certain that it is the desire, and I believe it is the practice, of the railway companies as a whole to share with their employees, particularly in an emergency of this kind, every advantage which they have gained for themselves.'[13]

It was to prove the hardest and most prolonged task of the officials of the N.U.R. throughout the war to prevent a serious deterioration of the standard of living of railwaymen. It was like someone trying to keep his place by running up a downward moving escalator. In this case, at the end of the war the runner was a little lower down than he had been at the start!

Increases in food prices immediately followed the declaration of war. In London the price of bread rose at once by $\frac{1}{2}$d to 6d a quartern loaf. By February 7, 1915, it had risen to 8d. By the middle of January 1915, castor sugar, which had been selling at 2d a pound early in 1914, was costing $3\frac{1}{4}$d. Since the start of the war flour had gone up from 1s 8d a stone to 2s 6d, butter from 1s 4d a pound to 1s 6d, cheese from 9d to 11d and bacon from 10d to 1s. By the beginning of January 1915, the Board of Trade estimated that food prices had risen by 19 per cent in the large towns and 17 per cent in small towns, when compared with the previous July. Early in February 1915, *The Times* correspondent estimated that the calculation of 19 per cent for January was 'well below' the figure for February. The most alarming increases were in the prices of eggs which rose over 60 per cent between September 1914, and January 1915, and fish which rose 51 per cent in price over the same period.[14] Although by the truce agreement of October the promise had been made by the Union leaders that 'no new arrangements' would be made with the companies or the Conciliation Boards, it was only to be expected that, faced with these rapid increases in the cost of living, the rank and file would demand an increase in wages. Nor was it in the national interest that railwaymen should 'waste away' like the little girl in the German nursery rhyme who wouldn't eat up her porridge. The *Railway News* admitted that the lower paid grades of men especially must have been experiencing some difficulty in making ends meet, and expressed 'surprise that the large number of men concerned should have shouldered the burden for a considerable period without complaint.'[15]

It was the rapidity in the rise of the cost of living which explains why the increases in wages took the form of a nationally negotiated war bonus rather than increases in the basic rates negotiated through the separate conciliation boards for each company. In view of the fact that in the past it had taken months to negotiate agreements through the boards, and since six weeks' notice had to be given of any intention to end the Conciliation scheme of 1911, it was deemed imperative to by-pass the entire conciliation machinery. The South Eastern and Chatham Railway had shown the way out of the difficulty. In November and December this company had awarded some of its employees a war bonus to meet the increased cost of living. The carters, who were not included in the award, wrote to Mr J. H. Thomas asking him to intercede on their behalf.

Mr Thomas was quick to seize upon the idea of a war bonus as a relatively simple solution of a pressing problem. Before Christmas he sounded the opinions of two of the most influential of the railway directors, Sir Guy Granet and Sir Sam Fay. They expressed sympathy with the plight of the men but asked: 'Where is the money to come from?' To resolve this difficulty the indefatigable Assistant Secretary used part of the Christmas holiday to interview Mr Runciman, the President of the Board of Trade.[16] The meeting on February 4th between Messrs Bellamy and A. S. Williams (N.U.R.), Messrs Hunter and Bromley (A.S.L.E. & F.) and Sir Guy Granet and Mr William Clower (General Managers' Committee) was the outcome of these exploratory talks. The day before the wage negotiations commenced a specially summoned E.C. of the N.U.R. had instructed its representatives to demand a flat rate of 5s a week increase in wages for all grades. The managers, having been given an assurance that the Government would meet three quarters of the cost of any increased award, were prepared to make an offer but for a long time would not advance above 2s. Eventually they conceded the alternatives of a flat rate increase of 2s 6d a week or an increase of 3s for those earning less than 30s and one of 2s for those whose earnings exceeded 30s. The unions settled for the 3s and 2s on the grounds that this was fairer to those most feeling the pinch. The agreement was signed in the Midland Grand Hotel, St Pancras, on February 12, 1915.

Although Messrs Bellamy and Williams were subjected to severe criticism for accepting less than 5s and for their failure to get anything for the youths under eighteen, the shopmen, the women or the staff of the District and Underground Railways of London or the Railways of Ireland (which had not been taken over at the beginning of the war), the settlement went some way to alleviate distress even if it did not compensate the men entirely for the rise in the cost of living.

The immense significance of what had happened on February 12th, was not immediately apparent to men involved in the struggle to make a meagre increase in pay cover the greatly increased cost of necessities. For the first time there had been a nationally negotiated settlement of wages on the railways. It was also the first national wage negotiation conducted by railway trade unions directly with the representatives of the companies. A great stride forward towards full union recognition had been taken. The procedure followed constituted an extremely important precedent. Before the war ended seven other increases were conceded, raising the total bonus (later known as war wage) to 33s a week for adult males.[17] The habit of wage negotiation at a national level was so firmly ingrained by 1919 that it was never abandoned. The negotiations in February 1915, had spelt the death knell to wage settlements on a company basis. The ground was being prepared for the national standardization of wage rates which came soon after the Armistice.

The particular method of a flat rate increase related to the rise in the cost of living had the effect of raising the wages of the poorest paid grades proportionately more than the wages of the skilled and better paid men. The porter who was paid 18s a week before the war was paid 51s in February 1919—an increase of 183·3 per cent. The wages of the permanent-way man rose from 20s to 53s or by 165 per cent in the same period. At the other end of the scale, the guard of an express train who earned 40s in 1914 was paid 73s in 1919—an increase of 82·5 per cent whilst the express drivers' wages rose from 48s to 81s, or only 68·7 per cent. Before 1914 all drivers earned at least twice as much as porters; some earned more than two and a half times as much. In February 1919, drivers' wages were not more than 60 per cent above those of porters. The relative position of the footplatemen was to some extent restored by the award of August 1919, but the consistent pressure exerted by the N.U.R. through the war years had raised the lower paid railwaymen from the ranks of the sweated workers into the group of the better paid among the unskilled in 1919.

The story of the negotiations for increases in the bonus through the war years is one of constant pressure (on the E.C.) from the rank and file at Branch and District Council meetings to wring more concessions from the companies. A report from Maze Hill Branch on October 1, 1915, was typical of many—'Members up in arms and trouble brewing unless an increase is forthcoming.'[18] A member of Crewe No. 1 branch in an impassioned letter wrote that:

'After over a year of war we are not able to supply our children with that which is so necessary to rear them up strong and healthy, while to see one's wife growing paler and thinner through lack of nourishing food makes one pause and wonder whether it is possible to carry patriotism too far.'[19]

A feature of the period was the growing influence of the District Councils and of Vigilance Committees such as that active in the Liverpool area from April 1915, onwards. Many of the active members of these bodies believed that the union was now so large that the officials were inclined to lose contact with the rank and file. The evidence of profiteering in food and essential supplies was mounting and causing an increasing restlessness among those harassed by the struggle to make ends meet. The fact that the price of tea fell from 4s a pound to 2s 8d immediately the Ministry of Food stepped in to control supplies, was regarded as evidence that the complaints of profiteering were justified.[20] So long as they were convinced that the Government was acting belatedly and half-heartedly against the profiteers the rank and file were prepared to follow the lead of the left wingers in the District Councils and not to be content with the compromise wage settlements the officials negotiated.

Before the war the E.C. of the N.U.R. had power by the rules to initiate, conduct *and settle* claims for improved conditions of hours, wages, etc. A sign of the increased influence of the rank and file during the war was the decision of the Bath A.G.M. in 1916 by 38 votes to 19 that:

'Any arrangements with reference to the question of the hours, wages or machinery for settling general movements of railwaymen considered by the E.C. with the railway companies' representatives should be ratified by the Annual or Special General Meeting.'

The rules were altered to give effect to this decision at a Special General Meeting in London on August 25, 1916.[21]

Earlier that summer the Liverpool Vigilance Committee had issued a circular urging the branches to call upon the General Secretary '. . . to at once summon a special meeting of the E.C.', so that that body could give the necessary six weeks' notice to terminate the truce and give effect to the demand for the 10s a week rise in wages.[22] The E.C. took the action recommended in July. A strong minority of the delegates at the Special General Meeting on August 26th favoured the handing in of strike notices because of the refusal of both the Prime Minister and the Railway Managers Committee to meet the E.C. on the need for an advance in the bonus. After keen discussion the idea of a strike was rejected by 36 votes to 16 with 7 abstentions. Instead it was resolved to call another Special General Meeting if the Railway Managers still refused to act.[23]

The men in the South Wales district who had supported the proposal for strike action then determined to strike on their own if, by Sunday, September 24th, no settlement had been reached. There was no shadow of doubt that they meant business, which was why the Government at last intervened. The E.C. was asked to attend an important conference at the Board of Trade. The importance of the occasion may be gauged from the fact that the Minister of Munitions, the President of the Board of Trade, and the Minister of Labour were present together with Sir William Robertson representing the Army. No sooner had the railwaymen arrived than they were delivered a lecture to the effect that the position of the lads at the front was so serious that there must not be a stoppage 'even for one hour'. At this point Mr J. H. Thomas jumped up to inquire of Sir William Robertson:

'Whether it would not have been better, if the position was so serious, that the railway companies should be called in so that they should be told their responsibilities as well as the railwaymen?'

This dramatic intervention so exposed the one-sidedness of the Government's case that pressure had to be brought on the railway directors to make a better offer. An addition of 5s to the war bonus operative from September 16, 1916, was the result.[24]

During the two remaining years of the war the members of the union were to witness, on the one had, the rise of Mr J. H. Thomas to a position of prominence and authority in national as well as union affairs, and, on the other, the increasing challenge of the District Councils and Vigilance Councils to the supremacy of the E.C.

There could be no mistaking Mr Thomas's rise to eminence. By June 7, 1916, ill-health had obliged Mr J. E. Williams to hand in his letter of resignation as General Secretary. Within a month of writing the letter he was dead. In the election which followed in the closing months of the year Mr Thomas beat his nearest rival, Mr A. Bellamy, by 107,333 votes to 32,772. The new General Secretary had twice served on the E.C., had been President from 1904–6, Organizing Secretary from 1906–10, M.P. for Derby and Assistant Secretary since 1910. The large vote in November 1916, was a reflection of his widespread popularity. At forty-two he was now at the height of his powers.

His popularity was, if anything, increased when he informed the A.G.M. in London on June 21, 1917, that on the occasion of the formation of the coalition government the Prime Minister had sent for him and offered him the post of either Minister of Labour or Pensions Minister, and that he had twice refused the offer. The persistent Lloyd George then asked him if he would submit the proposal to the E.C. He again declined. Later on he was again approached, this time to become Food Controller. In the week of the London A.G.M. he was asked whether he would consider a proposal to go to the Local Government Board to establish the Ministry of Health. In dramatic fashion he told the sixty delegates that 'not even the Premiership itself would be acceptable if it necessitated severing (his) connection with the Union'. He had asked Lloyd George whether acceptance of the office carried with it 'power to abolish pauperism and to establish a Ministry of Health' which would deal with 'every phase of the life of the people'. The Premier had replied that because of the war this was not possible. Mr Thomas immediately replied that he was not going 'to accept £5,000 a year for a dead office' and that he would not go into any office that was 'merely a sinecure'. He concluded by saying:

'I have been guided solely by my love for my Society and my love for my class. Unless and until I am absolutely sure I can do something for the people of this country no office or honour will tempt me from the work I am engaged in.'

One can detect in this important statement both an element of sincerity and an element of calculation. The General Secretary cannot have been unmindful of the fact that the knowledge that he had refused a £5,000 a year post would serve to bind many members more closely in their allegiance to him. There can at least be no mistaking the immediate impact of the speech. It was greeted with loud and prolonged cheering.

What Mr Thomas did *not* tell the A.G.M. was that on December 7, 1916, when the formation of a coalition Government was under discussion, he had had a conversation in a London taxi with two men, Thomas Jones and Joseph Davies, who were later to play a prominent part in Lloyd George's Secretariat. They discussed whether or not J. H. Thomas should join the new Government, and they all agreed that if he was asked to join the Council of Four (or War Council) he should accept, but that if he was merely offered a post as Cabinet Minister he was to refuse. On the following morning (December 8th) Mr Thomas phoned Davies from Unity House confirming that he would adhere to the verbal agreement of the previous evening. When Arthur Henderson called at 121 Bowes Road, Palmers Green, that evening to deliver, in person, Lloyd George's offer of the Ministry of Labour or Pensions *without* a seat on the War Council, Thomas's refusal of the offer was consistent with the undertaking he had given a few hours earlier.[25]

In the last year of the war Mr Thomas was offered and accepted a seat on the Privy Council. It was an action which was severely criticized by Messrs Black (Covent Garden) and Watson (Liverpool No. 4) at the Edinburgh A.G.M. on June 21, 1918. They contended that for Mr Thomas to accept an honour from those 'diametrically opposed' to the interests of the working class was inimical to the interests of the railwaymen. Mr Thomas succeeded in convincing forty-two of the sixty delegates that his acceptance of the honour had not interfered with his freedom to criticize the Government. Only six delegates felt strongly enough to vote for a resolution criticizing the General Secretary's action.[26]

War weariness and disgust at the Government delay in dealing with profiteering contributed to a strengthening of the influence of the District Councils and Vigilance Committees in 1917 and 1918.

In the campaign for increased wages terminating in an addition of 5s to the war bonus in April 1917, the London District Council, whose Secretary was the energetic and sincere Mr W. T. A. Foot, played a prominent part. On March 4th it organized what was described as 'a meeting of the rank and file' in the Albert Hall, London. Although there were no speakers of national prominence to draw a large crowd, the organizers nevertheless succeeded in filling the hall with 10,000 railwaymen who unanimously demanded that the E.C. should negotiate a 10s rise. Mr E. Charles of the South Wales District Council, who spoke of 'the smouldering anger of the men against the rapacity and greed of the food profiteers', quoted Board of Trade figures to prove that food prices had risen by 95 per cent since July 1914. On the other hand the railwaymen's total bonus at that time was only 10s or less than 40 per cent above the average pre-war wage.[27] It was partly because of extreme reluctance to call a railway strike while the country was at war that Mr Thomas was able to persuade the Special General Meeting on April 11th to accept the 5s which he said was the utmost that could be obtained.

Increasingly from the summer of 1917 the district council leaders were stealing the initiative which many members thought properly belonged to the E.C. itself. A group of twenty 'progressive' delegates to the 1917 A.G.M. in London met informally before the official opening of the conference to discuss the policy they would support in relation to each important item on the agenda. Two months later the first conference of the representatives of District Councils and Vigilance Committees was held at Anderton's Hotel, Fleet Street, London, when fifty-five delegates attended. They agreed to urge all branches to demand an ending of the industrial truce and to urge the E.C. to open negotiations for a 20s a week rise in wages. They favoured the N.U.R. being represented equally with the employers on the Railway Executive Committee and set up a sub-committee to draft a new National Programme for implementation after the war. Branches were urged to submit their proposals for the National Programme, not to the E.C. or the General Secretary, but to Mr Foot, the Secretary of the sub-committee.

Matters came to a head at the Special General Meeting at Leicester at the end of November 1917. In particularly tough negotiations earlier in the month Mr Thomas and the E.C. had been endeavouring to persuade the railway managers to concede a 10s rise. On November 22nd, Mr Thomas told the sixty delegates that they had not been successful in obtaining more than 5s. The meeting decided that the employers' offer was 'altogether inadequate' to meet the needs of the men and instructed the E.C. (by 51 votes to 8) to resume negotiations for a 'substantial increase'.

As soon as Mr Thomas took the matter up with the managers, however, Mr Walker, their secretary, wired back that he saw no object of a further meeting unless the men were prepared to accept the 5s. Mr Thomas therefore took the extreme step of calling uninvited at No. 10 Downing Street and demanding an interview with Lloyd George. He told the Prime Minister that something would have to be done to avert a strike since the men were adamant that the award was not enough. Lloyd George replied that he was, that evening, going to the Western Front where the condition of things was 'never so black' and he could not stop to deal with the railway crisis. Mr Thomas, with Lloyd George's permission, then phoned Mr Stanley, the President of the Board of Trade, from No. 10, but could not persuade him to ask the companies to resume negotiations.

When Mr Thomas reported back to the S.G.M. the situation looked very black. Some of the delegates were advocating a strike. Mr Thomas pleaded with the meeting not to resort to extremes. He said he would not have 'the leading of a railway strike on his conscience', and, rather than have that happen, he was 'prepared to slide out' of his position as General Secretary. A few hours later he saw Mr Bonar Law, deputizing in the absence of Lloyd George, and told him that it would put the S.G.M. in an 'untenable position' if they were to be called upon to accept the 5s after having once rejected it. The companies also saw the danger of control of union affairs passing from the hands of Mr Thomas and the E.C. to those of the more extreme elements in the Divisional Councils, and they agreed to a resumption of negotiations on November 26th.

The feelings of Mr Thomas may well be imagined when news came through immediately afterwards that the Liverpool and Birkenhead men had started a 'go slow' movement and had issued circulars to the branches to persuade them to follow suit. The London District Committee followed this up with organizing a mass meeting for a 20s advance in wages at the Willesden Hippodrome and the publication of a circular advocating 'drastic action' from December 3rd if the demands were not conceded. His fury with the radicals must have been all the greater when Mr Walker wrote on December 27th that the managers could not resume negotiations until the Liverpool and Birkenhead men had resumed normal working. He submitted the position to the E.C. which decided to recall the S.G.M., this time to London, to pass judgment on the rebels.

Although six days before, at Leicester, the delegates had turned down a resolution condemning the unofficial actions of the Vigilance Committees and District Councils, on November 28th at Unity House they began to see the force of Mr Thomas's arguments. Speaking with intense feeling he declared: 'Either you have to repudiate Liverpool . . . or you are going to say that Liverpool is going to run the Society. Either the E.C. and yourselves have to control our union or there is going to be chaos.'

A resolution repudiating the action of the Liverpool and Birkenhead men and demanding that they resume normal working was then carried by 50 votes to 10. The delegates felt less strongly about Mr Foot and the London District Council. Their action was repudiated by the narrower majority of 35 votes to 24. The worst of the crisis was then over. In quick succession the rebels agreed to resume normal working, the managers agreed to resume negotiations and the S.G.M. agreed to accept the extra shilling (making 6s in all) that these negotiations yielded. Mr Thomas said that these (November 1917) negotiations were 'the longest and most painful' he had ever had to face.[28]

The repudiation of the unconstitutional action of two of the divisions did not mean an end to the agitation, since the economic difficulties in which the discontent was born continued to exist. The smouldering conflict between the radicals in the branches and the General Secretary and the moderates on the E.C. flared up again in the summer of 1918. On June 4th, a fortnight before the A.G.M. was due to meet at Edinburgh, the Liverpool Vigilance Committee issued a circular inviting about twenty 'progressive' delegates to attend a pre-conference meeting at Melbourne Hall, Melbourne Place, on the morning of the 17th. The conveners declared that their object was not to circumvent the instructions delegates had received but to 'obtain unity of action on matters of policy' on which they were agreed. In a special debate on the subject Mr Thomas joined issue with his critics challenging their right to divide the delegates up into 'progressive' and 'non-progressive' groups. A number of the delegates who had attended the meeting declared that there was nothing secretive about it and that they had told their branches of their intention to attend. They had not discussed anything subversive, but had dealt with such important issues as the 8-hour day, eyesight tests, etc. Mr Thomas was making a storm in a teacup. This time the voting was closer. Thirty voted for a resolution condemning the Liverpool Committee; but the rebels mustered twenty-four.

The last battle of the war on the wages front was fought out in September 1918. Throughout the year the District Councils had been demanding an end to the truce and a forward policy on wage demands. At a conference attended by the representatives of twenty-six District Councils held in London on January 27th, the delegates were unanimous in demanding that the E.C. should end the truce and reopen negotiations with the companies. Early in September the E.C. had asked the managers for a rise of 10s but after days of negotiation had failed to persuade them to give more than 5s. A Special General Meeting on September 13th had rejected this offer by a very large majority and had declared that it would not accept anything less than 10s per week and a war wage for women equal to that for men. They did agree to the setting-up of a committee on which both the Government and N.U.R. were to be represented to regulate future war wages proportionately to the rise in the cost of living. The E.C. reopened negotiations and persuaded the managers to back-date the offer to August 10th and to permit the shopmen to have the 3s 6d award of the Committee on Production, but could not persuade them to advance the war wage by more than the 5s already agreed on. The S.G.M., meeting again at Unity House on September 19th, was persuaded that everything possible had been done, and decided to accept the offer.

In South Wales, where some munition workers were earning eight or nine pounds a week, there was strong resentment at the decision of the E.C. and the S.G.M. to accept less than the 10s demanded. On the night of September 22nd and 23rd, locomotivemen of both A.S.L.E. & F. and N.U.R. branches struck work in protest. Twenty-four hours later the strike had spread to London and Shrewsbury and parts of the London and North Western Railway system, but was still largely confined to locomotivemen. On the 24th, Mr Thomas addressed a very stormy meeting at Cardiff and pleaded with the men 'for God's sake to make amends' and get themselves 'out of an intolerable position before it was too late'.[30]

The General Secretary felt worn out and at the end of his tether. In a mood of extreme depression on September 26th, he sent in his letter of resignation in which he expressed his view that the strike was 'as wicked as it was dangerous' and that the policy of those who led the strike ought to 'be challenged and fought'. The letter had the desired effect. The E.C. at a special meeting declined to accept the proffered resignation.[31] By September 27th most of the strikers were back at work. 840 branches passed resolutions urging the General Secretary to reconsider his decision.[32] On October 9th, in a second letter to the E.C., Mr Thomas wrote that in view of the 'unique expression of confidence' in him from so many branches he had agreed to withdraw his resignation.[33] The last wage crisis of the war was over. In any case the odds against the strikers were heavy. The Government acted promptly in the emergency. The Board of Trade on September 25th obtained from Mr Justice Salter an interim injunction prohibiting the A.S.L.E. & F. and the N.U.R. from paying strike aliment. In the meantime, 2,400 men of the City of London Rifles and the London Rifle Brigade, had been sent down to Newport to keep the trains running if this proved to be necessary.[34]

Reviewing the whole of the war period it would be true to say that the majority of the men showed great restraint in wage demands. This is shown in the fact that at the end of the war, although wages had risen by 33s, representing a rise of 117 per cent over the average wage of July 1914, the cost of living had risen by 120 to 125 per cent in the same period.[35] All branches had members serving on the Western Front and were undoubtedly influenced by such appeals as that contained in a 'letter from the trenches' written by a member of Crewe No. 2 branch:

'Perhaps those who have not been out here scarcely realize the disastrous effect a railway strike would have, and that by the stoppage of transport of guns, ammunition, food, reinforcements, etc., the strikers would indirectly, but none the less surely, sell our lives to the Huns.'[36]

Compared with this, the argument that it was unpatriotic and contrary to the interests of railwaymen at home and in France to permit a fall in the standard of living, had less potency when it came to the question 'to strike or not to strike?'

III

As the railways of Ireland were not taken over by the Government at the beginning of the war the Irish railwaymen did not benefit from the early war bonus awards. By September 1916, the men employed by the Dublin and South Eastern Railway declared that if the E.C. failed to negotiate a

10s a week rise on their behalf it should order a strike throughout the railways of Ireland. The men warned that if the E.C. did not call the strike, they would do so themselves. This brought the President (Mr Bellamy) and Mr Thomas to Dublin post haste to negotiate with the directors of all the principal companies. It was admitted that since the beginning of the war wages had risen by as little as from 1s to 3s and that there was a strong case for an increased bonus. The directors, however, pleaded that they could not afford to be more generous since coal and materials for maintenance were costing them more, and unlike the other railways in the Kingdom, they had received no financial assistance from the Government. On his return to Westminster, Mr Thomas told the House of Commons that on the Irish railways hundreds of men with families were earning as little as 14s a week. He pleaded with the Government to take over the Irish lines and help the companies to pay a living wage. Mr Runciman, the President of the Board of Trade, stalled for many weeks until the Irish railway workers compelled his intervention. They declared their intention to strike on December 18, 1916. Then at last the Government acted promptly. Just before Christmas it announced that it would take control of the Irish Railways. The companies followed with the award of a bonus of 7s on December 29th.[37]

The Irish railwaymen never caught up with their English brothers in respect of the war bonus. Since only one in six of them were organized and the cost of living had not risen so much as it had on the other side of the Irish Channel it was an understandable situation. It did not prevent a number of Irish members holding the opinion that their English brothers were content to let them fend for themselves.[38]

Although over 4,000 women had been employed on the railways before the war they had not been admitted to membership of the A.S.R.S. or N.U.R. When asked for a ruling on this question in the summer of 1913, Mr Williams had decided that women were not eligible and the E.C. had upheld his view. There was one woman on the books of the union in 1914 but this was through the accident of her name being Jesse.[39] But by the end of the war over 55,000 women were employed on the railways and it was impossible to ignore such an important section of the labour force. At the A.G.M. in Nottingham in June 1915, the appeal against the E.C.'s ruling of 1913, supported by the Birmingham District and from branches at Bath, Batley and elsewhere was upheld by 33 votes to 23 and it was agreed that women be admitted to membership of the Union. The A.S.L.E. & F. did not admit women members until 1924.

The concern of the officers of the union in the early days of the war was that the companies would make the cheaper labour of women a permanent substitute for that of the men who had enlisted in the Army. The E.C. therefore, in June 1915, instructed the sub-committee which negotiated the war bonus with the managers, to obtain a promise that all former employees of the companies who had joined the forces would be reinstated after the war in positions no worse than those they had occupied before July 1914. Such a promise was obtained from the companies on July 21, 1915. It was a further cardinal principle of the union that women in each grade of the service should be awarded the minimum rate of pay for men employed in that grade. This was the policy, so Mr Thomas told the Special General Meeting at Leicester in 1917, because the union did not admit that women's employment was of a permanent character. Temporary labour of all kinds was paid the minimum rate and therefore women should receive the minimum. To have admitted their permanence would have been to have jeopardized the position of the men. Some of the companies, however, were not at first prepared to pay even the minimum rate for the grade. The E.C. took such a serious view of this refusal by the companies that, on July 31, 1915, they instructed the General Secretary to cancel the truce agreement if he did not obtain a satisfactory reply from the Government or the companies within fourteen days. It was the only occasion during the war that the E.C. seriously contemplated jettisoning the industrial truce. The threat proved effective. On August 10th, Sir Sam Fay wrote on behalf of the leading companies agreeing to pay the minimum rate for the job for all women taken into employment since August 1914. Although at first the Scottish and London tube railways were not included in the agreement the President of the Board of Trade had persuaded their directors to fall into line with the other companies by August 19th.

Many of the rank and file did not accept the General Secretary's policy on women's wages. In May 1915, both the London, Sheffield, Chesterfield and Birmingham District Councils passed resolutions in favour of a policy of equal pay for women. They did not see why the desire to protect the jobs of those temporarily serving in the forces should prevent the union fighting for the rate for the job. The E.C.'s policy stood half-way between that of the General Secretary and the District Councils. It favoured the women getting the same war bonus as the men but did not advocate their being paid the same basic rates.[40]

The rise in the cost of living compelled Mr Thomas and the E.C. to ask the companies to extend the bonus to women employees. The companies never awarded as much to the women as they did to the men with the result that at the end of the war the total bonus for women was only 20s 6d compared with the men's 33s. When the union argued that the women were as adversely affected by rising prices as were the men the managers replied that the overwhelming majority of the women on the railways were either the wives or daughters of railwaymen and their responsibilities were not the same as those of men with families. The union representatives retorted that since women did the same work as men they were entitled to the same increases in pay. This was met by the argument that women's labour was not as productive as that of men.

With a surprising and questionable precision the managers claimed that women's labour was only three-fifths as productive as that of men and that this was particularly the case with ticket collectors. They employed women 'not because it was an economic proposition but because of the circumstances created by the war'.[41]

It is difficult to follow the managers' argument about ticket collectors. Some stations such as that at Maida Vale on the Bakerloo line were, as early as June 1915, entirely staffed and efficiently maintained by women employees. Could it have been the fact that the two ticket collectors on this station only collected three-fifths the number of tickets collected previously by men? Though it was not a gain measurable in economic terms, it was observed that there was 'a distinct improvement in the dress and manners of the men' on stations where women were employed![42]

That women were capable of possessing strong views of their own as to the adequacy of their pay was shown on the occasion of the strike of the London bus women in August 1918. A number of the women employed on the London Electric Railways struck work partly in sympathy with the buswomen but also to enforce their own demand for the same war bonus (25s) then being paid to railwaymen. A deputation of the women visited Unity House where they were interviewed by the E.C. which advised them to return to work on the understanding that the matter would be taken up with the Railway Executive Committee. This was done and within a few days an increase was granted to the women at the same time as that given to the men.[43]

IV

During the war some of the fuller implications of organizing men on an industrial basis began to be appreciated by officials of the N.U.R. The A.S.R.S. in 1913, had not had a single shopman member, for it had not been the policy of that union to recruit from the railway workshops. The G.R.W.U., on the other hand, had made the unskilled grades in the shops its main field of activity and it was most successful in recruiting them on the North Eastern Railway. Its officials at the time of fusion in 1913 had obtained a categorical assurance that the policy of the new union would be to recruit shopmen along with all other grades. Hence in the N.U.R.'s rules it was stated that 'any worker employed on or in connection with any railway in the United Kingdom shall be eligible for membership'.

There was undoubtedly scope for union activity in the railway workshops. Before the N.U.R. was formed, despite the fact that more than eighty craft unions had, over the previous forty years, been enrolling members, they had succeeded in organizing only 20 per cent of the 73,000 employed. Jurisdictional disputes hindered the recruitment of some of the men—there were ten different unions catering for fitters alone—whilst others remained unorganized because they were classified as unskilled or casual workers. Within six months of the fusion of forces the N.U.R. organizers had gone about their task of recruiting the shopmen with such zest that they had enrolled 30,000 of them. By the end of 1916 over 50,000 had joined.[44] The result, according to Mr Thomas, was that the N.U.R. was 'at daggers drawn with every craft union in the country'.[45] The N.U.R. leadership had by no means chosen to pick a quarrel with the craft unions. Mr Bellamy, speaking in the special debate on the question at the Bristol T.U.C. in 1915, challenged the leaders of the craft unions to prove that the N.U.R. had been guilty of poaching members of other unions. He claimed that the new recruits had been obtained from the non-unionized 80 per cent of the men. The result of the failure of the craft unions to organize these men in the past was that the rates of pay in the railway workshops were 'shillings a week less' than those of tradesmen of comparable skill outside the railway industry.

In an endeavour to sort out the differences of view on the organization of shopmen, the E.C. of the N.U.R. in June 1914, appointed a sub-committee to meet the craft unions' officials. When the parties met, the craft unions agreed to the N.U.R. proposal to summon, on September 29th, a conference of all trade unions concerned with the shopmen. Although the N.U.R. delegates attending the conference represented 40,000 shopmen, the craft unions refused to co-operate further unless the N.U.R. promised to refrain from enrolling any more men of these grades. Since such a proposal was entirely contrary to the constitution of the union, the N.U.R. delegation could not give the required promise. In December 1914, the E.C. endorsed the action of the delegation. The sub-committee then proposed a system of transfer between the N.U.R. and the craft unions, whereby all men employed by railway companies would be eligible for the N.U.R., but on leaving the railway service would transfer to the particular craft union catering for their trade. The craft union officers, meeting separately, turned down this suggestion and merely reiterated their intention of refusing to co-operate until the bigger union promised to abstain from further recruiting. This disagreement on policy continued throughout the war. At the A.G.M. of the N.U.R. in Nottingham in June 1915, the delegates endorsed the action of the E.C., but, on the recommendation of Mr Thomas decided not to risk any trouble with the Miners' Federation. By 41 votes to 11 they rejected a proposal to admit colliery railwaymen to the union.[46]

To add to the difficulties of the N.U.R. the Bristol Congress of the T.U.C. in September 1915, by the narrow majority of 1,300,000 votes to 1,100,000 upheld the view of the craft unions in claiming 'that any method of organization that seeks to divide the workmen from their fellows in the same occupation' (i.e. men in similar trades employed by private firms) 'is detrimental to the best interests of Trade Unionism'. This was reaffirming T.U.C. decisions of 1906 and 1907 but reversing decisions in favour of organization on an industrial basis passed at the Congresses at Sheffield, Newcastle and Newport in 1910, 1911 and 1912.

The unfortunate outcome of all these wrangles was that when the N.U.R. entered into negotiations with the Railway Executive Committee for the first war bonus in February 1915, and included the shopmen in the demand, Sir Guy Granet, for the companies, did not admit of its right to speak on their behalf. He said: 'It is useless our negotiating with you when the majority of the shopmen are not organized at all'. Mr Thomas then asked: 'Does that mean that when the majority of the shopmen are organized you will negotiate with us?' Whereupon Sir Guy Granet replied: 'I am not going to anticipate the future, but as businessmen we shall have to deal with circumstances as they arise.'[47]

Mr Thomas and the E.C. were not slow to take Sir Guy Granet's hint. At the Special E.C. meeting on February 13, 1915, whilst it was decided to accept the companies offer of 3s and 2s on the wages of conciliation grades, it was also resolved that the General Secretary should make arrangements for meetings of shopmen to be held 'to push their claim'. In March the sub-committee on shopmen's matters was able to report to the quarterly meeting of the E.C. that many mass meetings had been held and that they had helped to persuade the companies in many cases to extend the bonus to the shopmen. In past weeks there had been 'a tremendous increase' in the numbers of shopmen members of the N.U.R.

But in the meantime the craft unions had also bestirred themselves. In February 1915, they formed the Railway Shops Organization Committee mainly for the purpose of enlisting support from the T.U.C. for their claim exclusively to represent the railway shopmen.

The big effort of the N.U.R. that summer was the Shopmen's National Conference held in Birmingham on May 18th. The delegates rejected a proposal by Mr W. Dobbie for the establishment of Shopmen's Conciliation Boards and carried by 26 votes to 18 the resolution in favour of the setting up of Shops Committees.[48]

Later that summer Mr Thomas approached the leaders of the craft unions with the object of reaching an agreed programme of demands to place before the companies. The craft union leaders, however, preferred to declare to the Committee on Production that a dispute existed between themselves and the N.U.R. and that, under the Munitions of War Act, the matter should be referred to arbitration. They then proceeded to put their case separately to Sir George Askwith, the Arbitrator of the Committee on Production. On February 22, 1916, Mr. Thomas put before the Committee on Production the claim of the N.U.R. to be heard in negotiations between the companies and the shopmen. He declared that at that time the N.U.R. had 52,000 shopmen members which was a larger membership than that of all the other unions taken together. Sir George

Askwith, in an interview with Mr Thomas, would not recognize the right of the N.U.R. to represent the shopmen though he agreed to the claim for an increase in their wages.

Whilst these negotiations were proceeding, the N.U.R. Shops sub-committee had attended a conference convened by the Parliamentary Committee of the T.U.C. on January 18, 1916. Representatives of twenty-eight craft unions were also present. The N.U.R. delegation proposed that a joint committee of craft union representatives and the N.U.R. sponsored Shops Committees should be established to speak with one voice for all railway shopmen in negotiations with the employers. It was suggested that craft union members should pay a nominal contribution to the N.U.R. and in return should be entitled to strike and legal defence benefits. Although the conference agreed to form a Joint National Committee of representatives of both the craft unions and the N.U.R. it rejected the other proposals emanating from Unity House. The majority agreed to the following formula for union membership of shopmen: 'Craftsmen employees of railway companies who have served the recognized term of apprenticeship or who have worked at their trade five years shall be members of the respective craft unions. Those not coming within the foregoing definition shall be members of the N.U.R.' As the N.U.R. had by this time thousands of shopmen members who, by the definition proposed, would have had to transfer to craft unions, the E.C. was unable to agree to the new plan. Instructions were given to the sub-committee to try again to obtain agreement to the original N.U.R. proposals.[49]

Although there were many further meetings between the two sides, the differences between the craft unions and the N.U.R. remained unresolved. The chances of reaching agreement were lessened when, in April 1917, the A.S.L.E. & F. affiliated to the Railway Shops Organization Committee. As a result of these continued divisions and the failure of the N.U.R. to gain recognition from the companies of its right to speak for the shopmen, many men in these grades who had flocked into the union in 1914 and 1915 withdrew from membership in the later months of the war.

If the N.U.R. was to fulfil its aim of organizing *all* persons employed in the railway industry, the clerks and supervisory grades, some of whom were members of the Railway Clerks' Association (founded in 1897), would have to be considered. The N.U.R. had always expressed its willingness to consider fusion with the R.C.A. but during the First World War the initiative was taken by the Annual Conference of the R.C.A. at Chester in May 1917. The following resolution was then passed:

'That this Conference instructs the Executive Committee to enter immediately into negotiations with the National Union of Railwaymen, to consider conditions under which the two unions could amalgamate, and then issue particulars of such conditions to all members of the R.C.A.'

Naturally the E.C. of the N.U.R. welcomed the overtures of the clerks and at its special meeting on July 19th, instructed Mr Thomas to convey to them its willingness to discuss the question of fusion. A meeting was therefore arranged between the sub-committee of the two unions at Unity House on November 9, 1917. The negotiations conducted throughout the day were of a very friendly character, but they failed to end in agreement, the N.U.R. delegation failing to resolve a number of doubts expressed by the other side. One difficulty was that the E.C. of the R.C.A., which organized the supervisory grades, was perturbed by Mr Thomas's speech in the House of Commons on November 9, 1916, on the Constabulary and Police (Ireland) Bill when he declared against the railway police joining the N.U.R. Although he admitted that the bulk of the men wished to join the union, he took a stand against the majority of his own union in opposing their recruitment. Mr Walkden, the R.C.A. General Secretary, wanted to know whether the N.U.R. would fully co-operate in organizing the managerial and supervisory grades as well as the clerks, and whether it would also stand by these grades if the companies and/or Government opposed their recruitment in the N.U.R. The R.C.A. was averse to joining a Composite Conciliation Board scheme—which had been advocated by the N.U.R. in 1914 and 1916. Finally the R.C.A. wanted to know whether the other members of the N.U.R. were prepared to support the separate demands of the clerks who were at that time better treated with respect to holidays, pensions and salary increments than were most of the other grades.

The N.U.R. delegation endeavoured to reassure the clerks in both discussion and correspondence. There is no full record of the meeting on November 9th since it was decided not to take shorthand notes, but from the reply sent by the N.U.R. sub-committee to Mr Walkden on December 14, it is impossible not to regret the fact that the N.U.R. did not answer the specific enquiries made with greater precision and in greater detail. They declared that once fusion had taken place many of the difficulties envisaged by the R.C.A. 'would not arise'. They believed that 'the questions of Conciliation Board machinery would have to be reviewed in the light of future developments'. Their reply on the question of supporting specific demands of the clerical and supervisory grades was more satisfactory. They anticipated that, after fusion 'programmes would be so drafted as to secure better conditions for our members in a way which would meet their special requirements'. The whole of the membership would, if necessary, back up the claims of 'any section' of the railway workers.

Mr Walkden replied on December 21st, complaining that 'certain important and specific questions' put by his committee were not dealt with in the N.U.R. memorandum. He requested further information. When the E.C. of the N.U.R. met on December 27th they considered that the detailed answers had been given verbally during the discussions. They offered further meetings with the R.C.A. sub-committee but did not give in writing the detailed replies which Mr Walkden had requested. Finally on January 11, 1918, Mr Walkden wrote that his E.C. was 'somewhat disappointed' that the N.U.R. had not given the detailed assurances asked for. They felt that no useful purpose would be served by holding another meeting and had decided to consult their branches about the next steps to be taken. Although the E.C. of the N.U.R. at its special meeting on January 14th decided to inform Mr Walkden that it was still desirous of continuing negotiations, a special Conference of the R.C.A. held a few weeks later decided not to take any further steps towards fusion.[50]

A significant unofficial attempt to close the big loophole in a campaign for an industrial union—the survival of craft unionism in the shape of the A.S.L.E. & F.—was the formation early in 1918 of the Railway Workers' One Union Movement. This was the outcome of a very successful conference in London in February when representatives of branches of the N.U.R., A.S.L.E. & F. and R.C.A. were agreed on the need to complete the process of fusion of forces which had been so successfully started in 1913. At a meeting held in the Trades Hall, Bradford, on May 26, 1918, Mr J. E. Conlon of the A.S.L.E. & F. said that 'if they were going to fight and win they must have one army and one purpose'. Mr T. H. Gill of the R.C.A., then prospective Labour candidate for York, expressed similar views. It appears that for some weeks the speakers of this new organization were constantly in demand from branches of all three of the unions.[51]

It was a movement which was regarded by the leadership of the A.S.L.E. & F. as inimical to the best interests of locomotivemen. In consequence of the existence of a strong sentiment in favour of industrial unionism, the officials of that union found it necessary to keep the sectional union constantly before the minds of the footplate staff. Mr John Bromley, General Secretary, and some members of the Executive of the A.S.L.E. & F. in the summer of 1915 were guilty of an ill-judged and misguided attempt to discredit the leaders of the N.U.R. In a speech at Newport on June 27th, Mr Bromley asserted that his union did not receive the support from the N.U.R. in the negotiations for the war bonus that they were entitled to. He expressed regret that their beating 'did not come from the masters' side but from our own' (i.e. the N.U.R.). At another meeting the same day he insinuated that Mr Thomas was in league with the companies and that he had a free pass on the railways because this was the case. The verdict in a libel action brought by the officials of the N.U.R. against Messrs Bromley, Moore, Cooke and Gamble was given on April 17, 1917, by Mr Justice Darling in the King's Bench Division. The judge found that the defendants had conspired together to slander the plaintiffs and that they had slandered them. Damages of £150 each were awarded to Messrs Thomas and Bellamy, £50 to Mr Williams and £25 each to Messrs Lowth, Hudson, Cramp, Charles and Cuthbertson.

Another bid to gain the support of locomotivemen was made by the A.S.L.E. & F. in August 1917. On 16th of that month the Special Conference of the union resolved that unless the Government accepted the principle of an 8-hour day for railwaymen and agreed to implement it after the war, the union's membership would be called out on strike. On the following day, Mr Bromley was interviewed by Mr A. H. Stanley, the President of the Board of Trade, and assured him that the conference was very determined on the question. Four days later Mr A. H. Stanley wrote to Mr Bromley pledging the Government, the War Cabinet, and himself to continue the control of the railways for a time after the cessation of hostilities, 'so there would be an opportunity afforded within one month to bring forward a request for a shorter working day while the railways were under control'. He added that 'any reasonable request for a short working day would have the immediate and sympathetic consideration of the Government' once the war was over.[52]

Although the A.S.L.E. & F. claimed great credit in exacting this promise from the Minister and in achieving its implementation from February 1, 1919, the Executive Committee and many members of the N.U.R. felt that the action of Mr Bromley in the critical days of the summer of 1917 was irresponsible in view of the acute shortage of manpower on the railways and the difficulties experienced by the armies on the Western Front. They discerned in the move an attempt to attract publicity and to justify the continued separate existence of a craft union. In the Liberal Parliament of 1906–10, Mr Hudson, the N.U.R. M.P. for Newcastle had repeatedly introduced an 8-hour bill for railwaymen. The A.G.M. of the N.U.R. at Nottingham in June 1915, carried unanimously a resolution expressing 'an unshaken belief in the principle of the 8-hour day or 48-hour week for all railway workers' and urging 'Mr Hudson, M.P., to again introduce his bill at the earliest opportunity'. It also urged the members of the N.U.R. 'to use all their power industrially and politically' to secure this objective. The demand for the 8-hour day was also included in the Leicester programme of 1917. The members of the E.C. of the N.U.R. could scarcely be accused of dilatoriness on this question. On November 12, 1918—the day following the armistice—they resolved to end the industrial truce and enter into negotiations with the Government for the implementation of the programme adopted at the Leicester Conference.[53] It was the industrial power of the 416,000 strong membership of the N.U.R. which effectively guaranteed the introduction of the 8-hour day.

V

It was only to be expected that with the adoption of new methods of negotiation for pay awards the question of Railway Conciliation Schemes should sink into relative obscurity. Things might have been different had there been agreement between the A.S.L.E. & F. and the N.U.R. on what were the desirable characteristics of a conciliation scheme. Since, however, there were important differences of opinion on this question, it is understandable that trade unionists did not appear to be too distressed at the fact that conciliation boards in war time did not have the same importance that they had before 1914.

In October 1913, the N.U.R. indicated to the companies its desire to bring the 1911 conciliation scheme to an end on December 1, 1914—the earliest date on which this was possible. On the other hand, on November 6, 1913, the E.C. of the A.S.L.E. & F., which was reasonably satisfied with the Sectional Boards, wrote to the companies indicating that it was prepared to agree to the continuance of the existing scheme with 'certain slight modifications'. A meeting between the E.C. and the companies was suggested. The companies eventually answered by suggesting on March 3, 1914, to both the N.U.R. and the A.S.L.E. & F., that they should form a small committee of seven drawn from both unions to meet a committee of equal size appointed by the companies to negotiate a new conciliation scheme.

The E.C.s of the two unions met at Unity House on March 10, 1914, in an endeavour to reach agreement on a common policy to be put to the employers. Unfortunately, there was an argument about the procedure of the meeting at the outset. Mr G. Wride, the President of the A.S.L.E. &F., proposed that they should first discuss whether or not they should accept the employers' invitation. He said that there was no point in their acceptance unless they agreed on a programme. Mr Thomas said that for the first time in the history of railwaymen the companies had freely offered to negotiate with the unions. Surely the first step was to tell the companies that the invitation was accepted as it was something they had been fighting for all along. 'Surely,' he said, 'we should regard this as a red-letter day in the history of the railwaymen—as the day in which recognition was achieved.' But the A.S.L.E. & F. delegation were unmoved by Mr Thomas and the whole of the first morning was taken up in a discussion on this point.

On the two following days agreement was reached that questions of discipline and management, hitherto beyond the competence of the Conciliation Board, should be brought within the purview of the new board. It was also agreed that instead of the scope of the board being confined to those grades engaged in the manipulation of traffic, it should be widened to include all grades of railwaymen who expressed a wish to come into the scheme. Under the 1911 scheme the presentation of a petition signed by 25 per cent of the men in the grade affected the organization of a deputation to the managers had to precede the meeting of the Conciliation Board. The two sides found no difficulty in agreeing that such a procedure ought to be scrapped. One member of the meeting declared 'We have done with petitions and deputations'. The meeting, however, broke down on the vexed question of composite versus sectional boards. Mr E. Moore of the A.S.L.E. & F. showed how determined his union was to retain the sectional boards when he declared that it was 'practically the law of the Medes and the Persians', as far as they were concerned, that there could be 'no modification on the question of a separate board for locomotivemen'. The N.U.R. was equally firmly in favour of composite boards for each railway with elections to the boards being arranged on a departmental basis with power for grade matters to be considered by departmental representatives. This, it was claimed, would ensure every safeguard being given to particular interests. Mr Thomas pointed out that 104 of the 164 locomotivemen representatives on the Sectional Boards of the United Kingdom were members of the N.U.R. who were satisfied that their interests would be adequately protected in the proposed Composite Boards. When no agreement could be reached on the composition of the boards, Mr Thomas proposed that they should refer the matter to an 'independent arbitrator drawn from, say, the ranks of the Labour Party', but the A.S.L.E. & F. would not agree to this procedure. Thus it proved impossible to present a united front to the employers, and the two executives met the small committee of the employers separately on two successive days in April. No agreement could be reached before war broke out in August and by the truce of October 1, 1914, it was agreed that the 1911 scheme should continue in being subject to six months' notice being handed in by either side desirous to terminate it.[54]

In response to requests from 120 branches, in 1915 a sub-committee of the E.C. of the N.U.R. renewed negotiations with the companies to work out a basis for a new conciliation scheme. An amended scheme was approved by the E.C. at a special meeting on February 4 and 5, 1916. It was to operate for three years, after which it would be terminable at twelve months' notice. Sectional Conciliation Boards were to be retained but their number was to be limited to four per railway. Petitioning was no longer to be insisted upon where it could be shown that 25 per cent of the men affected had expressed their view in open mass meetings. In place of the impartial chairman there were to be two assessors, one being chosen from each side. Where these failed to agree they had power to nominate an umpire whose decision was final. The greatest weakness of the scheme was that it still did not include clerks, supervisory grades, police officers, hotel employees, seamen and dockers. The shopmen had already indicated that they preferred to be represented in shop committees. Another weakness was that the boards could still not deal with questions of discipline and management.

It was these weaknesses in the new scheme which helped to influence the delegates to a Special General Meeting held in the Essex Hall, Strand, London, on April 7, 1916, to reject it by 32 votes to 28. W. J. Abraham, Sheffield No. 2, declared that if the union accepted the recommendation of the E.C. they would still be 'perpetuating sectional negotiations and agreements'. He contended that since they now had a truly national organization and a national programme they should insist on national-level rather than company-level negotiations. Mr J. Sledge, of Exeter, expressed the same point of view even more forcefully, when he asserted that the scheme 'undermined the very basis of our organization, namely organization by industry'. He appealed to the delegates to realize 'the inconsistency as well as the futility of trying to build up on the one hand a big organization by eliminating the last vestiges of sectionalism', whilst considering the acceptance of machinery which was in 'absolute violation' of the principles on which the N.U.R. was based. Although Mr Thomas wound up the debate with a clever speech in which he appealed to the delegates to give the scheme a trial, a majority of the delegates saw the illogicality of the continuance of the sectional boards, and effectively killed the scheme. Mr Thomas speaking at Bristol a few days after the A.G.M. rightly declared that the decision to treat the railway companies as one unit constituted 'a revolutionary change from past practice'.[55]

VI

Throughout the war members of the N.U.R. showed their concern as responsible citizens with the momentous issues of the time, such as those of conscription of men and conscription of wealth, the prevention of profiteering, the protection of civil liberties and the nature of war aims and the peace settlement.

Mr Thomas was a firm believer in the voluntary principle in the recruitment of the armed forces. For nearly two years, until the Military Service Act was finally approved by Parliament in 1916, he opposed all attempts to introduce the conscription system. At the same time he was frequently to be heard at recruitment meetings. The E.C. likewise opposed conscription, taking the view that all the recruits needed could be obtained from volunteers. At its special meeting on January 5, 1916, it resolved: 'That any scheme involving the confiscation of the lives of men and leaving the material resources of the nation in the hands of a privileged class cannot be termed "National Service" and should therefore be opposed by the united forces of labour.' It further decided that unless the Government was prepared to 'immediately confiscate wealth of all description' including 'land, shipping, money and all other national assets' it would resist the conscription of men by every means within its power. At the Special Congress of the T.U.C. held in the Central Hall, Westminster, on January 6th, the N.U.R.'s resolution opposing the Conscription Bill was carried by 1,998,000 votes to 783,000. Ten members of the E.C. at its special meeting on April 25, 1916, favoured asking the miners to join with the N.U.R. in industrial action to prevent the introduction of the Act, but their proposal was defeated by the majority of the committee. Later in the year when the Bill had become law the E.C. recommended branches to concentrate on a campaign to secure the conscription of wealth. It set an example to the branches by writing to the Prime Minister asking for an interview with him on the subject of the control of prices. Mr Lloyd George would not agree to meet the committee.[56] Nevertheless Messrs Beardsley and Bebbington, the E.C. representatives on the War Emergency Workers National Committee, through reports to the press and through public meetings, helped to influence public opinion in favour of a policy of government control of food, coal and other prices. The failure of the Government to act with sufficient vigour against the shipping rings and the speculators in food and war materials was denounced. Part of the credit for the Government bestirring itself in these questions in the last year of the war must go to leaders of the N.U.R. who constantly emphasized the need for intervention from Whitehall.[57]

By the summer of 1917 thousands of members of the N.U.R. were advocating the early termination of the war on the basis of no annexations and indemnities. Mr Thomas told the Special Meeting of the E.C. in July 1917, that 'many branches' had passed resolutions in favour of an early peace. A proposal 'to summon a Special General Meeting of the Union for the purpose of ascertaining the views of our members upon the desirability of securing peace on the basis of no annexations and indemnities' found six supporters on the E.C. but was defeated. On the other hand, at the A.G.M. in London in June 1917, Mr J. C. Finch of Barry found the delegates unanimous in supporting his proposal that 'to ensure permanent peace' it was essential that labour should be 'adequately represented by representatives; appointed directly . . . on any body or bodies . . . engaged in the negotiation of the terms of peace'. It was resolutions such as this which led the statesmen in 1919 to establish the I.L.O. in the hope that this would help allay fears about the character of the peace settlement.

VII

A subject on which the members of the N.U.R. could hope to exercise a greater influence was the future organization of British Transport. It was not long before it was generally agreed that the 'national programme' drafted just before the outbreak of war—an 8-hour day and a rise of 5s on the basic rates of pay—was totally inadequate as a policy for the postwar period.

Although the members of the E.C. at its special meeting in July 1917, were agreed on the need for a redrafting of the national programme and on the necessity of the Special General Meeting for this purpose, it was the fifty-five delegates attending the Conference of District Councils and Vigilance Committees in August that gave the idea substantial publicity.

This London conference appointed a sub-committee, whose Secretary was Mr W. T. A. Foot, to draft a programme for the immediate post-war period. At its meeting on September 10th, the E.C. decided to summon both the A.G.M. delegates and the E.C. to a Conference on After War Matters at Leicester on November 20th.

Mr Thomas gave the Leicester Conference an admirable lead in his opening speech on the future of the industry. He told the delegates that they must have 'big ideas on this matter'. It was 'not a mere "railway" problem but a "transport" problem affecting the nation as a whole'. It would be 'nothing short of madness to talk of railway nationalization alone'. He showed the absurdity of the State taking over railways with a capital of £1,400,000 'and then allowing the highway to be used by private competitors with, perhaps, 40,000 or 50,000 motor wagons which have been specially built for the war and which are used for short distance traffic'. The result would be 'railways owned by the state, run by the state, and used by the state with a competitor really created as a result of the war, using the highways and roads of the nation without any charge upon them'. But, unfortunately, the 10-point programme of the Committee of District Councils (published in the *Railway Review* on October 28th) which formed the basis for the Leicester discussion, had nothing to say on the future of transport as a whole, though in other respects it had much to commend it.

The delegates were far more concerned to establish workers' control of their own industry than they were to devise a policy for the future of the transport industry. By the overwhelming majority of 74 votes to 1 they endorsed the first point of the District Councils' programme: 'That there be equal representation both national and local for this union upon the management of all railways of the United Kingdom.' Mr Thomas was very sceptical about the practicability of this part of the programme. He said that he was quite sure that they 'did not want the railways to be run by railwaymen'. If the sponsors of this part of the programme meant that, then they 'might as well at once close the shutters', because the 'interests of railwaymen were subordinate to the interests of the state'. Other people had interests in the railways and ought to have some say in their control. He believed that so long as every man felt he had a 'fair crack of the whip' and was being treated as a human being with an opportunity to have his grievances dealt with 'fairly and honestly', they could not reasonably ask for more. That the General Secretary did have these important differences of view with the majority of the members goes a fair way to explain the failure to establish any workers' participation in management after the war.

The conference, by the large majority of 52 to 6, reached the very important resolve 'that conditions of service be standardized for railwaymen upon all railways in the United Kingdom'. This conclusion was reached despite a vigorous intervention by the General Secretary who declared that the adoption of the proposal was quite out of the question. Some companies would be able to afford it but others would not and it was unrealistic to treat them all alike. However, the majority proposal was the logical next step forward from the war bonus and State direction of railways in the war and proved to be perfectly practicable.

The delegates were more evenly divided on the question of the future hours of labour on the railways. Although a substantive motion in favour of an 8-hour day and a 48-hour week was eventually carried by 63 votes to 2, there was a strong '6-hour day' party including Mr C. T. Cramp, who declared he was 'a 6-hour man'. Some of the delegates were suspicious that the Union officials, who declared that they had not got figures of the number of branches sending in resolutions in favour of the 6-hour day, and those favouring an 8-hour day, were keeping this information from them because it would have shown a large majority for the shorter hours. All the same, Mr J. Wilson of Newcastle-on-Tyne undoubtedly expressed the view of the majority when he declared that a 6-hour day 'was not within the range of practical politics'.

On wages the left wing favoured a policy of converting the war increases to permanent wages 'with an advance of 10s on pre-war purchasing value'. Their case was that railwaymen were notoriously underpaid before the war and the rise proposed would put them on a par with wages in other occupations. But the majority of the delegates were doubtful whether this objective could be achieved. By 40—31 they voted for a policy of conversion of war wages to permanent wages. Later, on a substantive motion, this proposal was carried by 64 to 1. The delegates were unanimous in supporting a guaranteed day and a guaranteed week and nearly unanimous (53—3) in support of the abolition of piecework, tonnage and bonus systems. By 40—23 they favoured double rates of pay for overtime and Sunday duty and were unanimous for time and a half rates for night duty. They recommended where footplate staff worked under a mileage system, 120 miles should constitute a day's work on passenger trains and 96 miles a day's work on goods trains, all miles run over and above the day's work to be paid for at an equivalent rate. Fourteen days' holiday with pay were demanded. There were to be no more 'hybrid' grades on the railways. Taking the advice of Mr Thomas, who said at the opening of the conference that 'every programme that is to be useful should be short', the delegates omitted reference to lodging away from home, free passes and the non-unionist question.[58]

As a programme concerned principally with working conditions it was a very good one and likely to enlist the enthusiastic support of the overwhelming majority of railwaymen. Its great weakness was the absence of any reference to the transport industry as a whole. In the last resort the ability of the railways to provide a living wage and reasonable working conditions for railwaymen would depend on the soundness or otherwise of the nation's policy for transport.

Within the narrower field of the ownership of the railways the union's policy was clearly stated on other occasions during the war. Since the A.S.R.S had passed a resolution on railway nationalization at the A.G.M. in 1894, the policy had been one of state control. Less than two months before the outbreak of the war the A.G.M. at Swansea had carried unanimously a resolution moved by the able left winger from Sheffield, Mr C. Watkins. Whilst reaffirming previous decisions in favour of state ownership, it emphasized that no public ownership 'would be acceptable to organized railwaymen' if it failed 'to guarantee them their full political and social rights' and to 'allow them a due measure of control and responsibility in the safe and efficient working of the railway system'. It should also 'ensure a fair and equitable participation of the increased benefits likely to accrue from a more economical and scientific administration'.

When Mr Thomas was approached by the 'leaders of several transport unions' who were anxious to discuss 'the future organization of the transport industry', the E.C. at its meeting on July 21, 1917, indicated its willingness to discuss such questions with the other unions. In December of the same year Messrs Cramp, Charleton and Henderson were appointed to meet an equal number of representatives of the Transport Workers' Federation to work out a policy for the future of the industry. They reported next March that they had considered reconstruction of the transport industry as a whole and had appointed Mr Robert Williams to be their secretary charged with keeping both bodies fully primed with information.

The District Councils and Vigilance Committees awoke to the need for a comprehensive transport policy too late to be able to influence the Leicester Conference. At their own conference in London on January 27, 1918, they approved a proposal emanating from the South Eastern and the Sheffield District Councils that 'in view of the development of an Army Transport Service during the war' and the danger that the whole of the motor lorries, buses, etc., might 'revert to private hands to be used for private interest and profit', a 'national state transport system should be inaugurated'. It was to include transport by water (sea, river and canal), rail and road services. As a 'natural corollary' to such a scheme the N.U.R. in conjunction with the Transport Workers' Federation was to form 'a National Transport Workers' Union to embrace all the employees engaged in the transport industry'.[59] It was a resolution as far sighted as had been the speech of Mr Thomas just over two months earlier. When the after-war programme was discussed at the A.G.M. in June 1918, there was an opportunity to insert a policy statement on the lines of the resolution of January 27th, but the opportunity was let slip. Thus the N.U.R. entered the peace with a clear programme for railway nationalization and workers' participation in management, but without any statement of aims for the co-ordination and control of the different forms of transport.

NOTES

1. N.U.R., E.C. Minutes, September and December 1914.
2. Stated by J. H. Thomas in a speech at the A.G.M. in London, June 1917, *R.R.*, June 22, 1917.
3. E. A. Pratt, *British Railways and the Great War*, Vol. 1, p. 194; N.U.R. General Secretary's Report to the A.G.M., May 1919.
4. *R.R.*, June 22, 1917.
5. *Railway News*, July 3, 1915.
6. *R.R.*, May 19, 1916.
7. *Railway Gazette*, March 10, 1916.
8. *Railway News*, July 3, 1915.
9. House of Commons, Parliamentary Debates 1918, Vol. 106, Cols. 391–2, May 15, 1918.
10. E. A. Pratt, *op. cit.*, Vol. 1, p. 41.
11. *The Economist*, September 19, 1914, p. 495.
12. N.U.R., E.C. Minutes, September 1914, R.51.
13. House of Commons, Parliamentary Debate, 1914, Vol. 68, Cols. 290, 301, November 16, 1914.
14. *The Times*, December 31, 1914, January 18, February 8 and 9, 1915, *Labour Gazette*, January 1915.
15. *Railway News*, February 6, 1915.
16. N.U.R., E.C. Minutes, February 3, 1915, Rs. 4 and 5.
17. The stages by which the bonus or war wage was raised 33s above the pre-war basic wages were:

February 1915	Man	3s or 2s	Boys	1s 6d (from June 1915)
October 1915		2s		1s
September 1916		5s		2s 6d
April 1917		5s		2s 6d
November 1917		6s		3s
April 1918		4s		2s
September 1918		5s		2s 6d
November 1918		3s		1s 6d

18. *R.R.*, October 1, 1915.
19. *R.R.*, September 24, 1915.
20. Sir Leo Chiozza Money: *Fifty points about Capitalism* (1919), pp. 42–3. The author had served during the war as Parliamentary Secretary, Ministry of Shipping and as Chairman of the Tonnage Priority Committee.
21. *R.R.*, June 30, 1916, and Verbatim Report of S.G.M., Essex Hall, Strand, August 25, 1916.
22. *R.R.*, June 30, 1916.
23. N.U.R. Verbatim Report of the S.G.M., August 25–26, 1916. *R.R.*, September 8 and 22, 1916.
24. *R.R.*, September 29, 1916.
25. N.U.R., A.G.M., London June 21, 1917, Verbatim Report of Statement made (in Camera) by J. H. Thomas, M.P., and Sir J. Davies, 'The Prime Minister's Secretariat', p. 19.
26. N.U.R., A.G.M., Edinburgh, June 21, 1918, Verbatim Report.

27. *R.R.*, March 9, 1917.
28. N.U.R., S.G.M.'s Leicester, November 22–24, and London, November 28–29, 1917, Verbatim Reports.
29. *R.R.*, October 6, 1918.
30. *The Times*, September 26, 1918.
31. N.U.R. Special E.C. September 25–27, 1918, R. 362.
32. N.U.R. Special E.C. October 10, 1918.
33. *R.R.*, October 18, 1918.
34. *The Times*, September 26, 1918.
35. Ministry of Labour, 18th Abstract of Labour Statistics of the U.K., B.P.P. 1926, Vol. XXIX, p. 147.
36. *R.R.*, September 17, 1915.
37. *Railway Gazette*, October 6, 13, 20, 27; December 8, 15, and 22, 1916. House of Commons, Parliamentary Debates, October 18, 1916. Vol. LXXXVI, Col. 673.
38. Report of Mr Rimmer, Organizer for Ireland to S.G.M. of the N.U.R., August 28, 1916.
39. N.U.R., E.C. Minutes, September 1913, R. 141, and statement of General Secretary, J. H. Williams.
40. *R.R.*, May 7 and 14, 1915. N.U.R., E.C. Minutes, March 1916, R. 47.
41. N.U.R., S.G.M., Leicester, November 22, 1917, Verbatim report of Mr Thomas's speech.
42. *Railway News*, June 12, 1915, *R.R.*, July 30, 1915.
43. *R.R.*, August 30, 1918.
44. T.U.C., Bristol, September 1915. Speech of A. Bellamy. J. H. Thomas's speech at Derby, December 17, 1916; *R.R.*, December 22, 1916. Cole, G. D. H., and Postgate R. *Trade Unionism on the Railways*, p. 74.
45. N.U.R., A.G.M., Nottingham, June 1915. *R.R.*, June 15, 1915.
46. *R.R.*, June 25, 1915.
47. *R.R.*, December 22, 1916.
48. N.U.R., E.C. Minutes, June 1915.
49. N.U.R. E.C. Minutes, March 1916.
50. Railway Clerks' Association. Special Report by the R.C.A. Executive Committee upon negotiations with the N.U.R. in respect of conditions under which the two unions might amalgamate, 1918. N.U.R., E.C. Minutes, January 14, 1918; March 11–16, 1918.
51. *R.R.*, May 17 and 31, 1918.
52. N. McKillop: *The Lighted Flame*, p. 113.
53. N.U.R., E.C., November 12, 1918, R. 398.
54. N.U.R. Report of a Joint Conference concerning a new Conciliation Scheme, March 10–14, 1914.
55. *R.R.*, June 13, 1916.
56. N.U.R. Special E.C., August 1916.
57. N.U.R., E.C., March 1915.
58. Speeches and resolutions taken from a Verbatim Report of the Special General Meeting of the N.U.R. on After-War Matters, Leicester, November 1917.
59. Decisions of a Conference of District Council, Joint and Vigilance Committees, Anderton's Hotel, Strand, January 27, 1918.

CHAPTER XV

1919—THE 'DEFINITIVE' STRIKE

'*At midnight on Friday, September 26, 1916, a number of private persons employed on the railways, having accumulated sufficient money to enable them to take a month's holiday, ceased working and went home. Their object was to make the community, which had seriously under-rated their labour, realize its value by experiencing the discomfort and loss which its withdrawal would cause.*'
George Bernard Shaw, in Daily News, October 3, 1919.

I

THE year 1919 was one of widespread industrial and social unrest. Major industrial conflicts, looming in the summer of 1914, were postponed 'for the duration'; but no sooner had the armistice been signed than long-shelved programmes of reform were presented to the employers with demands for quick satisfaction. Every day that year an average of 100,000 men were on strike. Dissatisfaction spread to the Army. From January 3rd, impatient at the delay in their demobilization, soldiers at Folkestone, Dover, Kempton Park and even Whitehall itself demonstrated and mutinied.[1] A music hall hit of the year was entitled 'What are we waiting for now?' It was sung with greater feeling if, at the same time, with less polish, in the public houses and army camps.

The actions and speeches of members of the Coalition Government intensified the distrust felt of the intentions of the employing classes. Only thirty-three days after the armistice, Lloyd George, making the utmost capital from his reputation as 'the leader who won the war', gained an overwhelming victory in the 'coupon' general election. The Government benches in the House of Commons were then filled with 'hard-faced men who looked as if they had done well out of the war'.[2] There were 179 company directors in the new Parliament compared with an average of 139 in the whole inter-war period.[3] The view of the new Parliamentary majority was that wartime control ought to be removed with all possible speed and that the 'inflated' wages of the war period would have to be reduced if

375

British goods were again to be made competitive in world markets. On November 7, 1918, Mr Churchill expressed this view when he declared that the 'only object' of the Coalition was 'to liberate the forces of individual enterprise, to release the controls which have been found galling' and 'to divest ourselves of responsibilities which the state has accepted in this perilous emergency'.[4] Lord Inchcape rightly commented that the country would have 'an uphill task to get back to the position which it occupied in 1914. Lord Claud Hamilton again displayed characteristic candour when he assured the shareholders of the Great Eastern Railway Company that 'the time was arriving when the Government must take off the velvet gloves they had worn too long'.[5]

Listening to the roar of protest against the continuance of controls the Government 'scanned the sky, trimmed its sails and ran before the storm'.[6] All the same there was no indiscriminate retreat. Although within eight months of the armistice the large majority of the controls had been lifted, the Sugar Commission and Wheat Commission were maintained in being, the price of both commodities being kept artificially low by subsidies. The continued control over these and other foodstuffs was one of the measures taken in readiness for a showdown with the unions. In the event of a railway strike the Government would be in a better position to organize the distribution of foodstuffs and break the strike.

The Cabinet made other preparations for a struggle with labour. In February Lloyd George returned to London from the Peace Conference in Paris specially to establish the nucleus of an emergency transport organization. Under the general guidance of the Home Secretary, Mr Shortt, the Food Controller was given ample powers under the Road Transport Requisition Order, 1919, on a state of emergency being declared, to requisition motor and other vehicles to carry food and other essential supplies to any of the sixteen divisional areas into which the country was divided. Shopkeepers were advised to build up their stocks.[7] The War Office, then under the leadership of Mr Churchill, sent a 'Secret and Urgent' letter to all army commanders instructing them to send weekly reports in the form of answers to questions such as:

'Will the troops in various areas respond to orders for assistance to preserve the public peace?
Will they assist in strike breaking?
Will they parade for draft overseas, especially to Russia?
Is there any growth of trade unionism?
Have any soldiers' councils been formed?
Is any agitation from internal or external sources affecting them?'[8]

The replies received influenced the Government in speeding up demobilization of the forces, whilst also providing valuable information on which units of the army were likely to prove most reliable to guard stations, bridges and signal boxes in the event of a railway strike. A short while afterwards all stationmasters were advised from the War Office that in the event of a strike they were to help soldiers on leave rejoin their units with all possible speed. They were to reassure the troops who might be disgruntled through the curtailment of their leave that not only would they be allowed to complete it when the emergency was over but that they would be given an additional seven days' leave as compensation for helping to maintain essential services in the emergency.[9]

II

Negotiations between the Railway Executive Committee and the railwaymen's unions on the national programmes of the N.U.R. and A.S.L.E. & F. made heavy weather from the start. The men were in no mood to be trifled with. From its ham-fisted treatment of labour relations at this time it seemed as if management was determined to pick a quarrel with the unions. From February 1st the 8-hour day for railwaymen came into operation. Yet on the very day of its introduction notices were posted up on the railway stations to the effect that the five minute break which had been allowed for forty years at 6 a.m. and 1.0 p.m. to enable men to wash their hands, had been cancelled. In the House of Commons, Mr Thomas declared that it was like conceding a man a £1 and then being determined to give him only 19s 11¾d. It was the kind of thing which generated a suspicion that all concessions were conceded with reluctance and that they were to be offset as much as possible by pettifogging restrictions.[10]

At a conference of the London District Council of the N.U.R. held in the Memorial Hall, Farringdon Street, on January 21st, delegates representing 180,000 members declared that 'drastic action' would be taken unless the 8-hour day was granted throughout the kingdom 'without equivocation'. They were as good as their word. When the manager of the London tube railways refused to include meal times in the eight hours, a strike of the tube workers started on February 3rd. Though Mr Hudson (acting as General Secretary in the absence of Mr Thomas at Berne) advised an immediate return to work, the E.C. took a different view and gave official recognition to the strike. Eventually, on February 7th, Mr Thomas and Mr Bromley, General Secretary of the A.S.L.E. & F. obtained a promise from Sir Albert Stanley, President of the Board of Trade, that under the new conditions of service, the companies had undertaken within the 8-hour day 'to offer all reasonable facilities to meet the ordinary physical needs of the men'. The strike was then called off.[11]

Because of the delay in the implementation of the rest of the national programme, Mr Thomas had considerable difficulty in restraining the men in the London and Liverpool districts from calling a strike; he held them back through the promise of discussions with the Railway Executive on February 12th. To his dismay he was informed by the railway managers at this meeting that they (the managers) had only been told eight days previously that they would have any say in the negotiations. They claimed that this was insufficient time in which to prepare their case. It was a situation which revealed either mismanagement or deliberate delaying tactics on the part of the Government.

In the last fortnight of February and first fortnight of March discussions took place with the Railway Executive on the remaining items of the Leicester programme. At the end of this period it was apparent that the managers' offers fell far short of the men's demands. The men asked for overtime payment at double the normal rates and were offered time and a quarter; they asked for fourteen days paid holiday a year and were offered seven days for those with over three years' service; to their demand for an equal representation with capital in management of the railways the reply was that no change was possible.[12] In the view of *The Times* the Railway Executive and the Board of Trade 'had been pursuing the usual policy of haggling over every point, trying to make the smallest possible concession and grudgingly giving way by degrees'.[13]

A Special General Meeting of the N.U.R. on March 14th expressed its 'utmost dissatisfaction and disgust' at the 'parsimonious manner' in which the union's demands had been met. The negotiating committee was told that since the national programme constituted 'the irreducible minimum' they should continue to confer with the Railway Executive and report back to the S.G.M. on March 20th. From all parts of the country there were signs of the increasing impatience of the rank and file. The Liverpool district was 'seething with discontent', and a mass meeting of 'several thousand men' held in Birmingham on March 15th carried with only two dissentients a resolution pledging full support to the E.C. in 'whatever action they deemed necessary'.[14] The growing seriousness of the situation was indicated by the decision of Mr Thomas to return to London from Paris where he had gone for talks with Lloyd George. He made the journey on March 19th in a D.H.9 open biplane which took two hours and ten minutes to reach Hendon. The S.G.M. which he attended the following day learned that no progress had been made in the negotiations with the managers and resolved by 43 votes to 16 to ask the Triple Alliance to support them in calling a national strike.[15]

Meeting at Unity House on the morning of the 21st, the leaders of the Triple Alliance decided against an immediate strike. They thought it better to see if the Government would concede to the Alliance what it would not concede to the railwaymen alone. They advised the members of the N.U.R. to continue at work and await the outcome of the new discussions.

The negotiations with the miners were in too unsatisfactory a state to allow the Cabinet the luxury of a showdown with the railwaymen at this point. Thus when the leaders of the Triple Alliance met Mr Bonar Law (deputizing for Lloyd George who was in Paris), Sir Albert Stanley and Sir Robert Horne (the Minister of Labour) at No. 10 Downing Street at ten o'clock on the following morning they found the Ministers in a conciliatory mood. Mr Bonar Law agreed that men working between 6.0 p.m. and 2.0 a.m. would be paid night-work rates and agreed to Mr Thomas's proposal to accept a joint deputation from the craft unions and the N.U.R. on shopmen's pay and conditions. Most important of all, Mr Bonar Law offered great hopes that the wages would be 'standardized upwards' to the level of the best paid man in each grade. He said:

'When we were discussing in the Cabinet the question of equalization, it was understood there must be equalization upwards. . . . We at once recognize that if we accepted that principle at all on the present conditions it would mean more money.'[16]

These concessions made the E.C. of the N.U.R. think again on the subject of the strike. They decided that three months' negotiations had achieved a guaranteed day and week, a week's holiday after a year's service, extra remuneration for night duty, time and a half rates for Sunday duty, time and a quarter rates for overtime, and a recognition of the principle of standardization upwards. Since 'only a few matters' remained for further negotiations they recommended the S.G.M. on March 27th 'to accept the Government's proposals as an interim settlement of the N.U.R. programme'. The sixty delegates at the S.G.M. agreed by a majority of 41 to 19 that the differences between the demands embodied in the Leicester programme and the achievement of the negotiating committee were insufficient to warrant calling the men out on strike. For the time being the crisis had passed.

It was recognized that union forces would have to be united if they were to hold Bonar Law and his colleagues to their promises. In May, Mr Thomas, with the authorization of the E.C., wrote to John Bromley proposing a joint meeting of sub-committees of N.U.R. and A.S.L.E. & F. to consider the possibility of concerted action to deal with the outstanding problems. In June the E.C. agreed that 'the whole question of industrial organization' should be discussed by the two bodies. As a result of the discussions which followed, the two unions were able to present a united front to the managers on the question of footplatemen's pay.[17]

Relations between the N.U.R. and the R.C.A. had been strained at the beginning of the year through the Clerks' Executive, in its zeal to get recognition from the Government and the Railway Executive, offering to clerks and supervisors in the N.U.R., a month's back-dated membership of the R.C.A. for every two months' membership in the N.U.R. Mr. Thomas had found it necessary to make a strong complaint to

Mr A. G. Walkden, General Secretary of the R.C.A. about this and to publicize the complaint in the *Railway Review*.[18] However, the R.C.A.'s claim to negotiate for the clerks and supervisory grades had been recognized by the Government on February 4th, and by the end of June relations between the two unions had sufficiently improved to enable sub-committees from each to meet on July 3rd and to agree on a programme of demands including a 38-hour week, twenty-one days' holiday a year, double pay for work on public holidays and many other items. Thus when the Cabinet and the Railway Executive were ready to try conclusions with the N.U.R. in September, the three unions were in closer harmony than they had been since August 1911.

The biggest task facing the union and company representatives when discussions were resumed on the last day of March was the standardization of grades and of their rates of pay. According to one estimate[19] there were 512 different grades in the railway service. There were differences in the rate of pay of men in the same grade employed by different railway companies. The objective was to bring down the number of grades to an irreducible minimum and to make the rates of pay and conditions of service the same in all parts of the kingdom. It was a formidable task and the two sides met on forty occasions between March 31st and September 26th in an endeavour to complete it.

The strain of the last months of the war, the heavy work involved in the introduction of the 8-hour day and the crisis at the end of March inevitably took toll of the health of the General Secretary. Mr Thomas had a breakdown by the second week in April and a special meeting of the E.C. decided to free him from official duties for three months and to 'suggest that he take a long sea voyage'. He followed their advice and sailed for an extended stay in the United States of America on May 10th. Mr Hudson took charge until his return in robust health on July 26th.[20]

In the early summer there were frequent signs in the union of the continuing distrust of the intentions of the Government and the companies. As news of the secret army orders concerning strike-breaking spread through the branches angry resolutions accumulated at head office. The E.C. reported receiving sixty of them by June 23rd. They demanded the withdrawal of the orders and the resignation of Mr Churchill. In July there was a strike of locomotivemen on the North Eastern where ten members of the union had been suspended for refusal to undergo a new eyesight test the company was introducing. The E.C. after visiting Newcastle to find out the facts, decided to wire the President of the Board of Trade asking for negotiations to establish a national eyesight test agreed by both the unions and the companies. The strike was called off when the directors of the North Eastern agreed to postpone the introduction of the new tests until after the conclusion of the discussions in London. One of the first jobs Mr Thomas was called upon to perform on his return from America was to represent the E.C. on a Government Select Committee on eyesight tests. Agreement on a new national standard test was eventually reached on November 4th.[21] The union was also perturbed at the Government's continuation of conscription and at its failure to withdraw British troops quickly from the intervention in Russia. A joint Special General and E.C. meeting held on July 22nd expressed 'absolute disgust at the apparent intention of the Government to mislead the country', on these vital issues. The meeting resolved that if the Government did not give satisfactory replies within seven days to the demand for the withdrawal of the armies of occupation from Ireland and Russia and to the demand for the ending of conscription, the union should recommend the Triple Alliance (due to meet the following day) to call its members out on strike. When the Conference of the Alliance was held, however, the majority of the delegates were in a more cautious mood and it was decided to recommend the constituent unions to find out whether their members approved of industrial action to achieve these political ends.

By the end of July, however, the situation from the Government's point of view was getting more under control. A strike of the Yorkshire miners had been settled by means of a compromise which was accepted in all the coalfields. This emboldened Lloyd George to declare in August that the Government had no intention of carrying out the majority recommendation of the Sankey Commission in favour of the nationalization of the coal mines. The smoother working of demobilization of the forces and the breaking of the Police Union strike in July brought confidence that the forces of order might be more reliable than had been feared earlier in the year.

One way of weakening the railwaymen's forces might be to settle on generous terms the claims of the locomotivemen in the hope that they would then be less inclined later on to back by strike action the claims of the other grades. By concentrating on the footplatemen's demands it was possible to reach a very favourable settlement on August 20th. The principle followed in fixing the rate of pay for drivers and firemen was 'standardization upwards', i.e. to the war bonus of 33s was added the highest rate of pay prevailing in each category in July 1914. Drivers were to receive a basic rate of 12s per day in the first year, rising to 15s a day in the eighth year. At the maximum this meant a weekly wage of £4 10s od compared with the £3 18s od the majority of drivers were receiving when the settlement was made. Firemen were to start at 9s 6d a day and to rise to 11s a day by the fifth year. For both of these grades overtime rates were to be paid on all runs exceeding 120 miles, every additional fifteen miles to qualify for an hour's overtime pay. Since both N.U.R. and A.S.L.E. & F. representatives agreed to the treatment of cleaners as 'apprentices' they did not insist on the principle of standardization upwards being applied in their case. However, the full 33s war bonus was included—with the most favourable peace time rates that could be discovered—for all fully trained workers in the locomotive department. It was a settlement which the historian of the A.S.L.E. & F. described as 'a charter of service unparalleled in the history of British locomotivemen'.[22] It remained to be seen whether this generous treatment would bring the split in the railwaymen's ranks that at least some members of the Cabinet hoped to produce. The E.C. of the N.U.R., though welcoming the agreement on behalf of the locomotivemen, realized that it was not a complete settlement of railway wages and declared that the final solution was 'dependent on a settlement of the wage rates of all other grades'.[23]

III

The main objective of the N.U.R. after August 20th may be simply stated. It was that the principle of 'standardization upwards', already applied in the case of drivers and firemen, should be applied to the other grades of the service, that the 33s war bonus should be added to the most favourable peace time wage. But what the Government had conceded so bountifully to the locomotive crews it withheld from the remainder. As the weeks passed by without any signs of progress dissatisfaction among the other grades spread rapidly. Inevitably the question was asked: 'If it was possible for the Government to raise drivers' wages to a level only enjoyed by about 3 per cent of them before August why has it not been possible to do the same for porters, guards and shunters?' What made it increasingly difficult for the officials of the N.U.R. to curb the impatience of their members was that in places like South Wales where railway shunters earned minimum wages from 46s to 60s a week, colliery-employed shunters working nearby earned a minimum wage of 76s for a working week an hour and a half shorter. Many railway platelayers were in a similar position of inferiority.[24]

By mid-September the members of the E.C. realized that unless a settlement of the claims of the rest of the men was made soon there would be a series of local and sectional strikes. They determined to avoid such a situation if it was humanly possible. On September 16th, therefore, a conference of the Railway Executive, the President of the Board of Trade (Sir Auckland Geddes) and the E.C. of the N.U.R. was held at which Mr Thomas urged that the discussions should be expedited. 'Do not let us have any more jumping off grounds', he pleaded. . . . 'If you say a minimum of £4 a week or whatever it might be, say it rather than saying £3 leading up to £4. That is the kind of thing I have in mind.' He thought that if he had that intimation 'it would save a lot of bother'. Sir Auckland Geddes promised the concrete proposals of the Government at 'a very early date', perhaps 'within a week'.[25]

The Minister's promise was fulfilled. The Government's proposals reached Unity House on September 19th. In an accompanying letter Sir Auckland Geddes wrote that: '. . . the proposals contained in the attached memoranda are not put forward as a basis for negotiation, but as a definitive offer of the Government.'

The Minister subsequently revealed that the word 'definite' had at first been used but that 'he had himself made the change in the draft of the letter' to limit the scope of the discussions. Though Mr Thomas had asked for precise proposals, the term 'definitive' was an unfortunate one. To the majority of the E.C. it meant 'final'—that the Government had reached the limit of the concessions it was prepared to make. *The Times* considered it a 'damning fault' of the Minister to have used it since it was 'a literary word used more often to give an impression of elegance than to express a precise meaning'; it was highly important in these 'intensely practical matters' that his meaning should have been made clear. But it was the content rather that the finality of the Government's offer which distressed the E.C. It was for the reason that the rates proposed would 'ultimately mean such a serious reduction' to many of the members of the N.U.R. that they would not be able to maintain 'a decent standard of life',[26] that the proposals were turned down. Under the Government's offer a porter then earning between 51s and 53s would receive 40s—a reduction of between 11s and 13s; a passenger guard would have had his wages reduced by anything from 4s to 7s a week; a ticket collector's wages would have come down by from 5s to 10s. Every one of the 100,000 men who before the war was earning less than £1 a week—those whom the Prime Minister himself on September 25, 1919, described as having been 'disgracefully paid'—would have experienced a cut in his income. From Mr Thomas's point of view the Government's 'definitive' offer was quite unacceptable since he knew that no agreement he signed would be worth anything unless it could carry the acceptance of the men. Ever since Mr Bonar Law had stated on March 22nd that standardization of wages 'would mean more money' he had been reassuring the men to this effect. Now, when after much delay, the Government produced its offer, 'it did not contain a solitary case where the promise of more . . . materialized'.[27]

Thus there was every justification for the note of urgency and concern in his statement to the press published on September 24th. He warned the public that there was 'trouble in the railway world', that in the talks with the Government they were 'rapidly approaching a crisis'. *The Times* attributed the new announcements to the fact that the General Secretary was 'a Welshman with the native love of the vivid and the dramatic' and . . . 'a taste for making the public flesh creep'. Much nearer the mark was the *Daily Herald*'s comment: 'Mr Thomas is talking business because he meant business. It is not bluff.'

The next three days were packed with activity. At 9.30 a.m. on the morning of Wednesday, 24th, the E.C. met and after further examination of the Government proposals, considered they were unacceptable. A message was drawn up for the dispatch to all branch secretaries, instructing them that unless they heard to the contrary in the interim, all members of the union were to strike at midnight on Friday. At the same time the offer from Sir Eric Geddes to discuss the dispute further with him at the Ministry of Transport was accepted and talks between the Minister and the E.C. took place there in the afternoon of the 24th and the morning of the 25th. Since no progress was made in these discussions, a conference was arranged with the Prime Minister and other members of the Cabinet including Sir Eric and Sir Auckland Geddes, Mr Bonar Law and Sir Robert Horne in the afternoon of Thursday 25th.

From the frequent negotiations on railwaymen's pay throughout the war Mr Thomas had never failed to produce a compromise settlement which, while not gaining for the men all they had asked for, had achieved enough to avert a strike. Lloyd George had gained a great reputation as peacemaker for his part in the settlements of 1907 and 1911. How was it that neither of them was able to repeat the performance in 1919?

In 1907 and 1911 Lloyd George was singleminded, anxious to produce a settlement, and concerned to enhance his reputation. In 1919 he was, as Prime Minister, performing a difficult balancing trick in trying to reconcile the demands of the right wing of his Cabinet—the Geddes brothers, Winston Churchill and Bonar Law—for the restoration of Britain's competitive position by a reduction in wages, with his own appreciation of the justice of the railwaymen's demand for an improvement on their 'disgracefully paid' position of pre-war days. In the eleventh-hour talks on the Friday morning he told Mr Thomas:

'Whatever we lay down with regard to the railwaymen, you may depend upon it, it is going to be claimed throughout the country; and therefore we have to consider not merely your case but the cases of all the other trades in the Kingdom.'

Those members of the Cabinet who were willing to face a fight with the railwaymen had told the Prime Minister that if he avoided a railway strike by means of concessions to the N.U.R. he would be creating a precedent which would make it difficult to avoid concessions to the demands of other unions. That the railwaymen's claim was a crucial one was also appreciated by Mr Thomas who answered the Prime Minister's statement with the remark:

'We feel equally that we are doing something for the rest of the workers.'

In the discussions which settled the strike of 1911, the men's leaders, though they had disagreed on many issues with those facing them at the conference table, had nevertheless respected them as men of integrity. Of

Mr G. H. Claughton, one of the companies' representatives on that occasion, Mr Alcock declared that 'his word was his bond'; of Mr A. R. Askwith of the Board of Trade the same writer declared he was 'the best mediator and arbitrator in disputes the world has ever had'.[28] In September 1919, however, the men had little confidence in those with whom they were bargaining. In February of that year, Sir Eric Geddes, on severing his connection with the North Eastern Railway, was at the receiving end of a 'golden handshake' worth £50,000.[29] Was this sum accepted on the understanding that he would undertake 'the office of state bailiff in the interests of the private companies over the difficult period of post-war reconstruction?'[30] To the members of the E.C. this minister seemed to combine 'the manner of a schoolmaster with that of a foremen platelayer'. This was the man who sat at the Prime Minister's elbow throughout the discussion resisting suggestions which might have led to a compromise. Near the conclusion of the talks, late on the Friday morning and not long before the 2.0 p.m. deadline when—according to Mr Thomas—it would be impossible to prevent the start of the strike, the Prime Minister appeared to offer a ray of hope. He said:

'The Government will not act on rigid lines, but will in the future, as in the past, be ready to consider and discuss anomalies and cases of hardship to any particular grades in the application of the percentage increase to be made.'

Mr Thomas clutched at the straw. He asked for clarification of this offer in the hope of finding a compromise which might justify calling off the strike. It was at this point that Sir Eric Geddes butted in with a 'whispered' aside—'We could not do that'—which Mr Thomas heard quite clearly and which caused him to comment that in that case there was nothing further to be said. When the Government's information officer and Mr C. T. Cramp were reading over the proofs of the verbatim report the following morning before its release to the press, Mr Cramp noticed that this episode had been left out; it was only after prolonged argument that he was able to secure its inclusion.[31]

Of Sir Eric's brother, Sir Auckland Geddes, the President of the Board of Trade, it may be said that as a University Professor of Anatomy he found as much difficulty in finding any real point of contact with the railwaymen as they did with him. The *Railway Review* complained that he indulged in 'lectures in elementary economics at the wrong moment' and that the negotiating committee disliked the experience of being 'alternately lectured and bullied' by men recently appointed to posts carrying a salary of £96 a week.[32]

Mr Bonar Law created the impression that he was on the side of the Geddes brothers and to say the least, not over-anxious to avert the strike.

When, at a late stage in the talks, Mr Lloyd George made what he called 'a new offer', a proposal that the reduction in wages should only operate after December 31, 1919, and then only if the cost of living fell below its September level of 115 per cent over July 1914, Mr Bonar Law, like a wet blanket, intervened with the comment: 'This is not new.' Mr Thomas certainly had not heard it before, he was convinced Mr Bonar Law's intervention had persuaded the members of the E.C. that the Government had nothing fresh to offer and that there was little use in prolonging the talks. To the railwaymen it seemed that some members of the Cabinet were pulling in a different direction from the Prime Minister, who was being prevented from treating the men's case seriously.

One of the men sitting beside Mr Thomas was Mr Anderson, a guard from Bristol, then being paid 64s a week by the Great Western Railway. Sir Robert Horne, Minister of Labour, sitting opposite him was about to have his salary raised from £2,000 to £5,000 a year by the Ministers and Secretaries Act, first introduced on August 5th by Mr Bonar Law, who was supported in the division lobbies by the Geddes brothers.[34] 'Standardization upwards' had been the rule for the pay of Cabinet Ministers as well as locomotivemen that month! A different rule seems to have been followed in September. All these Cabinet Ministers were arguing that Mr Anderson's wage should be reduced from 64s to 60s a week (compared with 31s pre-war). Sitting beside Anderson was a driver, Robson, whose wages on August 20th had been raised from £3 18s od to £4 10s od a week (compared with 39s pre-war). In view of such anomalies as these the railwaymen's lack of confidence in the Ministers and the consequent breakdown of negotiations can well be understood.

It was knowledge of these facts that caused Beatrice Webb to write in her diary that the strike had been '. . . desired, if not engineered, by the Geddes brothers, and subconsciously desired by the Prime Minister. The Geddes brothers represent the universal determination of the capitalists to reduce wages to pre-war level, a possible pre-war money level but in any case pre-war commodity value level.'[35]

IV

Within a few minutes of the return of the N.U.R. delegation from Downing Street the staff of the post offices in the Euston area were busy dispatching telegrams with the words 'Negotiations broken down; strike at midnight' to all the N.U.R. branches in England, Wales and Scotland, the E.C. deciding not to call out the Irish branches at least for the time being.

When the talks with the members of the Cabinet were taking place, the Executive of the A.S.L.E. & F. was meeting in London on the question of eyesight tests. A message was then sent through to Unity House: 'If you want help we are standing by.' When news of the breakdown in the talks reached them they passed a resolution which expressed the opinion that the Government's offer was 'totally inadequate to compensate the men for the work performed and to meet the existing cost of living' and promised 'any support necessary to bring this movement to a successful issue'. Shortly afterwards the A.S.L.E. & F. branches were informed by telegram:

'Executive decided to support N.U.R. Our members must strike at midnight tonight. Bromley.' Even though, as John Bromley told the vast meeting of railwaymen in the Albert Hall in London on October 5th, they felt there was no other possible thing they could do as trade unionists than 'to step in and help the fight' it was nonetheless a generous gesture, particularly in view of the fact that the locomotivemen had achieved a favourable settlement in August. Though as John Bromley also said they had 'simply lent a few battalions to the N.U.R. army', the support of the 57,000 members of the A.S.L.E. & F. was invaluable. Once the strike began the two E.C.s met jointly each day until the dispute was over. The Government's attempt to divide the railwaymen had failed.

Through the press and the cinema Lloyd George endeavoured to persuade the people that they were confronted by an 'anarchist conspiracy'. If it was a conspiracy planned long in advance the N.U.R. entered the struggle singularly ill prepared financially. Only £3,000 was immediately available. Considerable difficulty was experienced in realizing ready cash from its investments to make available to more than 2,000 strike centres the 12s a week and 1s extra per dependent child paid out to all those who responded to the strike call. The total funds of the union stood at £1,218,232 but of this £477,098 was tied up in the form of provident funds. In the words of the historian of the Trade Union Movement, 'only the prompt and cordial assistance of the C.W.S. printing department which got out the necessary supply of cheques in marvellously quick time, and of the C.W.S. bank which made the N.U.R. cheques payable at the several Co-operative Societies themselves, averted a breakdown'.[36] It has also been suggested that but for the prompt action of the local Co-operative Societies in honouring the vouchers issued by local strike committees the Government would have withheld ration cards and would have refused to release to strikers any of the food supplies it controlled.[37]

Shortly after the strike began the general secretaries of the two unions declared that the response to the call had been 'beyond all expectations' and that victory was assured.[38] The telegrams which flowed in to Unity House confirmed the confident statement of the leaders. Glasgow and the West of Scotland reported, 'All out to a man'; from Edinburgh came the message, 'All men and women out'; Exeter declared that the stoppage was 'complete'. Birmingham and district were 'solid'; Cambridge, 'One hundred per cent solid'; Carlisle was experiencing an 'Unprecedented stoppage'. Only from a few centres were there any indications of men continuing at work. At Gravesend three men remained at work; from Newport,

Isle of Wight, the telegram read, 'Three blacklegs; remainder out'; only the inspectors continued on duty at Southampton. With buoyant confidence the men at Bradford wired: 'Jimmy go to bed for a week. All well here.'

At Derby there were normally 130 trains a day but on the first day of the strike only three trains appeared. On the same day only two down trains were run from Victoria, whilst on the South Eastern lines traffic was entirely suspended and continental traffic was similarly held up. In the early days of the strike there was no steamboat service between Ryde and Portsmouth, the people at Ventnor in consequence not receiving any mail until the Tuesday (October 1st) afternoon. The brewing of beer practically ceased at Burton on Trent, as well as in Edinburgh, owing to a shortage of barrels; works and collieries were closing down in the Leeds area; coal miners were idle in South Wales. People who risked travelling in the few trains which were run often arrived at their destinations hours or even days late. An 'express' which left Aberdeen at 6.35 p.m. on Friday reached King's Cross at 6.25 p.m. the following Monday. From 2.0 p.m. on Saturday to 5.30 p.m. on Sunday it stood at York Station, where the boredom of the patient passengers was relieved by a strapping piper who strutted up and down the platform playing a medley of Scots airs. A party of soldiers returning on leave from the army of occupation in Germany, stranded at Derby, were sent on to Birmingham in taxis paid for by the local branches of the N.U.R.[39]

On no previous occasion had so many men and women whose names appeared in Debrett's Peerage offered their services for manual work on the railways. Lord Cholmondeley became a volunteer porter at Paddington where he might also have met the Earl of Portarlington, who was engaged in moving churns of milk or milking goats stranded for want of a train. The Duke of Manchester, the Earl of Lathom, Lord Herbert Vane-Tempest and Lord Drogheda were also there to lend a hand with the movement of goods or the collection of the tickets. It was reported that Lord Grimthorpe was 'doing the work of two ordinary men in the provinder department' at King's Cross where Admiral Sir Drury Wake and Sir Frederick Banbury also found employment. Lady Meux, wife of an Admiral of the Fleet, served as a ticket collector on the Great Eastern. On October 3rd, a band of volunteers from the Carlton Club went to Liverpool Street Station, offering 'to go out with the vans, and take whatever measures were necessary in case the drivers were attacked'. According to the *Morning Post* report they were mainly 'young majors and captains' who looked 'fighting fit'. Although twenty-four of them were sent out with the vans 'their appearance was enough; they had no adventures'. Lord Louis Mountbatten, then a Sub-Lieutenant at Osborne, drove engines for the Isle of Wight Central Railway, and although he was already more interested in motor cars than locomotives, Lord Montague of Beaulieu worked as an engine driver on the London–Bournemouth run. The nonconformist journal *British Weekly*, after it was all over, urged that the opportunity should not be let slip. The editor recommended that the country should 'get hold of these dukes and earls who helped us with the railways, and set them to work in some other manner'. There is no evidence of his proposal being taken up.[40]

A favourite occupation with many of the volunteers was exercising the railway horses and cleaning out their stables. This was largely as a result of newspaper reports that the animals had been completely neglected by the strikers. The *Daily Mail* reported: '. . . strikers walking away from railway stables and leaving the horses uncared for—without food or water'. The report was untrue. At the beginning of the strike, Mr Foot, the Secretary of the London Strike Committee, asked the E.C. what action should be taken. In a letter drafted by the E.C. and signed by Mr Thomas he was told that horses should be fed and watered, that men doing these duties were to be accompanied by pickets and that the work was to be done voluntarily. This was the procedure generally followed. From Knebworth, however, the strike committee reported that when the drayman started to feed his horses the stationmaster (who had not joined the strike) prevented him doing so, saying that he would not employ the man again if he had his way.[41]

Mr Winston Churchill as Minister of War ordered units of the armed forces to protect all railway stations, bridges and signal boxes. At Woking the Army had worked with a thoroughness not entirely warranted by the state of affairs in the town. The east end of the station was surrounded by barbed wire entanglements and a Lewis gun was mounted on a heap of sandbags. Units of the Royal Fusiliers and the Cameron Highlanders were stationed at Paddington and naval ratings occupied the Glasgow stations. The Minister's proposal to place machine guns at the entrance of tunnels was turned down by the rest of the Cabinet, but he was allowed to establish from October 3rd, wireless communication between some of the principal railway centres as a precautionary measure in case the telegraph wires were cut. The centres selected for this experiment on the Midland Railway were St Pancras, Wellingborough, Leicester, Birmingham, Derby, Rotherham and Leeds. It was reported that the spoken messages came through clearly except in Leeds. This would appear to be the first instance in Britain of the use of the radio to help break a strike.[42]

Members of the armed forces on leave or in units not employed directly in connection with the strike were encouraged to enrol as volunteer workers on the railways. If they did so they were given extra pay for the work ranging from 1s 9d a day in the case of privates to 6s in the case of officers of the highest rank.[43]

Despite these attempts to undermine the morale of the strikers by a show of force and by the employment of volunteers from the armed forces as strike breakers, the relations between strikers and the troops remained completely friendly—a state of affairs manifested by the holding of over one hundred football matches between the soldiers and the strikers for the benefit of the railwaymen's funds.[44] Three ex-servicemen's organizations, the Federation of Discharged and Demobilized Sailors and Soldiers, the Comrades of the Great War and the International Union of Ex-Servicemen, refused to lend an ear to the Government's appeal for volunteers. They would not take sides in an industrial dispute.[45]

The strike emergency committee set up by the Government under the direction of Messrs Roberts and McCurdy from the first day of the strike organized a motor transport centre in Hyde Park, London. In consequence the public and even the orators were obliged to seek their recreation elsewhere. As might be expected, the speakers did not allow their voices to go unheard; they found new 'pitches' in side streets near the park. Meanwhile the Government's emergency transport arrangements worked well. Over a thousand lorries were used to bring milk to London and to take out food to the provinces. The National Kitchens Division of the Ministry of Food fed 2,000 drivers each day in Hyde Park, the staff sleeping in the park to be on the spot to give breakfast to the drivers at six o'clock. Lorries were brought across from the army in France to augment the 25,000 already in use in the country. Units of the fleet were pressed into service to bring yeast to the east coast ports. By these means no part of the country suffered any serious shortage of food, though priority in the distribution of milk was given to expectant mothers and young children. *The Times* headline on October 1st read: 'Triumph of the Lorry'—an accurate summary of the state of affairs in that it had been shown that there were now available sufficient alternative means of transport to the railway to enable essential supplies to be carried to all parts of the country. Nevertheless the almost complete stoppage of goods and mineral traffic on the railways was slowly bringing the industries of the country to a halt.

It is arguable that at least as many people enjoyed the experience of the days of the strike as suffered from it. There was the adventure of trying out new forms of transport to get to work. A few bought motor scooters advertised 'as an excellent method of propulsion during the strike crisis' and as 'available for immediate delivery for the sum of £50'. Some commercial travellers took advantage of the boom in motor charabanc services. Throughout the strike there were services from London to Folkestone and Dover daily for 30s single. Those who could afford it and had the necessary courage went by air if their work required travelling longer distances. Hounslow Airport was exceptionally busy with 111 planes leaving for the continent in four days instead of the pre-strike average of three a day. On the other hand many Southend businessmen who cycled to work in London may well have lost all spirit of adventure after the first few miles and have envied those employed by the Customs and Excise Department who were provided with 3s 6d each to buy an evening meal and breakfast in town and were loaned mattresses and blankets by the Office of Works. Most employers required those who lived within a five mile radius to walk to work. People lost their customary reserve and begged for lifts. Many rode to work on carts, private cars or taxis. People filled lorries to capacity, even riding on the roofs of the drivers' cabs whence lines of human legs protruded like a fringe. People learned that a motor car's capacity had nothing to do with the number of its seats and that a motor cycle and side-car could be made to carry seven passengers.[46]

V

The nine days of the strike provided a good opportunity for members of the union to display their initiative in devising means of raising funds, publicizing the strikers' case and relieving the boredom by organizing entertainments. At Watford, news of the possibility of a national strike was received on September 24th and a mass meeting of the railwaymen of the district was held that evening in the Co-operative Hall where the strike committee was elected. On Friday (26th) another mass meeting was in progress in the same hall when the telegram signed by J. H. Thomas and John Bromley calling out the railwaymen was received. The strike committee was in session throughout that night and continued to sit throughout the dispute in relays, without a break. From midnight on Friday nearly 2,000 railwaymen ceased work, though those in charge of the horses saw that their animals were provided with food and drink. So great was the interest aroused in the town that hundreds of people were unable to gain admission to the Palace Theatre where a monster demonstration was held on the Sunday evening. The local Labour Party orchestra volunteered its services on this occasion to provide music before the start of the meeting. On Monday a football match—Locomotivemen v. Permanent-way men—was played on the Callowland Recreation Ground and a collection was taken for the Watford Peace Memorial Hospital. On Tuesday, accompanied by band, banners and a 'Cycle Brigade', the strikers marched to Rickmansworth where they were welcomed by the local strike committee. A meeting held that evening in the Kingham Hall, Watford, was again crowded out. The return football match between the Locomotivemen and the Permanent-way men was played on the Wednesday. On Thursday there was a grand march to St Albans described as 'a most imposing spectacle'. In the evening the Co-operative Hall was again filled to capacity by strikers, their families and friends who were interested to discover how much musical and acting talent had been lying dormant on the railway service of the locality. With apparently unflagging energy on Friday (October 3rd) the strikers, many of them accompanied by their wives and children, marched to Chalk Hill where they met the marchers from Wealdstone. After a strenuous game of football—Watford v. Wealdstone—the Watford strikers' wives provided tea for the Wealdstone marchers in the Co-operative Hall and an enjoyable day was rounded off by a concert and meeting in the Kingham Hall. On Saturday members of the strike committee with a staff of assistants gave out the strike pay, while the local printers distributed 500 loaves of bread and 165 pots of jam to strikers' children. That night there was another concert and meeting in the Co-operative Hall. If called upon again the singers might well have exhausted their repertoires, but fortunately for them the strike ended on the evening of the following day. At 9.0 p.m. that Sunday members of the strike committee speaking from the windows of the Co-operative Hall informed a crowd of several thousands of the successful conclusion of the strike.

Where ministers of religion were sympathetic to the unions, special services were held for the strikers. The Vicar of St Marks, Leicester, held a special service for the railwaymen of the city and confronted a packed congregation. In his address he quoted with approval the statement of his bishop that it was impossible to withhold 'admiration for the higher paid grades of the service who have stood by their less fortunate brethren'.[47] In other areas opportunity was taken to view some of the local sights which, for the very reason that they were close at hand, many had previously failed to visit. The Hartlepool 'anarchists' distinguished themselves with a spate of cultural activities, visiting among other places the historic pile of St Kilda, the local museum and the Church of St Mary Magdalene.[48]

In all districts the wives of the strikers worked wonders with diminished housekeeping money and backed their menfolk in the many social functions which occurred during the struggle. In the interests of domestic harmony it is to be hoped that the case of the wife of a Metropolitan railwayman who ripped the braid off her husband's trousers to prevent his recognition by the pickets and who accompanied him to work to make sure he did not join the strikers, was a unique one.[49]

VI

The 1919 railway strike was remarkable in that for the first time in a modern industrial dispute the fullest opportunity was taken by both sides to utilize the mass media for publicity purposes. The public was subject to a 'curious campaign of advertisement which continued during the strike—a campaign in which the railwaymen's funds competed against taxpayers' funds in part forcibly contributed by the railwaymen themselves, who thus paid for their own attempted defeat'.[50]

The Prime Minister opened the attack on the railwaymen on September 27th in a telegram to the Chairman of the County Council of Caernarvon apologizing for his inability to speak to the councillors as planned. In it he descended to a low level of abuse and innuendo. The strike, he asserted, was not one 'for wages or better conditions. The Government have reason to believe that it has been engineered for some time by a small but active body of men who wrought tirelessly and insidiously to exploit the labour organizations of this country for subversive ends. I am convinced that the vast majority of the trade unionists of the land are opposed to this anarchist conspiracy.'[51]

The daily newspapers—with the exception of the *Daily Herald*—then under the editorship of George Lansbury—seemed to vie with the Premier and with each other in their condemnation of the strike and the railwaymen's leaders. *The Times* called the strike 'an attack on the community, an attempt to starve them into surrender. . . . Like the war with Germany it must be a fight to a finish'. The public, so it claimed, were 'defending themselves now, as then, against an attack inspired by greed, ambition and lust for power'. The *Daily Mail* opined that 'public opinion' was 'dead against the strike'; the *Morning Post* held that 'never was a strike more wanton or more gratuitous'; the *Daily Express*'s story was of 'a little band of conspirators who forced their duped followers into a strike against the whole nation'. Even the Liberal *Daily News* declared that there was 'no shadow or semblance of excuse for a strike'.[52] It was apparent that unless quick action was taken to counter this campaign of vilification, the railwaymen's case might go by default and the strike would be lost through lack of sufficient public support.

The Joint Executives acted promptly. On the afternoon of Saturday, September 27th, the Labour Research Department was authorized to take charge of publicity for the men's case. Operating from the Labour Party headquarters at Eccleston Square, a small but able committee including, among others, R. Page Arnot, W. Mellor and Will Dyson, worked full time until the conclusion of the strike, organizing the publicity on behalf of the railwaymen. G. D. H. Cole was ill with influenza at the beginning of the strike, but helped later. The first job each day was to sort out newspaper cuttings taken from the national and provincial dailies into twenty-four sections. At 11 a.m. a conference of publicity workers was held to determine, in the light of the press reports and comments of the day, the best mode of counter-attack. Sub-committees for posters, press advertisements and meetings were in charge of these aspects of the campaign. Great wisdom was shown in refusing to waste time on Lloyd George's anarchist red herring. Instead, the department went straight to the attack on the subject of the Government's intention to reduce the wages of the railwaymen. As Mr Masterman so clearly saw 'they repeated one accusation and one accusation only, that the Government were proposing to reduce wages. And a Government accused of reducing wages is like a beetle on its back. It can only feebly and ineffectively cleave the air.' The Government could have outwitted the railwaymen only by a forthright declaration that they had no intention of reducing wages. 'This they could not do.' Instead they issued announcements of 'incredible foolishness'.

One dramatic episode in the propaganda war was the battle of advertisements in *The Times*. On three successive days the Government published a full-page advertisement of its case only to find that the strikers' case was also presented in a full-page statement paid for from the £1,500 a day which the N.U.R. allowed the L.R.D. to spend on its behalf. In a poster displayed by the Government on October 3rd, the claim was made that there would be no reduction in war wages except under a sliding scale based on the cost of living. The N.U.R. answer in *The Times* that day, was to quote Lloyd George's statement of September 25th that 'very large numbers' of the railwaymen 'were disgracefully paid' before the war and to add the comment that 'Disgracefully paid workers should be substantially *better off* than before the war, not merely as well off'. On the following day the Government published a detailed table of the wages it claimed to have offered the railwaymen but on a full-page advertisement headed: 'Who is speaking the Truth?' which backed on to the Government's advertisement in the same issue of the paper, the N.U.R. declared that it was 'not true' that the figures quoted overleaf were the Government's offer since those figures 'included the very war bonus which the Government was attacking'. It was such incidents as this that led the Liberal leader, Mr C. F. G. Masterman, to assert that towards the end of the struggle 'the railwaymen were having it all their own way'.

No doubt Lloyd George thought he would have the field to himself if he could influence the twenty million cinema viewers of the country by a film in which he stated the case against the strike. Accordingly on October 2nd the face of the Premier appeared on all the cinema screens of the country with the statement that the Government was 'not fighting trade unionism'. It was fighting rather 'to prevent the extremists of any industrial body from attempting to gain their ends by attacking the life of the community and so bringing untold misery on the lives of innocent people'. But if Lloyd George and his Cabinet thought that this time they had stolen a march on the N.U.R. they were very soon disillusioned. On the following day cinemagoers throughout the kingdom saw a short film of Mr Thomas, who in an accompanying message assured them that 'the railwaymen were not fighting the community'. His assertion that he had 'always held back strikes' was known to be true by those who had any knowledge of the wartime negotiations with the Railway Executive. Even more convincing was his claim that he was 'not captured by the extremists'. His statement ended with a brief appeal to all working people:

'If the wages of the railwaymen are reduced other trades will follow. This is only the first battle of the campaign and the Government has thrown all its weight against the men. We are out to prevent a return to pre-war conditions and we mean to win. It is your fight as well as ours and we want you to help us.'

The strike gave a fillip to labour journalism in the provinces. In addition to being the cause of publication of local strike bulletins such as *The Glasgow and District Strike Bulletin* it boosted the circulation of the local socialist and trade-union weeklies, *The Brighton and Hove Labour News*, the Birmingham *Town Crier*, the *Surrey and Hants Labour Record*, and the *Leicester Pioneer* either owed their origin to the railwaymen's struggle or were given a new vitality as a result of it.

The cumulative effect of this remarkably successful publicity campaign was that 'before the strike had ended the railwaymen had rallied nine-tenths of the industrial workers to their side' and that the number of their sympathizers was 'increasing by hundreds of thousands a day'.[53] The press, almost unanimous in its opposition to the railwaymen at the beginning of the strike, was obliged to heed the trend of public opinion and to consider more seriously the case being presented by the Labour Research Department on behalf of the N.U.R. *The Times*, which on September 27th had declared that the Government's wage offer was 'generous' and the union's demands 'unjustifiable' was conceding by October 3rd, that it was 'sufficiently apparent that the wages question has not been well handled by the Government'. It was 'satisfied that some hard cases would occur under the Government's proposals'. It now believed 'the whole question should be reconsidered with an open mind'. The *Daily Express* which on September 29th claimed that this was 'a strike against the whole nation' organized by a 'little band of conspirators who forced their duped followers' was carrying a headline on October 3rd: 'The railwaymen have a case'; the *Daily News*, finding on September 27th 'no shadow or semblance of excuse for a strike' was admitting, by October 6th, that the men's wages were 'not good enough. . . . The offer has got to be improved'.

Sir Eric Geddes's announcement on October 3rd that the pay the rail-waymen had earned in the week in which the strike started would be with-held from them, affronted the British sense of fair play. Some, like *The Economist*, felt 'it smacked just a little of Prussianism'. Even the *Daily Mail* which throughout had condemned the strike, told Sir Auckland in a headline to 'pay them what they have earned'.[54]

VII

The Government had lost the support of many of the public. Although the newspapers were reporting an increasing number of passenger train services on the main lines—largely due to the work of volunteers, many of whom were not improving the serviceability of the equipment in their charge—there was but a small trickle of goods traffic. By October 5th, the strike had involved a direct loss to the Exchequer of £10 million[55] whilst the cost to the nation in diminished production and exports must have been many times this figure. From the union's point of view also there were limits to the duration of the strike. A total of £251,860 was expended on strike pay and £16,355 on publicity.[56] At this rate the strike could have continued for another three weeks, but not beyond that time unless the railway unions were prepared to accept help from other unions on a much larger scale. A railway strike to be effective must achieve its objective in the first few days. Every schoolboy at some stage of his school life longs to be an engine driver. Many retain this longing on reaching manhood and only have an opportunity to fulfil their ambition on the occasion of a railway strike. Thus, after the point of maximum effectiveness has quickly been reached, every day in which the struggle is prolonged brings more trains into service. Owing to the unpleasantness of the work the coal mines are largely 'blackleg-proof'; the railways are not.

By this reluctance to extend the scope of the strike by the participation of other unions, Mr Thomas made it easier for the Government to come to a compromise solution when it found that the public were sympathetic to the men's case. Though gifts of money to the union funds, such as the £10,000 given by the Lancashire Weavers' Union, were accepted, both the E.C. and the General Secretary of the N.U.R. declined offers of sympathetic strike action by other trades.[57]

Another suggestion which Mr Thomas did not take up even though it was made by those he described as 'very responsible people', was that he should endeavour to persuade the King (who had motored down from Balmoral to London to be near at hand) to intervene and bring about a settlement. His reason for rejecting the proposal was that no constitutional issues were involved in the dispute which purely concerned railwaymen's wages and it would be unwise to create a precedent of royal intervention in industrial disputes.[58]

When Ernest Bevin returned to London on Monday, September 30th, after spending the first weekend of the strike in Bristol and South Wales he was confronted by demands from London busmen, tramway workers and dockers that the Transport Workers Federation should call its members out on strike in support of the railwaymen. He did not favour the proposal but he also saw the dangers, if the strike continued, of the railway unions 'stumbling into an ineffectual challenge to the power of the state'. He therefore persuaded the executive of the Transport Workers Federation at its meeting on the following morning to call a conference of 'all the other unions it could reach' to consider the situation even though the railway unions had not asked for their intervention in the dispute.[59]

After ascertaining that sufficient support for the venture would be forthcoming, the Executive of the Transport Workers Federation met the Joint Executives of the N.U.R. and A.S.L.E. & F. in the afternoon of the same day to inform them that the Caxton Hall had been booked for the following morning for a conference of the leading unions and the Labour Party to consider what action should be taken with regard to the railway strike. Messrs Thomas and Bromley were asked if they were willing to attend the conference to state the case for the railwaymen and they indicated their consent.

At 10.30 the following morning the two railwaymen's leaders explained the issues of the strike to over seventy delegates from such bodies as the Labour Party, the T.U.C. Parliamentary Committee, the Amalgamated Society of Engineers, the National Union of General Workers, the Railway Clerks' Association, the National Federation of Women Workers and many other trade unions. After they had stated their case the two railwaymen left and the conference proceeded to carry unanimously a resolution which declared that the fight was 'a purely trade union fight for wages and conditions'. They decided to send a deputation of eleven men, including such well-known figures as Arthur Henderson (representing the Labour Party), Harry Gosling, Robert Williams, Ernest Bevin and J. R. Clynes to wait upon the Prime Minister at three o'clock that afternoon.

Lloyd George listened to what the deputation had to say and then made a statement that it would be 'quite impracticable to continue negotiations until work was resumed'. He was, however, willing to see the E.C.s of the two railway unions who, together with the deputation of eleven, returned to No. 10 for a long conference with the Premier which lasted until after midnight. Later on Thursday, the Joint Executives of the two railway unions had further discussions with the Prime Minister when it was again made clear that although the Government was prepared to consider any anomalies which might arise in the implementation of the new wage programme, there was to be no resumption of the main negotiations on standardization until the men had returned to work. The Government also proposed that, after the full resumption of work a seven-day truce should be declared in which the period of stabilization of wages and the alleged unfairness of the wage settlement to different grades might be discussed. The railway union executives and the Prime Minister were, however, quite unable to agree on the conditions of the 'proposed truce' largely because the Government would give no indication of the basis on which there would be a wage settlement. It was quite clear by that Thursday evening that the Government were still thinking largely in terms of a surrender by the railwaymen and that a deadlock had been reached.

In the meantime the conference of the other union and Labour Party delegates had adjourned to the Memorial Hall, Farringdon Street, where the news of the breakdown was received with dismay. It deplored the fact that although 'for the first time in industrial history a responsible body of trade unionists voluntarily undertook the task of mediation' the Prime Minister and his advisers had adopted 'an irreconcilable attitude'. It considered the Government's terms were not merely harsh but such as no union could accept, and resolved to summon for the following Tuesday, October 7th, a National Trade Union Conference whose purpose would be to determine 'what form of moral and sympathetic support' should be given to the railwaymen. The members of the Downing Street deputation from the conference, on Saturday, October 4th, sent a signed statement to the Prime Minister in which they warned him that unless 'a more reasonable attitude' was adopted by his Cabinet 'it would be impossible to avert a widespread extension of the strike with all its consequences'. They were not guilty of bombast. Mr F. Bramley, Secretary of the Joint Advisory Committee of Trade Unionists and Co-operators, had attended the meeting which had drafted the letter and had informed it of plans agreed by the Co-operative Union for 'the utilization of the Co-operative Movement as the food distributive agency to members of trade unions' involved in any extension of the strike movement.[60]

Faced with the distinct possibility of an extension of the strike to other trades, the Cabinet at last capitulated. The trade-union conference deputation was interviewed by Mr Bonar Law on the Saturday afternoon when it was arranged that, subject to the consent of the railwaymen's executives, the deputation and the executives should meet the Prime Minister at 11.30 on Sunday morning. After discussions lasting until 4.15 in the afternoon, agreement was reached on a settlement of the strike. Near the end of the proceedings, when agreement was in sight, the mediators were in an anteroom while the railwaymen's executive were conferring separately. In high glee at the prospect of a favourable conclusion of the strike some of the more daring of the N.U.R. Executive sang 'The Red Flag' and the 'Internationale'—for the first time probably within the walls of No. 10 Downing Street. Mr Churchill, who was passing by the room at that moment, poked his head round the door and observed with a smile—'Harmony at last, gentlemen'.[61]

By the terms of the agreement that made this harmony possible, Sir Auckland Geddes's definitive proposals were—to use the words of *The Economist*—'discreetly buried'. Work was to be resumed forthwith; but this was on the understanding that wages were to be stabilized at their existing level until September 30, 1920, and that negotiations on the standardization of wage rates should be completed before December 31, 1919. No adult railwayman was to receive less than 51s a week so long as the cost of living stood at not less than 110 per cent above the pre-war level; the arrears of wages which had been withheld were to be paid; the unions agreed that their members should 'work harmoniously with the railway servants who have remained at or returned to work'. The Government and the unions agreed that no man should be prejudiced in any way as a result of the strike.

So confident was Mr Thomas of the prospect of a settlement that Sunday that he composed the telegram: 'Strike settled, return to work', at Unity House before leaving for Downing Street. At 4.15 p.m. he simply telephoned through to the office to dispatch the telegram to the branches.[62] It is significant that the railwaymen returned to work without knowing the details of the settlement; the receipt of the telegram was regarded as sufficient.

The popularity of the settlement was shown by the fact that only one branch, Ystrad, condemned it, a resolution to this effect being sent to the E.C. On the other hand the great rally at the Albert Hall, London, on the evening of October 5th, gave a great ovation to the leaders of the two unions. The crowded meeting carried unanimously a resolution tendering 'sincere thanks to the General Secretaries and Joint E.C.s for their untiring efforts on behalf of all railwaymen' and undertaking to accept the settlement arrived at between the Executive Committees and the Government. Mr C. T. Cramp, who took the chair, assured his hearers that they had won a battle not merely for themselves but also 'for the organized workers throughout the country'. Mr Thomas, who was very tired from the prolonged strain of the previous days, emphasized that the resumption of work should be 'without any trace of bitterness whatever'. 'We did not want to beat the Government', he said. An honourable settlement that justified the action of the men had been achieved.[63]

At its Special Meeting on October 15, 1919, the E.C. set up a subcommittee to organize a special collection on behalf of Mr Thomas. Collecting sheets were sent to all branches and a sum of £2,598 was raised, £2,000 of which enabled the General Secretary to purchase his house at 125 Thurlow Park Road, Dulwich, while the balance, after deduction of expenses, was to go to Mrs Thomas 'to be expended as and how she should think fit in the furnishing and decorating of their new house'.[64]

As a mark of appreciation of the invaluable assistance rendered by the A.S.L.E. & F. the E.C. of the N.U.R. presented illuminated addresses to Messrs Cooke and Bromley (Chairman and Secretary) and a suitably inscribed gold medallion to each member of the executive.

VIII

An important question remains to be answered. Why was the assistance of the Triple Alliance not sought by the General Secretary of the N.U.R.? At its meeting on September 25th, just before the start of the strike, the E.C. instructed him to notify the other members of the Triple Industrial Alliance of the position. Mr Thomas did not make the time to do this and the aid of the Miners and Transport Workers Federation was not invoked, although, as we have seen, the mediation of the latter was not declined. When the strike was over Mr Robert Williams, the Secretary of the

Transport Workers Federation, complained to his audience at a demonstration in Newport (Mon.), on October 19th, that 'the N.U.R. had not utilized the machinery of the Triple Alliance'. This he considered to be an 'error in tactics'. From a 'common courtesy standpoint' he believed the Triple Alliance should have been kept informed of the progress of the negotiations. The first the Triple Alliance heard about the negotiations was 'what they learned in the newspapers'. A member of the E.C. of the N.U.R. who happened to be in Mr Williams's audience at Newport reported what had been said to Mr Thomas. When the matter was discussed at the next meeting of the E.C. on October 23rd, feeling was very strong against Mr Williams for washing in public the dirty linen of the Alliance. Mr Thomas sent the resolution to Mr Williams and in a covering letter accused him of bringing before the public matters which should have been dealt with in secret by the executive of the Alliance. In a sarcastic and not very friendly reply, Mr Williams wrote that he was glad to have Mr Thomas's letter since it was the only evidence, since before the railway strike, that its writer remembered that the Triple Alliance was still in being.[65]

The truth of the matter was that Mr Thomas had no desire to extend the strike in any way if an honourable settlement could be achieved by the railway unions fighting alone. He told the Albert Hall meeting on October 5th that from the beginning of the strike he was 'determined to make the issue a wage question and nothing more'. He was afraid that if the railwaymen called for the assistance of other unions a dispute which began on the question of railway wages might end by having political and constitutional implications—a development to which he was strenuously opposed. Soon after his return from America at the end of July he had told his constituents at Derby that he was opposed 'to any section that attempts to hold the nation to ransom', that there had been an opportunity in December 1918, to change things by the ballot box and that it was wrong to think that you had only to 'down tools' to achieve any political objective such as overthrowing the Coalition Government.[66]

A further reason for the General Secretary's reluctance to invoke the aid of the Triple Alliance at the end of September was the N.U.R.'s experience of co-operation with that body earlier in the year. When the E.C. on March 21st called for strike action and notified the Alliance of this fact the meeting of the Alliance had advised the railwaymen to postpone the strike until another attempt was made with the backing of the leaders of the Alliance, to obtain a more favourable offer from the Government. The E.C. of the N.U.R. agreed to this proposal and eventually agreed to abandon the plan for a strike. When on July 23rd the N.U.R. delegation at the Caxton Hall Conference of the Alliance advocated strike action to compel the Government to abolish conscription and to put an end to military intervention in Russia and military intervention in industrial disputes, the majority had turned down the proposal and decided instead that the three unions should be advised to conduct a ballot of their membership to find out whether they favoured or opposed strike action. Hesitation grew. When the Alliance met again on September 4th it was decided to postpone indefinitely the holding of a ballot.

It was at this September meeting that Mr Thomas declared that if ever the N.U.R. was called to upon strike again it could never win 'if it gave the other side notice of its intentions'.

'You cannot blackleg the mines,' he continued, 'it is an entirely different thing. But with a transport service, if you give them an opportunity of having a depleted service in order to run certain public services and so on, so far as the railwaymen are concerned, it would be merely giving an invitation to the other side to prepare in order to defeat us. That is why we are opposed to a ballot.'[67]

Had the assistance of the Alliance been sought at the end of September the reply might have been another proposal for a ballot of the three unions. The very fact of holding the ballot would have given the Government time to prepare and would have weakened the chances of success of a railway strike. On the other hand the support of the Alliance was of value in gaining concessions from the Government in March, and an attempt on similar lines might have had a successful outcome in September. It had been the intervention of the Transport Workers Federation and other unions which had been a decisive influence on the Government on October 4th and 5th. But if the Alliance had intervened successfully to settle the railwaymen's claims it would have strengthened the position of those in the union who wanted to use that instrument for other than industrial disputes. This was a prospect which Mr Thomas did not relish. Pressure for a strike on the wages question was increasing and he preferred to seek a battle on his own terms and for his own union. If it had a successful outcome this would allay the discontent among railwaymen and make them less likely to embark on a general strike for political ends. If on the other hand the strike were a failure it would provide a salutary warning to the extremists of the unexpected strength of the Government.[68]

Whatever the motives for choosing to fight alone the outcome was a further weakening of the Triple Alliance. When the Government's main negotiations with the railwaymen were resumed after the strike the Government made proposals that the N.U.R. should be entitled to a share in the management of the railways.[69] The union tended to become pre-occupied with the question of the form that this participation in management should take, rather than with the question of joint action with the Triple Alliance to secure the nationalization of all forms of transport and of the coal mines. Events were to show that the prospects for united action on behalf of these demands in 1920 and 1921 were less bright as a result of what had happened in the autumn of 1919.

NOTES

1. T. H. Wintringham, *Mutiny*, Chapter X, pp. 305-27.
2. This was Stanley Baldwin's phrase. C. L. Mowat, *Britain between the Wars* (1955), p. 7.
3. Mowat, *op. cit.*
4. Quoted in W. A. Orton, *Labour in Transition* (1921), p. 173.
5. Lord Inchcape, quoted in R. H. Tawney, 'The Abolition of Economic Controls, 1918-21', *Economic History Review*, 1943, p. 29. Lord Claud Hamilton reported in *The Times*, February 8, 1919.
6. Tawney, *op. cit.*
7. Lloyd George, Mansion House speech, October 7, 1919, reported in *The Times*, October 8, 1919, and Lloyd George's Foreword to Glasgow, G., *General Strikes and Road Transport.*
8. *Daily Herald*, May 13, 1919.
9. Secret Memorandum issued by the Superintendent of the Line, London, Brighton and South Coast Railway, April 23, 1919.
10. House of Commons Parliamentary Debates, February 13, 1919, Vol. 112, Col. 341.
11. *The Times*, January 22, 1919. G. W. Alcock, *op. cit.*, pp. 529-30. N.U.R. Special E.C., February 6-14, 1919, Rs. 44, 52.
12. *The Times*, March 18, 1919.
13. From its leading article, March 22, 1919.
14. *R.R.*, February 21, 1919. *The Times*, March 16, 1919.
15. *The Times*, March 22, 1919.
16. Press Bureau Report on Conference at No. 10 Downing Street, March 22, 1919.
17. N.U.R. E.C., May 23, 1919, R. 211, June Quarterly Meeting, Rs. 287, 288.
18. *R.R.*, February 24, 1919.
19. A. I. Thatcher, *The 1919 Railway Strike*, p. 5.
20. N.U.R. Special E.C., April 15, 1919, R. 197. *R.R.*, May 16, August 1, 1919.
21. N.U.R. Special E.C., July 12-22, 1919. Special E.C. July 31, 1919. Joint Meeting of the E.C.s of the N.U.R. and A.S.L.E. & F., November 4-5, 1919. Alcock, p. 541.
22. N. McKillop, *The Lighted Flame*, p. 122.
23. N.U.R. Special E.C., August 21, 1919, R. 533.
24. J. H. Thomas, statement at meeting of E.C. of N.U.R. with Sir Eric Geddes at 6 Whitehall Gardens, September 25, 1919. Press Bureau Report.
25. Press Bureau Report of meeting on September 16, 1919.
26. Press Bureau Report of meeting on September 25, 1919. *The Times*, September 25, 1919. N.U.R. E.C. Resolution, September 24, 1919.
27. *Daily Herald*, September 29, 1919. Press Bureau Report, September 25, p. 35.
28. Alcock, p. 431.
29. House of Commons, Parliamentary Debates 1919, Vol. 114, Col. 1099, April 1, 1919.
30. *New Age*, October 2, 1919.
31. *R.R.*, October 3, 1919. Press Bureau Report, September 26, 1919, p. 69.
32. *R.R.*, October 3, 1919.
33. Press Bureau Report, p. 62.
34. House of Commons, Parliamentary Debates, 1919, Vol. 119, Cols. 281-306.
35. *Beatrice Webb's Diaries* 1918-24, edited Margaret Cole, p. 167.
36. S. and B. Webb, *History of Trade Unionism* (1920 Edition) p. 541.
37. K. G. J. C. Knowles, *Strikes, a study in industrial conflict*, p. 76.
38. *The Times*, September 30, 1919.

39. *The Times,* September 30, 1919; *Daily News,* September 30, 1919; *Dundee Advertiser,* October 2, 1919; *Isle of Wight Mercury,* October 3, 1919; *Derby Daily Telegraph,* September 29, 1919.
40. *Morning Post,* October 4, 6 and 7, 1919 *Daily Mail,* October 2, 3 and 4, 1919; *British Weekly,* October 9, 1919.
41. *Daily Mail,* September 28, 1919. *R.R.,* October 3, 1919.
42. *Daily Herald,* October 2 and 4, 1919; *Wireless World,* April 1920; *New Statesman,* October 4, 1919.
43. War Department Instruction 65/485 (F.5).
44. According to a statement of J. H. Thomas in his Foreword to Alcock's *Fifty Years of Railway Trade Unionism.*
45. K. G. J. C. Knowles, *op. cit.,* p. 134.
46. *The Times,* September 3, October 1, 2 and 3, 1919. Circular of Secretary, Customs and Excise, to heads of offices in London, October 2, 1919.
47. *Leicester Pioneer,* October 10, 1919.
48. *R.R.,* October 24, 1919.
49. *Daily Express,* October 2, 1919.
50. Mr C. F. G. Masterman in *Daily News* quoted in 'Report from the Labour Research Department to the N.U.R. on publicity work undertaken in connection with the recent strike, October 6, 1919'. I am also grateful to Mr R. Page Arnot for information about this work.
51. *The Times,* September 29, 1919.
52. *The Times,* September 27 and 29, 1919; *Daily Mail,* September 28, 1919; *Morning Post,* September 27, 1919; *Daily Express,* September 29, 1919; *Daily News,* September 27, 1919.
53. Mr C. F. G. Masterman quoted in A. Hutt, *Post War History of the British Working Class.*
54. *The Economist,* October 11, 1919; *Daily Mail,* October 4, 1919.
55. House of Commons, Parliamentary Debates, 1919, Vol. 120, Col. 275, October 27, 1919.
56. N.U.R. Report and Financial Statement for 1919. *The Times* Industrial Correspondent must have been impressed by the union's publicity effort since his estimate for its expenditure under this head was £200,000. Strike pay he estimated more accurately at £300,000. *The Times,* October 7, 1919.
57. N.U.R. Special E.C., October 24, 1919.
58. J. H. Thomas, *My Story* (1937), p. 91.
59. A. Bullock, *The Life and Times of Ernest Bevin* (1960), Vol. 1, p. 108. *Daily News,* September 29, 1919.
60. National Transport Workers Federation, Railway Dispute, 1919, 'Report to the Labour Movement of Great Britain by the Committee appointed at the Caxton Hall Conference, October 1, 1919'.
61. *Dundee Advertiser,* October 7, 1919.
62. J. H. Thomas, *My Story.*
63. Salisbury Agency; Verbatim Report of Meeting in the Albert Hall, October 5, 1919.
64. N.U.R. Special E.C., October 15, 1919, Rs. 690, 692. Special E.C., October 24, 1919, R. 795. Quarterly Meeting, March 1920.
65. *South Wales Daily News,* October 20, 1919. N.U.R. Special E.C., October 23, 1919, R. 702. *Daily Express,* November 28, 1919.
66. *R.R.,* August 1, October 10, 1919.
67. Report of the Conference of the Industrial Triple Alliance, Caxton Hall, September 4, 1919, p. 24.
68. See W. H. Crook, *The General Strike,* p. 260.
69. *The Times,* November 17, 1919.

CHAPTER XVI

THE RAILWAYS ACT, 1921

> *'Before the Ministry of Transport was set up I agitated and wrote articles urging that a Ministry of Transport should be set up in order that transport in this country should be nationally owned if possible, but that in any case that it should be co-ordinated and utilized for the benefit of the people as a whole and not for the benefit of private shareholders. . . . Our conditions in the future are bound up with the organization of the transport industry generally. Until the transport industry is better organized I may tell you I do not think it will be possible for us as workers to make any great advance.'*
> *C. T. Cramp, Industrial General Secretary of the N.U.R., speaking in the Empire Theatre, Bacup, October 10, 1920.*

I

THE strike of the early autumn of 1919 successfully frustrated an attempt to reduce railwaymen's wages. It did nothing to settle the much bigger problem of the future organization of the transport industry.

The policy of the N.U.R. for the future of the industry had been clearly enough stated even though the scope of the statement was too limited. When a large number of branches asked the E.C., nine months before the Armistice, to define the union's policy on reconstruction, the E.C. responded by passing unanimously a resolution demanding 'complete nationalization of all the railways in the United Kingdom with equal representation both national and local for the N.U.R. on the management',[1] but said nothing about the union's policy for transport as a whole. Though Mr Cramp and other leaders of the N.U.R. had shown a realization of the importance of road transport developments, it was Mr A. G. Walkden of the Railway Clerks' Association who was largely responsible for the drafting of 'A National Transport Services Bill' in 1918 which provided for national ownership of the principal means of transport and for 'the co-ordination of road, motor, aerial, coastal and steam packet transport services' with those of the railways and canals 'as part of a national system of transport services'. The Bill, which in its general principles fore-shadowed the Transport Act of 1947, was never considered by Parliament, but the attention it aroused and the publicity given to a resolution moved by another member of the R.C.A., Mr S. Lomax, at the T.U.C. in Derby in September 1918, had some effect on the declarations of members of the Coalition Government. The resolution, which was carried by a large majority, urged on the Government the desirability of the complete national-ization of the railways, and expressed the opinion of Congress that, with a view to the full development of the national resources, 'steps should be taken to bring all the other principal means of transport and communica-tions (e.g. canals, road motor vehicles, postal, telegraph and aerial services) into harmonious and co-ordinated working; the whole to be controlled by a Minister of Transport and Communications'.

There may well have been thousands of railwaymen among the more than five million electors who voted for the coalition candidates in the General Election of December 14, 1918, in the mistaken belief that their votes were votes for the nationalization of railways. All the indications were that the Government intended such a reform. Lloyd George, the Prime Minister, told a deputation from the T.U.C. on March 20, 1918, that he was in 'complete sympathy' with the general character of the proposal to nationalize the railways. He assured the deputation that 'they could not go back to the old system'.[2] Four days after the Armistice a Select Committee of the House of Commons had urged in its report that:

'The main railway systems of the United Kingdom should be brought under unified ownership and managed as one system if the question of the improvement and development of the internal transport facilities is to be considered from the standpoint of economy and efficiency.'[3]

Nine days before the election, Mr Winston Churchill who, as Minister of War, was a member of the Coalition Cabinet, declared that the Govern-ment had made up its mind to nationalize the railways. Questioned at a meeting of the Dundee Chamber of Commerce six days later, he expressed his view that it was 'highly improbable' that action in that 'vital matter' (railway nationalization) could be delayed 'until a Royal Commission has wandered about'.[4] Nor was Mr Churchill alone in such pronouncements. Another member of the Coalition Government, Mr George Barnes, Minister without Portfolio, told his constituents in the Gorbals that 'he was glad to see that the railways and canals were to be nationalized'.[5] Most people took these statements of Ministers of the Crown seriously. Only Mr H. Cosmo-Bonsor, Chairman of the South Eastern and Chatham Railway, expressed in public any doubts of the Government's intentions. He told the shareholders of his company just over two months later that 'they should always take the utterances of a gentleman who is standing for

Parliament with a grain of salt'.[6] His scepticism was justified. At that time the Cabinet had come to no decision on the future of the railways or of any other form of transport. On July 19, 1920, Mr Bonar Law (as Leader of the House) told Mr Clement Edwards that although the subject of the future of the railways had been discussed in the Cabinet 'on numerous occasions' no definite decision on the railway policy of the Government was taken until June 7, 1920.[7]

The Coalition Government successfully sidestepped the miners' demand for the nationalization of the mines by the appointment of the Sankey Commission. With equal success it sidestepped the railwaymen's demand for public control of transport by the introduction of the Ministry of Ways and Communications Bill.

Had the powers conferred on the Minister of Ways and Communications under the original bill been fully exercised, State ownership of all principal forms of transport would have been a reality. Section 4 of the Bill authorized the Minister:

'... to purchase by agreement or compulsorily and work the whole or any part of any railway, light railway, tramway, canal waterway or inland navigation, harbour or dock undertaking, the acquisition of which is, in the opinion of the Minister, expedient for improving facilities for locomotion and transport.'

Under the same clause the Minister could purchase or take on hire and lease railway wagons belonging to private owners and 'establish, maintain and work transport services by land and water'.[8] Sir Eric Geddes introducing the Bill to the House of Commons declared that it would be 'nothing short of criminal to let the old system of competition between light railways and roads, railways and canals and between different docks', go on. He was sure 'some measure of unified control of all systems of transportation' was necessary. This was the 'cold bath' the country had to take.[9] But if the Bill created the necessary machinery for State ownership and control it did not follow that a majority of the Cabinet were in favour of it being used. If Sir Eric Geddes seemed to be in favour of the cold bath because his experience of administering the railways serving the Western Front in the latter part of the war had shown him the advantages of unified control, the majority of members on the Government benches did not relish such a spartan regimen.

Although to the simple-minded a perusal of Clause 4 would lead to the clear impression that the purpose of the Bill was to establish common ownership of the principal forms of transport, according to one authority 'its real and rather artless purpose was admitted to be to give Sir Eric and his subordinates time to think'.[10] Confirmation of this estimate of the purpose of the Bill is to be found in the confession of the Minister designate (Sir E. Geddes) himself to Standing Committee B in the House of Commons on April 2, 1919, that he had 'not yet made up his mind how transport was to be organized in the future'.[11] Another useful purpose of the Bill might be to kill time while what one M.P. described as 'the very great political pressure in favour of nationalization'[12] eased and the fervent spirit in the Labour movement, manifest in the first months of the peace, died down.

While Sir Eric Geddes and his subordinates were thinking, the Railway Companies' Association, the Federation of British Industries and numerous Chambers of Commerce were acting. In the first week in January 1919, the Federation of British Industries, which at that time represented £4,000 million of capital, held a conference at which its policy for the period of reconstruction was determined. The meeting declared its unanimous opposition to the nationalization of the railways.[13] Even before Sir Eric Geddes's Bill was published, a Committee of Chairmen and General Managers of the main railway companies was constituted to ensure that the companies' point of view was not overlooked by the Cabinet. As a result of what its Chairman, Viscount Churchill, described as 'the determined and persistent efforts' of the Railway Companies' Association, the spectre of nationalization was effectively laid and the original Bill was amended almost beyond recognition. Viscount Churchill assured the shareholders of his company that the small committee of the Railway Companies' Association had been working 'in perfect harmony with the Minister' and that the 'arguments and representations' put forward by the companies had met with 'recognition on the part of the Government'.[14]

Most of the forty-five railway director M.P.s were to be found in the ranks of the 200-strong Unionist War Committee in the House which, a few days before the day fixed for the Second Reading of the Ministry of Ways and Communications Bill, resolved to press for a discussion of the Bill in the more critical atmosphere of a Committee of the whole House, rather than in the more sober atmosphere of Standing Committee B which was limited to seventy-five members. When Mr Bonar Law heard of this he asked a deputation of members from the Unionists' War Committee to meet him privately. He told the deputation that he would resign if they persisted in their demands. Although the Unionist back benchers dropped their proposal for procedural changes in the discussion of the Bill, faced with an opposition of such formidable proportions, the Government made even greater concessions. It was a member of the Cabinet, Mr Shortt, the Home Secretary, who, on May 6th, moved the deletion of the whole of the vital Clause 4. The proposal was accepted without a division though the Chairman of the Committee, William Brace, who was Under Secretary to the Home Office, had spoken in favour of the State purchase of railways and canals in the election campaign.[15] The House of Lords added its quota of deletions and amendments (including the sensible proposal to call the new Government department the Ministry of Transport instead of the Ministry of Ways and Communications) and a much mutilated Bill, a pale shadow of its original robust self, then passed its final stages without serious opposition.

It had taken just over six months to scotch the proposal for the nationalization of the principal means of transport; in another six months another of the principal proposals of the N.U.R.—the demand for workers' participation in the management of the railways—met a similar fate.

The members of the union who advocated that railwaymen should share in the management of their industry were not always agreed on the reasons for desiring the change. To some, workers' control was the complement to public ownership and the completion of the process of the expropriation of the capitalist. Mr Thomas and the right wing element in the union, on the other hand, were aiming at 'a better and saner policy of closer co-operation between capital and labour'. In a statement made early in 1921, Mr Thomas said:

'Many of our difficulties are caused by our not understanding the employers' point of view. If we are denied an opportunity of knowing their case, can you wonder that mistakes are made? The same is equally true from the point of view of employers.

Our conception of workers sharing in management is not that they should be merely Trade Union delegates whose only interest is in the wages and the conditions of the men. It means something much bigger than that; it means a genuine contribution by practical men towards the solution of the difficulty common to industry.'[16]

It was this safety-valve-of-discontent conception which found favour with Lloyd George, Sir Eric Geddes and other members of the Cabinet.

It was soon after the conclusion of the railway strike that Mr Lloyd George began to toy with the idea of railwaymen's participation in management. He summoned the E.C. of the N.U.R. to meet him at No. 10 Downing Street on November 13, 1919, and there were prolonged discussions on the form that joint consultation between management and the workers should take on the railways. It was an obvious attempt to propitiate the N.U.R. and to reconcile it to the proposed abandonment of nationalization. The first intimation the public gained of the nature of the proposals which had been agreed by both sides was contained in a speech given by Mr Thomas in Bristol on November 16th. Three trade-union representatives (two from the N.U.R. and one from the A.S.L.E. & F.) were 'to join the Railway Executive Committee with co-equal powers to the General Managers who sit there'. A joint board comprising five representatives of the General Managers and five of the unions was to be established to deal with wages and conditions of service—this was the precursor of the

Central Wages Board. Another body of thirteen members (four each from the companies, the trade unions and the public, with an independent chairman) was to hear questions on which the joint board failed to agree— this was the precursor of the National Wages Board. Whilst the proposal to set up Central and National Wages Boards provoked little opposition, and the Boards began to function early in 1920, the other proposal stirred up a veritable hornets' nest of opposition.[17]

The proposal that both manual and white collar workers should play a part in management was expressed in the Government's White Paper on the future of the railways, published in June 1920. In this it was stated that:

'... the Government are of opinion that the time has arrived when the workers, both official and manual workers, should have some voice in the management.'

At this stage the Government was proposing that the railways of England, Scotland and Wales should be grouped into seven companies each with a monopoly of the rail traffic of its region. The Board of Directors on each of these companies were to include a majority representing the shareholders and a minority of representatives of the employees 'of whom one third might be leading administrative officials'.[18] It can be seen that the Government was not proposing a revolutionary transference of power over railway capital to the railwaymen.

The railway trade unions in a joint statement, whilst deploring the abandonment of nationalization, gave qualified approval of the grouping scheme as a step in the right direction leading to great advantages in economy and efficiency of working, and approved 'in principle' the proposal that railway workers should be elected to the boards of management of the companies. They, however, reserved the right 'to criticize the details of the arrangement' when they came to be formulated. They believed that as the income of the railway shareholders was 'in effect guaranteed' under the Government's proposals there was no justification for a scheme which left their representatives in a majority on the boards of management. It was better that there should be representatives of the traders, the travelling public and technical experts in addition to the railwaymen members.[19]

Some railway directors were sympathetic to a policy of consultation with their employees for reasons similar to those given by Mr J. H. Thomas. Thus Mr Charles Booth, Chairman of the Midland Railway, favoured the establishment of advisory committees on which employees might be represented since their opinion 'in view of their practical experience' might well be 'of interest and value'. But he was at pains to reassure his shareholders that such proposed changes would 'not in any way affect the responsibilities of the directors in the direction or management of the undertaking'.[20] He was also exceptional, just as Mr Henry Allan of the

Caledonian Railway had been exceptional, in welcoming the proposal for nationalization 'accompanied by fair terms of purchase' as being 'decidedly advantageous' to the shareholders of his company.[21] More characteristic was the uncompromising opposition to the scheme expressed by Sir Frederick Banbury of the Great Northern Railway.[22] The Memorandum published by the Railway Companies' Association may fairly be taken as expressing the view of the overwhelming majority of directors and general managers. The Association announced that it would 'strenuously oppose any suggestion that directors elected by the workers shall be appointed to the Boards'. The proposal was 'quite unjustifiable', 'wrong in principle' and 'from every point of view objectionable'. For many decades the companies had refused to recognize the unions on the ill-founded assumption that such recognition would interfere with discipline and hence impair safe working of the railways. This had been their view in the crisis of 1911 and again on this occasion they cited 'questions of discipline' as the principal reason why appointment of worker directors was regarded as 'intolerable'. They also thought it 'entirely wrong' to 'interfere with the right of shareholders to choose their own directors'. As one might expect, the stand made by the leading general managers and directors was strongly supported by the English Railway Stockholders Protection Society which passed a resolution condemning the White Paper proposals at its first Annual General Meeting in December 1920. One indignant member of the Society who declared the plan to be 'perfectly monstrous' favoured the directors 'stopping the trains' in protest.[23]

It seemed at first as if Mr Thomas was going to cross swords with the companies on the question. Addressing a conference of the International Transport Workers' Federation on November 29, 1920, he said he believed that there was going to be 'a big fight in the next few months' because it was the intention of the N.U.R. to hold the Government to the promise that railwaymen would share in the management since on this matter they were 'absolutely united and determined'. The E.C.s of the N.U.R., A.S.L.E. & F. and the Railway Clerks' Association, meeting together a fortnight later at Unity House, affirmed their determination to secure for railwaymen 'a share in management and control'.[24] However, there were many signs that the railwaymen were far from being 'united and determined' on the question despite anything Mr Thomas may have said. Thoughtful critics of the scheme expressed in the *Railway Review* the opinion that the position of railwaymen representatives on the Boards of Directors, which would be running the railways 'primarily for dividends and only secondarily for the public service', would be untenable.[25] Mr Cramp expressed the view that if minority representation on the Boards of Directors had been accepted it would undoubtedly have prejudiced the Labour Party in its policy of nationalization.[26]

Mr Thomas most probably 'blew hot' at the International Transport

Workers Conference in order to improve his bargaining position with the companies. Always a believer in the value of personal negotiation, he engaged in friendly discussions with Viscount Churchill, Chairman of the Railway Companies' Association at the end of January 1921. He knew that the Government was surrendering its wartime control over the railways on August 15th that year and that it was only practical realism to secure the best possible negotiating machinery for the railwaymen by that date. He gave a hint of his change of front at a meeting in Hornsey early in February. In the next few months, he argued, the railways would either be handed back to private ownership or they would be nationalized. He ruled the latter proposition out 'because of the absence of common sense and intelligence among the workers themselves who, whilst holding up their hands in branch rooms in favour of nationalization, had returned to the House of Commons people who did not believe in nationalization'. Therefore 'one of the other alternatives had to be considered'.[27]

The ground having been prepared by Mr Thomas's personal initiative, a letter of invitation from the Railway Companies' Association to the executives of the three railway trade unions followed on April 23rd. The unions accepted invitations to attend discussions with representatives of the companies at the Railway Companies' Association headquarters at 35 Parliament Street, Westminster, on May 3rd. In the meantime a special meeting of the E.C. of the N.U.R. on April 29th decided to drop the idea of workers' representation on the Boards of Management and to work for the continuance of the Central and National Wages Boards.

In the Memorandum of Agreement which was the outcome of the talks with the companies, it was stated that both sides had agreed to the continuation of the Central and National Wages Boards subject to the right of either side to end the arrangement by giving a year's notice. For each railway after grouping they favoured the setting-up of railway councils, composed of representatives of both employers and workers, to consider problems of management and discipline (though the Boards of Directors would have the final say in all matters of business policy). The unions gained the important concession that their officials were to be entitled to represent the men in disciplinary cases, the long standing reluctances of the directors to submit to any interference with their powers in disciplinary matters being at last overcome. Both sides agreed to support the inclusion of the terms of this agreement in the Railways Bill shortly due for consideration by Parliament.[28]

It was scarcely to be expected that the Government would persist with a plan which now found favour neither with the companies nor the unions. In its Memorandum on the Railways Bill it stated that the proposal for the inclusion on the Boards of Management of representatives of the workers and the leading administrative officials had been abandoned as 'such representation was no longer desired by the trade unions representing the men'.[29] Sir Eric Geddes in introducing the Railways Bill to the House of Commons on May 26, 1921, said that he thought both companies and unions had 'made a mistake' in dropping the scheme but since they had now 'settled the matter between themselves' the Government accepted what was inevitable.[30]

At the A.G.M. of the N.U.R. early in July that year, Mr Thomas, who eight months earlier had forecast 'a big fight' to secure worker-directors, now pointed out how unsatisfactory such an arrangement would have been. He assured the delegates that 'the nominees of the men on the Boards of Management would have been mistrusted and hated and their position rendered impossible'. The four working railwaymen out of a total of twenty-one directors would not have been nominees of the unions but men from the railway companies' employment. Without goodwill on both sides the scheme would not have worked. The directors would have made the position an impossible one for the men.[31]

The importance of the agreement of May 3, 1921, cannot be over-emphasized. In the Parliamentary Committee on the Railway Bill it was described as 'an epoch-making document which is actuated by and which breathes a spirit of peace in the industrial world . . . a document of the most supreme importance as marking one of the greatest steps ever taken towards industrial peace'.[32] It certainly marked the beginning of a period of the closest co-operation between the union leaders and the railway companies. The spirit of this new phase of co-operation was admirably expressed by Mr Thomas:

'The scheme has been created not only in the hope of industrial peace but also of a genuine co-operation between the railway companies and the railway employees in the provision of the most efficient transport service possible.'[33]

As far as labour relations were concerned the Railways Act of 1921 merely brought legislative confirmation to already established procedures of negotiation. In Part IV, Paragraph 61, of the Act it was stated that:

'. . . all questions relating to rates of pay or conditions of service of men to whom this part of the Act applies shall, in default of agreement between the railway companies and the trade unions concerned, be referred to and settled by the Central Wages Board, or on appeal, the National Wages Board as reconstituted under this Act.'

Paragraph 63 of the Act outlined the composition of the Wages Boards:

'The Central Wages Board shall be composed of eight representatives of the railway companies and eight representatives of the employees. The railway companies' representatives shall be appointed by the railway companies. The employees' representatives shall be appointed by the Railway Trade Unions, four by the N.U.R., two by the A.S.L.E. & F. and two by the R.C.A.

'The National Wages Board shall be composed of six representatives of the railway companies, six representatives of the railway employees (two of whom shall be appointed by the N.U.R., two by the A.S.L.E. & F. and two by the R.C.A.), and four representatives of the users of the railways with an independent chairman nominated by the Minister of Labour. The four representatives of the users of the railways shall be nominated as follows: one by the Parliamentary Committee of the T.U.C.; one by the Co-operative Union; one by the Associated Chambers of Commerce and one by the Federation of British Industries.'

The N.U.R. caused to be written into the Act clauses safeguarding the rights of those railwaymen who were made redundant as a result of the grouping of the railways into four main-line companies (the Southern, Great Western, London and North Eastern and the London, Midland and Scottish Railways). Not only were such persons to be paid compensation for loss of wages but also for loss of prospective superannuation. A man or woman moved from the service of one company to that of another was not to be put in any worse position in respect of his conditions of service as a whole than he was in his previous employment.

It was such provisions as these that caused Mr Thomas to wax lyrical in praise of the Act to the delegates of a Special General Meeting of the N.U.R. at Unity House on August 12, 1921. He declared that the Bill was 'as near perfection as the brain of man can make a Bill in its passage through Parliament'.[34] Everything humanly possible, he believed, had been done to safeguard the interests of the members. Thanks to the N.U.R. at that time it certainly *looked* as if railwaymen would enjoy a security of tenure and regularity of employment not found in any other occupation outside state service.

Perhaps the high water mark of optimism, confidence and co-operation between management and the unions was reached at a Conference of Great Eastern Railway employees and executives held in the Cambridgeshire Room of Liverpool Street Station on August 25, 1921. The meeting had been called by the General Manager, Major General Sir Henry Thornton, K.B.E., and was the first time a general manager of a large railway company had issued a general invitation to his staff for a frank and friendly discussion of matters of mutual interest. He appealed to his audience of nearly 200 men for team work:

'A cricket team may be made up of the bowler, wicket-keeper and fielders, but unless they pull together they will not meet with success. The principle which exists in the field of sport exists likewise in the field of industry.'

The particular way in which Sir Henry wished his cricket team to pull together was in effecting economies in railway working. The costs of wages and coal had increased so greatly since 1913 that team work in increasing productivity was vital. Mr Cramp pleaded with the men to realize the companies' difficulties and to make it their business to co-operate with them, both the management and the men had got to realize that they must 'pull together'. Mr Wild of the A.S.L.E. & F. said that his union was 'specially pleased to render any contribution to the problems facing the companies . . . in order to make them successful concerns'. Mr George Latham, Assistant Secretary of the R.C.A. spoke in similar vein. Apparently Mr E. Wenlock, a rank and file member of the N.U.R., was the only non-cricketer present. He brought a jarring note into the proceedings by mentioning fifteen separate items of grievance on behalf of various grades, including the reduction in shed staff, the placing of shopmen on short time and the methods of discharging redundant platelaying staff. Despite this one discordant voice, the meeting carried with acclamation a hearty vote of thanks to Sir Henry Thornton for his initiative in taking the men into his confidence. In many respects the meeting typified the rosy hopes of the new era and the practical difficulties of their fulfilment.[35]

II

Given a prosperous railway industry in a prosperous economy and enlightened general managers of the calibre of Sir Henry Thornton, there was every prospect of a reasonably contented labour force. Parliament had, however, rejected the idea of a co-ordinated transport system run primarily as a service for the benefit of traders and travelling public, and had adopted instead the policy of unrestricted competition between the different forms of transport. In particular, the railways were to be run as commercial undertakings whose first consideration was the production of a profit for those who had invested their money in the companies. Within these limitations the railwaymen could expect to enjoy reasonable conditions of service only when the country's industries and trade were booming and then only until such time as the road haulage industry and the motor bus services became formidable competitors for goods and passenger traffic.

The hectic post-war boom of the British economy was disappointingly brief. It continued throughout 1919, reached its peak in terms of high levels of prices, profits and employment in the first half of 1920, and then collapsed. In 1921 and 1922 the country was experiencing an extremely severe industrial depression. In the short-lived boom period railwaymen's wages rose, but at a slower rate than the general rise in wages; in the slump their wages fell more slowly than the average. The explanation lies in the operation of the sliding scale agreement on the railways and the strength of organization of the N.U.R. which made possible a slower and more orderly retreat from the peak gains of the immediate post-war period.

Mr C. T. Cramp, who had carried out his duties as President with outstanding ability through the last year of the war and the first year of peace, was due to relinquish his office on December 31, 1919. It was a very widely held opinion that his services should not be lost to the union which had increased its membership from 267,611 to 481,081 since the outbreak of the war. With the re-election of Mr Thomas as M.P. for Derby in December 1918, it was realized that a large part of his time would inevitably be taken up with Parliamentary matters and that it would be an impossible task for him to cope adequately with the vastly increased volume of industrial business. In September 1919, therefore, the E.C. invited nominations from branches for a new post of Industrial General Secretary. At its December meeting, Mr Thomas informed the E.C. that 465 branches had nominated Mr Cramp and only 24 had nominated Mr W. L. Loraine, the only other candidate. When he informed Mr Loraine of these facts that gentleman had withdrawn from the contest. By a unanimous vote, therefore, the E.C. declared Mr Cramp to be the successful candidate. When the appointment was endorsed by the A.G.M. in July 1920, it was made clear that although Mr Thomas as Political General Secretary and Mr Cramp as Industrial General Secretary would work in double harness and receive the same salary (£1,000 a year each) Mr Thomas would be the supreme head of the union.

Concemore Thomas Thwaites Cramp had been born in the village of Staplehurst, Kent, in March 1876. At the age of 12 he had left school to work as a gardener for the village squire. Whilst he was still in his teens he had moved to Yorkshire to become a railway porter, first at Bradford and then at Masborough, where he joined the A.S.R.S. From 1907, when he attended the Birmingham All-Grades Conference, he came quickly into prominence. He was an A.G.M. delegate in 1909 and a member of the E.C. in 1911, and was elected President in 1917. A man of unruffled temperament, wide culture and great sincerity of character he was to devote the remaining fourteen years of his life to the N.U.R.

When negotiations on the wages question were resumed after the strike, Sir Eric Geddes proposed that the wages of all employees (apart from the footplatemen whose wages had been agreed in the previous August) should be standardized 'on the average'. The suggestion was that 38s should be added to what was the average wage in each grade in July 1914. The future trend of wages should be regulated by a sliding scale based on the cost of living. For every rise or fall of 5 per cent in the cost of living (the figure for July 1914 being taken as 100) wages for all grades should rise or fall by 1s. The number of grades in the railway service was to be reduced from 512 to 88.[36] The union's negotiating committee found the Government quite unyielding in its opposition to the principle of standardization upwards. Nevertheless Mr Thomas was in favour of accepting the Government's offer. He told a mass meeting of Birmingham railwaymen on January 4, 1920, that 'having regard to all the difficulties', it was the best settlement they could get.

The majority of the branches which notified Head Office of their views on the proposals were against acceptance. The Special General Meeting which met at Unity House on January 7th, whilst welcoming the principle of standardization of railway work, carried by 54 votes to 2 a resolution instructing the E.C. to reopen negotiations in order to achieve standardization upwards. By 54 votes to 5 the conference also rejected the idea that wages should be fixed by a sliding scale, because, it was held, such an arrangement would tend to stereotype the standard of comfort and prevent any improvement in wages based on an increase in productivity. The facts that the Government offer had nothing to say about shopmen's wages and conditions, or about the Irish railwaymen and that there had been no agreement to back-date the award to August 18, 1919, were also regarded as wholly unsatisfactory features of the proposed settlement.

In view of the firm rejection of the Government's offer and the seriousness of the situation arising from it, Lloyd George cabled Sir Eric Geddes and Sir Robert Horne from Paris instructing them to fly across to discuss the question with him. He wished to avoid another national rail strike and he therefore urged the ministers to compromise.[37] The negotiating committee met Sir Eric Geddes again, after his return, on January 13th, when his attitude was more conciliatory. In the final negotiations which came after the Cabinet had discussed the question on the following day, the Government agreed to include Ireland in the settlement and to work for the inclusion of all grades in the standardization programme. In view of the administrative difficulties involved in calculating back pay to August 18, 1919, a lump sum grant of £1 per employee was suggested. The principle of standardization upwards was not conceded. By the very narrow majority of 29–27, with three neutral, the Special General Meeting on January 15th, decided to accept the settlement 'under protest'. An amendment to refer the question of the sliding scale to a full delegate meeting of the Triple Alliance was the subject of an even closer vote. It was declared 'not carried', when 28 had voted for it and 28 against, with three neutral. Up to the very last minute it had been doubtful how the voting would go. It had required all the persuasive skill of Mr Thomas to prevent a further rejection of the Government's programme.[38]

Opinion in the union remained very divided on the merits and demerits of the sliding scale. Its opponents argued that it helped to kill the fighting spirit of the rank and file and blinded them as to their true relationship to the employing class. A contributor to the *Railway Review* declared that: 'In actuality the present standard has been secured by the strength of the organization, but this fact is hidden. . . . By agreement to a sliding scale we help to make it appear that the sliding scale *as such* secures and maintains the standard, and not the organized strength of railwaymen.' Mr W. W. Craik, then Principal of the Labour College, expressing a more anarcho-syndicalist view, argued that 'unrestricted freedom of movement was indispensable for a real advance of labour', and that the scale undermined this freedom. Mr Cramp, on the other hand, contended that its acceptance did not hamper freedom of action; it was a 'foundation' on which something better could be built in the future.[40] The most ardent supporter of the sliding scale was Mr Thomas who believed that it would be conducive to industrial peace.

Also written into the agreement was the important provision that standard or 'B' rates of wages would, in no circumstances, be allowed to fall below 100 per cent above the July, 1914, average rates for each grade however much the cost of living might fall. In January 1920, with the cost of living 125 per cent over July 1914, it seemed a remote possibility that retail prices would ever be less than double those of the pre-war period. The sliding scale was thus most unpopular in the first few months after its introduction when the general level of industrial wages, following rising prices and profits, rose more rapidly than did railwaymen's wages. That criticism died down from April 1921 onwards was due to the sharp fall in prices and industrial wages after that date. By January 1921 the cost of living had, to the surprise of many, fallen well below the 100 mark and from then onwards with the real wages of railwaymen improving relatively to those of other workers, controversy on the subject practically ceased.

Meanwhile the immense task of the simplification and standardization of grades was in most cases brought to a successful conclusion. Names which recalled the earliest days of railway working and an almost infinite variety of local customs disappeared from current usage in the interests of justice and efficiency. Into the grade of 'Porter, Grade 1' were merged fifty-three former grades including those of bathroom attendant, bootblack, cab attendant, carriage searcher, coal porter, cash box porter, dispatch bag carrier, dining room attendant, gongman, luggage labeller, luggage loader and storer, pillow attendant, passenger number taker, rug porter, train indicating board attendant, train label board porter (Great Western Railway only), train reporter and van washer. Into the new grade of 'Porter, Grade 2 were merged thirty-two more grades including those of caller up, lavatory porter, station cleaner, sweeper and tideman; whilst into the new grade of 'Stableman' were merged assistant horsekeepers, cellarmen, feeder grooms (North Eastern Railway), harness cleaners, hinds (North Eastern Railway), horse dressers, horse removers, manger washers and stable whitewashers. When the work was completed by August 1, 1921, it made much simpler the task of negotiating new wages and conditions of employment.

The first opportunity to test the new negotiating machinery of Central and National Wages Boards came in the summer of 1920. With the cost of living rising by 12 per cent in the first four months of that year, with doubts being expressed as to the adequacy of the index as a real measure of working class living costs and with workers in other industries receiving larger wage increases than those gained by railwaymen, the branches demanded negotiation for a rise of £1 a week for all grades. On April 6th, a special meeting of the E.C. decided to endorse this demand.[41] The Central Wages Board heard the appeal expeditiously but would not concede the advance demanded. Hence the claim was referred to the National Wages Board.

Before that body, on May 28th, Mr Cramp put the case for the railwaymen in the course of a brilliant survey of the responsibility and duties of the various grades. It was the first time an official of the N.U.R. had to state a case to convince representatives of the general public as well as those of the companies. The backbone of his case was that the wages paid at different levels of skill on the railways were well below those paid for labour of comparable skill and responsibility in other trades. Thus a locomotive driver in his eighth year of service in that grade was drawing an average of 15s a day, whilst the South Wales collier was paid 17s 1d; even the colliery labourer got 14s 9d. He called in as witness Mr D. Thomas, a platelayer of the Rhymney Railway, who said that he was earning 61s a week whereas the colliery platelayers who worked just the other side of a fence to the railway track were being paid £4 8s 9d. Mr Joseph Astle, a signalman who worked at Bristol Junction Station and had had twenty-eight years' experience in his job, said that his wages were 77s a week compared with the Bristol Police Constable's £4 18s 0d. Mr H. C. Charlton, for eighteen years a driver on the Midland Railway, declared that drivers earned every penny of this 15s a day for the footplate of a locomotive could be 'one of the coldest places in the world'. A Liverpool shunter, Mr H. Williams, pointed out that in 1919 one in every fifteen shunters were injured and one in every 425 killed and yet his wages at 70s a week compared unfavourably with the Liverpool Corporation labourer's £4 4s 0d a week.

The companies' spokesman, Mr S. A. Clower, contended that since July 1914 the railwaymen had made progress in their wages and working conditions equal to or better than that made by men in other trades. He stressed the cost of introducing the 8-hour day and declared that if the men's claim were met in full the companies would be obliged to raise passenger fares and freight rates by at least 40 per cent.

Early in June the National Wages Board published its report. The arguments of the companies on the subject of the cost of the railwaymen's demands were accepted. Recognition was also given to the companies' claim that both the arduousness of railwaymen's work and the cost of living were less in rural districts than in industrial districts. On the other hand Mr Cramp's claim that railwaymen were underpaid in comparison with men of comparable skill in other trades could not be denied. The increases proposed by the board of from 4s to 7s 6d a week in 'industrial' districts and from 2s to 3s 6d a week in 'rural' districts by no means eliminated the numerous anomalies that existed and there was to be no back-dating of the award which was to operate from June 14th.

At the A.G.M. in Belfast early in July, Mr John Marchbank, the delegate from Glasgow, moved the rejection of the National Wages Board Award as being 'totally inadequate'. He said that no proposal could be accepted as satisfactory which created a differentiation between members in rural and industrial areas. But as a result of the vigorous pleading of Mr Thomas an amendment to accept was carried by 42 votes to 18 and one more wage crisis was over though in thousands of households the problem of coping with a high cost of living still remained.

III

In 1920 the talk was of wage increases. In 1921, with the collapse of the boom and the extremely rapid deterioration in economic conditions, the big topic of discussion was how to resist a worsening of conditions.

In the course of that one black year the value of Britain's exports declined by 47·9 per cent and of her imports by 43·7 per cent. The monthly average production of pig iron which was 669,500 tons in 1920 fell to 217,600 tons in 1921. The numbers of the unemployed jumped from 691,103 in December, 1920, to 2,171,288 or 17·8 per cent of the insured population in June 1921.[43] The first annual report of the Ministry of Transport revealed that between August 1920, and August 1921, the total tonnage of goods carried on the railways had fallen by 15·28 per cent, whilst over the same period the number of passenger journeys (exclusive of those of season-ticket holders) fell by 21·03 per cent and the number of workmen's journeys by 38·09 per cent.

Only a few months before these disasters befell the country the National Wages Board in its award of June 3, 1920, had confidently asserted that:

'In practice security of employment for the ordinary railway employee extends beyond the guaranteed week and, provided he is able to perform his work, he is practically immune from the vicissitudes of short time and unemployment.'

The experience of tens of thousands of railwaymen in 1921 belied this statement.

The companies, knowing that they would have to stand on their own feet when the period of Government control came to an end on August 15, 1921, began a drastic paring down of expenses. Early in January that year the men employed in the goods yards of the Lancashire and Yorkshire Railway were approached with proposals for the suspension of the guaranteed week which they had enjoyed since it was established by National Agreement on April 6, 1919. The E.C. considering the company's application later in January, refused to agree to the proposal on the grounds that 'short time is no solution of the present unemployment'.[44] The company dropped the scheme for the time being, but along with the other companies began to dismiss large numbers of carriage cleaners, engine cleaners, drivers, motormen, rulleymen and others from their employment. Mr Thomas told his audience at a meeting in Hornsey on February 5th that there were nearly 20,000 railwaymen out of work, and later, Ministry of Transport returns showed that dismissals continued throughout the year, the 676,802 persons employed on the railways in March 1922, being 59,068 fewer than in the March of the previous year.[45]

On some companies' lines the youths were the first to feel the effects of the slump. On the Midland Railway a number of youths and young men aged 18–23 received forms of application to continue to work for the company as *juniors* although it was part of the National Agreement in 1919 that on reaching the age of eighteen, youths should be classed as men. Some companies simply dismissed those they did not want when they reached their eighteenth birthday. These important issues were discussed at a meeting between the Standing Committee of Railway Managers and representatives of the unions held in Parliament Street, Westminster, on February 7, 1921. The N.U.R. delegation urged the companies to abolish all overtime and all tonnage and bonus working in an effort to spread more evenly the decreased volume of work. The managers promised to do what they could; but traffic on the railways was shrinking rapidly. On April 26th, when the two sides met again the managers put forward a formal and definite request for the temporary suspension of the guaranteed weeks claiming that there were at least 33,000 redundant men on the books of the companies and that the miners' strike had caused further redundancy. The union delegations agreed to submit to their respective E.C.s a proposal that there be a temporary suspension of the guaranteed week as from May 2, 1921, in order to spread more evenly the existing volume of work. The managers, for their part, agreed that the men should be provided with not less than three days' work a week. The E.C. of the N.U.R. and the other unions agreed to these proposals shortly afterwards.

The most serious attack on the living standards of the railwaymen that year came from Scotland. Mr Cramp received a letter from the Scottish companies in May in which they proposed to reduce wages by the amounts granted under the National Wages Board Award of June 1920; to abolish payment for night duty; to abandon the 8-hour day and establish a 10-hour day for drivers and firemen, except in first class shunting yards; to classify young men as adults at the age of 21 instead of 18 and to operate drivers' mileage bonuses only after 150 miles instead of after 120 miles in the case of passenger trains.[46] This was a major frontal attack on the hard-won gains of 1919 and 1920, which if wholly successful would have driven Scottish railwaymen a large part of the way back to the pre-war working conditions. The E.C. considered this application on July 1st and again in September when a resolution to turn down, out of hand, the Scottish companies' demands, was rejected on the grounds that it was better that the negotiating committee should meet the companies and note what arguments they used preparatory to facing them again in the Wages Boards. In the meantime meetings of railwaymen were organized in all the principal centres of Scotland. Speaking at the Glasgow meeting on September 25th, Mr Cramp said that if he was faced with the 'irrevocable choice' between giving up the 8-hour day or the wage advances gained in June, 1920, he would forgo the latter.[47]

What made more difficult successful resistance to the Scottish companies was the decision of the A.S.L.E. & F. to come to terms with them quite independently of any decisions of the N.U.R. As a result of meetings held in Glasgow, from September 15th, the Associated Society signed an agreement with representatives of the Scottish companies on September 27th under which the wage increases (for footplatemen) gained in June 1920, were to be removed in two stages, 5s coming off on October 17th and a further 2s on December 1st. It was also agreed that adult rates of pay should start at the age of 21 instead of 18 and that 'such overtime as the exigencies of the service required' should be worked by the locomotive staff. The N.U.R. for its part, pursued delaying tactics, fighting the companies' case first before the Central Wages Board on December 5th, and then before the National Wages Board from January 11 to 19, 1922. At this last stage of the fight Mr Matheson, for the companies, claimed that with the wages of railwaymen still 170 per cent above pre-war rates the wage burden was grievous in the extreme 'and that unless it was lessened something would break'. He showed that goods traffic on the Scottish railways had fallen by over one third during the previous twelve months. Mr Cramp was able to point out that the companies' figures of financial losses were unreliable. In fact Sir Eric Geddes himself had told the House of Commons on May 30, 1921, that the companies had 'over-stated their case'.

Considering the state of the economy at the time, the Scottish railwaymen could consider themselves lucky when they read the terms of the National Wages Board Award on January 24th. The reductions in wages were to operate only if the cost of living fell. For every fall of five points in the cost of living, there was to be a reduction of 2s (instead of 1s as had been the case in the past) but there was to be no reduction beyond the standard rate of 100 per cent above the average wages of July 1914. The age at which adult wages were to be paid was raised to 20 and not 21 as the companies had suggested. The 8-hour day was still to be regarded as 'normal', but there was to be a 'spread over' to 9 or 10 hours where economy would accrue and where a man could be booked off for short periods in the course of the day. It was a tribute to Mr Cramp's advocacy of the men's case that two of the companies' representatives on the board would not sign the majority report but drew up a dissentient one of their own. When the recommendations of the National Wages board were debated at the S.G.M. of the N.U.R. on February 2nd, a minority of the delegates were against acceptance as they believed that, if the award were accepted, the English and Irish companies would follow close on the heels of the Scottish ones and would demand their pound of flesh. The majority of the delegates accepted the view of the leadership that it was the best settlement that could be obtained in the circumstances. The resolution for acceptance was carried by 60 votes to 16.[48]

The ink of the signatures on the Scottish case was scarcely dry when the N.U.R. received applications on February 8, 1922, from the English and Welsh companies for the revised conditions of service to be applied south of the border. A lot had gone on behind the scenes on the companies' side before that application was finally drafted. Earlier in the year deputations of employers had waited upon railway company representatives in the Railway Clearing House urging upon them the need for a drastic cut in railway wages. Members of the deputation bluntly told the railway managers that the men they were employing were in many cases receiving wages no more than 40 per cent above the pre-war level, but that no railwayman was receiving less than double his pre-war rate of wages. They promised to support the companies if they agreed to reduce railway wages between 16s and 20s a week. Such a move they regarded as imperative in order to reduce freight charges and fares. A strong minority of the railway managers, including those of the Great Northern, accepted these proposals as their own as they were determined to obtain something more substantial than the Scottish Award. The decision of the English and Welsh companies to apply for the extension to them of the Scottish terms was only carried by a narrow majority. Mr Thomas acquainted the delegates to the Special General Meeting of March 17, 1922, with these facts and used them as an argument against the delaying tactic of referring the application to the Wages Boards. The majority of the delegates seem to have taken the view that they should thank their lucky stars that more serious incursions into their working conditions had not been proposed, and that it was safer not to risk the publicity which a fight with the companies before the National Wages Board would involve. It was decided by 56 votes to 23 to accept the proposals put forward by the companies.[49] The settlement of these claims by no means marked the end of the railway companies' attacks on the improved conditions, established in 1919 and 1920, but in 1922, with the fall in unemployment from the abnormally high levels of 1921, and the improvement in goods and passenger traffic, the companies were in a position to pay increased dividends. When they resumed their demands for concessions at the expense of the men in 1923 it was for a somewhat different set of reasons.

IV

It was only to be expected that the crisis in the economy and in the railway industry would have its influence on the membership, financial position and form of organization of the union itself. Like the country itself, the union sank from a position of great prosperity at the beginning of 1920 to one of depression and gloom eighteen months later. When membership was at its peak early in 1920 it was little short of the half million mark; by the end of 1922 it had fallen to 337,000, as a result of the reduction of the railway labour force and the disappointment of others, still employed, at the failure of the union to prevent some deterioration in workers' conditions (even though the deterioration was much worse in other industries). After 1922 membership again recovered to top 400,000 before the general strike. It was, however, the financial position of the union which gave its leaders most cause for alarm in 1921. For the first time in the history of the railway unions, unemployment amongst the membership reached serious dimensions. In the whole of the period 1872–1914 the number of unemployed in the union had never reached a half of one per cent of the membership. The ¾d a week (out of a total contribution of 5d) paid by members had been more than enough to cover the 15s a week (Scale A) or 12s a week (Scale B) benefit paid to unemployed members. After the war, however, with the decision of the E.C. to pay all unemployed members 15s a week from January 31, 1921,[50] and with tens of thousands of members dismissed by the companies, the expenditure on relief of unemployment increased alarmingly. From the end of February, 1921, to the end of February 1922, the union paid out nearly £1 million in donation benefit and payments from a special unemployment fund.[51] In a vain attempt to keep the unemployment fund of the union solvent, the E.C. came to the unanimous decision on January 18, 1921, to impose a special levy of 6d a week per member employed, to help those who had lost their jobs. For many months, however, the calls on the fund exceeded the contributions made to it, particularly after the E.C. in March 1921 came to the very necessary decision to pay out 2s a week to each dependent child under 14 and to pay 2s 6d a day to members working short time through circumstances beyond their control. The response of the membership to the decision to raise a special levy was disappointing. Less than half of them paid it.[52] By October 1921, the union's credit balance was down to £318,000 (after deduction of a £262,000 overdraft and the funds held in trust and in the political fund). By a resolution from the Mirfield branch, carried at the Newcastle A.G.M. in July 1921, the Industrial

General Secretary was instructed to prepare a report on the expenses of the E.C. and the administrative expenses of the head office. At the Special General Meeting, which considered Mr Cramp's report at Unity House on October 7th, it was revealed that the expenditure of the E.C. in 1920 was 988 per cent above the level of 1914. Naturally enough, in the branches sweeping statements were being made about the extravagance of the E.C., it being often overlooked that the membership had nearly doubled and prices had more than doubled in the period under consideration whilst the volume of legitimate business had greatly increased. Nevertheless the report stated that expenditure had been excessive and ought to be curtailed. Among the various economies recommended was the proposal that the payment of double expenses to members of the executive for Sunday duty should cease and that in future they should be paid at ordinary rates on these occasions. Too much money was being paid out for the holidays of men serving on the E.C. Delegates at the S.G.M. considered a resolution to reduce the size of the E.C. from twenty-four to twelve but eventually decided, in accordance with rule, to leave it to the E.C. to draft proposals for the consideration of the next A.G.M. The report had recommended that the extension building to Unity House then nearing completion at an estimated cost of £85,000 should be completed up to the point of making it weatherproof, but that no more work on interior fittings should be done and that a suitable tenant or tenants should be found willing to pay an economic rent for the lease of the building. The S.G.M. agreed to leave to the building sub-committee the implementation of these proposals. A proposal to reduce the number of A.G.M. and S.G.M. delegates from eighty to sixty was referred to the E.C. for further consideration as was a proposal to increase members' contributions by 1d a week. At this point Mr Thomas intervened with his contribution to retrenchment. He suggested the disposal of the union's motor car. The meeting turned down his offer by 52 votes to 23 as it was of the opinion that the car was 'necessary for the efficient carrying on of the union's work'.

By the summer of 1922, with some industrial recovery and a reduction in the number of unemployed, the crisis in the union's affairs had passed. Because 'the peak of the abnormal period had passed' the E.C. in June 1922, decided to discontinue the special unemployment levy.[53] Next month the A.G.M. at Bradford rejected proposals for the reduction in the size of the E.C. and the A.G.M. Gradually nervousness about the use of the extension building receded. By December 1921, the E.C. decided to accept the recommendation of the building sub-committee that the top floor of the new building should be used by the Union's Approved Society for insurance work, but deferred to March a decision about the use of the lower floor. In March caution still prevailed; the decision was postponed another three months. Finally in June it was resolved that the use of the remainder of the new building was justified and could be afforded.

The crisis of 1921 had given a severe shock to the union but it served as a salutary reminder that there was no lasting security under a capitalist economy and a largely unplanned transport system.

V

In the process of standardization of the wages and working conditions of different classes of railway employees the problem of reaching a satisfactory settlement was sufficiently great in the case of two large grades to merit individual treatment.

It was inter-union rivalry rather than the opposition of the employers which delayed a satisfactory solution of shopmen's questions. There were in the early 1920's over 600 workshops, running sheds and depots connected with the railways of England, Wales and Scotland and within them there were 1,500 different classes of workpeople and rates of pay. No wonder an arbitration court in July 1922, declared that 'the case is one of an extremely complex character'. It would have been a big enough job to simplify the grades and standardize the pay even with harmonious co-operation between the unions. Such harmony did not exist.

Generally speaking the craft unions had recruited a majority of the skilled craftsmen employed in the railway workshops, whilst the N.U.R. enrolled a larger proportion of the unskilled. The craft unions were therefore chary about accepting standardization of wages, as they feared it might mean reduced pay for the top men even though the vast majority of those employed in the shops were likely to benefit from such a change. The craft unions also thought of the men concerned as engineers, blacksmiths, coachbuilders and electricians, rather than as railwaymen. They believed they were entitled to receive the customary rate of pay earned by such craftsmen in each district of the country. Their slogan was 'Pay the district rate!' They denied the right of the N.U.R. to speak at all on behalf of the shopmen.

The N.U.R. view was that the shopmen were first and foremost railwaymen. Their possibility of obtaining regular work and a living wage depended upon the prosperity or otherwise of the railway industry as a whole. A great railway is a unity; it traverses innumerable districts, but the shopmen employed in these various districts are just as much the employees of the one big company and just as dependent on its prosperity for their livelihood as are the company's drivers, signalmen or guards. Mr Cramp summarized the industrial unionist viewpoint admirably when he wrote that:

'The fitter employed in engineering work outside of the railways is usually an employee of an undertaking which exists for the purpose of manufacturing and selling its products. . . . Now the main purpose of the railway company in building and manufacturing is entirely different.

O*

The material and articles which are produced are produced not for sale but for use; that use is for producing the one commodity which it has for sale, namely transport.'[54]

Until there was some authoritative ruling on the merits of these different policies and all the unions catering for shopmen were prepared to accept it, the railway workshops were bound to be a battlefield in the struggle between craft and industrial unionism. In his Presidential address to the A.G.M. of the N.U.R. in Belfast in July 1920, Mr W. J. Anderson said:

'The craft unions have in effect declared war on us, a challenge which the E.C. have been compelled to accept.'

An early sign of the war was the action taken by the craft unions in November 1919, when the N.U.R. had made application to the companies for an advance of 15s a week for railway shopmen. When a meeting with the companies' representatives was arranged to consider a programme which had eventually been endorsed by all the principal unions, the craft union representatives walked out of the room in protest as soon as the N.U.R. delegation entered.[55] The matter was then referred to the Industrial Court which recommended an advance of 5s a week.

A basic difficulty was that while the dispute between the N.U.R. and the craft unions continued the companies would not agree to the shopmen's claims being heard in the Central and National Wages Boards. After January 1920, other grades had access to the satisfactory machinery of negotiation; shopmen had not.

Recognizing the unsatisfactory character of this situation, the N.U.R. organized a National Conference of Railway Shopmen which was held at Unity House on May 11, 1920, for the purpose of devising improved machinery of negotiation for shopmen. Sixty delegates, together with the E.C. and the leading officials, attended. The conference endorsed a scheme drawn up by the Shops Sub-Committee of the E.C. Men in small workshops were to be represented by shop stewards elected annually by ballot. In the larger works there would be elected departmental committees whose members would choose representatives for general works committees. Shop stewards and general works committees on each main line company's system would then choose the members of a line committee dealing with questions of major importance. Finally the whole country would be divided up into districts from which, by ballot vote of all the shopmen in the area, men would be chosen to sit with the shops section representatives of the E.C. on the national shops committee.

From the beginning of May to the end of November 1920, the union organized over 100 meetings at which the shopmen's programme of a 44-hour week with a basic wage of £4 a week for unskilled, £5 a week for semi-skilled and £6 a week for skilled men was publicized together with the proposals for new machinery for dealing with shopmen's grievances.

When the N.U.R. shopmen's programme was submitted to the companies early in 1921, however, the representatives of the A.E.U. refused to attend and the companies then said that they could not negotiate with the N.U.R. alone. The E.C. of the N.U.R. then decided to refer the question to the Minister of Labour, while the Special General Meeting on February 15th decided to refer the question in dispute to the arbitration of the Industrial Court. Early in March Mr Cramp learned from the Minister of Labour that the Federation of Shipbuilding Trades and the A.E.U. had also agreed to arbitration by the Industrial Court. The E.C. then proceeded to draw up suitable terms of reference for which it quickly gained the approval of the Ministry of Labour and the railway managers; but there were more tedious delays. When the E.C. met on May 20th, it was resolved that, failing a satisfactory reply before May 26th from the Minister of Labour as to the date of the hearing of the case by the Industrial Court, the committee would meet again at once to consider means of applying pressure on the Government. On May 25th it was learned that the A.E.U. had declared its unwillingness to submit for review the rates of pay and conditions of service of such of their members who were already in receipt of rates higher than the district rates.

It was because of obstacles of this nature that it was not until February 21, 1922, that the Industrial Court began to hear the case of the companies, the N.U.R. and the craft unions.

Mr Cramp stated with great clarity the reasons for organizing the shopmen on an industrial basis. He advocated that the number of grades in the shops should be reduced to eight; that there should be a basic rate of wages for shopmen, 100 per cent in advance of that obtaining in July 1914, the minimum being 69s a week; that a sliding scale, similar to that in operation for other grades should also be applied in the shops; that overtime should be paid at time and a half rates, whilst double pay should be given for night work and Sunday work; that there should be a guaranteed day and a guaranteed week and that all shopmen should have at least six days' annual leave with pay. The craft union representatives argued that the shopmen should be paid according to the district rate for their craft. They claimed to have a majority of the shopmen in their ranks and denied the right of the N.U.R. to represent them.

The Arbitration Court Award, Number 728, which was published on July 8, 1922, proved to be a remarkable vindication of the N.U.R. contentions regarding the character of work in the railway workshops and its advocacy of standardization of conditions. The conclusion was reached:

'That the principle of regarding railway service as an industry in itself is a sound one, and that the principle should be applied to the manufacturing side of the companies' activities.'

The members of the Court decided they had no 'obligation to adopt or follow the rates of wages agreed on or recognized by employers and workers in other industries employing similar classes of labour'. They further decided that 'a substantial advance' should be made towards standardization 'without however necessitating changes in rates of wages greater than should be loyally accepted by the side on whom in any particular case the burden may fall'. Under Schedule A of the report all the railway workshops were classified into five groups (the N.U.R. had advocated three) whilst in schedules B–E, rates of pay in each grade were specified. In matters of practical application the award of the Court had not gone as far as the N.U.R. would have liked it to go, but in its statements of principle and ultimate objective it completely endorsed the industrial unionist viewpoint.

Not all of the companies welcomed the award and the directors of the London and North Eastern Railway were not at first prepared to apply the award to all parts of their system. In consequence, shopmen in these districts were receiving wages well below those recommended by the Court. Thus plumbers were paid 41s instead of 46s. Cabinet makers received between 37s and 43s instead of 46s and there were many other examples. The E.C.s patience was becoming exhausted. It resolved at its July 1923 meeting to give the Directors of the London and North Eastern Railway fourteen days to apply Award No. 728 on the Great Northern section of the line. Failing the directors' compliance, a strike would be called.[57] At this stage Sir Montague Barlow of the Ministry of Labour interviewed members of the E.C. requesting that notices should be withdrawn so that he could have time to negotiate with the company and the craft unions. On July 30th, the E.C. acceded to his request, and accepted an offer of the London and North Eastern Railway directors to submit the matter to the arbitration of the Industrial Court.[58] Early in August Mr Cramp approached the craft unions for a meeting to concert plans to persuade the London and North Eastern Railway to adopt the award. When the N.U.R. met the delegation from the craft unions they found them reluctant to act. They said that if the award were implemented some of their members would suffer as a result. Although Mr Thomas emphasized that the vast majority of the shopmen concerned would benefit to the extent of a total of 'several thousand pounds a week', and although he proposed they should set up a small committee to work out a scheme by which none of the members of craft unions or N.U.R. would suffer, the craft union delegates would not agree. Shortly afterwards Mr Cramp told a meeting at Perth that 97 per cent of the Great Northern men would have benefited by the application of the award. It was not until April 15, 1924, that the Industrial Court ruled that it was 'advisable that decision number 728 should be adopted on the Great Northern Section of the London and North Eastern Railway'. In an effort to placate the company and the craft unions it suggested that the award need not be applied until March 1, 1925. The men from whom the award was withheld all those months showed an amazing patience.

Despite the fact that by its Award No. 728 the Industrial Court had brought about a greater degree of uniformity of wages and conditions of service for shopmen, the fact remained that they were still at a disadvantage compared with other grades. About 87 per cent of those employed in the railway service had access to valuable and easily available machinery of negotiation—Sectional Councils and Central and National Wages Boards operating since the beginning of 1920, whilst shopmen were still denied these opportunities of having their problems examined, despite the fact that the Industrial Court had ruled that shopmen were railwaymen. These were facts well understood in the N.U.R. whose A.G.M. at Crewe on July 4, 1923, carried unanimously a resolution couched in the following terms:

'This Congress places on record its considered judgement that there can be no permanent peace in the industry until all railway employees are enabled to have their rates of wages and conditions of employment negotiated through the same tribunal, so establishing equality of treatment, and providing for the solution of railway labour problems in a broad and comprehensive way.'

Although the resolution was described by Mr Thomas as 'an olive branch' to encourage a spirit of conciliation in the railway industry, it was not until August 15, 1927, that an agreement was reached for the setting-up of works and departmental line committees for shopmen with an established procedure for settling disputes. Local Departmental Committees and Sectional Councils had functioned for other grades since 1920.

Disunity on the trade-union side had led, before 1913, to the very patchy and incomplete organization of the shopmen. During and after the war the craft unions' refusal to recognize the right of the N.U.R. to speak on behalf of the shopmen and the refusal of the N.U.R. to abandon its interest, particularly in the hitherto largely unorganized unskilled and semi-skilled grades, resulted in this group of railway workers being often behindhand in respect of wages, conditions of work and negotiating machinery when compared with the other grades in the service. It was a clear illustration of what happened when a section of the workers in the industry were not organized on an industrial basis.

VI

In the immediate post-war years the signalmen were not plagued by inter-union disputes such as those which beset the shopmen. The United Pointsmen's and Signalmen's Society which had claimed to cater specially for this grade since its foundation in 1880 was merged into the N.U.R. in 1913. By 1920 the overwhelming majority of signalmen were members of the

N.U.R. On the other hand signalmen, by the nature of their work, are perhaps more widely dispersed than any other major grade in the service, with the possible exception of the permanent-way men. In no other grade on the railways is there such a varying quantity of work and responsibility. No two signal boxes are exactly alike in their construction and in the quantity and quality of work performed in them. At one extreme there are signal boxes which pass but a handful of trains daily; at the other are giant marvels of railway signalling engineering whose train records show the passing of nearly 2,000 trains a day. Some boxes pass only a moderate amount of traffic in winter but have a very heavy summer holiday traffic. In the early post-war years these very diverse working conditions were the breeding ground of a great diversity of opinions among signalmen as to the best method of standardization of wages and working conditions.

Amongst no group of railway workers was discussion of the post-war programme more widespread or more animated than amongst signalmen during the last months of the war. More vigilance committees were formed of signalmen than of any other grade. No sooner had the fighting on the Western Front ended than the activists in the Vigilance Committees organized—without the authority or co-operation of Unity House—a National Signalmen's Conference, held in Birmingham late in 1918. It was at this conference that a designedly attractive programme was drafted with the demand for an irreducible minimum of £5 a week for all signalmen and the grouping of the boxes into three classes.[59] All over the country meetings in support of this glittering programme were attended by enthusiastic 'bobbies'. A National Signalmen's Council was formed of those who had drafted the programme.

In the meantime the Traffic Sub-Committee of the E.C. (which included Signalmen) persuaded the E.C. to sponsor a scheme of classification of signal boxes on the basis of the number of lever movements carried out by the signalmen working in them. Lest it be imagined that the proposal—'The Marks System'—was a brand new one, it should be pointed out that as far back as November 23, 1886, at a meeting of Midland Railway employees held in Leicester, a signalman startled his hearers by declaring that on the previous night he had worked thirteen hours, during which time 148 trains had passed his box and over 2,000 lives had been entrusted to his care. He had written 3,500 figures and been responsible for 1,600 bell beats and 2,300 dial signals and had pulled over the levers 500 times. For the whole of this work he had been paid at the rate of 3½d an hour. The publication of his statement in the *Leicester Daily Mercury* on the following day set in motion a discussion in the correspondence columns of newspapers all over the world on the wages of signalmen and on the best means of rewarding signalmen according to their responsibilities.[60] The North Eastern Railway already had a marks system in operation by the outbreak of the First World War, but the other main line companies had varying and cruder methods of classification. It was argued in favour of the marks system that it was the best way—despite the fact that there were bound to be some anomalies—of rewarding a signalman according to the amount of work performed and the degree of responsibility undertaken.

As the E.C.'s plan in favour of the marks system met with a hostile reception in the Vigilance Committees it was decided officially to summon a National Conference of Signalmen to Unity House for May 13–14, 1920, to give the signalmen an opportunity of stating what they wanted. The sixty delegates decided by large majorities to reject the marks system and to support instead the grouping of the boxes into four classes drawn from the existing classification. Wages were to be £4 at the minimum and £6 at the maximum. They wanted every signalman employed in a 'heavy' box, on reaching 55 to have the option to transfer to a lighter box without loss of pay. Conditions made applicable to signalmen should also apply to relief signalmen. At the A.G.M. in Belfast two months later, however, the resolution to adopt the programme drawn up at the Unity House Conference and to forward it to the Minister of Transport, was defeated, and an amendment supported by Mr Marchbank and others that 'the standardization of signalmen's conditions shall be on a servitude basis', was carried by 46 votes to 14, the six signalmen delegates present all supporting the amendment.[61]

In the meantime the companies had been preparing a classification of boxes on the marks system. They told the N.U.R. negotiating committee (the traffic sub-committee of the E.C.—which included two signalmen— and the two signalmen representatives appointed by the A.G.M.) that they could put a marks system into operation from October 1, 1920. This could not be done as the N.U.R. delegation had to reveal that the union now favoured classification on a servitude basis. This was a vital turning point in the negotiations. It was perhaps the last opportunity there was of effecting a reasonably good settlement in terms of cash. In view of what happened later, there can be little doubt that it would have been better policy to have accepted the marks system and to have worked for an elimination of anomalies and for a reduction of the number of marks determining the particular class of signal box.

When representatives from the Signalmen's National Council met the traffic sub-committee of the union on November 5, 1920, to discuss the next moves, they decided that the wisest policy, all things being considered, would be to adopt the marks system, after all, with a classification of boxes into six groups. Through the mediation of the Ministry of Transport, a meeting was arranged with the companies for February 8, 1921, at the St Pancras Hotel. It took four more meetings from May 1st to August 2nd to complete the draft of conditions of employment. The E.C. finally gave its blessing to the plan on August 6th.

The Special General Meeting of the N.U.R. summoned to Unity

House on August 11th, considered this proposal for the division of the boxes into seven classes on the basis of the marks system as follows:

Class	Wages per week	Marks
Special	75s	375 and over
1st	70s	300–374
2nd	65s	255–299
3rd	60s	150–224
4th	55s	75–149
5th	50s	30– 74
6th	48s	1– 29

Samples of marks to be awarded included, for pulling or pushing a lever, one mark; for replacing a lever, one mark; for opening gates worked by a wheel, 5 marks, and for closing the same, a further five marks; for opening and closing a wicket gate 2½ marks each operation. There were additional marks for bell signals, for entries in the train registers, for trimming lamps, for cautioning drivers on entering a section of the line and for many other operations. A signalman in a busy box got no marks for being obliged to squeeze a sandwich lunch in between entering trains in a book, pulling levers and answering the telephone. Under the proposed classification there were only 811 men in the special class compared with 976 in Class 1; 1,936 in Class 2; 4,427 in Class 3; 9,910 in Class 4; 6,963 in Class 5 and 883 in Class 6.[62] This was a much heavier grouping on the lower classes than the signalmen had advocated.

After a discussion lasting for two days the meeting though 'strongly of the opinion that the conditions set out were not satisfactory to the men concerned' passed, by 56 votes to 18, a resolution asserting that it was in 'the best interests of the signalmen to accept the settlement in order to secure a national and collective basis'.

This agreement was undoubtedly far less satisfactory than those reached for other grades at an earlier date. The signalmen had discussed their programme more fully and for a greater length of time than other grades had done. They discussed it all through the months of the boom of 1919 and 1920, until finally they scrambled home with an agreement negotiated in the depths of the trade depression and finally accepted three days before the date on which the companies were to be freed from Government control and therefore free to suggest district agreements rather than a national one if it suited them. As Mr Thomas so often pointed out the conditions of service of other grades had been negotiated on a rising market; the signalmen's settlement was negotiated on a falling market. It was for these reasons that, under the new classification, 17,756 signalmen were to be paid less than £3 a week and that it was possible for Mr Thomas to declare that he did not believe there was a solitary signalman in the country who wholeheartedly approved the agreement.[63]

The reluctant approval given by the union on August 12th did not, as it happened, put an end to the matter. When the companies began to apply the scheme early in 1922 they quickly found that a great many anomalies were created. Their representatives discussed these difficulties with an N.U.R. delegation on February 14th when they proposed that the marks for the opening and closing of gates should be reduced, and that where they found that the marks system put a man into a lower classification than they felt his work justified, they should be free to upgrade him. Likewise, when they considered a man's marks were too high they should be free to downgrade him. Mr Cramp pointed out some of these anomalies to the delegates at the Special General Meeting on March 17th. The Haverstock Hill Box in London controlled four through-lines with no points. The next box to it, Carlton Road Junction, Kentish Town, controlled one of the busiest and most complicated junctions. In pre-war times these differences were recognized by the Carlton Road signalman being paid 37s and his Haverstock Hill colleague 31s, but under the new dispensation both men would receive 65s. The E.C. and the officials were therefore in favour of giving the companies the latitude they desired, subject to the right of the union to raise the subject of a man's classification at Sectional Council or higher level. The S.G.M. accepted this viewpoint, turning down a resolution to reopen negotiations, by 54 to 22, and carrying an amendment to accept the companies' proposals by 46 votes to 29.

All the evidence shows that dissatisfaction with the S.G.M. decision was widespread amongst the signalmen. Resolutions passed by Vigilance Committees in Crewe, Derby, Mansfield, Nuneaton, Port Talbot and Sheffield (to mention only a few cases) expressed strong disapproval of the action taken.[64] Alternative schemes for the classification of the signal boxes multiplied like rabbits. The Annual Meeting of the Signalmen's National Movement held in the Milton Hall, Deansgate, Manchester on August 26th and 27th, was told of six, and resolved to forward all of them to the Vigilance Committees and District Councils which would eventually inform a small committee of five which scheme they preferred. The scheme which commanded majority support would become the policy of the movement.[65]

When the companies renewed their attack on the wages and conditions of employment in 1923 and 1924 a minority of the signalmen were sufficiently discontented to form a breakaway union.

VII

The basis of the companies' claim for further economies at the expense of their staff was different in 1923 and 1924 from what it had been in 1921 and 1922. In the earlier period the sharp fall in the volume of their own business had prompted the economies. At the later date it was mainly pressure from manufacturers and traders for a reduction of freight charges which eventually induced the companies to attempt further inroads into the earlier agreements on wages and hours of work. On April 18, 1923, Sir Herbert Walker on behalf of the Railway Managers wrote to Mr Cramp in the following terms:

'The railway companies are being very strongly urged by all classes of traders to make a further reduction in conveyance charges in the general interests of the rehabilitation of the industry of the country. The railway companies cannot remain insensible to this constant pressure indefinitely and they are of opinion that some concession must immediately be made in the interests of trade generally and as a contribution towards the solution of the grave problem of unemployment.'[66]

In particular Sir Eric Geddes who left the Ministry of Transport in 1922 and was now spokesman for the F.B.I. was speaking of the imperative necessity for the reduction of transport charges.[67] The E.C. was not impressed. At its special meeting on April 26th, it instructed the negotiating sub-committee to tell the companies' representatives that it did not feel there was any justification for the new claims. They were aware of the fact that the companies' wages bill had been reduced by at least £43 million between August 1920 and March 1923.[68]

Early in July the detailed proposals of the companies were published. It was suggested that if and when the cost of living fell to no more than 70 per cent over 1914, the remaining war bonus should be entirely withdrawn; that the special payment for night duty performed between the hours of 10.0 p.m. and 4.0 a.m. should be cancelled; that the minimum pay rates for Sunday duty should be withdrawn and that instead men should be paid at time and a half rate for the number of hours worked. The most important of the proposed changes, however, was the recommendation that bonus rates for drivers and firemen in charge of passenger trains should operate after 150 miles instead of after 120.

The two sides discussed these proposals on July 17th, but as the N.U.R. delegation indicated they could not be accepted, the companies' claim was referred to the Central Wages Board which examined it at the end of September. As was generally expected, no agreement was reached at this stage and the claim therefore came before the National Wages Board in November. Whilst the board would not agree to the companies' proposal that the sliding scale should be abolished and that the war bonus should disappear, it did recommend reductions in pay for Sunday duty and the introduction of the new mileage clauses for footplatemen. These new conditions of service though regretted by the N.U.R., A.S.L.E. & F., and R.C.A. representatives on the National Wages Board were accepted by them all since all of them signed the report. The Executive Committees of all three unions also accepted the report, but whilst the N.U.R. Special General Meeting held on December 21st reluctantly agreed to endorse the decision—the voting was 59 to 20 in favour of the platform—the Annual Assembly of Delegates of the A.S.L.E. & F. decided to organize a ballot vote of the members of that union, to ascertain whether or not they favoured strike action, in the hope that this would result in the withdrawal of the new mileage clauses. By a 6–1 majority the Associated Society's membership showed its inclination to fight and the strike began at midnight on January 19, 1924.

In the view of Messrs Thomas and Cramp and the majority of the E.C. of the N.U.R., the strike was to be deplored because it would destroy confidence in the negotiating machinery set up in 1920. Representatives of all the unions had signed the agreement and all the unions should loyally carry it out, for once the tradition of loyalty to negotiated agreements was broken, then the companies could also refuse to operate any award of the National Wages Board they did not like. Members of the N.U.R. should carry out the decision of their democratically elected body, the S.G.M., which had endorsed acceptance. As far as the leaders of the N.U.R. were concerned, the statement made by the *Manchester Guardian* at the start of the strike that 'the comments of Mr Thomas and Mr Bromley make it quite clear that the A.S.L.E. & F. is fighting the N.U.R. quite as much as it is the railway companies', was widely regarded as an accurate summing-up of the situation.[70]

In reply to inquiries from many branches, a telegram was sent from Unity House on January 21st: 'Inform our members who may be picketing with the Associated, that this strike is for propaganda purposes against our union. All our men must resent this by remaining loyal to our union. They must stop picketing immediately and actively assist our members who are remaining loyal to our union's instructions. Signed, C. T. Cramp.'

On the other hand the Executive of the A.S.L.E. & F. could point to the fact that the decision to strike was made not by Mr Bromley but by an overwhelming majority of the membership in a ballot vote. Critics of Mr Thomas were asserting that ever since the December 1923 election had resulted in the formation of a Labour Government with Mr Thomas as its Colonial Secretary, he had been strongly opposed to any drastic action by the unions. Within a few days of the date of commencement of the strike he was due to sit next to the Prince of Wales at a banquet.

The effects of the footplatemen's strike were unevenly felt. At the time the A.S.L.E. & F. had 59,000 members divided between the three grades of drivers, firemen and cleaners, whilst the N.U.R. membership in the same grades numbered between 20,000 and 30,000. Generally speaking the stoppage was most complete where the A.S.L.E. & F. was strong, as in many districts of the Great Western Railway, whilst services were near normal where a large proportion of the locomotivemen were members of the N.U.R. as in parts of South Wales and the North East. On the South Eastern section of the Southern Railway, services were well maintained, whilst in the London area and Norwich areas of the London and North Eastern Railway there was a very serious curtailment of normal services. N.U.R. men were naturally loath to appear as blacklegs. Many accusations were made that they had blacklegged the A.S.L.E. & F. men, but the truth of the matter was that hundreds of N.U.R. men all over the country sat in the mess rooms all day because they had instructions from Unity House that where one of a team was an A.S.L.E. & F. man on strike and the other a member of the N.U.R., the N.U.R. man was not to go out or to find a substitute fireman. The very last instruction that Mr Cramp gave over the telephone in the course of the strike was to members at Dunston-on-Tyne asking whether three jobs done by A.S.L.E. & F. men before the strike should be performed by the N.U.R. men. The advice was that the jobs were not to be done. In the Nottingham area there was an ironical situation with N.U.R. men who had struck work from the start, in sympathy with the A.S.L.E. & F., trying to persuade local members of the 'Associated' to join the strike, whilst at Bristol N.U.R. drivers refused to work with firemen members of the A.S.L.E. & F. who refused to strike. Whereas in Mr Thomas's own constituency in Derby over 100 locomotivemen members of the N.U.R. joined the strike, at Saltley (Birmingham) 80 per cent of the driver and fireman members of the A.S.L.E. & F. were at work.[71] In some cases N.U.R. men who supported the strike at the start, had second thoughts and decided that it was best to obey the decision of the S.G.M. that men should continue at work. Thus at Hull 400 N.U.R. men who had joined the strike went back to work on January 21st.

It was claimed by the leaders of the N.U.R. that it would have been possible to obtain without a strike, all the concessions that the A.S.L.E. & F. obtained in the final discussions with the companies at Euston Hotel which led to the return to work after January 29th. The biggest concession made to Mr Bromley was that the changes for locomotivemen would be introduced gradually instead of suddenly, that from January 29th to the beginning of July 1924, mileage bonuses should be paid for runs of over 130 miles; between July 1924 and January 1925, the bonuses would operate after 140 miles; and after January 1925, they would operate after 150 miles. The companies also agreed to a classification of drivers on shunting duties more favourable to the men. On the other hand when the companies' representatives were interviewed by the General Council of the T.U.C. on January 19th, before the strike began, they gave an assurance that if the strike notices were called off an immediate meeting with the unions would be held 'with the view of considering and alleviating the hardships affecting individuals or groups'.[72] On January 29th, the companies alleged that their offer made ten days earlier embodied 'in essence' all the A.S.L.E. & F. had now received. The General Council, too, had urged John Bromley to accept the offer on January 19th. On January 24, 1924, Mr Cramp wrote to John Bromley reminding him that before the National Wages Board had met he, Mr Cramp, had twice (at Mexborough and Wakefield) appealed for united action in dealing with the companies' claims. Had these appeals been answered it was very probable that the strike could have been averted.[73] The locomotive sub-committee of the N.U.R. was certainly not slow in looking after the interests of the footplatemen members of the union. On the day following the ending of the strike it took Mr Cramp and the President (Mr John Marchbank) to interview a committee of the General Managers and it succeeded in amending and improving the settlement made by the A.S.L.E. & F. the previous day. In particular the managers promised to issue instructions that short terms of Sunday duty would be kept to a minimum.[74]

<h2 style="text-align:center">VIII</h2>

Whatever may be said in favour or against the strike itself, there can be no mistaking the fact that the cause of trade-union unity was greatly harmed by it. At the A.G.M. of the N.U.R. in Belfast in July 1920, the President, Mr W. J. Abraham, speaking of inter-union relations, expressed the opinion that 'a far greater feeling of friendship' existed between the A.S.L.E. & F. and the N.U.R. 'than ever before'. This feeling was manifested by the appearance of Mr Thomas and Mr Cramp on the platform on the occasion of the A.S.L.E. & F. Annual Assembly of Delegates in May 1920 and Mr Bromley's similar appearance at the N.U.R. Annual General Meeting in July. Since then, however, there had been a growth of criticism on both sides. By 1923 abusive articles were appearing in the *Locomotive Journal* and the *Railway Review*. For a time after the 1924 strike, relations were so bad that the letters from Mr Cramp to Mr Bromley went unanswered. Some of the N.U.R. rank and file argued that it would have been better, once the rank and file of the A.S.L.E. & F. had decided to support a strike, to have recalled the delegates to the N.U.R. Special General Meeting so that they could consider what action they should take in the light of the new circumstances. It might have been possible in this way to have avoided the bitterness which came through the N.U.R. members continuing on duty whilst members of the A.S.L.E. & F. were on strike.

The policy of the leadership of the N.U.R. in the footplatemen's strike presented a golden opportunity for the malcontents amongst the signalmen to get busy and organize a sectionalist union. One of the ablest regular contributors to the *Railway Review* since the war had been Mr A. E. Rochester, a signalman employed on the Great Western Railway. With his lively, witty and well informed articles he had led the campaign against the marks system and the settlement of August 12, 1922. As far back as

August 1921, he had warned that it was 'being whispered loudly that the only way' was 'to re-establish a separate union for signalmen'. At the time he had denounced such suggestions as 'pernicious' since they 'would be merely carrying out the hope and intentions of the railway directorates' and would be 'hailed with glee by the sectionalists in the locomotive department'.[75] In January 1924, however, he submitted an article, written while the strike was in progress and entitled 'Impeach the "Leaders"'. It is scarcely surprising that the editor of the *Railway Review* refused to publish it. Neither did it improve Mr Rochester's chances of remaining a member of the N.U.R. when he took the offending article to John Bromley who needed little persuasion to agree to find the money for its publication as a leaflet. The tone of the statement is exemplified in the first two sentences in which 'the impeachment of Messrs Cramp, Marchbank and Thomas' was demanded. He accused that 'unholy trinity' of conduct 'prejudicial to good order and discipline, of shamefully abandoning their post in the face of the enemy, and of wilful, deliberately planned treachery towards a neighbouring unit during an attack'. He argued that owing to the 'distinct change of circumstances' caused by the decision of the rank and file of the A.S.L.E. & F. to strike, the N.U.R. Annual General Meeting delegates should have been summoned so that the strife between the unions might have been avoided. He foretold a growth of sectionalism and declared that 'even the signalmen' would be 'given furiously to think'.

In the *Railway Review* the editor wrote of legal proceedings being instituted against Mr Rochester so that when he (Mr Rochester) received a request from the E.C. to attend before that body to explain his conduct he declined the offer. On March 8th, however, he received a further request to meet the E.C. which said that a complaint had been made against him by Shepherd's Bush and other branches and that he should therefore attend to answer the charges. This he did. Outside of the Board Room at Unity House when the interview was over he asked the office manager if he could be paid his expenses. He was told 'There are the stairs; get down them'. In a fit of temper at being summoned to appear before the governing body of the union and then being so summarily treated, he struck the office manager in the face and proceeded into the Board Room, demanding to see Mr Cramp who was obliged to call a policeman to have him ejected from the building. Earlier he had taken an uncompromising line with the E.C. 'refusing to cut out one comma' of his leaflet.[76]

Had more tact been used in dealing with Mr Rochester, it is possible that the whole incident would have been forgotten and his talents retained for the benefit of the union. He told the A.G.M. at York on July 10th, when they were considering his appeal, that he had approached Mr Thomas in the Colonial Office before the publication of his leaflet. He claimed that if that gentleman had said 'Let's have a chat as to what had happened', things 'might have been different'. Instead he was given a brusque unfriendly reception. When he saw Mr Cramp after the publication of the leaflet, he said, 'Some people say I have hurt the N.U.R. If you will show me the way I will put matters right in an article in next week's *Railway Review*.'

But Mr Cramp did not consider this enough. He wanted Mr Rochester to make a public apology. That he was not prepared to do.

By the time the A.G.M. delegates assembled at York in July, it was almost certainly too late to repair the damage. Mr Rochester was given a very fair hearing with ample time to justify his actions, but only fourteen delegates voted for the appeal against his expulsion from the union, whilst fifty-five others upheld the action of the E.C. in expelling him.[77]

About a month earlier, thirteen men had met at the house of Mr Charles Breton at 11 Ranleigh Road, Paddington, and had decided to form the Union of Railway Signalmen. Discontent with the working of the marks system as well as some sympathy with Mr Rochester in view of his treatment at Unity House led to this unfortunate event. When the National Council of the National Signalmen's Movement met at Ipswich on May 11, 1924, it elected a sub-committee of five to wait on the E.C. of the N.U.R. to persuade its members to approach the railway managers for a meeting to discuss the abolition of the marks system. Though the deputation was advised to attend at Unity House on June 6th for the purpose of meeting the E.C., on appearing at the appointed time, it was kept waiting for two hours and was then told that its application had been referred to the Traffic Sub-Committee. Only two of the five members of the deputation (the secretary of the National Signalmen's Movement not being one) were seen by the sub-committee.

In the meantime, a prominent member of the National Signalmen's Movement, Mr George Richards, met Mr J. Bromley who told him that he was certain that the A.S.L.E. & F. would offer a substantial loan of money to any group of signalmen who decided to form a new union. The first accounts of the U.R.S. show that £1,000 was so 'borrowed'. A further £2,000 was 'borrowed' later.[78]

Fortunately the volume of support for the new union was meagre. Out of the signalmen in the country less than 250 had joined the U.R.S. by June, 1925. The 'bobbies' for all their grumbles about the marks system and the shortcomings of the leadership of the N.U.R., were rightly sceptical of the ability of the new organization to pay the benefits it offered. For a subscription of 6d a week it was offering a pension of 2s 6d a week to all with five years' paid up membership, out of work benefit of £1 a week for twelve weeks and strike benefit of 25s a week plus 2s a week for each dependent child. This was almost tantamount to accepting money under false pretences. The majority of the leadership of the National

Signalmen's Movement issued a manifesto of loyalty to the N.U.R. in August 1924:

'We stand by the old motto—"The interests of one are the interests of all", and consider the policy the new union advocates a suicidal policy entirely opposed to real working class progress. . . . The fact is patent to all willing to see that the enormous concessions granted to railwaymen during the last eleven years are solely due to the immense power that the N.U.R. has been able to wield.'[79]

Mr Cramp had no liking for litigation. When he received an undertaking from Mr Bromley that he would not dispatch further copies of the leaflet 'Impeach the Leaders' to the branches of the A.S.L.E. & F. for distribution, he regarded this matter as closed.[80]

IX

After the retreats experienced since 1921, increasingly the rank and file were expressing the opinion that it was time to call a halt. Not only were reductions in wages and (in some cases) lengthening of hours, increasing the arduousness of railway work; for some their work was also becoming more dangerous.

A particularly obnoxious form of economy was that of some companies increasing the 'lengths' for which gangs of platelayers were responsible, or reducing the number of men in a gang or increasing the number of extraneous duties the members of a gang were called upon to perform. When economy was the order of the day, gangs which were under strength due to sickness were sent out without substitutes being provided for the sick men. The work carried great responsibilities. A contemporary ganger described it:

'Every day brings its own work. Slacks in the top, crooks, slack bolts, loose chair fastenings, loose keys, weeds, washy places in the road bed, weak places in the fence, holes in the cart roads, mud to scrape up and remove, points to clean and oil.'[81]

If, for any reason, the number of men in a gang was reduced or the length of track for which the gang was responsible was increased, the standard of maintenance of the permanent way was likely to fall. In 1923 and 1924, this happened, and the number of railway accidents arising from defects in the permanent way increased. The Annual Report of the Minister of Transport for 1923 showed that the number of derailments—418—had increased by 30 per cent over the average of the two previous years. Rule 273 of the Companies' Rule Book made it clear that each ganger or foreman was responsible for the appointment of a competent lookout man to warn members of the gang of the approach of trains. When the companies understaffed the gangs, the foremen were more reluctant to release a man solely for the purpose of undertaking lookout duties, and in consequence, Mr Cramp felt obliged to issue a circular to all branches reminding permanent-way men of their rights under the rule. And yet the toll of fatalities to the permanent-way men continued. One well-informed veteran of this grade informed the author in July 1960 that he could recall seven men killed—most through a temporary lapse of thoughtfulness but some indirectly through the pursuit of economies—within a stone's throw of a bridge of signals just north of Clapham Junction.[82] It was working conditions such as these which brought discontent with the policy of retreat and increasing insistence on a new campaign for improved conditions.

An article by Mr A. E. Rochester 'Let's Ask for More', published in the *Railway Review* on June 15, 1923, led the way. He pointed out that the companies had increased their dividends in 1922, whilst their reserve funds had mounted from £17½ million in 1913 to £121 million in 1923. One of the railway managers, Mr Sam Fay, had been indiscreet enough to declare that the financial position of railways had 'never been as sound' as it then was 'since railways were first instituted'. The branches followed with demands that the E.C. launch a new all-grades programme, and eventually, at its quarterly meeting in June 1924, the E.C. in response to requests from 'numerous branches', instructed Mr Cramp to draw up a programme which would include demands on behalf of the shopmen.[83] There followed in July grade conferences of the supervisory staff, signalmen and others to draft programmes, that for the salaried and supervisory grades being jointly agreed between the R.C.A. and the N.U.R.

The all-grades programme of December 1924, included the demand for the restoration of the 120-mile limit as the normal daily run of passenger drivers with provision of proper breaks for the taking of food and a basic daily wage of 16s for drivers, 12s 6d for firemen and 6s to 10s for cleaners. For signalmen more marks were demanded for many actions performed in the box, with a 6-hour day for those men whose marks exceeded 349. For guards and all traffic grades there was to be an allowance of 30 minutes for meals within the working day. The hours of permanent-way men were to be limited to forty-four a week, while their gangs were to be kept up to pre-war strength. Porters' wages were to be raised from 60s to 63s a week and ticket collectors' from 69s to 71s. Improved rates of pay were suggested for dining car staff, goods and cartage staff, dock staff, women carriage staff and all the clerical and supervisory grades. Twelve working days were suggested in place of six for holidays and pensions for all permanent-way staff on reaching sixty years of age were proposed.[84]

In the meantime both the N.U.R. and the A.S.L.E. & F. had appealed to the Wages Boards to prevent the coming into operation on January 1, 1925, of the 150-mile rule in the mileage clause for drivers. Before the National Wages Board on December 18, 1924, Mr Thomas pointed out the increased weight of the trains and the increased responsibilities of the enginemen as reasons for retaining the lower mileage limit. Mr Clower, for the companies, said that the traders of the country had 'been for a long time pleading with the companies for help'. They said that railway wages were at an abnormally high level compared with the wages paid in other industries. The award of the National Wages Board on December 19, 1924, augured ill for the prospects of favourable hearing for the all-grades programme in the following year. The board ruled that having regard to all the circumstances, it would not be desirable to make any alteration in the mileage payment agreement.[85]

No sooner had the campaign for the all-grades programme got under way than the companies countered with their own programme of proposed economies and wage reductions. When the negotiating committee of the union met the general managers on February 3, 1925, and Mr Cramp put the case for the improvements demanded, Sir Ralph Wedgwood replied that in view of the fact that the settlement of the union's claims would cost £45 million, the companies were compelled to refuse to agree to any part of the programme. Then he produced the companies' alternative programme for the reduction in wages of all conciliation grades by 4s a week in London and industrial areas and 6s a week in rural areas. He said that they would consider claims on behalf of shopmen only if all unions concerned supported them.

The E.C. meeting on February 6th, to consider this impasse resolved to take the case, including that for the shopmen, through the Wages Boards and to call a Special General Meeting if this proved necessary.[86]

Early in July the companies published their revised proposals with as principal features a 5 per cent reduction in all salaries and wages (directors and officers included!). The sliding scale agreement was to continue and railway workshops were to be restored to full-time working.

When it came to the point, the case for the shopmen was not put before the Wages Boards. Mr Thomas told the delegates of the A.G.M. at Southport in July 1925, why this decision was made. The companies could argue that the National Wages Board was not, by its constitution, entitled to consider shopmen's claims. If the N.U.R. had persisted in lumping the shopmen's claim together with the others they would have been ruled out of court and the companies would have proceeded to make their claim for reductions without any defence being put up by the N.U.R. He confessed that in the summer of 1925 'it did not seem the happiest moment to choose even to put up a case at all' for the all-grades programme and he and Mr Cramp therefore resolved that the best tactic was 'deliberately to play for delay'.[87]

In November the rival claims came before the National Wages Board, Mr Clower arguing the case for the companies and Mr Cramp justifying the N.U.R.'s new programme. The result was a stalemate. The board, in its report on December 9th, was 'not satisfied that in the present circumstances a sufficient case' had 'been made by the railway companies for a reduction in the base and current rates' of wages. On the other hand it felt 'unable to entertain any of the applications made on behalf of the trade unions'.

What circumstances prevented the acceptance of even a single major item of the all-grades programme? The answer lies in the growth of road competition and the deflationary depression in industry. The members of the board were obviously impressed by Mr Clower's statements about road haulage competition. In the report it was admitted to be a 'serious menace to the railway industry'. Mr Clower had told the board that the total number of motor licences had increased by 124 per cent or 830,000 since 1922, and that the number of commercial road vehicles had grown from 131,866 to 216,966 in the same period. The board in its report agreed that it was unfair that the road hauliers were 'in a position to select the traffic for which they cater and to vary their charges to meet the circumstances of each particular case' whereas 'the railway companies are common carriers and have no such freedom'. It was also unfair that although the railway companies contributed £7,826,503 or about 19 per cent of their net revenue to the local rates, much of which contribution went towards road maintenance, they were not permitted a free use of the roads. The companies were 'thus put in a position of assisting to subsidize a formidable and increasing competition', a state of affairs which 'might not to be allowed to continue'.[88]

What the report did not state was that Parliament had in 1922 turned down a Bill 'to empower the London and North Western, the Midland, the Lancashire and Yorkshire, and the Furness Railways to provide and use road vehicles', although Mr Thomas had written to *The Times* on February 16, 1922, declaring that the companies in this request had 'the backing of the whole rank and file of the railway workers'. One reason for the rejection of the railway companies' Bill was given in the report of the Select Committee of the House of Commons which investigated in 1921 the question as to whether the railways should be given powers to compete on more equal terms with road hauliers. The report signed by Mr J. H. Balfour Browne, K.C., Mr Arthur Watson and Sir Thomas Williams stated that:

'One of the objections to the granting of general powers to the railway companies to carry goods by road was that it would have the indirect effect of increasing the power of the railway workers' unions—and that in the event of another railway strike it would be more difficult for the

Government to cope with such an emergency by reason of the greater power of the N.U.R. and by the diminution of the number of independent carriers on the roads.'[89]

In the 1925 Christmas box from the National Wages Board—a flat 'no' to demands which were in themselves reasonable and moderate enough— the members of the N.U.R. were brought sharply against the limitations of the post-war transport policy of the nation.

With the failure of the Transport Workers' Federation in 1920 to secure an 87s a week minimum wage for lorry drivers and the breakdown of negotiations in the Joint Industrial Council for the road transport industry due to the employers' desires to substitute local for national negotiations, the stage was set for a rapid deterioration of working conditions in road transport.[90] The competition of owner-occupiers and small firms with the larger concerns led to a reduction of road carriage charges at the expense of tolerable conditions of working for the drivers and at the expense of the wages of railwaymen who were being denied improvements due to the rail- way companies' loss of orders.

The interdependence of road and rail transport workers was recognized by the E.C. of the N.U.R. On March 1, 1923, it took part in a joint meeting with the Executive of the Transport and General Workers' Union when Ernest Bevin explained that employers in the road transport industry were demanding reductions in wages and increases in hours and unless the two unions co-operated in strengthening the organization of road transport workers, railwaymen as well as lorry drivers would be the victims of an attack on their standard of living. The meeting agreed that joint commit- tees of the N.U.R. and T. & G.W.U. should be established in the localities to set about the work of unionization of the road transport labour force. Mr Cramp, carrying out the decision of the March E.C. of the N.U.R., sent a letter to all the branches asking them to report on what they were doing in response to these earlier decisions. Although 197 branches reported that they had set up, or were in the course of creating, local committees in collaboration with the T. & G.W.U., it was clear from the replies of other branches that the task was not an easy one. Two hundred and sixty-nine branches had no road transport members while ninety others had taken no action because they had been unable to obtain the co- operation of other unions. In Scotland, the Scottish Horse and Motormen's Association would not co-operate, and on the North East Coast the General Workers' Union was the stumbling block. Not until the Road Traffic Act of 1930 was there effective limitation by statute of the hours and conditions of work of the lorry driver, and in the seven years following Bevin's speech to the two executives, the railwaymen, as well as those employed in the road haulage industry, increasingly felt the drawbacks of its absence.[91]

X

The settlement achieved by the N.U.R. for the Irish railway workers in 1923 is the greatest monument to the value of the union in this period. Despite the Civil War and the Partition and the economic decline resulting from these events, the union was able to secure for the Irish railwaymen most of the important gains obtained for their brethren across the Irish Sea. It was a triumph of skilful bargaining in the face of formidable obstacles.

At the beginning of the First World War there were thirty-two railway companies in Ireland with a combined mileage less than that of the Caledonian Railway. That most of them paid their way even if they did not yield handsome profits was largely due to the fact that the shareholders were rewarded 'at the expense of those employed'.[92] At the time these companies were placed under U.K. Government control in December 1916, the majority of Irish railwaymen were paid less than 14s a week. Following its practice with the other railway companies in the kingdom, the Government agreed to subsidize the war bonuses given to the men employed by the Irish companies. Consequently by 1920 the anomalous position was reached that in some cases the war wages of Irish railwaymen (or bonuses received, 1914–20) were equal to three times the standard or pre-war wage rates. It is not surprising in view of these gains that in the 120 branches of the N.U.R. in Ireland there were 20,000 members.[93] With Irish railways due for decontrol on August 15, 1921, at the same time as the freeing of the other lines, it seemed very doubtful whether these improvements would be maintained; and this was reckoning without the additional complications caused by the invasion of the Black and Tans, the acts of violence based on religious differences and the establishment of two rival governments in the country.

The N.U.R. soon felt the effects of the unsettled condition of Ireland. In August 1919, the Irish patriotic party, Sinn Fein, which had returned its candidates in every constituency except four (outside of Ulster) in the December 1918 General Election, was 'proclaimed' by the British Government, and in March 1920, General Sir Nevil MacReady was appointed Commander-in-Chief in Ireland with the task of restoring order. For nine months the I.R.A. had been conducting a campaign of violence and boycott directed against the pro-British Royal Irish Constabulary and the armed forces of the Crown. The part played by the irregular British forces or Black and Tans in resorting to all means, fair or foul, in a vain attempt to suppress the rebellion, has been described as 'the greatest blot on the record of the coalition'.[94] Munitions and supplies for the Black and Tans were entering the country through Dublin and Irish railwaymen were expected to handle them. In May 1920, 400 members of the N.U.R. belonging to the Dublin (North Wall) branch, without asking for, or receiving, the sanction of the E.C., refused to unload munitions. The stoppage of the traffic in Dublin led to the virtual closing of the port of Holyhead and the prospect of dismissal for hundreds of railwaymen there. Although the E.C. had not sanctioned the strike of the Dublin men, it was perturbed at the purely repressive policy by the Coalition Government. At a Special Meeting on May 20th, it instructed Mr Thomas to bring about a full delegate meeting of the Triple Alliance at the earliest possible moment so that constructive proposals could be suggested to the Prime Minister.[95] When it met, the Triple Alliance decided that the question of the attitude of British labour towards the production and handling of munitions of war for Ireland and Poland 'was so important as to warrant consideration by the organized trade-union movement as a whole'. It wanted a special conference of the T.U.C. to be called.

When this special conference assembled on July 13th, Mr Thomas opened the debate on Ireland, whilst Mr Cramp moved, and the President of the N.U.R., Mr W. J. Abraham, seconded, a resolution calling for a truce, the withdrawal of the British army of occupation, and the summoning of a special Irish Parliament 'with full Dominion Powers in all Irish affairs'. The resolution was carried by 1,953,000 votes to 1,759,000 and the N.U.R. could claim credit for having taken the initiative within the Labour movement on these important questions and of having given the Government some constructive proposals.[96]

In the meantime, in accordance with another decision of the E.C.,[97] Mr Thomas had persuaded the Prime Minister to grant him and his Executive an interview at No. 10 Downing Street on June 3rd. Mr Thomas warned Lloyd George that he would never bring peace to Ireland 'by merely reinforcing the military'. He believed 'the Government could bring to a conference table the people who would bring peace to Ireland' and he urged that this should be done.[98]

As far as the more immediate and limited question of the North Wall strikers was concerned, the E.C., whilst calling upon them to resume work, at the same time decided to call a conference of Irish branches with the members of the E.C. in attendance.[99] The Dublin men did not return to work until December 31st, after they had received an assurance from Sir Eric Geddes that none of the strikers would be penalized in any way, but the Conference, which met in Bristol, was quickly convened on June 16th. With 'nearly complete unanimity' the seventy-eight delegates carried a resolution which declared that the 'murders and outrages' then occurring in Ireland 'were the inevitable result of the Government's failure to govern Ireland in accordance with the wishes of the people'. The resolution condemned 'outrages by all parties' and urged the Government 'to prevent provocation' by ceasing the supply of munitions to Ireland. It requested Mr Thomas to arrange an interview with the Prime Minister at which he (Mr Thomas) would be accompanied by a deputation of North and South Ireland railwaymen delegates from the conference.

The interview with Lloyd George on June 21st seemed to be fruitless. In response to Mr Thomas's proposals for a truce and the withdrawal of the Black and Tans the Premier said that 'if it was a question of setting up an independent Irish Republic' it could only be accepted if they were 'absolutely beaten to the ground'. If Abraham Lincoln had 'faced a million casualties and a five years' war rather than acknowledge the independence of the Southern States', the Coalition Government would 'do the same thing'. Mr Thomas told the Premier that of course 'Your troops could wipe out the Irish people' but that this would 'not even then have contributed anything towards the solution' of a problem which would have become 'still more difficult and dangerous'. Constructively, he suggested that if Lloyd George agreed to send no more munitions pending the meeting of the English and Irish T.U.C.s they, the delegation, 'would do everything possible to prevent crime and outrage' and they believed this would lead to a return to work by the North Wall strikers. The Premier would not budge. He told Mr Thomas that the Cabinet had 'really got to be absolutely adamant'.[100] Nevertheless it is reasonable to suppose that the N.U.R. played some part in bringing about that change of mind in the Premier which led to the treaty with the Irish Free State in 1922.

The physical damage to railway property and the damage to trade caused by the Civil War prompted the Irish railway companies to think in terms of drastic reductions in wages and lengthening of hours of labour once Government control was ended. The Irish managers declared that from August 15, 1921, wage cuts of between 18s and 20s a week would be introduced, whilst the working day would be increased to ten and, in some cases, twelve hours. The outlook seemed very black for there was no conciliation machinery in Ireland such as had been established in Britain before the war. There was, however, one weakness in the Irish managers' position; the Minister of Transport had promised the Irish companies £3 million as their share of the £60 million total compensation to the railways of the kingdom agreed to by Parliament to cover arrears of maintenance accruing during the period of Government control.

Mr Thomas seized upon this weakness. He told the Irish managers he would see to it that they did not get their money. When the Chief Government Whip in the House of Commons heard of this he was nonplussed. He stopped Mr Thomas in the lobby and said, 'I understood that this was agreed.' Mr Thomas replied, 'Yes, there is an agreement between the Minister of Transport and the Irish Railways, but there is no agreement with us. You can pass it over our heads and defeat us by a majority, but it is not going through the House unless the Irish railway companies are prepared to set up machinery to deal with their men just as the English railway companies have done to deal with theirs.'

After this the Cabinet agreed that they would not proceed with the matter until Mr Thomas consented to the conditions under which the

£3 million was granted. Up to that point the railway managers had shown a certain indifference to the question of negotiating with the N.U.R., but faced with the loss of their compensation, they wired Mr Thomas and, as a result, an interview was arranged in a room in the Ministry of Transport building. The manager of one of the largest of the companies, the Great Northern Railway of Ireland, a certain Mr Bagwell—with whom the present writer claims no affinity in blood or in ideology—being completely opposed to union recognition, refused to attend the meeting. The other thirty-one managers, however, agreed to the establishment of Conciliation Boards on which the Railway Trade Unions would be represented, with appeals going to an Irish Railway Wages Board on which would sit five T.U. and five company representatives. The arrangement had the blessing of the Government. Mr Bagwell, being a man of principle, agreed that his company should forgo £200,000 (its share of the £3 million) rather than come into the scheme.

Although the companies had agreed to accept the new machinery for negotiation on wages, they still demanded reductions in wages which the rank and file and the Irish Council were not prepared to accept. Hence it was agreed that their claims should be submitted to an arbitration court over which Mr W. Carrigan, K.C., presided. For nine days the case for the Irish railwaymen was ably argued by Mr Thomas, Mr J. Gore (a member of the E.C.) by Mr R. Hennessy of the Irish Council and by Mr J. Bermingham, the Irish Secretary of the N.U.R. The Carrigan Award of September 10, 1921, provided for reductions in wages according to a sliding scale and confirmed a 6s reduction made by the companies in August. It also continued the assertion that it was 'not possible consistently with the solvency ... that the 8-hour day should be maintained on the Irish railways'.

The Irish Council, though disliking the award intensely, recommended the temporary acceptance of the wages clauses on condition that the 8-hour day was kept intact; but the companies insisted on the implementation of the whole of the award. Its efforts at compromise having failed, the Irish Council then decided to fight. It issued a circular calling for an unofficial strike of Irish railwaymen from January 15, 1922, unless, in the interim, the companies agreed not to apply the terms of the Carrigan award. At this stage the Governments of Northern Ireland and the Free State intervened and persuaded the Irish Council to withdraw the strike notices in return for an undertaking by the companies that they would not change existing working hours and conditions though they would reduce wages as planned. The Governments promised an inquiry into the state of the railway to be held within one month.

After long and strenuously fought negotiations between the N.U.R. (whose case was most ably conducted by Mr J. Gore), the A.S.L.E. & F. and the Irish companies, agreement was reached on February 17, 1922.

The unions secured the continuance of the guaranteed week. The principle of the 8-hour day was conceded though there was provision that 'where economy would accrue' men might be called upon to work a roster of nine hours a day, the extra hour being paid for at overtime rates. The men were to receive a week's holiday with pay. Some of the reductions in wages were to be restored. Although the agreement was to last only until the end of the year it was a remarkable achievement in the light of the condition of Ireland at the time.[101] The merging of the Irish Free State railways into three groups at this time had, no doubt, helped to make it possible.

Once the Irish Free State was formally recognized in March 1922, the question arose as to the whole future of the N.U.R. in that country. The Irish Transport Union was winning recruits from the railways and the membership of the N.U.R. fell in 1922 and 1923 so that it was down to 13,716 by 1924. In the spring of 1922 Mr Cramp visited Ireland to investigate the situation. He suggested to members of the Irish Council that they should organize a conference of the branches of the union to determine its future position in the country. They took his advice and called a conference in Dublin on June 25, 1922, sixty-six branches sending delegates. They decided to keep the organization in being, but demanded more local autonomy and suggested the Irish Secretary should invite the branches to submit their proposals for more autonomous working.[102]

In the light of these suggestions from Irish branches and the reports from Mr Gore who conducted an intensive membership and organization drive in the Free State throughout 1923, Mr Cramp made three important recommendations to the E.C. in December 1923. He considered that the time had come for the abolition of the Irish Council which had outlived its usefulness. Instead, there should be a negotiating committee of two men, one chosen from the Northern Ireland and one from the Free State. The man in charge of the Dublin office should be given a higher status and salary than that of an organizing secretary and there was a case for appointing two organizing secretaries to help him. The Special General Meeting, later that month, accepted Mr Cramp's report and instructed him to put it into operation. Thus by 1924 the organization in Ireland was considerably improved.

The Irish railway workers had reason to congratulate themselves on the wisdom of their decision to maintain the N.U.R. in their country when, early in 1924, Mr Cramp, together with Mr J. Kenny of the Dublin Office, successfully resisted, before the Irish Railway Wages Board, the companies' proposals for a worsening of rates of pay and conditions of service. In fact it was largely due to an appreciation of what had been done by the N.U.R. at this time to maintain decent standards of wages and hours that the work of the union in the Southern part of Ireland was not finally ended until December 31, 1952.

P

NOTES

1. N.U.R. Quarterly E.C., March 1918, R. 155.
2. *Railway News*, April 13, 1918.
3. 2nd Report of the Select Committee on Transport, November 14, 1918, P.P. 1918, IV, p. 471.
4. *The Times*, December 6 and 11, 1918.
5. *The Times*, December 7, 1918.
6. Reported in the *Railway Gazette*, February 21, 1919, p. 315.
7. House of Commons, Parliamentary Debates, 1920, Vol. 132, Col. 17, July 19, 1920.
8. Ministry of Ways and Communications Bill, May 18, 1919, P.P. 1919, II, p. 351.
9. House of Commons, Parliamentary Debates, 1919, Vol. 113, Col. 1768, March 17, 1919.
10. Article on 'The Ministry of Transport', *The Times Special Railway Number*, August 15, 1921.
11. *The Times*, April 3, 1919.
12. The words were those of Mr G. Balfour, M.P., *Daily Telegraph*, March 18, 1918.
13. *Daily Telegraph*, January 6, 1919.
14. A.G.M. of the Great Western Railway, February 19, 1920, reported in *Railway Gazette*, February 27, 1920, p. 308.
15. *The Times*, June 13, 1919. N.U.R. General Secretary's Report, 1921, p. 16. *The Times*, December 3, 1918.
16. *Manchester Guardian Commercial*, February 17, 1921.
17. *Financial Times*, November 14, 1919; *Financier*, November 29, 1919; *R.R.* November 21, 1919.
18. Cmd. 787.
19. The Railway Trade Unions Joint Committee: Memorandum on the proposals of the Ministry of Transport as to the future organization of transport undertakings in Great Britain and their relation to the State as outlined in the White Paper, Cmd. 787.
20. Midland Railway, A.G.M. Derby, February 19, 1920. Reported in the *Railway Gazette*, February 27, 1920.
21. *Railway Gazette*, February 21, 1919, p. 328.
22. *Daily Herald*, December 2, 1920.
23. *Yorkshire Post*, December 18, 1920.
24. *The Times*, November 30, 1920, January 15, 1921.
25. Article by 'Optometer', *R.R.*, May 20, 1921.
26. N.U.R. Industrial General Secretary's Report, 1921.
27. *Hornsey Journal*, February 11, 1921.
28. *R.R.*, May 20, 1921.
29. Cmd. 1292, 1921.
30. House of Commons, Parliamentary Debates, 1921, Vol. 142, Col. 357.
31. *R.R.*, July 15, 1921.
32. Cited in an article by Felix J. C. Pole, General Manager of the Great Western Railway, *The Times*, Railway Number, August 15, 1921.
33. J. H. Thomas, 'Labour Organization on British Railways', in *Modern Railway Administration*, Vol 2, p. 234.
34. *R.R.*, August 26, 1921.
35. *R.R.*, September 16, 1921.
36. *The Times*, January 5, 1920.

37. *The Times*, January 12, 1920.
38. *R.R.*, January 16, 1920.
39. R. Holder in *R.R.*, February 27, 1920.
40. *R.R.*, February 6, 1920.
41. N.U.R. E.C., April 6, 1920. R. 269.
42. *R.R.*, June 16, 1920.
43. C. L. Mowat, *Britain Between the Wars*, pp. 125–6. *R.R.*, November 25, 1921.
44. *R.R.*, January 21, 1921.
45. *R.R.*, February 11, 1921, December 8, 1922.
46. *R.R.*, September 23, 1921.
47. *R.R.*, September 30, 1921.
48. N.U.R. Quarterly E.C., December 1921. *R.R.* February 3, 1922. N.U.R., S.G.M., February 2, 1922, Verbatim Reports.
49. N.U.R., S.G.M., March 17, 1922, Verbatim Report, p. 17. *R.R.*, May 12, 1922.
50. N.U.R., S.G.M., October 7, 1921. Speech of J. H. Thomas. Special E.C., February 11, 1921. R. 96.
51. Statement made by J. H. Thomas at Birkenhead quoted in *R.R.*, March 10, 1922.
52. *R.R.*, October 14, 1921.
53. N.U.R. Quarterly E.C., June 1922. R. 200.
54. Article on 'Industrial Unionism', *R.R.* September 7, 1923.
55. *R.R.*, July 9, 1920.
56. *R.R.*, May 14 and 21, August 27, 1920. N.U.R. Quarterly E.C., December 1920.
57. N.U.R. E.C., July 1923. R. 394. *R.R.*, July 27, 1923.
58. N.U.R. Special E.C., July 30, 1923. Rs. 406, 404.
59. E. Stanley, *Signalmen and their Movement*, *R.R.*, July 10, 1925.
60. Information conveyed in a letter from Charles Harris, a retired signalman, Leicester No. 1 branch, N.U.R. *R.R.*, June 22, 1923.
61. N.U.R. A.G.M., Belfast, July 1920, Verbatim Report, *R.R.*, July 23, 1920.
62. N.U.R. Special E.C., July 15, 1921.
63. N.U.R., S.G.M., August 11, 1921, Verbatim Report.
64. *R.R.*, August 4, 1922.
65. *R.R.*, September 8, 1922.
66. National Wages Board: The Company's Case; the N.U.R.'s reply; The Board's Decision, November 1923; Mr Cramp's speech, p. 76.
67. *R.R.*, June 15, 1923. R. 205.
68. N.U.R. Special E.C. April 26, 1923, R. 205. *R.R.*, May 18, 1923.
69. N.U.R. letter to all branches signed by J. H. Thomas and C. T. Cramp, January 18, 1924.
70. *Manchester Guardian*, January 19, 1924. The leader writer of the *Daily Dispatch* (January 23, 1924) made a similar assertion.
71. *R.R.*, February 8, 1924. *Daily Herald*, January 22, 1924.
72. Memorandum issued as a result of a conference between the Railway Companies and the T.U.C., January 20, 1924.
73. *R.R.*, February 1, 1924.
74. N.U.R. letter No. 53, January 31, 1924.
75. *R.R.*, August 19, 1921.
76. I am indebted to Mr W. Loeber of Wood Green Branch, N.U.R., and the late Mr L. Bishop, of Willesden No. 4 branch, for loan of documents including 'Impeach the Leaders' and 'My Expulsion from the N.U.R.', by A. E. Rochester, and 'A Rank and Filer's Point of View', by J. Eggleston.

77. N.U.R. A.G.M., York, July 10, 1924, Verbatim Report.
78. U.R.S. *Opinion*, Vol. 5, No. 7, July 1951; *R.R.*, June 12, 1925.
79. *R.R.*, August 22, 1924.
80. *R.R.*, May 16, 1924.
81. *R.R.*, June 20, 1925.
82. N.U.R. E.C. Quarterly Meeting, March 1923, R. 530. My thanks are due to Mr Clift of Battersea No. 1 branch, N.U.R., for this information. Examples of companies' economies at the expense of the gangs given in *R.R.*, December 5, 1924.
83. R. 394.
84. *R.R.*, December 12, 1924.
85. *R.R.*, December 26, 1924.
86. N.U.R. E.C., February 6, 1925, R. 89.
87. N.U.R. A.G.M., July 8, 1925, Verbatim Report.
88. *R.R.*, November 20, 1925, National Wages Board Report, December 9, 1925, para. 37.
89. Report: A Departmental Committee on Road Conveyance of Goods by Railway Companies, B.P.P. 1921, Vol. XVII, p. 394.
90. A. Bullock, *The Life and Times of Ernest Bevin*, Vol. 1, p. 144.
91. N.U.R. E.C., March and December, 1923.
92. These words are taken from a report of a Commission on Irish Railways set up by the Provisional Government of Ireland. *R.R.*, November 24, 1922.
93. Statement by J. H. Thomas reported in *R.R.*, August 26, 1921.
94. C. L. Mowat, *Britain Between the Wars*, p. 65.
95. N.U.R. Special E.C., May 20, 1920, R. 339.
96. N.U.R. Quarterly E.C., May 31–June 5, 1920, *R.R.*, July 16, 1920.
97. R. 407, June 1920.
98. *R.R.*, June 11, 1920.
99. R. 409, June 1920.
100. *R.R.*, June 25, 1920.
101. *R.R.*, March 10, 1922. N.U.R. Quarterly E.C., March 1922.
102. N.U.R. Quarterly E.C., September 1922.
103. N.U.R. Quarterly E.C., May 1924.

CHAPTER XVII

THE RAILWAYMEN AND THE MINERS— THE GENERAL STRIKE

'We have not chosen lightly. Let none think
It is for any man an easy thing
To lead his women to starvation's brink
Or face for his own children suffering.'
'Tomfool' of the Daily Herald, *quoted in* The British Worker, *No. 1,*
May 5, 1926.

I

FROM May 3 to 13, 1926, there was fought the longest, most complete and most costly strike in the history of British railways. And yet, paradoxically, whilst every other strike before or since was fought in support of some demand of the railwaymen themselves, only this—the greatest—struggle had nothing to do with their own immediate objectives.

If to many it would appear most remarkable that the N.U.R. should have drained its resources, both human and financial, on behalf of the miners rather than the railway workers, it is worth remembering that often the greatest sacrifices are made for partly altruistic reasons. A great upsurge of public sympathy for 'poor little Belgium' in August 1914 induced hundreds of thousands of young men to enlist; the attempt of the mine owners to impose wage cuts led to a great upsurge of sympathy for the miners in 1926.

Nevertheless the railwaymen's decision to support the miners was not hastily made. An examination of the records of the railway unions for such years as 1912, 1920 and 1921 would soon reveal how closely interwoven were the interests of those who mined the nation's coal and those who carried it over the railway network. The first general miners' strike in Britain, which lasted for fourteen weeks in the spring of 1912, had brought

453

unemployment to nearly 200,000 railwaymen and part-time working to many thousands more. By the time the miners returned to work the cost to the A.S.R.S. of supporting its members who were the innocent victims of a dispute in another industry was £94,000.[1] As a result of this experience, active trade unionists on the railways reached the conclusion that something ought to be done to prevent the recurrence of such a catastrophe. In March 1912, the E.C. of the N.U.R. was receiving many appeals from branches to organize a boycott of the carriage of blacklegs, troops and coal whilst the coal strike lasted.[2] As we have seen in another chapter, the Annual Conference of the Miners' Federation in October 1913, decided to instruct its executive committee to approach the other big trade unions 'with a view to co-operative action and the support of each others demands'. The next step was taken when the Executive Committees of the N.U.R., the Transport Workers' Federation and the Miners' Federation met in April 1914, and agreed that the presidents and general secretaries of the three bodies should draw up a working agreement, the principal aim of which would be that each big union would seek the support of the two other members of the Triple Industrial Alliance before embarking on any big movement, either defensive or aggressive. The First World War intervened before the arrangements could be completed, but all three partners of the alliance had ratified the agreement by the end of 1915.

Within three months of the Armistice the Conference of the Miners' Federation had been held at Southport and had passed resolutions in favour of the nationalization of the mines, a 30 per cent increase in wages and the introduction of the 6-hour day. When the Coalition Government, which was still in control of the mines, gave an unsatisfactory reply to these demands, the miners by a six to one majority in a ballot vote decided in favour of a national strike to begin on March 15, 1919. It was at this point that Lloyd George intervened decisively to prevent a major industrial conflict. Fearing that the miners might successfully enlist the support of their partners in the triple alliance, he informed the miners' leaders that, if they would postpone the strike, there would be a 'full and free investigation' of conditions in the mining industry with the presentation of an interim report on wages and hours by March 20, 1919. By a narrow majority, a delegate conference of the Miners' Federation held on February 26–27, 1919, decided to suspend for a fortnight the starting of the strike. The interim report of the Royal Commission under Mr Justice Sankey on March 20, 1919, recommended an increase of wages of 2s a shift and the reduction of the working day from 8 to 7 hours. Recommendation IX was rightly regarded as the most significant part of the report. It read:

'Even on the evidence already given, the present system of ownership and working in the coal industry stands condemned, and some other system must be substituted for it, either nationalization or a method of unification by national purchase and for joint control.'

On the following day, March 21, 1919, Mr Bonar Law, on behalf of the Government, wrote a letter to the Secretary of the Miners' Federation in which he expressed his pleasure in confirming his previous verbal assurance 'that the Government were prepared to carry out in the spirit and in the letter the recommendations of Sir John Sankey's report'.

Confronted with this categorical promise, the delegate conference of the miners on March 26th accepted the interim report whilst the abandonment of the strike plan was authorized by postal ballot of the membership shortly afterwards.

When the fuller, second report of the Sankey Commission appeared on June 20, 1919, it was again seen that a majority of the Commissioners— seven out of thirteen—recommended nationalization of the coal mines even though the three mine owners and two industrialists were opposed. By August 1919, with demobilization more advanced, the police strike beaten, and the locomotivemen's claims met, Lloyd George felt that the Government position was stronger. On that day he informed the House of Commons that it was not proposed to nationalize the mines. This announcement provoked Mr Vernon Hartshorn, the Welsh miners' M.P., to declare that the miners of the country would say that they had been 'deceived, betrayed, duped'. By the autumn of 1919 the spirit of militancy in the labour movement had died down so that both the T.U.C. deputation to the Prime Minister on behalf of the miners' demands and its 'Mines for the Nation' campaign, started in December 1919, were fruitless.

In the interim, before the next crisis in the mines developed in the summer of 1920, the railway strike had been fought, the Central and National Wages Boards had been set up and the railwaymen had achieved a guaranteed week and guaranteed day.

Although the miners had obtained an increase in wages on March 29, 1920, owing to the rapidly rising cost of living, three months later they put in a claim for a further rise coupled with a proposal for the reduction in the price of household coal. Negotiations with the Government broke down, however, on the question of relating increases in wages to increases in output (the datum line) and after a miners' ballot had shown a large majority in favour of strike action, notices were handed in to expire on September 25, 1920.

As a miners' strike was bound to affect the railways and as a moral obligation to support a Triple Alliance partner was recognized, a Special General Meeting of the N.U.R. was called for September 21st to consider what action the union should take.

At Unity House, when the S.G.M. opened, both the general secretaries expressed opposition to strike action in support of the miners. Mr Thomas painted a grim picture of the consequences of a sympathetic strike. He claimed that whereas a miners' strike could last seven weeks, the funds of the N.U.R. would undoubtedly be exhausted within three weeks. It would be 'madness' to ask the railwaymen to strike unless they were sure of a good response; otherwise they would be 'merely inviting those who were loyal to the union to sacrifice themselves'. If they struck they would have to be prepared 'not for an industrial strike or even an industrial up-heaval' but 'for a revolution'.

The caution of the leaders might have been cast aside if the feeling in the branches had been strongly in support of action on behalf of the miners, but the delegates revealed some uncertainty and division of opinion amongst the members they represented. Mr Powell of Blaina said that many who attended the branch meetings in his district felt that 'it was unfair for them to be called upon to support workers who were already better paid than themselves' whilst Mr Dimmock from the Belfast area spoke on much the same lines. Mr Vincent, from Southampton, said that in his district the prevailing opinion was that the guaranteed week would save the railway-men's living standards. Although Mr Hall of Hull, Mr Marchbank from Glasgow and other delegates declared their branches supported the miners, Mr Cramp was able to show that only 106 branches out of 1,530 had replied—admittedly at short notice—to a head office inquiry as to whether the N.U.R. should strike in support of the miners, and that forty-eight out of the 106 had requested that a ballot of the members should first be taken, whilst another seven branches were against any action at all. Only fifty-one branches, or just under half those sending replies, were in favour of an immediate strike. It was therefore a comparatively easy task for Mr Thomas to persuade the delegates to defer a decision until after he had spoken to the meeting of the Triple Alliance summoned for the following day.[3]

At the Holborn Town Hall on September 22nd, Mr Thomas convinced the miners and transport workers' delegates that they would not get support in a strike until further attempts at reaching a settlement had been made. Later that day—twelve months after, to the day and hour, the momentous meeting on the eve of the railway strike—he was pleading with Lloyd George at No. 10 Downing Street that the miners' claim for an increase of 2s a shift was justified. His pleadings were of no avail; the Government was not prepared to make concessions.

In view of his failure with the Premier, Mr Thomas had a much harder task to persuade the delegates of the adjourned S.G.M. at Unity House on September 23rd, that a sympathetic strike was unwise. His speeches were more emotional, more extravagant and more defeatist than they had been two days earlier. He said 'that if the railwaymen were to take the plunge it would be the end of the Society' and that he doubted whether 50 per cent of the membership of the N.U.R. would come out. In view of the breakdown of all attempts at negotiation, the delegates were torn between an inclination to support the miners by striking and doubt about the degree of support for the strike among the rank and file. The debate was on the following resolution:

'That this S.G.M., having fully considered the miners' claims and being satisfied that they are reasonable and just and should be conceded, regret that the Prime Minister has definitely refused to concede same. We are satisfied that everything possible has been done by the Triple Alliance to endeavour to bring about a peaceful settlement, and having regard to the circumstances, we are compelled to recognize that to allow the miners to fight this issue on their own would not only be an act of treason but of suicide. We therefore decide that should the miners, at their adjourned meeting today, decide to give effect to the strike ballot on 25th instant our members in Scotland, England and Wales must cease work at 12 midnight on Saturday, 25th instant.'

The intense division of opinion among delegates on this momentous question was reflected in the voting. The motion was defeated by 28 votes to 27, with two Irish delegates neutral and two delegates absent.[4]

Although the hesitancy shown by the railwaymen contributed towards the postponement of the coal strike it did not prevent its occurrence. 'The datum line' strike of the miners began on October 16, 1920. The E.C. of the N.U.R. quickly appreciated the new situation. They realized that a complete stoppage of work in the mines would have immediate repercussions on the volume of traffic and employment on the railways. At its special meeting held on the day in which the coal strike began it decided to summon another Special General Meeting of the union for October 20, 1920.

Less than a month after the delegates of the S.G.M. on September 23rd had turned down the proposal for sympathetic strike action on behalf of the miners, the same group of delegates, on October 21st, after a prolonged and keen debate, carried by 33 votes to 24 a resolution which instructed the General Secretary to inform the Prime Minister that unless the miners' demands were met or negotiations resumed by October 23, 1920, the railwaymen in England, Scotland and Wales would be called out on strike.[5] The explanation of this switch of opinion lies in the fact that the delegates were all too well aware that the guaranteed week would not be retained if the miners' strike continued. Thousands of railwaymen would, in any case, experience unemployment or short-time working. Despite Mr Thomas's prophesy of a 'bloody upheaval' if a strike were called, the waverers among the delegates concluded that since many of their workmates were bound to suffer from the effects of the coal strike, there was little for the railwaymen to lose in supporting John Marchbank's appeal that they should be loyal to the miners and to the Triple Alliance.

That same evening, a telegram was sent to all N.U.R. branches:

'Special General Meeting instructs all members to be prepared to cease work at 12 midnight Sunday next, unless you hear to the contrary—Cramp.'

The Press made much of the fact that the telegrams were sent out under the name 'Cramp' alone and not under the two names 'Thomas and Cramp'. It was asserted that during Mr Thomas's absence in Prague before October 20th, Mr Cramp had exerted his influence in favour of the strike resolution and that he had tried to 'rush it through', despite the well-known fact that Mr Thomas was wholeheartedly opposed to extreme measures. It is true that Mr Thomas told Mr Vernon Hartshorn in the House of Commons the day after the passing of the strike resolution that he had gone to the extent of telling the delegates that he would not lead them if they decided to strike; but it is not true that Mr Cramp took advantage of the earlier absence of Mr Thomas to rush through a policy with which he knew his colleague was in disagreement. Mr Cramp had, in fact, taken no part in the discussion and on the day the resolution was carried at Unity House he was busily engaged elsewhere negotiating improved conditions for shopmen.[6]

When the Miners' Federation Executive met on the morning of Saturday, October 23, 1920, two important letters awaited its consideration. One was from Mr Cramp reporting the S.G.M.'s decision to strike in their support; the other was from Lloyd George inviting them (the miners) to meet him on Sunday, October 24th, at 10.0 a.m. The indefatigable Mr Thomas had been to see the Premier on the previous evening and had discussed the new situation with him.

When the executive committees of the Miners' and the N.U.R. met later that Saturday afternoon, the miners requested that the strike should be postponed until the outcome of the negotiations with the Government had been seen. Back at Unity House in the evening, the E.C. of the N.U.R. 'having regard to the miners' request' resolved unanimously 'that the notice to cease work be in the meantime suspended'.[7]

Lloyd George's measures to deal with the crisis, taken swiftly and cleverly, were partly conciliatory and partly repressive in character. The conciliatory side of the settlement, virtually completed by October 28th, was the granting of an immediate increase of 2s a shift to the miners with prospective additional increases proportional to increased output of coal. Though the result of the ballot vote of the miners announced on November 3, 1920, showed a small majority against the acceptance of the Government's offer, the rule required a two-thirds majority for strike action to be taken and, in consequence, the men were instructed to return to work on November 4th.[8] The repressive side of the Premier's response to the crisis was the passage through Parliament between October 22 and 28, 1920, of the Emergency Powers Act which gave the Government power to declare a state of emergency during which regulations might be issued by orders in Council and troublemakers speedily punished in courts of summary jurisdiction. It was hoped that the quick passage of this Act might help to bring second thoughts to men favouring the calling of a General Strike. It was to have its uses in 1926.

The unfortunate feature of the settlement of the autumn of 1920 was that it was only operative up to March 31, 1921, and the whole question of miners' wages and the future of the mines was bound to rise again. To make matters worse, the Government suddenly announced on February 22, 1921, that decontrol of the mines would come into effect on March 31, 1921, instead of on August 1st of that year, which was generally thought to have been the original intention. The reason for the sudden volte face on the part of the Government was that the system under which the profits and losses of the different collieries had been pooled under Government control since 1916 and wage adjustments fixed on a national basis, had been profitable to the Exchequer whilst high export prices had prevailed in 1919 and 1920. It ceased to be profitable when the bottom fell out of the export market as a result of the recovery of European coal production and the payment of reparations in the form of coal by the German Government. By January 1920, the operation of the profits pool was costing the Exchequer between £14 and £15 millions a month. As a result of the Government's action, the coal owners were suddenly obliged to try and make each colliery self-supporting at a time of trade depression, unemployment and falling prices (including falling prices of coal). As the wages bill in each colliery comprised at least 70 per cent of the cost of working the mines, the colliery owners met the new situation by proposals for wage reductions. A few days before Government control ended notices were posted up at the collieries of the wages the owners were prepared to pay from April 1st. The miners were faced with the ending of the system of nationally determined wages from which they had benefited over the last five years and with reductions in weekly wages varying with the profitability of such mining districts. In the South Wales area, where the mines were least profitable to run, some miners were faced with the immediate halving of their wages. In Nottinghamshire the reductions were to be between 10 and 25 per cent. Only in the profitable Yorkshire coalfields were wages to be virtually untouched; in fact some of the lower paid men were promised small advances.[9]

The coal strike began on April 1, 1921, because the miners would not accept a return to district wage settlements which would bring miners in the poorer coalfields to a near starvation level, whilst neither the coal owners nor the Government would accept the constructive proposal of the Miners' Federation for a National Wages Board similar to that set up for the railways the year before, and a national pool of profits. The Miners' Executive admitted that the economic position of their industry was serious, and its members were prepared to agree to a uniform reduction of wages of 2s a shift provided that wage negotiation at a national level was returned.

The E.C. of the Miners' Federation pleaded with the colliery owners and with Sir Robert Horne, the Chancellor of the Exchequer, but found both parties determined to return to district wage settlements with all that this implied. The Government would not entertain the idea of a subsidy. Therefore, on the morning of Thursday, March 21, 1921, Mr Frank Hodges, Secretary of the Miners' Federation, told a meeting of the Triple Alliance (the E.C.s of the N.U.R., Transport Workers' Federation and Miners' Federation) summoned to Unity House, that the Miners' Executive had decided to ask the Alliance to give them whatever help lay within their power. It was the first time that one of the partners of the Alliance had made such a definite request. Later that day the E.C. of the N.U.R. considered a resolution moved by Mr Dobbie and seconded by Mr Gore that a general strike should be called for midnight on April 8, 1921, unless a settlement in favour of the miners was reached before that date. A majority of the committee, however, felt that there was need for the rank and file to be informed more fully of the issues involved before they were committed to a strike, and the resolution was turned down in favour of an amendment to summon a Special General Meeting of the union for Wednesday, April 6, 1921.[10]

There could be no mistaking the fact that the active members of the N.U.R. were deeply sympathetic to the miners and felt that their cause was a just one. Many also argued that unless the partners of the Triple Alliance stood together they would be defeated piecemeal. If decontrol of the mines was to be followed by wage reductions in April 1921, what would be the consequence of decontrol of the railways in the following August? Nevertheless many of the delegates to the S.G.M. were full of doubts. Mass meetings had been held in many districts on Sunday, April 3, 1921, and delegates from Croydon, Southampton, Bristol, Barnsley, Staveley and elsewhere reported poor attendance and uncertainty as to the best means of supporting the miners. On the other hand delegates from the South Wales, Manchester and Glasgow areas reported strong feeling in favour of a sympathetic strike. The prolonged and earnest discussion at the S.G.M. centred round a 'militant' resolution moved by John Marchbank and a more cautiously worded amendment which had the support of Mr Thomas. The resolution, in pledging the full support of the N.U.R. to the miners, called for 'a national stoppage of work'. The other railway unions were to be notified of the strike decision whilst there was to be a request to the Transport Workers' Federation for a meeting in order that 'joint and simultaneous action' should be taken. The amendment which made the calling of the strike *conditional* on the Transport Workers' taking joint and simultaneous action reflected opinion in many branches that it would be foolhardy for the railwaymen to strike if the dockers, bus drivers and lorry drivers continued at work. When it came to a vote, the amendment was rejected by 31 votes to 29 but the resolution was declared 'not carried' by the Chairman when it was announced that the voting in this case was 30 for and 30 against. When, after this, Mr Thomas told the meeting he had drawn up a statement for the Press which declared that the conference had come to a 'unanimous decision' to support the miners, there was a spontaneous burst of laughter from the delegates. Mr Thomas assured them that in one sense it was true, but the wording was designed 'to put the wind up the Government'. On the following day it did not take long for the meeting to agree to a compromise resolution which pledged the N.U.R. 'to support the miners by a national stoppage of work, provided that a sufficient guarantee . . . be given by the Transport Workers' that they will take similar action, and that this decision . . . be put into operation jointly and simultaneously'.[11]

The next step to meet the executive of the Transport Workers' Federation was taken later that same day (Friday, April 8th) when agreement was reached on the following statement:

'This joint meeting of the E.C.s of the N.U.R. and Transport Workers' Federation gives notice to their several employers and to the Government that unless negotiations are reopened between the Miners' Federation, mine owners and Government, the full strike power of the Triple Alliance shall be put into operation as from Tuesday next, midnight'.

Faced with this evidence of determination on the part of the Triple Alliance the Government showed signs of alarm. By Royal Proclamation the armed forces of the Crown were mobilized and thousands of volunteers enlisted in a Special Defence Force. At the same time negotiations between the miners and mine owners were reopened on the basis of a Government subsidy of limited duration to make possible the more gradual introduction of the proposed wage cuts.

All these emergency measures failed to deter the Alliance, although the date of commencement of the strike was postponed from April 12th to 15th (midnight) whilst the discussions on wages were resumed. The miners stood pat in their insistence on national wage settlements and the crisis was as acute as ever on April 14th.

Almost at the eleventh hour, on the day before the Triple Alliance strike was due to commence, a group of coalition M.P.s met in the House of Commons to hear a statement from the Chairman of the Mining Association on the extent of the wage cuts proposed. The magnitude of the reductions startled them and helped to influence them to invite Frank Hodges to put the point of view of the miners to them and other M.P.s that evening. At the meeting Hodges put forward the miners' case with great eloquence and clarity. A host of questions followed. In his answers to a number of them the miners' Secretary appeared to indicate that he would be prepared to consider a temporary return to district wage agreements. Then someone said:

'Will the Triple Alliance support Mr Hodges's actions?'

Mr Thomas, who had that evening had dinner with Mr Hodges, Vernon Hartshorn and others, immediately stood up and declared:

'Yes, I am quite sure the Triple Alliance will support Mr Hodges's action.'[12]

Although it was past eleven o'clock at night, the news was considered so important that it was thought justifiable to send a message to Lloyd George immediately, informing him of the change in the situation.

Neither Mr Hodges nor Mr Thomas spoke with the authority of those they represented. 'Black Friday' and the split in the Triple Alliance arose from the fact that whereas Mr Hodges's statements were repudiated by the Executive of the Miners' Federation on the following morning, Friday, April 15, 1921, Mr Thomas was able to gain the support of the E.C.s of the N.U.R. and the Transport Workers' for his actions.

Lloyd George acted quickly to remove the danger of a Triple Alliance strike. On that 'Black Friday' morning the Miners' Executive received an invitation from the Premier to attend further discussions on the basis of Mr Hodges's suggestions of the previous evening. At a full meeting of the Triple Alliance held at Unity House that morning Mr Thomas and a majority of the executives of the railwaymen and transport workers tried to persuade the miners to accept the invitation. The situation at that meeting has been vividly described by Mr Page Arnot.

'When J. H. Thomas indicated that the strike might not take place if the miners persisted in their previous decision, the miners knew that they were in danger of being abandoned by their allies; and showed that they knew; it was not a harmonious hour.'[13]

After retiring from the meeting for over an hour and a half to consider the matter, the miners eventually returned to indicate that they could not accept the Premier's offer. After that there were one or two speeches which quickly swayed the conference. Mr Thomas, who had on many previous occasions expressed to the E.C. and the S.G.M. of the N.U.R. a very poor opinion of the negotiating abilities of the miners' leaders, said, on this occasion, that by repudiating Mr Hodges's statements they were rejecting all chances of a settlement. It was such declarations as these which persuaded a majority of those present at the meeting to leave the miners to fight their battle alone. At three o'clock that afternoon (Friday, April 15th) Mr Thomas ran down the steps of Unity House to tell the waiting reporters that the Triple Alliance strike was cancelled.

When the executives of the Transport Workers, N.U.R. and A.S.L.E. & F. met at Unity House on the following morning they issued a statement in explanation of the previous day's decision. They claimed that in view of the 'confusion' which confronted the Conference of the Alliance on the Friday morning, 'no reasonable hope remained of securing the spontaneous and united action of the three bodies which was so essential to give the Miners' Federation the assistance they sought'. A 'partial and hopelessly incomplete' stoppage would have weakened the power of the three unions without helping the miners.

Many members of the N.U.R. were far from satisfied with this explanation of the decision taken on Black Friday. Mr Thomas received critical and abusive letters after every settlement in which he was involved but, on his own confession, he received 'far more than the usual number' on this occasion.[14] In the branches opinion was sharply divided. Whereas from places as far apart as Edinburgh, Eastleigh, Gateshead and Cheltenham, branch resolutions strongly condemned the leadership, and the Manchester District Council with 23,000 members demanded the resignation of Mr Thomas, in other centres such as Guildford, Leeds No. 1 and Nuneaton, the sense of relief that there was to be no strike outweighed the sense of guilt at the suggestion of disloyalty.[15]

It was all very well looking for a scapegoat and putting the blame on Mr Thomas for what was widely regarded as a dishonourable retreat. Had the S.G.M. delegates been united in a determination to call a sympathetic strike it would have been much harder, if not impossible, for Mr Thomas to have made the announcement he did on the afternoon of Black Friday. There was heavy and rapidly increasing unemployment at the time of the crisis. By contrast with those in many other occupations the railwaymen were enjoying a guaranteed week. A few days before the strike was due to commence a railwayman in a mining district passed by with his lorry load of goods a long queue of men waiting to enter the labour exchange. One of the unemployed men called out: 'I shall be doing that job next week mate'.[16] It was incidents such as these which tended to make railwaymen hesitate about the sympathetic strike; and it was the cautious outlook of the rank and file as well as the conservatism of the leaders which led to the collapse of the alliance. All the same, it is very likely that if the strike call had not been rescinded there would have been a great demonstration of trade union solidarity which could have been utilized to obtain better terms for the miners.

At the A.G.M. in Newcastle early in July 1921, the frontal attack on the leadership of the union was led by Mr Sherwood of Wakefield who moved an amendment which expressed regret at the decision to cancel the strike. He claimed that that decision had 'killed the spirit of the best men in the union'. Coal miners on the Barnsley seam, who, under the mine-owners' plan were to have had an *increase* in wages, were prepared to come out on strike in support of a policy which included a general *reduction* of miners' wages by 2s a shift spread evenly throughout the country, but the refusal of the N.U.R. to maintain solidarity had led to a bitter feeling between the miners and railwaymen. Although Mr Cramp conceded that it might have been 'better to emerge from the fight . . . defeated for the moment but united altogether by bonds of common suffering and endurance, than to go back into a shameful security', he cast very grave doubts on the adequacy of the machinery of the Triple Alliance. He predicted that there would be further failures unless there was a joint policy right from the commencement of any movement. The Alliance, or something like it, would have to be entirely reconstituted. After Mr Thomas had asserted that the outcome of the strike would have been the destruction of trade unionism for 'many years to come', few could be found to support Mr Sherwood's amendment which was rejected by 60 votes to 16. The leadership was also under fire from another quarter. Mr J. Gore of the E.C., a man who was to serve with distinction as President of the Union from 1928–30, opened a debate on the division of responsibilities between Mr Thomas and Mr Cramp and pointed to some of the difficulties which arose from two general secretaries being responsible for the conduct of the union's affairs. He said the E.C. had 'felt very keenly' the action of Mr Thomas in opposing a Triple Alliance strike in August 1920, and arguing that there should have been a ballot vote of the members after the S.G.M. had voted in favour of the strike. Mr Thomas should confine himself to the political side of the movement just as Mr Cramp was solely concerned with the industrial side. When, at the end of the debate, he was reluctantly persuaded to intervene, Mr Cramp admitted that once or twice in the past 'in a friendly way' he had suggested to Mr Thomas that he should concentrate on political matters. Despite the fact that, at the beginning of his speech, Mr Gore emphasized that 'he was not leading an anti-Thomas policy', it was perhaps inevitable that Mr Thomas should take it all personally and give a strongly emotional reply. In the end the critics made very little headway. A resolution deploring the attempt of the E.C. to disturb in any way the existing division of labour between the two secretaries and appreciating the 'magnificent services' of both was carried by the large majority of 53 to 26 with one neutral. Mr Thomas had achieved another outstanding personal triumph.[17]

Although they had failed to obtain the support they had asked for from their partners in the Triple Alliance, the miners stayed out on strike until obliged to return to work on the basis of district wage settlements on July 1, 1921. The N.U.R. attempted one gesture of solidarity during this three months' struggle. On April 22nd the E.C. agreed to impose a ban on the movement to commercial users of British coal from colliery sidings and foreign coal from the ports. Coal destined for domestic use and for hospitals was not to be subject to the embargo.[18] It can scarcely be claimed that this gesture was of any material assistance to the miners. On June 17th the *Railway Review* reported that 'N.U.R. members all over Britain had failed to carry out the embargo', and that coal was being moved 'freely and smoothly over the railways'. Part of the reason for the failure lay in the fact that local N.U.R. branch officials were given the obviously tricky task of determining which of the coal was 'black' and which was not. Furthermore, the rank and file were more accustomed to receiving instructions issued nationally and in many areas they declined to obey those merely issued locally. To make matters worse, 300 members of the N.U.R. who did loyally operate the embargo were dismissed by the railway companies. Although they were all reinstated shortly afterwards, their misfortune did not encourage their fellows to observe a ban which was far from complete and effective. On May 31st the E.C. of the N.U.R. in conjunction with the E.C. of the Transport Workers' Federation, which had been a party to the scheme, decided that the embargo should be lifted in view of its lack of success and the threat to the continued employment of union members.[19]

The years of comparative peace on the coalfields of Britain between 1922–4 provided a breathing space during which the admitted imperfections in the Triple Alliance might have been removed. Ernest Bevin of the Transport Workers' was perhaps more alive to the need for changes than any other leader of the Alliance. Speaking at a mass meeting in Gloucester in August 1921, he said:

'The weakness of the whole structure was the preservation of the autonomy of the unions. They would not have mass power and mass action and sectional autonomy however much they tried.'[20]

The general secretaries of the N.U.R. agreed that this was a weakness of the Alliance but they had a different set of priorities. When, in July 1922, the A.G.M. of the N.U.R. considered a proposal to affiliate to the Transport Workers' Federation (as the A.S.L.E. & F. had just decided to do), Mr Cramp said that they wanted first of all 'to secure the amalgamation of their own people' and until they had the Associated Society and the Clerks joining with them, it would be unwise to make other alliances as it would only give the sectional societies 'an additional motive for remaining outside'. The delegates therefore rejected the resolution to affiliate to the Transport Workers' Federation by 64 votes to 12, but carried an amendment to conduct a referendum of the branches on the question. In March 1923 it was disclosed that of the 994 branches which sent in replies 465, with a membership of 118,629, favoured affiliation, compared with 511 branches with a membership of 130,964 which were opposed to the scheme and eighteen branches with 2,692 members who were neutral.[21]

It was not until March 1924, that a conference was called for the purpose of reorganizing the Transport Workers' Federation. In view of the division of opinion in the N.U.R. on the subject of full scale affiliation, the union's representatives at the conference were given a watching brief only. Their report was read by the E.C. in April 1924. Three months later the A.G.M. at York carried by 78 votes to 1 a proposal that the N.U.R. should affiliate to the Transport Workers' only on behalf of those 3,000 members (mostly trimmers, tippers and teamers) who came under the Shaw Award of 1920, but that full affiliation should await the achievement of closer unity among railway workers.

The same attitude was taken up by the N.U.R. when plans were considered for a revised form of industrial alliance in June 1925. Not only the transport workers and the miners, but also the engineers, were brought into these discussions which had for their aim the bringing together 'for offensive or defensive purposes the whole of the workers engaged in transport, mining and engineering'. Although at its June 1925 meeting, the E.C. of the N.U.R. 'heartily endorsed' the object of the discussions, it re-affirmed its belief that 'complete unity among unions directly affected by the separate and important industries was a first essential'. It stuck to this viewpoint when the matter was again considered in September and November. A conference of all the unions involved (including the A.S.L.E. & F.) held in the Essex Hall, London, on November 5, 1925, would not accept amendments in favour of union amalgamation on an industrial basis put forward by the N.U.R., and, in consequence, Mr Cramp was instructed by the E.C. to write to the other parties concerned that his union had 'no alternative but to refrain from being parties to the alliance'.

The chances of the conditions laid down by the N.U.R. being fulfilled seemed very meagre at that particular time. Bitterness resulting from the locomotivemen's strike of 1924 still remained. Mr Cramp told the A.G.M. at Southport in July 1925, than when, at one of the conferences about the proposed alliance, he had suggested that 'the various unions should work amicably together', Mr Bromley, General Secretary of the A.S.L.E. & F., rose immediately to say that he supposed Mr Cramp's remark was intended for his union, and that as far as he was concerned, he would never work with the N.U.R. again. The N.U.R. had not written to the Associated Society for a considerable time, but when they did write they received no answer.[22]

The negotiations to set up a new industrial alliance had not been completed when the coal industry was confronted with another major crisis. With the ending of the Ruhr strike and the stabilization of the German currency under the Dawes Plan of 1924, European coal production revived and export prices of British coal again collapsed. As they had done in 1921, the coal owners sought to offset falling prices and profits by slashing the wages of the miners. On June 30, 1925, they announced that wage reductions of between 13 per cent and 48 per cent of the existing wages would be introduced a month later. They were prepared to offer better terms only if the miners agreed to increase their working hours from seven to eight per day. The guarantee of a minimum wage—a characteristic of an agreement made in 1924—was to disappear under the new proposals. Later the news that the miners had rejected the new conditions caused little surprise in the labour movement.[23]

On July 10, 1925, the Executive Committee of the Miners' Federation met the General Council of the T.U.C. to explain the employers' terms and to state its case for obtaining the support of other trade unionists. The General Council, without hesitation, completely endorsed the refusal of the Miners' Federation to meet the owners until the new proposals had been withdrawn and it set up a special committee of nine members to watch developments and devise practical means of rendering assistance to the miners.

That more than the livelihood of the miners alone was at stake was made manifest at the time. The country had recently returned to the gold standard at the pre-1914 rate of exchange with the dollar, a decision which involved the maintenance of high interest rates and the depression of wages. On the day before the coal owners' notices were due to expire, i.e. July 30, 1925, the following dialogue took place when the Miners' Executive met Mr Baldwin, the Prime Minister:

Miners: 'But what you propose means a reduction in wages.'
Prime Minister: 'Yes. All the workers in this country have got to face a reduction of wages.'
Miners: 'What do you mean?'
Prime Minister: 'I mean that all the workers of this country have got to take reductions in wages to help put industry on its feet.'[24]

At a joint conference of the representatives of the N.U.R., A.S.I..E. & F., R.C.A. and the T.G.W.U., sponsored by the special committee of the T.U.C. and held on July 29, 1925, plans were drafted for enforcing an embargo on the movement of coal. Next day the following set of instructions were sent to all branches of the four unions co-operating in the scheme:

1. Wagons containing coal must not be attached to any train after midnight on July 31st, and after this time wagons of coal must not be supplied to any industrial or commercial concerns or be put on the tip roads at docks for the coaling of ships.
2. All coal en route at midnight on Friday to be worked forward to the next siding suitable for storing it.
3. Any coal either in wagons or stock at a depot may be utilized at that depot for the purpose of coaling engines for passenger and goods trains but must not be moved from that depot to another.

4. No imports of coal are to be handled from July 31st. Coal export: tippers and trimmers will cease work at the end of the second shift on July 31st.[25]

Had the occasion arisen for the implementation of these instructions it is highly probable that the embargo would have been more effectively enforced than had been the case in the spring of 1921. The union executives had learnt something from the mistake then made and the new instructions were more precise and were issued with full authority of the governing bodies of four powerful unions. More important was the contrast in the morale of the workers in the two periods. The coal embargo of 1921 was a half-hearted attempt at face saving after the debacle of Black Friday: the embargo of August 1925 looked like being the beginning of a determined counter offensive of labour to a new round of attacks on wages.

In the event the new embargo was never put to the test. The spirit of determination which was being displayed by the T.U.C. and the trade-union executives caused the Cabinet to resolve at its special meeting on July 30th, to attempt measures of pacification. After there had been further meetings between the Prime Minister, the coal owners and the Miners' Executive it was announced, early on Friday, July 31st, that a subsidy was to be granted to the coal industry for a period of nine months to enable a Royal Commission to make a full inquiry. A cartoon in the current number of *Punch* hinted at the extent of the Government's surrender but a few days after Mr Baldwin had bluntly declared that 'the Government would not grant any subsidy to the industry'. It depicted the Premier in his library surrounded by the members of the Cabinet diligently searching for a substitute for the word 'subsidy'.

As a result of these concessions, the coal owners' proposals for wage reductions were withdrawn and the projected coal strike was called off. Later, on July 31st, all N.U.R. branch secretaries received the following telegram:

'Miners' stoppage cancelled. Members must convey all traffic as usual. Cramp.'

The words of the *Daily Herald* poster—'Red Friday' were to become the enduring and fitting title to the events of July 31, 1925.

II

Although the immediate reaction of labour to the news of Red Friday was a spirit of exultation, it was quickly appreciated by the more far-sighted that the settlement of July 1925 provided no more permanent a solution to the ills of the industry than did the earlier settlements of 1921 and 1924. When the period of the subsidy came to an end on April 30, 1926, the Government was completely opposed to its renewal. The Cabinet granted it in 1925, so Mr Baldwin admitted, for the principal reason that it was not yet fully prepared for a 'showdown' with the unions. In May 1926, it was prepared. The presence in the Cabinet of a hard core of resolute opponents of any compromise with the miners—a group which included Mr Churchill, Sir William Joynson-Hicks and Mr Neville Chamberlain—and the determination of the miners' leaders to stand by their slogan of 'Not a penny off the pay, not a minute on the day' made conflict certain.

Once more the mine owners offered as their 'solution' to the problem, brought to a head by the withdrawal of the subsidy, a general reduction in wages varying in amount from district to district. The reductions originally proposed ranged from 20 per cent up to even 30 per cent or 40 per cent. In Durham, for example, hewers were to have 2s 10d taken off a wage of 9s 9d a day and labourers were to lose 2s 6¾d from a wage of 7s 6½d. The final offer made by the owners after the lock-out had begun on April 30th, was for an 8-hour day in place of the existing seven hours with a minimum wage of 20 per cent above 1914 compared with the then average of 33½ per cent above 1914.

It was these harsh terms and the Government's refusal to do anything to mitigate their severity which convinced the thousand-strong conference of trade-union executives which met in the Memorial Hall, Farringdon Road, London, on Friday, April 30th, that not only were the miners morally justified in resisting any further worsening of their conditions, but that the whole labour movement was threatened with a general offensive against the existing standard of living. Whilst these delegates waited for a total of more than eight hours—including two adjournments—whiling away the time by singing, the Industrial Committee of the T.U.C. was engaged in the final discussions at No. 10 Downing Street in an attempt to find a compromise making possible a return to work on the coalfields and a last minute abandonment of the plan for a general strike. It was not until just before midnight that this committee reported back to the union executives at the Memorial Hall. Mr Thomas, who was the sole railway-man representative on the Industrial Committee, told the meeting that the coal owners' final offer was one which 'would have meant such degrading terms', that he refused 'to believe there was any decent minded man or woman who would tolerate them'. In the talks with the Prime Minister he had failed in his main plea for a postponement of the lock-out notices which, he claimed, were inimical to calm and reasoned negotiation. He told his audience how hard he had laboured to find a peaceful solution:

'My friends, when the verbatim reports are written, I suppose my usual critics will say that Thomas was almost grovelling, and it is true. In all my long experience—and I have conducted many negotiations—I say to you, and all my colleagues will bear testimony to it, I never begged and pleaded like I begged and pleaded all day today.'[26]

At 12.30 p.m. the following day, Saturday, May 1st, the union executives met again in the Memorial Hall to vote on whether or not they approved the 'proposals for co-ordinated action' drawn up by the General Council of the T.U.C. The N.U.R. vote was included in the large majority in favour of the Council's plan. The count revealed that executives representing 3,653,527 members voted for the strike compared with a total opposition vote of 49,911. The executives also agreed to hand over to the General Council of the T.U.C. 'the conduct of the dispute' although it was not clearly under-stood by all the unions whether this did or did not include the right of the General Council to make a settlement of the mining dispute. It was left to the individual unions involved—and not all trade unions were called upon to strike at the outset—to issue orders to their members concerning the withdrawal of their labour.

Although at the Memorial Hall, the E.C. of the N.U.R. had pledged the full support of the members of the union in the forthcoming struggle, it was at the same time determined to retain full control on matters of policy. In the resolution carried unanimously at its meeting at Unity House on May 1st, it was decided 'in conjunction with the other unions affected, to instruct members to cease work in order to assist the miners to secure a satis-factory settlement'. The same resolution, however, ended with the words: 'So far as the conduct of the dispute is applicable to our members, this E.C. must retain autonomy'. In a branch circular posted on the following morning Mr Cramp explained why the executive could not place the union 'unreservedly in the hands of the General Council in so far as the dispute is concerned'. The fact was 'that many points arise on railways which the General Council could not be expected to understand'.

The relevance of this decision was soon apparent. Whilst the branch circular was still in the post, the E.C. was anxiously considering a recom-mendation it had just received from the General Council that 'a voluntary service should be set up to maintain food and essential supplies for the people'. After a careful consideration of the whole question, the unanimous decision was reached 'to request the General Council to review the position', the opinion of the E.C. being 'that all rail and transport workers should effect a complete stoppage'. Joint meetings with the executives of the A.S.L.E. & F. and R.C.A. had already been arranged as a result of an E.C. resolution passed on May 1st, and there was little difficulty in obtaining the consent of these bodies to the policy of a complete embargo on transport. By Monday, May 3rd, negotiations between the three railway unions, the Transport and General Workers' Union and the Advisory Committee of the T.U.C. had resulted in agreement in favour of a complete stoppage of all transport services. The E.C. of the N.U.R. later that day noted with satisfaction these developments and resolved to instruct the members of the union to co-operate with all other transport workers in their locality to ensure the success of the strike. Just over two months later, Mr Cramp explained bluntly and honestly the reasons for this decision which, he said, might 'seem very cruel'.

'If you were going to have a strike which should be effective . . . you have to shut down everything in the way of transport which might compete with railways. If you are in a war you have to fight with both hands. If once you start to play about with transport and arrange for food trains to run or food lorries, you are whacked straight off.'[27]

Once it had been agreed to try to stop all forms of public transport, it was all the more necessary for the T.U.C. to establish some system of communication between London and the provinces so that orders could be speedily delivered from Eccleston Square and reports be received in the opposite direction. On the eve of the strike (May 3rd) Mr Cramp received a request that the N.U.R. should send one representative to the T.U.C. to help set up 'a scheme of communications'. Brother Starling was sent. This, presumably, was the best that could be done, there being no Brother Pigeon on the E.C.

It was not union policy to stop supplies to hospitals. The E.C. decided to advise N.U.R. representatives on local strike committees to make arrangements 'according to circumstances' for the conveyance of food and other essential supplies to the local hospitals.[28] Rumours similar to those which had arisen on the occasion of the railway strike in September 1919, that the union was opposed to the feeding of the railway horses, were unfounded. In a circular to all branches on May 2nd, Mr Cramp wrote that the E.C. had decided that 'the strike committee in each area should make their own arrangements for the animals to be fed during the period of the dispute'.

Ironically, the union's officers were to some extent hoist with their own petard by the firmness of their resolve to stop all public transport. On May 7th, the E.C. 'having considered the difficulty respecting the hire of a car for the conveyance of our officials and the likelihood of increasing difficulty in this direction', instructed the Finance Committee to 'purchase a good and efficient motor car at once to enable our officers to carry out the necessary work they are called upon to perform'.

III

After the Memorial Hall meeting had voted overwhelmingly in favour of giving support to the miners, every branch secretary of the N.U.R. received, on the morning of Saturday, May 1st, a telegram bearing the following message: 'Executive instructs all our members not to take duty after Monday next. Arrangements to be made locally so that all men will finish their term of duty at their home station on Tuesday morning. Circular in post. Cramp'.[29] In the meantime the last attempts of Messrs Thomas, Pugh and Swales of the T.U.C. General Council to reach agreement with Mr Baldwin and his two Cabinet colleagues, Sir Arthur Steel Maitland and Lord Birkenhead, had failed late on the Sunday night, due to the Cabinet's decision to make the strike of the N.A.T.S.O.P.A. men at the *Daily Mail* a pretext for ending discussions. Next morning a further more lengthy telegram was sent to every branch of the N.U.R. advising members to act on the instructions already given as the stoppage now appeared 'inevitable'. After ordering that 'no trains of any kind must be worked', the message ended with the warning that members should 'allow no disorderly or subversive elements to interfere in any way' and that, if they had confidence in the union representatives, loyalty would 'ensure success'.

From midnight on Monday, May 3rd, the engine fires were raked out, the wheels stopped turning, and the station platforms, signal boxes and goods yards were deserted. The response to the strike call was unprecedented. More railwaymen came out in sympathy with the miners on May 4, 1926, than had struck in support of their own demands on September 26, 1919. During the next ten days thousands of telegrams were received at Unity House reporting the transport situation in every part of the country. With almost monotonous consistency they told of the remarkable unanimity and loyalty of the membership. Sheffield, Cardiff, Newcastle-upon-Tyne and the Manchester District all reported 'Response magnificent'; Bristol, Grantham, Toton, Masborough, Huddersfield, Leeds and Aberdeen reported 'All solid', whilst Plymouth reported an 'Unexampled discipline' from the 2,000 railwaymen on strike in that area. From only a few branches were there any indications of men in the conciliation grades remaining at work. Tring reported 'only one man at work', whilst from Chester came the news that 'all members except five' were on strike. On May 6th, another wire indicated that but five out of the thousand men of the locomotive grades employed at Camden Town were still at work.

Local strike bulletins confirmed the truth of messages sent by telegram. Stratford's Labour Bulletin of May 11th, under the heading 'Out to a Woman', reported that all the carriage cleaners at the Wimbledon Park Railway Depot had ceased work. The Grantham Joint Strike Committee News Sheet, published the same day, recorded that at Peterborough the only men at work were a relief signalman and four drivers, two of whom were time expired, and that there was no staff on duty between Sandy (Beds.) and King's Cross. From Nottinghamshire the Newark and District News Sheet, also on May 11th, showed that there were 383 on strike compared with eighteen, including clerical and supervisory grades, still at work. On May 9th, the official bulletin of the T.U.C. reported that there were only ten non-strikers on the whole of the Great Western Railway line from Evesham to Paddington. The telegrams sent to all branches from Unity House of May 5th—'All reports show position solid as a rock'—and on May 8th—'Stoppage 100 per cent efficient. Be sure and maintain our position. You cannot improve it'—were not a form of whistling in the dark, necessary to keep up the spirit of the membership, but a faithful representation of the true position as far as the N.U.R. was concerned. Among the membership of the A.S.L.E. & F. the response was, if anything, even more complete. According to the official journal of that Society 'there were not fifty members out of 50,000 who failed to answer the call'.[30]

The weakest link on the railways was the position with regard to the clerical and supervisory grades. Nevertheless, Mr A. G. Walkden, the General Secretary of the R.C.A., reporting on what he described as that Association's 'first real baptism in a general withdrawal of labour', declared the response of the membership to be 'most encouraging'. Three thousand new members were recruited in the first days of the strike. By May 10th, his office had received reports from nearly 100 branches which in most cases deemed the state of affairs to be 'highly satisfactory'. But if Mr Walkden's claim that 'the overwhelming majority of the clerical and allied grades were standing four square with the other workers' was true on May 6th when it was made, it was scarcely true on May 12th when only 55 per cent of the R.C.A. membership were on strike.[31]

The magnificent solidarity of the membership of the N.U.R. was encouraged by the hard work and efficiency of the staff at Unity House. The daily telegrams sent to every branch were much appreciated and helped greatly to maintain a high morale. Forty-one thousand of them were dispatched in the first fortnight of May. The telephone inquiries to the office were so numerous that a roster of four men was arranged for each of the four telephones connected with the external exchange. Of the 4,825 cheques sent to branches, only three were mislaid, with the result that in general members of the N.U.R. received their strike pay more promptly than did other strikers. A number of stranded railwaymen made their first real acquaintance with Unity House when they called asking for advice on how to reach their homes. All of them were put in touch with some form of transport going in the required direction. (It did not pay to be fussy.) To those who had benefited from these services Unity House was known as Dr Barnardo's.[32]

On the rare occasions when the cheque from headquarters was delayed, the local Co-operative Society lent generous assistance. The Secretary of the Kilwinning branch was greatly worried when no cheque had arrived by the morning of Saturday, May 8th. He was therefore much relieved to receive a telegram from Mr Cramp adivising him to contact the management of the local Co-operative store. Mr Scott, the Manager, was most helpful and quickly advanced the sum of £111 which enabled the Branch Secretary to face with equanimity the 109 members—an all-time record attendance for the branch—and pay each man his aliment at the rate of 4s a day. Afterwards the members joined lustily in the singing at the concert that had been arranged for that evening.[33]

In a number of districts members of the N.U.R. displayed their initiative by producing special railway strike bulletins. Among these were Punch (Brighton), the Oxford Railway Bulletin, the Stobcross N.U.R. Bulletin, the Victoria Signal, the Wigan Railway Bulletin and the York Railway Bulletin. Elsewhere they played their full part in contributing witty comments on the railway situation to the papers produced by the trades council or council of action of the area and to the *British Worker* published by the T.U.C. On May 11th, the 'Willesden (Central) Council of Action Strike Bulletin' noted: '*The British Gazette* (Mr Churchill's anti-strike official newspaper) announces that the vital services are getting better each day. But auto-suggestion won't run railways'. The *Preston Strike News* No. 3 (May 10th) under the heading 'Things we would like to know' asked if, 'After the blackleg amateur signalman at Ribble sidings had failed after trying for forty-five minutes to get an engine into the sidings and out again, the engine went into the shed disgusted?' In an ironical comment on the slowness and infrequency of the train service on the District Line in London the *Westminster Worker* commented: 'We understand that luncheon cars are to be put on trains running between Westminster and Blackfriars'. The St Marylebone Bulletin on Saturday, May 8th, reported 'that a train which left Manchester on Tuesday at 9.30 a.m. . . . arrived at Marylebone at 10.15 a.m. yesterday'; while from the Grantham Joint Strike Committees News Sheet on May 11th came the report that 'the railway crossing gates were given a ride to Peterborough from Helpston on Saturday'. Since means of communication were scanty during the strike, the publications of the strike committees were sometimes used to convey urgent messages. Bulletin No. 3 of the Midland District Council of the N.U.R. issued in Nottingham on May 7th contained this statement:

'The Toton No. 2 Branch reports that Mr A. P. of Alfreton No. 2 left Stapleford about 4.0 p.m. on May 5th. His wife will be pleased to learn of his whereabouts.'

It is to be hoped that the general strike was not, in this case, being used as an excuse for desertion. Occasionally sensible, practical household hints were included. The editor of the St Marylebone Bulletin on May 9th advised his readers to:

'Keep the home fires burning by destroying all your household refuse especially vegetable parings, tea leaves and everything likely to become offensive if not consumed.'

One outcome of the shortage of newspapers during the general strike was the increased attention given to the B.B.C. news bulletins. The Managing Director of the B.B.C., Mr John Reith, whilst desirous of keeping his organization free of direct Government control, at the same time believed it right that every assistance should be given to Mr Baldwin's administration in its attempt to defeat the strike. When the company was accused, after it was all over, of partiality on the side of the authorities, the official explanation given was that 'complete impartiality during the emergency was, in the circumstances, not to be expected'. On occasions the news bulletins revealed an excess of zeal to report a drift back to work, insufficient care being taken to check the accuracy of reports received. One of the tasks of the rank and file of the N.U.R. therefore, was to correct misleading or mistaken reports. On the one o'clock news on Saturday, May 8th, the announcement was made that seven sets of enginemen had that day reported back for duty with the Great Western Railway at Oxford. Members of the Oxford branch quickly investigated and found the reports to be false. They immediately notified Unity House and a denial of the B.B.C.'s statement appeared in the T.U.C. Official Bulletin No. 7 on May 10th. But the biggest howler came in the 5.30 p.m. B.B.C. news bulletin on Sunday, May 9th, when it was claimed that at Immingham there were fourteen food ships in the river and six in the docks and that the transport situation in that area was satisfactory. There was another quick check up by N.U.R. men on the spot who found that the actual position in the area was that there were no ships in the dock and none in the river. Since the previous Monday only two ships had entered the dock. In this case the T.U.C. distributed large numbers of specially duplicated leaflets which corrected the mis-statements of the B.B.C. and stressed the importance of strikers not being misled by reports given over the radio or printed in the *British Gazette*. Vague statements suggesting, at times, a disinclination of railwaymen to continue on strike and at other times giving an impression of a large scale return to work, were made in a number of the bulletins. At 9.30 p.m. on May 7th, the announcer said that 'it would appear that a good many railwaymen would like to return to work'. Two days later according to the 9.0 p.m. bulletin there 'appeared to be a tendency for railwaymen to return to work in various parts of the country'.

These statements were misleading if they led the public to believe that there was an appreciable return to work by men in grades concerned with the movement of traffic. It will be appreciated that there are some limitations to the efficiency of a railway system which is not provided with drivers, firemen, guards, signalmen, shunters and porters; and whilst at no time in the strike was there a 100 per cent withdrawal of labour on the railways, the situation was not far short of this among the conciliation grades on May 4th, and had not changed appreciably by May 12th. The

Ministry of Transport files for the locomotivemen revealed the following as the extent of the drift back to work:

Railway	Total Staff	Men available for duty	
		May 5th	May 12th
Great Western Railway . . .	6,206	79	104
London, Midland and Scottish .	14,671	93	273
London and North Eastern Railway	11,500	94	127
Southern	7,044	?	238

The extent of the wavering amongst signalmen was as follows:

Railway	Total Staff	Men available for duty	
		May 5th	May 12th
Great Western Railway . . .	4,843	384	584
London, Midland and Scottish .	11,871	901	1,152
Southern	2,940	?	534

The General Council of the T.U.C. was unable to reconcile the statements made in B.B.C. news bulletins with the reports it had received and thought that the big claims made were 'on the basis of a staff consisting in the main of supervisory grades, clerks, and more or less isolated railwaymen in the rural areas'.[34]

The solidarity of the men on strike is all the more remarkable in view of the sustained attempt by Government, B.B.C. and railway companies to persuade them to return to work. Much was made of the argument that the general strike was an illegal challenge to the constitution of the country. When this appeal failed to convince, personal letters and telegrams were sent to individual railwaymen instructing them to report for duty at specified times and places. Mr Cramp who, in a letter to the branches, reported the receipt of these messages, did not know who had been responsible for sending them. They were certainly ineffective.[35]

In so far as the companies had more men to employ on May 12th than they had had on May 4th, this was largely due to the enrolment of volunteers. There was no lack of enthusiastic would-be engine drivers from the earliest days of the strike. Shunters and permanent-way men were more difficult to obtain. Only a small percentage of those volunteering were in fact competent to take over duties without some preliminary training. The London, Midland and Scottish enrolled 21,807 volunteers but only employed 7,662 of them. The Great Western enrolled 5,620 persons in their recruiting office (the General Meeting Room) at Paddington but only utilized 2,234 of them. Although it recruited elsewhere on the system, the total number of amateur drivers employed at the end of the strike was only

760 compared with the normal complement of 6,202, 97·6 per cent of whom were still on strike on May 14th. Volunteer signalmen recruited at Paddington were sent to nearby Royal Oak where they were given a day's course of instruction comprising two three-hour lectures with an examination at the end of the day. They were then handed a textbook which had been specially prepared for the emergency. Just over 200 men were thus trained and sent to work in signal boxes. The company normally employed nearly 5,000 men in this grade. Training was also given to 138 volunteer shunters and seventy-four guards at Paddington, and although a few others were trained at other big centres, it is extremely doubtful whether more that one-twelfth of the normal labour force of about 7,000 men in these two grades was available for duty on the company's lines.[36]

Included in the volunteers were members of the aristocracy, some of whom had had experience of service in the 1919 railway strike. Among these was the Earl of Portarlington, who was to be seen at work on Paddington Station on both occasions. Lord Herachell drove a train in the Isle of Wight and Lord Monkswell acted as a signalman at Marylebone.

Despite the fact that some of the volunteers were men who had had previous experience of the type of work they undertook during the general strike, it must not be imagined that the companies' normal working rules were operative until after May 14th. With signal boxes only partially and spasmodically manned it was not possible to conform to the normal rules for safety of operation. The following instructions were issued for the benefit of volunteer drivers:

'Engine drivers are hereby informed that they are not to take any notice of the ordinary railway signals, but a very close watch must be kept at all signal boxes at either side of the line, and also on the line upon which they are working, and when they are required to stop their trains a red flag will be shown from the window of the signal box or by a man standing on the railway. When a red flag is shown, engine drivers must stop at once, and find out from the person giving the red flag stop signal what is required of them, and must on no account make any movement, either forward or backward, until they are told what to do.

'Engine drivers must only proceed slowly when travelling along curves in the railway.

'. . . When a train is stopped for any reason when travelling between stations, the driver must not start again until the guard gives him the green flag signal to do so, and the engine driver must then make quite sure that the guard is in the train and is not left behind.

'Engine drivers must keep a good watch for gates across the railway.

'It is only intended to run trains during daylight, but should a train, through delay, be on the line when it is dark, a red light waved from side to side will take the place of the red flag shown as the stop signal.'[37]

The thoughtful concern for the well being of the guard is an interesting feature of these instructions!

The sort of adventure that some train passengers experienced during the strike is illustrated in this report of a local businessman's journey from Hull to Selby in Yorkshire:

'The train was manned by the usual volunteer personnel in sweaters and plus fours, and all went well, though necessarily very tardily, until Staddlethorpe Junction was reached. Here the line divides into two branches, one leading to Selby and the other to Saltmarshe and Goole.

'The train was pulled up and the amateur driver was solemnly assured by signalmen of a similar type that the junction points were set in the direction of Selby. A fresh start was made, but in the course of time the businessman looked through his window and was alarmed by the unfamiliar scenery. The train was again pulled up when it was found that it had in fact reached Saltmarshe. With a fine disregard for all Board of Trade regulations prohibiting this mode of procedure for trains conveying passengers, it was propelled backwards to Staddlethorpe Junction for resumption of the journey.'[38]

It was often difficult to find suitable employment for those volunteers whose enthusiasm exceeded their technical knowledge. At a reunion dinner of Great Western Railway volunteers held in the Piccadilly Hotel on May 19, 1926, Viscount Churchill, the Chairman of the Company, told the story of an 'important volunteer for whom work could not at first be found'.

'He willingly accepted the task of oiling the points along the line. He was provided with a can of oil, and then nothing was heard of him for three whole days. On the fourth day a telegram was received at headquarters from him. It came from Bristol and read: "Please send me more oil." '[39]

It is an ill wind that blows nobody any good. Whilst the basic industries of Britain suffered losses as a result of the strike, those persons who gained their living as beauty specialists and manicurists experienced an unprecedented boom. Under the headline 'White Hands Again' the *Evening Standard* on May 18th, reported a 'rush to the Turkish bath establishments, skin specialists, manicurists, hairdressers and other purveyors of personal charm' by 'men and women strike volunteers including members of society and professional people' who were 'still endeavouring to remove traces of the grime of industrial warfare'. A leading manicurist told the reporter that his firm was 'very, very busy with women patrons and quite a number of men also, whose hands showed the effect of severe manual labour during the past ten or twelve days'.

How adequate were the railway services provided by voluntary labour? It is important to know the answer to this question, for it was claimed by the spokesmen of the railway companies that by the end of the strike services were beginning to approach much nearer to the normal. In the memorandum issued by the London, Midland and Scottish Company on June 2, 1926, it was claimed that 'had the T.U.C. not called off the general strike when they did there is little doubt that the company would very shortly have been in a position to deal effectively with all railway business offering'.[40] Even the railwaymen's leaders seem to have accepted something like this interpretation of events. On the night of Monday, May 10th, John Bromley, General Secretary of the A.S.L.E. & F. declared that unless the general strike was called off there would be 'thousands of trains running'. The result would be a 'debacle'. 'It is no good, we cannot go on any longer,' he said. Ben Turner of the National Union of Textile Workers and a member of the T.U.C. General Council wrote in his diary during the closing hours of the strike:

'During Monday night spoke to Cramp at top of steps about it being desirable strike should not go on above the week out. He declared also it must not go on much longer. Tuesday, Thomas saying ditto. Our reports are weakening 4,000 trains running, etc. Report Bristol docks weakened, Southampton strikers weakening, etc.'

After it was all over Mr Thomas said, 'The criticism is—Why did we not go on? We could not have gone on.' In an article he contributed to *Answers* in January 1927, he wrote that 'there was a wonderful service of trains on all lines in the Kingdom within a short while of the strike being called'.

The belief that the volunteers were on the point of re-establishing the train services to something like their normal pattern was, however, a myth. The following figures issued by the railway companies themselves show the extent to which volunteer labour had been able to meet the nation's needs for goods and passenger services:

Company	Passenger trains as a percentage of normal		Goods trains as a percentage of normal
	First day of strike	Last day of strike	Last day of strike
London, Midland and Scottish	3·8	12·2	3·0
London and North Eastern Railway	3·5	12·8	2·2
Great Western Railway	3·7	19·2	8·4
Southern	5·1	19·1	?

It is facts such as these which led the historian of the general strike to reach the very definite conclusion that 'the railway companies failed in their attempt to run an efficient railway system without railwaymen'.[41]

It is, of course, reasonable to assume that had the strike continued, the number of trains run would have continued to increase—up to a point. But it is also reasonable to assume that the arrears of maintenance (due to the fact that railway shopmen were not at work) would have reached serious dimensions. An increasing number of trains had been run, but often to the serious detriment of the locomotives. A driver from the London and North Eastern Railway noted, on his return to work at the Stratford depot, 'engines with buckled buffer beams and no buffers; some with great holes in their tanks and others with burnt and scored boilers'.[42]

It is largely due to the fact that the trains run were only a fraction of the normal number that there were not more accidents during the period of the strike. According to the then Minister of Transport, the railway companies, between May 4th and 14th, reported six accidents involving the deaths of four persons and the injury of thirty-five others. If these figures were complete, it was remarkable that the *British Worker*, in its issue No. 7 of May 11th, was able to report five serious passenger train accidents within thirty-six hours of dawn on May 10th. The most serious accident occurred at St Margarets, Edinburgh, on the afternoon of May 10th, when a number of wagons were being shifted from the 'up' to the 'down' main line and a passenger train, coming from Berwick and manned by a volunteer crew, crashed into them, killing three of the passengers and injuring fifteen others. Within a few hours of this disaster, at Bishops Stortford a goods train, coming from Cambridge, crashed into a passenger train which was standing in the station, derailing the goods engine and two of the passenger coaches and causing the death of one person and injury to three others. The Report of the Ministry of Transport Inspector, Lieutenant-Colonel A. H. L. Mount, on this accident stated that the disaster was to be attributed primarily 'to the failure of the volunteer driver of the goods train to realize the speed at which he was travelling, to the lack of explicit instructions to the traffic staff with regard to the preservation of the allotted time interval and to the lack of permanency in telephonic communications between stations'.[43] The system of requiring volunteer signalmen to phone through to the next manned signal box up the line to ascertain whether the line was clear before sending a train on, should have worked satisfactorily but in this instance both the driver and signalman were careless and failed to observe the emergency regulations. Had the number of trains increased much beyond the figure achieved at the end of the strike it seems very probable that there would have been a greater accident rate.

A remarkable feature of the strike was the orderliness of the strikers. Mr Cramp's advice to N.U.R. members wired to the branches on May 3rd —'Maintain perfect order'—was almost everywhere strictly observed. In a number of areas the police had occasion to compliment the N.U.R. on the good conduct of the members. Thus the Chief Constable of Hartlepool

J. Marchbank, General Secretary, N.U.R., July 1933–January 1943

PLATE 9

C. T. T. Cramp, Industrial Secretary, N.U.R., January 1920–August 1931. General Secretary, August 1931–July 1933

J. B. Figgins, General Secretary, N.U.R., September 1947–March 19

PLATE 10

J. Benstead, C.B.E., General Secretary, N.U.R.,
January 1943–September 1947

wrote to Mr Pounder, an N.U.R. official of the district, a letter of appreciation of the men's 'exemplary conduct during the strike'.[44] The sight of 'young bloods' lightheartedly manning the locomotives and guards' vans could be very provoking and yet on May 13th, the B.B.C. was able to announce that during the whole period of the strike 'the total casualties arising from disturbances and accidents are less than those caused in the recent fracas between Royalists and Police in Paris on Joan of Arc Sunday'.[45]

The sight of volunteer platelayers at work was too much for Mr T. A. of the Croydon No. 1 branch of the N.U.R. On May 8th, whilst on picket duty, he got over a fence and tackled three of them, taking a hammer from them and chasing them away. This impetuous act cost him two months' hard labour and the permanent loss of his job. Mr J. G., at Shipley, charged with throwing a stone at a passing train, was given one month's hard labour. The severest sentence inflicted on an N.U.R. member was one of four months' imprisonment, plus one week's hard labour, given to Mr J. B. of South Lambeth Branch. He was in a noisy crowd on the evening of May 7th when a policeman came straight to him and arrested him. He was later convicted on police evidence of 'obstructing the police; assault and wilful damage'. The local N.U.R. secretary believed him innocent and claimed that the police merely 'picked on' this member to make an arrest and to serve as a salutary warning to the rest of the crowd. But these cases were exceptional. Of nearly 400,000 members of the N.U.R. on strike only 174 were arrested. Of these, fifty-four had their cases dismissed, fourteen were found not guilty, fifty-four were given fines, mostly of £1 or £2, thirty-four were imprisoned, eleven bound over to keep the peace, whilst ten cases against the remainder were withdrawn.[46] The more serious case of the attempted derailment of the *Flying Scotsman* on May 10th did not involve railwaymen. Eight young miners were, on July 1st, convicted for this offence at the Newcastle Assizes and given sentences of from four to eight years' penal servitude.[47]

V

In view of the fact that Mr Thomas was more influential than any other man in bringing about the ending of the strike it is worthwhile examining his reasons for recommending—along with his colleagues on the General Council of the T.U.C.—the return to work on May 12th.

In December 1926, and January 1927, Mr Thomas contributed a revealing apologia for his actions in the previous spring in a series of articles published in *Answers*. In them he emphasized his thorough dislike of the general strike—'Never once . . . did I waver in my views, my certainty that disaster lay in adopting the last resort of a general strike as a way out of the labour troubles of the time'.

It may then be questioned why he did not speak against the majority at the momentous Memorial Hall meeting on April 30th. He frankly explained the reasons for his silence.

'What would have been the lot of the leader who, at that moment, had stepped forward and said: "You are all wrong. Your enthusiasm and your loyalty, one to the other, counts for nothing. You are being betrayed. I alone of all your leaders can see further than next week, or next month. Beware you are rushing to your doom."

'I tell you frankly that a situation had come along in the early days of May last year when no leader in the land who came forward with advice like this would have been listened to. He would have been scorned and execrated. . . .

'That is why I did not resign. I did not resign because I felt certain that I could do far more good by staying in than by going out. . . . Would it have been a brave thing on my part to have walked out of my party at that time and said: "Get on with it yourselves. You know that I disapprove of a general strike?"

'Perhaps it would. But it is my humble view that I did a far braver thing by staying with my army than by scuttling away from the field of battle. I remained because I felt convinced that I could assist to avert great dangers to the State and to my own folks.'

There was no doubt in Mr Thomas's mind that once the Cabinet had chosen to reject the General Council's claim that the general strike was merely a sympathetic strike in support of the miners and had chosen instead to pronounce it a challenge to the constitution, the eventual outcome could never be in doubt. The Government would, if necessary, arrest the strike leaders and call upon the armed forces of the Crown to deal with any disturbances. Since he believed the General Council would have to abandon the struggle sooner or later, he considered it best to end the strike at the earliest suitable moment before the unions were further weakened and their legal powers curtailed.

Mr Thomas's opportunity came when he received a phone call on the afternoon of Thursday, May 6th, from Sir Herbert Samuel who had that day returned to England from the Continent in the hope that he might be useful as a mediator in the dispute.[48] When the two men met in the Reform Club shortly afterwards, Mr Thomas readily agreed to ask the Negotiating Committee of the T.U.C. to meet Sir Herbert Samuel. The Cabinet, whilst not being opposed to the attempt to reach a settlement, at the same time made it clear that it held no brief whatever for any proposals which the Chairman of the Royal Commission might be prepared to make. So that there should be no doubt about the Cabinet's position, Sir Arthur Steel Maitland wrote to Samuel that it was 'imperative to make it plain that any discussion which you think it proper to initiate is not clothed in even a vestige of official character'.

Nevertheless Mr Thomas arranged for the Negotiating Committee to meet Samuel in the Bryanston Square House of his (Mr Thomas's) mining magnate friend, Sir Abe Bailey. The discussions there continued from Friday, May 7th to Monday, May 10th, the miners' leaders not knowing about them until the Saturday, and not being invited until the concluding stages on the Monday. In the end the Negotiating Committee was persuaded by Mr Thomas to accept the Samuel Memorandum which proposed that there should be no revision of miners' wage rates until a plan for the reorganization of the mines had been assured. There was to be no reduction of wages of the lowest paid men and no resumption of negotiations until the lock-out notices had been withdrawn.

On the evening of Monday, May 10th, at a joint meeting between the General Council of the T.U.C. and the miners' leaders, Messrs Thomas and Bromley tried their utmost to persuade the miners to agree to a return to work on the basis of the Samuel proposals. When they failed in this they threatened to take their men back to work if the miners did not comply, but Herbert Smith seemed unperturbed. He simply said: 'Take them back'.

Faced with this blunt refusal Mr Thomas then had less difficulty in persuading the General Council on Tuesday, May 11th, to prepare for a return to work without the miners. Some of its members might have been more hesitant about coming to this decision had they not been led to believe that the Cabinet was prepared to negotiate on the Samuel proposals. Ernest Bevin was certainly misled into this belief for he wrote to the branches of his union:

'You may take it from me that we, who were not on the Standing Committee, were assured that the Samuel document would be accepted, that the lock-out notices would be withdrawn and that methods of resumption would be discussed forthwith.'

At a final meeting on Tuesday night the General Council presented the miners with what amounted to an ultimatum that they must either return to work with the main body of trade unionists or continue the struggle on their own. When both Herbert Smith and Arthur Cook asked what guarantees there were that the Samuel proposals would ever be carried out, Mr Thomas replied: 'You may not trust my word, but will you not accept the word of a British gentleman who has been Governor of Jerusalem?' (Samuel).

After retiring to consider the question, the miners' leaders reported back to the General Council just after midnight that they regretted that, as the Samuel proposals included plans for a reduction in the wages of many miners, they could not accept them.

At 12.20 p.m. on Wednesday, May 12th, a deputation from the T.U.C. General Council waited on the doorstep of No. 10 Downing Street. They were admitted to see the Prime Minister and some members of the

Cabinet who were with him only when they gave an assurance that they had come for the sole purpose of calling off the strike. The formalities lasted less than fifty minutes during which time no mention was made of the Samuel proposals. Mr Thomas politely raised, in an indirect way, the question of the possible victimization of the strikers. He said to Mr Baldwin:

'We trust your word as Prime Minister. We ask you to assist us in the way you only can assist us by asking employers and all others to make the position as easy and smooth as possible because the one thing we must not have is guerrilla warfare.'

Only Ernest Bevin persisted in trying to get a definite assurance from the Premier that the strikers would be protected against victimization, but he was 'gently rebuked' and the deputation, bewildered and dismayed, were in the street again by ten past one. Bevin's comment on the interview was: 'Thousands will be victimized as a result of this day's work.'

v

There were two general strikes, not one, in May 1926. The first was fought under the direction of the General Council from May 4th to the 12th inclusive, whilst the second—a spontaneous refusal by the rank and file to return to work until better terms were promised by their employers—lasted a further two days.

On the evening of Saturday, May 8th, Baldwin, in a broadcast speech, not only denied that the Government was fighting to lower the standard of living of the miners or any other section of the workers; he also claimed that he was a 'man of peace' who promised to secure 'even justice between man and man'. On Wednesday evening, May 12th, he made a further broadcast speech in which he declared that 'our business is not to triumph over those who had failed in a mistaken attempt'.

The spirit of conciliation which was revealed in at least a part of Baldwin's speeches was not, however, to be reciprocated by some of the employers who preferred to take their cue from a Government statement issued on Wednesday (12th):

'His Majesty's Government have no power to compel employers to take back every man who has been on strike, nor have they entered into any obligations of any kind on this matter.'

It was the attempt of these employers to use the opportunity of the General Council's defeat to impose reductions in wages or renunciation of trade-union membership as a condition of reinstatement that brought the second general strike into being.

The railway companies felt that they had a legitimate complaint. The men's labour had been withdrawn on May 4th without the stipulated notice being given. The only notification they had received was a letter sent by Mr Cramp on May 1st in which he stated that 'in accordance with the decision arrived at at a Conference of Trade Union Executive Committees convened by the General Council of the T.U.C., it had been arranged to take steps in conjunction with the Transport Workers' Unions to call upon N.U.R. members to cease work on Monday 3rd (May)'. The general managers at once replied that this was 'an instruction to the men to break their contract of service with the company',[49] and that the union would be held 'responsible for the consequences'.

During the strike there were already indications that difficulties might be experienced in securing the reinstatement of the strikers. Mr F. J. C. Pole, General Manager of the Great Western Railway, who on May 7th published a statement in which he concluded that the 'only' explanation of the strike was that there was 'a deep conspiracy against the State', two days later issued a circular entitled 'Reinstatement of Strikers' to all the departmental managers of the company.

The instructions were as follows:

'Until further notice, men on strike who offer to return to work may be re-employed provided that their services can be utilized in any capacity, but no man who is known to have taken a leading part in organizing or carrying on the strike, nor any supervisor, is allowed to resume duty without explicit instructions from this office.

'A period will be reached when sufficient staff will have returned to work to enable a satisfactory service to be maintained, but the injury to trade is expected to be so serious that for some considerable time work will not be available for the normal staff. When 50 per cent of the staff at any station have resumed duty any other man allowed to return must be handed a notice that he has broken his contract.'

On Monday, May 10th, whilst the General Council of the T.U.C. was pleading with the miners to accept the Samuel Memorandum, the railway general managers were in conference drafting their terms of settlement of the strike. Minute number 21 of the meeting summarized their policy for the resumption of work:

1. The railway companies ought not to be put under any general obligation to re-employ persons on strike except as and when they are actually required for the conduct of the business of the companies.
2. The re-employment of any person is to be on the understanding that the railway companies do not surrender their legal rights to claim damages arising out of the strike from strikers and others responsible.

3. The railway companies to be at liberty to refuse to re-employ any person who has been guilty of acts of violence or intimidation, or who has wilfully damaged the property of his employers immediately prior to going on strike or whilst on strike.

4. The railway companies ought not to be committed to the re-employment of Stationmasters, Goods Agents and others who, having held positions of special responsibility, have joined in the strike.

Although these decisions were not known to the railwaymen's leaders at the time, it is clear that their attempted enforcement would mean that the return to work was likely to be an occasion for resentment and bitterness.

Meeting at Unity House on the afternoon of May 12th, the E.C. of the N.U.R. heard the news of the General Council's interview with members of the Cabinet. Still believing that the Government had given an undertaking at least to examine the terms of the Samuel Memorandum, it felt that the surrender had been 'on terms' and that the advice to return to work should be obeyed. All branches were therefore informed by telegram that afternoon:

'Trades Union Congress notify strike called off. Members must present themselves for duty at once. Keep me advised if necessary. Cramp.'

When that night and early the following morning the men presented themselves for duty the trouble began. At Lincoln the men were told that no instructions had been received from the company regarding their reinstatement.[50] Members of the R.C.A. at Glasgow reporting for duty were told that they would only be allowed to resume if they would agree to sign a statement that they were returning to work 'unconditionally'.[51] They refused to start work. On the Tyneside, at Edinburgh, Sheffield, Doncaster, Cardiff and many other places, as soon as the men discovered that the companies were not offering a general reinstatement, there was a spontaneous refusal to resume working. Rumours began to spread that in some places the companies had refused to take men back except at reduced rates of pay. These rumours were denied in a statement made by the Railway Information Bureau and broadcast on a B.B.C. news bulletin at 4.0 p.m. on May 13th. Every man taken back by the Great Western Railway was asked to sign the statement: 'You are hereby engaged on the understanding that you are not relieved of the consequences of having broken your service with the company'. London and North Eastern Railway employees were asked to sign a similar statement.

News of these difficulties soon reached the E.C. of the N.U.R. Later that afternoon (Wednesday, 12th) it was agreed to accept the request from the A.S.L.E. & F. for a 'joint three' meeting of the railway unions to consider questions of reinstatement. Next morning the three executives met at the A.S.L.E. & F. headquarters at 9 Arkwright Road, Hampstead. They carried unanimously a resolution which declared that the railway companies were 'not complying with the expressed desire of the Prime Minister that no vindictive action should be taken by the employers', and which instructed members 'not to return to work until the terms put forward had been withdrawn'. It was further decided to take up the matter with the companies with a view to removing 'difficulties' in regard to reinstatement.

To preserve unity and moral leadership whilst the strike continued, a Railway Unions' National Strike and Negotiating Committee comprising four representatives from each of the three unions, was set up.

Mr Cramp told a Press conference on the morning of Thursday, May 14th, that the railway companies were putting obstacles in the way of the return of the men to work and that 'the railwaymen would not stand for it'. He based this statement on the reports received from hundreds of branches within the previous twenty-four hours. The overwhelming majority of these were of the kind received from Grantham: 'Position absolutely solid', and Gloucester: 'Position fully maintained'—revealing no important break in the men's disciplined allegiance to the union.

The three general secretaries promptly composed a letter which they sent to the Secretary of the General Managers' Committee. It read:

> Joint Executive Committee,
> 9 Arkwright Road,
> Hampstead, N.W.3.
> May 13th, 1926.

Dear Sir,

Arising out of difficulties which are being experienced in the matter of the reinstatement of our members, our respective committees in joint consultation have been compelled to call upon all our members to continue the stoppage.

We are naturally anxious to bring the dispute to a speedy conclusion, and in order to accomplish this we suggest a speedy meeting between yourselves and our representatives at the earliest possible moment.

Kindly favour us with an early reply and oblige,

C. T. CRAMP, J. BROMLEY, A. G. WALKDEN.

There was a quick response. At 4.30 that same afternoon the Railway Unions' National Strike and Negotiating Committee was in conference with the general managers.

It was not an easy task for the unions to secure even tolerable conditions for the reinstatement of the strikers.[52] When their committee met the managers for the first time at 4.30 p.m. on Thursday, May 13th, its members were presented with a statement of the companies' proposals:

1. Those employees of the railway companies who have gone out on strike to be taken back to work as soon as traffic offers and work can be found for them.
2. In order to facilitate the early return of all men possible:
   (a) The guaranteed week for those classes of employees covered by the agreements with the railway companies to which the N.U.R. are parties, to be suspended forthwith, but to be restored as soon as traffic becomes normal.
   (b) Work available to be distributed as far as reasonably possible so as to equalize the number of days work for each man.
   (c) The companies, as far as possible, to arrange holidays during the suspension of the guaranteed week.
3. Each person as taken back to be reinstated in the position he held prior to the strike.
4. Each weekly paid person who has gone on strike to forfeit a week's wages at normal rates. Each monthly paid person to forfeit one fourth of a month's salary.
5. This arrangement is not to apply to:
   (a) Persons who have been guilty of violence or intimidation.
   (b) Persons in supervisory grades, including stationmasters, goods agents and clerks in special class and class 1; but each case is to be separately considered and decided by the companies.

The trade unions agree that each man who left his work without notice has broken his contract of service, and that the companies do not by reinstatement surrender any rights that they may possess.

Whilst the discussion on points 1 to 3 was not prolonged, since it was appreciated that no settlement of the coal dispute was in sight, and the volume of goods and mineral traffic was bound to be much below normal for some time, the union representatives strongly opposed the suggestion that each man should forfeit a week's pay (in addition to that not received during the strike) and that persons in the supervisory grades should be excluded from the terms of the settlement. The argument continued all that evening until ten o'clock when it was decided that it would be better to adjourn until half past ten the following morning.

Although the companies re-drafted the offending section 5(b) and specifically promised not to reduce the salary of any man they removed to a new position they asked the unions to undertake:

(a) Not again to instruct their men to strike without proper notice, and
(b) That stationmasters, goods agents and others holding positions of special responsibility should be excluded from any future strike.

The unions were further asked to deposit £100,000 as security for the observance of this clause.

In order to bargain for the removal of the security provisions, the unions conceded the right of the companies to move men in supervisory and top class clerical grades to new positions on condition that the companies supplied the unions with a list of names of the men it was proposed to move by the following Monday (May 18th) and that the men concerned should have an opportunity of having an advocate to present their cases to the general managers. As a further concession to the companies, the unions agreed to give 'no support of any kind to their members who take un-authorized action and to recognize that supervisory employees in the special class should not be encouraged to take any part in the strike'. The proposal of the companies which caused the greatest resentment, however, was that of withholding a week's wages from the men. In this case the union representatives were firm in their refusal to accept the companies' plan. In fact the meeting broke up with the general managers being told that the strike would continue unless the men were paid for the work they had performed. In the absence of the union representatives, the managers phoned the chairman of the four companies who agreed at a joint meeting with the managers to give the railwaymen their back pay.

When the union leaders were notified of the companies' decision they returned to the meeting and signed an agreement at 4.30 p.m.

Since the settlement of May 14, 1926, was to influence the lives of railwaymen for many weeks to come it is necessary to state its terms in full:

1. Those employees of the railway companies who have gone out on strike to be taken back to work as soon as traffic offers and work can be found for them. The principle to be followed in reinstating to be seniority in each grade at each station, depot or office.

2. The trade unions admit that in calling a strike they committed a wrongful act against the companies and agree that the companies do not by reinstatement surrender their legal rights to claim damages arising out of the strike from strikers and others responsible.

3. The unions undertake:
   (a) Not again to instruct their members to strike without previous negotiations with the companies.
   (b) To give support of any kind to their members who take any un-authorized action.
   (c) Not to encourage supervisory employees in the special class to take part in any strike.

4. The companies intimated that, arising out of the strike, it may be necessary to remove certain persons to other positions, but no such person's salary or wages will be reduced. Each company will notify

the union within one week the names of the men whom they propose to transfer and will afford each man an opportunity of having an advocate to present his case to the general manager.

5. The settlement shall not extend to persons who have been guilty of violence or intimidation.

Signed on behalf of the General Managers' Conference:

FELIX J. C. POLE, H. G. BURGESS, H. A. WALKER, R. L. WEDGWOOD, R. H. SELBIE.

On behalf of the Trades Unions:

J. H. THOMAS, C. T. CRAMP, J. BROMLEY, A. G. WALKDEN.

In a broadcast speech commenting on the settlement Mr Thomas declared: 'It is an agreement which in my judgment is not only satisfactory, but will set an example for others fo follow'.[53]

He was more aware than most of the financial difficulties of the N.U.R. and of the dangers to the funds of the union of a continuance of a strike. At a later date he claimed that it was the N.U.R.'s 'loyalty to the railway clerks' and the feeling of a moral obligation to them 'that caused him to sign the agreement'.[54] He meant that he believed a continuance of the strike would have jeopardized still further the chances of the clerks' reinstatement.

When the branches of the N.U.R. received a telegram in the early evening of June 14th: 'Complete reinstatement secured without penalties. All members should report for duty immediately. Full details to follow. Cramp', some, such as the branches at Sunderland, Middlesbrough, South Shields and Holyhead, decided to stay on strike until they learned more details. The Darlington men, after deliberations lasting nearly twenty-four hours, decided to return to work. The vast majority reached a similar conclusion. Mr Cramp endeavoured to allay the doubts and answer the criticisms in a branch circular on May 17th. He showed how the continuance of the miners' strike made immediate resumption of full working difficult and claimed that Clause 2 of the agreement was 'merely a statement of the position from the legal standpoint'. Nevertheless a mood of despondency prevailed and there was much criticism of the leadership.

Everywhere the ending of the strike was followed by part-time working and unemployment for many men. Shopmen returning to work at Barrow were told that they could be given only four days' work each week until further notice. The same fate befell most of the shopmen at Crewe and at Derby.[55] Thousands of locomotivemen, shunters and goods guards were entirely without employment. Only on the Southern Railway was there at first a practically complete reinstatement of the staff. Within a week the Government had requested that company to cut down its train services in order to conserve stocks of coal and the General Manager was asking for a suspension of the guaranteed week.

Because of these happenings, the joint E.C.s of the three unions asked the general managers to discuss the whole situation with them, and lengthy meetings were held on May 20th and 21st. The outcome was the agreement of May 21st, supplementary to that of May 14th. By it the guaranteed week was suspended except for those men who did not take part in the strike. Not less than three days' work was to be provided for each man and more would be provided when circumstances made it possible. Where the work available did not permit of three days' work a week what was available was to be shared by men working so many days one week whilst others, unemployed that week, would be taken on the following week. Men who could not be offered even this amount of work had their names put on waiting lists for re-employment when the situation improved.[56] This agreement was extended to include the Clearing House staff and clerical staff on June 2nd.

In the hope of obtaining the sympathetic intervention of the Government in the matter of railway employment, Mr Thomas wrote to the Home Secretary, Sir W. Joynson-Hicks on June 4th. The reply he received four days later was revealing as showing the hostility to labour characteristics of some members of the Cabinet at that time:

Sir,

I have your letter of the 4th inst. My sympathies are certainly with the man who returned to work before the strike was called off, though I need hardly say that my sympathies are greater with those who did not strike at all.

The Prime Minister's idea, I believe, was to get as many men back as possible, but you probably know that it is perfectly clear that the railways were frightfully overstaffed; no one in their service really worked his hardest and I think that some result of the recent strike will be either that they will work with less men or that if the total number are employed they will not be able to have full-time work.

This is only my private view but everybody knows that the facts were as I have stated.

Yours faithfully,
W. JOYNSON-HICKS.

Whilst the need for short-time working could be understood, though disliked, the greatest resentment was felt at the companies' treatment of the 'Clause 4' cases—the men in positions of special responsibility in the clerical and supervisory grades who had joined the strike and who were to be transferred to new posts. In accordance with the promise made on May 14th, the companies sent the three unions lists of the names of men it was proposed to move. The total number of men involved was ninety-four. The Southern Railway was the most lenient, only proposing to transfer three men, whilst the Great Western Railway list contained thirty-two names and the London, Midland and Scottish list thirty-one. Had the companies adhered strictly to the letter and spirit of the agreement of May 14th there would have been less cause of complaint, but when it became apparent that men were being transferred to new and lower-paid posts situated long distances away from their homes, and when the numbers involved exceeded those included in the companies' original lists, it was naturally concluded that some of the officials were being vindictive.

The three executive committees, therefore, resolved at a meeting on June 24th to ask for a conference with the companies to try to get more humane treatment of the men involved. When their request was granted and the two sides, the trade unions and the railway staff conference, met on July 2nd, the unions complained of the downgrading of salaried and supervisory staffs and of the practice of the London and North Eastern Railway endorsing the history records of their staff with detailed indications as to their attitude to the company during the strike. Mr Thomas contrasted the evidence of discrimination with the resolution (No. 530) of the E.C. of the N.U.R. on May 22, 1926, passed in reply to a suggestion from some branches that steps should be taken to penalize members who remained at work during the strike. It was unanimously resolved 'to instruct all officers that no action of a vindictive character' should be taken since it was a time for reconstruction when action of a 'vicious character' would be out of place. Mr Walkden for the R.C.A. complained that 1,500 of that union's members were not yet reinstated and that the companies were refusing to hold meetings of the departmental committees and sectional councils. Mr Clower, for the companies, said that in many cases men were not reinstated because there were no jobs available; he promised full inquiry into all the representations put forward.

Some anomalies and abuses were removed as a result of this vigorous protest, but it was still possible for the editor of the *Railway Service Journal* to write in August 1927: 'Today, fifteen months after the general strike, cases are still outstanding. In Scotland no clause four case has been settled satisfactorily on either the London, Midland and Scottish or London and North Eastern companies'. Even on the Southern Railway, whose record was generally the best of the four, men in the clerical and supervisory grades who asked for promotion received as a reason for the refusal of the request the retort: 'Well, you were disloyal in 1926 weren't you?'

It was not until April 11, 1927, that the full guaranteed week was restored on the railways. The long delay was not due to any lack of effort on the part of Mr Cramp or the E.C. of the union. It was not until November that the lock-out on the coalfields ended, and the goods and mineral receipts of the companies had declined sharply in the year 1926. When the joint three E.C.s met the railway managers on December 21, 1926, they were told that in view of the traffic conditions of the time, the immediate introduction of the guaranteed week would mean the discharge of a large number of men who were partially employed. The E.C. of the N.U.R. decided not to accept the companies' proposal to pay to each person an *inclusive* weekly amount (including overtime rate and Sunday pay) not less than the weekly *rate* of pay. It preferred to wait a little longer in the hope that the full guaranteed week conditions would eventually be restored.

A full agreement for the restoration of the guaranteed week was reached at a meeting between the three E.C.s and the general managers in London on February 16, 1927. After February 21, 1926, the companies promised weekly earnings to all employees of not less than four days' pay at ordinary rates. From March 14, 1926, five days' pay was guaranteed, whilst from April 11th the full working week was to be guaranteed for all conciliation, clerical, supervisory and other staff.[57]

Even for those who were lucky enough to have a full working week before April 1927, working conditions were often far from normal. A locomotive-man who was employed at this time writes:

'On the railways we were burning imported coal, coke and green logs. With varying results. Oil burners were hastily fitted on main line engines but the oil fuel supplied was of poor quality, in fact, it resembled thin tar. These engines were dubbed "tar pots" and much time was lost owing to the shortage of steam.'[58]

Changes such as these brought new problems for the shopmen, signal-men, shunters and guards as well as for the footplatemen.

VI

It was one of those English rarities—a warm, sunny summer day. Mr Thomas was with his family on the beach at Weymouth during one of the few brief spells of relaxation from the worries of an Annual General Meeting. He had completed most stages of the tricky ritual of undressing preparatory to a bathe when he discovered, with dismay, that his bathing costume had been taken from the place where he had hung it up to dry. In the emergency someone quickly found a bathing slip which he put on gratefully. He had not been in the sea many minutes, however, when he realized with even greater dismay that the bathing slip had completely disappeared. His daughter swam vigorously to the shore whilst he sat discreetly on the bed of the ocean. Another bathing costume was produced, but he was unable to get it on. Eventually he had to be towed beachwards on a raft with his back towards the shore until, reclothed in his normal attire, he was able to face the large crowd of holidaymakers who had been enjoying their free entertainment.

If, for a time, Mr Thomas was naked in the sea, it was not his habit 'to go naked into the conference room' and the A.G.M. at Weymouth in July 1926, was to prove no exception. It was expected that the keenest debate would be at the 'inquest' of the principal officers of the union on their conduct during the strike and their acceptance of the terms of re-instatement on May 14th. Thousands of railwaymen were still unemployed or only partially employed and it was inevitable that some of the delegates would feel that Mr Thomas bore the chief responsibility for this state of affairs. There were not lacking signs of discord even before the conference began. Mr Thomas had taken exception to some statements which Mr Dobbie, the President of the Union, proposed to make in his annual address. Mr Dobbie referred to Mr Baldwin 'as the "man of peace" who had always been engaged in fighting the workers' and who 'gained his ends by posing as a friendly disposed opponent' in contrast with the 'blunt but more straightforward methods of his Cabinet colleagues'. He (Mr Dobbie) expressed himself proud 'to have taken part in the great fight' which had been 'the means of rousing the class-conscious spirit of the workers'. Mr Thomas pleaded with him to delete these parts of this speech, but he declined to do so.

On Tuesday, July 6th, when the great debate on the general strike took place, Messrs Figgins, J. Henderson and Loeber led the opposition to the platform. Because the special T.U.C. conference on the general strike had not yet taken place, their proposal was that the full-scale N.U.R. discussion of the subject should be postponed until six weeks after the T.U.C. had met when a Special General Meeting of the union should be summoned with a better chance of the delegates being well informed on the facts.

Mr Thomas in a vigorous defence of his past actions declared that he had 'no regrets' and that all he had done was 'to try to make the best of it to find an honourable settlement to save as much from an inevitable wreck as could be done'. Anyone who believed that the strike could have continued for any lengthy period was not only 'not conversant with the facts' but was putting forward a view which was 'contrary to all their knowledge and experience'. The dramatic moment of the debate came when Mr Thomas read a Communist Party document of June 4, 1926, to all Party N.U.R. 'members' instructing them which resolutions on the agenda of the forth-coming conference they were to support. He also read private letters (which by some means had come into his possession) exchanged between three of the delegates—Messrs Figgins, Loeber and Wadge. In them they had arranged to meet before the A.G.M. to consider their tactics. He then appealed to the delegates 'to take no notice of delegates who had received their instructions from outside bodies', and to defeat Mr Figgins's resolu-tion.

The Political General Secretary's appeal to union loyalty and his skilful tactics had their effect. The delegates rejected Mr Figgins's motion by 54 votes to 23, whilst an amendment which had the support of the platform—'That having heard the report in relation to the calling off of the General Strike by the T.U.C. we accept the explanation given'—when put as a substantive motion, was carried by 52 votes to 25. The critics had failed once again in their challenge to Mr Thomas's leadership but they had gained the support of about a third of the delegates.[59]

VII

The General Strike was not only the most prolonged strike in which the N.U.R. had been involved, it was also the most expensive. On May 1, 1926, the total assets of the union had just topped the two million pounds mark. At the end of December 1926, they had fallen to £580,001 8s 0d.—the lowest figure in the union's history apart from its inaugural year, 1913. The cost of the strike benefit paid out from May 4th to 15th was £935,000, whilst, if the expenditure of the branches during those twelve days is added, the immediate cost of the strike was over £1 million. The indirect cost to the union was even greater. Up to April 11, 1927, when the guaranteed week was restored, the union had disbursed £1,564,277 in unemployment benefit to its members. Mr Thomas told the delegates of the Labour Party Conference at Margate on October 12, 1926, that, at that time, 45,000 N.U.R. members were unemployed and 200,000 others working a three-day week.[60]

Without the assistance of the C.W.S. bank the expenditure of such colossal sums would not have been possible. In the early days of the strike the trustees of the N.U.R. deposited with the bank securities to the nominal value of £1,143,345 2s 7d on which £950,000 was allowed as an overdraft. On May 8th another parcel of deeds of a nominal value of £469,209 15s 8d was handed in on which a further overdraft of £350,000 was obtained. The C.W.S. bank charged bank rate (then at 5 per cent) on these overdrafts whereas the other banks would have charged from ½ to 1½ per cent over the bank rate on such loans.

That by December 31, 1927, the assets had mounted from £580,001 8s 0d to £859,568 16s 10d was due to an economy of management, a relative freedom from industrial strife and the raising of additional revenue.

At the end of May 1926, the E.C. reluctantly decided that it could not pay donation benefit to men who were working only three days a week. At its December 1926 meeting it reached the unanimous decision that men who had received £11 5s 0d or more in donation benefit since May 4th, could not be paid any more until after they were re-employed and had completed at least twenty weeks' work and union contributions.

There were on the books of the union approximately 10,000 ex-railwaymen members—men who had been railwaymen but who had transferred to other occupations. The E.C. felt obliged to discontinue, from the beginning of 1927, the payment of donation benefit to such of these members who were out of work as a result of the strike since they had cost the union £30,000 and had paid in only £1,083 in contributions in the course of 1926.

At the same time the income of the union was improved by the E.C. decision to raise contributions of all members by 1d a week as from January 1, 1927, and to call for a special levy of 3d a week per member for the year 1927 only. Those members who could pay the levy in a lump sum of 13s at the beginning of the year were encouraged to do so! The levy produced a total of £141,132 2s 11d towards the recovery from pawn of the union's securities. To sugar the pill, the E.C. at the same time decided to discontinue the voluntary levy of 1d a week per member on behalf of the miners.

After 1929 the depression in trade had the effect of slowing up the rate of recovery of union funds, and it was not until June 1937, more than eleven years after the General Strike, that the then General Secretary, Mr John Marchbank, was able to report a favourable balance (£2,037,993) which exceeded that of May 1, 1926.[61]

The financial position of the A.S.L.E. & F. following the strike was even more serious than that of the N.U.R. The R.C.A. emerged from the struggle in the sunniest position of the three railway unions owing to a decision of the 1921 A.G.M. to raise the membership subscription to 1s a week, and the ready response of the membership after the strike to make a voluntary lump sum contribution of £1 a head. Mr Walkden reported to the Press on November 25, 1926, that his union had not had to realize money on any of its investments.

The R.C.A. apart, the financial difficulties of the unions after May 1926 were bound to limit their bargaining strength. The advocates of a policy of co-operation with the management, among which both the general secretaries of the N.U.R. were included, could point to the low state of the unions' funds as an argument against any further resort to industrial warfare and in favour of an attempt to gain the goodwill of the managers. Mr Thomas told the thousand railwaymen of all 'grades' from porters to directors who attended a Lord Mayor's Banquet on June 20, 1926, that 'peace was essential to industry'.[62] He told the delegates at the A.G.M. of the N.U.R. three weeks later, that 'he looked upon the negotiations following the General Strike as commencing a new era' and he wrote in the *Railway Review* on September 16, 1927, that there was 'scarcely a single question arising in the course of railway employment which may not be freely discussed between the management and the representatives of the men'.

The managers reciprocated this desire for industrial peace. Mr H. G. Burgess, the General Manager of the London, Midland and Scottish in a circular to his staff issued immediately after the strike claimed that the future held the 'promise of returning prosperity'.

'We cannot exact the fulfilment of that promise (he wrote) unless we all pull together. It is for the spirit of co-operation that I appeal to the whole of the staff.'[63] At the same time Sir Herbert Walker, General Manager of the Southern Railway, wrote to his staff:

'We all serve the same company, all belong to the same enterprise and our interests—the interests of the Southern Railway—are identical. Let us go forward together looking, as the Prime Minister has said, to the future.'[64]

Unfortunately, the future belied 'the promise of returning prosperity' and in the circumstances of diminished company revenues through growing road competition, followed, after 1929, by business depression, the policy of co-operation was subjected to severe strains.

NOTES

1. J. H. Thomas, Speech in the House of Commons, May 11, 1927, quoted in *R.R.*, May 20, 1927. R. Smillie, Article on the Triple Alliance in the Labour Year Book, 1915.
2. *R.R.*, March 8, 1912. A.S.R.S. Quarterly E.C. June 1912.
3. N.U.R., S.G.M. September 21, 1920, Verbatim Report.
4. N.U.R., S.G.M. September 23, 1919, Verbatim Report.
5. N.U.R., S.G.M. October 20, 1920, R. 5.
6. The editor of the *Birmingham Post* of October 25, 1920, had written of 'the railway strike so wantonly threatened by Mr Cramp and his followers'. Whilst the *Evening Standard* on October 22nd stated that Messrs Cramp and Williams had succeeded in persuading the delegate conference of the N.U.R. to declare a sympathetic strike. For Mr Cramp's denial see *R.R.*, November 5, 1920.
7. N.U.R., S.G.M. October 23, 1920, R. 13.
8. R. Page-Arnot, *The Miners*, Vol. 2, pp. 270–1.
9. C. L. Mowat, *Britain Between the Wars*, p. 121.
10. N.U.R., E.C. March 31, 1921, R. 300 and amendments.
11. N.U.R., S.G.M. April 6, 7 and 8, 1921, Verbatim Report.
12. J. H. Thomas, speech at Central Hall, Derby, May 1, 1921, reported in *R.R.*, July 1, 1921. R. Page-Arnot, *The Miners*, Vol. 2, p. 315.
13. *R.R.*, April 22, 1921.
14. *Daily Herald*, April 16 and 25, 1921.
15. *R.R.*, May 6, 1921.
16. N.U.R., A.G.M. Newcastle, July 1921, Verbatim Report.
17. N.U.R., E.C. April 22, 1921, R. 317.
18. N.U.R. Industrial General Secretary's Report 1921, p. 27. Special E.C. May 31, 1921, R. 379.
19. *Gloucester Journal*, August 20, 1921.
20. N.U.R., A.G.M. July 1922. S.G.M. March 28, 1923, Verbatim Reports.
21. R. 643.
22. N.U.R., A.G.M. Stockport, July 10, 1925. Verbatim Report, pp. 40–1.
23. R. Page-Arnot, *The Miners*, Vol. 2, p. 263.
24. *Daily Herald*, July 31, 1925.
25. N.U.R. Circular No. 344, to all branches, July 30, 1925.
26. Julian Symons, *The General Strike*, pp. 42–3.
27. N.U.R., A.G.M. Tuesday, July 6, 1926, Verbatim Report of Proceedings on 'General Strike', pp. 24–5.
28. N.U.R., E.C. May 7, 1920, R. 506.

29. I am indebted to Mr Frank Taylor of Richmond Branch, N.U.R., for loaning me a complete file of telegrams he received during the strike.
30. *Locomotive Journal*, June 1926.
31. General Council of the T.U.C. Strike Bulletin Nos. 4 and 7. C. T. Cramp's statement, N.U.R., A.G.M., July 6, 1926, Verbatim Report, p. 61. Nottingham Strike Bulletin No. 2, May 8, 1926, kindly lent by Driver L. Palpass of Middle Furlong Road, Nottingham.
32. *R.R.*, May 21 and June 4, 1926.
33. Minute Book, Kilwinning Branch, kindly lent by Mr Kenneth Close, Secretary.
34. Figures and the General Council's statement taken from Julian Symons's: *The General Strike*, pp. 209–10.
35. N.U.R. Branch Circular M7JMC/493, May 11, 1926.
36. Great Western Railway booklet: *The General Strike*, pp. 23–4 and Appendix 4. London, Midland and Scottish figures published in *The Railway Gazette*, June 11, 1926, p. 761.
37. Quoted in *R.R.*, May 28, 1926.
38. Quoted in Julian Symons's: *The General Strike*, p. 97.
39. *Railway Gazette*, May 7 and 14, 1926, p. 670.
40. *Railway Gazette*, June 11, 1926, p. 761.
41. Julian Symons: *The General Strike*, pp. 207–8, 96 and 100.
42. Typescript account 'Vaporisings of a Locoman' by Buffer Beam, kindly lent by Mr F. L. Button, 8 Connaught Road, Leytonstone, E.11.
43. *Railway Gazette*, August 27, 1926.
44. *R.R.*, May 28, 1926.
45. News Bulletin, 10.0 a.m., Thursday, May 13th.
46. N.U.R., E.C. September 1926, p. 63.
47. *Railway Gazette*, July 9, 1926, p. 64.
48. This summary of the negotiations between May 6th and 13th is based on the accounts given in Julian Symons's: *The General Strike*, pp. 187–90 and 203–7 and Alan Bullock's *The Life and Times of Ernest Bevin*, pp. 325–37.
49. Statement contained in a letter from F. J. C. Pole, General Manager of the Great Western Railway Booklet 'The General Strike', published by the Great Western Railway, p. 11.
50. B.B.C. News Bulletin, 1.0 p.m., Thursday, May 13, 1926.
51. *Scottish Worker* (Glasgow), May 13, 1926.
52. Details of negotiations for the railway settlement taken from the Great Western Railway publication: 'The General Strike'.
53. Quoted in *Railway Gazette*, May 14th, p. 665.
54. *R.R.*, July 9, 1926, reporting Mr Thomas's speech at Weymouth on Sunday, July 4, 1926.
55. *British Worker*, No. 11, May 17, 1926. (Last issue.) *Sheffield Daily Telegraph*, May 18th.
56. N.U.R. Circular to Branches, May 22, 1926.
57. N.U.R.,E.C. December 1926,Rs. 1400,1470 and 1471.*R.R.*, February 25,1927.
58. Buffer Beam: 'Vaporisings of a Locoman', p. 150.
59. Details about the debate taken from N.U.R. A.G.M. Tuesday, July 6, 1926, 'Verbatim Report of Proceedings on the General Strike'.
60. Labour Party Report of the 26th Annual Conference, Margate, October 10 to 15, 1926, p. 198.
61. N.U.R. Report and Financial Statement for 1937.
62. *R.R.*, July 8, 1926.
63. *Yorkshire Post*, May 18, 1926.
64. *R.R.*, May 28, 1926.

CHAPTER XVIII

1927-33: BACKS TO THE WALL

A. G. Walkden (Secretary, Railway Clerks' Association):
   Is it not the duty of all responsible people in this world to make things better for those who are coming after them?
Sir Ralph Wedgwood (General Manager, London and North Eastern Railway):
   I am talking in a strictly business sense.
A. G. W.: That is how we should live, is it not?
Sir Ralph: In our private lives?
A. G. W.: No, in all our capacities!
Sir Ralph: No, I am afraid you had better argue with the Board.
A. G. W.: May I argue with the Board? I should be very glad to come and talk with them. Is it not a part of our duty, at any rate, to make things better for those coming after us?
Sir Ralph: I think in matters of business—I am talking of big business—we are responsible to our shareholders!
National Wages Board Hearing on the Railway Companies' claim to reduce railwaymen's wages by 10 per cent, December 1932.

I

IN the years 1927-33 bleak times were experienced by many of those who sought to gain a livelihood on the railways. In respect of wages and working conditions the story is one of almost uninterrupted retreat, the union officials fighting a prolonged rearguard action to save as many as possible of the basic improvements achieved in the national settlements of 1919-20.

There were two main reasons for the setbacks of these years. The first was the intensification of road competition in the carriage of passengers and goods—a challenge which became the principal concern of the railway companies in the years 1927-30 when bus and road haulage services were virtually unregulated by Parliament. The second was the decline in industrial production which became serious in the summer of 1930 and continued until the summer of 1933. It brought with it a sharp fall in the railway companies' revenues from the carriage of coal, other minerals and general merchandise traffic. The policy of government and of private employers in meeting the economic crisis by wage reductions, by reducing demand for goods, served to aggravate the unemployment problem. As the number of unemployed soared to its peak of 2,955,000 in January 1933, the railway companies' revenue from passenger traffic sank to its lowest point in the inter-war period.

Of these two main influences the depression of the country's basic industries had the most serious effect on the ability of the railways to continue profitable operation; but in the first few years following the General Strike it was perhaps inevitable that attention should have been focused on the rapid expansion of motor transport. The number of buses and coaches in Great Britain increased from 40,118 to 52,648, or by more than a quarter, in the four years between the General Strike and the passage of the Road Traffic Act in 1930. The rise in the number of goods vehicles on the roads from 257,123 in 1926 to 348,441 in 1930, was proportionately greater.[1] The loss of passenger traffic to the buses was most serious on journeys of up to ten miles. A special study of London Midland and Scottish Railway revenue from passenger traffic for the period 1923-7 revealed that receipts from journeys of up to ten miles declined by 27 per cent, on journeys of between 11 and 20 miles by 23 per cent, on journeys between 20 and 50 miles by 7 per cent, whilst on journeys of over 50 miles there was an increase of 2 per cent.[2] Other companies suffered more seriously from the competition of coach traffic which was growing with great rapidity in East Anglia, the Midlands and the Home Counties in the later 1920's.[3]

The living standards of railwaymen were threatened not only by the abstraction of passenger traffic by the bus and coach companies, but also by the existence of sweated labour conditions on the newer forms of transport. A deputation from members of the Transport and General Workers' Union to the Glasgow magistrates in December 1927, urged that before bus owners were granted licences to operate in the city, they should be required to give an undertaking not to employ their drivers and conductors more than eight hours a day. Some firms, it was alleged, were working their men from fourteen to seventeen hours a day without relief.[4] Delegates to the A.G.M. of the N.U.R. in July 1929, gave instance of bus drivers in Wales employed for a weekly wage of between 25s and 30s a week, with no fixed hours, no payment for overtime, and no extra pay for Sunday duty.[5] In sober terms the Royal Commission on Transport in 1930 reported that the wages and working conditions in the bus industry 'left much to be desired'. There were 'firms whose profits represent(ed) to a considerable extent the difference between the wages paid and the conditions obtaining, and the wages which should be paid and the conditions which should obtain if proper standards were maintained'.[6]

The extent of the road hauliers' encroachments on railway goods traffic is more difficult to measure for the reason that the business was divided between some 30,000 operators who were engaged in a chaotic free-for-all struggle for survival, until the Road and Rail Traffic Act of 1933 brought some semblance of order into the industry by the introduction of a system of licensing. But all the Railway Companies' General Managers were agreed that the road hauliers were skimming off the cream of the hitherto profitable traffic in high value goods on the main trading routes. The character of much of the competition in goods traffic the railways had to face was lucidly described in a memorandum submitted to the Royal Commission on Transport in June 1930:

'The owner driver has usually been a newcomer to the trade who has acquired a lorry. He has little business experience, knows little of the cost of running a lorry over a series of years and has no appreciable organization for obtaining traffic. He probably starts with a promise of obtaining traffic from certain people. As soon as a run is accepted he has got to get back to his base, and is almost forced to accept any rate that may be offered, and is certainly tempted to canvass for traffic at a rate which will obtain the traffic irrespective of whether it is a paying proposition in the long run for himself. The same thing applies even in his home town if work is slack, and it is accentuated if his vehicle be bought on the hire purchase system, under which he has to obtain substantial cash receipts at any cost in order to meet his instalments. The only way in which the small man in this position can keep going is to increase his hours of labour and try and make man and machine do an abnormal amount of work. . . . The result is overwork for the owner or driver; machines in bad conditions; and often danger to the community through tired men being on the road when they ought to be in bed.'[7]

Sir Maxwell Hicks, a leading authority on the road haulage business, told the Royal Commission that he knew of a 'reputable firm' whose drivers were regularly scheduled to sleep in their lorries on the road every Monday, Tuesday, Thursday and Friday night in order to complete their stint of 700–800 miles a week. He said that it was a practice on the main roads of England for 'a great many drivers' habitually to sleep at the side of the road.[8] The rates of pay of road motor men bore unfavourable comparison with the rates paid by the railway companies for a similar type of work. Motor van drivers employed by private firms on the Liverpool–London run in 1928 were paid 35s 6d a week without any proper rest period or lodging allowance or overtime payments. Motor drivers employed by the London, Midland and Scottish Railway in the same period were on a wage rising from 54s to 74s for a week of 48 hours, whilst any overtime duty was paid at enhanced rates.[9]

It was becoming increasingly evident that the maintenance of a decent standard of living for railwaymen depended upon the establishment of tolerable conditions of employment for the road transport workers. It was no longer sensible to think of railwaymen's wages as being determined solely by conditions within the railway industry considered in isolation.

II

Old habits of thought die slowly, often surviving into an age when they no longer reflect the realities of daily life. This appears to have been the case both in the railway company board rooms and in the union conferences. For many decades before the First World War the railways had enjoyed a virtual monopoly of goods and passenger transport over the longer distances. It was therefore understandable in the early 1920's some railway directors should consider road transport competition of only limited importance whilst A.G.M. delegates and Executive Committee men should continue to confine their calculations to conditions of work on the railways.

It is true that Mr J. H. Thomas had warned the Leicester Conference in November 1917, that the problem was 'not a mere railway problem but a transport problem' owing to the fact that road transport competition would be intensified after the war, and that early in 1918 the Conference of District Councils and Vigilance Committees had urged the inauguration of a national State transport system which would include water, rail and road services;[10] but these far-sighted statements found no reflection in the resolutions of the unions' annual conferences until a decade had passed We have seen that in the year 1922 the companies endeavoured to obtain Parliamentary powers for their operation of extended road transport services.[11] However, when Parliament laid down onerous terms for the granting of these concessions the companies abandoned their Bill and it was not until six years later that they tried again.

Paddington No. 2 Branch of the N.U.R. submitted a resolution to the Belfast A.G.M. in July 1920, that the union should appoint an advisory committee of at least five members to examine the rates of pay and conditions of service of road motor transport workers. This Committee would then report to the E.C. recommendations for safeguarding the standard of living of both rail and road workers. The proposal was cold-shouldered by Mr Thomas from the platform when, with a wave of his hands, he assured the delegates that he had been in touch with the companies' general managers on the question and they had convinced him that there was no cause for alarm. With this reassurance from the General Secretary, the delegates rejected the Paddington resolution by 18 votes to 14. Two years later, Mr H. W. Lane, a motor driver from Paddington, tried again with a similar resolution which he considered particularly appropriate in view of the consideration by Parliament of the Companies' (1922) Bill for road powers. After another decisive intervention by Mr Thomas, the resolution was withdrawn. The same fate befell resolutions from the Essex District Council for an approach to be made, through the T.U.C., for an amalgamation of all transport unions and from London No. 2 branch for an approach to the newly formed Transport and General Workers' Union with a view to fusion.[12]

After the General Strike it was Mr Thomas who at the meeting of the General Council of the T.U.C. on December 20, 1927, moved the acceptance of the invitation from Sir Alfred Mond, head of I.C.I., to a series of discussions between the T.U.C. and leading employers on the subject of industrial peace.[13] Consistent with this advocacy of class collaboration in industry as a whole, was Mr Thomas's policy of co-operation with management in the railway industry. Thus, whilst he dominated the affairs of the union until his appointment as Lord Privy Seal in the Second Labour Government in June 1929, the policy of the N.U.R. for road transport largely took the form of a backing of the railway companies' efforts to secure a square deal for the railways.

The supreme governing body of the union—the A.G.M.—at first gave solid support for a policy of co-operation with the management. At Bristol in July 1928, a motion in favour of a policy of industrial peace was carried by the substantial margin of 64 votes to 16, despite the pleading of Mr W. R. Webster, a Finchley signalman, who argued that the policy of industrial peace was the method whereby the employers sought to render the trade unions impotent in the struggle against wage reductions.[14]

When, therefore, the four main line companies introduced Railway Road Transport Bills in Parliament in the spring of 1928 the leaders of the N.U.R. gave them every possible support. Speaking at the Willesden Hippodrome on February 19, 1928, Mr Thomas claimed that it was of 'paramount importance' to railwaymen that the N.U.R. members in the House of Commons should join 'hand in hand' with the Companies' spokesmen in piloting the Bills through Parliament.[15] The rank and file of the union were urged to keep the Minister of Transport well informed of their views. The Minister could not complain of lack of guidance. By March 9th he had received 26,500 postcards, although it is not disclosed what proportion of these came from railwaymen.[16] Not all of them would have been in favour of the proposed legislation. A minority of members of the union opposed the giving of support for the Railway Companies' Bills on the grounds that there had been no A.G.M. mandate for such a policy. The most outspoken opponent of the official line was Mr J. B. Figgins of Glasgow who argued that the policy of the union was the nationalization of the railways and that Mr Thomas had no right to make representations to the Labour Party in favour of increasing the powers of the companies.[17]

Nevertheless, by the close of 1928 all the railway companies had acquired power to own, operate or take financial interest in goods and passenger road transport concerns. Within a year of the Bill's becoming law, the railways had acquired a controlling interest in a large number of bus and coach companies principally in the Tilling and British Electric Traction groups. By 1932 the railway companies had invested £9,500,000 of their capital in bus or coach undertakings operating a total of 13,000 passenger vehicles.[18] Investment in road goods haulage was a much slower process, mainly for the reason that in this branch of the industry concentration of control had not proceeded so fast or so far. However, by August 1933, a controlling interest had been acquired in two of the largest road haulage firms, Carter Paterson and Pickfords.[19]

Once the railway companies were operating bus services in a big way the chief concern of Mr Cramp, the Industrial General Secretary, was to establish as favourable terms of service for the busmen as were gained for the railwaymen by the national settlements of 1919–20. In December 1928, the E.C. decided to appoint a sub-committee to meet the representatives of the railway companies to explore the whole question of the effect of taking over of private bus services.[20] At the first meeting with the companies on December 20, 1928, the N.U.R. raised the questions of the recruitment of busmen, the negotiating machinery and the conditions of employment. The companies volunteered to bring full-time bus workers within the negotiating machinery provided for under the Railways Act of 1921—a proposal which naturally found favour with the union representatives. It required but a few more meetings before signatures were appended to a 'Memorandum of Agreement' between the four main line companies and the N.U.R., dated April 9, 1929. Rates of pay were specified for London, Industrial Areas, and Rural Areas. They coincided as closely as possible with the rates of pay of railway company men previously doing a similar type of work. The standard hours of work were to be 48 per week exclusive of mealtimes; but owing to the peculiarities of the bus schedules, particularly in the country districts, provision was made for 'spreadover' turns whereby men might be called upon to work more than eight hours (but not more than twelve hours) in one day whilst not exceeding 48 hours in a week. Each man on completing a year's service was to be entitled to a week's holiday with pay.[21]

When the agreement was debated at the A.G.M. in Southampton that summer, some opposition was expressed by Mr W. McAdam, a goods guard of Glasgow No. 8 branch, who complained of the spreadover turns which obliged men to be at work for excessively long spells of duty. Examples were cited of the companies violating the agreement; men employed by the Great Western Railway and London and North Eastern Railway before April 1929, were now experiencing a deterioration of their conditions of service. But Mr Cramp argued that once the railway companies had obtained road powers it was imperative for the union to get 'quickly off the mark' in order to bring the road transport workers under the umbrella of the N.U.R. and its machinery.[22] He believed that 'the people who had set up the machinery would be the people who would obtain the members'. These arguments convinced the majority of the delegates who endorsed the official policy by 58 votes to 20.

The difficulty was that at this stage there was no agreement with the Transport and General Workers' Union. The E.C. of that body had opposed the granting of road powers to the railway companies,[23] but once the bills were passed it decided that the busmen employed by the railway-controlled companies should still be recruited into membership. In September 1928, Ernest Bevin wrote to Mr Cramp explaining his executive's decision and requesting a conference with the N.U.R. on the subject. Mr Cramp replied asserting the right of the N.U.R. to recruit all men on railway-owned buses, but the E.C. of the N.U.R. at its September 1928 meeting agreed to confer with the other union. For many months the negotiations between the two unions were deadlocked through the insistence of the T. & G.W.U. on its claim to organize *all* transport workers and the N.U.R.'s insistence, reiterated at a meeting of the E.C. on October 23, 1928, on organizing 'men employed on railway-owned road vehicles'. Since the foundation of the union in 1913, Clause 1 of Rule 9 had read: 'Any worker employed on or in connection with a railway is eligible for membership of this union.'[24]

At a joint meeting of representatives of the two unions held in Transport House on August 22, 1929, the T. & G.W.U. delegates accused N.U.R. branches of 'poaching' their union's members. It is true that in a circular sent to all branches of the union on June 5, 1929, Mr Cramp had urged branch secretaries to 'leave no stone unturned to get men into membership'; but the circular also stated that an applicant employed in the road transport services could not be accepted into membership unless the railway company had a financial interest in the bus company. No member of the T. & G.W.U. could be taken into membership until such time as his transfer had been ratified by the national joint committee of the two unions.[25] At Transport House, the N.U.R. delegation said that their branch secretaries' only 'offence' was in approaching men to find out whether they belonged to a union or not. Despite this, the meeting broke up with the agenda not completed, the T. & G.W.U. delegation stating that 'the N.U.R. was guilty of poaching and of an unfriendly act towards the T. & G.W.U. and that there could be no basis of relationship between the two unions'. Back at Unity House, the E.C. of the N.U.R. regretted the 'precipitous attitude' of the other union and re-asserted the right to enrol non-unionists employed by the railways and members of any organization twenty-six weeks in arrears in subscriptions.[26]

As no further meeting of the two unions took place in 1929, the E.C. of the N.U.R. came to the unanimous decision in December of that year that, unless the other side agreed to further meetings, it would regard the

National Joint Committee as defunct. By 16 votes to 8 it decided that if the deadlock continued the union would take fully paid up members of the T. & G.W.U. into membership and immediate benefit.[27]

The absence of an agreement benefited neither union. Membership fluctuated violently and organizers lacked confidence, having no clear area of operation. It was a difficult enough task to recruit busmen into a trade union without having that task made more difficult through inter-union rivalry. When Mr Cramp interviewed a bus proprietor who was not taking kindly to the idea of negotiating with the N.U.R. he was told:

'My great objection in the first place is that these men called a meeting to consider joining the union and never asked me to attend.'[28]

The experience of the Midland District Council in trying to organize the busmen of the area may be taken as illustrative of the difficulties of the time.[29] The Secretary of the Council wisely decided to meet representatives of the neighbouring District Councils to pool ideas and work out a plan of campaign. Such a meeting was held at Leeds on September 21st, when the delegates decided that no definite line of propaganda could be undertaken until there was a clear understanding with Head Office on their area of recruitment. Attempts were being made from Sheffield to recruit the employees of the Trent Motor Traction Company into the N.U.R. at a time when 85 per cent of the men belonged to the T. & G.W.U. which had established a signed agreement on the conditions of service with the company.[30] When thirty delegates of the Midland District reported their experiences to a special conference held at Clowne on February 2, 1930, the delegate from Worksop said that one depot dues collector had resigned for fear of victimization, whilst his successor complained that he was being brow-beaten by the company's inspectors to abandon the job. The delegate from Creswell told of 'a crop of dismissals, suspensions and fines'. The local officials in this area urged the E.C. to reopen negotiations with the T. & G.W.U. so that the two unions could co-operate in solving a difficult problem instead of treading on each others' toes. A resolution to this effect was also passed at a meeting of the Sheffield and Chesterfield District Council on October 23, 1929.

Stirred into action by such promptings, the E.C. of the N.U.R. tried a different approach. At its meeting in February 1930, it decided 'to request the T. & G.W.U. to meet . . . and discuss ways and means of forming a Transport Workers' Union', the General Secretary, in his letter, was to make clear that the purpose of the negotiations would be 'to form an organization of all engaged in the transport industry'.[31] At the next meeting, however, the committee learned, with regret, that the T. & G.W.U. could not agree on such an objective. Despite this rebuff, support for the idea of one transport workers' union continued amongst the rank and file of the

N.U.R. and, as a result, many further attempts were made to persuade Mr Bevin and his executive to change their minds. The A.G.M. at Folkestone in 1932 carried the following resolution by the large majority of 67 votes to 4:

'That this Congress is of the opinion that the present policy of the N.U.R. and the T. & G.W.U. fighting each other for membership is a waste of time and money for both organizations and can lead to no satisfactory results for either. Further, owing to the altered conditions of transport in general consequence of the growth of road motor transport, we instruct the E.C. of the N.U.R. to take the initiative in trying to form one union for all transport workers.'

Although the further negotiations which were the outcome of this resolution were conducted in a friendly spirit, there was no hope of Ernest Bevin agreeing to the N.U.R. plan. On June 2, 1933, he wrote to Mr Cramp to say that:

'The proposal for amalgamation would involve the breaking up of this union (the T. & G.W.U.), and it must be obvious to your E.C. that as such it represents an impossible proposition.'

The negotiations, simultaneously conducted, for a merger with the Associated Society and the R.C.A., were equally barren of results. Whilst Mr Cramp's comment at the A.G.M. at Ipswich, in July 1931, that the feeling between the three railway unions was 'better than he had ever known it in their history', was undoubtedly true, Mr Walkden, on behalf of the R.C.A., wrote on August 31, 1932, that his union could not take part in a conference on fusion though it favoured 'a friendly and joint working agreement', whilst John Bromley, for the Associated Society, wrote that his union was not prepared to go further than a 'working arrangement'.[32]

Still not disheartened, the delegates at the Special General Meeting of the N.U.R. in August 1933, advised by their President, Mr W. Dobbie, that the railway workers could not hope to win an industrial struggle 'unaided and alone', and warned that, under the Trade Disputes Act of 1927, they could not expect much help from other transport workers separately organized, since sympathetic strikes were illegal, decided to continue to strive for the objective of one union for all transport workers. They appointed a sub-committee of six (three from the S.G.M. and three from the E.C.) to find a way of meeting the difficulties.[33]

A very important working agreement was reached between the N.U.R. and the T. & G.W.U. in June 1932, on the division of spheres of influence in the organization of the busmen. It was the result of the labours of the joint committee of the two unions. Fifty undertakings were listed as coming under the jurisdiction of the Transport Workers and eleven—the Southern Vectis, Hants & Dorset, Devon General, Western Welsh, Mansfield & District Traction, Wilts and Dorset, Southern National, Lincolnshire Road Car Co., East Midland Omnibus Co., and North West Road Car Co.—as coming under the jurisdiction of the N.U.R. Decision on organization of the men in the employment of other companies was deferred, although in the case of the Ribble Motor Services there was to be joint recruiting. Negotiation on conditions of service and rates of pay were to be conducted by the union agreed as responsible for organization of the men. There was to be no poaching! With regard to Road Haulage, the N.U.R. undertook 'to render all assistance possible in the enrolment in the T. & G.W.U. of men employed by contractors outside railway work'. In a circular to N.U.R. branches Mr Cramp explained that the division of responsibility amongst the bus companies was based on the existing preponderance of membership. At the time of the signing of the agreement, Mr Bevin's union had, outside of the metropolitan area, 22,240 busmen members compared with 4,705 in the N.U.R.[34]

Whilst the efforts to reach a settlement with the T. & G.W.U. were proceeding, the N.U.R. redoubled its efforts to perfect the organization of busmen employed by companies subsidiary to the railways. The E.C. meeting on July 17, 1931, decided to enlist suitable members of N.U.R. branches for the task of recruiting non-unionists in the bus garages. Fifty full-time canvassers were appointed in the following autumn.[35]

For union organizers and special canvassers who gave their attention to road transport organization the situation bore some comparison with the pre-1914 situation on the railways, with the union struggling to obtain recognition in the face of the resistance of the managers and the occasional victimization of the men.

During 'Cowes Week' in 1931, with King George V and Queen Mary present to watch the yachting races, a strike of the employees of the Southern Vectis Omnibus Company suddenly started on August 8th. A driver and conductor had been summarily dismissed on July 25th, on a charge of breach of discipline—they had responded only slowly to the orders of a bus inspector peremptorily given—and the General Manager of the Company, Mr Dobson, had refused to grant an inquiry. Since the Southern Railway owned 50 per cent of the shares of the company a large number of the men had been recruited into the N.U.R.

The members of the E.C. decided that the strike was concerned with an important matter of principle—the right of men to a fair hearing when threatened with dismissal—and they therefore decided to give it official backing. The men were not strictly entitled to strike benefit as they had been so recently organized, but because the dispute was regarded as an important precedent and likely to influence the attitude of busmen all over the country on the question of whether or not to join the N.U.R., the E.C. decided not only to pay the men the normal allowance of 24s a week, but also to grant them an additional 6s a week. Three separate appeals were made to all N.U.R. branches to make a voluntary collection among the members on behalf of the Southern Vectis men. The importance given to the dispute is shown by the fact that both Mr Cramp and Mr Dobbie, the President, addressed meetings of strikers on the Island.

Although the strike dragged on until November 16, 1931, the company remained adamant in refusing to grant a hearing to the dismissed men. The reason for the defeat, despite the splendid morale and comradeship of the 100 strikers, was largely the failure of the majority of the drivers to come out in support of the overwhelming majority of conductors who had stopped work. It was easier for the management to replace the conductors than it would have been to find new drivers. Owing to the fact that the company would not re-employ the strikers after the dispute had ended the union continued to pay strike benefit. In June 1932, there were still fifty-three of the men who had failed to obtain alternative employment, and the E.C. therefore decided to grant them £39 each (i.e. 52 weeks at 15s a week) to enable them to seek employment on the mainland. The dispute cost the union a total of £5,437 15s 6d, but an important demonstration had been given of the N.U.R.'s determination to back up to the hilt what were regarded as the just demands of rank and file busmen.[36]

By 1932 conditions of employment began to improve with some of the bus companies. This was partly the outcome of the passage of the Road Traffic Act of 1930 under which a system of licensing of bus and coach services by area traffic commissioners was introduced. Under Clause 93 of the Act such licences could be withheld where the rates of wages and conditions of service of the employees were inferior to those working for employers under Government contract. It was the existence of this statute which made easier the negotiation of a series of agreements between the N.U.R. and the leading railway-controlled bus companies, such as the agreement signed with Ribble Motor Services on January 26, 1932.[37] Nevertheless there was still a long way to go before the conditions of employment in the bus industry could be standardized on a national basis. It was not until the foundation, in June 1940, of the National Council for the Bus Industry that national agreements of the same type as those secured on the railways in 1919-20, were obtained. But of that more hereafter.

III

The failure of the Government to co-ordinate road and rail traffic or to introduce any effective legislative control over road transport before the 1930's meant that by 1928 the railway companies were suffering serious depletion of their revenues. In 1927 the railways were deceptively busy though the increased freights of coal and general merchandise which were largely due to the backlog of orders arising from the general strike and the prolonged coal strike in 1926. Shortly before the A.G.M. in July 1928, however, Mr Thomas was informed in private conversation with the General Managers that the companies' receipts on the first half of 1928 were down by £4,100,000 compared with the corresponding period in 1927, and that in the years 1923–26 more than £31 million had been taken from reserves for dividend purposes with a consequent loss of income from interest on reserves of £1,556,700 a year.[38]

Mr Thomas, at Bristol, gave the A.G.M. delegates an alarming picture of the financial situation of the companies. With all his experience he did not remember the union being faced with so serious a situation as it then was. The London and North Eastern Railway had £47 millions of their capital on which they were 'unable to pay a copper dividend'. If this situation continued, then railway stock could no longer qualify to be included in Trust Securities and that would be disastrous from the point of view of working-class organizations. He knew of one society which had invested a quarter of a million pounds of 'working-class money' in railway securities. He therefore posed the question: How were they going to answer the inevitable demands of the railway companies for wage reductions?

Since 1920 the invariable procedure had been to negotiate through the Central and National Wages Boards; but he did not advise following this precedent since before these bodies they would have to convince the representatives of business and of the general public. The traders were all saying that the cause of the railways' difficulties was the 'high rate of railwaymen's wages'. His view, therefore, was that if they had to go through this machinery with the existing national agreements 'nothing could save them'. The idea of a strike he rejected as he claimed 40 per cent of the railwaymen were non-unionists! He therefore suggested that the union should negotiate on the basis of a percentage contribution for a temporary period with the higher paid grades sacrificing a larger percentage than the lower paid ones. In return he would insist on shopmen—who were at the time plagued by widespread part-time working and many dismissals—should be given a guaranteed week. By 60 votes to 14, congress endorsed the plan of the E.C. negotiating directly with the companies, provided that any sacrifices made should be spread over the whole staff and that any proposed agreement be submitted to an S.G.M. before ratification.[39]

On July 18, 1928, along with the executives of the R.C.A and the Associated Society, the E.C. were informed by the general managers of the companies' detailed proposals which they suggested should operate from the end of that month. They included the withdrawal of the remaining war bonus; the cancellation of all enhanced payments for night duty,

Sunday duty and overtime, and the temporary suspension of the guaranteed week and guaranteed day and in lieu thereof a guarantee to each man of weekly earnings from all sources of not less than his standard week's wages.

Nothing less than a frontal assault on the major gains of the immediate post war period was being attempted.

The executives of the three railway unions met at Unity House on July 23rd and reached the unanimous conclusion to reject the proposals. When they met the general managers again on the following day, Mr Thomas said that the companies' plan was unacceptable because the burdens would be unevenly spread between the different grades. Goods workers and clerks would be unduly penalized by the cancellation of enhanced rates for night duty, and permanent-way men would suffer through the cancellation of special rates for Sunday duty. The union leaders then asked the general managers whether they had any alternative proposals. After a brief retirement, the managers returned with the proposition of a general 5 per cent cut in wages and the abolition of the war bonus, but with a guaranteed 5-day week for shopmen. When they were told that this was impossible, they came back with a suggestion of a 3¾ per cent cut. At this stage the N.U.R. made an offer of a 2½ per cent cut, which the companies finally accepted after Mr Thomas had seen them during a break in the discussions and had said: 'Before you come in again you may take it we will not budge from 2½ per cent. You may take that as absolute.'

On July 27th, the executives of the three railwaymen's unions unanimously agreed to the final compromise plan which included a 2½ per cent reduction of wages of all staff (including the shopmen) the arrangement to last for one year and to be thereafter terminable by three months' notice given by either party. The deductions were to start on August 13, 1929. The companies undertook that at all places where sufficient work was available, full-time working would be restored in the workshops. Where full-time working was not possible men would be employed five full days and a short Saturday morning. The ninety-two directors of the four main line railway companies who between them enjoyed an income of £104,500 a year were also to be subjected to a cut of 2½ per cent on their salaries.[40]

At what was to prove his last statement on a wage settlement to a General Meeting of the union, Mr Thomas gave the delegates assembled at the Memorial Hall, Farringdon Street, London, on August 9, 1928, a brilliant survey of the negotiations, and convinced all but three of the eighty delegates that the only possible policy was acceptance. G. Berry of Manchester No. 13 and A. Udale of Crewe voted against the resolution approving the draft agreement, whilst J. Hayward of West Bromwich 1 remained neutral.[41] Mr Thomas explained his failure to achieve a percentage reduction which varied with income to the opposition of the R.C.A. to anything other than a flat rate reduction on all incomes.

Mr Thomas told a *Daily News* reporter that the agreement which was to bring to the companies a saving of £3 millions a year was 'the best ever made'. It was 'the most important document signed in British industrial history'.[42] Sir H. Walker, General Manager of the Southern Railway was somewhat more restrained in his approval. Commenting that it was the first time an agreement had been reached under which 'men voluntarily surrendered part of their wages in order to help the railway companies in very difficult circumstances', he expressed the hope that it would 'be an example to other industries'.[43] It was.

The overwhelming vote of confidence given Mr Thomas is explained by the fact that delegates who had feared the loss of the war bonus, the guaranteed day and week and special rates of pay, were greatly relieved to learn that all these fundamental gains of 1919–20 had been saved. Sympathy for the hard-hit railway shopmen led them to welcome the promise of fuller employment for this grade. But cutting railwaymen's wages would not bring back lost traffic to the railways since the sum saved was earmarked for dividends and not for the reduction of freights and fares. The supposed 'remedy' was liable to aggravate the disease through the fact that a sizable reduction in railwaymen's wages was bound to accelerate the general decline in the nation's purchasing power.

Although the long-term prospects of the companies were not hopeful, there was some recovery in goods traffic in 1929, though receipts from passenger traffic slumped sharply. The big question at the A.G.M. in Southampton early in July 1929, was whether the union should give notice to terminate the 'economy' agreement of July 27, 1928. A year's experience of its operation had put the delegates in a much more critical frame of mind than they had been the year before. Mr J. R. Rodgers, the signalman who moved the resolution favouring the termination of the agreement, complained of excessive overtime working in the traffic departments, whilst Mr W. McAdam, the goods guard who seconded, stressed that to reduce wages was no solution to the financial problems of industry. Mr Cramp pointed out that the companies' receipts for the first twenty-five weeks of the year showed that the Great Western Railway and London and North Eastern Railway had improved their position, but the Southern Railway and London, Midland and Scottish Railway were worse off by comparison with the previous year. He prophesied the companies would say that it was impossible to grant the men relief when the companies were in little better position than they had been in the previous July. But Mr Cramp lacked the persuasiveness of Mr Thomas (who was busy elsewhere as Lord Privy Seal with special responsibility for tackling the unemployment problem). The delegates were convinced that the recent repeal of the Passenger Duty which would save the companies £6 million a year

S. F. Greene, General Secretary, N.U.R., February 1958 (Acti from November 1957)

PLATE II

J. S. Campbell, General Secretary, N.U.R., March 1953–November 1957

An incident in the National Railway Strike 1911. Flagging messages from the Golden Gallery of St. Paul's, London

PLATE 12

Great London Railway Strike, 1911. Removing goods under police protection

and that the exercise of their recently acquired road powers would soon put them in a healthier position. By 76 votes to 3 they opted for boldness and an attempt to restore the 2½ per cent wage cut.[44]

When the E.C. of the N.U.R. approached the other railway unions to prepare for joint negotiations with the companies, the Associated Society favoured a delay in the belief that the financial position of the railways was improving. But since the R.C.A. was for a speedy approach, Mr Cramp did get in touch with the general managers who suggested a meeting on September 24th. On that date the companies argued that their wages bill in 1929 was likely to be higher than it had been in 1928 despite the cuts, as the shopmen were more fully employed and more overtime was being worked. Though the deficiency from the standard net revenue of £51 million a year was likely to be less than in 1928 it would still be in the order of £7 million. Mr Cramp argued that the road services were bringing in more revenue and that conditions would improve, but he was unable to persuade the general managers to agree to an immediate removal of the wage reductions. After separate consultations had been held with the other two unions on October 11, 1929, it was agreed to accept the companies' suggestion that the cuts should continue to operate until May 13, 1930, when they would be restored. Thereafter the companies would not come forward with any further proposals for economies for a period of at least six months, i.e. until November 13, 1930.[45]

At the S.G.M. held in the Memorial Hall on October 25, 1929, there was a strong body of opinion among the delegates in favour of terminating the 1928 agreement and bringing the issue before the National Wages Board. It was argued that it was better to go down fighting than to acquiesce in the continuance of a lower standard of living. The fact that the railway labour force had been reduced by 35,000 in the preceding twelve months was the subject of adverse comment. After a keen debate, the resolution to reject the companies' standstill proposals was lost by 35 votes to 45 and an amendment for acceptance was carried 45 to 35.[46]

Those who had hoped that by November 13, 1930, the railways prospects would be brighter were quickly disillusioned when they read the companies' returns. The net revenue of the four main line companies sank from £45·8 million in 1929 to £38·5 million in 1930. All the same, the delegates at the A.G.M. at West Hartlepool on July 8, 1930, considered that attack was the best form of defence, and they instructed the E.C. to draft a programme particularly designed to benefit the lower-paid grades and the shopmen, and to report back to a S.G.M. to be summoned not later than October that year. The E.C. carried out the task assigned to it, placing in the forefront of the new programme the demand for a minimum wage of £2 10s 0d for all adult employees together with the consolidation of the existing war wage of the shopmen. They demanded that all hybrid grades such as that of porter-guard should be abolished, and that there should be a guaranteed day and week for those grades not so far entitled to it. All grades should have twelve days' holiday with pay.

At the time the S.G.M. was summoned to the Memorial Hall in London on October 24, 1930, no official notification had been received from the companies of any plans to alter the conditions of service, but the September number of the *Great Western Railway Magazine* had contained a statement by the General Manager, Sir Felix Pole, that as soon as the truce expired the companies would insist on a reduction of wages. The delegates were therefore advised by Mr Cramp to consider what were the best tactics to follow. They decided to go ahead with the programme for improvements. By 53 votes to 21 they agreed to suggest a minimum wage of £3 a week in place of the £2 10s 0d submitted by the E.C., and by 49 votes to 22 added the recommendation that shop workers should be placed under the same machinery for negotiations on wages and conditions of service as the conciliation grades. Finally by 50 votes to 27 they decided to refer the amended programme to the Executive Committee so that it could be 'presented at the most favourable opportunity'.[47]

As Sir Felix Pole had accurately foretold, the companies began to demand further economies as soon as the 'truce' expired. Details of their proposals were first received by the executives of the three railway unions at a meeting with the general managers at the Midland Grand Hotel, St Pancras, on December 10, 1930. As the unions could not accept the case the companies had made, the claims of both sides were referred to a meeting of the Central Wages Board on December 19th. Since the two sides found it impossible to agree, the case was passed on to the National Wages Board in January 1931.

Before that body, Mr W. E. C. Lazenby, for the companies, claimed that the railways were 'hampered by the burden of excessive wages costs and undue rigidity in the conditions of service'. Specifically, he contended that although at that time the cost of living stood only 55 per cent above the level of July 1914, conciliation grade wages were 120 per cent above July 1914, and salaried grades incomes were 200 per cent over the pre-war figure. Since the railway industry was no longer a sheltered one, the workers must be prepared to accept only what was economically possible for the industry. The companies needed reduction of costs to the extent of £11 million a year. Since night work was not paid at enhanced rates before the war, and was (he claimed) no more arduous than work by day, it should be paid at the same rate as work by day. Extra payment for Sunday duty should disappear, since to satisfy the demands of the public they should extend their Sunday services. The existing conditions of service stood in the way of such extension. Extra payment for overtime should be made only when work was done in excess of the standard weekly hours. To place the companies 'in a better position to concede reductions in rail charges' there should be a cut of 6s a week in the wages of adult males provided that no man received less than 38s a week. Women workers and juniors should have their wages reduced by 3s a week whilst salaried workers' incomes should be cut by between £10 and £15 a year.

The union's case against the companies' proposals and in favour of the improvements suggested by the S.G.M. was ably drafted by Mr W. J. Watson of the Head Office Staff and skilfully presented by Mr John Marchbank, the Assistant Secretary. He showed that to make percentage comparisons between railway wages in 1913 and 1931 was unfair, since it was generally agreed that the wages paid to railwaymen before the war were scandalously low. Far from it being the case that railwaymen's wages were too high, he showed that the minimum of 40s a week which many permanent-way men and porters were paid, was too low. Mr S. Rowntree in his book *The Human Needs of Labour* had shown that with a diet in which porridge, skimmed milk, bread and margarine, cheese and cocoa figured prominently, a man with a wife and three children would need £1 18s 3d a week if 9s 6d was included for rent and 2s for insurances. This sum included no allowance for coal, soap, beer, tobacco, furniture or holidays. In the awards of the Trade Boards (set up to fix wages in the underpaid 'sweated' trades) over the period 1919–30 the average minimum wage awarded was 48s 10d a week and yet 100,000 railwaymen were being paid less than 46s a week.

When it came to the time for cross-examination of the witnesses before the Board, Mr Lazenby suffered from a severe attack of cramp. The Industrial General Secretary, who was a member of the trade-union panel of the Board, asked him whether in the event of the companies' application succeeding it was their intention to reduce freights and fares. Did the companies want the £11 million for this purpose or for the payment of increased dividends? Mr Lazenby said it was not possible to give a definite answer, it was needed to meet 'the whole economic position'.

On March 5, 1931, the National Wages Board decision was published. All men employed in the conciliation grades were to have their wages reduced by 2½ per cent provided such reduction did not result in a weekly wage of less than 40s. There was to be an additional 2½ per cent cut on the amount by which a man's wages exceeded 40s. Salary earners were to receive a basic reduction of 2½ per cent plus a further 2½ per cent reduction on income in excess of £100 a year. The new rates of pay were to come into effect on the first pay day after March 26, 1931, and were to remain in operation for a year. The Trade Union and Co-operative representatives on the Board issued a minority report in which they expressed the view that the problems of the transport industry could only be solved along the lines of comprehensive national organization of all forms of transport under public ownership and control.[48]

The case of the shopmen was settled by direct negotiations instead of by the Industrial Court. Mr Cramp favoured the direct approach because he knew that the main aim of the companies was to eliminate what remained of the war wage—the 4s 6d a week by which the day workers' wages in the railway workshops exceeded the rate paid in many other engineering establishments—and he was afraid that the Industrial Court might recommend the removal of this 'anomaly'. Negotiations with the companies stuck at the point of a $4\frac{1}{6}$ per cent cut, or 10d in the £, a situation which both the craft unions and the N.U.R. eventually accepted in return for a further promise from the General Managers to maintain full-time working as long as it was humanly possible.[49]

Many of the delegates who assembled for the S.G.M. in the Memorial Hall on March 19, 1931, had received the proposed terms of settlement for shopmen only on the previous day and had had insufficient time to consult their constituents. It was therefore decided to adjourn for one week so that meetings could be held in all centres on Sunday, March 22nd. Thus when the delegates returned to the Memorial Hall on March 26th, they had a recent and clearer impression of rank and file opinion.

In the circumstances it is not surprising that the meeting, by 49 votes to 31, carried a motion reaffirming the justice of the union's claim for better conditions, but accepting the National Wages Board award and the settlement for shopmen 'in the interests of peace in the industry'. The only real alternative was a strike. There was a little disagreement with A. J. Niven of Edinburgh who said that it was abundantly clear that 'there were no guts in the membership for a strike' at that time. To reinforce this John Marchbank pointed out that both the R.C.A. and the Associated Society had accepted the award, the latter partly because of a 1s a week increase granted to engine cleaners. He believed that 'not 50 per cent of the railwaymen in the country were members of the N.U.R.' Mr A. Ridout from Cardiff reported that 8 out of 12 branches in his area were against a strike since in the Great Western Railway area there were only five blast furnaces at work out of forty-five and there were men waiting for work who would 'jump like a shot' for a regular job on the railways at £2 a week. The principal support for an unsuccessful resolution for a new approach to the companies with a view to raising the minimum wage to 50s and removing spreadover turns, came from the Irish delegates and from Manchester, Birmingham, Swindon and Bristol. Mr G. McClounie, of Glasgow No. 5 Branch, believed it was time they dug their heels in; but he was the only Scottish delegate against the acceptance of the award.[50]

Although the wage reductions introduced in August 1928 had also been applied to the employees of the Metropolitan Railway, workers on the London Underground, whose finances were more prosperous than those of the main line companies, managed to escape any worsening of their conditions at this time. After the publication of the National Wages Board Award in March 1931, however, Mr Cramp received a letter from Lord Ashfield, head of the Underground Railways, warning the union that though they were not immediately demanding economies they claimed the right to do so if the position warranted it.[51] At the end of the year formal notice was given by Lord Ashfield to terminate the existing agreements on wages and conditions of service for Underground workers. The purpose was to secure a reduction on wage rates. No wonder the editor of the *Railway Review* in the last issue of the year wrote: 'The best we can do with the year 1931 is to forget it, there is nothing exhilarating about it to record.'

The negotiations with the management of the Underground Railways extended through the first six months of 1932. Lord Ashfield at the first meeting with the unions on January 18th had asked for a general reduction of 2½ per cent, plus 2½ per cent of all money earned in excess of 40s, plus a further 2½ per cent from those receiving more than £750 a year. The unions had no hesitation in rejecting these proposals. But as the decline in receipts continued in the spring and early summer, the demand from the employers' side for the implementation of the cuts intensified. The E.C. therefore decided to hold two mass meetings of the men at the Memorial Hall on June 21st to mobilize opposition. Unfortunately, there was not as much 'mass' in the meetings as the organizers had hoped; less than a hundred men turned up to the morning meeting and under two hundred to the evening meeting—a fact which made strike action seem a less feasible proposition. Since the majority present at both meetings were in favour of the E.C. continuing negotiations for the best possible agreement, this was done until a final settlement was reached on July 20th to come into operation on September 3rd. The reductions were agreed as originally put forward by the management in January, with the very important exception that no employee was to be reduced to a wage of less than 50s a week.[52] The reductions were to apply to bus men as well as to traffic and clerical grades.

To offset this retreat the union could congratulate itself that it had gained acceptance to all its proposed amendments to the London Passenger Transport Bill which received Royal Assent on April 13, 1933, and which contained provisions for the setting up of a Negotiating Committee with the representatives of the London Passenger Transport Board and six representatives of the three railway trade unions. A Wages Board of similar composition, with the addition of an independent chairman, was to take over negotiations if the Negotiating Committee failed to reach a settlement.[53] Mr J. H. Thomas claimed that he had threatened to resign from the Labour Government if Mr Herbert Morrison, the Minister of Transport, did not set up this machinery for which the craft unions and Transport and General Workers' Union had no great enthusiasm.[54]

If 1931 had nothing exhilarating about it, 1932 had even less to commend it. In that year the net revenue of the four main line companies at £27·2 million, fell to the lowest level of the inter-war period. The condition of the railways was described in a report of the Railway Pool Committee, in August 1932, which told of 'A vital national industry stricken, during a period of unexampled depression, up to a point which threatens exhaustion'. The number employed on the railways, by the end of March 1932, had fallen to 597,971, which was 17,621 less than in 1931 and 104,091 less than in 1925.[55] The *average* earnings of conciliation grades had fallen as a result of the National Wages Board Award of March 1931, from 65s 10d to 61s 8d whilst shopmen's average earnings fell from 68s 5d to 65s 4d.[56] Symbolical of the depressed state of the industry was the closing down of the London, Midland and Scottish steel works at Crewe in September with the immediate loss of employment for more than 400 men.[57]

Despite the failure of the earlier wage cuts of 1928–9 and 1931 to solve the problems of the industry, the railway managers attempted to secure even more drastic reductions in 1932–3. The National Wages Board Award of March 1931 continued to apply throughout 1932 although either side was at liberty to call for its abandonment from March 5, 1932. The E.C. of the N.U.R. did not do so, being aware of the difficulty of convincing the Board of its case in view of the country's economic position; the companies did not do so at first as they were preparing plans for more far-reaching economies.

By September 1932, however, the companies' plans were ready. Mr Cramp received the inevitable letter of invitation and the E.C. agreed, along with the executives of the other railway unions, to meet the general managers on the 28th of that month. They then learned that the companies wished to replace the existing cuts by a cut of 10 per cent on all wages and salaries, except that no worker was to receive a wage of less than 38s a week. The reductions proposed were so substantial that even those members of the N.U.R. executive most prone to accept a compromise felt that it was impossible to accept them. On October 13th, the unanimous decision was reached to advise the companies that the union was unable to accede to their request.[58] A proposal to advise branches and district councils to set up area and district strike committees, though not carried, found support from six of the twenty-four members of the committee. Indicative of the new spirit of determination to resist any further encroachments on the railwaymen's standard of living was Mr Dobbie's statement to a meeting at Newport (Mon.) that they would not step back any further 'unless forced back by defeat in the most fierce industrial struggle that has taken place in the country'.[59]

After there was failure to reach any agreement at a meeting of the Central Wages Board to consider the companies' case on October 27th, the union intensified its propaganda. 2,500,000 leaflets were printed and circulated amongst members and the general public and Mr Cramp drafted a newspaper article, copies of which were enclosed in a circular to all branches with the suggestion that secretaries endeavour to secure publication of the article in local newspapers.[60]

The prolonged battle of wits between Sir Ralph Wedgwood and Mr John Marchbank took place before the National Wages Board in Thames House, Millbank, London, during eleven days of November and December 1932.

Sir Ralph Wedgwood, for the companies, pointed out that railway receipts for the first forty-six weeks of 1932 were over 9 per cent down compared with the corresponding period in 1931 and that the main reason for this unfortunate state of affairs was 'the slump in heavy industry', although he gave the imposition of tariffs on imports and the loss of lighter, more profitable goods traffic to the roads as additional reasons. The return on ordinary stocks had fallen from an average of 3·97 for the four companies in 1929 to an average of 0·95 in 1931. As a result of this decline in profits the industry was being starved of capital, development was stunted and extensive schemes of improvement were 'indefinitely deferred'. The 'creeping paralysis' from which the railways were suffering could only be arrested if speedy steps were taken to relieve them of 'the burden of overwhelming costs'. The reduction in wages proposed would bring a saving of £4½ millions a year additional to the £3,660,000 a year saved under the award of March 5, 1931. For the welfare of the industry some adjustment was needed in the respective shares of the shareholder and the wage earner; the shareholders' share of the net product was too small and the wage earners' share too large. The railway companies desired to increase the shareholders' share of the net product.

Mr John Marchbank said that it could be stated with certainty that the companies' proposed minimum wage of 38s a week was 'not a figure on which men and their families could live decently'. He could cite cases of men, whose homes had already been broken up (with the minimum wage at 40s) through their inability to maintain their wives and families. The Public Assistance authorities in Cardiff and Lanark gave greater sums of money to families of six persons than the railway companies were proposing to pay in wages to thousands of their employees. He challenged the conception that the payment of dividends should take precedence over the payment of salaries and wages to those whose lives were spent in earning such dividends. Only approximately £275 million of the railways' total capital of £1,095 million was in the form of ordinary stock. The remaining £819,500,000 was in the form of debenture and preference stock more than two-thirds of which bore interest of 4 per cent or over. By comparison, holders of £1,920 million-worth of recently converted war loan stock were only receiving 3½ per cent interest. On £150 million of Treasury Bonds only 2½ per cent interest was paid. He suggested that the railway companies should 'write down' their capital, as Vickers Ltd. had done in 1925. In conclusion he claimed that the difficulties of the industry could not be solved by continued depression of salaries and wages. They could only be solved by 'a reorganization of the whole means of transport'.[61]

On January 13, 1933, the National Wages Board issued no less than six reports, thus revealing how divided its members were in their reactions to the companies' claim. As was to be expected, the report written by the railway companies' representative favoured the full implementation of the general managers' plan; but a second report from the representatives of industry and commerce also thought the companies' claim should be conceded in full. Henry J. May of the Co-operative Union and Arthur Pugh of the T.U.C. were responsible for the third and fourth reports which, like the fifth, written by the representatives of the railway unions, expressed opposition to any further wage reductions. Finally, the Chairman, Sir Harold Morris, K.C., in view of the failure of the others to agree, for good measure, added a report of his own which he hoped might be accepted by both sides as a fair compromise. In it he accepted the fact that the wages of railwaymen before the war had been too low and that the new conditions of 1919–20 had, with justice, been introduced to remedy the position. On the other hand, he felt that 'the grave difficulties of the companies justified a departure from the standards fixed by the national agreements' and he therefore proposed that in place of the deductions made in March 1931, wages should be cut by $4\frac{1}{8}$ per cent with a further cut of $4\frac{1}{8}$ per cent in respect of all incomes over 50s a week. He suggested that 40s should be the minimum below which a man's wages should not be reduced. His suggestions, if adopted, would save the companies up to £1 million a year compared with the £4,600,000 they were claiming.[62]

Within a week of the publication of the National Wage Board findings, the companies decided, with reluctance, to accept Sir Harold Morris's report as the basis of a new wage settlement on the railways. The view of the union was that in the Board there had been no majority for the companies' application, or any part of it, and that therefore they were under no obligation to accept the chairman's proposals. On January 24, 1933, the E.C. came to the unanimous conclusion to reject the $4\frac{1}{8}$ per cent cut. The executives of the other railway unions were of like mind.[63]

Since no way was found of resolving the deadlock, the situation throughout 1933, therefore, was that the economies first introduced at the expense of the men in March 1931, continued, but the companies were frustrated in their attempt to impose fresh burdens. So long as the National Wages Board was prepared to concede at least a part of their claims, the companies were satisfied to utilize the existing machinery of negotiation. It was a different matter to come away empty-handed after the presentation of a lengthy and well-prepared case. On March 3rd, therefore, in a joint letter to the railway unions, the four general managers gave formal notice, under the provisions of the 1921 Railways Act, to withdraw from participation in the Central and National Wages Boards after the stipulated twelve months had passed in March 1934. They had 'no desire to depart from their established policy of discussing labour questions with the unions' and they recognized the mutual advantages arising from the work of the Local Departmental Committees and Sectional Councils, but they had found that a tribunal constituted on the lines of the National Wages Board had 'inherent defects' which they could no longer accept.[64] Thus was brought to an end one of the most important instruments of conciliation established after the First World War.

As a partial substitute for the economies at the expense of railwaymen's wages, three of the companies went ahead with their scheme for a railway pool for eliminating redundant labour and avoiding competitive waste. Initially the brainchild of the general managers of the London, Midland and Scottish Railway and the London and North Eastern Railway it was, in 1933, extended to include the Great Western Railway. Traffics of the companies which were competitive were to be pooled and receipts were to be divided on the basis of the actual division of traffic in the years 1928-30 inclusive, unless a company could show good reasons why its proportion of the receipts should be increased. At the earliest opportunity after the plan of the companies was announced, Mr Cramp appeared before the special committee of the House of Commons on June 28th to object to the absence of any definite agreement for safeguarding of staff from sudden dismissal. The companies argued that it would be impossible to differentiate between those members of staff who would be dispensed with 'in the ordinary way' and those whose services were no longer required by reason of the operation of the scheme. But under pressure, they gave a written undertaking not to dismiss any person who had been taken in employment before July 1, 1932, so long as this did not debar them from accelerating the age of retirement or transferring men to lower paid jobs.[65] The prompt intervention of the union had prevented any serious aggravation of the problem of redundancy, though on the Great Western Railway there were complaints that locomotivemen were being retired at an earlier age than was usual. In the country as a whole, however, nearly 9,000 more men were being employed on the railways in March 1934 than in March 1933.

One reason for the failure of the companies to enforce their further economies at the expense of railwaymen's wages in 1933 was a stiffening of the *organized* opposition within the union to any further concessions. For some years, the only organized opposition to the official policy on wages was conducted by the Railwaymen's Minority Movement, a branch of the Communist-led National Minority Movement founded in 1924. Under the energetic and capable direction of its Secretary, Mr W. C. Loeber, a carriage cleaner of Wood Green Branch, the R.M.M. had kept alive the spirit of resistance to the wage reductions and other aspects of the economy drive. A spate of printed and duplicated weekly bulletins appeared: 'The L.M.R. Rebel'; 'The Midland Rail Special'; the 'St Pancras and Somers Town Headlight'; 'The King's Cross Star'; 'The Underground Depots Bulletin'; 'The Hornsey Star' and 'The Northern Star' (Bradford) are some examples. Membership of the R.M.M. was open to persons of all political parties (or none) who made an initial payment of 1s. There was no subsequent regular subscription. In the period 1930–32, however, the movement suffered from several disabilities. It was declared a proscribed organization by the T.U.C. and the N.U.R. and its active supporters were thus disqualified from contesting union elections. The policy of the Communist Party of Great Britain to counter the bans by 'secret membership' was misguided and caused much confusion in the ranks of the movement. The name—Railwaymen's Minority Movement—was also a stumbling block; few persons relish belonging to a permanent minority! The sectarian attitude and left-wing jargon of some of the publications tended to isolate the militants from the rank and file. A typed statement issued at the beginning of 1933 admitted 'The Minority Movement is still largely isolated from the mass of the 600,000 railwaymen'.

In the course of 1933 a complete reorganization took place. The name of the movement was changed to 'The Railwaymen's Vigilance Movement' thus recalling the work of the numerous vigilance committees which had functioned during the years 1916–25. The inaugural meeting of the new organization was held in Stratford Town Hall on January 22, 1933. A new policy of working *through* the constitutional means offered by the railway unions, the Local Departmental Committees, Shops Committees, Sectional Councils, instead of through ad hoc depot committees which had tended to *rival* the established institutions, was introduced, with a much greater measure of success. The Second Annual Conference of the Railwaymen's Vigilance Movement held in London in February 1934 was attended by 151 delegates, 55 of whom came from N.U.R. branches; 26 from branches of the A.S.L.E. & F.; 2 from branches of the R.C.A.; one from the A.E.U.; 4 from the Busmen's Rank and File Movement and the remainder from Depot or Local Vigilance Committees.

Throughout 1933 and subsequent years, increasing support was aroused for this movement's policy of the restoration of the wage cuts, the abolition of the New Entrants Clause which from 1926 on had deprived all new entrants to the industry of the cost of living bonus, and a national basic wage of 50s a week. Mr Loeber, who had taken a prominent part in the reorganization of the left-wing opposition to official union policy, travelled up and down the country organizing the groups. Of his experiences in the early 1930's he writes:

'I lived mainly on bread, cheese and pickled onions over the week-ends, and slept in queer places; upturned kitchen tables, on the floor and in railway carriages, but was thoroughly satisfied with the results obtained.'

Among members of the union who were supporters of the Railway Vigilance Movement may be included Mr J. B. Figgins of Glasgow, who was General Secretary of the N.U.R. from 1947 to 1953; Messrs W. Jefcoat, J. MacMillan, A. Ridyard and F. Donlon, who became members of the E.C.; Mr W. Ballantine, who was later elected Assistant General Secretary, and Messrs J. Matheson, J. Shearer and W. M. Williams who became N.U.R. organizers.

The movement obtained central direction through a new eight-page monthly publication, *The Railway Vigilant*, the first number of which appeared in January 1933. This largely replaced the spasmodically produced local bulletins and at times its circulation rivalled that of the *Railway Review*.

Although the economic circumstances after 1933 were more favourable for the restoration of the wage reductions of the period 1928–33, there can be no doubt that the Railwaymen's Vigilance Movement helped to stimulate political consciousness and to revive a militant spirit within the union.[66]

IV

The financial difficulties of the British Railways were trivial compared with the embarrassment experienced by some of the Irish railways in the period 1929–33. It was a feature of the great economic depression of these years that prices of foodstuffs and raw materials fell more sharply than did the price of manufactured goods. The Irish Free State, depending to a much greater extent for its prosperity on agriculture than was the case with Great Britain, was thus severely hit by the decline in world prices. Northern Ireland's prosperity was undermined through the slump in the ship-building industry. It is, therefore, not surprising that the application in 1928 from the Irish Railway Companies (with the exception of the Belfast and County Down Railway which had previously been authorized to reduce wages by 10 per cent) was for a more substantial reduction of labour costs than that recently put into operation on the British Railways. The claim was for a 10 per cent reduction from the wages of the conciliation grades and a 5 per cent reduction from the salaried staff. It was first considered by representatives of the three railway unions and the Irish companies at the St Pancras Hotel, London, on September 21, 1928. The unions were unanimous in rejecting the proposals.[67] Before the Irish Railways Central Wages Board the companies suggested that the cuts should be applied in two instalments, the first to operate immediately following the decision of the Board and the second to follow three months later. But no agreement was reached. There was still no agreement when the appeal was passed on to the Irish Railway Wages Board on January 31, 1929. Eleven members of the Board—the majority—expressed the opinion that the reductions would 'not materially benefit the companies, and would further divorce the efforts of the employees from concentrating on improved working and popularizing railway transit with the public'. They therefore refused to authorize the proposed economies. A minority of six members of the Board on the other hand, were of the opinion that the companies' case had been established and that their request should be granted.[68] The first attempt to economize at the expense of labour on the Irish Railways had failed.

Through much of 1930 the discussions were centred round the drafting of a new scheme for negotiating machinery. This was the outcome of the companies' intimation to the unions in June 1929 that they wished to terminate the agreement with regard to the then existing machinery.[69] With the Irish Wages Board reconstituted, the Irish companies tried again in November 1930. In a letter to Mr Cramp they declared that their financial situation was 'so grave that they must obtain some relief at once by reduction of labour costs'. Eventually, after the companies had claimed 10 per cent, the Irish Railway Wage Board, early in June 1931, recommended a reduction of $4\frac{3}{8}$ per cent from the wages of the conciliation grades (with a minimum wage of 40s) whilst clerical and supervisory workers were to lose $2\frac{1}{2}$ per cent, with a further $1\frac{1}{4}$ per cent in respect of all earnings over £100 a year. The award was to operate from May 9, 1931, was to last for at least twelve months and was to be terminable on the giving of three months' notice by either side. Both a special conference of Irish members held in Dublin, and the E.C. agreed to accept the award as a regrettable necessity.[70]

Since the business of the Irish companies deteriorated rather than improved, within a year of the E.C.'s acceptance of the 1931 award, the companies were requesting further meetings with the unions. When the two sides met at Unity House on August 2, 1932, the railway managers stressed the 'extreme urgency' of the financial situation and suggested that wage rates should come down to not more than 100 per cent above the pre-war figure. (At the time of the negotiations it was estimated that Irish railway wages stood at 140 per cent above the 1914 level.) The alternatives suggested were a 'simple' cut of 20 per cent or reductions in two stages; 15 per cent to come off from the end of November 1932, with such subsequent reduction as would be necessary to bring wages down to 100 per cent above 1914 rates. The wages of clerical and supervisory staff should come down in two instalments of 10 per cent and 5 per cent. When the newly constituted Irish Railway Negotiating Committee failed to reach agreement, the claim was considered by the Irish Railway Wages Board which recommended a flat rate 10 per cent reduction on the wages of all grades to operate from the first pay day after December 26, 1932. A minority report, opposing these recommendations, was signed by the union representatives on the Board.[71]

Among the Irish membership there was strong opposition to these drastic proposals and the E.C., recognizing this, decided to call a special conference of Irish members in Dublin on December 18, 1932. An all-Ireland strike might have started there and then had not the Government of the Free State decided to grant a subsidy (to last until April 30, 1933) equal to the savings the companies would have obtained through the operation of the 10 per cent cuts during that period. The Government of Northern Ireland was less generous, but it did persuade the companies in the six counties to delay the enforcement of the cuts until January 23, 1933.

When the negotiating committee of the N.U.R. met the representatives of the companies operating in Northern Ireland at Belfast on January 20th, they were informed that the majority decision of the Irish Railway Wages Board would be applied from January 23rd, and that no further postponements were possible. The day after the wage reductions began, the executives of the three railway unions met together in Unity House where they decided to inform the four Northern Ireland companies that, unless negotiations were reopened before that date, a strike would be called at twelve noon on Monday, January 30, 1933. In a last-minute effort to avert the strike, the Associated Railway Companies of Ireland, a body representative of the companies in the Free State as well as those in Northern Ireland, agreed to a meeting with the unions in Belfast on January 27th. But since the only modification the companies were prepared to make was to suggest a minimum wage of 34s and a reduction in two stages of 5 per cent each for those earning under 40s instead of an immediate 10 per cent reduction, and since these were regarded as insufficient by the unions, the meeting failed to prevent the outbreak of the strike. The unions were prepared to go as far as accepting a cut of $5\frac{5}{8}$ per cent until April 30, 1933—to allow more time for negotiations—but they were not prepared to concede any more.[72]

The strike in Northern Ireland which began promptly at mid-day on January 30th, was practically complete as far as the traffic grades were concerned, although as a result of a last-minute decision of its Belfast branch, the R.C.A. stood aloof whilst advising its members not to do any of the work of the strikers. It was decided to call out all the employees of the Great Northern Railway of Ireland although one third of that company's mileage was within the Free State. Only three miles of the Londonderry and Lough Swilly Railway's track was in Northern Ireland but all the men employed on this line, also, were brought out since it was considered impossible, on the same company's lines, to order some to strike and others to stay at work. Of the 6,415 employees of the four companies, 3,478 were members of the N.U.R., though this figure included the bus workers, most of whom stayed at work in defiance of union policy. The 2,765 members who did strike were joined by 1,037 non-unionists.[73]

The N.U.R. officially gave every possible backing to the strikers. In order to be in the midst of the battle, the E.C. met in Belfast for most of February. On 3rd of that month it resolved to award strike pay of 24s a week irrespective of a man's length of membership. On the 10th it decided to grant an additional 6s a week, from February 18th, to members still on strike. Three separate appeals were made by Head Office to the branches in Great Britain for voluntary donations on behalf of the Irish strikers,[74] but the response was very disappointing. Even with additions made from some branch management funds the total only reached £5,803 8s 2d by August 1933, or a little over 4d a member.

Despite the fact that on many of the lines the strike was remarkably complete—no train reached Newry from Belfast until February 15th and there was no train on the Londonderry and Lough Swilly line until February 14th,[75]—the union was obliged to accept humiliating terms of peace on April 6th. The companies promised to reinstate the men in order of seniority; wages on conciliation grades were to be cut by $7\frac{1}{2}$ per cent and of clerical and supervisory grades by 10 per cent. During 1933 holidays would be taken without pay. The reductions were to operate until May 1, 1934, and could be continued for a further year if the companies, in March 1934, found that their financial position warranted their continuance. A further agreement, with similar provisions, was signed between the unions and the Associated Irish Railway Companies on April 17, 1933, under which the economies already applied in Northern Ireland would be extended to the Free State lines on May 1, 1933, and would operate for at least a year.

Of the strike in Northern Ireland Mr Cramp said that at the start he knew it was impossible to win 'all out', but this was one of the times when they had to fight even though they knew they could not win. The two circumstances which helped to convince him of the impossibility of victory were that on the Northern Counties Railway they were £66,000 down 'on sheer working' without any question of dividends. The other lines were in a scarcely better position.[76] Mr Andrews, the Minister of Industry and Commerce for Northern Ireland, lacked both the personality and the constitutional powers to secure any Government intervention on behalf of the railwaymen. Once the strike had started, the odds against the strikers grew daily. The clerks employed on the Great Northern Railway were called upon to help with the handling of goods and forty members of the R.C.A. were sent home for refusing to do the work of other grades.[77] Army lorries were used to take to work Dublin businessmen who normally travelled on the Great Northern (Ireland) Company's lines.[78] Most of the bus drivers remained at work, but John Marchbank told the S.G.M. in August that there were six drivers for every one who ceased work.

Although some delegates criticized the leadership for failing to call out all Irish railwaymen, Mr Cramp countered with the comment:

'You could have the whole of Ireland standing still from the railway transport point of view and they would still be able to feed themselves and live.'[79]

A nation-wide railway strike had fewer terrors in Ireland than it would have had in heavily industrialized England.

From the point of view of L.S.D. the irony of the strike was that it was fought over a sum of £4,200 spread over a period of four months. Had the 10 per cent cuts proposed by the Northern Ireland Companies been operative from January to April inclusive, the saving would have been £9,600. Had the 5⅝ per cent cut the union conceded been put in operation, the saving would have been £5,400.[80] £4,200 represented the difference between these two figures and may be compared with the total cost of the strike to the union which was over £60,000.[81]

Irish delegates at the A.G.M. in Morecambe in July 1933, were angry that the E.C. and the other unions had signed the April agreements terminating the strike, without consulting the Irish members at a delegate conference, in the same way as the membership across the water was consulted when a new settlement was reached for the employees of the four main line British companies. By a majority of 79 votes to 1 the delegates upheld the Irish branches' repudiation of the April settlements and demanded the summoning of a special conference in Ireland to reconsider methods of resisting the wage reductions and restoring full employment on the railways. Such a conference was held in Dublin on August 4, 1933, but it was unable to exact better terms from the companies. The S.G.M. in London on August 29th by 43 votes to 28 accepted the Irish settlement 'under protest' and called for the setting up of a joint committee composed of the Irish representatives on the E.C. and representatives from the branches 'to go into the question of alleged redundancy with a view to the displacement of volunteer labour and the restoration of work to victimized members'. They had a hard task. A month later 599 members in Ireland were still out of work in consequence of the strike.[82] But the wise decision to give Irish members a greater degree of autonomy in the conduct of their affairs helped to restore confidence in the union.

v

One positive outcome of the many debates at all levels, on the companies' claims for wage reductions and worsened conditions of service, was the growing conviction among many members of the union that the remedy for their ills could not be found within the narrow confines of the railway industry. It was to be sought in the broader sphere of transport policy as a whole. This gradual maturing of a more comprehensive policy can be seen in the public resolutions of annual general meetings and in the development of concerted action with other trade unions.

It is true that a resolution passed by the A.G.M. in July 1927, referred to 'the chaotic condition of the road transport services' and to the need for 'a co-ordinated policy between all forms of transport', but a perusal of the speeches in the debate gives one the strong impression that many delegates would have been highly embarrassed if asked to explain more fully what was meant by a 'co-ordinated policy between all forms of transport'.

In January 1929, Mr Cramp, on behalf of the N.U.R., submitted a memorandum to the Royal Commission on Transport. It was a very sketchy document of sixteen brief paragraphs occupying one printed page, foolscap size. Paragraphs 1–5 outlined the origin and purpose of the N.U.R. The following seven paragraphs explained the unfair position in which the railways were placed in competition with the roads. The positive policy of the union for the future of public transport was confined to sixteen lines in paragraphs 14–15 which are worth quoting:

'In the view of the union, the first step to be taken should be the nationalization of the railways, and such road motor transport as is ancillary thereto, which could be accomplished with little practical difficulty, followed by an extension of municipal transport facilities.

'After this had been done, the Government would be in a better position to proceed to effect a nationally controlled and co-ordinated system of transport. It is necessary to create a community of interest so far as transport is concerned, and if the nation owned the principal means of transport, that is the railways, the Government would be in a better position to effectively control the remaining means of transport in the general interest of the nation.'

It is scarcely possible to excuse the brevity of the memorandum by claiming that it served merely as an introduction to Mr Cramp's verbal evidence. When asked by Sir William Lobjost the question:

'Have the railway unions formulated any scheme for the co-ordination of national control?'

Mr Cramp replied:

'No . . . we have no detailed scheme. One usually finds in practical affairs that it is best to get agreement on the principle, and when once the principle is agreed, to fit in details.'

When asked by Lord Northampton:

'Have your two unions (i.e. the N.U.R. and A.S.L.E. & F.) ever come together and discussed the question of nationalization?'

Mr Cramp was obliged to answer:

'No, we have not met to discuss the details of the question. If you can assure me that the matter is likely to become an urgent political question we certainly will.'[83]

By contrast, Mr A. G. Walkden's 60-paragraph memorandum on the future organization of transport was more penetrating and detailed and foreshadowed much of the legislation passed between 1930-47. It is to be regretted that leaders of the three railway unions did not exchange views before presenting evidence to the Commission. Had they done so and shown a united and well-informed determination to secure a reorganized transport system, they might have given the members of the Commission the courage of their convictions. As it was, the Commissioners, in their final report, whilst admitting that 'the nationalization of railways alone—leaving other transport in other hands—would certainly not produce any real co-ordination of transport', did not discuss the national ownership of all the principal means of transport since this could not be done 'without raising political differences of a party character'.[84] Thus the most that could be recommended was a series of piecemeal reforms, and it was not until 1947 that a more comprehensive solution was attempted.

At the A.G.M. in Southampton in July 1929, which closely followed the union's submission of evidence to the Royal Commission, Mr W. R. Webster moved a resolution on public transport which was more precise and detailed than had been the resolution passed two years earlier. It requested the (Labour) Government '. . . to take the necessary steps to bring rail road and air transport under national control in a single unit—each branch to be complementary instead of competitive—in order that the transport industry may be developed on the most efficient and economical lines'.

After having the blessing of Mr Cramp and other speakers, the resolution was carried with acclamation. A year later congress was content to congratulate the Government on its effort, through the Road Transport Bill, to secure 'a measure of control over road transport as a step towards complete national organization of transport'.

The real turning point, when the union passed from the phases of pious and somewhat vaguely worded resolutions, to a phase of energetic intervention with the Government and close co-operation with other transport unions, came in the spring of 1931. The acceptance by the union in March of that year of the most serious encroachment so far made in the national settlements of 1919–20, brought home to the membership the imperative necessity for legislation for the future development of transport as a whole. When the National Wages Board findings were published on March 5, 1931, the trade-union representatives on the Board included with their Minority Report an important Addendum worded as follows:

'Modern requirements make further co-ordination imperative, and the present inquiry has reinforced our opinion that only along the lines of comprehensive national organization of all forms of transport under public ownership and control can the problems of the transport industry be overcome.'[85]

That same spring a special committee of members of the executives of the three railway unions drafted a resolution which was carried by the T.U.C. in the following September. It urged the Government to take 'immediate steps to acquire on fair terms the railways and other transport undertakings to place them under a National Transport Authority'.[86] On May 19, 1931, a deputation from the special committee called upon the Prime Minister (Ramsay MacDonald), Mr Herbert Morrison (Minister of Transport), Miss Margaret Bondfield (Minister of Labour) and Mr Tom Johnston (Lord Privy Seal) at No. 10 Downing Street, and urged the implementation of their resolution. The Prime Minister promised a further interview after the matter had been considered. This interview did not take place. Owing to the financial crisis and the formation of the National Government in September 1931, the chance of a further sympathetic hearing had gone by. There were, however, further meetings of the special committee of the three unions, and the E.C. of the N.U.R. in December 1931 urged its representatives on the committee to 'unceasingly pursue the matter with the Government'.[87]

Thereafter, the policy of the union, which before the year of the $2\frac{1}{2}$ per cent wage cuts (1928) was largely confined to railway matters, was consistently and firmly for 'a comprehensive national organization of all forms of transport under public ownership and control'.[88]

Although the N.U.R. was not asked to send a delegation to the Conference on Rail and Road Transport under the chairmanship of Sir Arthur Salter in 1932, the union welcomed the Committee's recommendation that all road goods vehicles should be required to have licences which would be conditional, not only on the payment of the appropriate contribution towards annual road costs, but also on 'the observance of proper conditions as to fair wages and conditions of service'.[89] When many of the recommendations of the Salter Committee came to be embodied in the Road and Rail Traffic Bill in 1932 (enacted in the following year), the E.C. of the N.U.R. worked in close harmony with the executive of the

T. & G.W.U. in endeavouring to secure improvements in the Bill. After joint meetings held at Unity House on October 20 and 27, 1932, both unions sent memoranda to the Minister of Transport. Mr Cramp, on behalf of the N.U.R., urged that the Bill should include more definite proposals concerning wages and conditions of service which should be fixed in negotiations between the trade unions and the employers, or failing agreement at that level, by an Industrial Court. He deplored the fact that the transport industry was to be left to the 'vagaries of competitive enterprise' since this would inevitably lead to 'inefficiency and waste'.[90]

The experience of the years of wage cuts and industrial retreat, though a chastening one, had been valuable in compelling the union to think out afresh its policy for national transport. It was thus better prepared to meet the opportunities which came with the formation of a Labour Government with a clear majority in 1945.

VI

One outcome of the formation of the National Government in August 1931 was the resignation of the Political General Secretary of the union, Mr J. H. Thomas. In June 1929, when Ramsay MacDonald asked Mr Thomas to join the Labour Government as Lord Privy Seal with special responsibility for tackling the problem of unemployment, Mr Thomas accepted, and both the E.C. and the A.G.M. were unanimous in offering their congratulations.[91] In accordance with the precedent set in 1923–4 Mr Thomas was granted leave of absence, without salary, during the period the Government was in office, but his allowance of £250 a year as an N.U.R. M.P. continued until August 1931.[92] His salary as Lord Privy Seal was £5,000.

A sub-committee, appointed by the E.C. to make recommendations on how the work of the head office should be reorganized during Mr Thomas's absence, suggested that Mr Cramp should take charge of both Political and Industrial Departments and should be assisted in this work by Mr John Marchbank, both men to be paid £100 extra a year in view of their added responsibilities. These plans received the unanimous endorsement of the E.C.[93]

When on August 23, 1931, the Labour Cabinet was divided on the question of whether or not to impose a 10 per cent cut in unemployment pay, Mr Thomas sided with the Prime Minister and the nine other Cabinet Ministers who supported the imposition of the cuts. Ten members of the Cabinet refused their consent. Mr MacDonald then asked all the Ministers to hand in their resignations. The Labour Government had come to an end. On the evening of the following day (Monday, August 24th) when the public learned for the first time of the formation of a National Government, Mr Thomas was with the E.C. for over three hours, giving its members an informal statement about the financial crisis and the reasons that had prompted him to accept Mr MacDonald's offer of the post of Secretary for the Dominions in the new Cabinet.[94] Mr Cramp was on holiday at the time of the Cabinet crisis, but soon after his return to the office he received a phone call from Mr Thomas at Hove, asking him whether he would be prepared to take Mr Dobbie, the President, down to Hove with him for an informal talk. Mr Cramp consented. On the following day the three men 'talked it over' on the beach. Mr Thomas was loath to sever his connection with the union, but at the same time felt that he would be a 'coward and a cad' if he did not support Mr MacDonald. Mr Cramp clearly stated the alternatives. Since the T.U.C. and the Labour Party had decided to oppose the National Government, if Mr Thomas was determined to stay in the Cabinet, he must either resign from the office of Political General Secretary of the union or face the prospect of being dismissed for not obeying the union's rules.[95]

Mr Cramp decided to summon a special meeting of the E.C. for August 31, 1931, and to invite all the union's M.P.s to attend. The meeting carried unanimously the following resolution:

'That this E.C. having considered the position arising out of the formation of the new Government and also the decision of the Parliamentary Labour Party to become the official opposition, decide to instruct our Parliamentary representatives to conform to such decision and to act in accordance with Rule 21, Clause 10, Section C.'[96]

Since Mr Thomas did not feel that he could conscientiously accept the decision, he performed what he described as 'the most painful task' of his life, and wrote his letter of resignation to the President the same day. The members of the executive were unanimous in accepting the resignation and in placing on record their 'appreciation of the services rendered to the railwaymen of the country by Mr J. H. Thomas'.[97]

At the time of his resignation Mr Thomas was fifty-six years of age. Under the rules of the N.U.R. Employees' Superannuation Fund, he was not due to receive a retirement pension in 1931. Had he decided to remain as General Secretary and to resign from the Cabinet he would have been entitled to receive a £500 a year pension from the union in 1935. Some members of the E.C. thought it nevertheless desirable to award Mr Thomas £500 a year from the General Fund of the union. For some years past the union had maintained a Special Pension Fund fed from the profits on the sale of goods at head office. At the time of Mr Thomas's resignation this fund amounted to £1,772, and was being used to pay pensions to Mr Hudson, Mr Chorlton and a few other officials who, by decision of the E.C., had been *obliged* to retire on reaching the age of sixty, but who, for one reason or another, were not entitled to pensions from the staff Superannuation Fund. By 17 votes to 7, however, the E.C. rejected the resolution of Messrs Pounder and Benstead to make a special concession to Mr Thomas; by a like majority it carried an amendment moved by Ryan and Figgins: 'That consequent upon the resignation of Mr J. H. Thomas from the position of Parliamentary General Secretary and his position in connection with the Employees' Superannuation Fund, this E.C. decide that his position is governed by the Rules of the Employees' Superannuation Fund and instruct that he be treated in accordance with same.'[97] Since the E.C.'s acceptance of this amendment meant that Mr Thomas would receive no pension from the union, he decided to appeal against it to a general meeting (as he was perfectly entitled to do) and to issue a circular to all branches stating his case. Inevitably the E.C. determined not only to send to each member a printed statement of the political events that had brought about the resignation of the General Secretary, but also to issue a circular explaining the viewpoint of the committee on the subject of the pension.[98]

Mr Thomas's appeal was considered by a Special General Meeting of the union, held in the St Bride's Institute, London, on October 29 and 30, 1931. Between 10.0 and 11.30 a.m. on 30th the delegates listened to Mr Thomas's emotional speech in complete silence. There was no applause and no interruptions. In the course of his speech he recounted how as General Secretary he had saved the union 'thousands of pounds' by his financial and administrative reforms. He pointed to his wife, son and daughter who were sitting in the hall and said: 'Why should they be allowed to suffer after all I have done for the railwaymen?' His speech ended, questions came like a salvo from all parts of the hall. He conceded that at such time as he retired from the Cabinet he could claim a pension of £2,000 a year but that he would 'see them damned' before he would 'pauperize himself' to do it. His services had been to the union and from 'no other source' would he draw a pension.[99]

Despite this impassioned appeal, only five delegates out of eighty— Messrs Banks, Franklin (later President of the N.U.R.), Miller, Proctor and Ward voted to grant the appeal, whilst a resolution endorsing the decision of the E.C. was carried by 75 votes to 5.

The minority would undoubtedly have been larger, had it not been for Mr Thomas's front page article in the *Railway Review* on August 28, 1931, in which he defended the Cabinet decision to reduce unemployment benefit by 10 per cent and had it not been for the way in which he presented his case to the delegates at the S.G.M. In the course of his speech he had warned his hearers of the consequences of the rejection of his appeal:

'If you do not put on record that you do value past services, in whatever way you do it, I can see nothing but disaster for this union. Think of the reaction with the railway companies and the action of your membership....

The issue you have to determine is ... whether you as a union can dare to take the risk—I put it as high as that. You are the guardians of hundreds of thousands of railwaymen throughout the country, who will be affected by your decision to an extent you little dream of.'[100]

In the afternoon discussion which followed Mr Thomas's return to the Dominions Office, a delegate, Mr E. T. Cozens, expressed the feelings of many when he said:

'He dared you to turn down his appeal because of the effect on the membership. I resent being held up to ransom in that manner.'[101]

Mr Cramp defended the decision of the E.C. in a soberly-worded statement. He claimed that the only real parallel to Mr Thomas's case was that of Richard Bell who, through a difference of policy with the union, resigned from the post of General Secretary in December 1909, and received back his contributions to the Staff Superannuation Fund (as Mr Thomas would do) but had not received a pension. Mr Jim Campbell of Glasgow No. 7 Branch, who ultimately was to occupy the same General Secretary's chair for so long tenanted by Mr Thomas, conceded that Mr Thomas had, in the past, rendered services to the union 'which would have been worthy of great commemoration and gratitude' but that by his one action in 'handing over the working classes to a reactionary government' he had cancelled out the services he had rendered. Finally, another Scotsman, Mr R. Clark of Dundee tried to point a moral.

'The Thomases have risen on the crest of a particular wave of Capitalist Society, on a particular wave that has been semi-prosperous when the railway companies were able to grant certain concessions to the railwaymen. That time has gone. A thousand Thomases will not improve your conditions in the future.'

Although the majority against Mr Thomas was, perhaps, larger than feeling amongst the membership would have warranted, there was no doubt that the decision of the E.C. and the A.G.M. had the backing of the majority of the branches. Mr Cramp told the E.C. in September that he had received messages from 213 branches endorsing its action compared with 69 which contained votes of confidence in Mr Thomas. If some may have considered the union's decision ungenerous, it ought not to be forgotten that the members were still smarting from the biggest-ever reduction in their wages, imposed but a few weeks before.

VII

At its first ordinary meeting following the resignation of Mr Thomas the E.C. decided that Mr Cramp was now the 'Chief Officer of the union', but they left it to the S.G.M. to determine whether the post of Parliamentary General Secretary should be abolished or not.[102] On November 1, 1931, that meeting by the substantial majority of 61 to 15 with four abstentions, decided to abolish the post and to instruct the E.C. to make the appropriate alterations in the rules. The experiment of the union's affairs being conducted by two General Secretaries working in double harness had been brought to an end after eleven years.

The General Election of October 27, 1931, proved disastrous from the point of view of N.U.R. representation in Parliament. For the first time in thirty years no member of the N.U.R. (or A.S.R.S.) sat in the House of Commons. Mr J. H. Thomas was elected with an increased majority at Derby, but the E.C. had withdrawn his name from the official panel of candidates at the end of August.[103] The other six official N.U.R. M.P.s were all defeated.

After this disaster Mr Cramp seriously considered the possibility of accepting nomination for Parliament. Until Mr Dobbie was returned to Parliament in a by-election at Rotherham in February 1933, the General Secretary found it a 'serious handicap' that railwaymen had no voice in Parliament.[104] Although Mr Cramp said that, on balance, he favoured the idea of his acceptance of nomination for Parliament, the delegates at the A.G.M. in July 1932 decided otherwise. By 44 votes to 36 they rejected the proposal that a S.G.M. should 'review the position of the General Secretary as regards his eligibility to represent the union in Parliament'.[105] Mr Cramp did not appear to be unduly disappointed.

Less than two years after Mr Thomas's resignation Mr Cramp was dead. He was addressing a meeting of the E.C. at ten minutes past four on the afternoon of July 16, 1933, when he suddenly collapsed as a result of a cerebral haemorrhage. Although he remained conscious for an hour and a half after the seizure, he died at 3.0 a.m. the following day at a nursing home in Beaumont Street, London.

Ever since, one day in his 'teens, an I.L.P. cyclist had handed him a copy of Edward Bellamy's *Looking Backward* and he had read it with avidity, 'Charlie' Cramp had been a convinced socialist. In the course of thirteen years' management of the industrial affairs of the union he had become less extreme in his views. Nevertheless it was inevitable that many of those he met, whether on the opposite side of the table at National Wages Board meetings or at N.U.R. branch meetings should have on occasion disagreed with him violently. The unanimity of the tributes to his integrity of character, printed in a special supplement to the *Railway Review* on July 21, 1933, was therefore all the more remarkable. Mr A. Oliver, the Treasurer of the union wrote that 'his dignified presence charmed many and offended none'. Mr A. G. Walkden wrote that 'he had no rancour or bitterness in his nature' and was one of the most kind-hearted and generous men he had ever known.

It had been Mr Cramp's thankless task during eleven out of thirteen years of office to have to strain his utmost to hold back the companies' attacks on the favourable settlements made in 1919 and 1920. Only once— in 1920, at the very outset of his career as Industrial General Secretary— was he fortunate enough to be able to return from a meeting of the National Wages Board with an agreement for better wages and improved terms of service in his pocket. His passing marked the end of an important phase in labour relations on the railways. The year of his death saw the end of the chapter as far as negotiations through the National Wages Board were concerned. It also saw a change for the better (if only somewhat temporarily) in the railway companies' finances and the beginnings of a slow economic recovery for the nation. Finally, the era of completely unrestrained roads goods haulage competition came to an end with the passage of the Road and Rail Traffic Act in 1933. Had he not worn himself out in the struggles of the difficult years 1922–32, Mr Cramp would have gained some of the credit for the restoration of better conditions in 1935–7.

NOTES

1. *Basic Road Statistics* and C. Douglas Campbell, *British Railways in Boom and Depression*, p. 66.
2. Wilfred Smith, *Economic Geography of Great Britain*, pp. 620–1.
3. C. E. R. Sherrington, *Hundred Years of Inland Transport*, p. 330.
4. *Daily Herald*, December 20, 1927.
5. N.U.R., A.G.M., Southampton, Verbatim Report, July 5, 1929. pp. 4 *et seq.*
6. Final Report, p. 94.
7. Royal Commission on Transport: Minutes of Evidence, June 25, 1930. Memorandum 58, para. 12.
8. *Ibid.*, Q. 14,888.
9. *R.R.*, January 20, 1928.
10. See p. 370 above.
11. See p. 443 above.
12. N.U.R., A.G.M., July 1920, Item 19. A.G.M. 1922, Items 45 and 41. See also N.U.R., S.G.M., August 30, 1933, Verbatim Report, p. 119, speech of Mr H. W. Lane.
13. A. Bullock, *The Life and Times of E. Bevin*, Vol. 1, p. 398.
14. *R.R.*, July 13, 1928.
15. *R.R.*, February 24, 1928.
16. *R.R.*, March 9, 1928.
17. *R.R.*, February 17, 1928.
18. *Modern Transport*, October 28, 1933.
19. *R.R.*, August 11, 1933.
20. N.U.R., E.C., December, 1928, R. 938.
21. N.U.R., E.C. Minutes, June 1929, p. 136, Appendix I. H.O. Circular dated April 11, 1929.
22. N.U.R., A.G.M., Southampton, July 1929, Verbatim Report.
23. *The Times*, February 2, 1928.
24. N.U.R., Special E.C., October 23, 1928. R. 745.
25. N.U.R., H.O. Circular O/3291/RT/939/June 5, 1929.

26. N.U.R., E.C., September 1929, p. 137, Memorandum of Joint Meeting between the N.U.R. and T. & G.W.U., Transport House, August 22, 1929 and R. 737.
27. N.U.R., E.C., December 1929, Rs. 975, 976.
28. N.U.R., A.G.M., West Hartlepool, July 9, 1930, Verbatim Report, p. 15.
29. I am indebted to Mr S. J. Eite, Secretary of the Midland District Council, for the loan of documentary material on the organization of road transport workers over the period 1929–36.
30. Letter from the Secretary of the Sheffield, Chesterfield and District Council to Mr Cramp, October 2, 1929.
31. N.U.R., E.C., February 1930, Rs. 46 and 47.
32. N.U.R. Special E.C., July 19, 1933, A. Bullock, *The Life and Times of Ernest Bevin*, Vol. 1, p. 555.
    N.U.R., S.G.M., August 30, 1933, Verbatim Report, p. 88–90.
33. N.U.R., S.G.M., London, August 29–30, 1933, p. 11.
34. N.U.R., E.C., March 1932, p. 146 and Appendix K, pp. 232–37.
35. N.U.R., E.C., July 17, 1931, R. 600. H.O. Circular, September 2, 1931.
36. This account is based on N.U.R., E.C. Minutes, August 7, 1931, Rs. 630 and 648, August 22nd, R. 658, November 12th, 17th, R. 983.
    R.R., November 20, 1931. N.U.R., E.C., June 1932, R. 466, December 1932, R. 466, December 1932, p. 27 and *Isle of Wight County Press*, August 8, 15, 22 and 29, 1931.
37. N.U.R., Special E.C., March 30, 1932.
38. *R.R.*, August 3, 1928.
39. N.U.R., A.G.M., Bristol, July 1928, Verbatim Report, pp. 72 *et seq.*
40. *Liverpool Post*, July 28, 1928.
41. N.U.R., S.G.M., London, August 9, 1925, Verbatim Report.
42. *Daily News*, July 28, 1928.
43. *The Times*, July 28, 1928.
44. N.U.R., A.G.M., Southampton, July 4, 1929, Private Session, Verbatim Report.
45. N.U.R., E.C., October 11, 1929, R. 751. Agreement with companies reproduced in full in E.C. Minutes, December 1929, Appendix 'D', p. 134.
46. N.U.R., S.G.M., London, October 25, 1929, Verbatim Report, pp. 6 *et seq.*
47. N.U.R., S.G.M., London, October 24, 1930, Verbatim Report, pp. 4 *et seq.*
48. *R.R.*, Special Number, January 1931. *R.R.*, January 23, 30, March 13, 1931. United States Department of Labour, Monthly Labour Review, Vol. 32, p. 159, May 1931.
49. H.O. Circular S/1627/1357, March 18, 1931.
50. N.U.R., S.G.M., March 19 and 26, 1931, Verbatim Report.
51. N.U.R., H.O. Circular M7/351/1395, April 21, 1931.
52. N.U.R., Special E.C., January 7, 1932. R. 4. Special E.C., February 22, 1932, February 1932, p. 12. E.C., June 15, 1932, R. 857. Special E.C., June 28 and 29, 1932, p. 9. Special E.C., July 19–21, 1932, R. 870; *R.R.*, July 29, 1932.
53. N.U.R., E.C., December 1932, p. 170.
54. See Mr Thomas's speech at the S.G.M. of the N.U.R., St Bride's Institute, Fleet Street, London, October 30, 1931, Verbatim Report, p. 10.
55. *Ministry of Labour Gazette*, October 1933.
56. *R.R.*, September 16, 1932.
57. *R.R.*, August 19, 1932.
58. N.U.R., Special E.C., October 13–15, 1932, R. 1, 332.
59. Quoted in *Railway Gazette*, October 28, 1932, p. 523.
60. N.U.R., General Secretary's Report to the A.G.M., 1933, p. 16.

61. *R.R.*, December 16, 1932, Special Supplement. United States Department of Labour, Monthly Labour Review, Vol. 36, May 1933, pp. 1086–9.
62. *R.R.*, January 20, 1933.
63. N.U.R., E.C., January 24, 1933, R. 25.
64. N.U.R., E.C., March 1933, p. 101.
65. *R.R.*, July 1, 22, September 30, 1932. H.O. Circular M7/1078/1676, May 30, 1932.
66. I am much indebted to Mr W. C. Loeber for the loan of copies of the *Railway Vigilant* and other publications of the Railwaymen's Minority Movement and the Railwaymen's Vigilant Movement and for a written statement from him on the work of these two organizations.
67. N.U.R., E.C., September 1928, Rs. 691, 692.
68. N.U.R., E.C., March 1929, Appendices 'C' and 'F', pp. 147 and 157.
69. N.U.R., E.C., June 1929, p. 70.
70. N.U.R., H.O. Circular to Irish branches M7/1R/118/1422, June 10, 1931; E.C. June 1931, R.595.
71. N.U.R., E.C., July 1932, pp. 43–6, Special E.C., December 1, 1932; *R.R.*, December 2, 1932.
72. N.U.R., E.C., January 30, 1933, p. 18.
73. N.U.R., E.C., December 1933.
74. N.U.R., H.O. Circulars dated February 10 and 21, March 10, 1933.
75. *Irish Daily Telegraph*, February 14, 15 and 17, 1933.
76. N.U.R., S.G.M., London, April 4, 1933, Verbatim Report, p. 87.
77. *Irish Daily Telegraph*, February 22, 1933.
78. *Irish Daily Telegraph*, February 4, 1933.
79. N.U.R., S.G.M., London, April 4, 1933, Verbatim Report, p. 88.
80. *Irish News and Belfast Morning News*, February 13, 1933.
81. N.U.R., A.G.M., July 7, 1933, Verbatim Report, p. 426, Statement by Mr Cramp.
82. N.U.R., S.G.M., London, August 29, 1933, Verbatim Report, pp. 7 *et seq.* E.C., September 1933, p. 80.
83. Royal Commission on Transport, Minutes of Evidence, Part III, January 16, 1929, Qs. 1680, 1857.
84. Final Report, para. 536, sub-sections CXXI and CXXV.
85. *R.R.*, March 13, 1931.
86. N.U.R., E.C., June 1931.
87. N.U.R., E.C., December 1931, R. 308.
88. N.U.R., A.G.M., Folkestone, July 1932, Public Resolutions, p. 126. Re-affirmed with slightly different wording at A.G.M., Morecambe, July 1933, Public Resolutions, p. 84.
89. *The Times*, August 18, 1932.
90. N.U.R., E.C., December 1932, pp. 164–7.
91. N.U.R., E.C., July 10, 1929, R. 447. A.G.M., Southampton, July 2, 1929, p. 68.
92. N.U.R., E.C., July 10, 1929, R. 447. His allowance was in accordance with the E.C. decision R. 293 of May 1920.
93. N.U.R., E.C., July 10, 1929, R. 450.
94. C. L. Mowat, *Britain Between the Wars*, p. 392; *Daily Herald*, August 25, 1931.
95. This account is based on the Verbatim Report of the S.G.M. held in the St Bride's Institute, Bride Lane, Fleet Street, London, October 29–30, 1931.
96. N.U.R., Special E.C., August 31, 1931, R. 665.

97. *Ibid.*, R. 669 (amended).
98. *Ibid.*, R. 670 and September E.C., R. 946.
99. N.U.R., S.G.M., London, October 30, 1931, Verbatim Report, p. 27.
100. *Ibid.*, pp. 36 and 26.
101. *Ibid.*, p. 48.
102. N.U.R., E.C., September, 1931, Rs. 945 and 943.
103. N.U.R., Special E.C., August 31, 1931, R. 668.
104. N.U.R., General Secretary's report to the A.G.M., Folkestone, July 1932, p. 5.
105. N.U.R., A.G.M., Folkestone, July 1932, R. 64c.

CHAPTER XIX

UNCERTAIN RECOVERY: 1934-9

'The old boast that private enterprise or private capital can finance itself and can be self-reliant without intervention by the state is no longer true. The state has to prop up private capitalist undertakings in order that they can function.'
The Rt. Hon. Herbert Morrison, M.P. *(later Lord Morrison) speaking in the House of Commons on December 10, 1935, on the Railways (Agreement) Bill under which the Government guaranteed principal and interest on railway securities valued at £26½ million.*

'It may be doubted whether much of the diversion from rail to road will ultimately prove to be in the public interest or indeed, in the long run, in the interest of cheaper transport.
'Whatever doubts may be cast on the feasibility of planning industry as a whole, there can be no doubt that in the sphere of transport a far greater degree of planning is eminently desirable.'
From The Times *(Leading Article), February 25, 1935.*

I

WHEN the traffic receipts of the railways began to show a welcome improvement in the summer of 1933 the N.U.R. lacked both a General Secretary and a machinery of negotiation with the railway companies through which some of the benefits of improved trading might be passed on to the railwaymen. On this occasion finding a good General Secretary presented few difficulties; the establishment of a satisfactory negotiating machinery was a more prolonged and arduous task.

Few active members of the union can have had much doubt about the outcome of the election of a successor to Mr Cramp. John Marchbank had proved to be a very competent assistant secretary since his election to that office in 1925 and he was the best known of the candidates. His closest rival for the vacant post was a member of the Head Office staff, Mr W. J. Watson, whose talents had been employed in briefing the union's spokesmen for the meetings of the National Wages Board. Mr W. E.

Loeber stood for the programme of the Railwaymen's Minority Movement and the fourth candidate was Mr B. Dupree, a shunter from Swansea. When the result of the contest was published in the *Railway Review* on December 15, 1933, it was seen that in a poll in which less than half the membership voted, Mr Marchbank had obtained a clear majority over the combined vote of his opponents:

J. Marchbank	82,283
W. J. Watson	32,058
W. C. Loeber	7,025
B. Dupree	3,155

The new General Secretary, who was nearly 51 years of age, had started his working life as a shepherd boy in his native county of Dumfriesshire, but in common with many enterprising lads of his generation, had joined the railway service whilst still in his teens. Not long after, in 1906, a diligent branch secretary had persuaded him to join the A.S.R.S., John Marchbank helped to found the Buchanan Street, Glasgow (No. 4) branch of the union. Thereafter he served as Branch Secretary (until 1921), E.C. member (1916–18) and President (1922–4) before becoming right-hand man to Mr Cramp. Immaculately dressed, debonair and a great favourite with the ladies, he was at the same time a man of dynamic energy and determination. He was at his best in wage negotiations with the companies, never failing to make the utmost use of the well-prepared briefs drafted by the Head Office staff. In politics he was a consistent supporter of the moderate element in the Labour Party, being a vigorous opponent of all proposals for a 'united front' with the Communists.

Joseph Henderson, the goods guard elected by the A.G.M. in July 1933, to serve as President of the union from January 1934, was a man of very different character. He had a quiet, unassuming manner but impressed everyone with his sincerity and fair-mindedness. Besides serving both as A.G.M. delegate and E.C. member, he had been a member of the Carlisle City Council since 1919 and had been the first Labour Mayor of that city in 1927–8.

After informing the railway trade unions by letter in March 1933, that they intended to withdraw from the Central and National Wages Boards the companies were in no great hurry to suggest an alternative scheme of negotiation. By the unanimous decision of the A.G.M. at Morecambe on July 6, 1933, the E.C. of the N.U.R. was warned that it should 'refuse to consider any offer of new machinery less favourable to the railway trade unions than the machinery provided in the Railways Act of 1921'.[1] At a meeting with the representatives of the companies held on December 19, 1933, there was a general discussion of the problem but no tangible proposals were submitted by either side.[2]

Early in the following year, however, the companies submitted their proposals. They suggested that there should be five levels at which negotiations could be conducted; the Local Departmental Committees; Sectional Councils; Railway Staff Conference; Railway Staff National Council and Railway Staff National Tribunal. The first three stages were to be broadly similar to those established under the Railways Act of 1921, and the chief difference between the Railway Staff National Council and its predecessor, the Central Wages Board, was a nominal one. It was at the final stage of the negotiating machinery that the most radical changes were envisaged. In place of the cumbersome National Wages Board, the companies proposed the setting up of a three-man Tribunal comprising one nominee of the three railway unions, one of the companies and one agreed to by both parties. 'Relatively unimportant matters affecting the individual or a small group' were to be settled at the lower levels of the negotiating machinery. Time would not be wasted by referring such matters to the Tribunal which would confine itself to discussion of issues of national importance. In practice, where applications for changes in rates of wages and conditions of service affecting a large number of men would not be settled by direct negotiations, they would be referred to the Railway Staff National Council. If this body could not reach agreement, a final settlement was to be reached at the Railway Staff National Tribunal.[3]

The reason why discussions between the representatives of the companies and the three railway unions on the new proposals dragged on intermittently throughout the whole of 1934 was that the unions found the companies' scheme inferior to the old scheme of negotiation in four important respects. The three-man Tribunal was to be composed of persons without special knowledge or experience in railway matters; its deliberations were to be held in private; its decisions were to be binding on both parties and its scope was more restricted than that of the National Wages Board in that it could not deal with matters concerning individuals or small groups. Mr Marchbank expressed the hope to the A.G.M. delegates in July 1934, that 'they were not going back to a system that left it in the hands of one or two people' to determine their destiny. In no circumstances was the N.U.R. prepared to accept the Tribunal's decisions as binding.[4]

Early in 1935, however, the General Secretary was able to report to a special meeting of the E.C. that in further discussions with the companies just before Christmas and on January 8th and 16th, difficulties had been overcome on 'two very important points of principle' and a detailed scheme of negotiating machinery had been provisionally approved by the union's negotiating committee. Through the fact that, before each new discussion with the companies, the representatives of the three unions had met together and agreed on a common policy, the general managers deemed it wise to make concessions, especially as the Joint Executives of the unions had, on July 12, 1934, decided to inform the Ministry of Labour of the deadlock then existing. In return for the unions conceding that matters concerning individuals or small groups should not be dealt with by the Tribunal, the companies agreed that the hearings of this body should be held in public if the parties so desired and that its findings should not be binding on either party.[5]

After the combined executives of the three railway unions had met on January 21st and had recommended acceptance of the new scheme, the E.C. of the N.U.R. summoned a Special General Meeting of the union to be held in the West Central Hall, Alfred Place, London, on February 20, 1935.[6]

John Marchbank, in a strong speech urging that the action of the union's negotiating committee be endorsed, explained to the S.G.M. delegates that an attempt had been made to bring the railway shopmen within the main negotiating machinery, but the companies' representatives had said they were not prepared to discuss a scheme covering *all* railway employees and they did not consider the other thirty-seven unions with an interest in railway shopmen would be willing to forgo the existing arrangements for this grade. The N.U.R. representatives had, however, succeeded in inserting a loophole in the wording of the new agreement. The relevant sentence read:

'The staff to whom the machinery of negotiation shall apply shall be all persons regularly employed in the grades coming within the national agreement listed in Part VII . . . *or subsequently listed* by consent of the parties to this agreement.' (Our *emphasis*.)

This clause would allow for the subsequent inclusion in the scheme, not only of the shopmen, but also of other grades such as the dining-room staff and seafaring staff.[7]

The General Secretary claimed that the Tribunal would now be an acceptable body through the fact that its composition had been modified by the decision to appoint not more than six Assessors, three of whom were to be railway officials nominated by the companies and three members or officials of the railway trade unions, one to be nominated by each union. The Assessors, who were to give advice when requested to do so by the Tribunal, were not to sign decisions. Since with respect to 'all four cardinal points of principle' on which the union had voiced objections, the companies had made substantial concessions, he recommended the few scheme as one 'which, taken on the whole, was an improvement' on that instituted in 1921.[8] Forty-seven out of the eighty delegates agreed with him and with the resolution, moved by Mr H. Vincent, J.P., of Southampton, which stated that although it was to be regretted that shopmen were not included, the new machinery provided 'a reasonably fair basis' on which future negotiations could be conducted. A minority of the delegates were influenced by the argument of Mr H. F. Shepherd of

Forest Gate who claimed that 'there never could be an unbiased chairman' and that the whole scheme was 'a subtle way of bringing in compulsory arbitration'; but the amendment to reject the proposals and reopen discussions with the companies was defeated by 47 votes to 32.[9]

Thus on February 26, 1935, John Marchbank and Joseph Henderson, on behalf of the N.U.R., added their signatures to the 'Memorandum of Agreement for a Machinery of Negotiation for Railway Staff' which was to come into operation on March 1, 1935. Five stages of negotiating machinery were now established including: (a) the Local Representatives and Local Departmental Committees at a station or depot for discussion of such matters as arrangement of working hours, meal breaks and holidays; (b) Sectional Councils on each railway to consider the local application of national agreements and to devise improved methods of working; (c) direct discussions between the companies and the trade unions on national wage levels and conditions of service; (d) the Railway Staff National Council which would, as John Marchbank said, mainly act as 'a pillar box' for forwarding matters (that had first been raised in the direct discussions) to the last negotiating body; (e) the Railway Staff National Tribunal.[10]

II

The progress of the railway companies after 1933 may be compared with that of a drunken man moving, in the main, in a forward direction, but at times making no appreciable progress and at other times even lurching backwards before resuming an unsteady advance. If total net receipts of the four main line companies and their ancillary undertakings be considered as the yardstick of the industry's prosperity, then 1933, 1934, 1936 and 1937 were years of substantial improvements; 1935 and 1939 were years of little progress and 1938 a year in which there was a big lurch backwards. Always the improvement in railway business was at a slower rate than the recovery of the economy as a whole. Thus in 1935 the United Kingdom's industrial production increased by 4 per cent but gross railway receipts rose by only 1 per cent.[11] The roads were taking a larger share of the increased traffic than were the railways.

Because the recovery of the railways was such a slow and patchy one it was not until August 15, 1937, that the trade unions were able to negotiate the complete restoration of the wage cuts. It took but a few days of negotiation in the National Wages Board in January and February 1931, to introduce the wage cuts; six and a half years of persistent effort were required to restore them.

By the early months of 1934 there could be no mistaking the upward trend of railway business. Whereas in the first half of 1933 traffic receipts were down by £2,750,000 compared with the corresponding period of the previous year, in the second half of 1933 they were £2,646,000 *above* the corresponding period in 1932. The improvement continued throughout 1934. *The Economist* commented that railway stocks which had been 'friendless' in the spring of 1933 now presented 'an irresistible appeal to all sorts and conditions of investors' being the 'most popular of all recovery stocks'.[12]

The E.C. of the N.U.R. was not slow off the mark. At its quarterly meeting in March 1934, soon after the railway returns for 1933 were published, it decided to ask John Marchbank to seek an interview with the railway companies with the object of the restoration of the wage reductions. The other railway unions were informed of the decision so that concerted action could be taken.[13] A joint meeting of the three trade-union executives, held on April 10th, was unanimous in the view that the companies should be pressed to effect a full restoration of the pre-1931 conditions. At the first meeting with the unions on April 16th, however, the companies' representatives declared that the financial position had not improved sufficiently to make these concessions possible, though they would give careful consideration to the unions' claims. At a second meeting with the companies on May 24th, a fuller exchange of views took place, Mr Kenelm Kerr conceding that the reductions were only intended to be temporary, but arguing at the same time that the position was still much worse than it was in 1930.[14] Having read of the increased interest paid on the stocks of the London, Midland and Scottish, London and North Eastern Railway and Southern Railway and the maintenance of a steady 3 per cent dividend on the ordinary shares of the Great Western Railway, the union executives were not satisfied with the answers given by the companies, and at a joint meeting held at Unity House on July 12, 1934, they decided to seek another discussion with the general managers. When this discussion took place in the Midland Hotel, St Pancras, eight days later, Sir Ralph Wedgwood, for the companies, suggested that the unions should wait until the returns for 1934 were published in February or March 1935. The unions could not accept this delaying tactic and the meeting broke up without any agreement being reached.[15]

Back at Unity House, a special meeting of the N.U.R. Executive, held on July 23rd, decided to summon a Special General Meeting of the union for August 8, 1934. They were guided by the unanimous decision of the A.G.M. at Aberystwyth on July 3rd that 'failing a satisfactory and early settlement' with the companies they were to reassemble the delegates in London.[16]

John Marchbank told the delegates in London that the cost of restoring all the cuts would be £4½ million. The companies had argued that their net revenues were still £5 million short of what they were when the cuts were first imposed. He was willing to fight if 'what they were going to fight for was there to be got', but the railway returns were not the sorts of figures they could be 'over jubilant to fight on'. If they struck work there 'would be no road stoppage' and many of their members would be walking the streets after it was over. He supported a resolution, moved by Mr E. Kelly of Leeds, instructing the E.C. again to interview the general managers in order 'to secure the best offers possible for the lower paid grades—adults in receipt of 50s a week or less'. After a long and earnest discussion, congress defeated by 52 votes to 25 an amendment instructing the E.C. to try again to obtain the full restoration of the cuts including those imposed on the shopmen, failing which the companies were to be sent an 'ultimatum' of strike action, taken in conjunction with the other two unions, within one month. Mr Kelly's resolution for a compromise settlement was then carried by 51 votes to 26. Despite the claim of one delegate, Mr Ridyard, that the rank and file were looking for a bold lead, the majority were influenced by their knowledge of apathy in many districts. Mr Jenkins, the delegate from Burry Port, said that only thirty-six railwaymen had turned up to a 'mass meeting' held at Newport (Mon.) and only forty-one to another 'mass meeting' at Swansea. Mr H. Vincent of Southampton said that the reason why many railwaymen in his area were more concerned about working overtime than the restoration of the cuts, was that there were between 3,000 and 4,000 unemployed men in the area on transitional benefit who might fill the places of railway strikers. A delegate from Hull said that his own brother was waiting for him to 'chuck his job up' so that he (the brother) 'could take it on next morning'. Whilst it might have proved true, as Mr J. Grierson of Stockport suggested, that if they took upon themselves 'the spirit of the pioneers' apathy would have been conquered, most delegates agreed with their General Secretary who said he had not found men 'boiling over with enthusiasm to take to the streets'.[17]

All the same, the delegates might have had second thoughts had the negotiating committee come back empty handed from a further meeting with the companies' representatives on the morning of the following day (August 9th). The fact was that the companies were concerned that the N.U.R., R.C.A. and A.S.L.E. & F. were acting in unison in their demand for improvements; they 'were reluctant to face the prospect of a permanent loss of traffic to the roads',[18] and they were in a better position to afford some concessions to the railwaymen than they, at first, endeavoured to make out. *The Economist* advised investors in railway stocks that they should not overlook the extent to which 'policy' had determined the character of the companies' interim dividends in July. All except the Great Western Railway had 'deliberately under-distributed their earnings'. The financial correspondent of *The Times* considered the dividend distribution to have been 'exceedingly conservative'.[19] The companies therefore agreed to the removal of the second $2\frac{1}{2}$ per cent deduction (on earnings over 40s) in two stages, half to come off from October 1, 1934, and the other half from January 1, 1935. The improvement would apply to shopmen and the salaried grades as well as to the conciliation grades and would cost the companies £1,055,000. The agreement was to last for a year from October 1st. The initial 2½ per cent reduction and the reduced rates of pay for overtime, Sunday duty and night duty were to remain.

When the S.G.M. delegates considered the companies' offer that same evening from 7.45 to midnight, the number who still favoured an attempt being made to win back all that had been lost in 1931 was appreciably less than it had been the day before. An amendment in favour of strike action on behalf of the full restoration of cuts to the grades earning under 50s a week, was defeated by 61 votes to 17. After John Marchbank had warned that there would be no unanimity for a strike amongst the three railway unions since the R.C.A. had already decided against this form of protest, conference by 45 votes to 33 carried a resolution accepting the companies' offer 'without prejudice to any further applications' the union might decide to submit.[20] Possibly a further approach to the companies might have brought more concessions. The industrial correspondent of *The Times* believed that in view of the railway directors' reluctance to take the risk of a strike the union leaders had shown 'commendable moderation' in their policy.[21]

Although the companies had promised, on August 9th, that the concessions would be extended to the shopmen, the details had to be worked out in a meeting of the National Railway Shopmen's Council on the following day. In response to the unions' request for the full restoration of the 4⅙ per cent cuts introduced in 1931, the most that the companies would concede was to substitute a 3⅓ per cent cut from October 1, 1934, and a 2½ per cent cut from January 1, 1935, for the higher rate then in operation. The companies promised that, apart from holiday periods or 'circumstances of an exceptional character', they would ensure shopmen the equivalent of five full days' work a week.

The acceptance of these terms by the S.G.M., meeting in London on August 13th, was a near thing largely because of the phrase 'or circumstances of an exceptional character' which concluded the wording of the agreement. Many delegates felt that these words gave the companies a very big loophole to put the shopmen on short time whenever there was an economy drive. An amendment to refer back the agreement in order to secure the deletion of the offending words was, however, defeated by 43 votes to 37 and the resolution for acceptance carried by a similar margin.[22]

Nineteen thirty-four proved to be an even better year than seemed likely at its commencement. The introduction, in the summer of 1933, of third-class 'Monthly Return' tickets with return fare at the ordinary single fare of 1d a mile, had given a welcome boost to the receipts from passenger traffic. The net earnings of the railways' ancillary business—steamer services, bus services, etc., nearly doubled in 1934 and the improvements were reflected in more generous dividend distributions early in 1935.[23] Understandably, branches of the union were urging the executive to keep up the pressure on the companies. In December 1934, forty-eight of them demanded that if the other unions would not agree to a new approach to the companies the N.U.R. should 'go it alone'. The E.C. acted promptly. The General Secretary was told to consult the other unions for a concerted attack on the remaining cuts.[24] But owing to the need to await the outcome of the Annual Conference of the A.S.L.E. & F., it was not until July 12, 1935, that agreement was reached with the other two unions to confine the representations to the companies to the cancellation of the cuts in wages and worsened conditions of service introduced in February 1931. Not until September 25, 1935, was it agreed that each union should post simultaneously to the Secretary of the Railway Staff Council, a letter requesting discussions.[25] The first meeting with the companies was therefore not held until October 22, 1935, when the proceedings seem to have been largely limited to an exchange of documents. At a second meeting, Mr Kenelm Kerr, for the companies, brought more papers in an endeavour to show that there was no justification for making any changes. The unions were not convinced. Conferring separately the same day, they decided to demand a meeting with the general managers.

The union representatives finally got to grips with the general managers on January 7, 1936. Mr Marchbank argued that in the engineering and other industries the wage reductions imposed at the time of the economic crisis had since been restored; that the cuts in railwaymen's pay were supposed to be temporary, but it was now five years since they had been introduced; that the well-being of those who manned the railways should take precedence over the claims of the shareholders and that the companies could afford the concessions demanded. Mr Kenelm Kerr contended that owing to the increased cost of the materials the companies used, the improvement on their financial position was only a slight one. If the unions insisted on pressing their full demands they were likely to be met with a completely negative response. The union leaders said they would think it over. Meeting separately at Unity House on January 16th, they decided to drop their 'all or nothing' approach and instead to bargain for as much as they could get from the companies. They did not think it would be a wise policy to appeal to the Railway Staff National Tribunal.

A provisional settlement was reached after three meetings with the general managers on March 10, 16 and 25, 1936. Mr Kenelm Kerr said that the companies could not offer more than £600,000 and that their decision to offer that much was only reached by a majority vote. The Chairman of the London and North Eastern Railway, Mr Whitelaw—whose board of directors thought that a further *reduction* in railwaymen's wages was justifiable—had favoured referring the union's claim to the Railway Staff National Tribunal, but had been over-ruled by the others.

The union representatives therefore agreed to recommend to their members the acceptance of the companies' suggestion that the £600,000 should be spent in restoring from June 1, 1936, *half* the remaining 2½ per cent deductions.

The proposals could only be put into effect if the supreme governing body of the union accepted them. On March 26th, the E.C. decided to summon an S.G.M. for May 12th and to recommend to the delegates the acceptance of the companies' terms. The delegates, who met in the Conway Hall, London, decided otherwise. Though they turned down by 46 votes to 33 a proposal that, in the event of the failure of further direct negotiations with the companies, strike notices should be tendered, they rejected more decisively—by 57 votes to 23—the resolution for acceptance of the companies' offer. Instead they carried by 49 votes to 31 an amendment instructing the E.C. to resume negotiations and report back to the S.G.M. No doubt, in rejecting the strike weapon, the delegates were influenced by the fact that the dispute was all over the price of a packet of cigarettes. Mr W. T. Bason, a signal linesman earning under 50s a week, said: 'This 6d and this 1¼ per cent is not worth striking for.' On the other hand the delegates felt that the companies could afford to pay up. Earlier that year, in a test case, the House of Lords had ruled that the Southern Railway had been over-assessed for rating purposes to the tune of £1,103,131 a year since April 1931, and it had since been learned that the four main line companies would be entitled to a total windfall rebate from overpaid rates of £12,993,558. Compared with this, the full satisfaction of the unions' claims would cost the companies £2,970,000 a year.[26]

One reason why the further meeting with the general managers, which occurred on June 12th, was completely barren of results was that the Annual Assembly of Delegates of the A.S.L.E. & F. had deserted the 'united front' of the three railway unions that had hitherto prevailed. Mr Squance, their General Secretary, was instructed to press for what Mr T. Pocock, a N.U.R. veteran, called 'the Utopian programme' for a 6-hour day, double rates for Sunday duty, and other improvements. The claims were to be taken to the Tribunal if necessary. Now that the unions were fighting for different programmes, the companies were more confident that, through the negotiating machinery, they could successfully resist the demand for a full restoration of the pre-1931 conditions. Hence, after passing through the Railway Staff National Council on June 18th, the claims were considered by the Railway Staff National Tribunal between July 15th and 20th.

When, with characteristic clarity and competence, John Marchbank presented the union's case to the tribunal, he emphasized the increased productivity of labour on the railways. The annual engine mileage covered per locomotive had increased by 1,086 miles since 1929, permanent-way gangs had been amalgamated so that there were fewer lengthmen per mile of track, and manually operated signal boxes had been amalgamated into larger ones worked by electricity. Far from benefiting from these improvements, the railwaymen had experienced a slower rate of promotion. Owing to the fact that there were in 1936 over 6,000 fewer men in the locomotive departments than there were in 1929, it was taking about eight years longer for men to reach the top grades, and there were many drivers of over 50 years of age who had been 'put back' to the grade of fireman and were shovelling tons of coal daily. In a strong plea for the restoration of the pre-1931 rates of pay for overtime and Sunday duty, he pointed out that the old Great Western Railway, Taff Vale and Caledonian Railways paid better rates (time and a half) for Sunday duty from 1912 onwards than had been paid by the four main line companies since 1931.[27]

The drawbacks of Mr J. H. Thomas's policy of self-sacrificing co-operation with the companies was seen when Mr Kenelm Kerr, in his reply, harked back to the union's voluntary acceptance of wage cuts in 1928 and 1929.

'The unions,' he said, 'have twice voluntarily accepted as the justification for the relief a level of net revenue, which low as it was then in relation to the standard revenue (the £51 million standard set under the Railways Act of 1921), was nevertheless higher by £9¾ million and £8 million than the 1935 level which they now argue does not call for any relief at all.'

The weakness of a policy of basing wages on the fluctuating net revenues of the companies, instead of on the need of railwaymen for a reasonable standard of living was thus revealed. Since after 1934 the cost of living was rising at a faster rate than the net revenues of the companies, the logic of Mr Kenelm Kerr's argument would lead to a gradual worsening of railwaymen's living standards.

Sir Arthur Salter and the two other members of the Tribunal in their Decision No. 1, published on July 27, 1936, did not agree that the companies were unable to afford some concessions. They recommended that, from August 16, 1936, a deduction of 1¼ per cent from all earnings should take the place of the 2½ per cent till then operative. There were to be no deductions from earnings of less than 40s 6d a week. The standard rate of time and a quarter for overtime was to be restored in place of the time and one eighth instituted in 1931, but there were to be no changes in the Sunday and night duty payments. There were to be corresponding improvements in clerical workers' pay. The arrangements were to continue for at least a year.[27]

The S.G.M. of the N.U.R. held in the Memorial Hall, Farringdon Street, on August 11, 1936, by a majority of 53 votes to 26 decided to accept the Tribunal's findings. Delegates were influenced by the decision of the shopmen at a meeting of the Railway Shopmen's National Council on June 12th to accept the partial restoration of the remaining cuts and by the overwhelming vote of 67-4 of an S.G.M. of the N.U.R. on June 17th, to endorse that decision. The only real alternative to acceptance of the Tribunal's award was a strike, and there was little evidence of support for extreme action in the branches whose members believed that the risk of loss of employment after a stoppage was greater than in 1926. A shopman delegate from Glasgow said that thousands of men were 'hanging on to their jobs by the skin of their teeth'.[28] Could such men be expected to risk all for a sixpence a week rise?

The A.S.L.E. & F. gained absolutely nothing from its separate approach on behalf of the locomotive grades only. In their Decision No. 2 of December 29, 1936, the members of the Tribunal did not add a penny to any of the wage rates or take off a minute from the length of the working day. They said that it would be impossible to limit concessions to one department and that if the reforms advocated by the Associated Society were made generally applicable, the cost of their introduction—£50 million—would be prohibitive.[29] They did, however, concede one very important question of principle. If the improvement in the net revenues of the railways continued 'railway employees should obtain a share in the improvement without waiting for the large increase in railway profits that would be required before the Standard Revenue (£51 million) can be reached'.

The same S.G.M. of the N.U.R. which had accepted Decision No. 1 of the Railway Staff National Tribunal reaffirmed a resolution in favour of a 50s minimum wage for railwaymen passed at the A.G.M. a month earlier. As soon as the Railway Accounts for 1936 were available, the E.C. was to press for the introduction of the 50s minimum, together with the full restoration of the wage cuts.[30] Thus, when the executives of the three railway trade unions met at Unity House on March 12, 1937, the N.U.R. urged that they should make a concentrated and united effort to persuade the companies to grant these two important concessions. But although the executives of the other two societies agreed to demand the full restoration of the cuts, they would not agree to join a campaign for the 50s minimum wage. Instead, the Associated Society (which had few members earning less than 50s a week) decided to ask for twelve days' holiday a year for locomotivemen, the cancellation of provisions for extended rosters and the introduction of a guaranteed day for those called out on Sundays. The R.C.A., on behalf of the clerical and supervisory grades, asked for a 36-hour week and improved rates of pay for night duty.

As no progress was made in the earlier stages of the negotiations, John Marchbank presented the N.U.R. case to the Tribunal on July 20, 1937. He showed that since the wage reductions were introduced in 1931, the companies had saved a total of £21,891,000 at the expense of the railwaymen. In 1936 they had allocated more than £12 million to reserves, mainly as a result of earmarking the rate rebates for this purpose. This was well in excess of the £5 million taken from reserves in the more difficult years 1931–5. In the first half of 1937 their traffic receipts were over £3½ million greater than in the corresponding period of 1936. And yet 120,000 railwaymen were in receipt of basic rates under 50s a week despite the fact that in the revised édition of his book, *The Human Needs of Labour*, Mr Rowntree had shown that a minimum wage of 53s was needed by a family with three children. The cost of living was rising. It was becoming increasingly apparent that the minimum adult rates paid to railwaymen were, in many cases, not adequate to provide the necessaries of life.[31]

Mr Kenelm Kerr did not agree. He questioned the value of Mr Rowntree's book. 'Difficulties of inadequate nutrition did not arise primarily from lack of means' but from 'unwise choice in marketing and insufficient skill in cooking!' He taunted the unions which never ceased demanding the co-ordination of transport, for failure to co-ordinate their own demands. The R.C.A. had not included in their programme a demand for a 50s minimum wage. If it was possible for a clerk to live on less than 50s a week, he suggested it should be possible for a porter or lengthman to do so.[32]

Fortunately, for the railwaymen, 'a little meat came on the shelf during the hearing' (to borrow John Marchbank's colourful phrase). On July 28th the Railway Rates Tribunal granted the request of the companies to raise their charges by 5 per cent. In making its award the Tribunal must have taken this decision into account along with the rating rebates and the Government's guarantee of capital and interest on a £26½ million loan to the railways in 1936.

In its Decision No. 3, published on August 9, 1937, the Tribunal yielded to the demands made conjointly by the unions, but conceded very little in response to the demands made on behalf of the members of individual unions. The 1¼ per cent deduction from earnings was to cease from August 16, 1937, when the standard rates of payment for overtime (time and a quarter by day, time and a half by night); night duty (time and a half) and Sunday duty (time and a half) would also be restored. Although the claim for a 50s minimum was rejected on the grounds that its cost (at about £3 million) would be 'prohibitive', the strength of the N.U.R. case on behalf of the poorly paid grades was recognized. All adults in receipt of a base rate of less than 45s a week were to have a rise of 1s a week, whilst those whose base rate was 45s were to have a rise of 6d a week. The basic rates of the handful of men with under 40s a week were to be raised to 41s. The bill for these improvements would come to £2,700,000 a year. By contrast the cost of the concessions made to the R.C.A. and A.S.L.E. & F. would amount to only £200,000. This was to pay for the day's holiday awarded for work performed on Whit Monday or August

Bank Holiday, and for the compensation paid to clerks for long spells of night duty.

At the S.G.M. held in London on August 19, 1937, Mr Figgins spoke in favour of the rejection of the Tribunal's award. He believed that the country had reached 'the peak of trade recovery' and that if they did not go all out for the 50s minimum in the 'immediate present' there would be very little prospect of getting anything in a year's time. Events were to prove him right. The delegates, however, were impressed by the fact that the other unions had refused to co-operate in raising the minimum wage. They could see that, if it came to a strike, the N.U.R. might have to fight alone. They, therefore, turned down by 68 votes to 12 a proposal to reject the Tribunal's award and to reopen the campaign for the full implementation of the N.U.R. programme. A resolution to accept the award and to instruct the E.C. at the earliest opportunity to press the claim for the 50s minimum was carried by a similar margin.[33] The delegates were unanimous in recording their appreciation of the General Secretary's skilled presentation of the union's case at a time when he was much below par in health. He delivered his four-hour speech to the Tribunal with one eye covered with a shield. The head office staff was also congratulated for working 'very willingly night after night, up to midnight on some occasions', preparing the union's case.

Owing to the speedier and uninterrupted improvement in the passenger traffic receipts of the London Passenger Transport Board, it proved possible to restore the wage cuts in the London area at an earlier date than was the case with the main line companies. The first improvement was introduced at the same time as the agreement was reached with the main line companies, viz. August 1934. The second deduction of $2\frac{1}{2}$ per cent, i.e. on those earning over 40s a week, was restored in two stages; at the beginning of October 1934, and at the beginning of January 1935.[34] Full restoration of the remaining deductions from earnings resulted from discussions between the unions and representatives of the board held on December 18, 1934, when Mr Pick, for the employers, proposed that from the beginning of April 1935, the first $2\frac{1}{2}$ per cent deduction should be reduced to $1\frac{1}{4}$ per cent and that from the first pay week in July the remaining $1\frac{1}{4}$ per cent should be restored, thus completing the return to the position as it was before July 20, 1932, when the deductions were first imposed in London. The E.C. of the N.U.R. was unanimous in accepting this offer, but at a further meeting with the board on January 8, 1935, Mr Pick agreed to advance to the beginning of June 1935, the date for the full restoration of the cuts. The E.C. had no objections![35] For the L.P.T.B. staff the cuts had come a year later and were fully restored two years earlier than was the case with the men employed by the main line companies.

On the other hand the Irish railwaymen must have envied the steady progress of the main body of British railwaymen towards the final removal of the companies' economy cuts. The coming to power of De Valera in the Irish Free State in 1932, and the subsequent severance of many constitutional links with the United Kingdom, led to a five years' trade war between the two countries. By a British Treasury order of July 12, 1932, duties of 20 per cent were imposed on Irish live animals, meat, poultry and dairy produce entering Great Britain. The Free State quickly retaliated by imposing equally heavy duties on British coal, cement, iron and steel.[36] Inevitably there were serious repercussions on the volume of business and hence the profitability of Irish railways. On the largest Irish railway, the Great Southern, receipts from livestock traffic fell from £426,321 in 1931 to £273,396 in 1933.[37]

De Valera's Government acted more promptly than did the Government of Northern Ireland to meet the transport crisis. Under the Irish Railways Act of 1933, ownership and operation of all the railways situated in Southern Ireland was handed over to the Great Southern Railway Company whose directors were reduced in number to seven and whose capital value was scaled down. Ownership of the principal road transport undertakings was at the same time concentrated in the hands of three concerns only, The Dublin Tramways, The Great Southern Railway Company and the Great Northern Railway Company. One result of this rationalization of the transport system of the Free State was to ease the financial difficulties of the railways whose accounts remained in a healthier state than those of the companies operating north of the border.

The parlous condition of the finances of the Northern Ireland railways was partly the outcome of the fact that no less than eleven companies owned or operated the 649 miles of standard gauge and 124 miles of narrow gauge lines open to traffic in this small piece of territory. Competing with them (in 1932) were seventy-five separate bus undertakings running a total of 775 buses and employing nearly 8,000 men. Inevitably several of the smaller railway companies found it quite impossible to run at a profit. In the spring of 1934 the Great Northern Railway was running at a loss of £6,000 a week. The small Sligo, Leitrim and Northern Counties Railway was running at an annual loss of £15,000 and had not purchased a locomotive since 1918. The Londonderry and Lough Swilly Railway Company was only able to continue operations with the aid of a subsidy from the Northern Ireland Government. Even in the years 1928–32 the working expenses of the three principal railways in Northern Ireland had absorbed 91 per cent of their total receipts.[38]

Early in 1934 the Government of Northern Ireland asked Sir Felix Pole (of Great Western Railway fame) to conduct an investigation into the transport of Northern Ireland and to make a report on its future organization so that it should serve 'the best interests of the public'. On May 1, 1934, a political sub-committee of the E.C. of the N.U.R. submitted a scheme to Sir Felix Pole for a Northern Ireland Central Transport Board which would acquire the whole of the road and rail public transport undertakings in the area. The nine-member board, which would include representatives of the road transport and railway transport trade unions, as well as transport experts, would have responsibility for providing adequate transport services in the six counties.[39] This radical proposal was not accepted by Sir Felix Pole. In his report, published in July 1934, he declared that since six of the Northern Ireland railways also operated in Irish Free State territory it would not be practicable to transfer ownership of these lines to a State Board. But he did recommend that all road transport undertakings (except those owned by Belfast Corporation) should be transferred to a Northern Ireland Road Transport Board, and this recommendation was embodied in the Road and Rail Transport Act of 1935.[40]

Consequently the Northern Ireland railways continued to compete with each other and with the buses, and they continued to lose money. The railwaymen helped to foot the bill. Instead of the cuts of 1931-3 being restored, additional cuts were imposed. On the Sligo, Leitrim and Northern Counties Railway they were raised from the 10 per cent to 20 per cent on June 17, 1935. Only in February 1938 were they brought down again to 15 per cent.[41] In November 1934, the Board of Directors of the Londonderry and Lough Swilly Railway proposed a reduction of 25 per cent in the wages of the 151 men employed by the company. The negotiating committee of the union protested strongly—until they were shown the company books—when they quickly settled for a $22\frac{1}{2}$ per cent reduction. On this line the best that it had been possible to achieve, in small stages, by the outbreak of the Second World War was a reduction to $16\frac{1}{4}$ per cent.[42] Elsewhere in Northern Ireland the railwaymen were subject to a deduction of 10 per cent from their wages and salaries from May 1, 1934. Three years later this had only been brought down to $7\frac{1}{2}$ per cent.[43]

Only the men employed on the Great Southern Railway ever seemed likely to win back a full restoration of the 1931 rates of wages. Although they had to suffer a $7\frac{1}{2}$ per cent reduction in earnings in 1934, this was brought down to 5 per cent in January 1936. The Irish Railways Wages Board, in June 1937, recommended a further reduction to $2\frac{1}{2}$ per cent. A year later the same board ruled that the remaining $2\frac{1}{2}$ per cent should be restored in two stages—$1\frac{1}{4}$ per cent from July 1, 1938 and the last $1\frac{1}{4}$ per cent from January 1, 1939. Within sight of the winning post, the men were beaten by a sudden worsening of the company's financial position. Instead of starting 1939 with a clean slate, they faced a demand from the directors for the re-imposition of the $7\frac{1}{2}$ per cent deductions introduced in May 1934. Only a determined stand by the union prevented this relapse coming into effect. The outstanding $1\frac{1}{4}$ per cent deduction did not disappear until December 1939.[44]

III

On the other side of the Irish Sea, with the wage cuts at last out of the way, the union was able to concentrate on a long overdue campaign to raise wage standards and working conditions to levels above those of 1931.

When the national agreements had been drawn up after the First World War, the signalmen had been the last numerically large group to obtain a standardization of their terms of employment. In 1937 when the union was in a position once more to campaign for improvements it was the signalmen's cause that was first taken up.

One reason for this decision was that the men of this grade had never been very satisfied with the marks system standardized throughout the country under the agreement of 1922. The number of anomalies and injustices seemed to increase with each year that passed. Although plenty of antiquated signal boxes survived, modernization of this branch of the industry proceeded more rapidly than in any other. At the big termini small boxes were demolished to be replaced by large power-operated ones. When the new Waterloo signal box with its 309 levers was opened in 1936 it replaced six smaller ones (Waterloo 'A', 'B', 'C' and 'D' and Vauxhall East and West). Motor-operated points worked in conjunction with illuminated diagrams, and electrically operated remote control systems were the other principal innovations. The signalman was becoming more of a brain worker; the wearing strain of intense concentration took the place of the labour of pulling heavy levers. Since the productive efficiency of the signalman was increasing, fewer men of this grade were required by the companies. The number employed fell from 29,203 in 1921 to 23,392 in 1937. Such changes led some 'bobbies' to demand a thorough overhaul of the marks system, whilst others wanted its outright abolition and its replacement by wage scales based mainly on length of service.[45]

It was always the proud boast of the N.U.R. that more could be achieved for the different grades in the railway service by their working within an all-grades union than by the formation of sectional unions. Within the N.U.R., grade organizations are given free rein to advance their own interests provided they do not act to the detriment of the main body of railwaymen.

It was for these reasons that the A.G.M. at Ipswich in July 1931, carried unanimously a proposal that a National Signalmen's Conference should be summoned. Each District Council was to choose a delegate and there was to be a delegation from the A.G.M.

When the conference met in the West Central Hall, London, on December 21 and 22, 1932, the main theme of the discussion was whether length of service or marks earned provided the most suitable basis for payment of signalmen. Eventually the delegates rejected by 17 votes to 12 a proposal that pay should be on a servitude basis modified by the number of marks earned, and carried, by the narrow margin of 15-14, a resolution in favour of the continuance of the marks system.

A much larger conference, attended by 250 signalmen in London on May 7, 1933, defeated by 132 votes to 81 a resolution for the abolition of the marks system. Instead it proposed 'a scale rate for all signalmen starting at 50s for the first year and rising by 2s 6d a year to 60s, with an addition to the scale of 2s 6d per week for every 50 marks per hour made'. National Signalmen's Conferences were held annually thereafter.

From their deliberations it was clear that it was a modification of the marks system rather than its abolition which found most favour with signalmen in the 1930's.[4]

So that it should be well primed with information when the time came to make demands of the companies, the Head Office sent all branches a Questionnaire on August 1, 1934. Details of the method of allocating marks in power-operated signal boxes and other facts about modernization of signalling methods were requested.

Owing to the slow pace of restoration of the economy cuts of 1931, it was not until February 1937 that the Railway Staff National Council considered the N.U.R.'s programme for modifying the signalmen's agreement of 1932. The union's claim was for wage rates rising from 50s a week in a class 7 box with up to 49 marks an hour, to 80s from the second year of service, in a class 1 box with between 300 and 349 marks an hour. In addition a new, special rate of 80s a week of six 6-hour shifts was demanded for those working in boxes with a rating of over 350 marks an hour. The signalling of permanent-way motor trollies was to be awarded marks on the same basis as for trains; five marks were claimed for working manually operated generators for remote control of signals and points and various other modifications were suggested. A man working in a box which became reclassified at a lower level of marks should continue at his old (higher) rate of pay until he was found another post with a similar classification to that to which he had become accustomed.

Owing to the Tribunal's preoccupation in 1937 with the union's claim for the final restoration of the 'cuts' it was not until the summer of 1938 that it gave attention to the N.U.R.'s claim on behalf of signalmen. When, at last, time was found for the hearings a very careful investigation of the union's case was undertaken.

So that they should be more closely conversant with the facts, the assessors visited a number of signal boxes belonging to three of the main line companies in the greater London area.

John Marchbank again gave a masterly summary of the men's arguments for improvements in the rates of wages. He contended that signalling efficiency had been greatly increased and that the men were entitled to reap some of the benefit from their increased productivity. He showed that when automatic signalling replaced manually operated signalling on the

Euston-Watford section of the London, Midland and Scottish in 1932, the number of signal boxes was reduced from twenty-one to eight and the number of men employed from fifty-seven to thirty-seven. Far from the change increasing the number of better paid men, it was accompanied by an increase in the number and proportion of men in the not so well paid hybrid grade of porter-signalmen.[47] With the modernization of equipment the duties of signalmen, relief signalmen and train regulators became more responsible and the strain of their work was increased.

In resisting the claim, the companies maintained that new capital expenditure on the installation of more up-to-date signalling equipment had absorbed a large part of the savings resulting from the reduction of the number of signalmen employed. They asserted that the proportion of men in the better-paid posts had increased.

In its Decision No. 4, dated July 29, 1938, the Tribunal admitted that its recommendations were limited to 'comparatively minor adjustments'. The reasons why no more ample award was made was a financial one. The immediate cost of the full implementation of the union's demands would be a million pounds; the final cost would be much more. The increases proposed would raise signalmen's wages by an average of 22 per cent. This would completely disrupt differentials as between signalmen and other grades, and it would, in practice, be impossible to avoid making upward adjustment of other wage rates. Hence the Tribunal claimed that 'no general increase in wages was justifiable or practicable'. It did admit that the strain of working in the largest signal boxes had increased, and it therefore conceded an extra 2s 6d a week for men working in boxes with 500–700 marks and a further 2s 6d a week where marks exceeded 700. An extra mark was to be awarded where one lever operated two or more sets of points, motor trollies were to be classed with trains for mark-earning purposes, and there were to be other minor improvements.

The union's opinion of the adequacy or otherwise of the award was clearly enough shown in the verdict of a Special General Meeting held in London on September 23, 1938. By 79 votes to 1 the meeting decided to reject Decision No. 4 on the grounds that 'the application would not serve the best interests of the signalmen members'. The E.C. was advised that, should the companies endeavour to implement the Tribunal's recommendations, a further S.G.M. was to be summoned at once.

The fact that by its decisions 2 and 4 the Tribunal had twice rejected claims for a substantial advance in the wages of separate sections of the railway labour force on the grounds that improvements could not be confined to one group, greatly strengthened the position of those in the N.U.R. who maintained that the correct policy was to campaign on behalf of an improvement for all grades.

Even before the Tribunal had given its decision on the signalmen's appeal, the A.G.M. at Plymouth in July 1937 had directed the E.C. to do its utmost to persuade the companies to grant the 50s minimum wage and to mobilize support in the branches for this policy.[48] At its special meeting on April 5, 1938, the E.C. drafted a six-point programme which, it considered, would provide a suitable basis for common action with the other unions. Pride of place was given to the demand for the introduction of the 50s minimum wage, whilst the other items included the abolition of spreadover turns; twelve days' holiday with pay; the abolition of extended rosters; a minimum of four hours' pay for those called on to do Sunday duty and short Saturday turns for men obliged to work five long turns and one short.[49]

On May 4 and 16, 1938, the executives of the three railway unions discussed these, and other proposals, but could not agree on a common programme of demands though they were unanimous in asking Sir Arthur Salter to continue to act as Chairman of the Tribunal.[50]

Thus, when the unions met the general managers at the Charing Cross Hotel on October 12, 1938, each executive submitted separate demands. They were all told that it was 'quite impossible' for the companies to grant any of the requests so soon after substantial concessions had been made under the Tribunal's Decision No. 3.

Since direct negotiations with the companies had failed to produce any positive results, the E.C. decided to submit the N.U.R.'s claim to the Railway Staff National Council, and the other unions followed suit. Learning of their moves, the general managers asked for further discussions before the Council was due to meet. Undoubtedly their purpose was to try to dissuade the unions from proceeding with their claims, for at the informal meeting held in response to this request on November 8th, they warned that if railway traffic receipts continued to fall, the companies would be obliged to put in a counter claim for a *reduction* in wages. The aggregate loss of gross revenue in the first forty-four weeks of 1938 had been over £5 million. Since October 1, 1937, when they had been granted the right to raise their charges by 5 per cent, the companies had been losing more traffic to the roads and the anticipated increases in revenue did not materialize.[51] But the union leaders would not agree to drop their demands or to be content with direct negotiations. Hence the claims were considered by the Railway Staff National Council on November 14th. Here, as usual, there was deadlock.

Thus on January 24, 1939, John Marchbank was again endeavouring to convince the members of the Tribunal of the soundness of the union's case for a 50s minimum wage. He revealed that of forty-six awards made by various Government-sponsored Trade Boards in recent months, only three were for basic rates of wages below the base rate on the railways.[52] There were still 101,000 railwaymen with a base rate of under 50s and 58,000 of these took home average weekly *earnings* of less than that amount. In support of the claim for twelve days' paid holiday he showed that railwaymen in Norway, Australia, New Zealand, South Africa, Italy and the U.S.S.R. all had more than the seven days' paid holiday enjoyed by British railwaymen. A report of a Parliamentary Committee on Holidays with Pay in April 1938 had urged that paid holidays should be of longer than a week's duration. In anticipation that it would be pleaded for the companies, that they could not afford the £2½ million needed to meet the six demands of the N.U.R., he urged that the Tribunal should base its decision on the essential justice of the claims. It was wrong 'to reject legitimate claims of those employed in order to provide interest on redundant capital'.[53]

Mr Derbyshire, for the companies, made the usual pleas of poverty for rejecting *in toto* the unions' demands. He argued that a minimum wage of 50s would remove many existing wage graduations which 'were intended to reflect differences in work or seniority'. Merely to implement a 50s minimum and leave it at that would place nearly 40 per cent of the conciliation staff on one and the same rate of pay. The claim was in reality 'a disguised claim for a 9s a week rise for all conciliation grades'.[54]

The Tribunal agreed with the N.U.R. on some important points of principle, but its award conceded very little in terms of hard cash. It was admitted that as wages approximated to or fell below the point at which they did 'not suffice for reasonable human needs, the case for maintaining or improving the rates of wages became stronger', especially if railway wages were at a lower level than 'the standards in existence in industry generally'. On the other hand, 'it was not to be expected' that a Tribunal which less than two years previously had secured 'the maximum improvement that then seemed justified' should feel able to recommend large additional concessions at a time when 'the financial position and prospects were so very much worse'. However, there was 'a strong case for making an increase in the lowest rates of pay a first claim' as soon as the financial position made any substantial concession possible.[55] The only concessions made by the Tribunal were to grant men called out for Sunday duty a minimum of three hours' pay at the Sunday rate, and to limit spreadover duty to ten hours in most cases, though to permit its extension to twelve hours where the only alternative would be 'unjustified waste of time and expenditure'.

The delegates at the S.G.M. held in the Conway Hall, London, on April 3 and 4, 1939, had no hesitation in rejecting the award. The vote was 63–15, on a motion declaring the Tribunal's Decision No. 5 'unacceptable'. A resolution to give the companies twenty-eight days to concede the 50s minimum wage, and for the union to hand in strike notices if they did not comply, was defeated by the comparatively narrow margin of 43 votes to 35. (A new delegate, Mr Sidney F. Greene, a porter from Paddington No. 2 branch, voted with the minority.) By a larger margin (49–29) Congress agreed to an amendment simply instructing the E.C. 'to again approach the companies with a view to opening negotiations to secure a minimum base rate of 50s a week'.

In the first quarter of 1939 the gross receipts of the four main line companies were *down* by as much as a quarter of a million pounds a week on the corresponding period of 1938. The Tribunal had given its verdict with these depressing facts in the back of the minds of its members. By the second quarter of the year there was a complete reversal of fortune as the Government's re-armament programme was put into effect and railway goods traffic mounted in volume. By August 1939, traffic receipts were a quarter of a million pounds a week *greater* than those of a year earlier.[56]

In obedience to instructions received at the S.G.M., the E.C. at its May 1939 meeting considered the best tactics for a new approach to the companies. In view of the fact that the A.S.L.E. & F. had already decided to press on with its own demands, it was considered to be 'futile' to try to persuade them to co-operate in a campaign for the 50s minimum, and John Marchbank was asked to pursue the N.U.R.'s claim independently of the other unions.[57]

When the companies' representatives met the negotiating committees of the three railway unions at the Charing Cross Hotel on June 30th, the six-man N.U.R. delegation had a pleasant surprise when they heard the spokesman for the R.C.A. declare that his union considered the N.U.R.'s claim for a 50s minimum so completely justifiable that his union was prepared, for the time being, to drop all its demands in order to lend support to those men earning less than 50s a week. The Associated Society representative, on the other hand, repeated the case for the locomotive grades they had presented to the Tribunal earlier in the year. Despite the common front of the N.U.R. and R.C.A. on behalf of the lower-paid men, Sir James Milne made no promises of improvements. All he would do was promise 'careful consideration' of the demands.[58]

Although a large majority of the A.G.M. delegates at Clacton early in July 1939, were earning over 50s a week, they carried 'with acclamation' a resolution endorsing the action of the E.C. in concentrating on the single demand of a minimum adult wage rate of 50s. In the debate, Mr S. F. Greene warned the companies that the men's patience was 'not ever-lasting'.[59]

By the end of July the marked upward tendency in railway receipts could no longer be denied. At a further meeting with the unions, held in the Charing Cross Hotel on the 28th of that month, the companies' representatives announced that they had decided to increase the minimum rate of pay for adult male conciliation staff to 45s. This would raise the rates of pay of porters, Grade 2, and Goods Porters, by 4s a week in most areas, engine cleaners would receive an additional 3s a week and there would be many other upward adjustments, affecting a total of 15,000 men, including the shopmen.[60]

The delegates who met in London for the S.G.M. on August 11, 1939, were far from satisfied with the companies' offer, but they turned down, by 55 votes to 25, a resolution for strike action to obtain the 50s minimum wage. An amendment instructing the E.C. to continue to press the claim with the companies and to report back to the S.G.M. 'at the earliest possible date' when put as a substantive motion, was carried by 76 votes to 1. A resolution of thanks to the R.C.A. for its generous gesture in temporarily dropping its own claim in order to support the claim of the N.U.R. was carried unanimously.

Had it not been for the rapid deterioration in the international situation and Britain's declaration of war against Germany on September 3rd, a national railway strike would have been a strong possibility in the late summer of 1939. Through dissatisfaction with the way its claims had been treated by the Tribunal in its Decision No. 5, the Associated Society decided to call all its members out on strike at midnight on August 26th, and was only dissuaded from putting this decision into effect after lengthy interviews with the Minister of Labour on August 24th and 25th.

Many of the S.G.M. delegates of the N.U.R. were also in a very militant mood when they reassembled in London on August 22nd and were told by John Marchbank that the companies had refused to make any further concessions. Thirty-two of the delegates voted for strike action. The majority, however, believing that the N.U.R. case was 'an unanswerable one' resolved to submit it to the Tribunal 'without undue delay'. Before the Tribunal had time to meet, Hitler's armies had invaded Poland, and the N.U.R. entered the period of the Second World War, as it had done the First, with a substantial wage claim unsatisfied.

Owing to the steadier improvement in traffic receipts in the London area the men employed by the London Passenger Transport Board were able to obtain more substantial improvements in wages and conditions by September 1939, than was the case with the men employed by the main line companies. On August 25 and 26, 1936, a special conference of conciliation grade staff employed by the board drafted a comprehensive programme of demands. The E.C. at its December 1936 meeting decided to submit to the board an abbreviated version of the August Conference programme, but it included most of the important items such as a minimum wage of £3 a week, a 6-hour day and 36-hour week, time and a half rates for all doing duty between 10.0 p.m. and 5.0 a.m., overtime at time and a half rates, double time for Sunday duty; a general increase in wages of 3s a week; improved mileage rates for locomotivemen and a new and improved scale of pay for signalmen.[61]

Although the board received these proposals on April 26, 1937, there was a delay owing to its dispute with the London busmen, and the negotiating committee did not meet until June 25, 1937. Since claims had also been submitted conjointly by the N.U.R. and R.C.A. on behalf of the

clerical grades and since the cost of the proposed concessions to conciliation and clerical grades would come to £2½ million, Mr Pick (for
the employers) said it was impossible to concede them.[62] Apart from the
expense, the difficulty was that the proposals were 'in excess of those submitted by the same unions to other transport undertakings with which the
board was in close partnership'. The board could not consider this new
programme until the main line programme, then awaiting the consideration
of the Tribunal, was 'cleared up'.

The executives of the three railway unions, at a joint meeting held later
the same day, thought it wise to defer the matter until after the publication
of the board's accounts for the financial year 1936-7. A special N.U.R.
delegate conference of forty-one men employed in the board's railways,
meeting on November 27, 1937, agreed that it was best to shelve the comprehensive programme for the time being in 'favour of the E.C. continuing
negotiations to obtain the utmost improvement in the wages of the lower-
paid grades'.[63]

The outcome of this decision was an agreement between the board and
the three railway unions signed on February 28, 1938, whereby all conciliation grade employees earning less than 46s a week were to receive an
increase of 4s a week from the beginning of the year 1938 and a further
increase of 2s a week from January 1, 1939. There was to be a scaling upwards of many other rates of pay. A special E.C. meeting on March 5,
1938, approved the changes. Throughout 1937 and 1938 the N.U.R.
endeavoured to obtain a twelve-day annual holiday for all conciliation
staff. On June 18, 1937, the union's representatives managed to squeeze
from the board an additional three days' paid holiday on top of the
existing week, but in March 1939, the E.C. was obliged to admit that it was
impossible to obtain more through the existing negotiating machinery.[64]
That they were not more successful was chiefly due to the refusal of the
main line companies, on grounds of the cost, to grant their conciliation
grades twelve days' paid holidays.

IV

The union had good cause to be proud of its achievements on behalf of
the busmen in the years 1934-9.

To begin with, it seemed an almost impossible task even to obtain
recognition of the union by the companies, let alone negotiate wages and
conditions of service. John Marchbank told the A.G.M. delegates on
August 14, 1934, that it had taken 'many years of trade-union agitation to
break down the opposition of the Tilling and B.E.T. Groups even to
receive trade-union representatives and discuss matters'. A man employed
by the Devon General Omnibus Company was 'stood off' until he was
prepared to assure his employers that he was not a member of the N.U.R.

Quick intervention by the union had brought about his unconditional re-instatement, but the attitude at first displayed by the company was indicative of the fact that the employers had not yet come to value co-operation with the union.[65] More than a year later, Mr S. E. Claxton, a delegate at the S.G.M. in London bemoaned the fact that, despite the union's attempt to establish separate working agreements with eight bus companies 'practically every one of these efforts had failed'.[66] For a time, from January 1934, the only company with whom the union had an agreement was Ribble Motor Services. It was not surprising that in the summer of 1934 there were only 2,472 busmen members of the union.[67]

By the spring of 1937 there had been a remarkable improvement. Henry Harold Clay was able to tell a conference of busmen, jointly sponsored by the T. & G.W.U. and N.U.R. and presided over by John Marchbank in Leeds on February 10, 1937, that there were only five bus undertakings in the country 'of any size' with whom one or other of the unions had not got an agreement.[68] In his report to the A.G.M. in July 1937, John Marchbank gave details of settlement on rates of pay, conditions of service and union recognition negotiated by the N.U.R. with United Automobile Services, the Lincolnshire Road Car Company, East Midland Motor Services, the Devon General Omnibus Company, the Mansfield District Traction Company and Ribble Motor Services (in the last case a confirmation of an earlier agreement) during the past twelve months. The N.U.R. had established 'conclusive agreements' with nine out of the twelve companies with which it was concerned.[69]

What had made this quick transformation possible? One important influence was the closer co-operation established between the N.U.R. and the T. & G.W.U. In March 1935, the Sheffield and Chesterfield District Council of the N.U.R. proposed to the E.C. that a conciliation board be set up for the road passenger services. When the subject was discussed at a meeting of the Joint Passenger Committee of the two unions on July 26, 1935, the two E.C.s were advised to form a Bus Federation in which both organizations would co-operate to secure the three main aims of 100 per cent trade unionism amongst the busmen, properly regulated national conditions of service and loyal observance of the division of territory for recruitment of members. John Marchbank was recommended as Chairman and Harold Clay as Secretary of the new organization.[70] The E.C. of the N.U.R. quickly gave wholehearted support to the plan which came into operation that summer.[71] Thereafter the organizers of the two unions worked harmoniously in the different districts, accusations of 'poaching' died down and a successful recruitment drive was conducted. Ernest Bevin and John Marchbank co-operated in lobbying the Minister of Transport on road passenger and goods service questions.[72]

The situation was changing very rapidly. John Marchbank told the S.G.M. delegates in November 1935, that he 'did not believe it was possible to have standardized pay for busmen' because 'the conditions were not the same throughout the country'. Fifteen months later he was admitting to the conference of busmen at Leeds that 'some suitable national machinery' would have to be set up to deal with the wages and conditions of busmen as a whole.[73] At the outbreak of war the two unions were within striking distance of achieving this aim. By June 14, 1940, the National Council for the Bus Industry was an accomplished fact.

In the 1930's more than 5,600 men were employed in the dining cars, restaurants and hotels owned by the four main line companies. Since there was no national agreement or any kind until July 1937, there was no uniformity in the rates of pay or hours worked, but most restaurant car staff worked at least sixty hours a week for an average wage of 26s and tips. They received no extra pay for overtime worked, but many men refused to take the rest days to which they were entitled. Some justified such overworking by stating that, without it, they would be taking less than 30s home to their wives. The N.U.R. had tried to bring these men under the machinery of the National Wages Board, but had failed, partly because only 60 per cent of those employed on the Great Western Railway, London and North Eastern Railway and London, Midland and Scottish and only 50 per cent of those employed by Fredericks Hotels Ltd. on the Southern Railway, belonged to the union. In 1933, John Marchbank did not believe the men would strike for better conditions even if called upon to do so.[74] Even as late as July 1937, in his report to the A.G.M. the General Secretary admitted that 'the opposition to complete recognition of trade-union activity was very hard to break down'.

The only solution was to increase union membership as a first condition for fighting for union recognition and a national agreement on wages and working conditions.

A small beginning was made in April 1932, when ten delegates attended a national conference of restaurant car staff held in London. A programme including a 10s a week increase in wages, a reduction of hours to forty-eight per week, with time and a quarter rates paid for work between 10.0 p.m. and 4.0 a.m. and time and a half for Sunday duty and twelve days' holiday with pay, was unanimously agreed.[75] At a further, better supported, national conference, held on July 27, 1936, the union's executive was urged to seek an agreement with the companies on the programme drafted in 1932. Consequently the negotiating committee of the union submitted the proposals to the Railway Staff Conference on January 21, 1937, and eventually signed an agreement with the representatives of the Great Western Railway, London, Midland and Scottish and London and North Eastern Railway, for uniform wages and conditions of restaurant car staff on April 12, 1937. It fell far short of the demands formulated in 1932 and did not apply to men working for Fredericks Hotels Ltd., on the Southern Railway. The men's hours were to be limited to 120 a fortnight, Sunday duty was to be paid at time and a third rates and special compensation was to be given to attendants working on dining cars where customers were consistently close-fisted in their tipping habits! In addition pay for cooks on some of the busier cars was to go up to 65s a week and new grades of Assistant Attendant and Junior Assistant Attendant were to be established.[76] This 1937 agreement was important as laying the foundations for the more comprehensive and valuable agreement of June 1940.

The difficulty in making headway on behalf of those employed in the railway hotels and restaurants, was the decided anti trade-union policy of the Hotels and Restaurants Association. For some years the companies would not recognize the right of the N.U.R. to negotiate conditions of service for these men, and eventually, in the spring of 1937, John March-bank raised the question with the Ministry of Labour. The companies then agreed to meet the union to discuss a machinery of negotiation and on September 28, 1937, after a full review of the position made in conference with the negotiating committee of the N.U.R., the companies agreed to recognize the union's authority to bargain on behalf of the men. Whilst this understanding was not immediately fruitful in respect of improvements in working conditions, it was valuable as a foundation for the June 1940 agreement.

By 1938 the 51,000 shopmen members of the N.U.R. were discontented with the negotiating machinery through which their wages and conditions of service had been settled during the past eleven years. The A.G.M. at Southport in July 1938 endorsed the opinions expressed at National Conferences of Railway Shopmen by carrying by 54 votes to 23 a decision that 'notice be given to the railway companies of the intention of the N.U.R. to withdraw from the National Railway Shopmen's Council' and that matters in dispute should be dealt with by direct negotiations between the union and the companies. By the time the union's negotiating committee met the employers to discuss the N.U.R.'s proposal, however, the war had started and the companies suggested that the matter be deferred.[77]

V

Throughout the 1930's a large number of N.U.R. members took an active part in the political life of the country both at local and national level. In 1935 John Marchbank was proud to report that the mayors of nine boroughs and the chairmen of twenty-three urban district councils were members of the union. In addition there were no less than 1,168 members who were councillors and aldermen, 388 who were J.P.s and 157 who were members of public assistance committees.[78] Some of the branches with the best record of public service were those in the Lambeth and Battersea area. Between 1938 and 1960, the Borough of Battersea had as Mayor no less than seven different members of the N.U.R. In 1956, Mrs Cooper, the wife of the Chairman of the Battersea No. 2 branch, was elected to this office.[79]

As the shadows of war darkened it was inevitable that active branch members and A.G.M. delegates should become concerned at the rapidly deteriorating international situation. Even if they had not become aware of the menace of Fascism through reading their newspapers, A.G.M. delegates at Hull, in July 1936, had the industrial consequences of Fascism revealed to them by the address of Mr Eddo Fimmen, the fraternal delegate from the International Transport Workers' Federation. He showed that the number of men employed on the Italian railways had been reduced from 240,000 in 1922 (when Mussolini came to power) to 132,000 in 1935. Locomotivemen who had been lucky enough to keep their jobs had had their working week increased by more than $6\frac{1}{2}$ hours and their pay reduced by between 35 per cent and 40 per cent. Other grades had suffered wage reductions of up to 27 per cent. Fascism, he said, was also the greatest danger to peace, and the working class 'nationally and internationally' had 'to hammer out a new policy with regard to fighting the war danger'.[80]

Members were reminded of the danger of Fascism in Britain through the slander suit lodged by Sir Oswald Mosley against John Marchbank arising from a speech the latter had made at Newcastle-on-Tyne on July 14, 1934. The General Secretary alleged that Sir Oswald was preparing to overthrow by force the constitutional government of the country. The case was heard in the King's Bench Division between February 3 and 7, 1936, when the jury found in favour of the Fascist leader but awarded him damages of only $\frac{1}{4}$d, and ordered each side to pay its own costs. Railwaymen and other trade unionists and co-operators contributed so generously to a voluntary Testimonial Fund on behalf of John Marchbank that he did not have to meet any of the £5,517, which was his bill for costs, out of his own pocket.[81]

The A.G.M. at Morecambe in July 1933, believed that the best method of combating Fascism was the creation of 'a highly disciplined and organized working class schooled in militant socialist principles'. It instructed the E.C. 'to spread information regarding all forms of capitalist dictatorship by the publication and effective distribution of a constant stream of suitable and up-to-date literature'.[82] Although the General Secretary circularized all branches, including with his letter samples of the available T.U.C. and Labour Party literature, Mr C. W. Evans of King's Cross No. 2 branch (President of the N.U.R. 1958–60) complained to the S.G.M. on August 16, 1934, that the E.C. had been dilatory in implementing the resolution passed at Morecambe, and he carried his resolution of protest by 40 votes to 31. Consequently the E.C. stepped up its activity, sending to all branches on September 7, 1934, a special letter entitled 'The Menace of Dictatorship' and enclosing with it three anti-Fascist pamphlets.

A militant minority of the A.G.M. delegates, from 1933 onwards, urged the view that the best way to defeat Fascism was to create a united front of all working class political organizations in the country. On July 5, 1933, Jim Campbell (General Secretary, N.U.R., 1953-7) told the A.G.M. delegates that unless they 'did away with divisions and dissensions' the same thing would happen in England as had recently happened in Germany. But his resolution 'to co-operate with all working class bodies . . . to defeat the aims of the employing class' was lost by 49 votes to 31 after Mr Cramp had warned that, once they joined with the Communists, there would soon come a time when the legally elected Government would 'be suppressed and bodies of commissars would tell' (them) 'what they had to do'.[83] The 31 votes collected at Morecambe in 1933 proved to be the high watermark of achievement of the left wing at pre-war conferences. Though similar resolutions were moved at all subsequent annual meetings except that of 1934, the maximum vote achieved in favour of co-operation with Communists and other left-wing parties was the 23 mustered at Clacton in July 1939.

One striking fact about the public resolutions passed at the conferences held between 1935 and 1939 was their manifestation of the union's complete lack of confidence in the National Governments of Baldwin and Chamberlain. At Plymouth, in July 1937, the left-wing delegate, W. C. Loeber, must have been somewhat nonplussed to find his resolution of support for the Republican Government in Spain criticized for its 'mildness', though he was, no doubt, gratified to find the voting unanimous in its favour. The following July, at Southport, Congress approved unanimously a resolution deploring 'the unprovoked attacks of the Fascist powers on Abyssinia, Austria, Spain and China' and calling 'upon all nations for collective security, to give reciprocal guarantees of mutual assistance in the case of aggression, these guarantees to be laid down in a treaty freely concluded between equals based on the Covenant of the League of Nations'.

Some might have expected that the union would support, as a corollary to the resolutions in favour of collective security, measures for strengthening the country's defences. In fact, most of the decisions seemed to be of the opposite tendency. In 1935-6 Baldwin's Government consulted the T.U.C. concerning the drafting of a schedule of reserved occupations. On January 3rd, the E.C. of the N.U.R. instructed John Marchbank to inform the T.U.C. that it was 'opposed to the scheme as creating a dangerous precedent' and implying 'support for the National Government's defence scheme'.[84]

When, early in 1938, the railway companies appealed to members of the N.U.R. to attend A.R.P. classes, the members of the Glasgow No. 5 branch objected on the grounds that the scheme was only nominally voluntary. John Marchbank advised them that they 'could not reasonably refuse to co-operate with the railway companies' and the E.C., more sympathetically, considered 'the question of attending training classes was one for the men to determine for themselves'.[85] Glasgow No. 5 did not consider this a strong enough lead and was successful at the A.G.M. in July 1938, in carrying, by 54 votes to 23, an appeal against the E.C.'s decision of the previous March. Influenced by this strong expression of feeling, the E.C. at its special meeting on August 11, 1938, carried unanimously a much stronger resolution worded (in part) as follows:

'This organization cannot advise any of its members to take part in schemes that are now in existence, and we are determined to protect the interests of any of our members who may refuse to take part in the scheme.'[86]

If challenged with inconsistency and 'lack of responsibility' in voting for collective security, but, at the same time, refusing to vote for military and civil defence preparations, many delegates would have justified their action by quoting another resolution, carried by 55 votes to 22 at Clacton in July 1939:

'National unity is impossible and undesirable behind a Chamberlain Government, and we therefore demand a more uncompromising fight against the so-called "National" Government as an essential step to real security.'[87]

Others would have emphasized that they were not opposed to *voluntary* efforts for defence but that they were opposed to any kind of conscription. In taking this stand they would quote the N.U.R. opposition to conscription in the First World War. With the sound of gunfire of battleships out in the North Sea punctuating the delegates' speeches, Conference at Clacton on July 5, 1939, carried with only two dissentients, a resolution strongly condemning 'the introduction of conscription for life' which was 'in strange contrast with the failure to conscript the wealth necessary to pay for the defence of the country', and praising 'the pronounced success of the voluntary system'.[88]

A few weeks earlier the E.C. had had to decide its policy for a special conference of T.U. Executives summoned by the T.U.C. for May 19th to consider means of averting war. With only Donlon against, it decided to advocate:

'Complete opposition to the Government in the operation of their Military Training Bill and the mobility of labour during war time, even to the extent of a general and national strike.'

As Ernest Bevin passed by members of the N.U.R. Executive, seated at the front of the conference hall, he commented sarcastically:

'You fellows can't strike to get a 50s minimum wage, let alone to stop a war.'

Nevertheless, Mr J. H. Potts, the recently elected President of the N.U.R., moved—'That this meeting of Executive Committees consider the question of calling a General Strike as a last effort to oppose military and industrial conscription.' The resolution was defeated by 4,172,000 votes to 425,000. Since the membership of the N.U.R. at that time was 364,653, the E.C. was only able to win an additional 60,347 votes from the other unions.[89]

Within four months Hitler's armies had invaded Poland and Britain was at war.

NOTES

1. N.U.R., A.G.M. July 6, 1933, Verbatim Report, p. 318.
2. N.U.R., Special E.C. December 20, 1933, p. 150.
3. Report of a Special Joint Committee on Machinery of Negotiation for Railway Staff, 1933–4, 27 pp. Bound with N.U.R. Proceedings and Reports, 1934.
4. N.U.R., A.G.M. July 4, 1934, Verbatim Report, p. 23.
5. N.U.R., Special E.C January 17–19, 1935. Special Joint Meeting of the three T.U. E.C.s, July 12, 1934.
6. N.U.R., Special E.C. January 21, 1935, R. 53.
7. N.U.R., S.G.M. February 20, 1935, Verbatim Report, p. 17.
8. *Ibid.*, p. 16.
9. S.G.M. February 21, 1935, Verbatim Report, p. 72.
10. See N.U.R. *Machinery of Negotiation* (82 pp., 1954), Chapter 4, pp. 26–40 for a full statement of the negotiating machinery agreed on February 26, 1938.
11. *The Economist*, August 1, 1936, p. 227.
12. March 3, 1934.
13. Rs. 205 and 206.
14. N.U.R., E.C. June 1934, p. 102.
15. N.U.R., Special E.C. July 23, 1934, p. 46.
16. N.U.R., A.G.M. July 3, 1934, R. 116.
17. N.U.R., S.G.M. August 8, 1934, Verbatim Report, pp. 10 and 15, 51–88.
18. *The Economist*, August 18, 1934, p. 304.
19. *The Economist*, July 18, 1934, p. 174 and August 4, 1934, p. 231. *The Times*, August 11, 1934.
20. N.U.R., S.G.M. August 9, 1934, Verbatim Report, pp. 55 *et seq.*
21. *The Times*, August 11, 1934.
22. N.U.R., S.G.M. August 13, 1934, Verbatim Report, pp. 6 *et seq.*
23. *The Economist*, March 23, 1935, p. 649; March 7, 1936, p. 515.
24. N.U.R., E.C. December 1934, R. 1125.
25. N.U.R., E.C. September 1935, p. 32. Special E.C. September 25, 1935, p. 2.
26. N.U.R., S.G.M. May 12, 1936, Verbatim Report, pp. 7, 23, 54. R.S.N.T. Decision No. 3, August 9, 1937, Minutes of Proceedings, p. 7.
27. R.S.N.T. Decision No. 1, July 27, 1936, Minutes of Proceedings, p. 72.
28. N.U.R., S.G.M. June 17, 1936; August 11, 1936, Verbatim Report.
29. *Locomotive Journal*, February 1937, p. 92. R.S.N.T. Decision No. 2, December 29, 1936, p. 6.
30. N.U.R., S.G.M. August 11, 1936, R. 6.

31. R.S.N.T. Decision No. 3, August 9, 1937, Verbatim Report, pp. 9–18.
32. *Ibid.*, pp. 72, 96.
33. N.U.R., S.G.M. August 19, 1937, Verbatim Report, pp. 97, 134.
34. N.U.R., E.C. September 1934, R. 789, p. 127.
35. N.U.R., Special E.C. December 19, 1934, R. 1227 and p. 13 and Special E.C. January 11, 1935, R. 38.
36. C. L. Mowat, *Britain Between the Wars*, p. 431.
37. N.U.R., Special E.C. May 18, 1934, p. 17.
38. *R.R.*, May 4, 1934. N.U.R., Special E.C. May 4, 1934, p. 9. 'A Transport Experiment in Ulster', *The Economist*, January 29, 1938, p. 211.
39. N.U.R., E.C. June 1934, p. 117.
40. *R.R.*, August 3, 1934. N.U.R., E.C. June, 1935, p. 157.
41. N.U.R., E.C. July 1935, p. 25, R. 735; February 12, 1938, R. 55.
42. N.U.R., E.C. June 1939, p. 173.
43. N.U.R., E.C. May 4, 1934, p. 10, R. 320.
44. N.U.R., Special E.C. May 4, 1934; September 1937, p. 8; June 1938, Appendix L, p. 310; September 1938, pp. 184–5; December 1939, p. 201.
45. J. W. Morris, 'Signalmen and Electrification', *R.R.*, September 3, 1937.
46. N.U.R., A.G.M. July 8, 1932, Verbatim Report, p. 32; N.U.R., E.C. March 1932, pp. 318–72. *R.R.*, May 19, 1933.
47. R.S.N.T. Decision No. 4, July 29, 1938, Minutes of Proceedings, p. 58.
48. N.U.R., A.G.M. July 14, 1937, Verbatim Report, p. 19.
49. N.U.R., E.C. April 5–8, 1938, R. 515.
50. N.U.R., Special E.C. May 16, 1938, and H. O. Circular M/8/2/6D/3451. E.C. June 1938, p. 150, R. 847.
51. *The Economist*, November 12, 1938, p. 332.
52. R.S.N.T. Decision No. 5, February 28, 1939. Minutes of Proceedings and Documents submitted to Tribunal, N.U.R. Document No. 4.
53. *Ibid.*, Minutes of Proceedings, p. 100.
54. *Ibid.*, p. 62.
55. *Ibid.*, pp. 228–9.
56. 'The Railwaymen's Case', *New Statesman*, August 26, 1939, p. 303.
57. N.U.R., E.C. June 1939, R. 940, p. 172.
58. N.U.R., Special E.C. June 30, 1939, p. 14.
59. N.U.R., A.G.M. July 4, 1939, Verbatim Report, p. 13.
60. For full details see N.U.R., Special E.C. July 29, 1939, pp. 54–6.
61. N.U.R., E.C. December 1936, pp. 149–51, R. 1560.
62. N.U.R., Special E.C. June 30, 1937, p. 3. E.C. September 1937, Appendix L, p. 301.
63. N.U.R., E.C. December 1937, p. 167.
64. N.U.R., E.C. March 1939, R. 385.
65. N.U.R., S.G.M. August 14, 1934, Verbatim Report, pp. 46 *et seq.*
66. N.U.R., S.G.M. November 18, 1935, Verbatim Report, p. 52.
67. John Marchbank's statement to S.G.M., August 14, 1934.
68. *R.R.*, February 19, 1937.
69. N.U.R., General Secretary's Report to the A.G.M. July 1937, pp.21–49.
70. N.U.R., E.C. September 1935, Appendix A.
71. N.U.R., E.C. March 1935, p. 97; July 1935, p. 34 and R. 746.
72. Statement by John Marchbank, N.U.R., S.G.M. November 18, 1935, Verbatim Report, p. 57.
73. N.U.R., S.G.M. November 18, 1935, Verbatim Report, p. 55. *R.R.*, February 19, 1937.
74. N.U.R., A.G.M. July 1933, Verbatim Report, pp. 249 *et seq.*

75. N.U.R., E.C. June 1932, p. 301, Appendix P, April 29, 1932.
76. N.U.R., E.C. June 1937, p. 12.
77. N.U.R., A.G.M. July 1938, R. 105. E.C. December 1939, p. 433, Appendix S.
78. N.U.R., General Secretary's Report to the A.G.M. June 1935, p. 10.
79. I am indebted to Mr Clift of Battersea No. 2 branch for this information.
80. N.U.R., A.G.M. July 7, 1936, Verbatim Report, p. 28 and *R.R.*, January 3, 1936 for I.T.W.F. Report on conditions of employment in Italy.
81. N.U.R., General Secretary's Report to the A.G.M. 1936, pp. 81–2 and 1937, p. 106. *R.R.*, February 14, 1936.
82. Quotations are from R. 67(b) carried by 49 votes to 31 at the A.G.M.
83. N.U.R., A.G.M. July 5, 1933, Verbatim Report, p. 200.
84. N.U.R., E.C. January 3, 1936, R. 6.
85. N.U.R., E.C. March 1938, R. 374.
86. R. 1032.
87. N.U.R., A.G.M. July 1939, R. 100.
88. N.U.R., A.G.M. July 5, 1939, Verbatim Report, p. 26.
89. N.U.R., E.C. May 16, 1939, Rs. 1072–3. Report of Proceedings of the 71st Annual T.U.C., Bridlington, September 4 and 5, 1939, p. 265. Bevin's statement reported by Mr F. Donlon of Manchester who was present at the conference when it was made.

CHAPTER XX

THE SECOND WORLD WAR, 1939-45

'Hon. Members have often read how hard it is to sail a ship in convoy, without lights, through a north Atlantic storm. Perhaps they have not thought what work is like in a railway marshalling yard, in the blackout, on a stormy winter night.'
Mr P. J. Noel-Baker (Parliamentary Secretary to the Minister of War Transport), House of Commons, May 5, 1944.

I

IN the days and weeks immediately following September 3, 1939, the railway workers were more forcefully reminded than were most of the people of Britain of the fact that the country was at war. In three days of early September, no less than 3,823 special trains were run to carry 1,334,358 evacuee children from congested urban areas. By mid-September two million others had made their own arrangements for evacuation, most of them going by rail. By October 5th, 102,000 troops with full equipment had been entrained for Southampton, their embarkation point for the continent.

The sudden imposition of a rigorously enforced blackout made particularly trying the task of all those railwaymen whose work was performed out of doors. Trainmen and shunters considered their working conditions unusually difficult, but Mr E. G. Bowers, a motor-driver delegate to the A.G.M. at Morecambe in July 1940, must have given men of these grades second thoughts, as well as causing them amusement, when he declared:

'Since the war no locomotiveman or signalman has had to suffer what the motor driver has had to suffer in doing his job during the blackout. The only time you can see anything or know that you have met something is when you hit it.'

Fogmen maintained that their job was the most uncongenial of all. Their one source of consolation—the brazier fire—was taken away from them at the outbreak of war. The fires were restored after a few weeks of the 'phoney war', but when air raids were intensified in the late summer of 1940 it was feared that the glare from them might invite enemy attacks, and some Yorkshire branches of the N.U.R. wanted the Government to order the replacement of open fires by covered-in ones. The delegates to the A.G.M. in 1942 did not agree. There were no closed-in type fires available, and they considered the slight risk of machine-gunning from the air preferable to the misery of freezing in the dark.

Even those grades not so adversely affected by the blackout were not allowed to forget that the country was at war. In consequence of a strict rationing of petrol, by February 1940 long-distance road haulage of goods was reduced to less than 75 per cent of the pre-war mileage, whilst the increase of coastal shipping freights by 33 per cent by May 1940 (compared with an increase of only 10 per cent of rail freights), caused a substantial diversion of traffic to the railways.[1] Many of the fittest men had been called up for service with the armed forces, with the result that those who remained were expected to work overtime to clear the lines. To make matters worse, at the end of January 1940, many parts of the country experienced the heaviest snowfall within living memory. London had 25° (F) of frost on January 28th, and two days later a 'rescue' train which went to dig out a passenger train stranded between Manchester and Sheffield, itself got into difficulties and sent for another rescue train to rescue it. *The Times* reported that the railway staff were working long hours under 'unprecedented conditions' to give travellers and traders the best possible service.[2]

In those early months of the war railwaymen worked conscientiously and, when necessary, performed remarkable feats of endurance, but they had no great enthusiasm for the war. Before the invasion of Poland, the A.G.M. of the N.U.R. had repeatedly expressed distrust of Neville Chamberlain's policy in relation to Nazi Germany. With the men of Munich still in power, it was not to be expected that the distrust would be removed overnight on September 3, 1939. In December 1939, the members of the E.C. were unanimously of the opinion that the issuing of a manifesto stating the peace aims of the Labour Movement was 'long overdue'. They asked the General Secretary to inform the Executive of the Labour Party accordingly. Ten out of the twenty-four members of the union's executive were in favour of summoning a 'World Conference for Peace', but were outvoted by the remainder who considered the plan 'not practicable'.[3] In March 1940, the E.C. feared the 'switching' of the war to the U.S.S.R. It resolved to inform the National Council of Labour that it took 'strong exception' to its decision to send a delegation to Finland which was then engaged in war with the U.S.S.R. since 'such actions were likely to bring about an extension of the war front'. Even after the Government had been reconstituted, following Dunkirk, the A.G.M. on July 2, 1940, urged 'as a matter of public confidence and national morale that cabinet ministers and other persons in high office associated with the previous government's policy of appeasement, be at once removed from office and their places filled by men whose reliability . . . is proved by their antecedents'.[4]

Confidence in the Chamberlain Government was certainly not increased when the terms of the financial settlement with the railway companies were announced in a White Paper on February 7, 1940.[5] The companies had demanded the guaranteeing of their standard revenues of £51 million which was the unachieved target under the Railways Act of 1921, but few persons, apart from the railway directors, regarded this claim as anything but unrealistic and unreasonable. Instead, the Government guaranteed the four main line companies and the London Passenger Transport Board a minimum net annual revenue of £40 million, which was a sum equal to the *average* net revenue of the companies for the three fairly prosperous years of 1935–7, together with the *actual* revenue of the L.P.T.B. for the year ending June 30, 1939. If the railways carried anything over the guaranteed £40 million they were to be allowed to keep all the excess up to £43¼ million, but beyond this they were to share with the Exchequer any excess up to £56 million. It was a settlement exceedingly favourable to the shareholders. *The Economist* found it 'impossible not to conclude that the companies had been treated too generously' and urged that it was 'a sound principle that nobody should be allowed to make windfall profits out of the war', whilst at Westminster, Mr Herbert Morrison deplored the fact that, as a result of the White Paper, the market value of railway stocks had risen by 'at least £100 million'.[6] Had the agreement been continued beyond the autumn of 1941, the companies, as a result of the handicaps imposed by the Government on their competitors, would have earned the £51 million which they had found it impossible to achieve in any year of peace.

Dunkirk brought many changes. The E.C. was engaged in a prolonged discussion on such matters as an appeal from five railway bridge painters to be granted a 'dirty work allowance', when news was received of the Government's decision to evacuate the British Army from France. The union quickly co-operated with the Railway Executive Committee in forming a pool of 186 trains from the four main line companies to convey such men as were rescued from the beaches to the reception camps in England. It was a remarkably successful operation, particularly in view of the fact that the R.E.C. had no advance knowledge of how many men were involved or when the trains would be required.

On May 28, 1940, at the height of the national emergency, the General Council of the T.U.C. summoned a special conference of union executives in London. The E.C. of the N.U.R. was at one with the other executives in endorsing 'the action of the General Council in giving its full support to the necessary measures that must be taken to protect our people . . . by organizing the entire resources of the country and striving to the utmost to defeat the forces of aggression'. Full support was also given to the 'solemn pledge to the fighting forces' that 'all industrial resources' would be used to provide the forces with the arms and ammunition they needed.[7]

Confidence was increased when the Labour leaders were brought into the Government in June 1940, and when a new, less extravagant, settlement was made with the companies in the following year. Profiteering on the railways was reduced. From January 1, 1941, the Churchill Government guaranteed the railway companies a fixed annual sum of £43 million. All net receipts in excess of this figure were to revert to the Treasury. Costs of capital replacement were to be shared equally between the Government and the companies. Under the agreement, between January 1, 1941, and December 31, 1944, the Government received back no less than £176 million from the pooled revenues of the companies.[8]

With accumulating evidence of the determination of the new Government to prosecute with more vigour the struggle against Fascism, railwaymen endured the terrors of the blitz with stout hearts. From the time that the first bomb to damage railway property fell at Melton Ross Siding on the London and North Western Railway between Lincoln and Grimsby on June 19, 1940, to the last 'buzzing' of a V-bomb, there were 9,239 instances of damage to the railways by enemy action. Nearly half the instances were crowded into the six months of June–December, 1940.

At the outbreak of war instructions were received that trainmen and signalmen were to continue on duty during an air raid—goods trains were to proceed at 10 m.p.h. and passenger trains at 15 m.p.h.—but that men in other grades were to take shelter when the air raid warning was sounded. During the first nine months of the war when there were comparatively few alerts, such an arrangement did not seriously hold up railway operations, but it proved impossible to continue it during the period of the blitz. At meetings between the representatives of the companies and the three railway unions held on September 10, 1940, it was agreed that, in future, essential work should be carried on after the warning siren had sounded until an enemy attack was imminent; work was to be resumed when the immediate danger was past without waiting for the public 'all clear' signal. All branches of the union were notified of these decisions in a circular issued on September 27, 1940, but in very many places railway staff had followed the new procedure ever since the Dunkirk crisis. The difficulties of working under conditions of intensified enemy attack were shown by the fact that during October 1940, marshalling yards in the London area experienced an alert almost every night, with the result that out of 382 hours of darkness shunting had to be carried on in complete darkness for 299 hours.[9]

Under the new conditions much greater risks had to be undertaken if the vital work of maintaining communications was not to be interrupted.

One Friday night during the blitz a number of time-bombs were dropped in the Brent and Cricklewood area of London. On the following day it was decided to allow goods trains, but not passenger trains, to pass the unexploded bombs, but early on Sunday morning the signalman on duty was offered a passenger 'express' train which, in accordance with instructions, he refused to pass. When he rang up the control point to discover why the request had been made, he was given quite a shock when he was told: 'Oh, that's all right, you can let the train through, it's only conveying railway workmen.'[10]

The extension of the war to the Soviet Union in 1941, for some time intensified the shortage of locomotives and rolling stock in Britain. In the autumn of 1941, 151 2-8-0 locomotives were sent to Persia to assist in the conveyance of arms to the U.S.S.R. The result was that goods and passenger trains in Britain were lengthened. Express passenger train weights on the East Coast routes increased from 450 tons to 650 tons, whilst coal trains of 1,400 tons were being pulled on the London, Midland & Scottish.[11] At the same time it was realized that the stupendous efforts of the Russians were greatly lessening the volume of German air attacks on Britain. Appreciation of the heroic resistance of the Russian people was expressed by the union in a practical way, when, on October 6, 1941, the E.C. decided to contribute £1,000—the first of a number of contributions—to the National Council of Labour Fund for medical relief in Russia.

As an outcome of a decision taken at the quarterly meeting of the E.C. in September 1941, the ex-President of the union, Mr J. H. Potts, left the United Kingdom on February 10, 1942, on a goodwill visit to the U.S.S.R. Mr Anthony Eden, the Foreign Secretary, had endeavoured to dissuade the E.C. from supporting this enterprise on the grounds that the journey would be a difficult one and accommodation was very scarce in Kuibyshev. But neither Mr Potts nor the E.C. were to be deterred. The journey to Murmansk via Iceland was indeed an arduous one, taking thirty-two days. Because of repeated enemy air attacks and the groaning of cracking ice floes Mr Potts got very little sleep, but he felt that the warm welcome he received more than offset the hardships of the voyage. He was sure that his pledge given to the Presidium of the Russian Railwaymen's Trade Union in Moscow at the end of March 1942, that the members of the N.U.R. would do their utmost to help the Russians in their fight against Fascism, was a great inspiration to his hearers, and he was pleased to see Mr Tarasov, the Russian Railway Union President, proudly wearing on his tunic alongside the Order of Lenin, the N.U.R. gold medallion he had recently received. Friendly relations have existed between the two unions ever since.[12]

II

In 1938 a sub-committee of the E.C. was set up to explore the possibility of finding a new head office site for the union. Visiting no less than sixteen possible sites in and around London made a welcome diversion from office routine, but only in one case, some almshouses at Wood Green on which the present Town Hall stands, did the committee come near to effecting a purchase. Negotiations fell through when the sellers asked for a larger sum than the £25,000 the union was prepared to offer.

In the autumn of 1940 there was a far more urgent problem of finding alternative accommodation. Branches were warned on September 30, 1940, that there would be 'considerable delays' in dealing with correspondence owing to the depletion in the Head Office staff and the interruptions caused by air raids. Later that month the E.C. decided that in future it would 'remain in session until bombs can be heard dropping or gun-fire can be heard in the vicinity'[13] and the office staff adopted a similar policy. A sub-committee of the E.C. was in the meantime given the task of finding alternative accommodation.

When Head Office staff and members of the Executive Committee arrived to work at Unity House on the morning of Friday, October 11, 1940, their entry to the building was barred by the police. A time-bomb had fallen in the rear of the building the previous night. It was not possible to reoccupy the building for another twelve days, during which time temporary accommodation was provided at Dilke House, Malet Street, London, W.C.1, through the generosity of the National Union of Shop Assistants, Warehousemen and Clerks. Early in November, Castle Priory, Wallingford, a three-storey Queen Anne mansion, standing in thirty-six acres of ground and with a very pleasant frontage on the Thames, was purchased by the union for £11,000. Encouraged by further contributions from the Luftwaffe, the transference of the office departments was expedited and the move was completed by November 18, 1940. The N.U.R. Approved Society offices remained at Unity House and the General Secretary and other officers of the union continued to do much of their work there after the worst days of the blitz had passed.

The A.G.M. at Edinburgh in July 1944 gave the General Secretary *carte blanche* to bring back any of the Head Office departments he thought necessary, and on February 8, 1945, the E.C. adopted Mr Benstead's recommendation to return 'the major portion' of the staff to Unity House. This was done in time for the E.C. to hold its May meetings there. On June 29th, the Finance Committee reported the sale of Castle Priory to the Oxford Co-operative Society (acting on behalf of a group of Co-operative Societies) for £16,000. The E.C. turned down a suggestion, made by Reading No. 1 branch, that Castle Priory should be made an orphanage for children bereft of both their parents, as it has always been the policy of the union to give monetary assistance to the orphans of its former members.

The location of the Head Office at Wallingford was certainly consistent with the efficient conduct of the union's business. The rise in membership from 349,542 to 409,826 during the war was one indication of this.

Pessimistic members of the N.U.R. had said that it was impossible for a General Secretary to serve his time and retire in accordance with the rules on reaching the age of 60. When the delegates to the A.G.M. at Blackpool on July 16, 1942, praised their chief officer for his work for the union and expressed their best wishes for his retirement in the practical shape of a cheque for £270, John Marchbank was careful not to say too much as he still had six months to serve. He was well aware of the fact that two of his predecessors had died at their posts; two had been dismissed and the other two had resigned as an alternative to dismissal! But January 1943 came and went without mishap. Through John Marchbank's example, the post of General Secretary held less terrors for ambitious members of the union in the future.

John Marchbank's successor was 45 years old John Benstead, a Peterborough man who had been educated at the King's School in that city before becoming a clerk at the Headquarters Offices of the Great Northern Railway in London in 1911. After wartime service with the Royal Navy, he was employed from 1920–35 in the Great Northern Railway's District Manager's Office at Peterborough where he joined the N.U.R. on March 3, 1920. Thereafter he served as branch secretary from 1922–38, Eastern District Council Secretary from 1923–9 and executive committee member from 1930–32. In an election for the post of organizer in 1935 he came first out of fifteen candidates, and on the retirement of G. W. Brown as Assistant Secretary in December 1939, he was elected to fill the vacant post. His victory in the contest for the post of General Secretary in 1942 was a decisive one:

J. Benstead	63,120
W. J. Watson	17,683
W. T. Proctor	5,534

W. J. Watson was the same W. J. Watson who had been runner-up to John Marchbank in 1933. W. T. Proctor was a veteran of the Pontypool branch who had served as an A.G.M. delegate. If he followed his predecessor's example and reached retirement age, John Benstead had one advantage over his closest rival—he could offer the union fifteen years' continuous service as General Secretary, whilst Watson could offer but a third of this time. The new General Secretary, though less flamboyant than his predecessor, impressed everyone with his confident command of the facts and his ability as a speaker.

Other important wartime changes in the leadership of the union were the success of the left-winger Jim Figgins in the election for the post of Assistant to the General Secretary in 1943—he defeated the Finchley signalman W. E. Webster in the final count by 40,011 votes to 30,277—and the election of a more moderate man, Mr Sidney Greene, as organizer in March 1944, when he defeated Mr G. W. Brassington (later elected Assistant General Secretary) by 32,461 votes to 27,219.

III

One of the toughest problems which occupied the attention of these new officers of the union and the E.C. was how to overcome the wartime shortages of manpower and materials without too great a sacrifice of union principles.

When approached by the Minister of Transport before the war on the adequacy of the railway track and rolling stock to deal with the increased traffic that a war might be expected to bring, the companies replied that they were confident they could meet, with their existing equipment, all extra demands likely to be imposed on them.[14] After September 3, 1939, these assurances were soon proved to be ill-founded. The consequence of the companies' improvidence was the existence of serious transport bottlenecks, particularly in 1943, and the placing of an excessive strain on the railway labour force.

To meet the growing shortage of locomotives, the companies ceased to scrap those due for retirement and endeavoured to effect repairs more rapidly. At the end of 1943 the London, Midland and Scottish Railway had 491 locomotives which in peacetime would have already been on the scrap heap. Thus in addition to the difficulties caused by the blackout, footplatemen had to contend with more 'temperamental' engines requiring more tactful nursing. The situation was improved by the end of 1944 when 450 Ministry of Supply Austerity 2-8-0 locomotives and 400 locomotives loaned from the United States of America were in service. Nevertheless repair work presented difficulties owing to the fact that about a fifth of the workshop staff were employed making munitions and armaments.

By the summer of 1943 the ton mileage of merchandise traffic and passenger mileage were practically double the pre-war level and yet, by this time, more than 100,000 men, mostly under 25 years of age—the reservation age for most grades—had joined the armed forces. The deficiency was ultimately more than made good by the retention of staff beyond the normal retirement age, by the employment of women and by the occasional employment of prisoners of war and members of the armed forces.

It was as early as January 26, 1940, that the union's negotiating committee heard a request from the companies for the retention of the older men.

Mr Halliday of the London and North Eastern Railway reported that there were a number of depots where, as a result of the shortage of staff, men were working up to twenty hours a day. It was a false economy, for becoming fatigued, they were more frequently absent sick. Early in February 1940, therefore, the E.C. agreed to the retention in service of men due for retirement, provided that the posts they should have vacated were declared vacancies and were filled by men promoted from lower grades.

Before the war approximately 26,000 women were employed on the railways of Britain; by D-Day in 1944 the number had risen to 114,000. It was a development which, by and large, took place with the full co-operation of the union. The main concern of the union's negotiating committee when an important meeting took place with the companies' representatives at Euston on May 10, 1940, was that women should be employed in the 'starting' grades only and that they should be paid at the men's rate for the job. The companies would not agree to these conditions at first, but at a further meeting on June 28, 1940, they promised that every effort would be made to find men to fill vacancies, but that in the event of women being employed, they should be confined to the starting grades and, in the case of the conciliation grades, should be paid the rate for the job after serving a probationary period of thirteen weeks at a wage slightly below the pay for a man. The E.C. gave its unanimous approval to the scheme the same day.[15] A month later the E.C. agreed to the employment of women as storekeepers in the workshops and as dining-car attendants, subject to their wages, after a probationary period, being the same as men's (except that they had a lower war wage addition). At a meeting with the London Passenger Transport Board on March 10, 1941, the negotiating committee consented to the employment of women in the grade of porter-signalman, but was more dubious about the request that lift-women should be employed in the Underground. They believed that the less women had anything to do with mechanical equipment the better! The E.C. later resolved:

'With regard to the lift women, we agree, provided the women are not called upon to attempt to interfere with the mechanism of the machine rooms of the lifts in the case of failures.'

However, it was not long before women were performing, with great competence, jobs hitherto only regarded as suitable for men. Mr D. Lauder, a shopman delegate to the A.G.M. at Carlisle in July 1943, said:

'We have many women driving cranes in foundries, handling hot metal in a very short time—a job which many male members were not prepared to tackle without some months of experience. We have women working in the forges, either driving the hammer or working the machines. We have women in the railway shops carrying pretty heavy loads and carrying out their duties quite efficiently, performing duties . . . without which the war effort could not be carried on.'

Despite this, the women in the workshops had to serve a much longer probationary period—thirty-two weeks—than was the case with the conciliation grades, before receiving the man's rate of pay.

When an appeal was made to the companies to pay women clerks the rate for the job, the reply received in March 1942 was that since the managers had been unable to find any industry where the principle of equal pay for equal work was applied, they did not see why they should apply it on the railways. In view of the companies' attitude, the A.G.M. at Carlisle carried 'with acclamation' a declaration in favour of equal pay for equal work.[16]

As the labour shortage became more acute in the summer of 1943 it became necessary to employ women in other than the starting grades. In particular, a large number of women signalmen and guards were employed. The male members of the Connah's Quay Branch of the N.U.R., whilst as courageous as any in the face of attacks from hostile aircraft, found that their courage failed them when confronted with the task of travelling long distances alone in the guard's van with alluring women trainees. The Traffic Sub-Committee of the E.C. sympathized with the harassed male members of the branch and arranged for a special meeting with the Officer for Labour and Establishment Questions of the London, Midland and Scottish on November 25, 1943, when it was agreed that, as a general rule in the future, women should be trained in pairs.

If guards were sometimes shy of sharing their vans with members of the opposite sex, the same reticence was not shown by branch secretaries and organizers in recruiting women to the union. A delegate to the A.G.M. in July 1943 declared that it 'was easier to interest some of the female members in the N.U.R. then it had been in the past to interest some of the male workers'. In his report to the A.G.M. in 1944 John Benstead stated that there were 50,865 women members of the union, which was a fine achievement in view of the fact that many women clerks were members of the R.C.A.

Even with the addition of this sizeable army of women recruits the railways were still faced with a shortage of labour which reached as large a figure as 13,000 persons in October 1943.[17] By the application of the Essential Works Order to the railways from October 9, 1941,[18] the drift of labour *from* the railways to better-paid employment was stopped. It was a far more difficult task to attract youths *into* the service. Owing to the shortage of footplatemen, youths still in their teens, taken on as cleaners, were employed long hours as firemen under conditions which violated Acts of Parliament passed since 1920 to safeguard the health of young employees.

The official historian of War Transport considered that 'the main difficulty in recruiting labour for railway work was that pay and conditions were proving very unattractive especially compared with the new munitions industries'.

The N.U.R., recognizing this fact, endeavoured to make it a condition of the union's acceptance of the Essential Works Order that the companies should introduce a minimum wage of £3 a week exclusive of any war bonuses. The negotiating committee argued 'that if railway workers were to be precluded from seeking other or remunerative employment outside the railway service, then an adequate rate of pay should be granted', but the companies declined to accept this argument and after a fruitless appeal to the Minister of Labour himself on September 15, 1941, the union had to accept the Essential Works Order without achieving the £3 minimum basic wage.[19]

One indication of the acute labour shortage was a report received by the E.C. on January 4, 1944, from Shildon No. 2 branch that a number of Italian prisoners of war were to be employed on shunting duties. Since the General Secretary had had no previous notice of the companies' intention, he was asked to seek an immediate meeting of the Railway Staff Council and to urge the companies not to employ the Italians until the matter had been discussed. When the companies' representatives, at a meeting with the union at the Charing Cross Hotel on January 19, 1944, undertook to inform the Local Departmental Committees whenever they intended to use P.O.W. labour, and undertook not to reduce in grade any British railwayman, the union representatives gave their consent to the plan.[20]

In the event few Italians were employed. The Railway Executive Committee decided that during the emergency it would be better to use British troops. On January 26, 1944, it notified John Benstead that for 'a short period' and 'in order to relieve acute traffic congestion at various important points', men from the Railway Operating Division of the Royal Engineers who were mostly ex-railwaymen, would be employed by the companies. At a joint meeting of the executives of the three railway unions held on January 27th, it was agreed that, subject to certain financial and other safeguards, the employment of the troops should be approved. At a meeting he had with the union on February 10th, the Minister of War Transport was able to agree to these conditions and in the next few weeks a total of 1,001 men were seconded from the army for employment with the companies.

It took the experience of the war years to teach the Board of Trade what a vital part in a railwayman's working life is played by that rude disturber of well-earned rest, the alarm clock. By 1943 members in many branches were experiencing considerable difficulty in buying new alarm clocks or having old ones repaired. John Benstead, therefore, wrote to the T.U.C.

stressing that to those who worked turns of duty 'round the clock' and were not awakened by 'callers up', an alarm clock was an essential part of household equipment. Thus prompted, the T.U.C. urged the President of the Board of Trade to allow a greater importation of these articles than had been the case. Consent was given, and from the early summer of 1944 members of the N.U.R. and the other railway unions were given top priority in purchasing the scarce supplies. There was such a rush to buy that the Board of Trade was obliged to insist that only those whose conditions gave genuine cause for alarm would be granted permits.

A wartime issue which, according to J. H. Potts, aroused a greater feeling of resentment than any question of wages, was the obligation of railwaymen to perform firewatching duties.[21] After the blitz of the autumn of 1940, when many buildings were destroyed by fire, the Rt. Hon. Herbert Morrison, M.P., the Minister of Home Security, was concerned to establish adequate fire precautions for the future. At meetings held to discuss the question on January 23 and February 4, 1941, the companies' representatives told the E.C. that although the men called upon to do firewatching in addition to their normal duties would be provided with cooking facilities, they would be provided neither with food nor the extra money to purchase it (except in the few cases where such payment was already made). The E.C. refused to accept these conditions. It was felt very strongly that the companies were being parsimonious and that some payment, at least to cover extra expenditure on food, ought to be made. The view of the rank and file, some of whom, as a result of firewatching, were away from home three days at a stretch, was forcefully expressed by an A.G.M. delegate, W. N. Hayter, who said:

'Apparently your first duty is to protect your place of employment and you are expected to leave your own home, your wife and family to the mercies of the blitz!'

The general managers, on the other hand, considered that the union was acting unpatriotically in not immediately co-operating with the fire protection arrangements.

Negotiations were prolonged. Through the determination of the E.C. the companies gradually made concessions. On February 25, 1941, they offered to re-imburse firewatching staff for bus or train fares incurred, and to grant an expense allowance of 3s for meals. As the E.C. remained unimpressed, on March 7th the offer was increased to a total of 4s 6d for periods over ten hours' firewatching. As the E.C. still regarded the payment as inadequate, John Benstead was summoned to the Ministry of Transport on April 21st to be told by the Permanent Secretary that the action of the union had prevented the application to the railways of the Fire Prevention Business Premises Order (No. 69) of January 1941. The

General Secretary defended the action of the executive, giving reasons for its determined stand. A few days later he received a letter requesting the attendance of a delegation to meet the Ministers of Transport and Home Security and the Home Secretary on May 2nd. The members of the negotiating committee, sent in response to this request, were not overawed by the array of Ministers confronting them. They stressed that the N.U.R. was not opposed to the performance of firewatching duties, but that members were dissatisfied with the standard of amenities provided (e.g. the sleeping accommodation, facilities for making hot drinks, etc.) and with the amount of the allowances. This exchange being inconclusive, a short while afterwards, John Benstead received from Lord Leathers, Minister of War Transport, a letter which, after some preliminary soft soap, ('the minister recognizes the desire of railwaymen of all grades to render to their country the same devoted service in frustrating the attempt of the enemy to destroy our resources by fire'), announced the companies' decision to increase the allowance by a further 1s 6d, making 6s in all, where spells of duty in excess of twelve hours were performed. Back at Unity House, the E.C. whilst recording that its efforts had caused the companies to increase their offer by 100 per cent, still regarded the payments as 'inadequate and shamefully unreasonable'. Though members were advised to accept the new conditions, the General Secretary was instructed to convey to the Prime Minister, Lord Leathers and the General Council of the T.U.C., the executive's strong disapproval of the 'dictatorial attitude of the Minister of Transport'.[22]

The payment of aircraft spotters was settled more amicably. As a result of negotiations which were conducted spasmodically through the summer of 1941, the E.C. eventually accepted, on October 30, 1941, the companies' offer of a minimum payment of 65s exclusive of war wage addition to full-time spotters.

The circumstance of many men working unusually long hours or being employed as spotters or firewatchers made necessary the provision of proper canteen facilities on the railways. In peacetime the fact that the railways had made far less adequate provision of canteens than had most factories did not attract much attention. The war spotlighted the deficiencies. Liverpool No. 5 branch took the initiative in urging the E.C. to make representations to the companies, but when the question was considered at a meeting of the Railways Staff Conference on July 30, 1941, the companies' representatives said that the demand for more canteens 'was no doubt due to a desire on the part of the staff to supplement the ration allowed them under the rationing scheme'. They 'could offer no hope ... of greatly increasing the number of canteens'.

After further direct negotiations with the companies had produced meagre results, a joint A.S.L.E. & F. and N.U.R. conference with the companies on April 10, 1942, resulted in agreement on an application

T*   585

being made to the Ministry of Food for increasing the number of railway canteens providing full meals. The R.C.A. also joined in on August 5, 1942, when the unions met the Rationing and Food Prices Committee of the T.U.C. to urge speedier action. A branch circular posted on November 6th reported some progress but showed how much still remained to be done. At the beginning of September there were eleven canteens which offered full meals service to a total of only 6,385 staff. There were thirteen other canteens which provided a more limited service and work had been authorized for the erection of another forty-three. Undoubtedly the slow progress was partly due to the shortage of building labour and materials and the difficulty of obtaining 'A' priority for the schemes which had passed the blue-print stage.

A consideration of the adequacy of the railway canteen services naturally led on to an examination of welfare services as a whole. At its March Quarterly Meeting in 1944, the E.C. considered a resolution from the Hull Divisional Council of the N.U.R. which deplored the lack of proper lavatory accommodation as well as the inadequacy of the medical services and canteen services on the railways in the area. At the June Quarterly Meeting the E.C. decided to be better informed of the facts by asking branch secretaries to fill in a questionnaire. Through this medium, 118 branches and two District Councils had, by the beginning of 1945, complained about such matters as the absence or inadequacy of washing facilities, cloakroom accommodation and first-aid equipment. Mr W. S Walters of Birmingham No. 16 branch, persuaded the A.G.M. at Edinburgh on July 8, 1944, to instruct the E.C. to take the necessary steps 'to have made applicable to all premises and undertakings on the railways of the United Kingdom, the Factory Acts'. His experience led him to believe that railwaymen were 'accommodated worse than any section of the workers in Great Britain'. Where he worked there were 2,000 men employed. For drying their hands after washing they were provided with only two clean towels every twelve hours. There was no doctor or trained nurse available. Following the A.G.M. resolution, John Benstead persuaded the T.U.C. to write to the Minister of Health to urge him to bring the railways within the scope of the health and welfare provisions of the Factory Acts. By the end of 1945, however, the Sub-Committee of the E.C. had reached the conclusion that it was best to agitate for improvement through the Local Departmental Committees and that where local representations had failed the companies had been 'approached and in many cases satisfaction secured'.[23]

IV

As the cost of living rose by 31 per cent during the war a major part of the union's activity consisted in negotiating with the companies' improved rates of wages to ensure at least that there was no deterioration in the standard of living (apart from that which was inescapable due to the circumstances of the war).

Eight separate additions to the basic rates of wages were secured in the war years. Four of these came from Decisions Nos. 6–9 inclusive of the Railway Staff National Tribunal, whilst the other four were obtained at a lower level of the negotiating machinery.

The first award under the Railway Staff National Tribunal Decision No. 6 of October 18, 1939, was the outcome of a N.U.R. claim lodged before the outbreak of the war for a 50s minimum for all railwaymen. The Tribunal's decision to grant the 50s minimum to men of the four main line companies working in London, but to limit the minimum to 48s in other 'industrial' districts and to 47s in rural districts, was reached without regard to the new wartime circumstances and must therefore be regarded as being in a separate category from the other wartime awards. The subsequent advances negotiated on behalf of the conciliation grades may be summarized as follows:

Date of Award	Operative from	Negotiating Body	Amount of Award	Aggregate war wage
8.2.40	1.1.40	R.E.C. Staff C'tee	4s od	4s od
31.5.40	3.6.40	R.E.C. Staff C'tee	3s od	7s od
15.5.41	6.1.41	R.S.N.T. 7	4s od	11s od
9.3.42	9.3.42	R.S.N.T. 8	4s 6d	15s 6d
9.12.42	24.6.42	R.S.N.T. 9	5s od*	16s od
18.6.43	26.4.43	R.E.C. & Unions	4s 6d	20s 6d
20.4.44	17.4.44	R.E.C. Staff C'tee	5s od	25s 6d

The increases were extended to those employed on the London Passenger Transport Board rail services and were in each case also applied to the shopmen, the men employed in electric power generating stations and other ancillary services controlled by the Railway Executive Committee. It was agreed in advance by both parties that the wartime awards of the Tribunal should be binding. Thus the union was spared the expense of a succession of Special General Meetings called to consider the proposed increases. Increases in the basic scales of the salaried and supervisory staffs were awarded at the same time as those given to the conciliation grades and they amounted to £66 6s od a year for adult males, by the end of the war. The war wage given to women was below that of men in all grades, reaching an aggregate of 21s 6d in each case.

In the early months of the war the E.C. vacillated between attempts to raise the basic peacetime rates of wages and attempts to compensate for the rising cost of living by securing war wage additions.

*This advance *absorbed* some of the earlier advances made under R.S.N.T. Decision 7.

No sooner was the Tribunal's Decision No. 6 put into effect than the rank and file began to demand further wage increases. W. H. Marshall, a chief lineman from Cross Gates, told the S.G.M. in London on November 9, 1939, that there was not one of the eighty delegates who would deny 'that his wife had been at him because of rising prices'. In the early months of 1940, therefore, the efforts of the E.C. were concentrated on a demand for an increase of 10s a week to offset the increase in the cost of living. It succeeded in obtaining 7s of this in two stages within six months.

When a similar policy of seeking special war advances was pursued in the second half of 1940, the E.C. met with no success. When the negotiating committee met the R.E.C. on February 4, 1941, it was taken aback when Sir R. Wedgwood informed it that since 'wages had to be approached from a national standpoint more than had been done previously', the companies were not able to make any offer but suggested the men's claim be referred 'to some body of a national character'. The truth of the matter was that the Coalition Government was, by this time, dissatisfied with Chamberlain's, February 1940, Agreement with the companies and feared the inflationary effects of further wage increases to the railwaymen. Thus when the negotiating committee met the R.E.C. again on February 11, 1941, it learned that Sir R. Wedgwood had recently seen the Minister of Transport who had recommended the submission of the men's claim to an 'independent tribunal'. The union's executive naturally regarded this as a major change of policy which could have serious repercussions, and it therefore secured an interview with the Minister of Transport—the Rt. Hon. J. T. C. Moore-Brabazon, M.C., M.P.,—on February 20th. Confronted with the straightforward question as to whether the new policy of the R.E.C. had been proposed at the instigation of the Government, the Minister frankly admitted that this was the case. He argued that since the Government took control of the railways through the R.E.C. at the outbreak of war, the companies were no longer 'valid negotiators' who would themselves bear the cost of wage increases. Neither was the Government a 'valid negotiator', since it was a third party, the travelling public and the traders, who would be ultimately called upon to pay the cost. For these reasons the wage claim should be subject to the arbitration of a body representing the traders and the public.

The executives of the three railway unions were united in opposition to the new proposals. At a joint meeting on February 28th, they decided to press the claim through the established negotiating machinery, and John Marchbank was instructed by the E.C. of the N.U.R. at its March 1941 meeting to write to the Prime Minister to inform him of the union's determination to maintain the existing negotiating machinery. These prompt actions were effective in quashing the Government's proposals. At a meeting held at the Ministry of War Transport on May 22, 1941, the union's negotiating committee was informed that the Minister had decided to make no changes, and that 'the practice followed prior to the last application would continue in the future'.[24] The Government thereafter was content to let well alone.

After Newport No. 8 branch had persuaded the A.G.M. at Swansea, in July 1941, to concentrate on the demand for a £3 a week minimum basic wage (irrespective of any war wage additions) the E.C. was obliged to change its tactics. At its meeting on October 9, 1941, it decided that 'no claim for any additional war advance should be made pending developments in respect of the claim for £3'. But when the R.S.N.T. considered the claim in February and March 1942, it avoided a decision on the basic peacetime rates but resolved instead to grant an increase of 4s 6d on the war wage.

In his Presidential Address to the A.G.M. in 1942, Mr F. J. Burrows, J.P., expressed the view that it would not be in the best interests of the union to pursue the minimum wage policy. It was better to obtain flat rate additions to the existing rates. The testing time, he claimed, would come after the war when the union's policy should be—'What we have we hold and must improve upon'. The majority of the membership agreed with him, and this policy was followed during the ensuing three years.

Through this intelligent use of the union's bargaining strength the increase in railwaymen's wages more than kept pace with the general increase in wages. Between September 1939 and April 1944 (when the last war wage addition was obtained) railwaymen's basic rates (including war wage) rose by 56 per cent. The comparable figure for all industries and services was 44 per cent.[25] Munitions and engineering workers were better paid than railwaymen but the *relative* position of railway wages improved during the war. John Benstead told the A.G.M. at Carlisle on July 12, 1943, that railwaymen were getting 'the highest war wage of any principal industry in the country'. On the other hand the increase of *earnings* of the conciliation grades (65 per cent) was less than the national average (79 per cent); only the shopmen kept pace with other tradesmen in this respect. It was also to be remembered that railway wages recovered more slowly than did wages in industry as a whole in the five years before the outbreak of the Second World War.

The war brought substantial improvements in the pay and working conditions of the Hotels and Refreshment Room Staff employed by the railways. In December 1938 the E.C. had sent a questionnaire to the branches asking for detailed information on conditions. A sub-committee sifted the replies and presented detailed reports on the situation in the refreshment rooms and hotels in April 1939. There were no less than 68 adult grades employed in the refreshment rooms and 150 male and 45 female grades in the hotels. There was no uniformity even within one company's system, and there were instances of individual hotels being divided into sections and wings, each of which possessed its own peculiarities respecting methods of grading and sharing out tips. There were complaints of excessive hours; irregular meal breaks; no guaranteed booking-off time; poor food; poor dormitory accommodation; inadequate rest room accommodation and the absence of payment for overtime, night duty or Sunday duty.

When the union's negotiating committee discussed its programme of uniform rates of wages, a 10-hour maximum working day, payment for overtime and Sunday duty and many other improvements, with the companies on January 18, 1940, the general managers replied that cost of standardization would be such as to make the hotels 'entirely unremunerative'. But at further meetings in February, March and May 1940, important concessions were made, and on June 17th, the negotiating committee provisionally accepted an agreement which shortly afterwards received the unanimous approval of the E.C. As from June 3, 1940, a scale of minimum wages for the different grades of hotel and refreshment room staff was put into operation on a uniform basis throughout the country. There were still many demands unsatisfied—particularly the refusal of the companies to allow the establishment of Local Departmental Committees in railway hotels and refreshment rooms—but it was a big step forward, and patient negotiation was to bring further improvements.

On the other side of the Irish Sea, in the early years of the war, the employees of the Sligo, Leitrim and Northern Counties, the Belfast and County Down and the Londonderry and Lough Swilly Railways were granted rises in wages which mostly took the form of a reduction in the amount of the cuts imposed in the earlier 1930's. On the Belfast and County Down Railway the cuts were eliminated by the end of 1940, but it was well into 1943 before the men employed by the Londonderry and Loch Swilly Railway had their wages restored to the level of the early 1930's. South of the border, all wage cuts had been eliminated on the Great Southern Railway by the end of 1939 and the men received their first war bonus (2s 6d) on April 29, 1940. There were further small additions before Emergency Powers Order No. 166 came into operation on April 8, 1942, after which further increases were granted only after the previous consent of the Ministry of Industry and Commerce of the Government of Eire had been obtained. Though further wage advances were authorized they were always well below the amounts applied for. The majority of Irish railwaymen at least escaped having to work in the difficult conditions of the blackout but, in contrast with the conditions in Great Britain, there was a drastic curtailment of services particularly on the Great Southern Railway's lines.

Ever since the National Conference of Busmen had been held in Leeds in February 1937, the N.U.R. and the T. & G.W.U. had made strenuous endeavours to establish national negotiating machinery for busmen's wages. The circumstances of the war made possible the early fulfilment of this aim. When the General Secretaries of the two unions wrote to the Secretary of the Omnibus Owners Association in the autumn of 1939, requesting discussions, they were told that these were impossible as the bus companies lacked the constitutional powers to negotiate a national agreement. An approach was therefore made to the Minister of Labour who responded by inviting the two sides to attend discussions at the Ministry. So successful were these talks, that a meeting of the Bus Federation held in London on December 15, 1939, was able to consider a draft constitution for 'National Council for the Omnibus Industry'. At a later meeting of the Federation, held on January 23, 1940, it was argued that there should be a panel of sixteen members on each side of the Council and that the trade-union panel should be composed of eleven members of the T. & G.W.U., three of the N.U.R. and one of the N.U.G.M.W. At its February meeting the E.C. of the N.U.R. endorsed these proposals and decided that the union should be represented by the General Secretary and two members of the E.C.[26]

At the inaugural meeting of the council held at the Ministry of Labour in London on June 14, 1940, John Marchbank was elected Vice-Chairman. That Ernest Bevin strongly supported the new venture was indicated by his presence at the meeting to give a speech of welcome. A further milestone was reached at the second meeting on June 26, 1940, when it was agreed to award a war bonus of from 4s to 7s to all male workers employed by the concerns represented on the council. There were proportionately smaller increases for women and youths.

Though there was now a national negotiating machinery there was still a long way to go before there was national uniformity in wages and conditions of service. The best that could be achieved in the war years was some uniformity in the war bonus advances. However, on January 28, 1944, Mr Harold Clay, Secretary of the Employees' Side of the Council wrote to the Employers' Secretary, requesting the establishment of a nation-wide settlement of wages and conditions of service. At a meeting of the council held on March 14, 1944, Mr Clay countered the employers' argument that there could be no national uniformity because of great local variations in costs of operation, by saying that there were the same variations of cost on the railways which had had a nationally negotiated scale of wages for twenty-five years.

Undoubtedly one of the obstacles to an agreement was the fact that only 63 out of the 4,702 operators of public service vehicles were represented on the Council. Although the 63 controlled 18,000 out of 35,000 public service vehicles (apart from those owned by Local Authorities and the L.P.T.B) the employers in the Council feared that after the war 'receipts would fall and costs would not', and they feared competition from the concerns as yet uncontrolled by the decisions of the Council. It was not until after the war was over that these fears were overcome.[27]

V

A.G.M. delegates were accustomed to debating resolutions on the need for one union for all railwaymen, but the resolution of the Paisley branch debated on July 17, 1942, at Blackpool, seemed to be particularly apposite. During the preceding six months both the N.U.R. and the Associated Society had applied for an increase in the war wage. The companies would not concede more than 4s a week and the Executive of the Associated Society, in the belief that this was the best that could be done, accepted the offer. The A.G.M. of the N.U.R., however, on July 9, 1942, resolved to press the union's claim for 10s, if necessary to the Tribunal. The delegates naturally considered these differences of approach to the problem of wage negotiations to be deplorable and were in unanimous agreement with the members of the Paisley branch that the 'policy of the A.S.L.E. & F., the R.C.A. and the N.U.R. fighting each other for membership' was 'a waste of time and money'. The E.C. was instructed to 'take the initiative in trying to form a union for all railwaymen'. After the vote was taken John Benstead did not sound too hopeful. He said the attempt would be made 'at the risk of getting another rebuff'.

At first it looked as if his pessimism was justified. Both W. P. Allen (General Secretary of the Associated Society) and C. N. Gallie (General Secretary of the R.C.A.), in their letters of reply, rejected outright amalgamation. But the approach led to important discussions being held. The joint meeting of the three executives held at Unity House on January 12, 1943, was later described by John Benstead as 'one of the most harmonious, if not the most harmonious', he had known. When the executives met again on February 18, 1943, it was agreed (a) that all future wage claims should be subject to joint consultation between the three unions before they were submitted to the companies; (b) that machinery should be devised to facilitate the co-ordination of the policies of the unions in matters 'of common interest to railwaymen' and (c) that to ensure smooth and friendly working, attacks upon each organization were to be discountenanced. Finally, at their meeting on March 25, 1943, the executives approved a Constitution for 'A National Joint Committee of the R.C.A., A.S.L.E. & F. and N.U.R.'

The Joint Committee, which was 'consultative and advisory in character' was to comprise the President and General Secretary and four other representatives from each of the three unions (making eighteen members in all), and had the aim of creating 'the maximum amount of unity of purpose on matters of common interest to the three unions, e.g. important matters for negotiation with the railway authorities; legislation affecting railways or railway workers; and other matters where agreement is desirable'. The E.C. of the N.U.R. at its special meeting on April 8, 1943, was unanimously in favour of the new scheme.

The experience of the second half of 1942 had helped to convince the three executives of the advantages of closer unity of working. It was not until November 11, 1942, that the N.U.R.'s claim for a 10s increase in the war wage was heard by the Tribunal, which published its decision on December 9, 1942. The award was a shilling more than the companies had been prepared to offer; but in the interim the Associated Society had lodged another claim. By the award (R.S.N.T. Decision 9) the members of both unions received a small advance. In both unions there was a strong feeling that if they had acted together they might well have got more at an earlier stage in the negotiating machinery.

Relations between the unions continued to be friendly throughout the remainder of the war years. Mr F. J. Burrows, J.P., President of the N.U.R. at the A.G.M. on July 6, 1944, 'for the first time in the history of the Conference' welcomed a fraternal delegate from the Associated Society, Mr W. P. Allen, who assured the delegates that his 'good friend Benstead' and he were so long acquainted that they would not 'fall out over silly things'. Seven days later Alderman Percy Morris, fraternal delegate of the R.C.A., got a warm-hearted response from the same audience when he confessed 'without shame' to having helped many a signalman to achieve the desired number of marks on D-Day (when a census of work was taken) by 'ringing up and asking him the right time half a dozen times'. The delegates were so impressed by the improvement in the atmosphere, that they asked the E.C. to make another approach to the other unions for an amalgamation in which the 'maximum amount of democracy' would be afforded to different grades. The outcome of the subsequent negotiations was disappointing to those who believed the time was ripe for the creation of one union for all railwaymen. Representatives of the other two unions told a meeting of the National Joint Council on January 9, 1945, that there had been 'no material change in their policy' since the subject was considered before the Council was formed, though good results had accrued from co-operation.[28]

At all levels of the organization members of the N.U.R. took a lively interest in political developments during the war years. The *Railway Review* twice published lengthy articles by Nehru and as early as January 1941 the Glasgow and West of Scotland District Council urged the E.C. to appeal to the T.U.C. and the Labour Party 'to endeavour to secure the release of Nehru and his comrades'. The E.C. complied with this request at its next meeting.[29] Treherbert No. 2 and fourteen other branches reminded the E.C. that the time had arrived to apply Freedom No. 3 of the Atlantic Charter—'They respect the right of all peoples to choose the form of Government under which they will live'—to the peoples of India. The E.C. resolved to notify not only the Labour Party but also the Prime Minister of its agreement with this policy.[30] On July 7, 1943, the A.G.M. at Carlisle was unanimous in urging the Government 'to immediately open up negotiations with the principal national representatives of India with a view to the establishment of an Indian National Government', and in December of the same year the E.C., prompted by Polmadie branch, demanded 'that immediate measures be taken to deal effectively with the famine in India'.

As soon as news was received of the appointment of the Beveridge Committee to review the national Social Services, the Executive appointed a sub-committee to draft detailed recommendations. At the March 1942 meeting the sub-committee's recommendation in favour of 'an all inclusive scheme to cover unemployment, sickness, maternity, non-compensatory accidents, invalidity, old age, blindness, death, widowhood and orphanhood', with a new Ministry created to administer the scheme, was adopted by 17 votes to 3.

A more immediate need, in the view of the delegates to the A.G.M. in July 1942 was the provision of more Nursery Schools. The Executive was directed to urge the Government to take over 'halls, public and private ... empty large shop premises, dwelling houses used as offices', etc., for temporary conversion to nurseries, pending the later erection of equipped nursery schools. Such action would, it was claimed, liberate 'a huge army of women for industry'.

VI

In a survey of wartime transport made in the House of Lords on October 27, 1943, Lord Leathers, the Minister of War Transport, declared that for the first time the country had 'evidence of the benefits of a fully coordinated transport system', and he did not think 'the industry would ever want to go back to the conditions prevailing before the war'. The railway companies were not slow in considering plans for the peacetime organization of transport. It was as early as 1942 that the Railway Companies' Association set up a commission to make recommendations for the future working of the railways. But an examination of the speeches of the chairmen of the four main line companies, delivered at the Annual General Meetings in March 1944, reveals that the future envisaged was of an intensification of private monopoly rather than a transference to public ownership and control. Each speaker harked back to the 'Square Deal' Campaign of 1939 and demanded that, after the war, railways should be given freedom in fixing charges and in selection of traffic, and equality of treatment with the roads in the incidence of track costs. Each welcomed the recent establishment of the National Road Federation among goods hauliers and envisaged the negotiation of an agreement with it on rates and conditions of service. There were also plans for the extension of railway companies' interests in air services.

A vigorous propaganda against public ownership was being conducted.

Gilbert Szlumper, onetime General Manager of the Southern Railway, speaking at a dinner of the Engineering Industries Association in London on January 25, 1944, said that:

'Nationalization would mean that a horde of black-coated, stripe-trousered young men, full of theory, would be playing at trains or lorries when their knowledge of transport was limited to the cost of a season ticket from their home town to Whitehall.'[31]

Clearly it was imperative that the N.U.R. should formulate its policy for the future of the industry.

The passing of a resolution on the need for public ownership and co-ordination of transport became almost a formality at A.G.M.s through the war. The resolution carried unanimously at Morecambe on July 4, 1940, may be taken as characteristic.

'This Congress notes that the circumstances arising from the war have compelled the Government to take over control of the railways and to impose a measure of co-ordination with all other forms of transport, owing to the serious waste and inefficiency involved in the competitive system under private ownership and control; Congress calls upon the Government to prepare plans for the future complete co-ordination of all forms of transport under public ownership and control, believing that the reconstruction after the war will depend more upon a sound transport system than any other factor.'

At the Labour Party Annual Conference at Westminster on June 17, 1943, John Benstead moved an N.U.R.-sponsored resolution calling for the appointment of a Royal Commission on Transport which would be instructed 'to submit a report within twelve months of the cessation of hostilities in Europe on the steps necessary to bring all forms of Transport under National Ownership and Control'. However, when the Chairman assured the N.U.R. delegation that the National Executive accepted the principle of the resolution, it was agreed that it should be withdrawn. This was a wise decision, for as Harold Laski, speaking for the National Executive, pointed out, the experience of the previous hundred years showed that when a Royal Commission was unanimous it took an average of nineteen years for its recommendations to become law, but that when there were majority and minority reports it took an average of thirty-three years for legislation to follow!

Of more value was the work of John Marchbank as Chairman of the Labour Party's Sub-Committee on Transport which in 1944 published a 23-page pamphlet entitled 'Post War Organization of British Transport' and John Benstead's work on the T.U.C. which published a report on the 'Public Operation of Transport' in the same year. Both reports recommended the setting up of a National Transport Authority which would be appointed by and bear responsibility to the Minister of Transport, and which would own and control the principal means of transport in the country. The groundwork having been prepared by specialized sub-committees, the Labour Party's Declaration of Policy 'Let us Face the Future', published in April 1945, as a programme on which to fight the General Election, included a demand for public ownership of inland transport and co-ordination of services by road, rail, air and canal.

Some members of the N.U.R. were concerned lest in the establishment of a national transport board, the interests of the workers in the industry be unrepresented and largely forgotten. At the A.G.M. in Edinburgh on July 4, 1944, Mr W. Ballantine moved an amendment to the usual resolution on public ownership. The E.C. was to go into the question of 'preparing a plan of organization for transport based on workers' control' and was to carry out a vigorous campaign in the country to gain publicity and support. But the majority of the delegates were satisfied to back the Labour Party's report, and turned down the amendment by 65 votes to 8.

The members of the N.U.R. were determined not to enter the post-war period without a detailed programme for improved pay and conditions of service. On a resolution of the Swansea No. 3 branch the A.G.M. at Carlisle on July 10, 1943, instructed the E.C. 'to go fully into the question of submitting items for a new National Programme for all grades including shopmen'. The proposals were to be submitted to the next General Meeting and there was to be 'no delay' in submitting them to the companies after the cessation of hostilities. At its meeting in August, the E.C. appointed a special sub-committee of one member chosen from each of the four departmental sub-committees, to receive suggestions from the branches and prepare recommendations. The four men told the E.C., when reporting back on April 4, 1944, that their proposals were 'not revolutionary in character' being largely a continuation of the principles which led to the national agreements of 1919–22. They were aiming at 'a high degree of uniformity and order out of the chaos of a vast and complex system that had grown up with the multiplicity of the railway companies'. Their main suggestion was for a sweeping reduction in the number of grades and their grouping into ten classes for pay purposes. The policy advocated for wages was a high minimum rate and a lessened gap between the minimum and the maximum. Thus the basic pay in Class 10 was to be £4 4s od and in Class 1 £6 os od. Hours of work were to be reduced to forty per week and twelve days' paid holiday to be taken in two consecutive weeks within the period May to September.

What were called Minor Recommendations included, among many others, the abolition of differences between 'London', 'Industrial' and 'Rural' rates of pay; the abolition of spreadover turns; overtime payments and night duty payments at time and a half, and Sunday duty at double time rates; payments for periods of sickness, and days off in lieu of work done on bank holidays.

The full programme, modified by recommendations from the departmental sub-committees was approved by the E.C. on April 20, 1944. The A.G.M. at Edinburgh in July 1944 decided to subject the document to a further vetting by a sub-committee of eight, four of whom were to be chosen from the A.G.M. and four from the E.C. By the time the programme was presented to the S.G.M. at Morecambe on November 7th, some changes had been made. The ten pay groups had been reduced to five and a demand for half-pay pensions at 60 with a minimum payment of £2 5s 0d a week, had been added. The rest of the draft remained substantially the same. After prolonged debate, the S.G.M. gave its approval to this carefully thought out and comprehensive plan for improving the peacetime pay and conditions of service of railwaymen.[32]

In December 1943, at the end of the busiest railway year of the war, the Prime Minister, in a message to the four main line companies, admitted that results such as the railways had achieved were won only by 'blood and sweat' and expressed the gratitude of the nation 'to every railwayman who had participated in this great transport effort'.[33]

Whilst railwaymen willingly gave their blood and sweat during the war, they believed that, once the long struggle was over, much of the distress which had been caused before 1939 as well as after it, could be avoided in the future, given the comprehensive planning of the main transport services of the nation. To discover what were the Coalition Government's intentions, a delegation comprising the President, General Secretary and two Executive members from each of the three railway unions waited upon Lord Leathers, Minister of War Transport, on April 24, 1945. Members of the delegation told the Minister that wartime experience had confirmed their opinion that there was 'an overwhelming case for the co-ordination of transport in all its various branches'. Lord Leathers, in reply, said that 'the Government had not made up its mind on this very important and complicated question'.[34]

Less than three months later, on July 5, 1945, the people of Britain were given the opportunity, for the first time in nearly ten years, to vote in a General Election. The overwhelming majority of railwaymen seized the opportunity to reject the uncertainties of Lord Leathers in favour of the firm promises contained in the Labour Party's 'Let us Face the Future'. On July 26th there was formed a Labour Government pledged to the 'public ownership and co-ordination of transport services by rail, road, air and canal'.

NOTES

1. C. I. Savage, *Inland Transport*, History of the Second World War, U.K. Civil Series, p. 51.
2. *The Times*, January 29-31, 1940.

3. N.U.R., E.C., December 1939, p. 299, Rs. 2566 and 2571.
4. R. 687 (amended).
5. Cmd. 6168 (analysed in Savage, *op. cit.*, pp. 123–5).
6. *The Economist*, February 10, 1940, p. 244. Hansard, Parliamentary Debates, February 13, 1940.
7. H.O. Circular 351/4125, June 12, 1940.
8. *The Economist*, September 6, 1941, p. 290. *R.R.*, April 20, 1945.
9. Savage, *op. cit.*, p. 201.
10. I am indebted to Mr Sidney D. Hoskins, Secretary of the London District Council, N.U.R., for this story.
11. Savage, *op. cit.*, p. 401. 'The Railways in War Time', *The Times*, January 6, 1942.
12. N.U.R., E.C., September 1941, Rs. 1779–80. December 1941, R. 2424. September 1942, p. 441, Appendix G.G. for Mr Potts's report of his 48 days' tour within the U.S.S.R.
13. N.U.R., E.C., September 1940, R. 2016.
14. Savage, *op. cit.*, p. 74.
15. N.U.R., E.C., June 28, 1940, R. 1378.
16. N.U.R., A.G.M., Carlisle, July 1943, R. 119c.
17. Savage, *op. cit.*, p. 422.
18. N.U.R., General Secretary's Report to the A.G.M. 1942, p. 31.
19. N.U.R., Special E.C., May 14, August 25 and September 16, 1941.
20. N.U.R., E.C., March 1944, Appendix D, p. 258.
21. T.U.C., Edinburgh, September 1941, Debate on Firewatching, p. 312.
22. N.U.R., E.C., February 5, 6, 15, 28, April 7, May 6 and 14, 1941. *Manchester Guardian*, June 7, 1941.
23. N.U.R., A.G.M., Edinburgh, July 8, 1944, Verbatim Report, p. 2. E.C., May 1945, p. 78. September 1945, p. 99 and December 1945, pp. 120–1.
24. N.U.R., E.C., February 5, 6, 15, 25 and 28, 1941; March and June Quarterly Meetings, 1941.
25. *Ministry of Labour Gazette*, April 1958, p. 132.
26. N.U.R., E.C., December 1938, R. 1732, June 1939, pp. 51–8. January 1940, R. 59; March 2 and 21, June 25, 1940. A.G.M. Agenda and Decisions, 1942, p. 68.
27. National Council for the Omnibus Industry. Minutes of meetings held on June 14 and 26, 1940, February 24, March 14 and April 14, 1944.
28. N.U.R., A.G.M., 1942, R.124. E.C., March 1943, Appendices C, p. 273, H, p. 300 and R, p. 327 and A.G.M. July 6 and 13, 1944, Verbatim Report.
29. N.U.R., E.C., March, 1941, R. 526.
30. N.U.R., E.C., March 1942, p. 245.
31. Quoted in *Railway Gazette*, January 28, 1944.
32. See N.U.R., S.G.M., Morecambe, November 7–10, 1944, Agenda and Decisions, pp. 2–47 for full programme.
33. Quoted—*R.R.*, December 31, 1943.
34. N.U.R., E.C., May, 1945, p. 83.

CHAPTER XXI

THE LABOUR GOVERNMENT AND THE
TRANSPORT ACT OF 1947

*'Open competition is too costly to contemplate, and it is likely to lead
to the breakdown of the public services, and no effective middle course
appears to be possible without subsidies. The complete co-ordination
of transport by means of a scheme of unification is the only way to
get the best possible service at the lowest economic cost.'*
Financial Times, *September 3, 1946.*

I

IT is common knowledge that the General Election of July 5, 1945,
resulted in a decisive shift of political power from the receivers of
rent, interest and profit to the wage and salary earners. In no industry
was this shift more dramatic than in the case of the railways. When
Richard Bell first entered Parliament in October 1900, as the sole representative of railway labour he was confronted by a group of no less than fifty-
three M.P.s who were railway directors. In the Parliament of 1935–45,
the number of railway directors in the Commons had shrunk to twelve,
but it was still greater than the number of railwaymen. After July 1945,
however, the thirty railwaymen M.P.s on the Labour Benches faced but
two railway directors on the opposition benches. Fifteen of the thirty
railwaymen were members of the N.U.R. Perhaps the most remarkable
achievement of any member of the N.U.R. Parliamentary Panel was A. J.
Champion's Labour gain in South Derbyshire where he romped home
with a majority of 22,950 in a three-cornered fight. The presence of these
railwaymen in the Commons was valuable, particularly in the debates on the
Transport Bill, but also in the distinguished service that some of them gave
in ministerial appointments. To give only two examples, J. B. Hynd as
Chancellor of the Duchy of Lancaster had wide responsibilities in Germany and Austria, whilst Joseph Henderson served with distinction as
Lord Commissioner to the Treasury. (He was raised to the Peerage in
1950.)

Whilst the election of fifteen members ensured that the N.U.R. case did not go by default, it was no guarantee that the legislation concerning transport was entirely in accordance with the policy of the union as the withdrawal of vital clauses from the Transport Bill, in the teeth of the opposition of all railwaymen M.P.s, was to demonstrate.

II

Since inland transport had been placed second only to fuel and power in the list of industries declared ripe for public ownership in 'Let us Face the Future', it was not a matter for great surprise when the Rt. Hon. H. Morrison, Leader of the House, told the Commons on November 19, 1945, that it was the intention of the Government to introduce, during the life of that Parliament, measures 'designed to bring transport services, essential to the economic well-being of the nation, under public ownership and control'.

In view of the fact that the N.U.R.—or its predecessor the A.S.R.S.— had advocated the nationalization of the railways ever since 1894, it is understandable that the Labour Government's decision was greeted with enthusiasm by the A.G.M. at Morecambe in July 1946. The resolution, which was carried unanimously, welcomed 'the contemplated legislation for the nationalization of transport' and stressed that the forthcoming Bill would only be regarded as satisfactory if it aimed 'at embracing and co-ordinating all forms of transport'.[1]

Seven months earlier the National Joint Committee (of the N.U.R., A.S.L.E. & F. and R.C.A.) at its meeting on December 7, 1945, decided to advise the new Minister of Transport, the Rt. Hon. Alfred Barnes, of 'the desire of the three unions to be consulted when his proposals ... have been prepared'. The Minister responded by inviting the unions to send representatives to meet him on January 30, 1946. The union delegations (including four representatives of the N.U.R.) came to the meeting armed with a seven-point memorandum which gave priority to the need for 'safeguards in any proposed legislation in respect of compensation for workpeople who may be displaced or otherwise disadvantaged'. The N.U.R.'s interest in those employed in docks, road transport and hotels was stressed. 'Workers representation on any national or regional authority set up' was essential; welfare services needed urgent improvement; existing pension rights of employees should be safeguarded and the existing negotiating machinery should be maintained pending agreement or improvements. Finally, it was 'strongly urged upon the Minister ... that the change over from private to public enterprise should not be unduly delayed'. There was no mention of methods of controlling road transport or of integrating it with rail services.

When the members of the N.U.R. reported back to the E.C. on February

5, 1946, they said that Mr Barnes was 'very sympathetic' to their case and had declared that he would welcome the 'fullest co-operation and association' with the unions 'as the policies developed'.

The omission of any reference in the Memorandum to a policy for controlling 'C' licences is to be regretted. It is true that, in the discussion, the Minister mentioned that he had previously met a delegation from the T. & G.W.U. and that he recommended that all the unions concerned in road transport should meet together to try to reach a common policy.[2] But when, in March 1946, the E.C. of the N.U.R. took the Minister's advice and approached both the N.U.G. & M.W. and the T. & G.W.U. for Joint Consultations, Mr Deakin, in his reply for the transport workers, caused an unfortunate delay by, at first, declining direct discussions with the railway unions. He suggested instead that there should be talks between the Minister of Transport and the General Council of the T.U.C. In May he did discuss road transport policy with the railway unions, but no joint memorandum was submitted to the Minister.[3] Had the three railway unions, at this early stage, included in their memorandum a strong recommendation concerning the radius of operation of 'C' licence vehicles, they would have made it harder for the Minister, at a later date, to yield to the pressure of business interests. As it was at this stage, Mr Barnes had no documentary evidence that the railway unions felt strongly on the question.

The representatives of the three railway unions met Mr Barnes once more, on September 24th, before the Transport Bill was published two months later. The long interview was largely taken up with a discussion on trade-union representation on the management, compensation rights of displaced workers and the unions' recommendation to end the separate organization of the London Passenger Transport Board.

After the Transport Bill had passed its second reading on December 18, 1946, four N.U.R. M.P.s (Messrs Dobbie, D. T. Jones, Popplewell and Proctor) who were members of the House of Commons Standing Committee 'B', persuaded Mr Barnes to agree to amendments to Clauses 99, 100, 102, 111 and 124 of the Bill. In a report sent to John Benstead on April 10, 1947, they wrote:

'In every case, except one, the amendments were accepted and incorporated in the Bill. In the case of one (to Clause 124) the Minister overlooked to append his name but it is anticipated the matter will be put right at the report stage.'

Most of these amendments were in Part VII of the Bill which dealt with conditions of employment, pensions and compensation to employees. Their main purpose was to safeguard the rights of those employed and to make more definite the obligation of the Transport Commission to promote welfare services.

At a later stage the union's M.P.s persuaded the Minister to amend Clause 67 to make it obligatory, instead of permissive, for the Transport Commission to prepare schemes for the integration of road and rail passenger services.

Ironically enough, the greatest damage sustained by the Bill in the Committee Stage was that inflicted by the Minister himself. On March 13, 1947, he announced his decision to remove clauses 56–8 inclusive which had limited the sphere of operation of most 'C' licence vehicles to a radius of forty miles from their operating centre. Mr Barnes surrendered to the demands of private traders, the more cautious members of the Cabinet and the Co-operative Societies which, according to Herbert Morrison, showed 'a distinct lack of enthusiasm about surrendering their large road transport fleets', and which, through the Parliamentary Committee of the Co-operative Congress, made representations to the Minister—himself a Co-operative Party M.P. In addition, Douglas Jay, M.P., had worked hard to persuade Mr Attlee to get the provisions about 'C' licences dropped from the Bill.[4] Although the Parliamentary Committee of the Co-operative Party on March 28, 1947, said that there was 'no truth whatever' in the assertion that it had demanded the removal of the offending clauses, it did admit asking the Minister to extend the mileage limit from forty to sixty miles.[5]

In the Parliamentary Committee, Mr D. Jones of the N.U.R., protested in the strongest terms against Mr Barnes's decision:

'One of the disturbing features about the removal of these clauses', he warned, 'is that we shall again see big industrial concerns operating under "C" licences, carrying in their own vehicles all the highly remunerative traffics which it suits them to carry, and handing over the difficult jobs and "returned empties" to the public service.'

Mr Barnes replied that the issue had 'got out of all proportion' from what he and the Government had intended. He made a solemn promise:

'If we have any evidence that it is being abused, steps will be taken to amend the Act, to put "C" licences into their proper place, so that they cannot abuse or undermine the public transport system.'[6]

In view of the fact that the Minister had made an even more explicit promise of a similar nature a week before, the N.U.R. M.P.s did not press their opposition to a division.[7]

In the meantime, on the day following the Minister's announcement, the E.C. of the N.U.R. reached the unanimous decision to ask the T. & G.W.U. to join in a protest. But when Mr Barnes saw a deputation of the two unions on March 30th he would not agree to insert new clauses in the

Bill concerning the 'C' licences. In any case he was not alone responsible. The decision to make this vital change in the Bill was upheld by a majority of the Cabinet of which he was not a member.

When Mr Barnes told the Commons on November 18, 1946, that the basis of compensation for the holders of the stock of the main line railways and the London Passenger Transport Board would be the stock-market valuations for November 1–8, 1946, or February–July 1945 (whichever was the most favourable to the stockholders), the first reaction of the leading financial newspapers was one of relief. The Financial Editor of the *Manchester Guardian* considered that the stockholders had come off 'reasonably well'; the *Financial Times* considered the terms 'not ungenerous'. It was only a short while later that the Government was subjected to a concerted attack both for making stock-market valuation rather than net maintainable income the basis of compensation, and for proposing that the rate of interest on British Transport compensation stock should be as low as $2\frac{1}{2}$ per cent. As far as is known, no prominent member of the N.U.R. subscribed to the view expressed by Sir Ronald Matthews, Chairman of the London and North Eastern Railway, that the terms being offered by the Government 'would bring a blush of shame to the leathery cheek of a Barbary pirate', or adopted the suggestion of a member of the audience at a Caxton Hall meeting addressed by Mr Harold Macmillan, M.P., that opponents of the award should chain themselves to the railings of the House of Commons.[8] The atmosphere in the Board Room at Unity House was, at least on this occasion, somewhat less heated. With only two dissentients, the E.C. endorsed the view of its Nationalization Sub-Committee that:

'The scheme of compensation, assuming the stock issued in exchange bears interest at the low rates now yielded by gilt-edged securities, should effect a large annual saving and we recommend support for the same.'[9]

The saving did not prove to be as great as the committee had anticipated. By January 1948, when the Government fixed the interest rate on British Transport Stock, owing to the fact that money market rates had risen above the low levels of 1945–7, the Government felt obliged to offer 3 per cent instead of the $2\frac{1}{2}$ per cent which had at first been suggested. The change meant that the sum which the Transport Commission would have to find annually in interest payments to the former railway stockholders, was increased from £25½ to £31 millions. To the extent of this increased annual liability, it became more difficult for the N.U.R. to negotiate better conditions of service for railwaymen in the years after 1948.

From the point of view of establishing co-ordination between road and rail services, the demand made by the railway unions in their first interview with Mr Barnes—that the transition to public ownership should take place as quickly as possible—had much to commend it; from the point of view of the ability of the Commission to pay its way, a delay of a year or two in the date of transfer might have had advantages. As Mr R. H. S. Crossman told the House of Commons on May 10, 1950:

'Mr Churchill who is sometimes frank . . . remarked the other day that we nationalized at the wrong time, by which he meant that if we had waited two years, at least two of the main railways would have been in the hands of receivers and we should have got them cheaper.'[10]

Far from it being a case of 'Nationalization on the cheap' as suggested by *The Economist*, in the light of the earning prospects of British Railways in the post-war years, the take-over was an unduly expensive one.

III

The British Transport Commission which began its operations on January 1, 1948, was controlled by a chairman and four other full-time and three part-time members. Through its subsidiary organizations—the Railways; the Road Haulage; Road Passenger; London Transport; Docks and Inland Waterways and Hotels Executives—it owned and operated the principal transport services of the country, although air transport and a substantial part of road goods haulage was outside its control. Under Section three of the Act, the Commission had the duty to provide 'an efficient, adequate, economical and properly integrated system of public inland transport and por: facilities within Great Britain for passengers and goods'. The properties of the Commission were 'to form one undertaking' from which the revenue earned was to be 'not less than sufficient for making provision for the meeting of charges properly chargeable to revenue, taking one year with another'.

The N.U.R.—unlike the R.C.A. and A.S.L.E. & F.—had a substantial membership employed by *each* of the six executives, which meant that any major programme of demands had to be advocated separately to each of six bodies. This tended to increase the volume of work undertaken by the E.C. and the Head Office. The bound volume of E.C. Minutes for 1948 contains 2,111 pages compared with 1,558 in 1938.

Despite the setbacks experienced during the passage of the Bill through Parliament, the members of the N.U.R. at special celebrations held in all parts of the country in January 1948, gave an enthusiastic welcome to the new venture. The London District Council organized a mass meeting at the London Coliseum on January 4th when the principal speaker was Jim Figgins, then acting General Secretary. More than a thousand persons attended a celebration dance sponsored by the Paddington No. 3 branch and held in the Porchester Hall on the last night of 1947. Meetings at Cardiff, Hull, Crewe, Edinburgh and many other places were well supported. The President of the union, W. T. Potter, voiced the feeling of many thousands of the members when he told a mass meeting organized by the Newcastle District Council: 'Take off your coats, roll up your sleeves and give of your best'.[12]

As far as the Minister of Transport was concerned, the delegates to the A.G.M. at Ayr on July 16, 1947, were prepared to let bygones be bygones and Mr Barnes was warmly applauded at the end of his speech to the Conference.

The evidence from the branches goes to show that the launching of the great new experiment in common ownership was greeted with idealism and much goodwill on the part of very many railwaymen.

Nevertheless, by the time the Labour Party relinquished the reins of office in October 1951, it must be frankly admitted that a large part of the goodwill and idealism had dissolved. By December 1950, when the Manchester and District Council requested that the E.C. should 'press for the removal of Mr Barnes from his post as Minister of Transport', the E.C. reacted very differently from the way it would have done four years earlier. Instead of letting it lie on the table, by 13 votes to 8, it decided to forward the resolution to the Minister.[13] Why had there been this decline of confidence?

IV

One reason was that railway wages lagged behind the general trend of wage rates after 1947. This relative decline was all the more noticeable by contrast with the gains that were made in the first two and a half years of peace. In his report to the A.G.M. in 1946 John Benstead wrote:

'I think that we can claim that during the past twelve months we have made more progress than we were able to achieve during the preceding quarter of a century.'

The catalogue of concessions obtained from the railway companies and the London Passenger Transport Board in the last months of their existence when they were still enjoying the Government's guarantee of net revenue of £43 million a year, does make impressive reading. None of the improvements were granted just for the asking. It was as early as March 20, 1945, that the N.U.R. submitted to the companies its 'National Programme' for improved wages and conditions of service on the same day as the other two railway unions presented their demands. Prolonged negotiations in the Railway Executive Staff Committee and directly with the Railway Executive Committee followed. By the beginning of August 1945, the companies announced that they had reached the limit of their concessions with a proposed increase in the basic wage of 5s 6d. As they did not regard this offer as adequate, on August 8th the members of the negotiating committee met the Minister of Labour who, later in the day, induced the companies to add 1s 6d to their offer. There was a last-minute hitch when the companies endeavoured to make the increase conditional upon the unions not presenting any further demands until the end of 1947. But after the E.C. had rejected these terms by a four to one majority, Mr Isaacs was seen again on August 9th and the companies were persuaded to withdraw their twenty-eight months' ban on further applications.

The agreement, which was made operative from July 30, 1945, raised basic wage rates from 77s per week to 84s in rural areas, from 78s to 85s in industrial areas, and from 80s to 87s in London, but it also increased the Sunday duty rate from time and a half to time and three-quarters, and extended the time during which time and a half rates would be paid for night duty from 10.0 p.m. to 4.0 a.m. to 10.0 p.m. to 6.0 a.m., this latter concession operating from February 8, 1946. From January 1, 1946, all men in the conciliation grades who had completed twelve months' service were to be entitled to twelve days' paid holidays instead of six. There were improved lodging allowances for train staff. For the salaried grades there were increases ranging from £10 to £15 a year and an increase in the annual paid holiday from twelve to fifteen days. Restaurant Car travelling staff had their hours reduced from 120 to 108 hours per fortnight, with increases in pay proportional to those obtained for the Conciliation Staff and a corresponding increase in Sunday pay rates from time and a half to time and three-quarters.[14] Bearing in mind the prolonged unemployment and under-employment of railway shopmen in the 1930's, the most notable gain from the Railway Shopmen's National Council Award Number 408, of September 1945, was the introduction of the guaranteed day and guaranteed week, although another important feature of the Award was the simplification of the wage rates. Thenceforward there were only three basic rates for shopmen—those applying in London, Class 'A' towns and Class 'B' towns—in place of the four existing previously.[15]

Important though these concessions were, they still fell short of the demands contained in the National Programme approved by the A.G.M. in July 1944, particularly in respect of the 40-hour week, the abolition of lodging turns, the consolidation of the 'war wage' with the standard rates of pay, and the elimination of the difference between 'rural' and 'industrial' rates of pay. The greater part of 1946 was taken up in a struggle to persuade the companies to grant these outstanding demands. Throughout the negotiations the N.U.R. worked in close collaboration with the other two railway unions. When little progress was made within the Railway Executive Staff Committee, representatives of all three unions met the Minister of

Transport on October 29, 1946, and on December 5th interviewed the Minister of Labour as well as Mr Barnes. In the meantime the E.C. of the N.U.R. on November 20th had announced its intention 'to bring this matter to a satisfactory conclusion, if necessary by strike action'. The combination of these pressures induced the general managers of the railway companies at meetings held on December 13th and 23rd to increase their earlier offer. They agreed to the consolidation of war wages with the basic rates, to the granting of improved rates of pay for hybrid grades such as porter-guards and to the payment of time and a half rates for bank holiday duty. Lodging turns for train staff were to be reduced to the minimum. The unions accepted these terms as a step in the right direction.[16]

The final spate of pre-nationalization improvements came on July 4, 1947, with the Report of a Court of Inquiry under the Chairmanship of Mr C. W. Guillebaud.[17] The continuing rise in the cost of living since the previous wage award of July 1945, prompted many branches to urge the representation of new claims to the companies. Liverpool No. 5 Branch, in December 1946, suggested a demand for an extra 10s a week, but on January 9th, the E.C. adopted the suggestion of its negotiating committee to ask the companies for £1 a week and the reduction of hours from forty-eight to forty. Once more the intervention of the Minister of Transport was sought to speed up the negotiations; but at the interview which took place on May 9, 1947, Mr Barnes pointed out that the railways were expected to be £32 million short on net revenue that year, that even to grant a 44-hour week would cost £15 million, whilst if the full programme were conceded, ordinary fares would have to be increased from $33\frac{1}{3}$ per cent to 80 per cent above the pre-war levels. The unions were not to be easily deterred. They saw Mr Barnes again on May 23rd, this time along with Mr Isaacs, who five days later announced the setting up of the Court of Inquiry.

The Minister of Labour took this way out of the impasse as John Benstead had made it crystal clear to him that the N.U.R. was not prepared to submit the claim to the Railway Staff National Tribunal. By an agreement reached between the trade unions and the railway companies on June 19, 1940, it was accepted by both parties 'that the decisions of the R.S.N.T. be final and binding' so long as the Condition of Employment and National Arbitration Order No. 1305 of 1940 remained in force. That order has not yet been revoked and it was the firm conviction of the E.C. that the Tribunal, one of whose three members was a nominee of the companies, would concede very little so long as it knew that its award would not be turned down.

John Benstead's evidence greatly impressed the Court of Inquiry. He showed that since the Essential Works Order had been lifted in August 1946, and railwaymen were once more free to move to other industries,

13,486 members of the permanent staff had left the railways for other jobs in the short space of six months. The reason for this was that wage rates in other industries were 68 per cent above those of August 1939, whilst the wages of railwaymen had risen by only 54 per cent in the same period. The railways were having to refuse traffic because 4,881 footplate staff and cleaners had left the service of the companies to take up better paid employment elsewhere, and sufficient suitably qualified replacements could not be found. In their report, the members of the Court of Inquiry stated that the railway unions had 'established a case for some improvement in the wage and salary scales throughout the industry in order to bring them more closely into relation with the general level which has already been established elsewhere'. They therefore recommended an increase of 7s 6d a week on the basic rate of pay, to be put into effect from the first full pay period after June 30, 1947. With regard to the claim for a 40-hour week, they offered a compromise. Since it was 'impossible to justify a 48-hour week against the march of events' they recommended that hours be reduced to 44 per week (with clerks working 42) from June 24, 1947. The concessions which were applied to the shopmen and the employees of the London Passenger Transport Board as well as to those employed by the main line companies, were approved by the E.C. on July 4, 1947, by 14 votes to 4, 'as an interim arrangement prior to the nationalization of transport'.[18]

On the strength of this award and the other concessions obtained since the end of the war, the union's twenty organizers and 1,600 branch secretaries (and other officers) succeeded in increasing the membership from 409,826 at the end of 1945 to 462,205 at the end of 1947. Further, in consequence of the repeal of the Trade Disputes and Trade Unions Act in 1946, the number of members contributing to the political fund of the union rose from 247,231 in 1945 to 363,422 in 1947.

From the time that the British Transport Commission took over the railway companies on January 1, 1948, the union encountered much heavier weather in its wages negotiations. During the period 1940–7 in which the Government guaranteed the net revenue to the companies, any deficit the companies might incur, partly as a result of wage increases, was made good by the Treasury. From 1940–5 the railways earned a substantial surplus over the £43 million net revenue they were guaranteed, but from 1946 they fell far short of the earnings of the wartime boom, and the Treasury had to pay out no less than £59,708,000 in 1947. Thus the increase granted the railwaymen in 1947 may be regarded as having been paid out of the Treasury subsidy. After January 1, 1948, however, the British Transport Commission was under obligation to pay its way 'taking one year with another'. Inevitably the Railway Executive viewed with much greater circumspection demands for increases in wages.

It was unfortunate that railway wages still lagged behind those of outside industry when the Labour Government published its White Paper on Personal Incomes, Costs and Prices in February 1948.[19] Except in cases where it could be clearly shown that productivity had increased or that an industry was undermanned, there was to be 'no further general increase in the level of personal incomes' so that the rise in prices might be checked and the volume of exports raised. In these circumstances, the task of the new General Secretary, Jim Figgins, to try to bring railway wages more in line with the level of outside industry was difficult enough. By his tactics he tended to make it a Herculean one.

When the A.G.M. at Wallasey in July 1948, instructed the General Secretary 'to prepare the claim for a flat rate increase for all workers', neither Jim Figgins nor the E.C. thought it essential to secure the support of the other railway unions before approaching the Railway Executive, and hence profitless negotiations between the N.U.R., the Railway Staff Conference and the Railway Executive continued throughout September and October of that year. Finally the E.C. decided to report the deadlock to an S.G.M. held in the Conway Hall, London, between December 21 and 23, 1948, when the delegates resolved that Mr Isaacs be informed that a dispute existed between the N.U.R. and the executives of the Commission. This time the Minister refused to set up a Court of Inquiry, supporting the view of the Permanent Secretary, Sir Robert Gould, that it was still the obligation of the union, so long as National Arbitration Order No. 1305 was not withdrawn, to resort to the statutory negotiating machinery. The N.U.R. asserted that this procedure was inappropriate since it alone was making the claim, but on the Railway Staff National Tribunal the other unions were also represented. To settle the question Mr Isaacs agreed that the N.U.R. should appeal to the National Arbitration Tribunal for a ruling. This body found that 'suitable means' existed for negotiation of claims which had, therefore, to be taken to Sir John Forster (the Chairman) and the other members of the R.S.N.T. After hearing Jim Figgins put the case for the N.U.R., and W. P. Allen (its Chairman) the case for the Railway Executive, the Tribunal published its Decision No. 11 with remarkable promptitude on March 18, 1949. Citing the White Paper on Personal Incomes, Costs and Prices, the financial position of the railways and the costs of the suggested wage increase as its principal reasons, it concluded that the union's claim had 'not been established'.[20]

An S.G.M. summoned to the Memorial Hall, Faringdon Street, London, on April 22nd, decided to ask the General Secretary to make immediate representations to the Prime Minister and the Ministers of Transport and Labour to receive a deputation from the union, which was to stress the dissatisfaction that existed, and to report back to the S.G.M. immediately. In the event, only Mr Isaacs saw the eight men chosen for the interview. After consulting his legal advisers, the Minister, at a second meeting on April 27th, said that the most hopeful approach for the union to make was to submit a completely new claim. Sir Robert Gould, his representative, had seen Sir Eustace Missenden of the Railway Executive and had impressed upon him the urgency of the situation. Jim Figgins told the S.G.M. delegates on the following day that the deputation felt that George Isaacs was someone who would give the railwaymen 'a measure of assistance'. Conference therefore agreed to take the Minister's advice. By 69 votes to 7 it was decided to make a new application, this time for an addition of 10s a week on all railway wages and salaries with time and a quarter rates to be paid for those obliged to work from twelve noon to midnight on Saturdays.[21]

At first the new approach proved no more profitable than the earlier one had been. After a number of preliminary exchanges, Mr Allen told the union's negotiating committee on May 19, 1949, that 'since it involved a flat rate increase for all grades' he could make no offer. Later the same day the E.C. decided to try to break the deadlock by means of a further approach to Mr Isaacs. This time the General Secretary's confidence in the Minister was not misplaced, for when the negotiating committee met him with his permanent officials at the Ministry of Labour on May 26th, Mr Isaacs said he would talk the matter over with Mr Allen. Five days later the E.C. was informed that the Railway Executive had 'definite proposals'. But on June 3rd when it learned that these were for the lowest paid grades only and were for a maximum increase of 3s a week, it was unanimous in rejecting them as 'totally inadequate'.[22]

The rank and file were becoming restive. From May 30th the staff at the London Road (Manchester) and Nine Elms Goods Depots began to 'work to rule'.

It was at this stage that the drawbacks of a policy of not consulting the other unions before presenting a wage claim were apparent. When they learned of the N.U.R.'s claim for a flat rate increase of 10s, the executives of the Associated Society, the R.C.A. and the Confederation of Engineering and Shipbuilding Trades (who represented about 35,000 out of the 130,000 shopmen—the remainder being members of the N.U.R.) were disturbed lest the differentials of the higher-paid grades were upset. They therefore decided to be represented at the N.U.R.'s meeting with the Railway Executive on June 21st in order to state their objections to the bigger union's demands.

These lamentable divisions were largely due to the dissolution, in July 1947, of the National Joint Council of the three railway unions, following accusations by the N.U.R. of Associated Society 'poaching' its members among the staff employed by the Manchester Ship Canal Company which since 1937 had recognized the N.U.R.'s exclusive right to bargain for its employees.

By June 28, 1949, the delegates summoned to an S.G.M. in London, reached the opinion that no improvement in the wages situation was likely until the union showed a stronger determination. By 66 votes to 13, therefore, it was decided to call upon all members from midnight on July 3–4, 1949, 'to cease working any tonnage, bonus or piecework schemes and to work strictly to rules and the 44-hour week' until such times as the union's just demands were met. The decision left a week for further negotiations, and Mr Isaacs made the most of it. Sir Robert Gould, asked to find a way out of the impasse, ruled that since there was no agreement between the parties on the terms of reference to the R.S.N.T. there could be no appeal to it, and the Minister would be at liberty to set up an independent inquiry on railway wages. In the light of this promising development, the E.C. decided to suspend the decision to work to rule and the A.G.M. meeting at Brighton, on July 9th, agreed to Mr Isaacs' proposal that the N.U.R.'s claims together with those of the other railway unions, should be submitted to a Board of Conciliation.

For three days from August 8th, Jim Figgins and Assistant Secretary Pounder expounded the union's case to Sir John Forster and the four other members of the Conciliation Board. It was pointed out that the cost of living had risen 11 per cent since the last wage award in 1947 and that the 10s increase claimed was barely sufficient to offset that rise. Impressive evidence was submitted to show that, because of the low wage rates, there was still a heavy drain of manpower from the industry making it necessary for over 48 per cent of the signalmen to work on their rest days. Because the union's case was such a strong one, the disappointment with the Board's report, published on September 8, 1949, was all the greater. And yet the decision (reached unanimously) 'that neither the claim for the flat rate, or any increase, nor the claim for enhanced payment for time worked on Saturdays was justified' is not at all surprising in the circumstances. There was no support at all for the N.U.R. from the other unions. The representative of the Associated Society said that his union was mainly concerned about pensions for railwaymen and was not therefore making any claim for an increase in wages at that stage, whilst the R.C.A. executive declined to back the N.U.R. because it was in the process of drafting its own charter for submission to the next A.G.M. of the Association. Jim Figgins told the S.G.M. on September 29th that when Mr Allen presented a document which showed that the average *earnings*—as distinct from wage *rates*—of railwaymen were over 134s a week, it had a 'devastating effect' on the independent members of the Board. It was in vain that Mr Pounder pleaded that whilst it was true that earnings had increased, this was 'largely secured by railwaymen working for longer hours than their colleagues in outside industry'. The Board tended to overlook the fact that thousands of men were not in a position to take home more than their basic rate of pay.[23]

One concession obtained from the Railway Executive on August 18, 1949, while the report of the Board of Conciliation was still awaited, was the abolition of the 'rural' rates of pay. This improved the basic rates of the

9,000 men in this class and was to operate from September 5th that year. The Conciliation Board itself made recommendation for three minor concessions, including a new marking classification for signalmen, increased 'on call' allowances for stationmasters, goods agents, etc., and a 42-hour week for stationmasters, agents, control staff and supervisors.

Inevitably, in the minds of the delegates assembled at the S.G.M. in London on September 29 and 30, 1949, these marginal improvements were overshadowed by the fact that in a period of sharply rising prices there had been no improvement in the basic rates of pay for over two years. By 63 votes to 16, conference registered its 'emphatic protest' against the Board's recommendations which, in view of the union's acceptance of the terms of reference, it had 'no alternative but to accept'. The same resolution instructed the E.C. to reopen negotiations immediately with the Executives of the Transport Commission 'with a view to an improvement in wages being obtained for low paid employees'. The aim was to see that no man was paid less than £5 a week. The General Secretary told the supporters of an amendment 'to work to rule and refuse overtime, piecework and Sunday working', that such a policy would 'considerably undermine' whatever little chance they had of 'economic recovery and political independence'. They must do nothing which would 'injure the chances of the Labour Party in winning the next General Election'.[24] The amendment was defeated by 62 votes to 17, with one neutral.

When the members of the E.C. came to consider how best to carry out the instructions of the S.G.M., they showed that they had learnt from previous mistakes. It was unanimously decided to convey the terms of the S.G.M. resolution to the two other railway unions 'with a view to a joint claim being made for an improvement for lower paid employees'.[25] Although the Associated Society would not agree to a joint meeting, on this occasion the R.C.A. gave some backing to the N.U.R.'s claim for a minimum rate of 103s a week in London and 100s in the provinces. It took from December 24, 1949, when the claim was first submitted to the Railway Executive, until August 15, 1950, when Decision No. 12 of the Railway Staff National Tribunal was published, for an increase to be negotiated. The Award, which became operative from September 1, 1950, was for an increase of 3s 6d on the basic rate, with certain consequential adjustments in rates above the lowest rates and with comparable adjustments for clerical staff.

That, on this occasion, quicker results were obtained was in part due to the absence of opposition from the other unions and in part to the Railway Executive's realization that some advance in wages would have to be conceded if the dangerous drift of labour away from the railways was to be arrested. The Tribunal's award was almost identical with the offer made by Mr Allen to the N.U.R. on July 7, 1950. (It was because of this offer that the N.U.R. had less hesitation on this occasion in taking the claim to the Tribunal.) That more was not obtained was partly due to the fact that 'wage restraint' was still the order of the day. Following on the devaluation of the pound on September 18, 1949, a special conference of Trade Union Executives and the General Council of the T.U.C. held in the Central Hall, Westminster, on January 12, had endorsed by a majority of 657,000 the General Council's Report on 'Trade Union Wages Policy'. This had advocated 'vigorous restraints on all increases of wages, salaries and dividends'. Although the N.U.R. opposed the report, its endorsement by other unions made the climate of opinion more hostile to the latest demands expressed for the railwaymen.

Throughout the negotiations of the first half of 1950 the union had made it clear that the claim for an increase for the lower paid men was made without prejudice to the long-standing case for an all round improvement in railway wages. Hence the A.G.M. in July 1950, decided that as soon as the Tribunal's Decision No. 12 was published, the General Secretary was to submit to the Railway Executive an immediate application for a 10 per cent increase for all grades, and was to inform the R.C.A. and A.S.L.E. & F. of the claim and to offer joint discussions with them.[27]

By the late summer economic conditions had improved and the T.U.C. had conceded the need for greater flexibility in wage movements. Hence by September 15th all three of the railway unions made application to the Railway Staff Conference for general increases; the N.U.R. for 10 per cent, the R.C.A. for 7½ per cent, and the Associated Society for improvement in the rates of wages of the locomotive grades. Mr Allen, for the Railway Executive, at a meeting of the Railway Staff National Council on November 7, 1950, offered to raise the basic rates in the Conciliation grades to 97s 6d per week in the provinces and 100s 6d per week in London, but tied to this concession the requirement that the unions should agree to help the Railway Executive introduce such economies as the elimination of the grades of 'caller up' for trainmen and of vanguards for road transport in the London area, and an increase in the number of lodging turns. The E.C. was prepared to discuss economies in a separate series of meetings, but objected strongly to Mr Allen's procedure of making the grant of improved rates of wages conditional on their acceptance. On November 30th, at a joint meeting of the three executives, it persuaded the other railway unions to join in a deputation to the Minister of Labour to persuade him to bring about the withdrawal of the 'objectionable conditions' laid down by the Railway Executive. At the Ministry of Labour, three separate attempts were made to reach agreement, but on each occasion 'both sides held definitely to their respective positions'. Just before Christmas the two sides met Mr Isaacs in the House of Commons where they agreed to refer the dispute to a Committee of Inquiry, but could not agree to the terms of reference, as Mr Allen insisted on tying up the plans for economy with the discussion of the wage claim. Mr Isaacs, therefore, decided that the terms of reference should be simply to inquire into the application for improved wage rates and make recommendations.[28]

Mr Figgins told the Court of Inquiry under the Chairmanship of Mr C. W. Guillebaud, that since 1947 not only had railwaymen's wage *rates* fallen behind those in comparable outside industry, but also that their average *earnings*, at 135s 9d a week, compared most unfavourably with the 145s 9d a week average of all other industries. In consequence there was a very rapid turnover of labour which interfered with that steady progress up the promotional ladder which was vital to the efficient working of the industry. That the union's case was an unanswerable one was shown by the fact that the Railway Executive was prepared to make a more substantial wage offer than it had done the previous July, and that the Court of Inquiry in its report of February 8th, recommended the acceptance of this offer of an advance of from 1s 6d a week in the basic rates to 7s a week in the higher grades, with some modification in favour of improved differentials for signalmen in Special Classes A and B, drivers and motormen in the highest grades and salaried staff in Special Categories A and B. The Court of Inquiry also recommended the adoption of Mr Allen's economy proposals. It believed that 'substantial and progressive' economies were necessary if the railways were to increase their revenue.[29]

When Jim Figgins, and the recently elected President of the N.U.R., Mr H. W. Franklin, saw the advance copy of the Report they were 'grievously shocked', especially by paragraph 267 in which the members of the Court declared that the proposed wage advances were 'in the nature of an advance or mortgage on economies to be effected in the future'. The wage increases proposed were in the region of a 5 per cent advance—only half the amount which the N.U.R. had considered the minimum necessary. The General Secretary in explaining to the S.G.M. on February 27, 1951, the reasons for the E.C.'s 19–1 rejection of the report a fortnight earlier, declared that to have accepted it with all that was implied in the future redundancy of staff, would have been 'an absolute disaster'. It was the first time in the history of the industry that the recommendations of a Court of Inquiry had been turned down by the union.

In the meantime the rank and file, particularly in Liverpool and Manchester, were expressing their disgust with the report by 'working to rule', and the E.C. decided on February 14th to seek the co-operation of the other two unions in 'an approach to the Minister of Labour and/or any other Minister (including the Prime Minister)'.

It was the newly appointed Minister of Labour, Mr Aneurin Bevan, who saw the representatives of the three unions at 4.0 p.m. on Friday, February 16, 1951. Jim Figgins warned the Minister that history looked like repeating itself. In 1911 the strike had begun in Liverpool and Manchester and had then spread to the rest of the kingdom. Once more, forty years later, there had been a withdrawal of labour and work to rule in the

Lancashire area. This would spread unless prompt action was taken. Mr Bevan promised that he would try to arrange a meeting between the unions and the Railway Executive at the latest on the following Monday (February 20th). He pleaded with the delegates from the N.U.R. to advise members of the union to resume normal working, but the E.C. (all of whose members were present at the meeting), after a brief withdrawal to consider the matter, told Mr Bevan that it could not issue such an instruction as, if this were done, the rank and file would feel that they were being deserted by their leaders. Thus the partial strikes and work to rule continued throughout the weekend.

At the meeting at the Railway Clearing House at 10.0 a.m. on February 20th, Mr Figgins found the new Chairman of the Railway Executive, Mr J. Elliot, 'a very adaptable fellow' who said he would not insist on the men going back to work as a pre-condition of negotiation since it was more important to create the 'proper atmosphere'. Despite the fact that the General Secretary in the course of three days' negotiations found Mr Elliot 'very helpful indeed' the improved offer made was not considered adequate by the unions and at 11.0 p.m. on Wednesday, February 22nd, negotiations broke down.

The unions immediately got in touch with Mr Bevan who agreed to meet them at 10.0 a.m. the following morning before he took part in a Cabinet meeting at 11.0 a.m. He must have put in a strong plea for an improved offer to the railwaymen, for, later that same day, he announced that there would be further advances in pay. When the Presidents and General Secretaries of the three unions met Mr Elliot on Friday (February 23rd) they were handed two documents. The first comprised detailed proposals for wage increases averaging $7\frac{1}{2}$ per cent, the second, entirely separate, was headed 'Measures for Increased Efficiency', and contained an assurance that the unions acknowledged 'the imperative need for the fullest co-operation with the Railway Executive in the elimination of waste of manpower, in increasing efficiency and improving productivity within the railway industry'. A special Joint Committee of the Executive and the unions was to be set up to promote these economies.

This was the improvement both in respect of the amount offered and in the separation of the document on economies from the wage settlement which enabled the E.C., later the same day, by the comfortable majority of 18–6, to decide to accept the Railway Executive's offer.[30]

Nonetheless the union had claimed 10 per cent, not as a bargaining counter, but as the minimum necessary to offset a 10 per cent rise in the cost of living and the improvement in wages in other industries since the previous railway settlement. The real wages of railwaymen were still well below what they had been in 1947. It is not surprising, therefore, that the same S.G.M. which on February 27, 1951, so warmly applauded the General Secretary for his presentation of the union's case in the recent negotiations, appointed a special sub-committee to draft, for the forth-coming A.G.M., a comprehensive scheme for new rates of pay and conditions of service for the industry.

The situation since nationalization was aptly summarized in *The Times* of ten days earlier:

'If railway charges are kept artificially low at the expense of the em-ployees it would appear that the railway workers are, in effect, sub-sidizing other industries.'

It was precisely because they knew that they were subsidizing industrial users of the railways and commuters that railwaymen felt resentment at the way the nationalized transport system was being managed.

V

Even before the lifting of the Essential Works Order on August 31, 1946, there was a persistent shortage of labour on the railways. Before 1938 one of the great attractions of the railway service (even when allowance has been made for much short-time working in the workshops) was the greater regularity of employment than was the case in many 'outside' industries. This advantage disappeared with the coming of full employment in the war and post-war years. That railway wages at times lagged behind other industrial wages in the inter-war period was a matter of no great concern to the general managers who could count on the attraction of regular employment to bring them an adequate labour supply. The changed circumstances of the post-war world were graphically described by an S.G.M. delegate, Mr W. S. Vosper, on April 21, 1949:

'A few years ago it used to be said by one of the delegates who was speaking for the railway groups that he did not care very much how many men left the railways so far as the platelayers were concerned, because he had only to go 'over the banks' and get men to come from the fields along by the railways. But that is not so today. Men are leaving the service, going over the fence and working for the farmers where they can get £5 a week plus the other incidentals.'

For more than a century it had been the policy of the railways to augment their labour supply by offering a shilling or two more than the farmers paid their labourers. Now apparently the situation was reversed. Men were leaving the railways for the better pay and more regular, more congenial, hours of labour of a host of other industries. By January 1951, men were leaving the industry at an average rate of 20 per cent of the staff each year or an average of a complete 'turn round' of staff every five years.[31]

Inevitably these conditions undermined the morale of those members of the permanent staff who had made the railways their career; they also greatly impaired the efficiency of railway operation and made refusals of orders for goods carriage a frequent occurrence.

In default of offering wages adequate to retain men on the railway service, the management resorted to a series of temporary expedients. With the railways short of 13,000 men at the cessation of hostilities, the Minister of Labour met the negotiating committee of the N.U.R. on September 19, 1945, and asked whether they were willing for German prisoners of war (in addition to the Italians already employed) and British servicemen, to be employed to mend some of the 150,000 wagons awaiting repair and help maintain the permanent way. The E.C. was not prepared to agree to the employment of the Germans, though it raised no objections to the continued employment of the Italians and consented to the repair of wagons in ordnance factories strictly as 'a temporary measure'. The constructive alternative, urged to the Minister at a further meeting on October 23rd, was to give the railwaymen still serving in the forces, class 'B' releases. Early in January 1946, Mr Barnes informed John Benstead by letter that about 6,000 railwaymen had been given the early release from the forces which the N.U.R. had suggested.[32]

The serious drawbacks arising from the undermanning of the railways were spotlighted in mid-February 1947, when, in consequence of heavy snowfalls and the immobilization of the coal wagons at the pit heads, power stations ran out of fuel, factories closed down and more than three million workers were temporarily unemployed. In the afternoon of February 12th, the E.C. received an urgent phone call from Mr Isaacs asking for the union's co-operation in moving 97,000 loaded coal wagons from the sidings. Messrs Figgins, Murphy and Donlon, who interviewed Mr Isaacs on the question, offered the full support of the members of the union, and shortly afterwards the E.C. gave its hearty endorsement. Railwaymen of all grades responded magnificently to the appeal and performed feats of endurance second only to those many had been called upon to perform during the war. By February 24th the number of loaded coal wagons awaiting movement had been reduced to 54,121 despite the continuance and intensification of the most severe weather.[33]

It was clear that it had been a railway wagon and manpower crisis as much as a coal crisis. But although the Minister of Labour exempted coal miners from the call-up he turned down the plea of the N.U.R. to extend the deferment of the call-up of locomotive, maintenance staff and train crews beyond March 3, 1948. Eventually after further representations had been made he agreed to extend the deferment to footplate staff only, until the end of 1948.[34]

In the meantime, early in July 1947, the E.C. agreed to the employment of Polish labour provided that these men were employed on the same rates of pay as Englishmen and provided there was no English labour available.[35]

Inevitably a larger proportion of women were employed on the railways than had been the case before the war. It was a development which was received with far less concern than had been the employment of women in the period of the First World War. In December 1947, the E.C. could not see eye to eye with the Cromer Branch which protested against the employment of female lavatory attendants on a seasonal basis on the grounds that this practice was 'sabotaging the national economy'.

At the end of February the members of the Cricklewood No. 1 and West Hendon Branches asked for a ruling from the E.C. regarding the proposed employment by the London, Midland and Scottish Railway of coloured men as shunters on the Cricklewood Down Sidings. It was unanimously decided that the General Secretary should inform the branches 'that we have no objection to the employment of coloured men in the railway industry'. They were further to be told that coloured men had been 'satisfactorily employed on the railways over a long period'.[36] By September 1950, when many more coloured men were being employed, especially on London Transport, the E.C. was receiving complaints from English railwaymen employed in the Goods Department at King's Cross that coloured men were being taken on above the starting grades and that if coloured men became senior to white men 'they would not stand for it'. After Assistant Secretary Jim Campbell had addressed a meeting of men employed in six London depots and the matter had been discussed at two meetings of the Railway Staff Conference, on April 13 and November 23, 1951, the opposition was placated, the union's policy of opposition to the colour bar was reaffirmed and the E.C. at its December 1951 meeting agreed unanimously to co-operation with the Railway Executive in the removal of obstacles to the employment of coloured persons.[37]

With the lagging behind of railway wages, the situation became more serious by the summer of 1951. At meetings with the unions on June 6th and 26th, the Railway Executive proposed that men employed in areas of labour shortage be asked to give up voluntarily one week's holiday, that more Italians should be employed on the permanent way and that men be retained in the service after reaching the age of 65. Mr H. McRitchie, a delegate from Salford to the S.G.M. on November 1st, caused loud laughter when he described the situation as follows:

'Men are to be retained over 65 years of age. If you could see them going to work at seven o'clock in the morning you would be amazed; one foot in the air and the other in the grave. They say "Keep going, brothers, and we will have Italian labour to help you out".'

Nearly four months before he had spoken, on July 10, 1951, the union's negotiating committee had agreed to Italian labour being employed not only on the permanent way but also in the signal and telegraph departments; to men being asked to relinquish a week's holiday provided they were paid additionally at time and a quarter rates; to wages staff being employed for a 48-hour week instead of the recognized 44 in some areas, provided they were paid time and a half rates for the extra four hours; and to the employment of men over 65 years of age.

These makeshift measures may have helped to relieve immediate labour shortages, but who could wonder if railwaymen gained the strong impression that their industry was being treated as the cinderella among major industries for whom the 'left overs' of the labour market were regarded as appropriate?[38]

VI

Such exalted hopes had been centred in the nationalization of transport by many of the union's stalwarts that disillusionment was, perhaps, inevitable when the expected improvements did not materialize very rapidly.

The prospects of the railways continuing to play a large and profitable part in the transport services of the country depended in no small measure on the degree of success achieved by the British Transport Commission in carrying out its statutory task of integrating road and rail services. If railways were to fulfil their appropriate task—the long-distance haulage of goods in bulk—the indiscriminate growth of long-distance road haulage had to be held in check. This Mr Barnes conspicuously failed to do.

At the very first meeting of the British Transport Joint Consultative Council (at which management and unions met to discuss matters not dealt with through the previously established negotiating machinery), held on January 25, 1949, Jim Figgins raised the subject of the decrease of goods traffic carried on British Railways which he attributed largely to the increase in the number of 'C' licensed vehicles by 196,000, or 63 per cent between December 1946 and December 1948. He urged that representations should be made to the Minister. At the second meeting of the Council both the Trade Union and the Transport Commission representatives agreed that Sir Cyril Hurcomb, the Chairman, should tell Mr Barnes of the Council's anxiety at the unrestricted growth of 'C' licences and its effects on the Commission's receipts. In the meantime Jim Figgins had interviewed Mr Barnes and reminded him of his earlier promise to amend legislation if the use of 'C' licences was excessive, but was told by the Minister that he was not 'unduly alarmed'. A deputation, with like purpose, from the Transport Committee of the T.U.C. was equally unsuccessful. Even when Mr H. Clay of the T. & G.W.U. produced before the Consultative Council detailed evidence of 'C' licence holders illegally carrying goods 'for hire or reward' and a memorandum was sent to Mr Barnes by the Council on May 10, 1951, the Minister took no action.[39]

Despite the failure to check the rapid growth of long-distance goods haulage by private carriers, there was still scope for the integration of the Road Haulage Executives services with the goods traffic of the railways. Mr Blee of the Railway Executive told a conference of the railway unions' representatives in October 1948, that the objective in this case was 'to use the road arm to focus into one station in each outer area traffic in such volume as could be made into train loads, so as to avoid triangular transit and the delay inherent in transhipment'.[40]

It was the Transport Commission's policy, intimated to the unions in a letter of May 20, 1949, to use Road Haulage Executive vehicles for zonal collection and delivery schemes from rail heads and for the trunk haul of regular streams of cross-country traffic and to use the railways for long-distance trunk haulage of large consignments; but as late as July 1950, Jim Figgins was obliged to admit that progress in the implementation of this plan had been 'very slow'.[41] The basic reason was that, although the principal officers of the N.U.R. saw the advantages of the scheme and strove hard to make it a success, the members of the union employed in the goods and cartage sections feared the loss of their jobs or a deterioration in their conditions of employment, when collection and delivery work was transferred from the Railway Executive to the Road Haulage Executive. It was very unfortunate that the Transport Commission's spokesman who attended the first discussions with the unions on May 31 and June 21, 1949, had no clear-cut scheme for compensation to those men who might become redundant. Had a comprehensive and clearly-worded promise of full compensation been issued and fully publicized from the start, a great deal of the subsequent delays might well have been avoided.

In the event there was resistance to the speedy introduction of 'pilot' integration schemes in East Anglia and other regions, and some Local Departmental Committees had refused even to discuss the Commission's plans.[42] The A.G.M. delegates at Brighton in July 1949, fearing redundancy, carried by 61 votes to 10, a resolution from the Sunderland No. 2 branch stating '. . . that railway cartage arrangements should definitely be under railway management'.[43] Thus at further meetings between the unions and the two Executives in London in October and November, the N.U.R. spokesmen were obliged to point out that on the question of zonal collection and delivery of goods the union's policy was in direct conflict with that of the Commission. However, after the Commission had made a more detailed explanation of its policy in a letter of November 14th, the E.C., at a special meeting a fortnight later, agreed to co-operate, and full agreement was reached on general principles early in February 1950.

Even then the battle was not over. At Morecambe on July 7, 1950, the A.G.M. carried by 42 votes to 28 an appeal against the E.C. decision of November 28, 1949, to co-operate with the Commission in its integration plans.[44] This was despite the impassioned intervention of Assistant Secretary, J. Campbell, who revealed that there was 'a tremendous amount of bitterness' in the other unions because of the past attitude of the N.U.R. Because he felt so strongly on the question, at a later stage of the Conference Jim Figgins took the unusual step of recommending to the Standing Orders Committee a reconsideration of the earlier King's Cross resolution. In the renewed discussions the General Secretary pleaded— 'If we do not make quick decisions now, more and more traffic will go to the roads'.

He argued that if the E.C. had not decided to continue in the discussions, the T. & G.W.U. would have had the field to itself. A motion to defer implementation of the King's Cross resolution and to instruct the union's representatives to attend an important meeting on integration on July 17th was then carried by 70 votes to 10.[45] It had been a triumph of courage and intense conviction over hesitations and fears.

A month later the S.G.M. in London by 43 votes to 34 realistically decided to rescind the King's Cross resolution.

Although good progress was then made with road-rail integration, there were still difficulties. In the first week of January 1951, staff at St Pancras, who were complaining about inadequate lighting in the loading bays and unsatisfactory arrangements for bonus payments, threatened to stop work from midnight on January 7th, unless the Railway Executive agreed to suspend the trunk conveyance of Road Haulage Executive containers by rail between St Pancras and Glasgow. When the threat was carried out, the E.C. by a majority of five to one, instructed the N.U.R. members involved to resume normal working. Mr Figgins told the Joint Consultative Council that he had done everything possible to persuade the men to stay at work, but the uncompromising attitude of the two Executives (who said that there could not be two separate pay scales for road haulage and railway cartage men) was at the root of the trouble. Eventually, on January 17th, after the Commission had promised to examine nine points of grievance arising from the integration scheme, a mass meeting of the men on January 17th voted for a return to work. Of the strike, Mr Benstead said that he knew of 'no other dispute for which there was so little basis'.

If the railways were to retain goods traffic and attract new business they needed to be able to guarantee speedy delivery. Early in 1949, Mr Allen became alarmed at the loss of orders and came to the conclusion that to speed up goods trains and advance delivery times it was necessary for train crews to do more 'lodging turns'. Here he came up against union policy.

Ironically enough, the sub-committee of the N.U.R. which drafted the National Programme in 1944–5 had not included the abolition of lodging turns in the original draft (mainly with a view to keeping the programme a simple one) but at a joint meeting held on February 8, 1945, the Associated

Society persuaded the N.U.R. committee to include it. Thus negotiations with the companies for the elimination of lodging turns began as early as September 20, 1945, and by the end of 1948, through the agency of a joint sub-committee comprising six representatives of the workers and six of the employers, their number had been reduced by 76 per cent.[47] It was for the very reason that so much headway had been made since 1945 that the proposal to increase lodging turns again in 1949 aroused so much opposition in some areas.

But it would be wrong to assume that feeling on this question was equally strong in all districts. Resentment was greatest on Tyneside, possibly because the lodgings offered on the North Eastern Region were less satisfactory than elsewhere. Mr C. Jones, a goods guard, told the S.G.M. on June 16, 1949, that he had recently had the experience of being obliged to get into a bed just vacated by a man with 'flu.[48] On the other hand there was little resistance to lodging turns by men on the Western to Midland Regions.

In the circumstances it is difficult to understand why there was at first such a united opposition to the re-introduction of the lodging turns, until it is realized that there was a fear of redundancy. G. Romilly, who investigated conditions on the spot, said that it had got about among the men that the Railway Executive considered it had 26,000 surplus staff. 'No railwayman,' he reported, 'wants either to be himself one of those 26,000, or by working overtime and lodging to make someone else into one.'[49]

The Railway Executive was far from tactful in its approach to the problem. Instead of saying: 'Let us consider together how we can speed up the delivery of goods', its spokesmen stressed the time wasted under the existing arrangements and said that there was no other way out than an increase in lodging turns.

Matters came to a head with the refusal of train crews at Gateshead, Heaton, York and other depots on May 22, 1949, to work the new timetables. Only ninety-six men were directly involved. Mr Allen had to withdraw, temporarily, some of the summer services. On May 24th, the E.C. was unanimous in its opposition to the introduction of new lodging turns. Members were 'to immediately cease taking part in unofficial Sunday strikes' but if the Railway Executive took action against any members refusing to work the turns, 'the whole resources of the union would be used, if necessary, to protect them'. A branch circular issued on the following day, whilst promising 'the full support of the organization' for those who refused to lodge, concluded *in block capitals* with an appeal to all members 'not to take part in any unofficial stoppage of work'.[50] Nevertheless the unofficial strikes continued, and on June 9th, Mr Figgins received a telegram from the Railway Executive asking what steps the E.C. proposed to take to secure the restoration of Sunday services. In reply, the E.C. instructed the General Secretary to ask for a meeting 'on the whole question of the principle of additional lodging turns'. When the two sides met on the following day, Mr Allen caused consternation by saying that unless the N.U.R. branch circular of May 25th (which he regarded as an incitement to the men to sabotage the new timetables) was immediately withdrawn, it would not be possible for him to attend the wage negotiations planned for the following day. The union's representatives retorted by saying that if Mr Allen's action became known it would greatly aggravate a difficult situation. Back at Unity House, the E.C. decided 'to seek the personal intervention of the Prime Minister to avert a national stoppage on all sections of British Railways'. But Mr Attlee merely passed the letter on to Mr Isaacs who said that he could only invite the executive 'to give . . . without delay, an undertaking . . . that the Sunday strikes would stop'.[51]

This proved to be the turning point. Mr Isaacs was informed of the steps taken by the E.C. to persuade the men in the North East to resume normal working, and an S.G.M., summoned to London on June 16, 1949, decided by 48 votes to 26 to rescind Decision No. 53 of the A.G.M. of 1947 (which had opposed all lodging turns) 'in view of the urgent need of attracting passenger and goods traffic to the railways'. Finally, a meeting of the E.C. on June 18th decided that the circular letter of May 25th was 'now no longer operative'. The attempt, over a period of two years, to enforce the Ayr resolution of 1947 had, as Jim Figgins admitted, 'created enormous difficulties'. Henceforward, as the S.G.M. resolution stated, it was the policy of the union to continue negotiations 'to eliminate unnecessary lodging turns', but there was no return to the extreme policy of the immediate post-war years.[52]

VI

The problem of British Railways after 1948 was as much one of poor morale as of poor wages. If by 1951 many railwaymen experienced disillusionment with the results of nationalization it was because they lacked any strong sense that the railways were *their concern* in whose future they had an important voice.

In the *Railway Review* of 1946, 1947 and 1948, hundreds of yards of column space were taken up by articles and correspondence on the subject of 'Workers Control'. Since the A.G.M. in 1914 had resolved that railway workers should be given 'a due measure of control and responsibility' in the industry, it had been the official policy of the union that nationalization also meant substantial representation of the workers on the board of management. The first A.G.M. to assemble after the Labour Government had been elected in 1945, was unanimous in emphasizing the view that 'workers' participation in its management is an indispensable requisite to ensure the success of a publicly owned transport industry'.[53]

In part, the later disillusionment sprang from the fact that 'workers' participation in management' meant different things to different people. The National Executive Committee of the Labour Party in its Report on the 'Post War Organization of British Transport' was not contemplating workers' control in the sense of trade-union or working-class nominees forming a majority of the management. The Report stated that the members of the Authority were 'to be appointed on grounds of their competence to conduct the affairs of the industry, and include representatives of the workers', for whom statutory provision was to be made.[54] Likewise the T.U.C. document on 'Public Operation of Transport', approved by the Blackpool Congress in 1945, stated that:

'The Chairman of the Authority would be chosen as being of proved ability in the conduct of large-scale undertakings.'

Other members were to be appointed at the discretion of the Minister 'solely on the grounds of their competence and ability, experience gained "on the job" or in the collective organization of the workpeople, being regarded, in respect of certain members, as an essential qualification'.

Despite the fact that many A.G.M. delegates understood 'workers' participation in management' to mean 'workers' control', during the vital period of transition, the General Secretary of the N.U.R. and the E.C. accepted the policy of the Labour Party and the T.U.C. John Benstead reminded his audience at a pre-conference rally held in the Arcadian Cinema, Morecambe, on June 30, 1946, that 'the trade unions did not control the railways in Russia. The control is placed entirely on the shoulders of the management itself'.[55] When the nationalization sub-committee of the E.C. met Mr Barnes on September 24, 1946, they asked that the railway unions 'should have the opportunity of submitting nominations for representation of the workers on the various Boards or Regional Committees', but emphasized that 'particularly on Boards at the highest levels, those appointed should be appointed on grounds of suitability for the job, and have independence and not be answerable to the nominating bodies but to the Minister'. There was no insistence on trade unionists constituting a majority on any governing body. The E.C. was unanimous in endorsing the action of its sub-committee.[56] The Minister himself was no advocate of workers' control. Defending his action in appointing only one trade unionist (John Benstead) to the British Transport Commission (which at that time had five members), he told the delegates at the A.G.M. at New Brighton on July 9, 1948, that 'nowhere in the world' had 'economic democracy in the fullest sense functioned successfully'. There had been a 'multitude of experiments' in the preceding hundred years, but they had all failed.

It was customary, in thanking a guest speaker, to make only complimentary remarks, but the recently elected General Secretary, Jim Figgins, whose views on this subject were markedly different from those of his predecessor, did not confine himself to pleasantries. Returning to the subject of workers' control, he said: 'It may have failed in the co-operative movement, but I am perfectly certain that we in the railway industry will not fail to solve the problem, because I know of no industry in this country where men have to display greater initiative'.[57]

Two days earlier in Public Session, Conference had reached a unanimous decision directly at variance from the views of the Minister. Reaffirming the belief that workers' participation in the control of the industry at all levels 'was a prerequisite for the success of the undertaking', it claimed the right for wages grades to progress to all supervisory and administrative positions and for workers' representatives to have 'equal rights' with the management in L.D.C.s, Sectional Councils, Works Committees, etc. The E.C. was to seek an interview with the Minister of Transport to give effect 'to the desires of the membership and the needs of the industry'.

The interview with Mr Barnes on September 28th was friendly but unprofitable. The Minister was not prepared to agree to 'so great a change as had been put forward by the union'.

In the meantime, on September 7th at the T.U.C. in Margate, Mr Figgins had spoken to a resolution which expressed concern at the composition of the Boards of the Nationalized Industries and stressed 'the necessity for greater workers' participation'. He believed that unless they could bring conviction to the rank and file that the Nationalized Boards were really in earnest in advancing the cause of nationalization, they were not likely to get that 'enthusiastic support and co-operation' by which it would be possible to make a success of nationalization. The resolution was carried.[59]

However, when the E.C. approached the Railway Executive to give practical application to the principles endorsed by the delegates at Margate, it was offered an elaborate scheme for consultation between management and staff which had much to commend it, but which was no substitute for the policy of joint control of the industry that the A.G.M. had approved. On January 17, 1949 Mr Allen wrote in reply to the N.U.R. claim for 'equal right of decision with the management by staff representatives on L.D.C.s, Sectional Councils, etc.', that 'in certain matters decision must remain with the Railway Executive if that body is to discharge its responsibilities under nationalization'.[60] The extent of the failure of the agitation is seen in the fact that there remained only one trade unionist on the Railway Executive which had seven members.

The annual meetings of the union remained as unshaken as ever in their belief in fuller workers' participation in management. In 1949, the meeting carried by 72 votes to 2 a resolution demanding '50 per cent workers' representation at all levels', and in the following year delegates were unanimous in instructing the E.C. 'to take immediate steps to secure greater participation by the workers in the management of the industry'. But no progress could be made. Mr Barnes re-emphasized that 'ultimate responsibility' would have to rest with the Railway Executive; the E.C. could only 'note the unsatisfactory reply of the Minister'.[61]

Ultimately the chief opportunity for extending workers' responsibility for management in the industry lay in the work of the Joint Training and Education Advisory Council which was an offshoot of the Transport Act; but this was a longer process, and in the meantime the truth of Sir Stafford Cripps's assertion to the T.U.C. on September 7, 1948 that 'you cannot impose efficiency' but that it can only be won by 'the enthusiastic co-operation of the workers', was never more manifest than on the railways.

VII

The appointment of John Benstead as full-time member of the British Transport Commission at the beginning of 1948 set in motion a re-organization of the management of the union. In the first place a new General Secretary had to be elected. The result of the ballot was the victory of Jim Figgins with the biggest majority achieved in any similar contest since the election of J. H. Thomas in 1916:

J. B. Figgins	74,826
S. F. Greene	16,388
J. S. Campbell	8,999
M. Pounder	5,842
J. Barker	5,472
F. E. Bell	5,388
J. T. Weighell	3,491

James Hugh Blair Figgins, who was nearly 55 years old at the time of his election, had been born in Largs, Ayrshire, the son of a small market gardener. The railways had been his career ever since he had left school at the age of 14 to become a junior ticket collector in Glasgow. He served his apprenticeship in union work as Branch Secretary of Glasgow No. 3 (later No. 7) branch, succeeding in that office another distinguished member of the N.U.R., James Campbell. He had been elected to the E.C. in 1931; was Road Transport Organizer from 1938 to 1940 and District Organizer for South East England from 1940–3, before being elected Assistant to the General Secretary. He was a man of intense sincerity and tenacity of purpose who remained throughout his life loyal to his ideal of international brotherhood. In the First World War he was a conscientious objector, and during and after the Second World War he was particularly zealous to maintain the international contacts of the N.U.R. Because Mr Figgins had associated with Communists in the Railwaymen's Minority

Movement in the 1930's and more recently had been in sympathy with them in opposition to a 'standstill' on wages, the *Railway Review*, in the course of the campaign for the election of a General Secretary, had asserted that he was a Communist. Mr Figgins therefore drafted a letter to Harry Pollitt in which he stated he was not a member of the Communist Party, and he read this letter and Pollitt's reply, endorsing the truth of his statement, to the E.C. which decided to make no formal resolution on the matter.[62]

A few months before Mr Figgins was elected General Secretary, the A.G.M. at Ayr in 1947 decided to abolish his old post of 'Assistant to the General Secretary' believing that it was better that, instead, there should be a second Assistant Secretary. As Mr W. J. Watson who had served with devotion as Assistant Secretary, died on July 6, 1947, it became necessary to fill the two posts. In the election of September 1948, Mr M. Pounder of West Hartlepool No. 3 branch, who was the same age as Jim Figgins, and Mr J. S. Campbell, late of Glasgow No. 3, but now of Doncaster No. 1 branch, were successful against three other competitors. Thus the union acquired new leadership just at the time the new Railway Executive was taking up its responsibilities.[63]

As far back as June 1944, the E.C. had supported a plan for the setting up of a Research and Records Section within the Movements Department at Head Office 'immediately circumstances permitted this being done'. But when the war ended there were so many other urgent matters to attend to that it was not until the S.G.M. of February 19, 1948, that a resolution which included this proposal was passed.[64] Before the Research and Records Section came into being later that year, it had been the practice of each Head Office Department to keep its own records—with varying degrees of completeness. On the frequent occasions since 1939 that it had been necessary for the chief officers of the union to present a case to the management for improved wages and hours, a great deal of extra labour had been involved in gleaning information from different departments. With the pooling of records in one section, not only was time saved but also there was a better opportunity to see problems in broader perspective. Had the change been made earlier the union would have been better equipped in 1946–7 to make a case with Mr Barnes for the effective control of road goods haulage.

Another important decision on organization made during the period of the Labour Government concerned the future of the union in Ireland. From the time of the establishment of the Irish Free State in 1922, the N.U.R. had been under attack from nationalists who urged railway and bus workers to join native Irish trade unions. But the organization of the Irish branches was, by a resolution of the S.G.M. on December 21, 1923, put in the capable hands of Mr C. D. Watters, who was assisted by two organizing secretaries (one of whom was withdrawn at the end of 1927). During the Second World War, with Eire remaining neutral, difficulties mounted, especially after the passage of the (Eire) Trade Unions Act in 1941 which provided that unions with headquarters in Great Britain were not to be given the exclusive right to represent any group of workers in negotiations with their employers. Matters came to a head in 1946 when the Coras Iompair Eireann (the transport trust which controls the rail and bus services of the Republic) announced its intention of withdrawing from the Irish Wages Board. The N.U.R. might well have left Ireland then and there had it not been for the decision of the Supreme Court of Eire that year that it was 'repugnant to the constitution' that foreign-based trade unions should be penalized as they were under the Act of 1941.

Given this new lease of life, the union decided at its S.G.M. in London on December 18, 1946, to set up an Irish Negotiating Committee of six persons to deal with all questions affecting wages and conditions which were referred to it, either by the General Secretary or by Mr Watters in Ireland. The Committee did not have power to call a strike, but in order to ascertain the views of the Irish members, a ballot was to be taken before the withdrawal of labour was authorized. The main purpose of the setting up of the Committee and the rules regarding a ballot, was to try to destroy the argument of the nationalists that by some decision of an executive body (i.e. the E.C.) sitting on the other side of the Irish Channel, the domestic economy of Eire could be strangled.[65]

One weakness of the decision made in December 1946 was that the new scheme was to be tried out for a period of five years only, after which the whole future of the union in Ireland would be reconsidered. This encouraged the nationalists to spread a rumour that the N.U.R. would be leaving Eire in 1951; hence it was inadvisable for young railwaymen to join the 'foreign union'.

A conference of representatives of District Councils held in Dublin on January 31, 1950, wanted more powers conferred on the Irish Negotiating Committee but was not in favour of severance of the ties with Great Britain. It was clear that the older membership was still very much attached to the N.U.R. However, the report of a sub-committee of four members of the E.C. released on May 15, 1951, commented on the widely held view in Eire 'that Irish citizens should belong to Irish Trade Unions'. It revealed that whilst older Irish railwaymen retained their membership of the N.U.R., the younger entrants into the transport service joined in ever increasing numbers 'one of the Irish unions based on Dublin'. Consequently the union's membership in Ireland (North and South) had declined from 9,681 in 1947 to 7,522 in 1950.[65]

Despite the fact that at a Conference held in Dublin on April 10-11, 1951, seventy-three out of the eighty-nine Irish branches represented had wanted the N.U.R. to remain in Ireland, the A.G.M. in Hastings, on July 11, 1951, after a five-hour debate in which all the Irish delegates had spoken strongly in favour of maintaining the union's connection with

Ireland, voted by 54–26 in favour of complete withdrawal from the whole of Ireland by the end of 1952. An association which had lasted sixty-six years was to be brought to an end. Apart from the difficulties of contending with a growing nationalism, the union had always found the Irish branches a financial liability. John Benstead told the conference that the net loss to the union over the years had been a quarter of a million pounds.[67]

In the case of the busmen employed in the United Kingdom, the task of the N.U.R. was simplified with the coming into force of a national agreement for rates of pay and conditions of service on February 14, 1946. It was at a meeting of the National Council for the Bus Industry held on April 21, 1944, that Mr Harold Clay of the T. & G.W.U. first submitted to the bus companies a draft agreement for nationally uniform conditions of service based largely on the existing municipal agreements. But agreement on these proposals was held up through the opposition of the British Electric Traction group of companies which preferred the continuance of rates of wages differing from district to district. At a meeting held on September 6, 1945, the representatives of 'independent' companies voted with the trade-union representatives for the acceptance of the scheme, but the five men present from the B.E.T. group opposed, and the chairman was obliged to declare the proposal 'not carried'. On the following day, therefore, Mr Clay, acting on behalf of all the unions, wrote to Mr Isaacs pointing out the deadlock which had arisen. The Minister of Labour persuaded the two sides to come together again, and by January 25, 1946, the companies all agreed to a national scale of wages but would not concede the unions' claim for £5 a week for a top-rate driver. Mr Isaacs therefore appointed a Court of Inquiry which presented its report on April 17th. There were to be two wage scales for drivers and conductors. In Group 1 drivers were to rise from 96s to 100s a week and conductors from 92s to 96s, whilst in Group 2 the rates were from 94s to 98s and from 90s to 94s. Though the recommendations of the Court fell short of what the unions had demanded, a National Conference of Busmen held in London on May 8, 1946, decided by an overwhelming majority to accept the awards. The new scales of pay came into operation on the first full pay day following February 14, 1946.[68]

The task of organizing the men and women employed in the Hotels and Restaurant Rooms was also simplified through the coming into force of the Wages Regulation (Licensed Residential Establishment and Licensed Restaurant) Order of 1948. After negotiations culminating in a meeting of the Railways Staff Conference on April 30, 1948, agreement was reached on the classification of Railway Hotels into three groups, A, B and C, for purposes of wage payments, and minimum weekly rates of pay were established for all grades. The agreement came into operation on April 19, 1948.[69]

VIII

In the six years of Labour rule after the war the political decisions of the union often tended to be critical of Government and T.U.C. policy.

Opinion in the E.C. and among A.G.M. delegates was strongly internationalist in character. Full contact was quickly established with the International Transport Workers' Federation. When that body sent an appeal in September 1945 on behalf of between 500 and 1,000 children of Dutch railwaymen who were rendered homeless by the war, the E.C. decided to contribute £1,500 and to invite, by branch circular, members in the South of England and home counties to take children into their homes. Over 300 offers were received. Later that year 235 of the children were placed in homes as far apart as Ashford (Kent), Southampton and Plymouth. The Portsmouth Medical Officer of Health reported an average gain in weight of over 12 lbs. per child in two months, which was 'the nearest approach to a twentieth century miracle we are likely to hear of for a long time'. The following March, the members who had helped the children received an invitation to visit Holland as the guests of the Dutch Railwaymen's Administration.[70] By 1950 regular invitations were being accepted to the West German Railwaymen's Union Conferences. At the same time the A.G.M. on July 3, 1951, passed with only two dissentients a resolution against the rearmament of Germany and Japan.[71] The E.C. accepted an invitation from the Polish Railway Workers' Union for three of its members to visit Poland in 1951.[72]

Whilst the E.C., in March 1947, rejected by 15 votes to 9 the suggestion of Warrington No. 3 branch that the foreign policy of the Government was 'at variance with Socialist principles', just over a year later an executive, little changed in composition, accepted a resolution from Manchester No. 12 branch which opposed the T.U.C. policy of withdrawal from the Communist-led World Federation of Trade Unions.[73]

The S.G.M. on December 21, 1948, discussed at length a letter sent by the General Council of the T.U.C. to the E.C. on October 27, 1948, urging the union 'to counteract every manifestation of Communist influence' and to take 'energetic steps' to stop the 'evil machinations' which threatened economic recovery. Conference found it impossible either to accept the policy in the T.U.C. document or to make an outright rejection of it. By 52 votes to 27 it rejected the resolution that 'no members of a proscribed organization shall hold office in the N.U.R.', but by 51 votes to 28 it also rejected an amendment that it would not be in the best interests of the membership 'to sanction a policy of discrimination either politically or on trade-union grounds against any section of the membership'. Since the attempts to rescind Decision No. 904 of the 1943 A.G.M. (in favour of the affiliation of the Communist Party to the Labour Party) and to refer the matter to a sub-committee, were also defeated (by 45 to 34 and by 41 to 38) it was presumed that the decision of the 1935 A.G.M. at Hastings, that Rule 9, Clause 14, of the N.U.R. book of rules was a sufficient guarantee of the interests of the union against those seeking to damage them. This provided for the expulsion of a member who, in the opinion of the E.C., attempts to injure the union.

In July 1950, at Morecambe, Conference delegates shared the deepening concern of the rank and file of the Labour Movement at the development of nuclear weapons. With only one dissentient, the meeting carried a resolution which expressed alarm '. . . at the decision of the Government of the United States of America to continue preparation for the manufacture of the hydrogen bomb, since it believes that the pursuit of such a policy must lead to the adoption of similar measures in other countries'.

The E.C. was to use its influence to urge the British Government to appeal to the United Nations with 'all the force and fervour' that the danger demanded, to secure 'the banning of hydrogen bombs, all atomic weapons and all stocks of such weapons, the branding of the first government to use such weapons as an aggressor, international control and inspection of the use of atomic energy and an all round reduction of all forms of armaments'.

It was by no means the last time that this all-important subject was debated at an A.G.M.

NOTES

1. N.U.R., A.G.M., Morecambe, July 1946, R. 17.
2. N.U.R., E.C. February 5, 1946.
3. N.U.R., E.C. June 1946.
4. H. Morrison, *An Autobiography* (London, 1960), p. 259. See also Mr Barnes's statement in the Third Reading debate, May 5, 1947, Hansard 1946–7, Vol. 437, Col. 38.
5. *Reynolds News*, March 30, 1946.
6. Standing Committee B. Official Report Transport Bill, 22nd Sitting, March 20, 1947, Cols. 1017–18.
7. *Daily Herald*, March 21, 1946.
8. *The Economist*, March 15, 1947, p. 391. *The Times*, November 19, 1946.
9. N.U.R., E.C. December 1946, R. 2498.
10. Hansard, May 10, 1950, Vol. 475, Col. 443, quoted in the Rt. Hon. Harold Wilson, M.P.'s 'The Financial Problem of British Transport', p. 31, 1951, a report addressed to the executives of the three railway unions.
11. *The Economist*, November 23, 1946, p. 836.
12. *R.R.*, January 9, 1948.
13. N.U.R., E.C. December 1950, R. 3222.
14. N.U.R., General Secretary's Report to the A.G.M. 1945, p. 12 and 1946, p. 14 and E.C. August 9, 1945, R. 1213.
15. N.U.R., E.C. September 1945, p. 213.
16. N.U.R., E.C. January 17, February 19, October 10, November 1 and 20 and December 1946, p. 369.

17. Cmd. 7161 of 1947.
18. N.U.R., E.C. July 4, 1947, R. 1622. Meeting with London Passenger Transport Board recorded in E.C. Minutes, August 7, 1947. The Railway Shopmen's National Council gave its approval on July 22, 1947.
19. Cmd. 7321 of 1948.
20. N.U.R., A.G.M. July 1948, R. 83. E.C. August 11, September 18, October 26, December 28, 1948. S.G.M. December 21, 1948, R. 8. E.C. January 7 and 17, 1949, R.S.N.T., March 11, 18, 1949, p. 5.
21. N.U.R., S.G.M. April 21, 22 and 28, 1949, Verbatim Report. See especially the report back of Jim Figgins on April 28th, pp. 4 *et seq.*
22. Railway Executives' proposals in Appendix R. E.C. Minutes September 1949, p. 603. E.C. Decision, June 4, 1949, R. 1673.
23. 'Report of a Board of Conciliation appointed by the Minister of Labour and National Service to assist in the consideration and settlement of certain problems relating to salaries, wages and conditions of service of the Conciliation and Salaried Grades on the Railways'. September 8, 1949. N.U.R., S.G.M. September 29, 1949, Verbatim Report, p. 14.
24. N.U.R., S.G.M. September 30, 1949, Verbatim Report, p. 5.
25. N.U.R., E.C. October 4, 1949, R. 2791.
26. N.U.R., E.C. November 29, 1949, R. 3131.
27. N.U.R., A.G.M. July 1930, R. 30.
28. N.U.R., E.C. December 1950, p. 188.
29. Court of Inquiry Minutes of Proceedings, January 11, 1951. Statement by Mr Figgins, p. 190. Report Cmd. 8154 of 1951, pp. 50–4.
30. This account of wage negotiations is based on Minutes of Proceedings and Documents submitted to the Court of Inquiry, January 4–11, 1951, and Report Cmd. 8154, February 13, 1951. N.U.R., S.G.M. February 27th, Verbatim Report of Mr J. Figgins's speech to the Conference, and E.C. Minutes.
31. Minutes of Proceedings of the Court of Inquiry, January 11, 1951. Evidence of Mr J. Figgins, p. 192.
32. N.U.R., E.C. Minutes, September 28 and November 8, 1945, Rs. 1724 and 1865.
33. *Railway Gazette*, March 7, 1947. N.U.R., E.C. February 13–18, 1947, R. 199.
34. N.U.R., E.C. June 23 and July 27, 1948.
35. N.U.R., E.C. May 7, 1947, R. 1121.
36. N.U.R., E.C. May 1, 1947, R. 1005.
37. N.U.R., E.C. September 1950, p. 279; December 1950, p. 183; June 1951, Appendix J. 40, p. A125; December 1951, Appendix D. 39, p. A139 and R. 3177.
38. N.U.R., A.G.M. July 11, 1951, Verbatim Report, p. 104. Speech of Mr J. Figgins. E.C. July 18, 1951; report of meeting with Railway Executive and R. 1885.
39. British Transport Joint Consultative Council Minutes of Meetings held on January 25 and April 1, 1949, and October 12, 1951. N.U.R., S.G.M. July 28, 1949, Verbatim Report, pp. 34–5. Speech of Mr J. Figgins.
40. *Labour Research*, December 1948, p. 223.
41. N.U.R., General Secretary's Report to the A.G.M. 1950, p. 17.
42. N.U.R., E.C. September 1949, Appendices Z and AA, and E.C. October 18, November 29, 1949.
43. N.U.R., A.G.M. 1949, R. 160.
44. N.U.R., A.G.M. 1950, R. 51.
45. N.U.R., A.G.M. July 19, 1950, Verbatim Report, p. 43.

46. N.U.R., E.C. January 8, 12 and 16, 1951, R. 56, and March 1951, Appendix M. 4, and British Transport Joint Consultative Council Minutes, January 26, 1951, p. 10.
47. According to Mr Allen at a meeting held on March 2, 1949. N.U.R., E.C. March 1949, Appendix UU.
48. N.U.R., S.G.M. June 16, 1949, Verbatim Report, p. 79.
49. *New Statesman*, July 16, 1949, p. 62.
50. N.U.R., E.C. May 24, 1949, p. 11 and R. 1574. *The Economist*, June 4, 1949, p. 1031.
51. N.U.R., E.C. June 7, 1949, p. 49 and R. 1683.
52. N.U.R., S.G.M. June 16, 1949, R. 5 and speech of Mr Figgins. Verbatim Report, p. 108.
53. N.U.R., A.G.M. 1946, R. 145a.
54. P. 5.
55. *R.R.*, July 5, 1946. In the Conference debate the following day, E. A. Arnold of Boston No. 1 Branch said: 'We want to have the workers in control, not as has been arranged in the mining industry'. Verbatim Report, p. 57.
56. N.U.R., E.C. December 1946, R. 2497.
57. N.U.R., A.G.M. July 9, 1948, Verbatim Report, pp. 71, 83.
58. N.U.R., E.C. December 1948, R. 2182.
59. Report of the 80th T.U.C., Margate, 1948, p. 371.
60. N.U.R., E.C. December 1948, R. 3151; March 1949, R. 113; and Appendices G and Q; April 1949, Appendix J.
61. N.U.R., E.C. December 1950, R. 3247.
62. N.U.R., S.G.M. December 21, 1948, Verbatim Report, p. 72.
63. N.U.R., E.C. October 8, 1948, R. 2225.
64. N.U.R., S.G.M. February 19, 1948, R. 5.
65. N.U.R., S.G.M. December 18, 1946, Verbatim Report, p. 47, R. 6.
66. N.U.R., Agenda and Decisions of the A.G.M., July 1951, pp. 121–41.
67. N.U.R., A.G.M. July 8, 1946, Verbatim Report, p. 61.
68. National Council of the Bus Industry. Minutes of Meetings held on April 21, 1944, September 6, 1945 and January 25, 1946. N.U.R., General Secretary's Report to the A.G.M. 1946, p. 36.
69. N.U.R., E.C. September 1948, Appendix V, p. 509.
70. N.U.R., E.C. September 1945, p. 238; September 21, 1945, p. 5; December 1945, p. 294; General Secretary's Report to the A.G.M. 1946, and E.C. May 1946, p. 253.
71. N.U.R., E.C. August 25, 1950, and November 10, 1950, p. 114.
72. N.U.R., E.C. March 1951, R. 845.
73. N.U.R., E.C. March 1947, R. 276 and December 1948, R. 2615.

CHAPTER XXII

THE TRANSPORT ACT, 1953, AND ITS AFTERMATH

> '*The nation has provided, by statute, that there shall be a nationalized system of railway transport, which must therefore be regarded as a public utility of first importance. Having willed the end, the Nation must will the means. This implies that the employees of such a service should receive a fair and adequate wage and that, in broad terms, the railwayman should be in no worse case than his colleague in a comparable industry.*'
> Interim Report of a Court of Inquiry into a dispute between the British Transport Commission and the N.U.R., January 1955.

I

THE Transport Act of 1947 had its weaknesses, but these should not blind us from recognizing it as a major work of constructive statesmanship. It would be equally foolish to ignore the outstanding achievements of the British Transport Commission in the period 1948–52. After 1951, the Conservative Government undermined the provisions of the 1947 Act, not because the experiment had been a failure, but because it was becoming increasingly successful. In the first four years of its existence the Commission was beginning to reveal the substantial advantages of transport co-ordination and planned development. But from the Conservative point of view, it was dangerous for the public to become too conscious of the advantages of socialized transport.

The publicly owned transport services of Britain earned operating surpluses of £165 million in the years 1948–51 inclusive. It was only after the deduction of interest charges on compensation stock (£176 million), capital redemption charges (£13½ million), Central administration expenses (£4 million) and freight rebates (£11 million) that the accounts of the British Transport Commission were in deficit. And the situation was improving, not worsening, at the end of the four years. In 1951 the Commission earned a small surplus of £100,00 after meeting all central charges. This encouraging improvement may be compared with the situation in 1947, the last year before nationalization, when the receipts of the four main line railway companies and the London Passenger Transport Board fell short of their operating costs by £16 million, a sum which, together with the £43½ million guaranteed net revenue, was met from taxation.

The favourable trend in the net receipts of the Commission was made possible by more economical operation of rail and road services. The efficiency of rail freight haulage is most clearly shown in the figures for net ton miles hauled per total engine hours in service. These rose from 461 in 1938 to 543 in 1948 and 595 in 1951. Freight carried on the railways in 1951, at nearly 285 million tons, was an all-time record and was achieved with 1,000 fewer engines than were in service in 1948. Average passenger train loadings in 1951 were also greater than pre-war, the Commission's Report for that year telling of improvement 'by more than a quater, public impressions to the contrary notwithstanding'. These results were obtained despite a decline in the numbers employed by British Railways from over 650,000 at the beginning of 1948 to under 600,000 at the end of 1951.[1] Even more remarkable was the improvement in efficiency of the Road Haulage Executive after its early teething troubles had been passed. It is true that from January 1, 1948 to July 1, 1952, freight rates charges by the Executive increased by 30 per cent—largely on account of the increased costs of labour and of fuel oil—but private hauliers' rates over the same period increased by 40 per cent. The Executive had a smaller proportion of administrative staff and a larger proportion of operating staff per vehicle than was the case with the private hauliers and this, together with its greater success in reducing the amount of empty running of vehicles, enabled it to increase its financial surplus from £1·1 million in 1948 to £3·2 million in 1951 and £8·9 million in 1953, the last year before its disbandment.[2]

All the signs were of increased efficiency of operation of the Commission's undertakings and an increasing effectiveness of its measures to co-ordinate road and rail goods services.

II

The defeat of the Labour Government in the General Election of October 29, 1951, brought to a halt these promising developments. With a clear majority of 17 over all their opponents, the Conservatives were in a position to give statutory expression to their very different views on transport policy.

The N.U.R. was still strongly represented in the new Parliament. Each of the nine members of the union's Parliamentary Panel who sought re-election was successful. The election of two non-panel candidates brought the total union representation up to eleven. Even in the General

Election of 1955 there were few casualties, as eight of the nine 'panel' M.P.s were again returned. The big set back for the group did not come until 1959 when the defeat of Messrs Champion, Jones and Sparks, by very narrow margins—in Champion's case it was twelve votes—reduced N.U.R. strength in Parliament to five—exactly one third of what it had been in 1945. The A.G.M. at Paignton, on July 7, 1953, carried unanimously a resolution expressing 'warm appreciation' of the work of the union's M.P.s in the debates on the Transport Bill of that year.

The history of Conservative transport policy in the 'fifties may be divided into two phases. In the period to the end of 1954 the unified undertaking painstakingly built up since the beginning of 1948 was partially dismembered under the provisions of the Transport Act of 1953. In the second phase, from 1955 onwards, through the Railway Modernization Plan and such measures as the Transport (Railway Finances Act) of 1957, which increased the Transport Commission's borrowing powers, a largely unsuccessful attempt was made to repair the damage inflicted a short while before. Predominantly 'free enterprise' governments in France and West Germany, over the same period, felt no necessity to sabotage public transport as a form of 'creeping Socialism'. Consequently their private road haulage was (and still is) restricted by legislation and 'the general rules under which competition is governed within the community' (i.e. the common market) 'do not apply to transport'.[3] Only in Britain was transport policy so bedevilled by politics that the solemn farce was enacted of a Government allocating with one hand £1,200 million to repair the damage inflicted, but two years earlier, by the other.

Even while the Labour Government was still in office a sustained attempt was made to undermine the most profitable of the Transport Commission's undertakings—British Road Services. On November 21, 1950, the House of Lords gave a second reading to a Bill, sponsored by Lord Teynham, which provided for the radius of operation of private hauliers' vehicles to be extended from 25 miles to 60 miles. Power of granting, extending and removing road haulage licences was to be taken away from the Transport Commission and handed over to local licensing authorities. But it did not prove possible to push this Bill through all its stages before the outcome of the General Election provided the opportunity for a more thoroughgoing assault on the public sector of transport.

In the summer of 1949 *The Commercial Motor* appealed to road hauliers to contribute to Conservative Central Office Funds.[4] Those who responded to this appeal would have been gratified to read in the King's Speech delivered within a fortnight of the Conservative election victory of 1951 the brief sentence: 'Proposals will be made to facilitate the extension of private road haulage activities.'

The White Paper, Transport Policy (Cmd. 8538) which followed in May 1952, outlined the new Government's plans for the future organization of the industry. In it it was asserted that the process of restriction of road haulage 'to avoid excessive competition between road and rail' had gone so far as to 'deprive trade and industry of the full advantages of modern road transport' and had 'driven private traders to provide their own road transport to an extent which would not otherwise have occurred'. The undertakings of the Road Haulage Executive were therefore 'to revert to private enterprise'. The 'excessive centralization' of the railways would be reduced by granting greater autonomy to regional administration.

In the view of *The Economist*, the White Paper could be described as 'a set of contrivances to make the resale to private bidders of lorries, now owned by the Transport Commission, look respectable'. The document was condemned as offering 'no study of any of the serious issues on Transport—the terms on which rail and road transport can live together, the public obligations each should assume, the nature of their costs and the best way in which they could be organized and managed'.[5] The E.C. of the N.U.R. found it 'unfortunate that political spite, and a complete lack of community interest, should cause the Conservative Government to propose legislation which, in the ultimate, will be detrimental to transport services as a whole and railways in particular'. It declared that it would 'not tolerate any worsening of railwaymen's wages and conditions' because of a 'lessening of railway revenues caused by this anti-public policy'. The National Executive of the Labour Party was urged to declare that, when a Labour Government was returned to power, it would 'compulsorily acquire all state property handed over to private individuals or companies ... without compensation of any description'.[6] It is, therefore, not surprising that when Morgan Phillips wrote to Jim Figgins on May 16th, asking whether the N.U.R. would be prepared to co-operate in a national campaign to resist the denationalization of road transport, he received an enthusiastic response.

In the meantime the Government presented its Transport Bill to Parliament on July 8, 1952. It was a measure which *The Economist* described as being 'virtually devoid of principles'. What was to happen to the railways was 'almost as obscure as the objects of a South Sea Company'. The Bill, which bore 'all the marks of haste, lack of fundamental thought and back bench pressure to secure a victory for "free enterprise" in road haulage', would be likely to 'promote confusion and inefficiency'.[7]

The reason for this strong condemnation was that the Bill provided for the disposal by a Road Haulage Disposal Board of the bulk of the Road Haulage Executive's vehicles to private bidders, thus depriving the Transport Commission of its most profitable undertaking and seriously threatening the viability of the transport services as a whole. Whilst maintaining the Common Carrier principle for the railways—the obligation to carry all goods presented for dispatch however unprofitable their carriage might be—it imposed no obligation of that kind on the road hauliers who were left free to vary their charges at will and to accept or decline traffic according to its degree of profitability.

It was scarcely to be expected that the A.G.M. of the N.U.R. held at Scarborough would give a warm welcome to the Bill. In public session on July 10, 1952, delegates gave unanimous support to a resolution which expressed 'profound regret' on the Government's decision to adopt a policy which would 'affect adversely the whole structure of transport'. The return of any part of nationalized transport to private enterprise would be an 'act of sabotage inspired by selfish sectional interests'. All workers in the industry were urged to unite to defeat the Government, and the demand, made earlier by the E.C., that the Labour Party, on resuming power, should restore to Public Ownership 'without loss to the community' any part of transport which was denationalized, was repeated in this resolution.[8]

In fact, Mr. Morrison had already declared in the House of Commons, on May 21, 1952, that:

'... if ... a Labour Government with a working majority is returned to Parliament, we shall return to public ownership such operable units as are necessary for a co-ordinated transport system ... we shall see to it that the public purse does not pay again for what has already been paid for out of the funds of public authority.'[9]

Partly because of pressure of other business but, one suspects, mainly because of the severe criticisms which had been made of its terms, the Government announced on July 10th that it would postpone further consideration of the Transport Bill until the autumn.

The respite afforded by the Summer Recess was used by the Minister of Transport, Mr Lennox Boyd, to remove some of the more obnoxious clauses of the Bill. In the debate in the Commons on May 21, 1952, Sir R. Glynn, the ex-Railway director member, from the Conservative benches, said that he had 'not met one person who approved the White Paper'. He criticized the Bill on the grounds that it took away from the railways 'any possibility of their ever paying'. The Minister, therefore, inserted into Clause 19 of the revised Bill (which appeared on November 5th) provisions giving the railways greater freedom to vary their charges, and exempting them from laws against the granting of undue preferences. The Minister met a criticism of the N.U.R. M.P.s that the railways were not being allowed to retain sufficient collection and delivery vans, by increasing from 4,000 to 5,000, the number of road vehicles the Commission was to be allowed to retain for the use of the railways.

Although the union had expressed the strongest possible opposition to the Government's proposals, the E.C. considered it wise to accept the invitation to the trade unions to consult him made by Mr Lennox Boyd in the House of Commons on May 21, 1952. At a meeting of the General Council of the T.U.C. on November 26th, Jim Figgins urged that when they saw the Minister they should stress that if the Railway Executive was abolished it should be made clear that wage negotiations should be continued on a national basis by the Transport Commission and not on the regional basis through the Regional Boards it was proposed to set up. The Minister agreed to this recommendation when he met a delegation from the unions in a committee room of the House on December 5th. When urged to alter the constitution of the B.T.C. to make it possible for more than one representative of the trade unions to be a member of the Commission, the Minister would not alter the wording of the Bill although he said it was 'not necessarily the intention to restrict trade-union representation on the Commission to one'. He did give the unions the dubious honour of the offer of a seat on the Road Haulage Disposal Board, but the offer was declined at a further meeting held on December 9th. At a third meeting, held three days later, Mr Lennox Boyd assured the members of the N.U.R. present that none of the arrangements made for pensions under Sections 95 and 96 of the Transport Act of 1947, would be altered. In the course of these consultations the trade unionists learned that the Transport Commission had recommended the disbandment of the Railway Executive.

In the meantime, in the House of Commons, Mr Ernest Davies largely demolished one of the main arguments used by the Minister in justification for his Bill. Mr Lennox Boyd had spoken of the Commission's 'huge fleet of road transport vehicles under the control of a massive and impersonal organization, unable to meet the resilient and flexible demands of a large trading community'. As a result 'in an effort to get out of these difficulties a large number of people in recent years' had taken out 'C' licences. But Mr Davies showed that the biggest increase in 'C' licences occurred *before* the B.T.C. began to take over road haulage vehicles in 1949 and that, thereafter, the number of new 'C' licences issued each month had fallen from the peak of 8,600 in 1948 to 5,064 in 1950, and 3,733 in the second quarter of 1952.[11] The lesson of these figures was that traders rushed to acquire 'C' licences when the 'C' licence clauses were withdrawn from the 1947 Bill, but that increasingly, as they sampled the services of the Road Haulage Executive, they found them satisfactory. This interpretation squares with the comment of *The Economist* that there was 'a growing body of evidence that hasty denationalization would disrupt the trunk road haulage services on which traders relied and which on the whole they found efficient and economical'.[12]

Nevertheless, as a result of the use of the guillotine, the Transport Bill was read a third time in the Commons on February 16th and, with the Royal Signature, became law on May 6, 1953. By its enactment the Road Haulage, Docks and Inland Waterways, Hotels and Railway Executives were abolished, the work of administration of these bodies being transferred to departments of the B.T.C. From the end of 1954, private road hauliers were to be freed from the restriction of the 25-mile radius of operation to which they had been subject since January 1, 1948. From October 1, 1953, the Commission was to take over the functions of the Railway Executive, but it was under obligation to prepare a scheme for the reorganization of railway management. This it did in the plan for regional boards announced in the Government White Paper in July 1954.

The effect of the introduction of the new measure on the finances of the Commission were not immediately felt. A £4,560,000 surplus was declared in 1952 and a further surplus of £4,200,000 in 1953, in both cases after deductions had been made for central charges and for capital redemption.[13] Thereafter from 1954 to 1956 the Commission continued to earn a working surplus but was increasingly in deficit after the payment of central charges. From 1956 onwards the railways, and from 1957 onwards, the Commission as a whole, experienced working deficits.

It would be wrong to attribute these depressing results solely to the introduction of the Transport Act 1953—though this did lop off the bough that bore the best fruit. Among the other factors which aggravated the decline in railway revenues was the rapid increase in the number of private cars licensed in Britain after the ending of petrol rationing in 1950—it rose from over four million in 1950 to over nine million in 1960. The increase in the number of 'C' licensed vehicles from 733,000 to 1,204,000 in the same decade played its part, together with the now unrestrained activities of the private hauliers, in reducing the railway's share of inland goods transport from 54 per cent of the ton miles carried in 1952 to 42 per cent in 1959. The fact that the railways were not in a position to increase capital expenditure fast enough to enable them to scrap obsolete equipment—their proportion of United Kingdom capital investment fell from 3 per cent in 1948 to 2 per cent in 1951—tended to weaken their competitive position. Throughout the 'fifties the cost of materials the railways used rose faster than did the charges the Commission was permitted to levy for the services it rendered. In December 1955, whilst wholesale prices were 249 per cent above the level of December 1938, freight charges had only risen by 175 per cent in the same period, and whilst retail prices in July 1957 had risen 165 per cent above the pre-war level, passenger rail fares had only increased by 110 per cent.[14] Politics also bedevilled the Commission's finances. In April 1952, after permission had been obtained from the Transport Tribunal to increase fares in the London Region, Mr Churchill intervened, just before the L.C.C. elections, to prevent the recommendation being put into effect. It was estimated that this and a similar intervention in 1956, lost the Commission at least £15 million in revenue.[15]

These were the grim realities which made so formidable the main task

September 1919—Great Railway Strike (Main Line Signals, Waterloo)

PLATE 13

May 1926. Miss Talbot, volunteer lorry driver

of the N.U.R. in this period—the maintenance of the standard of living of the railwaymen.

Whilst some of the measures introduced by the Government in the second half of the 'fifties were constructive, if long overdue, reforms, others were in the nature of stop-gap expedients. Neither succeeded in bringing the railways 'out of the red'.

The Transport Commission's Plan for the Modernization and Re-equipment of British Railways, published in December 1954, may be placed in the first of these two categories. Its purpose was 'to exploit the great natural advantages of railways as bulk transporters of passengers and goods and to revolutionize the character of the services provided for both'. Approximately £1,200 million was to be spent on an extended use of power signalling, centralized traffic control, the replacement of steam by diesel and electric power for locomotives, the fitting of continuous brakes for goods wagons, the replacement of many older-style marshalling yards by fewer, automatically controlled 'hump' yards, the mechanization of office equipment and many other improvements.

On July 6, 1955, the A.G.M. of the N.U.R. passed unanimously a resolution welcoming 'the modernization and re-equipment proposals of the British Transport Commission'. The meeting, however, warned that the response of the railwaymen would be 'conditioned by the attitude of the management in the matter of adequate safeguards and reasonable incentives'. So that the membership would be 'free to co-operate without fear of redundancy or reduction in grade, or a worsening of conditions of service', the E.C. was instructed to open negotiations with the Commission.[16] Jim Campbell got to the crux of the problem when he wrote:

'What has to be done is to convince the staff that their interests are adequately protected and, indeed, that the fulfilment of the plan is to their advantage.'

His task with the Commission was to persuade it that '... any man rendered redundant should retain his rate of pay until he regains his original status by reason of natural wastage or other means.'[17] Both sides needed a lot of convincing.

A year after the conference resolution welcoming the Modernization Plan, the delegates at the Annual Grade Conference of N.U.R. shopmen members carried unanimously a 'priority' resolution expressing great alarm at 'the policy of the B.T.C. in relation to the closing of shops and depots, the treatment of the staff concerned, also the placing of contracts with private firms, which leads to redundancy in railway workshops'. In the same month the union's annual conference, 'whilst appreciating the modernization and productivity proposals of the B.T.C.' was concerned for the future employment of railwaymen and instructed the E.C. 'to press for the immediate implementation of the forty-hour week'.[18]

(Lest it be charged that the rank and file did not welcome the Modernization Plan with unbounded enthusiasm, it needs to be pointed out that during the brief life of the Commission since the beginning of 1948, the number of railwaymen employed had declined by 86,000 *before* the publication of the Plan. It was likely to decline at an even faster rate during its implementation. Many thousands more would be obliged to uproot themselves and find new homes, sometimes far removed from their relatives and friends. Even for those with assured and more adequate professional incomes, such uprooting is often distasteful; for those, like many of the railwaymen, with incomes nearer the margin of subsistence, the change was more to be dreaded.)

On grounds of expense the Commission rejected the 40-hour week as a solution of the redundancy problem—it was not until 1962 that a further step in that direction was taken with the reduction of hours from 44 to 42 per week.

Securing an adequate redundancy agreement for the footplate grades was very much tied up with the question of the manning of diesel and electric locomotives. When negotiations between the B.T.C. and the unions on this subject opened in the spring of 1956 the prospects for an agreement seemed remote. Mr Allen argued that the general principle for the manning of the new locomotive should be 'one man only on the footplate'. The members of the negotiating committee of the N.U.R. said that this was 'not conducive to the safe working of the railways', though they added that 'there would be no difficulty in getting the men to accept new ideas if they could be assured that their position would be safeguarded'. By mid-July 1957, through concessions made by both sides, the main principles of an agreement were discernible, although it was not until December 18, 1957, that the final details were worked out and an agreement was signed. Single manning of the new locomotives was to be the rule on passenger trains where the distance run was not in excess of 200 miles or the distance between stops more than 100 miles. For freight trains fitted with continuous brakes, single manning was to apply for distances up to 150 miles provided the distance between stops was less than 75 miles. There was to be a 'physical needs' break between the third and fifth hours of running. As well as for the longer distance runs, double manning was to apply where the dead man's device was not fitted, where it was necessary to attend to steam heating arrangements, and during the hours between midnight and 6.0 a.m., except for trains scheduled to finish between midnight and 1.0 a.m. or to start between 5.0 and 6.0 a.m.[19]

The redundancy agreement for footplate staff which came into operation on September 2, 1957, was an amplification of earlier agreements and was designed especially to take into account changes brought about by the modernization plan. Drivers, firemen and cleaners who, owing to redundancy, had to be offered lower-rated posts were, under certain conditions, allowed to remain on their old rates of pay for a period of three years and during that time were to be entitled to receive any increments normally awarded. An agreement for compensation for loss of promotion in the footplate grades was approved by the E.C. on July 16, 1957. Firemen who completed ten years' service were to be paid the drivers' minimum rate. Those who completed fifteen years' service were to be paid the rate for a driver in his second year and those who completed twenty years' service were to receive the driver's maximum rate. Cleaners who completed ten years' service were entitled to be paid the minimum rate for a fireman.[20]

A new redundancy agreement for salaried staff and conciliation staff other than footplate staff was negotiated by May 1957. It contained the same basic principle that a member of staff declared redundant in his old grade was to receive his old rates of pay with any increments to which he was entitled, for a period of three years, provided he accepted any 'reasonable offer' of alternative employment in the railway service. Members of all grades who were still redundant after the expiry of three years were entitled to have their cases considered in the appropriate sectional council. If they were not satisfied with the treatment of their case the matter could be referred for discussion between the Regional Staff Headquarters and the Trade Union.[21] Because of the more complicated nature of the problem and the quicker pace of run-down of railway workshop employment, it did not prove possible to reach a redundancy agreement for shopmen until April 30, 1959. The Memorandum of Agreement then reached in the Railway Shopmen's National Council, included a similar three-year guarantee of pay to that given to the conciliation grades, but also included lump sum compensation payments for dismissed employees, varying from a minimum of two thirds of basic piecework rates for a fortnight for a man with between three and five years' adult service, to a minimum of two thirds of thirteen weeks' pay for a man with over thirty-eight years' adult service. Unemployment pay received was to be deducted from these lump sum payments.[22]

Although these arrangements, which the union had helped to negotiate, were in the 'copper handshake' rather than the 'golden handshake' class, they went some way towards reconciling the Transport Commission's staff to many innovations which involved the blocking of promotion or even the loss of employment.

Before the benefits to transport of the Modernization Scheme could be reaped the financial position of the Commission deteriorated further. In the White Paper 'Proposals for the Railways' published in October 1956, the Government proposed that 'for a specified number of years, broadly until the revenue account of the Commission is expected to be in balance', loans limited in total amount to £250 million should be made to the Commission from the Consolidated Fund.[23] The Transport (Railway Finances)

Act of 1957 gave effect to these proposals in that it allowed the Commission to obtain loans equal to any deficits incurred on Revenue account during the years 1956–62 inclusive. It also authorized borrowings to enable the Commission to pay interest on the above-mentioned deficit loans and to borrow further to pay interest on the capital borrowed for modernization. These transactions were undertaken during a time of credit squeeze. Thus on much of the money borrowed, the already financially overburdened Commission was required to pay interest of over 6 per cent. Although the amounts to be advanced were, in 1957, limited to £250 million, these proved inadequate, and under the Transport (Borrowing Powers) Act of 1959 the limit of borrowing was raised to £400 million.

The financial background to the union's struggle to maintain railway wages at a level sufficient to keep pace with the rise in the cost of living was aptly summarized by a writer in the *New Left Review*:

'The railways were borrowing money to pay the interest on the interest on the money borrowed to pay the interest on compensation stock.'[24]

This was the millstone round the neck of the Transport Commission which put such severe limits to its ability to pay adequate wages to its staff.

III

In the 'fifties the executive committee of the N.U.R. had a well deserved reputation for its moderation and sense of responsibility. That such a body should come to a unanimous decision in favour of a national railway strike on no less than three occasions—December 9, 1953, December 21, 1954, and January 29, 1960—is a measure of the seriousness of the wages problem on the railways during this period. On a fourth occasion, May 7, 1958, there was a majority decision in favour of strike action.

It is understandable that it proved an easier task for the Commission to meet the wage claims of the unions in the years 1951 and 1952, when it was making a financial surplus, than it was from 1953 onwards when its accounts were increasingly 'in the red'.

The increase of 8 per cent on all salaries and wages awarded by the Railway Staff National Tribunal in its Decision No. 13 of November 7, 1951, though falling short of the 10 per cent the N.U.R. considered necessary to offset the rise in the cost of living and to stop the drift of labour from the industry, was nevertheless the nearest approach to the full satisfaction of the union's claim of any of the awards made after 1945. There was also less of a time lag between the presentation of the claim and the conclusion of an agreement than was often the case. The claim was first submitted to the Railways Staff Conference on July 30, 1951, and the award was made operative from September 3, 1951. That such quick results were achieved was due not only to the state of finances of the Commission. On this occasion the three unions were united in their main demand for a 10 per cent rise in wages, though the Associated Society also asked for enhanced payment for Saturday afternoon duty, Sunday duty and Sunday-Monday turns of duty. The Tribunal met this last claim (in part) by granting flat rate increases varying from 2·0d to 5·0d.

Owing to the continued rise in the cost of living, the General Secretary informed the E.C. of the N.U.R. at its special meeting on April 7, 1952, that many branches had submitted resolutions asking the executive to demand a further increase in wages. The outcome was a joint meeting of representatives of the three railway unions on May 9th, when it was unanimously agreed to ask for a 10 per cent increase in wages and the substitution of a new agreement for Saturday afternoon working (an addition of half the time rates to the existing Saturday afternoon rates) for the one reached by R.S.N.T. Decision No. 13.[25]

On this occasion the time lag between the submission of the claim and the operative date for the award of the Tribunal was twenty-five weeks, compared with five weeks in the case of the previous claim. The Commission's case for resisting this further demand of the unions was that the only effective way of meeting a substantial increase in wage levels was to increase railway charges, and it was doubtful whether the passenger traffic could bear an increase in fares without a disproportionate loss of traffic. On the other hand, Mr Figgins had a very strong case when he told the Tribunal on October 6, 1952, that, compared with June 1947, the cost of living in May 1952, had risen by 35 per cent whereas railway wages had only risen by 16·1 per cent and during the same period the average rise in wages and salaries in outside industries had been 29 per cent. The award of the Tribunal, in its Decision No. 14, operative from November 1, 1952, was for a flat rate increase of 7s a week for adult males in the salaried and conciliation staff, with 5s 6d for adult females, 4s for junior males and 3s for junior females. It was not so well received in the branches as the previous award had been and it was unpopular with the Associated Society because it narrowed wage differentials.

When, in December 1952, the Earls Court branch suggested to the E.C. that since the 7s award 'solved nothing' it should seek the help of the other unions in demanding a 15 per cent increase in pay, the members of the Executive were in unanimous agreement with Jim Figgins that the claim would 'not have the slightest chance of success'. Four months later the response to a similar demand from the Bethnal Green Branch was different. The negotiating committee was asked to take up the matter with the other unions and, at a joint meeting on July 2nd, there was complete agreement to press the Commission for a 15 per cent increase. Both direct negotiations with the Railway Executive, and discussions in the Railway

Staff National Council, were barren of result so that the claim was forwarded for hearing by the Tribunal from November 9th to 11th, inclusive.

Jim Campbell, who put the N.U.R.'s case to the Tribunal, made much of the fact that current wages of railwaymen were lagging behind the wages of those with comparable skill and responsibility in other occupations. He showed that a passenger guard's maximum wage was £6 19s od a week, whilst a postman, aged twenty-eight, was paid £7 8s od. He cited a very long list of letters from experienced, qualified men in the higher grades of the railway service who had left their jobs for the better pay and more regular hours of work in other industries. His reporting of the case of a signalman who became a bookie's clerk because he thought the odds were in his favour, brought some light relief to the proceedings. But he spoke forcibly and with feeling on the subject of overtime earnings:

'The basic wage should provide for basic needs. Extra earnings for working on Sundays, rest days or overtime are legitimate penalty payments and it is unfair to quote them in opposition to an application for a wage increase.

'Many a railwayman is compelled to work on his rest day because of shortage of staff. Overtime is worked for the same reason. Is it fair to attempt to deprive him of a reasonable basic wage if he earns extra by working longer hours ?'[26]

There was also the point that there was 'no average man'. Many railwaymen were not in a position to take home more than the basic wage.

All these were strong arguments. But the railways were beginning to feel the pinch of the increase in goods haulage by private carriers who were by this time freed from the restraints of the 1947 Act. The Award (No. 15) made by Sir John Forster, K.B.E., A.C., and his two assistants on the Tribunal on December 3, 1953, reflected these new embarrassments of the Commission. Starting with the first full pay week following the date of the award, there was to be a 4s a week increase for adult males, with smaller increases for females and juniors.

This decision provoked the first major industrial crisis on the railways following the passage of the Transport Act of 1953. The E.C. of the N.U.R. in a unanimous resolution expressed its 'profound disgust at the total inadequacy of the amount recommended'. On December 9th it was unanimously agreed that members were to be called upon to withdraw their labour 'to enforce a fair and just settlement'.[27] Although a joint meeting was held with the other two railway unions on December 10th, they decided not to support strike action though they were in agreement with the N.U.R.'s point of view on the claim. In an effort to reach a settlement without a strike, the N.U.R. Negotiating Committee met the Chairman of the B.T.C. twice on December 11th. Sir Brian Robertson said that if the union accepted the award of the Tribunal he would be prepared, 'at the earliest opportunity, to review the whole wage and salary structure of the staff of the railways' with a view to correcting anomalies and giving added incentives where these were justifiable. He also wanted the unions to confer with the Commission to devise ways of increasing the railways' efficiency. But since Sir Brian quite frankly stated that it should not be supposed that the proposed review would 'produce a concrete result in the terms of a rise for anyone', the E.C. reached the unanimous decision to call a strike from midnight December 20, 1953.

At this stage the Minister of Labour, Sir Walter Monckton, intervened, and discussions were held in the offices of the Ministry in St. James' Square, London, on December 15th and 16th. Following these discussions, Sir Brian Robertson promised Jim Campbell that there would be a further increase in pay; but since the amount and the date of the increase were not specified, the executive by a majority of 13–10 decided to continue with the plans for a strike. When talks with the Commission were resumed, agreement was reached on new terms of settlement which included a promise that within two months of the operative date of the Tribunal's Award No. 14, there would be a further improvement of the standard rates of wages on a percentage basis. The settlement had been made possible after consultations between Sir Brian Robertson and the Cabinet. On December 17th, therefore, strike notices were withdrawn. The E.C. was unanimous in recording 'its deep appreciation of the attitude of the Press' which, with few exceptions, had by its 'sympathy' and 'encouragement' contributed considerably towards the satisfactory settlement'.[28] The subsequent discussions between the B.T.C. and the union resulted in an agreement on a general increase in wages of 6 per cent above the level existing before the publication of R.S.N.T. 14, i.e. the 6 per cent was to *include* the 4s awarded by the Tribunal. The new rates of pay came into operation from January 24, 1954.

The advance for the shopmen took longer to negotiate. Two months after men in the other grades had begun to take home bigger wage packets, Head Office was receiving indignant letters from shopmen branches complaining of the delay in reaching a settlement on shopmen's pay. The E.C., therefore, warned the Commission that the strike decision of the previous December was taken in order to secure a satisfactory increase for all the union's members, including shopmen. If the delay in fixing the shopmen's pay continued it would have 'no alternative but to give notice of a withdrawal of labour of all members of the N.U.R.'. The warning had its effect. By April 5th increases roughly corresponding to those conceded to the conciliation grades were negotiated in the Railway Shopmen's National Council.[29]

In this crisis the N.U.R. had stood on its own. By its strike threat, and by its determination to see the job through, it had gained a 6 per cent increase for all grades. For locomotivemen, the Associated Society was prepared to accept 4s and a promise. The N.U.R. fought for and won an increase of 10s for the top-rate driver. By campaigning for *all*, including the lowest-paid grades, the wages of the skilled men had also been advanced.

The policy of the union in the more prolonged negotiations in 1954 for a new wage and salary structure on the railways was consistent with its attitude during the December 1953 crisis. It was to establish a satisfactory minimum rate as the only sound basis for a satisfactory superstructure. It had a moral as well as a practical justification. In declaring that he would 'never be a party to a policy of favouring the few and to hell with the hindmost',[30] Jim Campbell was expressing the long established and ethically commendable tradition of the N.U.R. He ably summarized the practical advantages of the union's policy in an article in the *Railway Review*:

'A large differential over a low minimum can be of less value than a smaller differential over a higher minimum. When a trade union fights to increase the minimum rate, it is acting on behalf of the man at the top no less than the man at the bottom.'[31]

In the discussions which began in February 1954 on the new wages structure of the industry, the most that the Commission was prepared to offer was an increase of 2s 6d a week on the minimum rates and an increase of 4s 6d for the footplate grades. Since all three of the unions found this offer unacceptable, negotiations broke down by August 6th, but discussions were shortly afterwards resumed on the N.U.R.'s counter-proposals for an increase of 10s 6d on the basic wages with other pay scales rising to a maximum of £9 15s 0d. By August 17th, the N.U.R. and Transport Salaried Staffs Association (the R.C.A. had changed its name in 1951) accepted an improved offer of the Commission 'as a basis for discussion', but the Associated Society, which was far more concerned about maintaining differentials than increasing basic rates, found the proposals 'quite inadequate'. It announced that its claim would be submitted to arbitration. On October 4th, in order to keep in step with the other union, the N.U.R. also decided to submit its footplate staff claim to the same procedure.

Decision No. 16 of the Tribunal, published on November 15th, went some way towards meeting the claims of the N.U.R. and the Associated Society for their footplatemen members. But in the fortnight before its publication a large number of branches of the N.U.R. had expressed their profound dissatisfaction with the new wage proposals the executive had accepted for the other grades. On November 10, 1954, the E.C. therefore felt obliged to inform the B.T.C. that the settlement reached on October 12th was 'unacceptable to the membership'. It asked for a resumption of discussions on the basis of the claim made in July 1953—and still not fully met—for a 15 per cent increase for all grades. Since the Commission would not reopen negotiations on that basis, on December 6th, the E.C. sought an interview with the Minister of Transport, Mr Boyd-Carpenter, to see if he would help the Commission's finances by returning part of the £124 million profit the state had made from the railways between 1940 and 1947. Exactly a week later the Minister told the N.U.R. delegation that he would 'not consider anything in the nature of a subsidy to enable railway wages to be increased'. A week later still he informed the union that it was free to take its claim through all the stages of the negotiating machinery.

In the N.U.R. there was a strong feeling that when it came to a question of rewarding special skill, there were others to consider besides the foot-plate grades, and that it was unfair that skilled men in one department only should receive extra rewards. This was one reason for the executive's decision, reached on December 21st, to call a national strike from midnight on January 9, 1955.[32] Another reason was the conviction that the Tribunal was unlikely to be able to offer improved wage rates as the Commission was losing money at the rate of £500,000 a week. Some more radical solution was needed. In the *Railway Review* on November 26, 1954, Jim Campbell had quoted with approval an article in the *Financial Times* which advocated consideration of a Treasury subsidy for a limited period 'to bear some of the burden which would normally have fallen on the ordinary shareholders'.

Within forty-eight hours of the decision to call a strike, the Minister of Labour, Sir Walter Monckton, following discussions with Sir Brian Robertson, informed the N.U.R. that he proposed to appoint a Court of Inquiry into railway wages with instructions to make recommendations with the minimum of delay.

On December 30, 1954, Jim Campbell told the Court of Inquiry under Sir John Cameron, Q.C., that the decision to withdraw labour from January 9th 'had not been taken lightly'. Average wages in manufacturing industry were 22s 4d per week above those of the railways, with the result that many of the most skilled members of the staff were leaving the Commission's service. A branch secretary of the N.U.R. had recently been informed by one of the big motor works in East London that they had enough ex-railwaymen in their employment to run a railway of their own. Railwaymen were 'no longer content to sit on the sidelines watching other industries reap the benefits of a prosperity dependent on cut-price railway wages'. If the financial obligations which had been placed on the B.T.C. prevented their paying reasonable wages then 'some other way would have to be found'.[33]

Though the Cameron Committee, in its Interim Report of January 3, 1955, issued a reproof to the union for not again using the negotiating machinery, it said that there was reason for the executive's exasperation. The Commission was reproved for, at one and the same time, arguing that railway wages were reasonable and that it would pay more adequate wages if it could afford to foot the bill. In its most important recommendation— 'Having willed the end, the nation must will the means'—the Committee was echoing the claim made to it by the General Secretary of the N.U.R. that 'some other way would have to be found'. For these reasons, it said, negotiations ought to be resumed for improvements in the wage rates 'at the earliest moment' and 'with a sense of urgency'.[34]

On January 6, 1955, the E.C., having heard that the Government had adopted the report and that Sir Brian Robertson was willing to negotiate at once, decided by a majority of 20–3 to call off the strike.[35]

Within a fortnight, increases had been obtained for all the conciliation and salaried grades, which brought the wage rates to approximately 15 per cent above the level of December 1953. The porters' starting rate was raised to £6 11s 0d with increments bringing it up to £6 15s 0d after three years' service. The footplate grades benefited with the rest; the wages of adult engine cleaners going up by 6s, of firemen by between 5s 6d and 6s 6d and of drivers by 2s 6d. The wages of top rate drivers were now £9 15s 0d a week.

As had been the case just over a year before, a sympathetic Press had contributed to the victory. The *Daily Express* thought it 'scandalous' that the railwaymen were 'so poorly paid' and the *Daily Sketch* had 'every sympathy with the just claim of the underpaid railwaymen'.

The unilateral action of the N.U.R. had raised footplatemen's wages by several shillings above the level awarded in R.S.N.T. Decision 16, but the Executive of the Associated Society was not satisfied. It said the increases were too small, and declared, on January 25, 1955, that it would submit a claim for an additional 8s for locomotivemen to the Tribunal. After this claim had been turned down in R.S.N.T. Decision 17 on April 16th, the Society called for a footplatemen's strike on May 1st. Talks with the T.U.C. led to a suspension of the strike order on April 30th, but after the Society had rejected a proposal of the Minister of Labour, made on May 26th, that the N.U.R. and the A.S.L.E. & F. should meet under his auspices, as it had a similar offer by the T.U.C., a national strike of footplatemen began at midnight on May 28th, and lasted for seventeen days.

The policy of the N.U.R. in this new crisis was clearly stated in a branch circular issued on May 26, 1955:

'The N.U.R. is NOT in dispute with either the B.T.C. or the A.S.L.E. & F. with whom we are prepared to discuss the question at issue at any time.

'Division in the ranks of railwaymen can do nothing but harm.

'All members should report for duty in the normal course.

'Should members work with volunteers? The answer to this question is emphatically no!

'Members should do no work done by men engaged in the dispute.'

Most of the footplatemen members of the N.U.R. obeyed this directive. The B.T.C. stated that on June 8th, 11,273 drivers, firemen and cleaners reported for duty. The N.U.R. claimed 17,000 footplatemen members, but some of these were members of both unions. Some of the 17,000, being loath to be charged with 'blacklegging', stayed away from work.[36]

By the arbitration award of Lord Justice Morris of June 20, 1955, which was the outcome of the strike, the majority of those who struck work—the firemen and cleaners—did not get a penny piece more. The minority, viz. the drivers, had increases ranging from a shilling a week in the first year to three shillings a week in the third year. To achieve this the average driver must have sacrificed up to £25 in income (even allowing for £2 a week strike pay) in the course of the dispute.[37]

From the trade-union point of view the most deplorable consequence of the strike was the worsening of relations between the N.U.R. and the A.S.L.E. & F. At Taunton the Associated Society members of the railway choir refused to sing with the N.U.R. members; at Dundee and Perth in Scotland and in Stratford and King's Cross in London, some drivers and firemen, manning the same engines, refused to speak to each other throughout the shift. There was even a case of an Associated Society fireman who cleaned just his half of the cabin, refusing to touch the N.U.R. driver's side.[38] The customary telegram of fraternal greetings from the A.S.L.E. & F. was not received by the A.G.M. of the N.U.R. in July 1955 although ill-feeling had subsided sufficiently by the following year for the practice to be resumed.

The union had promised the Court of Inquiry under Sir John Cameron in December 1954, that it would co-operate with the management in an endeavour to increase efficiency on the railways. At a meeting of the British Transport Joint Consultative Council held on February 14, 1955, Jim Campbell, on behalf of the N.U.R., agreed to a proposal to set up a British Railways Productivity Council which was to initiate proposals for the best use of manpower and the more efficient use of modern machinery. The E.C. gave its unanimous approval to this development.[38] The new Council, which contained three N.U.R. members, soon got into its stride. By the end of its inaugural year it had initiated work study schemes and had made plans for railway staff to visit the most up-to-date workshops, marshalling yards, goods depots, docks, etc., at home and on the Continent.[39] The Council was soon making an important contribution to more efficient and economical working of British Railways.

Compared with the rumpus that had been caused over the negotiation of new wage and salary scales in 1954–5 the new agreements of the years 1956–7 presented fewer difficulties.

The 7 per cent increase in rates of pay offered by the Commission at a meeting of the Railway Staff National Council on January 19, 1956, and accepted unanimously by the E.C. on the following day, was the final outcome of a resolution passed at the A.G.M. in the preceding July. On the twin grounds of a rise in the cost of living and the still inadequate pay of the employees of the Commission, the E.C. was instructed to formulate a wage claim on behalf of all the members of the union. This was to be done jointly with the other unions, if practicable, but singly by the N.U.R. if the others would not co-operate.

When the approach was made to the Associated Society the reply received was that, as the question of wages was down for discussion at the forthcoming annual delegate conference, the Society was not prepared to meet the N.U.R. in the interim. Meetings with the T.S.S.A. on September 27th and October 20th were inconclusive because the Association's representatives said that they wanted more time to consider the question. On November 21st, therefore, the E.C. of the N.U.R. decided, with only one dissentient, to lodge a claim for a general increase of 10 per cent. At its same quarterly meeting the executive decided to ask the Commission to give women equal pay to that of men where they occupied positions normally occupied by male staff.[40] The union had much more rapid success with the general claim than it did with the special claim for women. The improvements offered by the Commission just over two months after the submission of the claim for an increase in wages, included not only the 7 per cent on the basic scale, but also the payment of time and a quarter rates for ordinary time, and time and a half rates for overtime workings, on Saturdays between 2.0 p.m. and 10.0 p.m. irrespective of the time the turn of duty commenced. The hours of duty of those salaried staff till then working a 44-hour week, were reduced to 42 hours, and leave was to be given in lieu of work performed on six Bank and Public Holidays.

The Commission gave way gradually on the question of equal pay for women. On October 3, 1955, it announced that it was 'prepared to agree, in principle, to the introduction by stages in respect of administrative, technical and clerical staff on British Railways of equal pay for equal work', but, on January 24, 1956, it was made clear that a number of important supervisory grades were to be kept as male preserves. They included stationmasters, goods agents, yardmasters, workshop supervisory staff and about a dozen others. At a meeting of the London Transport Executive Negotiating Committee on October 28, 1958, it was agreed that women employed in the conciliation grades on the same work as men were to be paid the man's rate of pay. It was not until January 22, 1959, that the E.C. was informed that the Commission had agreed to implement equal pay for most women employed on British Railways with effect from January 1, 1958. The London award was subsequently back-dated to the same time.[41]

Delegates would have thought something was very wrong if an A.G.M. went by without the adoption of a resolution about improved rates of wages. The 1956 A.G.M. at Great Yarmouth was no exception to the general rule. Unanimously congress instructed the executive to consult the other trade unions with a view to agreeing a common wage policy which would 'counter the attacks on the standard of living' but which would also take into account 'increased productivity and efficiency on the railways' which had not, so far, been reflected in wages. As it happened the Associated Society had already lodged a claim for a 15 per cent rise for footplatemen, and, in consequence, no joint meetings were held with that body. After two meetings with the N.U.R., the T.S.S.A. decided that the time was 'not opportune' for a new approach to the Commission. In the face of these frustrations the negotiating committee of the N.U.R. could not, at first, persuade a majority of the executive to endorse its suggestion of applying for a 10 per cent increase on all railway wages. When this majority was obtained, the claim was submitted to the Railway Staff Joint Council on November 19, 1956. A month later the Commission offered 3 per cent. The executive had no hesitation in rejecting this meagre advance and in deciding to press the claim through the further stages of the negotiating machinery.

By February 28, 1957, Jim Campbell was again putting the union's case to the Tribunal. As usual he had some startling facts to reveal. The basic rate paid to a carriage and wagon examiner, at £8 3s 6d a week, was sixpence less than the sum suburban borough councils paid their street sweepers. Postmen unloading mailbags at the main line termini in London were being paid £2 7s 0d a week more than senior parcel porters employed by the railways in the same locations.[42]

For the first time in the history of the negotiating machinery the findings of the Tribunal were not unanimous. In its Decision No. 20 published on March 19, 1957, the Chairman (Sir John Forster) and Mr A. N. Espley were agreed in recommending for the salaried and conciliation grades no more than the 3 per cent which they had recommended for the footplate grades in Decision No. 19, dated December 5, 1956, but Mr E. Hall, in a minority report, declared that the N.U.R.'s claim was 'fair and reasonable' particularly in view of the fact that productivity on the railways had increased. Considering the decision on the following day the members of the E.C. were of one mind in rejecting the Majority Report as an 'insult to railwaymen'. The General Secretary was to ask for an immediate meeting with Sir Brian Robertson to inform him of the executive's view.

There is no doubt that Sir Brian Robertson was willing to help, and in talks with Jim Campbell and the Negotiating Committee of the N.U.R.

on March 22, 1957, a compromise was reached. Rates of pay of all salaried and conciliation staff were to be improved by 3 per cent with effect from November 26, 1956, to March 3, 1957. Thereafter they were to be improved further so as to give an increase of 5 per cent (in substitution for the 3 per cent) on the basic rates paid before November 26, 1956. The justification given in the published Terms of Settlement for this further increase was that 'tangible results' and 'real increases in efficiency' had resulted from joint consultation 'in which the N.U.R. had co-operated at all levels'. It was the first time increased productivity had been cited by the management as the main reason for an increase in wages. The E.C. accepted the offer unanimously.[43]

IV

The Guillebaud Report of March 2, 1960, was conceived under the threat of one national railway strike and born under the shadow of another. When the claim for 'a substantial increase in wages' initiated by resolution No. 67 of the A.G.M. in July 1957, reached the Tribunal in March 1958, the majority of its members, viz. Sir John Forster and Mr A. J. Espley, in the Decision No. 21 of April 10, 1958, whilst conceding that railway wages were 'low in comparison with those cited ... in nationalized industries, public services and certain private undertakings', were not prepared to recommend any advance in railway pay. Although Mr. E. Hall, in a minority report advocating further discussion with a view to an improvement in the wage rates, did not see why the deficits incurred by the Commission on account of its modernization programme should be 'partially recouped through the worsening of the standard of living of the employees', the other two were concerned lest the cost of a further wage advance would 'seriously deplete the £250 million which had been calculated as necessary to cover the Commission's deficits for the whole of the period 1956–62 inclusive'.

This negative outcome from arbitration led the E.C. to approach the other two railway unions who agreed at a joint meeting on April 14, 1958, to seek further talks with Sir Brian Robertson. The Transport Commission's Chairman was, however, as circumscribed by the mounting financial deficits as the Tribunal had been. He did not feel able to make any offer, but he willingly accepted the suggestion of an approach to the Prime Minister. At the meeting with the representatives of the unions and the Commission, held in the afternoon of April 22nd, Mr Macmillan argued any further increase in wages could only be granted after there had been that further increase in productivity. Sir Brian Robertson felt that this warranted his giving a promise of a further wage increase in October but not before then. The E.C. did not consider this soon enough. After another interview in which it tried in vain to persuade Sir Brian to alter his views,

654

it decided on May 7, 1958, by a majority of 13–10, to call a national railway strike starting at midnight on Sunday, May 25th.

This was the threat which, following conversations at the Ministry of Labour, had a double outcome. On May 14th, Sir Brian Robertson offered the railway unions (a) an increase of 3 per cent in railway salaries and wages with effect from June 30, 1958; and (b) the setting up of an Inquiry to make a comprehensive examination of the wages structure. After Sir Brian had promised that discussions on the proposed Inquiry would start in August, the N.U.R. executive, by a majority of 17 to 6, decided to accept the compromise. There was to be no strike in the summer of 1958.[44]

All might have been well had it proved possible to establish the Committee of Inquiry quickly and for the Committee to present its report without delay. Neither of these things happened. It was not until August 25, 1958, that a meeting between Sir Brian Robertson and the unions was held to agree on the broad outlines of the inquiry, and it was not until December 2nd that all three members of the committee had been apponted. The next two months 'were occupied in planning the work and finding the staff to carry it out'.[45] In fairness to the committee, it must be said that it had a very big job on its hands. By its terms of reference it had to:

'... conduct an investigation into the relativity of pay of salaried and conciliation staff in British Railways covered by the machinery of negotiation for railway staff with the pay of staff in other nationalized industries, public services, and appropriate private undertakings.'

An inquiry of such scope had never been undertaken before. The ten investigation officers appointed by the committee collected a mass of information on the rates of pay and conditions of service in over thirty trades or occupations of such major importance as the Civil Service, the G.P.O., the Banks, I.C.I. Ltd., the Ford Motor Company, Unilever and the National Coal Board. At the same time they interviewed between 1,500 and 1,600 members of staff in 150 grades in the employment of the Transport Commission.

Ultimately the findings of the committee would be of immense value to railwaymen in demonstrating how far their pay had fallen behind the rewards common in other industries. But as 1959 dragged on the staff of the Transport Commission were becoming increasingly restive.

Understandably so. As *The Economist* pointed out, in the summer of 1958, they got a smaller increase than any other major industrial group. In the twenty-one months which elapsed before they received any more, at least sixty-one industries had granted improved rates of pay to their employees.[46] Already by March 1959, Mr Greene, who had become the General Secretary of the N.U.R. following the tragic death of Jim Campbell in November 1957, was receiving dozens of letters from branches and district councils of the union urging a new wage application through the normal negotiating machinery. The executive felt obliged to comply with these requests and submitted a claim to the Railway Staff Joint Council on May 6, 1959, for a substantial increase in wages and salaries. In the second half of the year 1959, this claim was taking its tortuous course through the established negotiating bodies at the same time as the Guillebaud investigators were compiling their mass of evidence.

Late in August Mr Greene tried to console the members of the executive by reporting that it was 'anticipated that the independent investigators would complete the investigation of railway grades early in September'. But autumn came and went and to the rank and file experiencing steadily diminishing real incomes, the report seemed as far off as ever.

By the New Year the patience of the men, particularly in the traditionally militant areas of London and Manchester, was coming to an end. On January 5, 1960, the executive of the London District Council called for a 24-hour stoppage in the London area to begin at midnight on January 31st. On January 17th, the Manchester District Council demanded that the national executive should call a national railway strike unless a favourable answer was received from the Commission for an immediate increase in pay.

Sensing that something would have to be done to alleviate the discontent, Sir Brian Robertson announced on January 11th that the Commission would be prepared, immediately on receipt of the Guillebaud report 'to discuss with the unions what interim action could be taken'. Any pay award which might be agreed at such discussions could be back-dated to January 11th. The E.C. seized the opportunity with both hands and instructed Mr Greene 'to seek an immediate meeting with the Chairman of the B.T.C.'. But this attempt to settle the immediate crisis ended in failure. When the representatives of the three railway unions met Sir Brian on January 29th, the Associated Society and T.S.S.A. representatives said that they were not anxious for an interim payment to be made. Believing that there was a strictly limited amount of money available for wage increases, they preferred to await the publication of the Guillebaud Report which they believed would recommend increased differentials for the skilled men. If a flat rate or percentage increase were granted before the report appeared, there might not be enough money left at a later date to give extra rewards to the top grades. Consequently Sir Brian had to tell the N.U.R. that he was unable to meet the demand for any increase in pay.

Meeting later the same day, the E.C. of the N.U.R. reached the unanimous conclusion that it had no alternative '. . . but to instruct members of the union to withdraw their labour from 12.01 a.m. on Monday, February 15th.'

The executive of the London District Council, meeting early on January 31st, recognized that united action was better than piecemeal stoppages.

It pledged full support for the national strike and recommended London branches to defer the one-day strike due to start that night. It appreciated that it might be difficult to prevent the token stoppage at such short notice.

In the event, most of the London Underground men stayed away from work on February 1st. There were only 85 trains, in place of the usual 493, to carry the 453,000 persons who normally left Central London by Underground for their homes in the suburbs. Thousands more motor cars jammed the roads. Rusty old bicycles which had not seen the light of day for years, were dragged out of garden sheds and dusted and oiled ready for emergency service. The A.A. called the congestion of vehicles in Central London 'the worst traffic chaos ever experienced'.[47] People had to wait so long on station platforms for the few trains that were running that they even began to talk to each other.

The episode of the one-day strike was a salutary warning. If such a colossal breakdown could result from an incomplete strike, confined to the Underground services, it was not difficult to imagine that it might well be impossible to reach London by any form of transport except shanks' pony in the event of a national strike. Consequently, furnishing stores were innundated with orders for mattresses and camp beds, and hotel switchboards were jammed by callers wanting rooms. Civil servants were told that they would have to walk to work if they lived within four miles of their offices.

In the meantime the N.U.R. completed preparations for the strike. On February 3rd, the executive decided not to call out the busmen, lighthouse keepers, watchmen, the safety men of the Sudbrook Pumping Station of the Severn Tunnel, and the hotel and refreshment room staff. Local strike committees were 'to co-operate with local management to avoid hardship or injury to railway animals or livestock in transit at the time of the strike'. Mr Greene informed the Press on February 7th that apart from provident funds the union had £2½ million, and with dispute pay at 36s the strike could last for five weeks.

But no one in a responsible position in the union wanted the strike if a satisfactory settlement could be reached without it. Thus the executive willingly accepted the invitation to meet the General Council of the T.U.C. on February 5th. After the meeting it was in unanimous agreement with the proposal that the General Council, acting on behalf of the three unions, should inform the appropriate authorities that 'an immediate percentage increase' would meet the N.U.R.'s claim.

On February 8th when they met the Finance and General Purposes Committee of the T.U.C., the N.U.R. representatives read a letter from Mr Guillebaud stating that the pay report would be submitted as early as possible in the week beginning February 29th instead of in April as had earlier been forecast. At 8.30 p.m. the same day, in the Charing Cross Hotel, Sir Brian Robertson told the negotiating committee that within one week of the receipt of the report he would make an offer of an interim increase back-dating to January 11, 1960. On the following day, however, the members of the executive were unanimous in their decision to inform the Commission that 'only an immediate substantial increase in wages and salaries' would meet the union's demands.

The settlement came at a meeting of the three trade unions and Sir Brian Robertson, presided over by the Minister of Labour, Mr Heath, on February 12th. With the active encouragement of the Government and an assurance from Mr Guillebaud that the proposal would be 'containable' within the Committee's findings, Sir Brian offered the unions a 5 per cent wage increase to be given early in March but to be back-dated to January 11th. The decisive contribution to the success of the negotiations had been made by Mr Guillebaud. His assurance that the 5 per cent could be absorbed within the increases the committee was likely to recommend, reassured the craft unions that the prospects for the improvement of their differentials were not impaired.

The Report, which was published on March 2, 1960, found that all railway wages were well behind those in other, roughly comparable, occupations. For the lowest-paid grades such as porters, it was suggested that an increase of 8 per cent would bring them into line with the wages paid for comparable jobs in outside industry. Other grades such as permanent-way lengthmen, relayers and shunters, whose wages were 'out of line' with the general run of railway wages, should be rewarded with an additional 5 per cent. Finally there were those, including drivers, motormen, guards, top class signalmen, and telecommunications staff, whose 'badly out of line' wages should be advanced by a further 5 per cent, making 18 per cent in all. For the salaried staff bigger increases than the basic 8 per cent were recommended for those supervising manual workers, for traffic controllers and for stationmasters (among others).

In a comment about amenities and welfare services, the committee noticed that on the railways '. . . provision for meals, rest rooms, sanitary facilities and the like are generally unsatisfactory, and frequently inferior to the standards prevailing in most other industries'.[48] If the railway pay crisis had done nothing else it had at least drawn attention to the unsatisfactory working conditions of many of the men. A letter in the *Daily Telegraph*[49] written by a top ranking signalman earning £9 6s 6d a week, pointed out that the writer had to bolt his sandwiches 'in between pulling levers, ringing bells and answering telephones' in connection with the 100 trains a shift that passed by the box. He asserted that 'nearly all signal cabins were not equipped with flush lavatories'. The Commission had spent over £17 million in the provision of new amenity blocks, storage accommodation, lengthmen's huts, lavatories, better lighting and other improvements since the beginning of 1951 but it was still a fact, as revealed by the Gowers Committee Report in March 1949, that the railways had a long way to go before welfare and amenity services approached the standards of the typical factory.[50]

It was not until June 24, 1960, that agreement on the detailed application of the recommendations of the Guillebaud Report was reached between the Commission and the unions. The delay had been tedious, but the new rates of pay were back-dated to January 4th. For a brief period railway wages were nearly, but not quite, on a par with wages for comparable jobs in outside industry. It was not long before they were falling behind again.

v

As far back as July 1922 the Romford branch of the N.U.R. persuaded the A.G.M. delegates at Bradford to instruct the executive to try to induce the railway companies to 'standardize the objects, contributions and benefits' of the forty different superannuation funds they sponsored. There was certainly a case for more uniformity. Some railway pensioners got as little as ninepence a week, a few received over a pound and many had nothing at all.

In December 1924 the union included in a national programme for both conciliation and shop grades the demand 'that provision be made for all grades to be granted a pension at 60'.

But the replies from the companies were invariably depressing. In October 1925, the Secretary of the Railways Staff Conference wrote that the question of pensions could not be discussed as it was 'a managerial and directorial matter'. The state pension scheme was involving the companies in additional expenditure of a million pounds a year and participation in a railway pension scheme would involve an outlay of several millions more. Until the revenue position of the railways improved, further expenditure was out of the question. After many unsuccessful attempts to persuade the railway directors to change their minds, the E.C. of the N.U.R. in September 1928, gave up the campaign for the time being. A month before, an S.G.M. in London, by an overwhelming majority, had agreed to railwaymen's wages being cut by 2½ per cent, and staff contributions to a pension fund would cost at least as much money as the sum sacrificed in wages to help restore the companies' financial position.

In 1933 the A.G.M. returned to the subject of pensions by directing the executive to examine the comparative merits and comparative cost of a £2 a week pension for all railwaymen on reaching the age of 60 and a Government pension to all citizens over 60. The Political Sub-Committee of the E.C. found that it would require a contribution of 6s a week during the working life of railwaymen to pay for a pension of £2 a week on retirement. Since this was out of the question, they recommended instead that the union should support the Labour Party (1930) plan for a £1 a

659

week pension for all at 60. When they reported back, Jim Figgins persuaded the E.C. to turn down their recommendation in favour of a state non-contributory pension of £2 a week at 60.

The division of opinion in the union between those who favoured concentrating on a railway pension scheme and those, like Jim Figgins and John Marchbank, who believed it was wiser to work for more adequate state pensions, should not mislead us into thinking that, but for these divisions, the companies could have been induced to sponsor an adequate pension scheme. They repeatedly stated that they could not afford it.

In the spring of 1947 the E.C. of the N.U.R. was protesting—in vain—about the railway companies' decision to reduce their ex-gratia pensions because the state old-age pension had just been raised to 26s a week.

After nationalization, it took nearly three years of hard bargaining between the B.T.C. and the unions before a workable plan for retirement pensions for railwaymen was agreed and came into operation, on October 1, 1954, under statutory instrument No. 898. What held up negotiations after thay had started early in 1951 was the reluctance of the Commission to promise to pay pensions to those who were over 45 when the scheme started, and the haggling over contributions and pensions. A further cause of delay was the reluctance of the Minister of Transport to approve the principle of the scheme. After his consent had at last been given, in March 1953, it did not take long to complete the business.

That the S.G.M., which met in the Victoria Halls, Bloomsbury Square, London, on October 13, 1953, solely for the purpose of considering the draft scheme, approved it by the large majority of 69 to 8, was in no small measure due to the determination and hard work of the General Secretary, who, after a clear and closely reasoned speech in favour of its acceptance, patiently answered 177 questions on details.

Under the scheme there were, in fact, two pension scales. Section 'A' scale applied to all full-time wage employees of the Commission, whilst the Section 'B' scale was confined to those included in a schedule of senior grades. Both schemes were contributory and membership of both was optional for existing employees but compulsory for those joining the Commission's service after October 1, 1954. In Section 'A', pensions, at 60 years of age, varied from 9s 9d a week to those over 52 years old at the inauguration of the scheme, to 30s a week for those who were in a position to complete forty years' service. Any man who chose to continue working could add 2s a week to his pension for each year of additional service up to the age of 65. Membership of Section 'B', which was in addition to, and not in substitution for, membership of Section 'A', was designed by the Commission to act as an incentive to staff to seek the more responsible posts. For a small additional weekly contribution there were additions of up to 10s a week on the pension. There were provisions under both scales for ill health retirement pensions and death benefits, and membership of the Section 'B' scheme was most sought after for the more generous scale of these allowances.

The main criticisms that were made at the S.G.M. were that the Section 'B' scale should have been made available to all wage employees irrespective of grade, and that the weekly pensions were too small. They certainly compared very unfavourably with post office and police pensions in Britain and with railwaymen's pensions in Holland, Belgium, Western Germany and France where weekly payments of up to half the wage earned at the time of retirement were common. However, Jim Campbell argued that half a loaf was better than no bread:

'Hundreds of old railwaymen retire each month. Should we say to them: "We will not accept the minimum of 9s 9d per week, it is unworthy? It is better to go off the railway with no pension at all?" I can hardly believe that any delegate would want us to say that.'

This argument undoubtedly had a great influence on the delegates.[51]

In June 1955, on the instructions of the E.C., Jim Campbell wrote to the Secretary of the Central Committee—the body which administers the fund—asking for the admission of women. The Commission would not agree. Because of the possibility of marriage and earlier retirement from the fund, women's membership, it was argued, would add greatly to the expenses of administration.

Women (over 25) were, however, included in the sick pay scheme which the N.U.R. helped to negotiate on behalf of all wage employees, including part-time staff, and which came into operation on December 1, 1956. Benefits included sick pay of from 30s up to 40s for from six weeks to twelve weeks in any one year, depending on the length of service. To save administrative expense, benefit was not payable on account of the first seven days of sickness.

For both pensions and sick pay schemes the patient unspectacular efforts of the head office staff and sub-committees of the N.U.R. executive had contributed greatly to improve the character of the arrangements finally negotiated.

Even before the outbreak of the Second World War there were complaints in the union about the character of the negotiating machinery established in 1935. In March 1945 before the war ended, valuable discussions were held with the companies in the Railway Executive Staff Committee. But because of the pressure of other business, a revised scheme was not agreed until the end of 1955, to come into operation on July 1, 1956. There were no fundamental changes from the machinery set up in 1935, but in order to speed up procedure, it was provided that minor issues of interpretation of national agreements should not ordinarily be carried beyond the stage of the Railway Staff Joint Council. A completely new

Section VII, headed 'Consultation between Management and Staff' reflected the concern on both sides to promote the more efficient working of the railways and the best use of manpower.[52]

On June 12, 1952, the Railway Executive, A.E.U. and N.U.R. agreed to a new machinery of negotiation for Railway Electricity Generating Staff replacing an earlier agreement of 1927. It provided for a National Railway Electrical Council with representatives of the unions and management, to deal with applications of a national character affecting wages, hours or other standard conditions of service. If agreement could not be reached at this level there was provision for reference of the matter in dispute to the Industrial Court.[53]

Throughout the 'fifties the annual grade conferences of bus workers, goods and cartage workers, permanent-way and signal and telecommunications grades, catering trades, locomotive and shed staff, shopmen, shunters and guards, signalmen, supervisors, docks and marine staff, and carriage and wagon grades served the extremely useful function of channelling complaints and formulating programmes.

VI

There were two changes in the leadership of the union during the 1950's.

As the rules of the union then stood, Jim Figgins was obliged to relinquish office as General Secretary on reaching the age of sixty in March, 1953. His energies had by that time been so used up on the service of the union and the Labour Movement that he did not long survive his retirement. He died on December 27, 1956.

Only three candidates were nominated in the election to choose his successor; Mr Jack Barker who had been a member of the union for forty-two years, and since 1948 had been employed at Head Office as Senior Organizer; Mr Sidney F. Greene who had stood in the previous election for the same post in 1948; and Mr James S. Campbell, Assistant General Secretary since 1948. The result of the election announced on February 13, 1953 was as follows:

J. S. Campbell	72,384
S. F. Greene	25,815
J. Barker	12,653

'Jim' Campbell, who was born in Glasgow on April 17, 1895, joined the A.S.R.S. on August 13, 1911, when he was in the employment of the Glasgow and South Western Railway as a lampman. In 1919, when he was appointed Secretary of the Glasgow No. 7 Branch of the N.U.R., he was one of the youngest branch secretaries in the country, but he filled the post with conscientiousness and ability for seventeen years. Before being elected full-time organizer in 1938, he had served with distinction on the Glasgow and West of Scotland District Council and had been an A.G.M., T.U.C. and Labour Party delegate and member of the Executive Committee. A man of integrity, humanity and good fellowship, he quickly won the esteem and affection of those, whether of the executive committee, head office staff, or A.G.M., who got to know him best. In the Board Room, feeling could run high and angry words be said, but 'Big Jim' bore no grudge against anyone, and within a few moments of the fiercest of arguments he would be joking and laughing with those he had most vigorously opposed. The 'Guvnor', as he was known at Head Office, would get far better results from a courteously phrased request than many a man who gave the most peremptory order.

The decision of the A.G.M. at Gourock in 1954 to give the full-time officers of the union (but not the Head Office staff) the option of continuing to work up to the age of sixty-five was a welcome one to the General Secretary who, under the old rules, would have had to retire in April 1955. He had no hesitation in deciding to continue at his post.

He was looking forward to five years more service to the union. As a result of the greatest domestic tragedy the union sustained in the course of its history, he was destined to complete only half that time.

Jim Campbell always believed strongly in maintaining and extending the international links of the N.U.R. During his brief period of office the E.C. accepted invitations from railwaymen's unions in Holland, Switzerland, Bulgaria, Yugoslavia, Poland, Rumania, W. Germany, the German Democratic Republic, Rhodesia, China and the U.S.S.R. for delegations to be sent to their annual congresses or for other occasions. In many cases exchange delegations were welcomed in London. After attending the merger conference of the A.F. of L. and C.I.O. in New York in December 1955, the General Secretary made a five-week goodwill tour of some of the principal railway centres in the United States where he made many new friends.

In February 1957 an invitation was received from the Central Committee of the Railway Workers Union of the U.S.S.R. for the N.U.R. to send a delegation of eight persons to spend three weeks in the Soviet Union. After the Budapest uprising of October 1956 the T.U.C. had advised affiliated unions against all exchange visits with organizations in the U.S.S.R. On November 13, 1956, the E.C. of the N.U.R. by a majority of 17–6 had endorsed a T.U.C. resolution condemning the Soviet intervention in Hungary.[54] Nevertheless, in March 1957, it was decided to accept the Russian invitation and to send a delegation of six persons including the President, the General Secretary, two members of the E.C. and two members elected by the 1957 A.G.M.[55]

It was whilst this delegation was in Stalingrad on November 4, 1957, that there occurred the terrible accident which caused the death of Tom

Hollywood (the President of the N.U.R.) and Jim Campbell. At 5.50 p.m. that day, while the motor car in which they were travelling was crossing Defence Square, it collided with a ten-ton lorry emerging from a side street. Tom Hollywood, who sustained a fractured skull and was rendered unconscious from the time of impact, never regained consciousness. Jim Campbell, who suffered from a broken leg and ribs and a damaged collar bone, remained conscious for many hours but died just before 10 o'clock on the evening of November 6th, nineteen hours before his colleague. The Russians did their utmost to save the two men. An ambulance from the nearby 3rd Stalingrad City Hospital was at the scene of the accident within three mintues of the crash. Though Moscow airport had been declared fogbound and no aeroplane had been allowed to leave it for many hours, an exception was made to allow specialists to fly to Stalingrad. When all efforts to effect recovery had proved unavailing, a special plane carried the bodies to London on November 9th.

It was altogether fitting that before leaving for the U.S.S.R. Jim Campbell's last important public speech, given to the Labour Party Conference at Brighton on October 2nd, should have been on the subject of Socialism which was, as he told the A.G.M. delegates at Hastings in 1955, a way of life he had 'imbibed with his mother's milk'. Moving the reference back of the Policy Statement 'Industry and Society', he advised the National Executive of the Labour Party to 'inject into the document the rich red blood of socialist objective'.

Though Tom Hollywood was less of a public figure than his distinguished colleague, he had given a lifetime of service to the union. Dignified, yet always approachable, he quickly put people in a good humour by his wry wit. Perhaps a more impressive tribute to his character than the hundreds of wreaths, was the silent lining of the road leading to the crematorium by all the men who had worked with him for so many years at the St Rollox Motive Power Depot in Glasgow.

The Executive Committee decided that the best form that a memorial to their two colleagues could take was 'making some contribution or addition to Manor House Hospital'. By the beginning of December, 1958, members of the union and friends had contributed £5,971 to a testimonial fund. This sum was made up to £7,500 from the central funds of the union and shortly afterwards the Tom Hollywood and Jim Campbell Ward of the hospital was opened.

On November 18, the E.C. appointed Mr Greene Acting General Secretary, pending the holding of an election for a successor to Jim Campbell. But although branches were given until February 24, 1958, to send in nominations, only the 511 in favour of Mr Greene were received, and on February 25th, the E.C. declared him elected and gave him best wishes for a successful term of office. Few men could have had a more varied and useful experience in the service of the union. Since starting work as a porter at Paddington he had been an A.G.M. delegate in the years 1937–9 and E.C. member from 1941–3. As an organizer during the years 1944–53 he had served in the Newcastle, Doncaster, Manchester, Cardiff, Bristol, Nottingham and London Districts and he also served as a Road Transport Organizer. When in 1953 he had headed the poll for the election of two Assistant General Secretaries he was declared to be the Senior Assistant General Secretary.

In elections held in October 1958, to fill the vacancies caused by Mr Greene's promotion and the impending retirement of Mr F. E. Bell, Mr G. W. Brassington of Newcastle (Staffs) was elected Senior Assistant General Secretary and Mr W. Ballantine of Perth No. 2 Branch, Assistant General Secretary.[56]

The A.G.M. at Morecambe in 1950 considered it 'vitally necessary in the interests of the organization' that a propaganda and publicity department should be set up at Unity House. But owing to a difference of view on the question of whether it was best to bring in an outsider, or promote an existing member of staff, the carrying out of this decision was delayed until June 1954, when Mr C. R. Sweetingham was promoted from the Movements Department at Head Office to take charge of this work. The success of the new venture was shown by the fact that, three years later, the forty members of the Industrial Correspondents Group of the Press presented Mr Sweetingham with a book of his choice in recognition of the fact that he had given them 'most help' during the preceding year.[57]

Because of the union's work on behalf of the many grades in the Transport Commission's service and the expansion of the Head Office Legal Department it was found necessary to extend Unity House upwards and on the Euston Road frontage. The work on the extension which was completed in March 1959, at a cost of £190,344, had dragged on for a period of five years. As a result of these improvements the staff had a much improved canteen, lighting was modernized and a lift was installed.

VII

The continuation of the cold war provided every Annual General Meeting with an opportunity to debate a major issue of foreign policy. On most occasions the decisions reached were Bevanite in character. The opposition to German rearmament, so strongly expressed at Hastings in 1951, was maintained in the following years. In 1954 Jim Campbell's speech from the platform urging the delegates to 'repudiate emphatically' the decision of the Parliamentary Labour Party to support the expansion of a new W. German army was greeted with prolonged applause. The resolution, which echoed these sentiments was carried by 75 votes to 2. Nevertheless one of the delegates who spoke strongly for the resolution and used as final argument these words:

'Next week we will have our brethren from the German Railway Union here. That is the crux of it. That is the test of German rearmament. Ask them whether they are in favour of the rearmament of Germany and see what they say'

must have been greatly embarrassed to hear Herr Kamp say, eight days later, '. . . it may be necessary that we have some sort of armament'.[58] This did not, however, deter Jim Campbell from telling the T.U.C. at Brighton on September 24, 1954, that the General Council was

'. . . clasping to the bosom of the British T.U.C. as comrades in arms, generals and leaders who, during the Second World War, connived, acquiesced in, and sometimes ordered the brutalities of the Nazi régime.'

When on July 3, 1951, the A.G.M. at Hastings carried with only two dissentients a resolution calling for the 'withdrawal of all foreign forces from Korea' the N.U.R. was one of the first British unions to make such a recommendation.

Decisions reached in the later 1950's showed that members of the union were being strongly influenced by the Campaign for Nuclear Disarmament. Delegates at Exmouth on July 7, 1958, carried by 46 votes to 31 a resolution which demanded the abandonment of nuclear tests, an end to the stockpiling of nuclear weapons and the abandonment of plans to establish missile bases in Britain. In the following year, under the shadow of an impending General Election, delegates by resolution endorsed the official multilateralist Labour Party document on 'Disarmament and Nuclear War' by 51 votes to 25, after the President, Mr C. W. Evans, had intervened in the debate to say that the amendment (in favour of unilateral disarmament) was 'being used as a weapon to split the Labour Party right down the middle with a view to seeing that the Tories are returned at the next General Election'. In 1960, after the General Election had increased the Conservative majority in Parliament, Conference was less ready to follow the lead of the platform. The resolution, which called for Great Britain 'to take a definite lead in world affairs by declaring its absolute abhorrence of Nuclear Weapons and its determination to take action to renounce them forthwith' also demanded 'the withdrawal of United States forces, nuclear weapons and warheads from British soil'. It was carried, on a recorded vote, by 39 votes to 38. It was not until the last name was read out that the fate of the resolution was determined. The atmosphere in the Conference Hall was electric.

The N.U.R. vote at the Labour Party Conference at Scarborough in October 1960, proved decisive in helping to carry the unilateralist motion of the A.E.U.

That year the N.U.R. also opposed Mr Gaitskell on another issue. The A.G.M. carried by 66 votes to 11 a Greenwich Branch resolution which reaffirmed the belief that common ownership is an essential objective of the Labour Party and that union policy should be 'to retain the present wording of Clause 4'.

Mr Gaitskell must have got more satisfaction from the decisions of the union's conference in 1961, which, on the subject of nuclear weapons, were again in line with official Labour Party policy.

VIII

The union's policy for the future of British Transport broadened and matured in the years following the passage of the Transport Act of 1953. Gone were the days when it had been rather narrowly confined to purely railway policy. In 1953 the N.U.R. succeeded in incorporating in the Labour Party policy statement on Transport a pledge that a future Labour Government would effect 'the removal of all restrictions which are aimed at preventing the British Transport Commission from developing a fully integrated public service of road and rail transport'.[59] At the Labour Party Conference in Scarborough on September 30, 1954, Mr Greene, on behalf of the N.U.R., moved a resolution that 'the Labour Movement should prepare in advance its legislative policy on transport in readiness for the future accession to power of a Labour Government'. The Rt. Hon. Herbert Morrison, M.P., on behalf of the National Executive, welcoming the proposal, promised that the whole question would be reviewed carefully by the Labour Party Executive in conjunction with the unions concerned and the T.U.C.[60]

In April 1956 the N.U.R. submitted a detailed memorandum to the Joint Labour Party/T.U.C. Sub-Committee on Transport. In February, 1958, the union submitted another detailed memorandum of thirty-seven foolscap pages on 'Legislative Policy for Transport'.

The proposals contained in these documents were amplified and re-emphasized in the N.U.R.'s printed 66-page booklet, 'Planning Transport for You', issued in October 1959. A total of 20,000 copies were issued for distribution to the branches of the union or sale to the general public. The authors of the booklet argued that responsibility for paying the interest on the Transport Commission's Compensation Stock should be undertaken by the Treasury. Two years later the Macmillan Government's Transport Bill proposed to do just that. It was not the policy of the union to establish 'a transport system under which every parcel . . . and passenger is bound to be conveyed by a service provided by the state', but it was essential that the policy of co-ordination of road and rail transport which made a moderately successful start in the years 1948–52 should be resumed, with modifications as were indicated by the lessons of experience. The authors believed that the main obstacles to the re-introduction and improvement of co-ordinated transport services would be 'political and not technical'. Confirmation of this view came shortly afterwards from an unexpected quarter. On December 10, 1959, within two months of being appointed

Minister of Transport, Mr Marples told the House of Commons that, before he took up his new post, he thought he knew the meaning of the words 'vested interest'. In the past decade it has been the intervention of such powerful groups as the motor manufacturers and the road haulage organizations that has undermined the viability of the public transport services to the detriment of the interests of the British people. Through the influence of such vested interests, the Government of the United Kingdom is still, in 1962, pursuing the will-o'-the-wisp of free competition in the hope that an efficient and economic system of transport will thereby somehow emerge.

Few would maintain that there is anything sacrosanct about the existing route mileage of British Railways. None would wish to restrain unnecessarily the use of the private car. But those who consider that the growth of automobile and air transport will shortly render railways obsolete should ponder the words of President Kennedy, who addressed the United States Congress on the subject of transport on April 4, 1962.

He warned that, despite an enormous expenditure on road improvements, the unprecedented multiplication of the motor car had resulted in 'clogged arteries in the most populous metropolitan areas' and 'the frustration of congested streets'. In consequence 'mass transportation continued to deteriorate and even to disappear' and 'important segments of the population are deprived of transportation'. He therefore recommended that Congress should vote $500 million as an emergency measure 'for the revitalization and needed expansion of public mass transportation . . . in the interests of national welfare'.[61]

If the rehabilitation of public transport has proved to be necessary in the United States of America, how much more will this not be the case in densely populated Britain!

In the first fifty years in the history of the N.U.R. so much time and energy was taken up in the necessary struggle, first to win recognition of the union and then to achieve and maintain tolerable wages and conditions of service, that it was inevitable that comparatively little attention should have been devoted to the broader questions of transport policy. At the same time there has been an ever-growing awareness of the need to think out a comprehensive transport policy and an increasing desire on the part of the membership to participate in the planning and management of the industry.

Whether or not there will be an opportunity for the fulfilment of these desires will be largely determined at Westminster. Should the Government of the United Kingdom, in defiance of the experience of the Governments of all other European states, persist in an endeavour to make commercial profitability the sole criterion for determining the size and scope of the railway system, and should it pursue this objective largely regardless of the views of those employed in the industry, it is likely that the N.U.R. will again be mainly preoccupied with the strenuous defence of the interest of the membership. If, on the other hand, it becomes the aim of government to give each form of transport the opportunity to fulfil the role for which it is technically and socially most suitable, the co-operation of the union can be expected in this more constructive endeavour.

In the years that lie ahead it is greatly to be hoped that in place of struggles against redundancy and declining living standards, new political conditions will allow the talents of the members of the N.U.R. to be employed in the constructive reshaping of the railways as a public service within the framework of a co-ordinated transport industry.

NOTES

1. British Transport Commission. Report for 1951, pp. 45–7, *British Railways Magazine*, August 1952.
2. British Transport Commission Reports, 1951, p. 19, 1953, p. 16A, and Hansard, Parliamentary Debates, Vol. 501, July 22, 1952, Col. 392, Speech of Mr J. Callaghan, M.P.
3. *The Times Review of Industry*, May 1962, p. 68.
4. See the speech of Mr J. Callaghan, M.P., November 12, 1951, Hansard, Parliamentary Debates, Vol. 493, Col. 739.
5. *The Economist*, May 10, 1952, p. 349.
6. N.U.R., E.C., May 9, 1952, R. 1286.
7. *The Economist*, July 12, 1952, p. 65.
8. R. 197.
9. Hansard, Parliamentary Debates, Vol. 501, Col. 517.
10. Hansard, Parliamentary Debates, Vol. 501, Col. 518.
11. Hansard, Parliamentary Debates, Vol. 501, Col. 482, and Vol. 507, November 17, 1952, Col. 1538.
12. *The Economist*, November 29, 1952, p. 603.
13. British Transport Commission, 6th Annual Report, p. 42.
14. Legislative Policy for Transport and British Transport Commission Finances, Memorandum submitted to a Joint Committee of the T.U.C. and the Labour Party by the N.U.R., February 1958, p. 7.
15. Report from the Select Committee on Nationalized Industries: British Railways, July 11, 1960, paras. 407–8, p. xci.
16. R. 238.
17. Both these statements are taken from the General Secretary's Report to the A.G.M., June 11, 1956, p. 6.
18. *R.R.*, July 13, 1956. N.U.R., A.G.M.
19. N.U.R., E.C., July 25, 1956 and September 1956, Appendix S. 9. June 1957, Appendix J.18; September 1957, Appendices S.40, S.54 and S.76; December 1957, Appendices D.2, D.40, D.43 and D.44. Final unanimous ratification by E.C. on December 19, 1957, R. 3601.
20. N.U.R., E.C., July 16, 1957. R. 1694.
21. N.U.R. 'Supplementary Redundancy Schemes; Salaried Staff and Conciliation Staff (Other than Footplate Staff), May 1957.
22. N.U.R., E.C., September 1959, Appendix S.16.
23. Cmd. 9880, 1956, p. 7, para. 25.
24. John Hughes, 'Railways and the Transport Muddle', *New Left Review*, May–June 1960, p. 20.
25. N.U.R., E.C., June 1952, R. 1324.

26. *R.R.*, November 13, 1953.
27. N.U.R., E.C., December 1953, Rs. 2946, 2947.
28. N.U.R., E.C., December 1953, pp. 140–5, Rs. 2949–60.
29. N.U.R., E.C., March 23, 1954.
30. *R.R.*, April 9, 1954.
31. *R.R.*, April 22, 1955.
32. N.U.R., E.C., December 21, 1954, R. 3517.
33. *R.R.*, January 7, 1955.
34. Interim Report printed in N.U.R. E.C. Minutes, March 1955, Appendix M.8.
35. N.U.R., E.C., January 6, 1955, R. 71.
36. *Railway Gazette*, June 17, 1955.
37. Terms of the Award printed in N.U.R. E.C. Minutes, September 1955, Appendix S.15. *The Economist* estimated that the majority of the drivers would have to work nearly twenty years before the strike would have been worth their while.
38. *R.R.*, June 24, 1955, Article by Dave Bowman. *The Economist*, June 25, 1955, p. 1117.
39. See N.U.R., E.C., December 1955, Appendix D.36, British Railways Productivity Council Summary of Proceedings at Meetings held on September 26 and November 2, 1955. E.C., March 1955, R. 170.
40. N.U.R., E.C., December 1955, Rs. 2794 and 2892.
41. N.U.R., E.C., March 1956, Appendix M.19; December 1958, Appendix D.38; January 22, 1959, R. 105 and June 1959, R. 1147.
42. *R.R.*, March 1, 1957.
43. N.U.R., E.C., March 22, 1957, R. 791.
44. N.U.R., E.C., June 1958, pp. 49–52.
45. Report of the Railway Pay Committee of Inquiry, March 2, 1960, p. 9.
46. *The Economist*, January 16, 1960, p. 189; N.U.R., E.C., March 1960, Appendix M.11.
47. *The Times*, February 2, 1960.
48. Report, paragraph 239, p. 41.
49. February 8, 1960.
50. I am indebted to Mr W. E. Webster of Barnard Castle for the signalman's letter. For welfare expenditure see Minutes of British Railways Joint Advisory Council for Welfare, October 8, 1958, E.C. Minutes, December 1958, Appendix D.21. Also E.C. Minutes, December, 1960, Appendix D.8.
51. This account is based on N.U.R., A.G.M., 1922, R. 32; E.C., September 1933, Report of the Political Sub-Committee, pp. 140–2; April 1947, p. 25; S.G.M., October 13, 1953, Verbatim Report, and E.C., September 1954, Appendix S.29 for text of Statutory Instrument 898.
52. N.U.R., E.C., November 13, 1956, R. 2854.
53. N.U.R., E.C., March 1957, R. 775.
54. Election figures in N.U.R., E.C., December 1958, Appendix D.11.
55. *R.R.*, May 17, 1957.
56. Full text of the Memorandum of Agreement is printed in N.U.R., E.C., June 1956, Appendix J.17.
57. Full text of the Agreement is printed in 'Machinery of Negotiation', N.U.R., April 1954, pp. 46–9.
58. N.U.R., A.G.M., 1954, Verbatim Report, July 6th, pp. 14, 24, July 14th, p. 56.
59. N.U.R. General Secretary's Report to the A.G.M., 1956, p. 5.
60. Labour Party 53rd Annual Conference, Scarborough, 1954, Report, pp. 154–8.
61. For the text of this speech I am indebted to the United States Information Office, London.

RAILWAYMEN AND WORKING-CLASS EDUCATION

by

FRANK MOXLEY

Editor of *The Railway Review*

The establishment of the N.U.R. arose almost as much from the ferment of social and economic ideas as from the need of railwaymen to organize and gain recognition by the management. Amalgamation of the railway unions into an industrial organization was an ideal motivated by the theory of working-class unity as a means of achieving working-class power.

This was a logical step. For shortly after its originator the A.S.R.S. was formed its leading members turned their minds to the mobilization of the means to fight what was then the opening of a great battle of ideas. Within the decade of the formation of the A.S.R.S. the *Railway Review* was launched as a weekly workers' newspaper.

And a great deal of the discussion which preceded the Birth of the Labour Party was conducted in the columns of the *Railway Review*. Its role as a socialistic party was however not then so clearly seen as later.

The establishment of the Labour Party, the Taff Vale struggle and the surge of new power as expressed in the election campaign and result of the 1906 General Election all were influenced by the boiling over of this powerful ideological tumult in which the A.S.R.S. played such a significant role.

It was early recognized by some, not all, that to be equipped to meet the challenge trade unionists must be well educated—but not necessarily in the pattern set by State educationalists. On the contrary. Those who recognized the true nature of this flexing of the intellectual muscles of the working-class also saw that working-class education would have to develop independently. Its purpose would be different. Its aims would be infused with the necessity of social change, and social change demanded a new educational function and direction.

When Ruskin College was opened in Oxford in 1899 by two Americans, Walter Vrooman and Dr Charles Beard, its aims as then stated made an appeal to the leaders of the A.S.R.S. And within a few years, 1907, the first two A.S.R.S. students were in residence.

But by that time the original founders of the College had withdrawn support and returned to the United States. It was then touch and go whether it would continue. But support came, not always, in the opinion of some, from the right quarter. Money was provided. Conditions were not immediately imposed. But during the very years that the first A.S.R.S. students began their studies it became clear that powerful influences were anxious that workers' education should be conducted according to their views.

This was remarkably manifested in an article in the *Railway Review*, published on January 5, 1906. It was written by Ruskin College General Secretary, Bertram Wilson and described the early scepticism of the University towards the establishment of what one national newspaper said was 'a college for Labour leaders'. Even *Punch* at the time published an amusing but imaginary interview with a Ruskin College student. It was significantly headed 'A Striking Experiment'. The Student's Union debated the subject of Ruskin College which it was suggested was to be 'an educational sausage machine for the turning out of Labour agitators'.

Mr Wilson and the Ruskin authorities were evidently extremely anxious to make Ruskin respectable, and acceptable to the important people in the country and the University.

Ruskin was, in fact, he wrote, 'for the young and intelligent artisan who is prepared to devote his energies to the good of his fellows, to help them in their social and educational work; for the young man who will accept office in his trade union or Co-operative Society'. He stressed the need for 'sound economic knowledge', and 'true ideals of citizenship'.

His emphasis on 'sound' and 'true' was explicable by his use of a long statement on the question by Professor Marshall.

The significance of Ruskin's anxiety to explain the aims—the new aims, because they were different from the founders'—was made evident by Professor Marshall.

'The present age,' Professor Marshall wrote, 'is indeed a very critical one, full of hope but also of anxiety. Economic and social forces capable of being turned to good account were never so strong as now, but they have never been more uncertain in their operation. Especially is this true of the rapid growth and inclination of the working-class to use political and semi-political machinery for regulation of industry.' He had in mind, of course, the ferment of ideas aroused by the establishment of the Labour Party, the awakening power of the trade unions and the results of the General Election of 1906.

For he went on 'the well-to-do may say wise things effectively, but they are not strong enough to do wise things that are difficult unless they can first get the working-class on their side'.

It was essential that the working-class should not be guided by 'unscrupulous and ambitious men, or even by selfish enthusiasts with narrow range of vision'.

Already, in Professor Marshall's view this sort had had too much of their own way. There was need for a larger number of 'sympathetic students who have studied working-class problems in a scientific spirit, and who, in later years, when their knowledge of life is deeper and their sense of proportion more disciplined, will be qualified to go to the root of the urgent social issues of their day and lay bare the ultimate as well as the immediate results of the plausible proposals for social reforms'.

There then was the general precept. It was, in effect, a declaration of direction which the ruling circles in the University and in the country thought would be best for working-class education to go. We shall see later that the A.S.R.S. played a leading part in putting forward a view which was based on the idea of independent working-class education.

Unity House, Euston Road, London. Headquarters of the Union since 1910

PLATE 15

Castle Priory, Wallingford. Temporary wartime Headquarters of the Union 1940–45

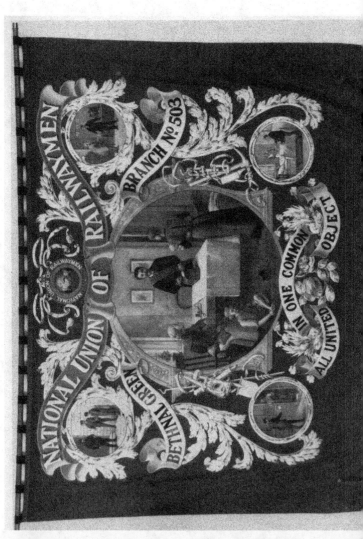

But the General Secretary of Ruskin College made it quite clear that he and the college authorities saw working-class education as did Professor Marshall.

Mr Wilson indeed said, 'Ruskin College will prove an excellent training ground for sympathetic students of social problems for whom Professor Marshall calls'.

This new policy was just getting into its stride the year the A.S.R.S. students started their studies. One of the students was Mr A. J. Williams, the son of Jimmy Williams, A.S.R.S. general secretary after Bell. Mr A. J. Williams later became a N.U.R. organizer. In a letter in the *Review* he wrote that complaints had been received 'from orthodox political and religious subscribers as to the advanced views held and propagated on these subjects by students'. The principal, Dennis Hird, was largely held responsible for the spreading of these 'advanced' views. 'And to satisfy the whims of these antiquated donors attempts were made in 1907 to substitute' Mr Hird's subjects, sociology and evolution, by 'others of a less progressive character, namely English Literature and Temperance.' This move was stopped by the opposition of the students. The college authorities, however, denied that they had ever intended to dispense with the teaching of sociology.

But further developments took place. In November 1907 Ruskin College, for the first time, had a visit from no less than the Chancellor of Oxford University, Lord Curzon, and a member of Hertford College. About the same time the college authorities complained that students were propagating socialism. When the new rules for 1908 were drawn up an additional clause was inserted to the effect that students were requested not to take part in any public meeting without the authority of the E.C. or the Faculty.

The students were immediately up in arms. Their opposition was successful and the clause was withdrawn.

Following the visit of the heads of the University the students again objected to what they believed was a move to bring about a tangible connection between Ruskin and the University. One immediate reason was the threat of a new system of examinations in embryo to accustom students to university type examinations. They thought this would lead to cramming. Anyway they were against anything which aided the suggested coalition because this would prevent Ruskin from retaining its individuality as a working-men's institution.

Once more the authorities of the college denied that they intended to sacrifice the independence of the college.

To the students these moves seemed the more regrettable in that by 1907 the college was largely paying its way. It had gained more and more support from the trade unions and the T.U.C. had thrown its considerable weight in with the college. In an appeal the T.U.C. said that now Labour was showing that it was determined to take its rightful position in the country, it more than ever needed the knowledge and training necessary to maintain that position.

Its success seemed to cause the University to pay more attention. But others were interested—those who had provided money to keep the college going. Among them were the Dukes of Fife and Norfolk, Lords Avebury, Crewe, Monkswell, Ripon, Rothschild, Tweedmouth, Northcliffe, Rosebery and Wolverhampton, the Right Hon. Sidney Buxton (father of the vice-principal of the college), C. B. Harmsworth, A. J. Balfour, Walter Runciman, Rupert

Y

Guinness and others of the same stamp—by no stretch of the imagination gentlemen who wished to see a change in the social system.

The situation became intolerable for many of the students. As they saw which way the college was going they began to organize classes themselves.

These classes were, according to the evidence of students who later recorded their impressions of these momentous events, better attended than the official lectures given in the College, with the exception of the principal's. There was clearly, in the years 1907–9, a growing division of opinion between the college authorities and the students on what should be taught. And more fundamentally, the whole purpose of the college was in dispute.

As we have seen above one view was that it should produce the kind of leaders who would suit the defenders of the status quo. The other, held by most of the students and the principal of the college that it should provide an educational spearhead for social change.

One student who wrote later in *Plebs* about these issues, concluded that the function of a Labour College 'should be the diffusion of ideas most likely to assist the Labour Movement generally'.

And in a statement published by the E.C. of the Plebs League on the Ruskin College dispute it was affirmed that 'a Labour College must be devoted to a particular training of men, already conversant with Labour difficulties, who have already proved their ability in local spheres of working-class activity'.

The principal of the College was undoubtedly a leading influence against linking Ruskin with the University. He deeply offended the authorities. They soon realized that if they were to get their way Dennis Hird would have to be removed.

That he was not the most discreet of men is clear from his rather tempestuous background. He did not make things better for himself by publicly, on the occasion of Lord Curzon's visit to Ruskin College, showing his contempt for the former Viceroy of India. That he was applauded by the students for snubbing Lord Curzon made a show-down inevitable.

The students, with outside help and some former students, in 1908 formed the Plebs League, and declared for 'a more satifactory connection of Ruskin College with the Labour Movement'. The magazine *Plebs* was started and Dennis Hird accepted the students' invitation to conduct it.

The Executive of Ruskin immediately met and ordered Mr Hird not to have anything to do with the *Plebs* movement. They also attempted to get at the students who were organizing it. The names of students helping were therefore kept out of the magazine.

The principal was told either to sever his connections with the *Plebs* or get out of Ruskin. He was in effect dismissed from the college. This sparked off one of the most remarkable episodes in the history of Oxford and was a turning point in the development of the Labour Movement. The students at Ruskin towards the end of March 1908 went on strike. They stayed away from lectures and refused to participate in the life of the college for a fortnight.

The national Press took up this unique occurrence and it was front-page news. Considering this was a revolt by about three dozen worker students at a little college in Oxford it received astonishing attention. But it proved how concerned were the authorities. In a sense, it justified the students' determination to bring out into the open a fundamental issue for the Labour Movement.

The A.S.R.S. were in some dilemma. Richard Bell was a leading member of the Executive of Ruskin College. He served on it for ten years. Some of the leading strikers were A.S.R.S. students. And a number of former students sent by the A.S.R.S. joined in the controversy. A letter from an old student was published in the *Railway Review* in 1909 under the nom-de-plume 'Young Engineman'. This was undoubtedly from George Brown, a member of Hull No. 2 branch who was later to become assistant general secretary of the N.U.R. In his letter he referred to a circular sent out by the students. He said if the facts were true it would materially alter the aims and objects of Ruskin 'which have mostly influenced trade unionists in persuading them to contribute to the funds'. The circular stated that the College Executive had claimed they had been forced to ask for Hird's resignation 'because he was unable to maintain discipline in the institution'. This, said the students, was so palpably false and absurd 'that it cannot be entertained for a moment by anyone who knows Mr Hird's authority with students'. They added that Mr Hird was the most capable teacher they had.

George Brown said that Mr Hird's offence 'seems to me that he is not quite as orthodox as he might be to suit the views of the Executive Council'. But on the other hand his work and his record were 'absolutely in the strictest accordance with the ideals and objects of the founders of Ruskin College and in strict conformity with the expectations of those organized masses of men who have given of their funds to carry out and further its objects'.

An editorial in the same issue of the *Railway Review* said, 'it would appear as if Mr Hird had been doing his work too well to suit that portion of the controlling board which leans in sentiment towards the owning classes.'

The governors, said the leader, were evidently afraid of the material that was being turned out and it was their desire to turn the course of lecturing into a channel which may be more comfortable for themselves. Students who saw the drift started a movement for democratic control of the College. 'They could see it drifting into the enervating influence of the University, being divorced from the intentions of the founders, and instead of training working-class leaders and tutors capable of holding their own with the opposite classes, becoming a patronized pulpit for the production of semi-political prigs. The students are to be congratulated on their attitude in refusing to submit.'

The *Review* was expressing a view which rapidly found agreement in A.S.R.S. branches and district councils all over the country. There was no doubt that the students and their sympathizers brilliantly beat the combined big guns of the University, the rich supporters of Ruskin College and those who wished to re-direct the course of the education provided.

Hull No. 2 Branch paid tribute to Hird's teaching and his work on behalf of Labour, and the Hull District Council said the College should be placed on a democratic basis. If the demands were not granted 'we shall feel constrained to do all in our power to bring about a withdrawal of trade-union support from the College'. Similar resolutions were passed by many other branches.

Allen Wells, of the Oxford branch, wrote in the *Review* at the end of April 1909. He said that a letter had been sent round branches saying the dispute was over. He was authorized, he said, to state that only the strike was over. The students were still agreed that the College was untenable to the Labour Movement and that a new and definite working-class structure must be established.

A former student, William Seed of Finsbury Park, London, said the trouble was that the College had appealed to well-to-do people for financial assistance on the grounds that young men who might otherwise become 'agitators' were taken into the institution and trained to be 'sound politicians'. He described the economics lectures, Mr Lees-Smith (later Professor) as one of the 'most hopelessly reactionary men I ever came across'. He commenced his lectures on Marx with, 'I have no wish to appear biased, but I cannot sufficiently express my contempt for such a system'. According to Mr Seed, the plea made by Sidney Webb for trade unionism, was dismissed by Mr Lees-Smith as 'a tissue of error'.

The E.C. of the College put the blame entirely on the Principal who they said was at variance on matters of general policy and administration. They denied emphatically that they were trying to destroy the independence of Ruskin College. And Mr Robert Young, Assistant Secretary of the A.S.E., replying to Mr Seed said that Labour leaders were not the creation of University or any other kind of college education; 'they are the creation of the movement they serve, and no amount of economics and sociology, orthodox or heretical, will qualify an individual for the position of a labour leader unless there is combined with education the power to inspire confidence and the ability, gained by experience, to lead and influence movements for the betterment of industrial and economic conditions'.

Robert Young had in fact addressed the A.S.R.S. conference at Sheffield prior to the resolution which first determined that the union would send students to Ruskin. It was obvious that influences within the A.S.R.S.—probably led by Bell—were angry at the way things had turned out. The E.C. minutes give only a hint of the undercurrents of the struggle.

In July 1909 the *Review* carried a strange article by Albert Mansbridge who had, with much more important men than himself, started the W.E.A. in 1903. This article was undoubtedly placed in the *Review* to try to influence the A.S.R.S. conference later in the year. The W.E.A. had played a leading role in trying to forge closer links between Ruskin and the University.

Mr Mansbridge's opening sentence was odd in the circumstances seeing that throughout the union there had been a wave of support for the striking students. He wrote, 'No body of working men have given greater support to the W.E.A. than the railway employees.' He claimed that in almost every town where the W.E.A. existed the A.S.R.S. branch was affiliated.

The following week Mr C. Watkins, an A.S.R.S. old student of Ruskin, made mincemeat of Mr Mansbridge and ended with this richly expressed comment.

'If Labour was class-conscious; if it accepted the scientific theory of the class struggle, and recognized that no progress is possible for a subject class; if it is realized that all compromise between these opposing classes resulted in the arrest of its own development; then the dangers that now beset the movement would vanish, and we should look upon all these arrangements between the class at the top and the class at the bottom as betrayals of our sacred cause, and treat those responsible for them according to their deserts.'

That the A.S.R.S. Executive were not completely convinced by the arguments is proved by their attitude to one of the A.S.R.S. students, Mr W. W. Craik.

Ruskin College complained to the A.S.R.S. about Craik's attitude to the students' movement. They told the union 'to bring influence to bear upon Mr Craik to abstain from his opposition or to remove him'. The E.C. refused to hear Craik's explanation and told him to adhere to the rules and government of the College. Before the June E.C. was also a long and detailed answer by the Executive of Ruskin College to the points made by the students.

At the September E.C., however, it was decided to invite a member from the Ruskin Executive and Craik. Professor Lees-Smith attended to 'explain the constitution'. After listening to Lees-Smith and Craik the E.C. decided that there were no good grounds for withdrawing support from Ruskin, 'and instruct our representative to the A.G.M. to endeavour to secure a larger measure of financial assistance being given to Ruskin College by this Society'.

An amendment by Edwards and Fagg recommending the A.G.M. to withdraw support from Ruskin was lost.

A further resolution was carried which, although supporting Ruskin College, questioned its administration. They had raised it with Professor Lees-Smith. He had assured them that steps were being taken to make the control more democratic.

Later the same year A.S.R.S. student Craik was suspended by the College authorities. The Principal, Dr Gilbert Slater, told the A.S.R.S. Executive that Mr Craik had been caught, with another student, trying to get into the College in the early hours of the morning. When the porter appeared they cleared off and did not come back until the next day. Craik, in a letter to the A.S.R.S. Executive, said that he was being victimized as others had also broken rules and not been so severely punished.

He added, however, 'I am not sorry to leave this institution, whilst at the same time regretting the circumstances, as for the past few months everything has been done to make life here unbearable, as well as for those students holding the same opinions as ourselves.'

They had applied to enter the new Central Labour College set up in Oxford under Dennis Hird in September 1909. The A.S.R.S. Executive nevertheless resolved that they saw no reason 'to interfere with the action of the Ruskin College authorities in maintaining proper discipline'. Craik's A.S.R.S. co-student resigned on health grounds but also because of 'the treatment accorded to Mr Craik'. The E.C. unanimously agreed to accept his resignation.

Certainly the hard-headed men of the Executive Council of the A.S.R.S. were not yet ready to embrace the new educational movement. They were not alone in their coolness to what the more frank regarded as a rather dangerous revolutionary movement bent on making trouble for the elected representatives.

Many had forgotten or never knew that the founder of Ruskin College quite clearly set out the function of the College. At its inauguration ten years earlier Walter Vrooman declared that 'the Ruskin students come to Oxford, not as mendicant pilgrims go to Jerusalem, to worship at her ancient shrines and marvel at her sacred relics, but as Paul went to Rome, to conquer in a battle of ideas'.

When most of the students acted on this maxim they were scattered by the people who should have been just as keen to cherish and develop this exciting idea.

At the A.G.M. of the A.S.R.S. in October 1909 at Leicester the delegates disposed of the doubts as far as the Society was concerned. Whatever evidence caused the E.C. to come to their conclusion a few months earlier, there was little of it left to influence the A.G.M. delegates. Motions from all over the country arrived for the agenda. The one from Toton No. 1 branch was debated. The motion regretted the recent changes made at Ruskin College, especially the deposition of Mr Dennis Hird 'who by his fidelity to principle and loyalty to Labour, won for himself the confidence and esteem of the working-class movement. We further decide to withdraw all further support from the College, believing that it has forfeited the confidence of the Labour Movement. We welcome the new Labour College in process of formation and decide to give it our support on condition that it is under the control of the Labour Movement, and instructs the E.C. if these conditions are fulfilled, to take up two annual scholarships in place of the present ones at Ruskin College'. The resolution was passed by 44 votes to 5.

The new College had stated its object: 'to train men and women for the industrial, political and social work of the organized Labour Movement, under the supreme control of the Labour organizations in the United Kingdom, and to assist in the establishment of similar institutions elsewhere.' The assumptions on which the new College was to work, however, were startling to those leaders of the Labour Movement who had barely begun to think beyond the Lib.-Lab. alliance. Even in 1908 the Labour Party 'allowed' Winston Churchill to be elected for Dundee. He was then a Liberal and newly appointed as President of the Board of Trade. There was a Labour candidate. But he was only supported by the Scottish Labour Party. It should also be realized that Marxism had made much less impact than had Fabianism. Indeed, out of fifty-one Labour and Lib.-Lab. members elected in 1906 who answered a questionnaire by the Editor of 'The Review of Reviews', Mr W. T. Stead, on the books they had found useful in their early days only two indicated any interest in socialist theory. The rest plumped for the Bible, then Shakespeare, Carlyle, Ruskin or Dickens.

It can be imagined how some of these would view the following:

'The Central Labour College is based on a recognition of the antagonism of interests existing between Capital and Labour. This produced a battle of ideas. The C.L.C. seeks to make the working class conscious of this antagonism for the purpose of removing it. It teaches social science from the point of view of Labour. It believes in the independence of Labour, industrially, politically and educationally.'

Perhaps this explains the slowness of the A.S.R.S. Executive in implementing the A.S.M. decision. Even after Bell resigned as General Secretary in February 1910, and dropped off the Executive Council of Ruskin College, things did not go any faster. The June 1910 E.C. meeting discussed the matter and decided they could not work with only a provisional committee of the C.L.C. And until a proper management committee was appointed, after the Annual Meeting of the C.L.C. in August, they could not take up two scholarships at the Labour College.

Hudson and Williams, the General Secretary, were elected to attend the first Annual General Meeting of the Central Labour College. At the September quarterly meeting they reported to the A.S.R.S. executive, who were still not satisfied that the conditions laid down by the A.G.M. of the union were being fulfilled. They came to this decision despite strong pressure from a number of branches to implement the 1909 A.G.M. Decision No. 94.

At Barry the following month, however, the delegates to the A.G.M. decided in no uncertain manner that the provisional committee of the Central Labour College 'answers all the requirements for democratic control'. The E.C. were instructed to transfer the remaining student at Ruskin College to the Labour College and appoint another student to the Labour College. They must also appoint two representatives to the provisional committee, said the A.G.M. by 47 votes to 2.

It was the following June 1911 that Edwards and the General Secretary were appointed to the Board of the Central Labour College. In September Edwards was also nominated as a Trustee. He later became Chairman of the C.L.C. Board.

That autumn saw the prising out from Oxford of the Labour College—by their University landlords. The college moved to Nos. 11 and 13 Penywern Road, Earls Court, London, which were bought on borrowed money for £1,800 at 5 per cent interest. Debts and removal expenses from Oxford caused a deficit of £400. The A.S.R.S. representative, Ernest Edwards, reported to the E.C. that the year's income was £753 against expenditure of £761. There were sixteen students in residence. Each student cost £52 a college year for board, lodging and education. Two hours each day had to be devoted to cleaning and other duties. There were no examinations. Studies included sociology, evolution, logic, rhetoric, economics and history. It proved to be the finest two years' training ever provided by a Labour College. Dennis Hird was the Principal.

There was a correspondence course department. One shilling was charged for each essay correction. There were also local classes being organized mainly by A.S.R.S. branches. Particularly strong were these classes in Lancashire—Rochdale, Bury, Oldham, Waterfoot, Radcliffe, St Helens, Warrington, Wigan, Liverpool and Birkenhead. There were also local classes in London and the mining valleys of South Wales.

During this time great efforts were being made to press forward the conception of industrial unionism which culminated in the significant if incomplete amalgamation of three of the railway unions into the National Union of Railwaymen early in 1913.

The interest in working-class education was undiminished even as these events took place. On the occasion of the N.U.R. fusion conference in London the Labour College organized a social evening to welcome delegates and 'to congratulate them on their work'.

At the Annual Meeting of the College in August of that year out of sixty-one delegates, thirty-four came from the N.U.R. Ernest Edwards of the N.U.R. was Chairman of the College Board. Frank Hodges—a former C.L.C. student and then S.W.M.F. Agent for the Garw District—was elected chairman of the Annual Meeting. In his opening remarks he said, 'As for the financial position of the college, it was a standing disgrace to the Labour Movement that such things as prize draws should be necessary to finance this most important activity of this movement.'

An appeal for financial assistance was made and the Executive of the N.U.R. agreed to lend £200. The union's trustees, however, were unable to pass the loan as it was contrary to the union's rules. However, the E.C. showed its support by advancing one year's scholarship fees (£104) in advance. The General Secretary, James Williams and Ernest Edwards were still serving on the College Board of Management.

At that year's Trades Union Congress an attempt to commit the trade-union movement to support of Ruskin College was defeated, mainly by delegates with allegiances to the Central Labour College.

No union supported the college more loyally than the N.U.R. This was acknowledged in an article in the July 1914 issue of the *Plebs* magazine.

That the college needed the help of such powerful unions as the N.U.R. and the South Wales miners was plain from the fact that the College was always in financial difficulty. It was evident that not enough students could be accommodated or the charges were insufficient. What was clear was that the staff, Dennis Hird was still warden, were far from generously rewarded.

A recommendation was made that the N.U.R. and the South Wales Miners' Federation should take over the property of the college and thus clear it from a bank overdraft of £2,300. A sub-committee of the two unions was appointed. The issue was brought before the Annual General Meeting of the N.U.R. at Swansea in July. It was there decided to increase the number of N.U.R. students from two to six and to advance the sum of £1,150 to meet the College's financial difficulty on condition the S.W.M.F. advanced the same sum. It was carried by 40 votes to 12.

At the S.W.M.F. Special Conference at Cardiff delegates voted 115 to 44 for acceptance of the N.U.R.'s proposal. They also drew up a scheme making provision for scholarships for the whole of the South Wales coalfield. The resolution was moved by A. J. Cook of Porth, a former student of the Labour College. Hird made an appeal to the delegates.

On August 3rd, the eve of the outbreak of the First World War, the college held its fifth annual meeting, at which there were fifty-seven N.U.R. delegates out of a total of eighty-nine. It was reported that owing to prolonged illness the work of Dennis Hird, the warden, had been successfully carried out by the sub-warden, former A.S.R.S. student W. W. Craik. The meeting was told that it had been a most critical year and time after time it had appeared that the college would close. On no less than four occasions financial salvation came through the efforts of the College Board Chairman, Ernest Edwards of the N.U.R. and President of the West Midland District Council of the union. He raised money be a benefit tickets scheme. N.U.R. branches throughout the country rallied to the support of the college, under the stimulation of a sustained propaganda drive by the *Railway Review*.

Giving a list of staff appointments and details of their pay—for instance, Craik as sub-warden and lecturer was on a nominal £40 a year—the annual report commented 'needless to say some of the salaries are greatly overdue'.

The College Board consisted of four representatives of the South Wales Miners and two of the N.U.R. Towards the end of 1915 the N.U.R. Executive decided that the expenses incurred by the Governors should be charged to the college.

During the previous year special efforts had been made to interest the railway Women's Guild in the work of the college. A typewritten lecture was prepared to be read out to branch meetings of the Guild. But the long-term aim was to persuade unions to provide sufficient money for scholarships for women trade unionists—and for the furnishing of a hostel for women students.

The range of the activities of the college may be judged by the fact that besides educating the small number of residential students, more than 2,000 students in local classes and through correspondence lectures were being taught by this tiny band of brilliant men and women. Whatever financial and administrative difficulties they had there was no paucity of zeal and skill on their part. If there was lack it was on the part of the rest of the trade-union movement which failed lamentably to give them adequate means to carry out their vitally valuable work.

The decisions of the N.U.R. and the S.W.M.F. to take over, at least the financial burden of the college, were not as easily carried out as passed. Lawyers advised that the rules of the unions would not permit control of the college. The joint sub-committee of the two unions could not find a satisfactory method of taking over the financial responsibility and the direct control and management of the college. They reported back to their executives that to give effect to the respective conference decisions it would be necessary to alter the unions' rules. The delay did not please the editor of *Plebs*, Mr J. F. Horrabin. In an editorial in the February 1915 issue he appealed directly to the N.U.R. rank and file to insist that the decision be carried out. He also said that although there may be some doubt about the legality of management and control there was no reason why the number of N.U.R. students should not be increased from two to six as had been decided by the A.G.M.

The S.W.M.F. in February 1915, at a special conference decided to accept the joint contribution with the N.U.R. to pay off the mortgage on the buildings of the college, and also to take over the maintenance and control of the college.

However, the future of the college was held in doubt pending the decision of the N.U.R. at a Special General Meeting in June. This was held in Nottingham on June 25, 1915. Mr A. Bellamy, the President, was in the Chair. The General Secretary, Mr J. E. Williams, had sent a note to branches saying that there had been difficulties in carrying out the previous year's A.G.M. decision. The E.C. had decided to convene a S.G.M. to consider the alteration of rule by adding to the union's objects, 'to make grants to and share in the management and control of the Central Labour College'.

Mr. J. H. Thomas, Assistant General Secretary, moved the alteration of rule. He outlined the differences between the N.U.R. and the S.W.M.F. The latter insisted on control of the college. The N.U.R. could not do this as the rules stood, which was why the E.C. had proposed the alteration.

Questioned on why the E.C. had not increased the number of students as they were instructed to do by the A.G.M., Thomas said the E.C. had asked for nominations. But they did not give effect to this because 'we were receiving letters from the college itself saying that the brokers were in'. Still, they had 'appointed four students' pending a decision on the future of the college.

In a second contribution, however, Thomas went into great detail about the financial difficulties he said were facing the N.U.R. He had no quarrel with handing over £1,300 to get the college out of difficulty. But he said 'you cannot take the responsibility of adding this Central Labour College to your liabilities'. He asked delegates to limit their liability, press that the Labour Movement as a whole should maintain the college, and support an amendment that would carry out such policy. Several delegates said Thomas had exaggerated the financial difficulties of the union. The amendment was lost by 47 to 4. The original change of rule giving the union the right to share in the management and control of the college was carried by 51 to 2.

At that year's A.G.M. of the college tribute was paid to the valuable work of the students, not only in the studies, but in the assistance they had given 'in the conduct of the domestic and general work of the college'.

Despite the war, provincial class work went on particularly in Lancashire, although George Brown, N.U.R. organizer and former Ruskin Student, was sedulously active in the Bristol area. The Liverpool District Council of the N.U.R. and the Midland District Council were being taught economics and the history of trade unionism by the sub-warden of the college, W. W. Craik. Of the four lectures-by-post classes held, two were under the auspices of N.U.R. branches, Carlisle City Branch and Wellington (Salop) respectively. The London District Council of the N.U.R. was then starting a highly successful course and was itself organizing classes in the London area with the assistance of the college.

Even the Women's Guild said: 'Two things—the war, and the delay in the taking over of the college by the Railwaymen and the South Wales Miners'— ought to have crushed us during the year, but neither succeeded in doing so.'

However, the ladies were proved wrong the next year. In 1916 the Military Service Acts threatened to, and ultimately did, carry off to the war the sub-warden and the secretary. The N.U.R. tried to obtain exemption for Craik but failed. The college ceased as a residential institution although the correspondence course department was kept going.

The controversy on the subject of working-class education went on in the columns of the *Plebs* magazine. In the November 1916 issue, Mr G. D. H. Cole wrote an article in which he said some wise things. He agreed, he said, with the main position of the Central Labour College, 'so far as working-class education is concerned, and I agree further that, in the attitude which it takes up towards elementary and secondary education, Labour must, and should, be guided by class bias.' As for the W.E.A. and its co-operation with the Board of Education and the universities, 'I am as ready as anyone can be to bid that connection goodbye. The sooner Labour can stand on its own educational legs, the better for itself and the worse for the capitalist system . . . I am only waiting till Labour is prepared to take over the W.E.A. and run it as a definitely Labour concern— and to pay for it.'

Another man, who was destined to reach levels rather higher than that of 'a working miner' which he was at the end of 1916, addressed an open letter to 'a Durham miner'. He told him that, 'up and down the country, the workers are beginning to see that education is the greatest step towards the winning of their freedom from wage-slavery. They look to social science to show them the way to that freedom which they have sought in vain by other means'. The man: Will Lawther.

The position of the sick Principal, Dennis Hird, presented a difficulty.

At the end of the year 1916, the N.U.R. refused to grant Hird anything in the nature of unpaid wages. The Executive did not consider they were responsible for any work performed previous to the union accepting joint control. Again in June the following year the N.U.R. turned down Hird's claim from the two unions for five years' salary at £100 a year plus travelling expenses between his home in Bletchley and London—a total of £565. They declared they could not pay debts incurred by the Central Labour College except those already acknowledged. A little later a decision by the A.G.M. of the N.U.R. to grant Craik £50 for his services was not paid on the ground that the remit was too vague.

After the war immediate steps were taken to get the college restarted. Craik was appointed acting-principal to take up his duties as soon as he was released from the army. The South Wales Miners, however, wanted Hird to be Principal again. The college governors were not in favour. The South Wales Miners asked to be allowed to speak to the A.G.M. of the N.U.R., which request was, of course, refused. These difficulties were soon, however, smoothed out and Craik was made Principal. The *Plebs*, prodding as usual, urged the Governors to reopen on May Day 1919. It was also reported that there had been over 200 applications from members of the South Wales Miners Federation for its eight scholarships. Among successful applicants for N.U.R. places was Tom Ashcroft of the Southport Branch who later became Principal of the college and subsequently editor of the *Railway Review*.

The N.U.R. examination paper for candidates was difficult, as the test set in June 1921 shows. Applicants had to write an essay on the question, 'What do you consider should be the functions of the Triple Alliance, and how should it be constituted in order to effectively discharge these functions?' This was followed by four questions: (1) Draw up a programme containing not more than four demands, the carrying into effect of which would, in your opinion, have an immediately beneficial effect on railwaymen. Give briefly, a reason in each case. (2) Of the two methods of Branch organization, branches of one grade or department, and branches of mixed grades, which do you consider to be best calculated to make for the efficient unity of the organization as a whole? (3) Give two reasons either for or against the regulation of wages on the principle of a sliding scale. (4) What do you understand by the following terms: The State, the proposed 'Miners' Pool', and a craft union.

Each candidate must have had two years' continuous trade-union membership, give evidence of elementary education, and pledge himself 'to place his services at the disposal either of his own organization or of the general Labour Movement, on the termination of his residence at the college.'

But independent working-class education was not waiting for the reopening of the college. Now classes were starting up and groups of them were forming themselves into colleges. The Scottish Labour College movement was quickly getting into its stride again. In September 1919 the Glasgow No. 7 branch of the N.U.R. asked for the appointment from members of ten part-time students at the Scottish Labour College. But the N.E.C. declined because of the close association with the London Labour College. A conference on I.W.C.E. at Wigan, attended by 200 delegates, decided to establish a Lancashire and Cheshire College. And in the North Eastern Area, Durham and Northumberland, a full-time lecturer for Labour College classes was appointed. In all this the small but immensely talented and energetic leaders of the Plebs League played a decisive part. In three years, 1918–20, Plebs sold 27,000 textbooks, 30,000 pamphlets, and 20,000 study outlines.

The magazine *Plebs*, surely one of the most remarkable small journals in the history of the Labour movement, was selling well. Its influence was strong. Ramsay MacDonald detested it and the whole movement it represented and stimulated. Earlier he had attacked the Labour College in his 'Syndicalism' and said the movement was the inevitable product of an attempt 'to send to breathe the atmosphere of Oxford a body of young workmen, able and ambitious, but not sufficiently prepared for the work given them to do.' And this man was a leader of the Labour Party.

The college reopened in September with twenty-nine students. Besides those from the N.U.R. and the S.W.M.F. (Central Committee Scholarships), other students were sent up by other miners' areas and from the Dyers' and Bleachers' Federation. A large number of applications for places had to be turned down.

In the middle of the following year a major development took place. A joint meeting of the N.U.R. and the South Wales Miners agreed to the plan outlined by College Secretary George Sims for the purchase of additional premises at Kew. The N.E.C. agreed with the S.W.M.F. to buy the property for £5,500. A month or two later in November the union agreed to give each student £45 a year allowance, to pay for necessary books and to allow third-class rail travel home at each vacation.

Glasgow and the West of Scotland District Council of the N.U.R., in March 1921 appealed to the N.E.C. for a grant of £100 to the Scottish Labour College which was then doing valuable work among large numbers of trade unionists. The E.C. gave half what was asked. Later that year the E.C. doubled the number of N.U.R. Scholarships to the London Labour College to twelve.

Other important moves were on foot involving the educational services of the whole trade-union movement. This was in line with the view of J. H. Thomas who had constantly urged the movement to participate in the work of the college. The issue of workers' education had always been a problem in the T.U.C., and it had never been resolved. Once again at the 1922 T.U.C. a resolution was carried instructing the General Council to co-operate with an Educational Inquiry Committee set up to consider the best way of educating trade-union members. The General Council were empowered to produce a comprehensive scheme for trade-union education, to take over the Labour College and Ruskin College and the educational set-up of the Iron and Steel Trades Confederation which included the Post Office workers, the railway clerks and the draughtsmen. No increasse in affiliation fees to the T.U.C. was permitted and the General Council were to have direct representation on the governing bodies of any college or institution taken over. The General Council met representatives of Ruskin College, Labour College, W.E.A., N.C.L.C. (which had been set up in October 1921), Scottish Labour College, Co-operative Union Educational Committee, and the Club and Institute Union. The representatives of the Labour College, and the others, approved the scheme provided it did not interfere or seek to alter their policies and outlook. Yet at that year's A.G.M. of the N.U.R.

a motion from Nine Elms No. 1 branch, calling for a scheme for the whole membership of the union, was defeated 27–41.

More and more attention was, however, being paid to the spread of educational facilities to the trade-union rank and file. The establishment of the National Council of Labour Colleges, following the Yardley (Birmingham) Conference, gave great impetus to the co-ordination and expansion of class work, and in *Plebs* the recognized organ of the N.C.L.C., the governors of the Labour College were urged to think more about the work for the rank and file. The N.U.R. branches and District Councils played a big role in the expansion of Independent Working-Class Education as they had done in the establishment of the Central Labour College.

Mark Starr, former student at the college and author of the widely read Plebs textbook, *A Worker Looks at History*, was lecturer for the N.U.R. South Wales and Monmouthshire D.C., classes in economics and in Industrial History. J. P. M. Millar, another student and later to become General Secretary of the N.C.L.C., had been busy with the Scottish Labour College which attracted many N.U.R. members. It was an N.U.R. member who first urged Millar to get into the movement.

At their March 1923 meeting, however, the N.U.R. Executive decided that the Chairman of the College Board of Governors should become a member of the National Executive of the N.C.L.C. The E.C. were not, on the other hand, prepared to allow N.U.R. students to exploit their position. In the summer of 1924 seven of the students offered their services as propagandists during the college vacation. The E.C. politely refused the offer as they did the application of six students for a grant of £10 each to help them to pay a visit to Russia during their holidays.

There was trouble when it was discovered the college was being used as the headquarters of an unofficial railway strike committee. Mr C. T. Cramp thought it serious enough to send a stern letter by special messenger telling them to stop using the college for such purpose. The Board of Governors told two representatives of the strike committee to remove themselves as early as possible. At the end of that year George Sims was sacked.

Tom Ashcroft, in September 1924, was appointed economics lecturer to fill the position vacated by Will Mainwaring who left to become miners' agent in the Rhondda. Early the following year W. W. Craik, the Principal, was suspended and then dismissed for misconduct and A. M. Robertson was appointed Acting Principal of the College.

In the background to these startling events the wheels of the proposed T.U.C. trade-union educational scheme went on turning slowly. At a meeting of the N.U.R.–S.W.M.F., it was agreed the college would be handed over to the T.U.C. providing the principles of independent working-class education were maintained. The N.U.R. Executive resolved in July 1925 that the two unions should each contribute £1,000 a year for two years and continue to send their usual complement of students. Another condition laid down by the N.U.R. was that the General Council of the T.U.C. should agree to proceed with the plans to develop the college's Kew property and the construction of new buildings. The General Council agreed to give the necessary assurances that the theoretical teaching in economics and historical sciences at the Labour College would remain upon its Marxian basis. This would be safeguarded by direct representation, in perpetuity, from the N.U.R., and the South Wales Miners, on the governing body of the college. Another condition laid down by the N.U.R. that the teaching staff be composed of individuals qualified to impart their teaching 'from the above theoretical basis' was also accepted by the T.U.C. General Council. However, with regard to the extension of the college at Kew, the General Council wished to add 'or at an equally suitable centre as soon as funds are available'. The N.U.R. Executive agreed. The meaning of this alteration became clear later when the Easton Lodge issue arose. The outline of the educational scheme was accepted by the 1925 T.U.C. Congress.

The pressure for an extension of educational facilities from branches and district councils never relaxed during this time. Equally the N.E.C. consistently confined their interest to the Labour College and its future. The South Wales and Monmouthshire D.C., issued a circular to its branches telling them it was in order for them to pay an additional halfpenny a quarter for each member out of the Branch Management Fund or the Branch Political Fund to finance a scheme with the N.C.L.C. However, at the December 1925 E.C. meeting, the District Council were told they were wrong. The union's rules did not permit such a levy.

At the A.G.M. in 1925 the Midland District Council tried to have a motion discussed which called for an educational scheme for all N.U.R. members. Each district council should deal with education in conjunction with the E.C. and employ their own full-time lecturer. All members would be obliged to pay for this at the rate of sixpence a year. It was ruled out by the Standing Orders Committee.

In the college the N.U.R. students had worries besides academic ones. Once their studies were over they had the problem of finding a job or getting back on to the railway. At that time the railway management were not of the firm opinion that Labour College 'graduates' would be better, even suitable, railwaymen when they left college. The N.U.R. had to fight many individual battles for reinstatement and they promised students they would try to get them their jobs back. But the E.C. stated: 'We cannot accept responsibility for their future employment, and candidates should obtain leave of absence to enable them to attend the college.'

However, if the T.U.C. had its way trade-union education would take a big sweep forward. Since the Scarborough Congress decision of 1925 there had been a remarkable development. The Countess of Warwick had offered her county house, Easton Lodge, to the movement through Arthur Pugh, Vice-Chairman of the T.U.C., for a trade-union college. This was in November 1925. Pugh reported to the T.U.C. Education Committee who visited Easton Lodge a few weeks later. The idea was to bring Ruskin College and the Labour College into Easton Lodge, each to pursue its own curriculum—an impossible scheme as was pointed out by Ruskin College although they agreed to come in. In the middle of January 1926 representatives of Ruskin, the Labour College, the Education Committee of the T.U.C., Lady Warwick, lawyers and architects met for a weekend discussion at Easton Lodge.

The General Council of the T.U.C., following a report of the Education Committee, sent a circular round all the affiliated unions telling them of the offer and saying it would mean a modification of the Scarborough decision. The new plan would also cost about £50,000 to put Easton Lodge into shape to serve as a college. Unions would be compulsorily levied to pay for this at the rate of one penny a year for each member for three years running. The unions were also expected to provide scholarships. So this was the new plan, and it called for many joint meetings between the N.U.R. and the S.W.M.F. There were also meetings with the T.U.C. Towards the end of the summer of 1926—it is remarkable that such an issue could have survived in view of the calamitous events a little earlier—the N.U.R. Executive were told that the T.U.C. had asked the opinion of the union's sub-committee 'as to whether we could in any way modify our policy with regard to the curriculum'. Later Walter Citrine, T.U.C. secretary, gave another assurance that the teaching and the staff would be maintained. The N.U.R. agreed and it was decided that the T.U.C. would take over the Labour College from October 1, 1926. By that time the college would have a new Acting Principal, Tom Ashcroft. Robertson had resigned.

It seemed then that the T.U.C.'s plans would be carried out and the Labour College taken over from the N.U.R. and the S.W.M.F. The General Council, however, were either not serious in their intentions or they seriously miscalculated the mood of the movement. The Easton Lodge scheme was crushed decisively by the 1926 T.U.C. Annual Conference. Delegate after delegate criticized the General Council. The burden was too great for most of the unions, said Arthur Henderson. The General Strike had gravely depleted their finances. Anyway, the General Council had not come out clearly on what they intended. The Woodworker's delegate, Mr Strain, who moved the reference back said the General Council had ignored the educational interests of the rank and file. The scheme, he said, would only meet the needs of a handful of students 'who some day may possibly become trade-union leaders'. Miss A. Loughlin of the Tailors and Garment Workers Union agreed with him. So did Herbert Smith of the Miners' Federation. W. J. Brown of the Civil Service Clerical Association thought that the events of the last few months proved that the leadership needed educating. Jack Tanner, A.E.U., wanted the money to be spent with the N.C.L.C., and Jack Jones of the General and Municipal Workers talked about men who had gone up to Ruskin dressed as workmen 'who have come back with haloes, dressed in plus fours, and immediately wanting to be general secretary of their union'. The reference back meant the scheme was dead. The Labour College was not taken over by the T.U.C. in October and the N.U.R. Executive were told at their December quarterly meeting that Lady Warwick had withdrawn her offer. The General Council informed them that they could not take over the college because of their financial position. However, as they had already been committed to provide scholarships to Ruskin they offered to give scholarships to the Labour College for 1926–7.

The N.U.R. decided to have a meeting with the South Wales Miners to tell them that it was 'not in the best interests of the union to continue part ownership and control of the college', when the union's liabilities to the present students were completed. They were also to sell the Kew property. Tom Ashcroft, the acting-principal, was designated principal, but there would be no guarantee of employment after July 1927.

That year's A.G.M. at Weymouth had narrowly defeated—voting was 33–35 —a motion from Kilmarnock No. 2 and thirteen other branches instructing the E.C. to arrange a national educational scheme with the N.C.L.C., and in January 1927 the N.C.L.C. put a scheme to the N.U.R. and the S.W.M.F. at a meeting in Unity House to link up the college with the classwork. The N.C.L.C. would take over the college providing the S.W.M.F. and the N.U.R. contributed £2,500 each a year. The N.U.R. in return would have six places for residential students and free access to N.C.L.C. classes for the whole of the membership. Millar of the N.C.L.C. said the College course could be cut from two to one year if students did preliminary work in part-time classes. Both meetings found the proposals unacceptable.

The Board of Governors suggested controlling unions make an attempt to bring other unions in by sending students and giving financial support. A week or two later representatives from the T.U.C. General Council, George Hicks, J. W. Bowen of the Post Office Workers and General Secretary Walter Citrine visited the College. They told the governors about their invitation to provide scholarships and handed over a cheque for £375 to cover the cost of five students. George Hicks was Chairman of a meeting called by the N.C.L.C. to discuss the future of the college. It was suggested that there should be a joint conference of the two controlling unions and the N.C.L.C. The college governors agreed to this but the N.U.R. Executive refused to participate. The S.W.M.F. said they would at first, but when the N.U.R. turned it down the Miners did the same.

Among the minor items which concerned the college, especially the Principal, provided some light relief. One student was charged with 'using abusive epithets and accusing officers of the college with making statements which were not true'. The Principal had been unable to deal with the matter because the student 'fell sick immediately after the alleged offence'. Things were put right when he apologized. A bit later one the students asked for facilities to see the film 'Ben Hur', 'in connection with their course on the origin and development of Christianity'. The governors said they had no objection at all to their going to see the film—at their own expense.

The summer of 1927 then proceeded on the assumption that soon this unique educational institution would be finally closing its doors at the end of the term. Once again, however, an N.U.R. Executive's decision was overturned by the Annual General Meeting. At Carlisle delegates stopped the closure of the college by 41 votes to rest of Conference. An appeal, by Warrington No. 2 and six other branches and the Glasgow and West of Scotland District Council, against the E.C.'s decision not to accept the N.C.L.C.'s solution to the problem of the maintenance of the college, was defeated, twenty-nine voting in favour. March-bank, the Assistant General Secretary, led the N.U.R. representatives at the meeting with the S.W.M.F. in Cardiff to consider how they were to keep the college open. Financial stringency notwithstanding, it is not without interest to note that the bank balance of the college was quite healthy. At June 17, 1927, for instance, it stood at £3,358 5s 6d.

The college governors asked the two controlling unions to select their students, and at the December meeting the N.U.R. Executive chose twelve from a list of fourteen applicants. After examination eight were finally chosen to reside at the college for the session January 1928 to July 1929. At the same meeting the E.C.

declined an invitation from Ruskin College to endow scholarships for N.U.R. members.

At the end of 1927 also the college governors appealed directly to the T.U.C. to help to make the college a national institution for the education of the workers. In May the following year the sub-committees of the N.U.R. and the S.W.M.F. met the T.U.C. Education Committee about the takeover of the college. On the maintenance of the curriculum the T.U.C. now asked the controlling unions to give up the college unconditionally. At the June 1928 E.C. meeting the N.U.R. agreed to hand over the college, unconditionally, but rather paradoxically, though shrewdly, added that the curriculum should not be changed except by a decision of the whole T.U.C., and this was reported to the S.W.M.F. at another joint meeting in Cardiff. Will Mainwaring, of the Miners, did not trust the T.U.C. to maintain the curriculum. Marchbank, however, did. The meeting decided to accept the T.U.C.'s proposal. The two unions also decided to sell the Kew property, an offer of £5,500 had already been made, and to divide the proceeds equally between the N.U.R. and the S.W.M.F. They also agreed to subsidize the college by £1,000 a year each for two years or alternatively guarantee twelve students a year each for the same period.

The General Council were chary of committing themselves too far again. Their report to the Swansea Congress said that to run a college for thirty students would cost £7,000 a year to be raised partly by scholarship fees and partly by direct contribution to the balance if needed. If the T.U.C. took over the Labour College it would mean a levy of ten shillings a year from every 1,000 affiliated members. It was a depressing proposal depressingly bare of any enthusiasm for the college as an invaluable workers' institution. No wonder it was referred back by an overwhelming majority. Thomas said he had always disagreed with the N.U.R. and the S.W.M.F. having to bear the burden. The only speaker who tried to divert the minds of the delegates into the most useful channel was Mainwaring, who stressed the importance of independent working-class education. Arthur Pugh said if it was referred back it would kill the scheme. It was indeed the fatal blow.

A joint N.U.R.-S.W.M.F. meeting on December 28, 1928, was told that as the T.U.C. had turned them down and other unions (seventy-one had been written to) had refused to help or send students, the S.W.M.F. would withdraw support and recommend closure in July 1929. At the June 1929 N.U.R. E.C., it was decided that as N.U.R. support was contingent on participation by the South Wales Miners, the college must indeed close. A little earlier the college staff, who were then under notice, made one last attempt to keep the college going. But the governors replied that 'no useful purpose would be served'.

The closure of the Labour College, as can be seen, had a mixture of causes. Financial difficulties played a part. But financially it was really a matter of the relative importance of expenditure rather than the total amount involved, which was not large. There were powerful influences in the two controlling unions, and in the movement as a whole, of the opinion that it was not right to educate a handful of workers so thoroughly and largely neglect the needs of the total membership. What was not fully realized was the aim of the founders of the college to provide a nucleus of trained workers to supply the intellectual stimulus for the bulk of trade unionists. The College did not help to further this aim sufficiently although class lecture notes and correspondence courses were started. The Plebs League, the propaganda body for independent working-class education, constantly complained about this. On the other hand, there was justification in the view, held by Thomas and others, that the burden of residential independent working-class education should not fall entirely on the shoulders of the N.U.R. and the South Wales Miners Federation. The failure of the rest of the trade-union movement to back up the magnificent lead given by the A.S.R.S.–N.U.R.–S.W.M.F. was the real cause of the closure of this remarkable institution. Nevertheless, in the relatively short time the college operated its achievements were astonishing. Whatever faults there were in the administration there is no doubt that the teaching and the teaching methods were brilliantly conceived, developed and executed.

If the college could have continued and expanded there is no doubt that the course of the Labour Movement would have been different.

However, it was evident that the establishment of the N.C.L.C., with the consequent competition for the limited funds the trade unions were willing to spend on education, meant that this specialized residential institution would lose sympathy and support. It is to the credit of the N.U.R. that the union consistently supported the college up to the final phase.

Once the college had gone, the way was then open for the N.U.R. to throw its considerable support into the continued effort for independent working-class education through the N.C.L.C. The A.G.M. at Southampton in 1929 instructed the E.C. to begin negotiations with the N.C.L.C. for a national scheme. In August a sub-committee of the E.C. met the N.C.L.C. A scheme was put forward by the latter, which would cost the union threepence a member a year, for the provision of facilities for classwork, postal courses and representation. Total cost would be £3,750. The E.C. asked for alternative arrangements and met the N.C.L.C. again at the end of October. Two schemes were submitted: one costing twopence a member for all facilities and the other costing one penny a member just for postal course facilities. Classwork could be arranged for districts at an additional cost of twopence a member. The proposals were referred to the 1930 A.G.M. which decided by 63 to 12 to affiliation to the N.C.L.C. at twopence a member, the cost to come out of the General Funds of the union. Incidentally, at the June 1930 E.C. the W.E.A. asked for support now the College had closed. The E.C. declined this request.

The great political and economic upheavals of the early years of the 1930's did not allow for much attention being paid to working-class education. The N.U.R. had its hands full. Membership of the union declined as men were sacked or driven from place to place like nomads. Despite the extremely trying conditions, however, the educational work of the union was not forgotten. The Executive Committee kept close watch on the working of the scheme with the N.C.L.C. and representatives played their part on National and Divisional Executives. After just over a year's efforts the Executive expressed their concern that the membership were not using the facilities of the N.C.L.C. in sufficient numbers. Circulars were sent out to branches urging members to attend classes and schools and to take up postal courses. One man very active in the work of education at this time was J. B. Figgins, later to become General Secretary.

And another was Jack Martin, a signalman from Manningtree, who subsequently was appointed Vice-President of the N.C.L.C.

At the 1932 A.G.M. there was an abortive attempt to get the union to share the money devoted to education equally between the N.C.L.C. and the W.E.T.U.C. Moved by York No. 3 branch, it was defeated 14 to 65.

The General Secretary the following year, 1933, called the attention of delegates to the unsatisfactory use members were making of N.C.L.C. facilities. They were at that time costing the N.U.R. £2,512.

It was, incidentally, in this year that the former principal of the Labour College, Tom Ashcroft, took over the editorship of the *Railway Review* from Willet Ball who had done as much propaganda work for the idea of independent working-class education as any man or woman.

During the next few years the educational work for the union's members was conducted by the N.C.L.C. in classes, day and weekend schools. In 1936 the N.C.L.C. asked the N.U.R. to increase its affiliation by one penny a member. The N.E.C. referred this to the A.G.M. which decided by 53 votes to 14 to agree to pay threepence a member a year to start from 1937. That year the N.U.R. paid on a membership of 337,000—a sum of £4,212. This was more than any other union. In fact for years the N.U.R. was the highest contributor to the funds of the N.C.L.C. Out of a total contribution of £13,865 the N.U.R. in 1941 paid over £4,000.

At the same A.G.M. another attempt was made to get the N.U.R. to support the W.E.T.U.C. 'Next Business' disposed of the issue. In 1940 it was raised again by the same branch, Lancaster No. 2. The motion received only four votes. The W.E.A. the same year asked the E.C. to receive a deputation. The reply was polite but decisive. In view of the policy of the union 'no useful purpose' would be served by seeing the W.E.A. There were more than 6,000 N.U.R. members studying with the N.C.L.C.

As the effects of the war began to be felt the number of students fell sharply. But participation in summer schools increased. The N.C.L.C. offered eighteen scholarships to the N.U.R. which were fully taken up.

With the end of the war in sight the trade-union movement was shaping up to the task of preparing for the great strides society, it was confidently believed, would take once the fascist reaction had been defeated. The N.C.L.C. revived the idea of a residential college for tutors, educational organizers and prospective trade-union officials. The N.U.R. had turned down a suggestion in 1942 that the union should sponsor another college. When it was raised again in 1944 the N.U.R. put up the suggestion that the T.U.C. should examine the possibility of a college. The E.C. thought the provision of a residential college should be the responsibility of the trade-union movement as a whole. This view was supported by the T.U.C., who undertook to look at the problem of trade-union education.

In April 1945 a new development took pace. The Co-ordinating Committee of the three Scottish N.U.R. District Councils held a highly successful weekend school in Edinburgh. Encouraged by this the Edinburgh and East Scotland District Council asked the E.C. for financial assistance to organize a week's summer school but were turned down because of the union's commitments to N.C.L.C. summer schools. An appeal against this decision at the A.G.M. was lost, only six voting in favour.

The T.U.C. General Council—N.U.R. General Secretary J. Benstead, was on the Education Committee—reported they were examining a proposal to have a non-residential full-time college as a war memorial to trade unionists. They hoped training courses would start soon. This would in effect be a 'T.U.C. training college in embryo'. As for the N.C.L.C.'s proposal, the T.U.C. declared that any such residential college must be 'under the undivided control of Congress'.

Despite the N.U.R.'s co-operation in the T.U.C.'s educational plans, the E.C. rejected an invitation by the T.U.C. Educational Trust to send students to a three-year evening course in trade-union studies at the London School of Economics.

With the approach of railway nationalization some sections of the union believed that the time was opportune to train workers for the takeover of control of the industry. At their December 1946 meeting the Executive Committee were asked by the Manchester District Council and the Sheffield and Chesterfield District Council to set up a permanent residential school for the purpose. Rather turning a blind eye the E.C. declined on the grounds that the question of training personnel would be considered in conjunction with the Nationalization of Transport Bill of 1946.

Rationalization of trade-union education was one of the main subjects at the 1947 Annual Conference of the N.C.L.C. It was recalled that the T.U.C. the previous autumn had carried a resolution from the National Union of Mineworkers and the A.E.S.D. (Draughtsman's Union) asking the General Council to set up a comprehensive trade-union education scheme under centralized control. The N.C.L.C. drafted a memorandum in favour of complete amalgamation of all existing workers' educational bodies. This was remarkable in that the N.C.L.C. had legitimate claim to being a highly successful organization. Indeed Arthur Woodburn, M.P., the President, at the 1948 annual conference, referred to the fact in the organization's thirty years over one million trade unionists had used the educational facilities provided by their unions through the N.C.L.C. The N.U.R. membership had a good record of participation. But not enough considering the N.U.R.'s financial contribution, which was why year after year the General Secretary's annual report to the A.G.M. contained an appeal to the membership to use these facilities. The issue of rationalization was again brought up at the Margate T.U.C. of 1948. In a very long report the General Council outlined the differences in outlook of the W.E.A. and N.C.L.C. and decided they could not express any preference. They could not see amalgamation being possible. The General Council could not recommend a centralized comprehensive educational set up.

The relatively hum-drum educational work with the N.C.L.C. went on with only slight variations. In 1949 the union had twenty-eight free scholarships to Summer Schools. There was also a Dutch summer school for which the union awarded six places. There were 183 applications.

But a new direction in workers' education was shaping up with the nationalization of the railways. The 1948 A.G.M. had asked the Executive to prepare a report on training and education in the railway industry and demanded action to remove all grade barriers to higher appointments. The following summer the E.C. reported that they were to co-operate in the British Transport Commission's training and educational schemes which was in line with the policy laid down by the E.C. in 1946.

As for the T.U.C. courses, the E.C. were reluctant to extend any facilities. They took the same attitude to a proposal from the Scottish T.U.C. that the union should help support Newbattle Abbey. In 1951, the T.U.C. decided to include in their autumn programme two one-week non-residential courses on Industrial Relations and Negotiations for trade union officers. The E.C. decided to take no action on the matter although twelve N.U.R. members attended the specialized course for shopmen.

From this discussion the E.C. in September 1952 initiated a brand new policy. They said that in view of the cost and value of the present facilities they proposed to examine the possibility of setting up, 'within our own organization', an educational scheme for the training of younger members in order that they may secure, 'for the benefit of the organization', education in such subjects as Branch Accountancy, Chairmanship, Agreements held by the union, Methods of organization, Rules of the union.

The cost of the N.U.R.'s educational work was estimated. In 1951, for instance, £4,561 was being paid to the N.C.L.C. and £2,725 to the T.U.C. for training courses. The expenditure on T.U.C. courses for the first half of 1952 reached the same total for the whole of the previous year and the N.C.L.C. were pressing for an increase in affiliation fees which would add a further £700 to the annual fee. If the N.U.R. scheme was adopted it would cost £4,200 for five courses. The E.C. in June, 1953, decided to adopt the new policy which would still allow for full affiliation to the N.C.L.C. But for two years the union would not pay for students at N.C.L.C. and T.U.C. summer schools. The union would run three fortnightly schools for two years in different parts of the country. Twenty students were to be selected from two E.C. areas in sequence. A Tutor-organizer and two assistant-tutors were to be appointed from within the union.

The first schools were held in 1954 at Wortley Hall, Sheffield, Lambton Castle Residential College, Chester-le-Street, Co. Durham and Thomas Hall University College of the South West, Exeter, under the control of Tutor-organizer Mr L. Watters, a member of West Ealing No. 1 and a retired member of Unity House staff. The two assistant tutors were Mr R. J. Tuck of Pontypridd and Mr J. Dunk of Grimsby No. 1 branch.

There was an appeal against the E.C.'s policy at the A.G.M. at Paignton from the North West of England District Council, Peterborough No. 2 and five other branches. It was defeated 21 to 53.

The schools attracted a large number of potential candidates, who, it was found, were usually already fairly well equipped as a result of their N.C.L.C. studies in classes and through postal courses. Choosing the students was, therefore, a difficult job. The two years' schools were 'very satisfactory', in the opinion of the E.C. But at their December 1955 meeting they decided that the character of one further school should be altered. A school designed to meet the needs of less-experienced branch secretaries was decided upon. Two others would concentrate on the structure of the union, industrial unionism versus craft unionism, 'and other N.U.R. activities'. The number of students for the branch secretaries' school would be twenty-four. It was decided that at the end of the 1956 series the union's educational policies should be reviewed. At the beginning of that year, however, the N.C.L.C. told the union that owing to increased costs they proposed to suspend their free summer-school places. The E.C. declined to agree to pay for students.

Rationalization of trade-union education was once again being discussed. It was one of the main topics at the annual conference of the N.C.L.C. in June 1956 and was related to the need for an increase in the finance available to carry on the work. At that year's A.G.M. a motion from March Branch asking that the N.U.R. summer schools be made permanent was lost, only five voting in favour.

At the beginning of 1957 the E.C. accepted a report of the Education Sub-Committee which recommended renewed participation in T.U.C. training college courses, certain T.U.C., N.C.L.C. and Labour Party summer schools, and that the N.U.R.'s own scheme should be discontinued on its present lines. They agreed to pay an increased fee to the N.C.L.C. A further report stated that the committee, in view of the T.U.C. decision in 1948 on rationalization of trade-union education, could see 'no useful purpose in pursuing this matter'.

At the S.G.M. in August, however, a motion from Peterborough No. 2 branch was carried unanimously and demanded that the E.C. use all influences to secure co-operation and co-ordination between all sections of the movement who were catering for working-class education—in short, rationalization.

At the Blackpool T.U.C. the President, Tom Hollywood, moved an N.U.R. motion asking for trade-union educational rationalization and this was remitted to the General Council of the T.U.C. on the understanding that the problem should be examined in the light of the conditions in 1957 and not 1947.

Still another report was prepared and accepted by the E.C. at the June meeting. In it there was a proposal for a special six-lesson N.C.L.C. postal course on the structure of the N.U.R. It was also recommended that District Councils organize day schools on branch book-keeping and the machinery of negotiation, and that a series of courses on branch administration for members appointed for the first time as branch secretaries be centrally organized.

A peculiar step was taken by the E.C. in August, historic in its way. For the first time for very many years the N.U.R. became associated with Ruskin College. The General Secretary of the College and the Principal had asked to see the Education Sub-Committee back in April. The result was that the N.U.R. decided to contribute £25 a year to the Ruskin College 'Trade Union Appeal Fund'. Arising from this decision the N.U.R. again, after nearly half a century, became entitled to have a representative on the governing council of Ruskin College.

By the time of the 1958 A.G.M. the General Secretary could report that the N.U.R.'s education scheme costing £13,000 was the most ambitious in the union's history. There were schools at national level for branch secretaries and for those doing work study and District Councils were organizing one-day schools on work study, negotiating machinery, etc. At the 1960 A.G.M. a Kettering motion, carried unanimously, decided that educational courses should be extended to include administration and finance of the railway system and to base this on the N.U.R. booklet 'Planning transport for you'. There was also a move to find out the facilities at universities and technical colleges for the study of transport. Branches were given this information and assured that Head Office would help with the necessary contacts to start new classes. District councils were authorized and urged to run more schools on transport subjects. Head Office undertook to pay the hall rent, provide tutors and meet reasonable costs of meals.

In 1962 the General Secretary reported to the A.G.M. at Margate that the schemes were going well and that the moves to rationalize trade-union education were almost completed. Following the N.U.R.'s motion at the T.U.C. in 1957 the General Council and the interested bodies met many times and thrashed out a plan which would see the end of the N.C.L.C. and the setting-up of a T.U.C. Educational Council. Some feel that this will close a fascinating chapter in the history of the working-class movement. Throughout this section we have been describing the struggle of independent working-class education to survive in the midst of financial stress and opposition. It may, of course, be thought that with the developments of the last few years of the period trade-union education has become much more independent but that its nature has changed so much that new forms and methods were needed. Whatever interpretation is given there is no doubt that the N.U.R. has played a distinguished and leading role.

GENERAL SECRETARIES OF THE UNION

1871/Oct. 1874	G. CHAPMAN
Oct. 1874/Feb. 1883	F. W. EVANS
Feb. 1883/Oct. 1897	E. HARFORD
Oct. 1897/Jan. 1910	R. BELL, J.P., M.P.
Jan. 1910/June 1916	J. E. WILLIAMS
June 1916/August 1931 ⎱	J. H. THOMAS, P.C., M.P.
Jan. 1920/July 1933 ⎰	C. T. CRAMP
July 1933/Jan. 1943	J. MARCHBANK
Jan. 1943/Sept. 1947	J. BENSTEAD, C.B.E.
Sept. 1947/March 1953	J. B. FIGGINS
March 1953/Nov. 1957	J. CAMPBELL
Feb. 1958/—	S. F. GREENE
(*Acting from Nov. 1957*)	

PRESIDENTS OF THE UNION

1872/73	DR B. LANGLEY, LL.D.	1928/30	J. GORE
1874/76	REV. CANON JENKINS, D.D.	1931/33	W. DOBBIE
1877/91	P. S. MACLIVER, M.P.	1934/36	J. HENDERSON, J.P.
1892/98	W. HUDSON	1937/38	W. T. GRIFFITHS, J.P.
1899/1901	G. THAXTON	1939/41	J. H. POTTS
1902/04	W. G. LORRAINE	1942/44	F. J. BURROWS, J.P.
1905/06	J. H. THOMAS	1945/47	J. E. BINKS
1907/09	J. R. BELL	1948/50	W. T. POTTER, J.P.
1910	E. CHARLES	1951/53	H. W. FRANKLIN
1911/17	A. BELLAMY, J.P.	1954/56	J. W. STAFFORD
1918/19	C. T. CRAMP	Jan. 1957/ Nov. 1957	
1920/21	W. J. ABRAHAM		T. HOLLYWOOD
1922/24	J. MARCHBANK	Feb. 1958/60	C. W. EVANS
1925/27	W. DOBBIE	1961	W. H. RATHBONE

Year	No. of Members	Total Income since Fusion	Paid for Legal Assistance	Unemployment Benefit		Trade Conferences, Conciliation Boards, and Expenses of Movements for Improved Conditions	Strike Benefit Paid
				Union Benefit	State Benefit		
		£ s d	£ s d	£ s d	£ s d	£ s d	£ s d
1872	17247	..	..	106 13 4	..	*1004 19 3	..
1873	15830	..	150 0 0	117 0 3	..	..	..
1874	14254	..	167 0 0	460 12 3	..	..	..
1875	13018	..	390 13 9	809 7 10	..	..	..
1876	13440	..	430 12 3	610 9 6	..	..	..
1877	12815	..	460 19 3	640 8 1	..	..	..
1878	13543	..	490 18 8	907 19 2	..	..	..
1879	11516	..	484 1 2	1311 0 4	..	..	..
1880	8589	..	183 16 2	785 14 7	..	..	..
1881	6878	..	804 12 0	586 6 0	..	48 6 0	..
1882	6321	..	544 1 4	479 18 3	..	158 5 0	..
1883	8077	..	493 10 4	370 4 10	..	109 10 9	..
1884	8460	..	391 11 2	427 12 7	..	163 1 9	..
1885	9052	..	311 8 4	515 15 6	..	74 8 1	..
1886	9609	..	378 17 7	551 15 6	..	274 5 11	..
1887	10830	..	1145 10 5	2068 5 9	..	386 13 11	6690 0 0
1888	12080	..	353 2 9	705 17 10	..	901 9 10	..
1889	19585	..	189 3 1	599 12 11	..	461 3 6	..
1890	26360	..	1803 11 9	1018 18 7	..	6743 18 0	..
1891	29820	..	1078 1 9	1762 6 1	..	4191 18 5	..
1892	30228	..	560 4 2	5663 13 7	..	1445 17 3	..
1893	33826	..	783 1 3	5046 7 9	..	4136 19 6	..
1894	40735	..	1267 10 6	2951 8 5	..	2048 12 0	..
1895	38119	..	745 13 1	3217 6 4	..	2260 13 0	..
1896	44709	..	840 1 5	2715 4 10	..	2528 13 3	..
1897	85928	..	930 5 6	3118 15 4	..	3643 2 11	..
1898	54426	..	2005 14 5	16331 12 7	..	6562 11 8	5812 10 8
1899	59819	..	1962 15 9	2882 19 11	..	2468 19 9	..
1900	62023	..	2507 3 0	3215 12 7	..	2611 18 5	3540 16 6
1901	55943	..	10793 4 2	3230 15 5	..	1485 3 3	..
1902	53453	..	13400 13 9	3153 11 5	..	1118 10 11	..
1903	52355	..	3795 10 5	3233 16 0	..	1739 18 3	23000 15 0
1904	53407	..	1980 0 7	3704 5 7	..	1768 14 8	..
1905	57462	..	2989 11 8	3965 1 11	..	1793 9 7	..
1906	70130	..	2097 10 0	3661 6 8	..	4057 19 2	..
1907	97561	..	7683 4 11	4227 11 7	..	4147 15 2	..
1908	80321	..	7598 16 11	8574 0 2	..	7413 19 10	..
1909	73571	..	14607 1 8	9017 17 4	..	16205 5 8	..
1910	75153	..	15154 11 3	8792 16 10	..	4573 9 1	..
1911	116516	..	7269 2 8	10560 2 10	Commenced	6461 17 8	29622 6 9
1912	132002	..	5669 17 5	94901 14 7	1912	6544 5 6	3564 5 5
1913	267611	213983 0 2	4470 15 10	9427 8 6	147 13 4	4549 17 10	7254 16 11
1914	273362	243401 2 6	6743 11 1	12814 6 5	638 7 6	2089 17 7	..
1915	307135	251014 4 6	4485 7 6	5077 0 4	166 5 9	2124 9 10	..
1916	340511	264180 15 7	7471 10 9	2367 9 4	57 9 0	2308 0 9	..
1917	401519	311810 13 11	9034 19 3	2225 1 7	28 16 4	2853 13 9	..
1918	416531	355626 1 9	5172 16 2	2609 18 9	52 13 3	4417 7 1	..
1919	481081	540378 19 9	6670 5 7	11933 14 7	31 18 0	5195 15 1	273411 13 3

* Specially raised by Levy.

AND TOTAL FUNDS AT THE END OF EACH YEAR SINCE 1872

Disablement		Deaths		Orphans			Benevolent Fund		Total Funds	Year
No. of Claims	Total Grants Paid	No. of Claims	Total Grants Paid	No. placed on Fund	Total Paid	No. of Children on Fund	No. of Claims	Amount Paid		
	£ s d		£ s d		(The Orphan Fund was established in 1880, and money received prior to that date was remitted to the Derby Orphanage, Derby)			£ s d	£ s d	
..	..	..	..			..	..	..	2569 2 0	1872
..	..	..	..			..	..	..	5028 10 5	1873
..	..	..	..			..	..	..	9393 5 0	1874
..	..	..	..	..	£81 0 0	..	..	..	12243 7 3	1875
..	..	..	..	..	180 17 0	..	..	..	16159 18 8	1876
..	..	..	..	..	100 16 10	..	..	..	18715 15 7	1877
..	..	..	..	..	101 4 1	..	..	..	22371 18 8	1878
..	..	..	..	..	76 7 0	..	..	..	24117 17 7	1879
..	2023 19 10	..	..	36	169 5 0	36	..	..	26013 9 7	1880
..	..	..	..	30	415 5 8	..	..	..	24525 3 0	1881
34	680 0 0	14	140 0 0	15	597 7 11	..	..	..	27176 9 6	1882
45	900 0 0	10	100 0 0	65	672 14 4	..	..	..	36932 4 5	1883
56	1120 0 0	17	170 0 0	106	791 2 4	..	..	..	42851 2 7	1884
61	1260 0 0	14	140 0 0	67	1155 15 8	..	..	..	50788 11 5	1885
65	1300 0 0	14	140 0 0	105	1467 3 4	..	..	..	55708 14 4	1886
44	880 0 0	12	120 0 0	118	1677 6 10	..	..	..	62186 8 11	1887
59	1180 0 0	82	420 0 0	100	1910 18 5	..	..	..	73733 17 3	1888
67	1340 0 0	93	465 0 0	143	2186 14 11	559	..	..	81763 11 6	1889
71	1420 0 0	98	490 0 0	126	2286 4 7	556	..	..	98114 10 7	1890
83	1660 0 0	182	910 0 0	193	2872 8 1	612	..	..	110584 9 3	1891
86	1720 0 0	167	835 0 0	246	3610 5 2	789	..	..	120826 16 3	1892
101	2020 0 0	194	970 0 0	272	3803 16 5	801	..	..	122870 12 8	1893
30	600 0 0	107	535 0 0	223	4257 11 6	964	..	..	140339 12 6	1894
81	1620 0 0	203	1015 0 0	274	5089 5 9	1068	..	..	158725 12 0	1895
88	1760 0 0	201	1005 0 0	264	5300 6 0	1150	..	..	178842 17 7	1896
100	2000 0 0	266	1330 0 0	369	5615 5 0	1351	..	..	197992 12 5	1897
97	1940 0 0	259	1295 0 0	273	6786 5 5	1355	..	..	199303 0 9	1898
115	2300 0 0	278	1390 0 0	379	6829 2 3	1676	..	..	224389 17 2	1899
99	1980 0 0	265	1325 0 0	347	8380 15 7	1728	..	..	245055 10 2	1900
113	2260 0 0	302	1510 0 0	430	8629 12 9	1878	..	..	264098 13 5	1901
130	2600 0 0	273	1365 0 0	341	8882 17 1	1886	..	..	279447 0 4	1902
146	3304 0 0	261	1305 0 0	342	9077 14 9	1789	..	..	278842 14 0	1903
157	3820 0 0	279	1395 0 0	347	9326 5 3	1949	..	..	305491 6 8	1904
165	4050 0 0	294	1470 0 0	320	9516 8 3	1865	..	..	330567 10 9	1905
171	4154 0 0	306	1530 0 0	309	9396 13 4	1838	..	..	362732 15 8	1906
199	5007 0 0	242	1710 0 0	337	9472 1 8	1806	Commenced		397168 12 11	1907
240	5889 0 0	341	1705 0 0	324	9457 9 9	1843	Jan. 1, 1908		423966 7 10	1908
294	6837 0 0	415	2075 0 0	319	9406 17 6	1815	3	75 0 0	429273 13 6	1909
311	7101 0 0	368	1840 0 0	306	9719 14 9	1872	13	175 0 0	441181 10 10	1910
343	8031 0 0	407	2035 0 0	348	9641 17 9	1883	6	60 0 0	437121 14 6	1911
326	7976 0 0	423	2115 0 0	290	9828 11 8	1839	12	120 0 0	379025 0 7	1912
327	7845 0 0	503	2515 0 0	393	9426 16 0	1845	1	10 0 0	476434 17 6	1913
357	8703 0 0	674	3370 0 0	558	10598 15 5	2023	14	170 0 0	574426 1 5	1914
285	7018 0 0	785	3923 0 0	721	11006 4 4	2433	8	130 0 0	680846 14 5	1915
271	6958 0 0	785	3925 0 0	626	12739 5 9	2553	6	100 0 0	812617 11 10	1916
336	8810 0 0	842	4210 0 0	672	13951 18 7	2891	8	110 0 0	982834 3 4	1917
281	7393 0 0	1398	6990 0 0	1397	14885 2 5	3857	6	110 0 0	1178586 5 9	1918
349	9823 0 0	1166	5830 0 0	1118	29624 18 8	4267	14	230 0 0	1188853 13 11	1919

continued overleaf

TABLE SHOWING THE NUMBER OF MEMBERS, BENEFITS PAID,

Year	No. of Members	Total Income since Fusion	Paid for Legal Assistance	Unemployment Benefit		Trade Conferences, Conciliation Boards, and Expenses of Movements for Improved Conditions	Strike Benefit Paid
				Union Benefit	State Benefit		
		£ s d	£ s d	£ s d	£ s d	£ s d	£ s d
1920	457836	676244 1 9	9187 5 8	26734 1 10	694 0 11	6535 10 4	7594 18 1
1921	386115	777794 2 0	8436 3 8	579123 7 9	115506 0 8	8010 14 9	3278 1 0
1922	337350	644635 10 4	8502 13 7	101427 13 4	105685 15 9	13067 3 4	104 0 0
1923	363230	576611 12 5	7341 17 7	27017 4 1	37761 13 11	15077 2 10	1081 13 4
1924	381099	628836 8 2	8855 9 1	23190 8 0	25812 2 3	28375 14 1	5170 7 6
1925	398596	691424 18 11	9956 7 8	43452 1 3	50132 18 2	19700 10 8	1206 5 9
1926	387540	893217 13 6	18871 6 3	629179 11 8	257813 12 5	15317 5 8	935086 17 0
1927	311740	729181 5 1	11838 1 5	31317 5 8	60573 11 9	10873 16 5	468 15 0
1928	308046	615834 7 8	12413 16 10	26835 18 5	56802 7 4	11174 19 7	..
1929	312879	554126 0 0	12123 7 8	12620 17 7	593 17 6	10935 8 3	..
1930	334835	580196 17 7	12286 18 3	47234 19 10	10 0 0	12302 13 0	9087 18 4
1931	295268	551928 11 1	11344 7 10	58977 13 4	..	16457 19 11	3062 11 8
1932	289925	536417 13 5	13315 16 6	65211 1 3	..	17570 4 10	4671 0 9
1933	275706	544891 16 2	10565 16 7	29248 10 9	..	17617 13 3	52878 15 6
1934	290273	542811 14 7	12842 10 10	9947 19 7	..	17124 17 10	92 8 0
1935	305972	554948 13 2	10316 1 4	7953 3 4	..	23771 4 3	..
1936	337848	593749 2 6	10526 6 7	6814 15 0	..	19294 10 2	..
1937	364356	635053 7 6	12185 15 6	5205 18 3	..	19705 16 10	944 0 0
1938	366659	674935 6 0	11839 13 9	22036 12 3	..	20217 8 11	3050 8 0
1939	349542	640445 4 10	15586 16 4	14518 15 1	..	20088 16 1	893 19 0
1940	361750	614183 17 5	21472 6 3	8863 12 8	..	20452 8 5	54 12 0
1941	377005	655550 19 2	24147 11 10	3643 15 4	..	25701 18 7	184 16 0
1942	394144	699701 15 11	19124 17 1	1789 10 3	..	27909 11 4	..
1943	405758	742775 17 8	21858 14 5	601 1 3	..	27107 7 0	328 16 0
1944	404355	759368 14 7	16026 8 8	755 12 9	..	28696 7 4	2 12 0
1945	409826	787475 6 10	17245 19 2	2244 10 9	..	31691 13 8	..
1946	452742	915611 4 6	20603 13 10	45037 15 3	..	37791 0 11	311 0 0
1947	462205	1072391 6 9	19158 8 11	9161 2 9	..	51679 14 6	2018 0 0
1948	454710	1025152 11 9	19083 9 1	2466 3 0	..	44804 19 5	761 16 0
1949	421197	985153 14 7	17350 14 3	3544 0 4	..	44290 9 9	368 0 0
1950	391799	932680 5 3	21925 3 8	1807 4 2	..	72513 12 4	1323 6 0
1951	396257	929445 14 6	19268 8 4	858 5 3	..	61099 16 1	2317 10 0
1952	397141	958053 12 10	21127 16 6	1225 12 9	..	61101 16 3	64 18 0
1953	378309	1063947 12 10	21728 14 1	980 14 6	..	53277 8 8	..
1954	371896	1092225 2 9	24432 3 5	507 2 2	..	53955 8 4	90 0 0
1955	367917	1107487 1 10	29607 15 8	191 16 6	..	57287 11 11	5025 6 0
1956	369379	1106994 11 1	37552 5 10	351 17 0	..	55708 19 3	..
1957	370576	1191803 9 5	39866 15 4	521 14 3	..	56648 10 7	25771 5 0
1958	355440	1200733 3 4	36407 17 10	1285 19 6	..	59279 13 2	48 12 0
1959	333844	1159792 11 6	39345 7 2	2535 5 6	..	57530 19 3	321 6 0
1960	333888	1186450 2 6	*45218 6 0	793 14 6	..	65576 16 4	..
1961	317036	1417844 17 11	66147 3 3	183 19 0	..	60836 12 8	5204 10 0
Totals		36428502 19 9	985259 5 11	2138855 8 0	712509 3 10	1503237 5 7	1425764 8 5

No. of Claims	Total Grants Paid £ s d	No. of Claims	Total Grants Paid £ s d	No. placed on Fund	Total Paid £ s d	No. of Children on Fund	No. of Claims	Amount Paid £ s d	Total Funds £ s d	Year
562	15234 0 0	1085	5425 0 0	954	36827 10 5	4857	4	75 0 0	1449989 7 10	1920
852	23551 0 0	1172	5860 0 0	871	34688 9 9	5323	10	215 0 0	1225803 5 2	1921
739	20416 0 0	1189	5945 0 0	907	39244 17 0	4880	8	160 0 0	1408736 12 11	1922
755	19937 0 0	1104	5520 0 0	879	40068 3 5	4956	7	150 0 0	1563018 3 9	1923
806	22388 0 0	1261	6305 0 0	883	41710 11 9	5062	2	20 0 0	1742576 5 3	1924
685	19117 0 0	1301	6505 0 0	900	42438 7 1	5146	12	255 0 0	1951796 6 3	1925
740	20339 0 0	1291	6530 0 0	891	43577 12 3	5649	8	190 0 0	580001 8 0	1926
843	23011 0 0	1362	6810 0 0	902	46050 5 9	5563	14	255 0 0	859568 16 7	1927
1501	41690 0 0	1289	6445 0 0	746	46036 19 0	6052	9	205 0 0	1035324 0 10	1928
1506	41549 0 0	1551	7755 0 0	859	45270 1 4	5885	8	165 0 0	1202098 5 10	1929
1328	36455 0 0	1425	7125 0 0	709	44678 19 0	5744	14	265 0 0	1296857 12 5	1930
1476	37861 0 0	1488	7440 0 0	687	44773 19 9	5720	15	305 0 0	1391683 16 7	1931
1787	46255 0 0	1475	7375 0 0	629	43866 12 7	5680	10	195 0 0	1483003 18 11	1932
2641	63874 0 0	1703	8515 0 0	691	42444 16 9	5426	11	200 0 0	1559856 5 11	1933
2093	51885 0 0	1671	8355 0 0	594	40533 11 6	5288	14	285 0 0	1713877 4 6	1934
2243	55897 0 0	1686	8430 0 0	548	38205 11 9	5073	21	475 0 0	1852507 2 4	1935
2343	58965 0 0	1846	9230 0 0	515	35346 1 8	4577	25	485 0 0	2037993 11 7	1936
2713	68949 0 0	1979	9895 0 0	598	32948 14 7	4296	13	255 0 0	2216105 0 5	1937
2604	67062 0 0	1860	9300 0 0	518	32074 19 6	4166	16	305 0 0	2391386 18 10	1938
2943	74820 0 0	1992	9960 0 0	472	29350 5 4	3712	9	220 0 0	2548495 18 3	1939
2809	75480 0 0	2416	12080 0 0	459	28249 17 4	3646	10	215 0 0	2708779 10 1	1940
2688	75538 0 0	2138	10690 0 0	362	26567 14 3	3347	16	250 0 0	2866722 6 10	1941
2747	75931 0 0	1927	9635 0 0	417	24611 5 10	3382	11	175 0 0	3074787 7 2	1942
2610	73606 0 0	2159	10794 0 0	357	22464 11 6	3146	14	215 0 0	3304330 18 11	1943
2514	72425 0 0	2250	11250 0 0	426	21566 18 1	2735	9	200 0 0	3516778 6 5	1944
2600	76716 0 0	2200	11000 0 0	308	20386 6 2	2683	14	310 0 0	3693760 3 11	1945
2746	79758 0 0	2286	11430 0 0	331	24375 15 5	2200	21	500 0 0	3939866 0 3	1946
2588	75122 0 0	2474	12370 0 0	384	23354 4 7	1974	9	230 0 0	4174179 14 0	1947
2585	72443 0 0	2369	11845 0 0	394	24823 4 4	2089	15	370 0 0	4488704 14 6	1948
2689	75649 0 0	2546	12635 0 0	338	24343 14 8	2042	6	150 0 0	4580263 10 9	1949
2669	74233 0 0	2518	12590 0 0	308	23785 16 7	2012	15	395 0 0	4778156 4 4	1950
2518	69049 0 0	2749	13745 0 0	244	22051 0 0	2023	10	245 0 0	4603455 16 5	1951
2421	68216 0 0	2500	12500 0 0	265	21733 12 6	2288	11	275 0 0	4799131 11 8	1952
2244	65309 0 0	2461	12305 0 0	288	26762 13 8	2037	17	410 0 0	5023253 11 3	1953
2703	68777 0 0	2579	12895 0 0	260	26311 6 9	1783	10	250 0 0	5343328 3 1	1954
2719	72040 0 0	2568	12840 0 0	262	26160 2 2	1734	20	495 0 0	5424671 18 2	1955
2901	78749 0 0	2665	13325 0 0	309	25843 6 9	1675	15	360 0 0	5461363 81 7	1956
2959	80809 0 0	2512	12560 0 0	320	27559 2 10	1877	12	300 0 0	5538230 11 3	1957
3249	86904 0 0	2660	13300 0 0	324	32661 14 0	1721	19	470 0 0	5803810 19 0	1958
3256	84077 0 0	2581	12905 0 0	217	32802 18 1	1642	9	235 0 0	5982692 10 6	1959
3218	85859 0 0	2339	11695 0 0	259	30572 3 9	1764	10	250 0 0	6124834 12 4	1960
3340	89351 0 0	2522	12610 0 0	232	27817 3 7	1753	3	75 0 0	6362273 9 11	1961
98335	2636960 0 0	..	479487 0 0	35066	1645945 13 9	..	597	12345 0 0	..	

SELECT BIBLIOGRAPHY

The following list is by no means exhaustive but it includes the main Parliamentary Papers and secondary works of value. Except where otherwise stated, the place of publication is London.

(a) STATUTES

Regulation of Railways Act, 1868 (Parl. Pap. 1867-8, iv, p. 511)
Railway Returns (Continuous Brakes) Act, 1878 (Parl. Pap. 1878, vii, p. 47)
Employers' Liability Act, 1880 (Parl. Pap. 1880, iii, p. 123)
Regulation of Railways Act, 1889 (Parl. Pap. 1889, vii, p. 221)
Railway Servants (Hours of Labour) Act, 1893 (Parl. Pap. 1893-4, iii, p. 407)
Workmen's Compensation Act, 1897 (Parl. Pap. 1897, iii, p. 697)
Railways (Prevention of Accidents) Act, 1900 (Parl. Pap. 1900, iv, p. 267)
Railways Act, 1921 (Parl. Pap. 1921, v. 1)
Road Traffic Act, 1930 (Parl. Pap 1929-30, iv, p. 111)
Road and Rail Traffic Act, 1933 (Parl. Pap. 1932-3, iii, p. 301)
Railways Agreement Act, 1935 (Parl. Pap. 1935-6, iv, p. 1)
Transport Act, 1947 (Parl. Pap. 1946-7, iv, pp. 531, 1023)
Transport Act, 1953 (Parl. Pap. 1952-3, ii, p. 565)

(b) OFFICIAL ACCOUNTS AND PAPERS

Return of weekly paid servants, during July 1886 and January 1887, on duty for more than twelve hours at a time, or who afterwards were allowed to resume work with less than eight hours rest (Parl. Pap. 1888, lxxxix, p. 437)
Similar returns for September 1889 and March 1890 (Parl. Pap. 1890, lxv, p. 827), for December 1890 (Parl. Pap. 1890-1, lxxv, p. 525), and December 1891 (Parl. Pap. 1892, lxx, p. 291)
Return of Railway servants killed by accidents in which movement of vehicles used exclusively on railways was concerned in each year 1884-93 (Parl. Pap. 1894, lxxv)
Return since 1884, name and date of accidents, railways on which occurred and passages in such reports relating to unduly long hours (Parl. Pap. 1892, lxx, p. 391)
Railway servants killed and injured by accidents in which movement of vehicles was concerned during years 1870, 1873, 1877 and 1880-92, computed number of servants on each railway and the proportion of killed, etc. (Parl. Pap. 1893-4, lxxix, p. 489; 1897, lxxvii)
Memorandum of the Board of Trade on Automatic Couplings (Parl. Pap. 1899, lxxxv, p. 695)
Earnings and Hours of Labour of Railway Service in 1907 (Parl. Pap. 1912-13, cviii, p. 1)

Railway Conciliation Scheme. Statement of Settlements regarding Questions as to Rates of Wages and Hours of Labour of Railway Employees that have been effected under the scheme for Conciliation and Arbitration arranged in accordance with the Agreement of November 6, 1907 (Cd. 5332 of 1910)

Report of a Court of Inquiry into Applications by the Trade Unions representing the employees of the Railway Companies for improvement in Wages and Reduction in weekly hours of work (Parl. Pap. 1946–7, Cmd. 7161, xiv, p. 303)

REPORTS OF ROYAL COMMISSIONS AND SELECT COMMITTEES OF PARLIAMENT

Regulation of Railways (Prevention of Accidents) Bill. Select Committee of House of Lords. Report and Minutes of Evidence (Parl. Pap. 1873, xiv)

Royal Commission on Accidents on Railways. Report, Minutes, etc. (Parl. Pap. 1877, xlviii)

Select Committee on Employers' Liability. Proceedings, Minutes and Evidence (Parl. Pap. 1876, ix, p. 669)

Select Committee on Employers' Liability Act Amendment Bill. Report (Parl. Pap. 1877, x, p. 551). Minutes of Evidence and Report (Parl. Pap. 1886, viii, p. 1)

Select Committee on Railway Servants (Hours of Labour)—
Minutes of Evidence (Parl. Pap. 1890–1, xvi)
Report and Special Report. Minutes of Evidence (Parl. Pap. 1892, xvi)

Royal Commission on Labour, Group B, Vol. III (Parl. Pap. 1893–4, viii)

Royal Commission on Accidents to Railway Servants, Minutes of Evidence, Appendices and Report (Parl. Pap. 1800, xxvii)

Royal Commission on Trade Disputes and Trade Combinations. Minutes of Evidence and Appendices (Parl. Pap. 1906, lvi, p. 137)

Royal Commission on the Railway Conciliation and Arbitration Scheme of 1907—
Report (Parl. Pap. 1911, xxix, part 1)
Minutes of Evidence and Appendices (Parl. Pap. 1912–13, xlv)

Royal Commission on Transport, 1930—
First Report, The Control of Traffic on Roads (Parl. Pap. 1929–30, Cmd. 3365, xvii, p. 835)
Second Report, The Licencing and Regulation of Public Service Vehicles (Parl. Pap. 1929–30, Cmd. 3416, xvii, p. 1895)
Final Report, The Co-ordination and Development of Transport (Parl. Pap. 1930–1, Cmd. 3751, xvii, 619)
Communications received from organizations, etc. (Parl. Pap. 1931–2, Cmd. 4048, xx, p. 873)

SECONDARY AUTHORITIES

THE RAILWAY INDUSTRY

C. D. CAMPBELL. *British Railways in Boom and Depression.* 1932

I. SAVAGE. *Economic History of Transport.* 1960

W. JACKMAN. *The Development of Transportation in Modern England* (1962 Edition)

R. BELL. *History of British Railways during the War 1939–45.* 1946
J. SIMMONS. *The Railways of Britain.* 1961
M. R. ROBBINS. *The Railway Age.* 1962

GENERAL TRADE UNION HISTORIES

G. D. H. COLE. *A Short History of the British Working Class Movement.* 1948
SIDNEY and BEATRICE WEBB. *History of Trade Unionism.* (1920 Edition)
A. BRIGGS and J. SAVILLE (Ed.). *Essays in Labour History.* 1960
E. J. HOBSBAWM. 'General Labour Unions in Britain, 1889–1914' in *The Economic History Review,* 2nd Series, Vol. I (Cambridge) 1949

RAILWAY TRADE UNIONISM

EDWIN PHILLIPS. *Full Report of the First General Delegate Meeting of the A.S.R.S. together with a concise history of the union from its commencement.* 1872
C. BASSETT-VINCENT. *An Authentic History of Railway Trade Unionism.* (Derby) 1902
A.S.R.S. *Souvenir History.* 1910
ROWLAND KENNEY. *Men and Rails.* 1913.
NATIONAL GUILDS LEAGUE. *Towards a National Railways Guild.* 1916
G. D. H. COLE and R. PAGE ARNOT. *Trade Unionism on the Railways.* 1917
G. D. H. COLE. *Workers Control for Railwaymen,* Workers Control Series No. 3. National Guilds League. 1921
G. R. RAYNES. *Engines and Men.* 1922
G. ALCOCK. *Fifty Years of Railway Trade Unionism.* 1922
R.C.A. *The R.C.A. and its Path to Progress.* 1928
N.U.R. *What Trade Union has done for Railwaymen and other Transport Workers.* Silver Jubilee. 1938.
N. MCKILLOP. *The Lighted Flame.* 1950
B. PRIBICEVIC. *The Shop Steward's Movement and Workers Control 1910–22.* Oxford 1959.
H. A. CLEGG. *Labour Relations on London Transport.* Oxford 1950

WORKING CONDITIONS OF RAILWAYMEN

LEONI LEVI. *Wages and Earnings of the Working Classes.* 1867
W. F. MILLS. *The Railway Service.* 1867
EDWIN PHILLIPS. *A voice from the signalbox.* 1874
W. R. CHAMBERS. *Railways and Railwaymen.* 1892
W. GORDON. *Everyday life on the railroads.* 1892
R.C.A. *Life of the Railway Clerk.* 1911
A Comparative study of railway wages in the United Kingdom and United States of America and other European Countries. Bureau of Railway Economics. Bulletin No. 34 (Washington D.C., U.S.A.), 1912
ALFRED WILLIAMS. *Life in a Railway Factory.* 1915
A STOKES. *Fifty years on the Railway: yarns by a Methodist Signalman.* Birmingham, 1936
INTERNATIONAL TRANSPORT WORKERS' FEDERATION. *The Working Hours of Railwaymen.* Amsterdam 1939

C. E. STRETTON. *Safe Railway Working.* 1887 and 1893

P. W. KINGSFORD. 'Labour Relations on the Railways. 1853–75'. *Journal of Transport History.* 1954.

STRIKES, CONCILIATION AND ARBITRATION

J. MAVOR. *The Scottish Railway Strike.* 1891

E. J. CROKER. *Retrospective Lessons on Railway Strikes.* (London and Cork) 1898

J. KEIR HARDIE. *Killing no Murder.* The Government and the Railway Strike. 1911

C. LEUBUSCHER. *Der Arbeitskampf der Englisher Eisenbahner im Yahre 1911.* Jena 1913

G. TAYLOR. *The English Railway Strike and its Revolutionary Bearings.* Chicago 1911

A. J. THATCHER, *The 1919 Railway Strike and the Settlement of January 1920.* 1920

LORD ASKWITH. *Industrial Problems and Disputes.* 1920

G. GLASGOW. *General Strikes and Road Transport.* 1926

J. SYMONS. *The General Strike.* 1957

BIOGRAPHIES AND AUTOBIOGRAPHIES

G. ALCOCK. *Life of John H. Dobson,* ex-organizer, N.U.R. 1921

ANON. *A Brief Biography of J. Baxter Langley, Esq., M.R.C.S.* 1867

E. HODDER. *Life of Samuel Morley.* 1889

F. A. CHANNING. *Memories of Midland Politics, 1885–1910.* 1918

BASIL FULLER. *The Life Story of the Rt. Hon. J. H. Thomas.* 1933

H. R. PHILLPOT. *The Rt. Hon. J. H. Thomas.* 1932

J. H. THOMAS. *My Story.* 1937

RAILWAY UNIONS AND POLITICS

W. FOREMAN. *Workingmen and Politics.* 1889

S. MACCOBY. *English Radicalism. 1853–86.* 1938

H. PELLING. *The Origins of the Labour Party.* 1954

F. BEALEY and H. PELLING. *Labour and Politics, 1900–06.* 1958

J. H. THOMAS. *When Labour Rules.* 1920

M. HARRISON. *Trade Unions and the Labour Party since 1945*

INDEX

aa

Printed in the United States
by Baker & Taylor Publisher Services